DICK TURPIN
AND THE
GREGORY GANG

DICK TURPIN
AND THE
GREGORY GANG

by
DEREK BARLOW

PHILLIMORE
London and Chichester

1973

Published by
PHILLIMORE & CO. LTD.,
Shopwyke Hall, Chichester, Sussex.

© Derek Barlow, 1973

All rights reserved

ISBN 0 900592 64 8

*Printed in Great Britain by
Redwood Press Ltd., Trowbridge, Wiltshire.*

PREFACE

In the course of research such as that which has gone into the making of this account, one must inevitably look to others for advice, assistance and information; and the extent to which these have been given in this case may be gauged from the amount of correspondence which has accumulated. I am grateful to all those who have contributed to that file, as indeed I am to those who were unable to help but who recommended me to persons who could; but in acknowledging many kindnesses shewn to me in over three years, it will, I hope, be appreciated that without record it would be impossible to recall the names of all those who have come to my aid when it has been sought.

It is appropriate however for me to mention separately Mr. F.G. Emmison, the former Essex County Archivist, whose interest and encouragement were formidable factors in bringing the discovery of the man behind the legend to the notice of the public.

Mr. J.H. Barry, H.M. Nautical Almanac Office, Royal Greenwich Observatory.
Mr. J.B. Bennett, Hon. Librarian, Essex Archaeological Society.
Mr. E.G.W. Bill, M.A., Librarian, Lambeth Palace Library.
Mr. F.G. Emmison, M.B.E., F.S.A., F.R.Hist.S., County Archivist,* Essex Record Office.
Mrs. P.M. Eteen
Mrs. N.K.M. Gurney, M.A., Archivist, Borthwick Institute of Historical Research, York.
Dr. W.O. Hassall, M.A., D.Phil., F.S.A., Deputy Keeper of Western Manuscripts, Bodleian Library, Oxford.

Mr. N. Higson, County Archivist, East Riding County Record Office, Beverley, Yorks.
Mr. P.E. Jones, O.B.E. LL.B., F.S.A., F.R.Hist.S., Deputy Keeper of the Records (London Records),* Guildhall.
Miss P.S. King, B.A., Assistant Archivist, Greater London Record Office (Middlesex Records).
Mrs. S. Kington, B.A., Librarian, London Museum.
Miss J. Laing, Meteorological Office, Bracknell, Berks.
Mr. W.H. Liddell, University of London, Department of Extra-Mural Studies.
Mr. W.R. Maidment, F.L.A., Borough Librarian, London Borough of Camden.
Miss B.R. Masters, Guildhall (London Records).
Mr. W.R.M. McClelland, F.L.A., City Librarian, Leicester City Library and Publicity Department.
Miss E.D. Mercer, B.A., F.S.A., Deputy Head Archivist,† Greater London Record Office (Middlesex Records).
Mr. E.L.C. Mullins, M.A., Secretary to the Editorial Board, Institute of Historical Research.
Mr. D.G. Neill, Assistant Librarian, Department of Printed Books, Bodleian Library, Oxford.
Mr. K.C. Newton, M.A., F.R.Hist.S., County Archivist, Essex Record Office.
Mr. A.N. Stimson, National Maritime Museum.
Miss M. Thompson, York.
Mr. O.S. Tomlinson, F.L.A., City Librarian, City Library, York.
Mr. R.R. Toole-Stott, Librarian, Treasury Solicitor's Office.
Mrs. J. Varley, M.A., F.S.A., Archivist, Lincolnshire Archives Committee.

* retired.   † now Head Archivist, Greater London Record Office.

I am also grateful for the facilities and assistance provided at the following:—

British Museum, Reading Room and North Library
Essex Record Office, Chelmsford
Greater London Record Office (Middlesex Records)
Guildhall Library and Record Office
Islington Central Library
Public Record Office.

The following were approached in connection with a search for a newspaper, the lack of which raised a particular problem, and although none of them possessed the edition in question, a complete set of negative replies obliged me to look at the problem from another angle and resolve it satisfactorily without the need for recourse to the elusive newspaper:

Dorothy W. Bridgwater, Assistant Head, Reference Department, Yale University Library, New Haven, Connecticut.
Annette Fern, Assistant Reference Librarian, University of Chicago Library.
John L. Hardesty, Editor of Publications, Union Catalog Division of the Library of Congress, Washington, D.C.
T.E. Ratcliffe, Reference Librarian, University of Illinois Library, Urbana, Illinois.
Eugene P. Sheehy, Head of Reference Department, Columbia University Libraries, New York.

Transcripts and extracts of records are quoted by permission of the following:

> The Corporation of London
> Essex Record Office
> Greater London Record Office
> East Riding of Yorkshire County Record Office

Extracts etc. of Crown Copyright material in the Public Record Office and other archives appear by permission of the Controller of Her Majesty's Stationery Office.

Printed material from contemporary sources in the British Museum appears by permission of the Trustees of the British Museum.

Key to abbreviations used in the footnotes

Beverley	East Riding of Yorkshire County Record Office.
Brit. Mus.	British Museum.
Essex	Essex Record Office.
Guildhall	Corporation of London Record Office.
Lincoln	Lincolnshire Archives Office.
Middlesex	Greater London Record Office (Middlesex Records).
P.R.O.	Public Record Office.
Westminster	Greater London Record Office (Middlesex Records).

Copyright (excepting Crown Copyright material referred to above) by Derek Barlow, 1970.

To my wife, my son, and my daughter, who each in their own way contributed something and made it possible, I dedicate with love this book.

Derek Barlow

CONTENTS

Book One—The Deerstealers *Page*

Chapter I
1731 Mar.–1733 June Waltham Forest. Keepers, deer- 3
stealers and others.

Chapter II
1733 June–Oct. Enfield Chase. Rewards. Game 13
laws. Murder.

Chapter III
1733 Dec.–1734 Sept. The deerstealers captured. Two 23
women. The course of Justice
perverted. Some deerstealers
released. Roll call of known
offenders. Deerstealing abandoned
for more profitable activities when
leader of gang captured and subsequently rescued from pillory.

Book Two—The Gregory Gang

Chapter I
1734 Oct.–Dec. Strype, Wooldridge, Gladwin and 43
Shockley, and Skinner robberies.

Chapter II
1734 Dec.–1735 Jan. Mason robbery and attempted 58
Justice Asher robbery.

Chapter III
1735 Jan.–Feb. Saunders, Sheldon, Reverend Mr. 70
Dyde and Widow Shelley robberies,
and an escape from the Clerkenwell
Bridewell.

Chapter IV
1735 Feb. Lawrence robbery and rape of 83
Dorothy Street. The Francis
robbery.

Book Three—John Wheeler the Evidence, and Archelaus Pullen, Constable

Chapter I
1735 Feb.   Wheeler and others taken. First   103
                           rough descriptions of gang.

Chapter II
1735 Feb.   The survivors disperse. The Savage   120
                           robbery. Newspaper leak of
                           detailed descriptions of the remain-
                           ing gang members. Second Skinner
                           robbery. Mrs. St. John robbed.
                           Some stolen goods recovered.
                           Turpin visits home. The Berry
                           robbery. A receiver and others
                           captured.

Chapter III
1735 Feb.   Some cases of mistaken identity.   137
                           Proclamation reward for capture,
                           and descriptions of those still at
                           large. Preparations for a rescue and
                           official counter manoeuvres.

Book Four—The Old Bailey Trials and a Remarkable Coincidence

Chapter I
1735 Feb.–Mar.   Trial of Fielder, Rose, Saunders and   151
                           Walker. Capture of John Lyndon
                           alias Samuel Gregory. A receiver
                           taken.

Chapter II
1735 Mar.   Walker dies. Rose, Saunders and   167
                           Fielder executed. Barnfield the
                           receiver dies. Those still at large.
                           Abortive attempt to effect rescue
                           of Jasper Gregory. His execution.
                           The survivors split up again.

Chapter III
1735 Apr.   Flight of Jeremy and Samuel Gregory and subsequent capture. Activities of Turpin, Rowden and Jones.   176

Chapter IV
1735 Apr.   Haines elopes with his mistress and is captured. John Lyndon released. More of Turpin &c. Trial of Mary Brazier.   185

Chapter V
1735 Apr.–June   Jeremy Gregory dies. Turpin &c. again. Samuel Gregory brought to London. Haines sent to Chelmsford. Samuel Gregory tried and executed.   195

Book Five—Turpin (part the first)

Chapter I
1735 July–Aug.   Turpin and Rowden, South of the River Thames. Haines' trial and last meeting with mistress before execution.   213

Chapter II
1735 Aug.–Nov.   Turpin and Rowden in same vicinity. Turpin visits his wife. Back South of the Thames again. Last robbery for some time.   222

Chapter III
1735 Dec.–1736 May   Mary Brazier transported. John Jones is captured and Turpin and Rowden disappear. Some popular fallacies demolished. Jones and Wheeler go to Chelmsford for Jones' trial. Macabre incident near Edgware. Daniel Malden escapes from Newgate.   228

Chapter IV
1736 May–Dec.

Malden escapes and goes to Holland. Turpin rumours. Rowden caught pushing counterfeit coins in Gloucestershire. Jones' sentence commuted. Rowden's trial and sentence in name of Daniel Crispe. Malden returns from Holland and is recaptured. More Turpin rumours. Wheeler released. Case for Turpin being in Holland. Jones transported.

240

Chapter V
1737 Feb.–Apr.

Letter from Turpin in Holland. His wife and two friends captured but Turpin escapes; the case for this event pointing to a reunion with his wife after returning from Holland. Meeting with Matthew King and Stephen Potter and their sojourn in Leicestershire. Elizabeth Turpin and one friend released but the other remains in Hertford Gaol. They see him here, they see him there.

256

Chapter VI
1737 Apr.–June

Turpin, Matthew King and Potter back in London. Mr. Major robbed outside *Green Man* at Epping. Search for a racehorse. Ambush in Whitechapel. John and Matthew King taken and Matthew wounded. Turpin and Potter escape. The part of Richard Bayes. Another escape for Turpin. Potter taken. Murder of Thomas Morris. Elizabeth King taken in attempting to retrieve horses. Turpin removes northwards, but reports of Home Counties

268

sightings and captures persist. Rumours of £200 reward. Proclamation drafted but not published. Matthew King dies.

Book Six—Turpin (part the second)

Chapter I
1737 June — Turpin arrives at Brough in the East Riding. Rowden discovered in Gloucester gaol. Further reports of Turpin's capture. Preparation for Rowden's removal to Chelmsford *via* London. Proclamation for Turpin's capture published. Appraisal of a contemporary Turpin pamphlet and its being the basis of some traditions.   299

Chapter II
1737 July–1738 June. — Potter to be sent to Chelmsford. Elizabeth Turpin's other companion released. Rowden passes through London to Chelmsford. Potter released and Rowden convicted at Chelmsford Assize. Dissertations on Turpin. Calendar of Turpin's movements between Yorkshire and Lincolnshire. Death of Wheeler. Rowden's sentence commuted to transportation.   316

Chapter III
1738 July–Sept. — Turpin steals a horse in Lincs. and gives it to his father in Essex. He returns to Lincs. to steal sheep and is arrested. He escapes and steals three horses and travels back to Yorks. His father committed for stealing the horse given to him by his son. Turpin sells two of the three horses.   331

Chapter IV
1738 Oct.–1739 Feb.   Turpin arrested for disturbing the peace and committed to Beverley House of Correction. Inquiries instigated in Lincs. Turpin removed to York Castle. The three Lincs. horses traced to Yorks.   344

Chapter V
1739 Feb.   Question of authenticity of published Turpin correspondence. Turpin writes to his brother-in-law. Local suspicions aroused that letter was from Turpin and witness sent to York to identify him. Official recognition of identity and report to Secretary of State. Attorney General thinks Turpin should be brought south. Another Essex witness goes to York.   355

Chapter VI
1739 Mar.   Examination of admissibility of charges being brought at York. Yorkshire intervention upon the question of trial venue, and decision to hold it at York. Turpin's father released and an old deerstealing rival convicted. Unexpected precautions taken to prevent Turpin's discharge if acquitted. The question of Turpin' real alias and his mother's maiden name resolved. Opening of York Assize, the indictments presented to the Grand Jury and the arrival of the day of Turpin's trial.   370

Chapter VII
1739 Mar.–Apr.   Trial, conviction and judgement. An examination of the evidence. Consideration of pirate version of   393

trial testimony. Post trial proceedings. Turpin's behaviour. Two confessions. His execution and subsequent events.

Appendix One   Claims   433

Appendix Two   The Legend of Dick Turpin's Ride   441
                      to York.

Appendix Three   The Print taken, 'From a Print in   449
                      the *Tyburn Chronicle* 1742'.

Select Bibliography   452

Index   455

LIST OF ILLUSTRATIONS

Plate		Facing page
1	Proclamation offering £10 reward for the capture of deerstealers	94
2	The Duke of Chandos's letter about deerstealers	94
3	Elizabeth King's information about the robbery of Ambrose Skinner by the gang	95
4	The Widow Shelley being roasted by the gang	95
5	Map of London and Westminster, showing Dagot's Farm	110
6	Newgate in the 18th century	111
7	New Prison, Clerkenwell in the 18th century	111
8	*Night Cellar* by Hogarth	142
9	Order for military escort to Tyburn	143
10	Part of Rocque's Map, showing the site of Tyburn gallows	158
11	*Cock Match* by Hogarth	159
12	Expenses claimed for bringing Samuel Gregory and another man to London	286
13	The imprisonment of Turpin's wife, Elizabeth	287
14	Turpin in his cave in Epping Forest	302
15	Turpin shooting Thomas Morris outside his cave	302
16	Map of the vicinity of Turpin's stay in Yorkshire	303
17	Information against John Palmer	334
18	Turpin identified in York Castle	335
19	The Attorney General's opinion that Turpin should be brought south from York	350
20	Sir Dudley Ryder	350
21	York Castle in 1750	351

BOOK ONE

THE DEERSTEALERS

CHAPTER ONE

I

ESSEX
We Henry Thompson, Henry Pater, Joseph Bastick, Thomas Hydes, John Leigh, John Wooton and John Peckover Keepers of the Forest of Waltham in the County of Essex severally make oath that diverse disorderly and idle persons have of late frequently both in the day time as well as in the night killed wounded and carried off several of his Majestys red and fallow deer within the said Forest of Waltham in defiance of us the Keepers thereof and do still persist in committing great abuses and frequently go in numbers together with fire arms and other dangerous weapons insomuch that the Keepers of the said Forest go in danger of their lives.[1]

THIS AFFIDAVIT was taken 5 March 1731 before John Goodere, J.P., and reflects considerable contempt on the part of the deerstealers for the game laws and the Keepers whose responsibility it was to enforce them; but of Dick Turpin's having been a deerstealer there is no more proof than there is for his having been a smuggler,[2] and at this particular point in time, if the Hempstead witnesses at his trial are to be believed, he was a butcher.

By the summer of 1734 however, Turpin was very much an associate of the men who had been deerstealers in 1731; and for him to have been allowed to join their throng suggests that he had been known and trusted by them for some time. As a butcher it would not have been difficult for him to dispose of the venison, and this was probably the extent of his involvement.

It took little more than a month for the authorities to act on the Keepers' complaint, and on 8 April the Duke of Newcastle, Principal Secretary of State for the Southern province, signed a proclamation which repeated the substance of the Keepers' complaint, offered a pardon to any accomplices who would betray their associates, and promised a reward of £10, payable upon conviction, to anyone bringing about the capture of a deerstealer.[3]

The proclamation was published in the *London Gazette* for 1 May 1731 and the stage was set for a drama which nobody could have anticipated might last eight years, and history was about to witness the birth of a legend. The public were ready for a little diversion: the newspapers ready to welcome sensational news. We were not actively involved in any war, our ministers on the continent plodded through fairly routine diplomatic missions, and George the Second, about to enter the fifth year of his reign, needed little encouragement for him to visit Hanover and leave domestic affairs to Caroline his Queen and the Lords Justices of the Realm. Even the Jacobites were between rebellions, quietly intriguing beyond the seas. And £10 proved to be so great an incentive to the Keepers that one of them actually contrived to capture a deerstealer.

> Henry Thompson, Under Keeper of New Lodge Walk in the Forest of Waltham ... did on the 24th of September 1731 at the great hazard and peril of his life apprehend *John Fuller* for killing a fallow deer in the said forest of which he was convicted and lay in gaol a year and stood in the pillory one hour for the said fact as appears by the certificate of John Goodere Esq., one of his Majesty's Justices of the Peace for the County of Essex.[4]

It took nearly two years and a significant increase in the reward offered before others were caught and convicted, but it is unlikely in view of later events, that the £10 reward discouraged them from Waltham Forest. But before we look at the next report of their activities there are some apparently odd and unconnected incidents to relate.

II

From about the autumn of 1731 to the spring of the following year, a fresh-faced young man, five feet seven inches high and about nineteen years of age, lived and worked as a farrier at Richard Taylor's smithy at Edgware, Middlesex. Sometimes a wealthy farmer from the same parish, a man who paid his employees generously, would send to the smithy for his horses to be shod; and young Samuel Gregory would go to Joseph Lawrence's farm at Earlsbury, observing when he did so that the farmer must be a very rich man to pay his employees so well.[5]

III

Thomas Rowden was a little man, stocky, with a round red face marked with small pockholes. He was aged about 26 in August 1732, and was by trade a pewterer. At least, this was his legitimate calling, but it appears that on the side he was not averse to making money; and between 10 and 12

August 1732 the authorities later came to suspect that he and John Gassey *alias* Gaskey might have been making their own at Christchurch in Southwark. Another companion of his, William Faulkener *or* Falconer, swore that he did, but this accusation was not made until the following year.[6]

IV

On 27 November 1732, the Court of Attachments of the Royal Forest of Waltham was held at the *King's Head* at Chigwell. During the proceedings John Wooton, one of the Keepers who had complained about the activities of the deerstealers in the previous year, brought before the court a gun which he had taken from Jeremiah Gregory, a person unqualified to possess a gun in the forest. Jeremiah was one of Samuel Gregory's brothers and Wooton was ordered 'he have the gun for his care in his office.'[7]

V

On the day following the proceedings at Chigwell, on 28 November 1732, John (or Henry) Deakins was present at a house in Chingford, Essex. Over a year later it was said that Jeremiah Gregory, Joseph Rose and John Coster, or one of them, fired a gun in his direction. It is possible that Deakins was subject to some such experience, because before the three men were accused of shooting at him, he had unfortunately died. The cause is not known; it may have been a wound or shock or even a natural death in no wise hastened by what happened in November. The significant point about this odd incident is that two of the men implicated were deerstealers.[8]

VI

Nearly three weeks later a similar but more immediately tragic incident occurred. On 16 December 1732 at about 6 p.m. John Boston was travelling the highway from Woodford and passing through Wanstead towards London when a shot was fired and a bullet penetrated his skull to a depth of three inches. He languished nine hours before he died, and then his body was taken to Woodford and an inquest held before Luke Dore the Coroner. The jury brought in a verdict of 'killed or murdered by a person or persons unknown', and, as in the case of Deakins, the matter was to all appearances forgotten.[9]

VII

In the Spring of 1733 Thomas Rowden was charged at the Assizes at Kingston-upon-Thames with counterfeiting ten half-crowns at Christchurch, Southwark on 10 August in the previous year; and that on the next day he counterfeited one half-crown and one shilling; and that on the day after that, 'he had in his possession in his dwelling house, one pair of moulds for striking English money.' John Gassey *alias* Gaskey, who was also charged on the first count, was described in the indictment as being 'At large', i.e. not found or arrested.

The witnesses sworn in court were, on the first count, William Falconer and John North, gent.; and on the second and third counts, Alice Falconer and John North, gent. Rowden put himself upon his country (pleaded not guilty) and was found not guilty and acquitted. A retrospective newspaper account, in describing another episode in his career, mentioned that he had been tried for coining on the evidence of his companion Faulkener, but Faulkener's evidence not being sufficient he was acquitted. Several years later Rowden was convicted of a similar offence and imprisoned. John Gassey *alias* Gaskey was not heard of again, but Rowden's erstwhile friend Falconer *or* Faulkener went his own way to share a somewhat dubious distinction with some of Rowden's other friends.[10]

VIII

The evidence of James Smith and Edward Saward, the two Hempstead witnesses at Turpin's trial, gives us some idea of Turpin's activities and whereabouts at this time. The trial took place in March 1739.

Smith, in reply to two questions from counsel, replied, "Tis about five years since I saw him', and, 'the last time I saw him, I sold him a grey mare, about five years ago before my brother died.' Very approximately, this would have been about the spring or summer of 1734. Asked how long Turpin had been set up as a butcher, Smith replied, 'I cannot tell he lived at .... in Essex, he left it about six years and after he kept a public house.' When asked if he had seen him after this, he replied, 'six miles from thence,' but this was before he had sold him the mare.

Since Smith's reply to the question about Turpin's term as a butcher was, 'I cannot tell ... ,' it must be inferred that the continuation of that reply should have read, 'he left it about six years ago,' which would have been in 1733, with a subsequent term as landlord of a public house from 1733 to

1734. This accords with conclusions drawn from other circumstances involving Turpin's association with the deerstealers, but for the moment we are particularly concerned with the place name omitted from Smith's testimony. In a footnote to the trial proceedings, the author states that the name was lost due to the uproar in court, but that it was thought to have been 'Boxhill or some such name.'

The name was not Boxhill, but something like it, and allowing for the name having been misheard, phonetic similarity and the fact that a place-name then might be spelt differently now, it appeared that Bookers Hill *alias* Bucket Hill *alias* Buckhurst Hill was the place most probably mentioned at the trial. But apart from being conveniently near to Waltham Forest (if not actually just within it at that time) and the area of the deerstealers' activities, there did not seem to be much else to recommend it. Buckhurst Hill is in the parish of Chigwell, and in 1738 and 1739 there was a John Turpin, innholder who lived there.[11] but it was clear from his will that if he was related to the Hempstead Turpins the fact would be very difficult to prove.[12]

Without corroboration the link between Boxhill and Buckhurst Hill remained a possibility, but in another version of the trial proceedings, a pirated version, the blank was filled in, and the place-name recorded was 'Booker's Hill'.

Now leaving aside the matter of piracy (this is discussed in the chapter on the trial itself) we are left with two accounts from different publishers (which even if piracy was *not* involved would perforce have been practically indistinguishable from one another), in which the later one supplied positive identification of a place only vaguely identified in the earlier one. Both editions appeared within a short time of each other in 1739, which leaves but two factors to consider,

(i) if the later account was an independent version, the place-name was included because the person who recorded it was in a better position to hear it than anyone else, and there would therefore be no reason to doubt that the place name was that which was given in testimony, and

(ii) if the later account was pirated from the original the inclusion of the place-name is explained by an obvious necessity to distinguish it from the other in such a manner as to make it appear authentic. If the latter factor applied, then the choice of Booker's Hill was governed either by the same process as that which guided the present author, or the publisher went to the trouble of establishing what it was that had been said at the trial; this would have not been particularly difficult in 1739 when a letter to James Smith at Hempstead (with perhaps some slight inducement) would have provided the answer within a short space of time. In any event, by whatever means two authors separated by 230 years arrived at the same answer, the fact that they did would seem to indicate a much more substantial relationship between Boxhill and Booker's Hill than mere coincidence. There can be very little doubt that Turpin was set up as a butcher, for some unspecified length of time which came to an end in 1733, at the place we now know as Buckhurst Hill.

There is one minor point about Smith's testimony and that is that if Turpin was 'set up' as a butcher, it would seem that he was financed by someone, possibly his father, in the purchase of his own shop, rather than that he was employed as a butcher by someone else.

Claims that Turpin was a butcher at Thaxted have undoubtedly originated from the description given of him in a reward notice which stated as much, but insofar as the information was obtained from one of his associates it is probable that the statement was not without some foundation. The argument is given some support by the possibility that a Thomas Turpin who married at Thaxted in 1726 (and presumably, from the fact his wife subsequently bore two children there, lived there some length of time) may have been one of Turpin's older brothers. On these grounds there is some case for Turpin having traded there, possibly before he went to Buckhurst Hill.

Documentary evidence of Turpin's marriage, other than the statement of one who knew him that he did marry, has not been found, and claims that the marriage took place in 1728 appear to have been based on the account by his earliest biographer, writing in 1739, that he married 11 or 12 years earlier. There is in fact no doubt at all that the greater part of anything which has been written about Turpin's early years originated in this particular work, and it is appropriate at this point to reproduce that part of it which leads up to him becoming an associate of the deerstealers:

THE LIFE OF RICHARD TURPIN

It is supposed the world naturally enquires after persons that have in any manner been rendered either famous or infamous; for which reason we think the account of a man who for some time past has been not only the terror but talk of a county that makes considerable figure in this nation, cannot be disagreeable. Essex hath been lately much alarmed at the enterprizes of Turpin, several families have suffered by him, and others, of Gregory's Gang, as our ensuing narration will relate.

Richard Turpin, who was executed at York on Saturday the 7th of April, 1739; was son of John Turpin of Hempstead in Essex, who put him to school to one Smith a writing master; from thence he was placed apprentice to a butcher in Whitechapel, where he served his time; he was frequently guilty of misdemeanours, and behaved in a loose disorderly manner; so soon as he came out of his time he married the daughter of one Palmer, and set up for himself at Suson in Essex, which is about eleven or twelve years ago; where (not having any credit in the markets, and no-body caring to trust him) he was reduced to a necessity of maintaining himself by indirect practices and accordingly very often used to rob the neighbouring gentlemen of sheep, lambs, oxen &c. particularly one time he stole a couple of oxen from Mr. Giles of Plaistow, which he had conveyed to his own house and cut up, but was detected by two of the gentleman's servants, who having a suspicion of him, from some information or other which they had received, went to his house, and seeing an ox slaughtered were confirmed in their suspicions, but in order to be further assured, enquired where Turpin sold the hides of his beasts, and being informed, that he generally sold them at Waltham Abbey, they went there, and were convinced on sight of the hides, that Turpin was the man who had stolen the oxen, and immediately returned to Suson, which he being apprised of, left them in the foreroom, jumped out of a window and made his escape, when he was gone his wife disposed of the carcasses.

Turpin having made his escape from Justice for that time, though by this means his character was blown, and he could never entertain a thought of returning to Suson, or following his trade of a butcher in that county, he immediately formed a design of commencing smuggler; for which reason, his wife having supplied him with what small matter of money she could raise, he took his way to the Hundreds of Essex, where he had not stayed long before he got into a gang of smugglers, he followed his new profession for some time with tolerable success; but at last Fortune took a turn, and he lost all that he had acquired; upon which not caring to run any more hazards, he thought it proper to try his luck some other way.

When people are inclinable to vice they seldom wait long for opportunities, which was the case with him, for no sooner had he left off smuggling than he met with a gang of deerstealers, who finding him to be a desperate fellow, and ripe for any mischief, made no scruple of admitting him to be one of them; but the Hundreds of Essex not being so proper for them as the other part of the country, they concluded to come up nearer to town and the forest, which they accordingly did, and robbed not only the forest of deer but several gentlemen's parks, and by that means got a considerable sum of money.[13]

Turpin was baptised on 21 September 1705 at Hempstead, the son of John Turpin. Before he was 11 or 12 years old he learned 'to make letters' with James Smith at a school, apparently in Hempstead. Again, according to

Smith, he afterwards worked with his father, who was at that time himself a butcher. From this fact it would seem that any further apprenticeship in that trade might have been superfluous, and although Turpin did live at Whitechapel during the winter of 1734–35 there is no corroboration of this having been his abode at any time before then. The vexed question of whom he married is more appropriately examined in another chapter, but it can be stated that the date of his marriage is not known. What is certain is that the remainder of Richard Bayes' introduction to Turpin's criminal career is an imaginative piece of fiction designed to fill an unrecorded gap. Suson, or Sewardstone (in the parish of Waltham Abbey, Essex) as it is now known, was frequented by Turpin and the rest of the gang of which he became a member, but again this was at a later date, and reliable evidence of his ever having been a butcher at Sewardstone is non-existent. That the Farmer Giles story may be fully discounted is shewn by the fact that Turpin operated quite openly as a butcher until 1733. He was never a smuggler and his role with the deerstealers (as they were until 1734) seems almost certainly to have been limited to that of receiver when he lived at Buckhurst Hill.

The Bayes' account is a curious mixture of fact and fiction hurriedly accumulated to satisfy the post-execution demand of a gullible public, but having been used as a basis for much that has been written since, the fiction has been perpetuated, and only by careful appraisal of all the facts now available will much of this be dispelled.

Edward Saward, in reply to similar questions to those put to Smith at Turpin's trial, said that Turpin came 'backward and forward' to Hempstead, and that he had seen him frequently until five or six years before, but never since. So it is probable that Saward did not see Turpin from about the spring or summer of 1733, possibly when Turpin ceased to be a butcher at Buckhurst Hill and left that place to keep a public house. The reason for giving up his trade as butcher was almost certainly the change in fortune of the deerstealers on whom he relied for cheaper supplies of meat than on the open market. The exact cause is not known, but it was either because the supply dried up or because Turpin was suspected of involvement with the deerstealers as receiver. The complete change in employment perhaps favours the latter theory as Turpin was able to obstruct enquiries which might have been made about a butcher setting up elsewhere; and in this respect it is possible to see some affinity with the story of Farmer Giles in which Turpin was obliged to give up his trade. Such distortion of the facts is not unusual in Bayes' account, and there are a number of instances where he describes incidents which might appear to have no foundation, but which on closer examination do contain elements which can be identified with factual incidents. We do know however that Turpin did not subsequently take up smuggling, but became instead the landlord of a public house.

The most popular choice for the house in question has been the one alleged to have been managed by his grandfather. '... Turpin, whose grandfather, one Nott, kept the *Rose and Crown* by the Brook (Bull Beggar's Hole), Clay Hill.[14] This was right on the edge of Enfield Chase, which figures prominently in the next chapter. Some authors have suggested that Bull Beggar's Hole was the place stated at the trial to have been 'Boxhill or some such name', but this would seem to be very contrived, and, insofar as in the context of the trial the reference was to the place where Turpin had been a butcher, misconceived.

Robinson's claim has not been substantiated by current research, at least not in such a way that would close it to question, but there are circumstances which will be dealt with later in which Turpin is shewn in association with a man called Robert Nott. It is also quite clear that Nott was known to Turpin's wife, a factor which distinguishes him from Turpin's usual associates and points to a closer relationship between them. Thus it may be that we do not need to look far afield from Clay Hill to locate the place where Turpin played 'mine host' to the travellers he would in later years unceremoniously rob.

IX

Finally there appears once more John Fuller the lonely deerstealer. He has stood in the pillory and served his year in prison, but he has not learned his lesson, for on 2 June 1733, he, 'killed and carried off [from Waltham Forest] one red deer.'[15]

Little more is known of Fuller, but being caught on his own on two occasions suggests that he may not have been connected with any larger company operating in the forest at this time. There is nothing which would link him with those deerstealers who were known to Turpin, and we can from now on more or less disregard the comparatively humble misdemeanours of this individual, and concentrate on the men Turpin did know and who were also active in the same month.

FOOTNOTES

1. P.R.O./S.P.36/22/166. Signatures different from text. Tomson, Hide, Lea, Wootton.
2. The two most popular traditions of Turpin having been a smuggler refer to his activities in the *Hundreds of Essex,* and of his having belonged to a gang whose headquarters were in the ruins of Hadleigh Castle.
3. P.R.O./S.P.36/23,f.15 (printed).
4. P.R.O./T.53/37,p.293.
5. Middlesex Sessions. Printed Proceedings Vol.I. Sessions Paper No.3, pp.75 and 76.
6. P.R.O./Assizes 35/173/5, Surrey, Winter 6 Geo.II 1732/3; and *Political State,* Vol.LIV, p.145.
7. *Rolls of the Court of Attachments of the Royal Forest of Waltham.* Vol.I, 1713–1748. Spottiswoode & Co. 1873.
8. P.R.O./Assizes 35/174/1, Essex. Winter 7 Geo.II 1733/4.
9. P.R.O./Assizes 35/174/17, Essex. Summer 8 Geo.II 1734.
10. P.R.O./Assizes 35/173/5, Surrey, Winter 6 Geo.II 1732/3; and *Political State,* Vol.LIV, p.145.
11. P.R.O./A.O.3/1229–1230, Wine Licence Revenue Registers.
12. Essex/1740/D/AER/33/39.
13. *Life of Richard Turpin,* by Richard Bayes of the *Green Man* on Epping Forest and Others in Essex, 1739.
14. W. Robinson's *History and Antiquities of Enfield,* 1823, Vol.I, p.58, n.2.
15. P.R.O./T.53/37, p.293.

CHAPTER TWO

I

THE DEERSTEALERS were not just a bunch of wild young men who intimidated the keepers by sheer weight of noise and numbers, whooping and shooting it up as they rampaged through the forest, for there was much more to it than bravado, and the 1st Earl Tylney, Lord Warden of Waltham Forest, must have intimated as much to the Lords Commissioners of the Treasury in his letter to them on 10 June 1733. This apparently has not survived, but its impact may be deduced from measures which were taken consequently. But first there is the event which happened at Enfield Chase, Middlesex, two days after Earl Tylney's letter.

This chase is but a few miles from Epping, and was governed in similar manner to Waltham Forest by a number of keepers under the Duke of Chandos. At that time there was little between the Chase and the Forest except the River Lea, but from an account given by three of the keepers of the Chase, it might appear that they were made of sterner stuff than their counterparts across this natural boundary.

> On Tuesday the 12th of this instant June 1733 seven deerstealers entered the said Chase with fire-arms, and killed several brace of male deer; but being pursued by the Keepers and others who came to their assistance, they fled and left behind them a horse, which was taken and delivered to James Cadwallader, Bailiff of the Chase.[1]

Not much resolution there, one might think, on the part of the deerstealers, in fact not much to connect this incident with Waltham Forest, except its proximity. But that was only part of the keepers' account, and in the meantime the Lords Commissioners were deliberating on Tylney's letter, which created quite a stir in Whitehall.

At a meeting at Treasury Chambers on 14 June 1733, the Secretary to the Treasury was instructed to write to the Earl of Tylney,[2] and on the following Tuesday two things happened which in retrospect appear a little absurd in their relationship to one another. Thus firstly we have John Scrope, the Secretary to the Treasury, replying to Tylney's letter.

19 June 1733

> The Lords Commissioners of his Majesty's Treasury being made acquainted by your Lordship's letter dated the 10th instant with the great destruction of his Majesty's deer in Waltham Forest by deer stealers who as your Lordship alleges continue to come daily in such numbers and so armed that without a good reward, people will not venture their lives in apprehending them; Their Lordships have commanded me to let your Lordship know that their Lordships shall be ready upon the apprehending and convicting of any such deer stealers to pay a reward of Fifty Pounds to the person or persons who shall apprehend and prosecute to conviction every or any such deer stealer. Your Lordship may please therefore to cause a proper advertisement hereof to be inserted and continued in such public papers as your Lordship shall think fit, and the said reward shall be punctually paid upon producing here proper certificates of the said convictions, and of the names of the person or persons who shall be entitled to the same.[3]

And secondly the continuation of the Enfield Chase saga.

> On the Tuesday following, being the 19th instant, a greater number of them, armed with guns, pistols and swords, came to the house of Colonel Robinson (Chamberlain of the City of London and Receiver for the County of Middlesex, who lives in one of the lodges belonging to the said Chase) and enquired for William Wood one of the Keepers aforesaid; and he having appeared to them and desired to know their business, they told him they come to blow his brains out, and set fire to the house; for which purpose they endeavoured to force open the gate; but not being able to do it, they got upon a brick wall at some distance, and fired into the court yard and gardens, to the great terror and danger of the said William Wood, and the servants of the said Colonel Robinson who were then in and about the house. From thence they went towards the house of Turpin Mason, another of the said Keepers, and meeting his son, a young man about seventeen years of age, in their way, they fired at him several times; but he being on horse back had the good fortune to escape. When they came to the house of the said Turpin Mason, and found that the doors were locked and all the family fled, they shot his dogs, and then went to a labourer, who was at work at some distance, and having beat him in a barbarous manner with their guns, they told him they were sorry they had not found the said Turpin Mason nor his wife or children for that they designed to have murdered them. Afterwards they went into the stable to look for the horse that had been taken from them the week before, and being told that he was in the custody of James Cadwallader, Bailiff of the Chase, who lives at Barnet Wells, they went directly thither, armed as aforesaid, and by force and violence took the said horse out of the bailiff's stable and carried him off.[4]

This was without doubt the Waltham Forest gang. There was in this area no other body of men so organised that when seven were routed they could come back with possibly double the number merely to wreak vengeance. Again there is a lot of shooting and bluster; but this time they gave the dogs short shrift, beat up a harmless labourer who happened to get in the way, and retrieved the horse taken from them the previous Tuesday.

It would be satisfying to be able to say that this time Dick Turpin was with them, that he had inspired in them a sense of grievance, doubly justified because one of the Enfield keepers not only bore the name of a hated Waltham keeper, but his own as well. But no, the bounds of coincidence would be stretched too far. There was no more tolerance of keepers who thwarted the gang in Enfield than there was later for those who did so in Waltham. Mason assisted in depriving the gang of one of their horses and this was sufficient reason for threatening his life and that of his family. Had Dick Turpin been riding with the gang at this time it would have still been impossible to ascribe any other motive to their actions than one of vengeance, but he was probably still cutting meat during that violent summer.

We now know why it was necessary to increase the incentive for capturing these men. And Tylney was not slow in taking up the Treasury suggestion to advertise in the newspapers, the substance of their letter to him being reproduced as an offer of a reward as an inducement to capture deerstealers in Waltham Forest.[5]

The Enfield Keepers, having more recent experience of events which had occurred in Waltham decided that they too would apply for a little incentive. Thus, two days later, the information from which two extracts have already been given was written; and in concluding the same it is interesting to note the influence of the *Gazette* advertisement.

> ... The said Keepers do further inform, that a great number of deer stealers, supposed to be at least twelve or fourteen, do almost daily assemble together, and enter his Majesty's said Chase of Enfield with fire-arms and other dangerous weapons, and have killed and carried off great numbers of fallow deer in defiance of the said Keepers of the said Chase; and that they threaten to murder the said Keepers and others, and to destroy all the deer on the said Chase and set fire to the same; in so much that it is dangerous for his Majesty's subjects to pass through or near the said Chase about their lawful business and employments ... It is therefore humbly prayed, that his Majesty will be graciously pleased to order such a reward for apprehending and convicting of deer stealers on Enfield Chase, as is offered for the apprehending and convicting of those who have for some time past infested his Majesty's Forests of Epping and Waltham.
>
> The information of Turpin Mason, William Wood and William Crew, Keepers of his Majesty's Chase of Enfield. Taken 25th June 1733.[6]

The Duke of Chandos meanwhile had not been idle, and just over a week later he enclosed the Keepers' information in his letter to Baron Harrington, Principal Secretary of State for the Northern Province.

Cannons July 2: 1733.

> When I had the honour to wait on your Lordship, you were so good to acquaint me, you would lay before his Majesty, an account of the havoc which the deer stealers make in his Chase of Enfield; it is indeed grown to such a height, that unless there can be a stop put to it, the Chase will be all destroyed; I enclose in this the information the Keepers have given, which they are ready to attest upon oath, and entreat your Lordship will be pleased to move his Majesty, that the same reward which was promised for the taking and convicting of any of the deer stealers on Epping Forest, may be allowed in behalf of Enfield Chase; This has had a very good effect in the former, and it is to be hoped it will have the same in this.[7]

Apart from the fact that Chandos seemed unaware that from the moment Tylney wrote to the Treasury the Waltham Forest gang turned its attention to Enfield Chase, this request was not unreasonable; but the letter is a little confusing when Chandos says that the reward had had a good effect in Waltham Forest. The advertisement had only been published a week, and, despite the irony of the transfer of activities to his own domain, it was insufficient time on which to base the effect of the reward. His keepers however, were not bothered again.

Harrington did act on Chandos's letter, but not before two more days had passed and six of the Waltham Forest keepers had become encouraged to make their first significant arrest.

II

On 4 July 1733 the odds were in favour of the keepers of Waltham Forest by six to three, and inevitably perhaps, the three succumbed. William Mason Snr., William Mason Jnr., Thomas Mason, Thomas Hebborn, Thomas Hide and Henry Pater captured Abraham Downham, Robert Woodward and John Field. A fortnight later, on or about 18 July 1733, the three Masons and Henry Pater captured Joseph Rose who 'in company with the three above named did kill and destroy great numbers of deer in his Majesty's forest.' Of these four, the only one for whom descriptions can be provided are Field; who was a tall man, and Rose, a fresh coloured man, about five feet eight inches high, aged between forty and fifty, and who, in common with Samuel Gregory, was a blacksmith. These four men appeared before Carew Mildmay, Verderer of Waltham Forest, and John Goodere, Ranger of Waltham Forest, both of them Justices of the Peace for the County of Essex, and being 'examined and found guilty were legally convicted of killing and destroying great numbers of deer and committed to Chelmsford gaol.'[8]

Our understanding of the laws governing deerstealing offences, and the methods by which offenders were dealt with, is aided by one such Justice of the Peace as convicted Downham, Woodward, Field and Rose in his book on the functions of his office:

Game: Section I: Of Deer.
There have been many laws from time to time enacted against deerstealers; which being not so much altered, as inforced by the subsequent statutes, except only in increasing the penalties, it may be proper to insert them all in their order; and the rather, because an offender, as it seemeth, *may still be convicted upon any one of them;* and it is generally provided, that such conviction upon one statute, shall be as a bar to all the rest.

9. The next act is in 13 C.2 c.10. [An Act to prevent the Unlawful Coursing, Hunting or Killing of Deer] by which it is enacted, that if any person shall unlawfully course, kill, hunt, or take away any red or fallow deer, in any forest ... where deer are or have been usually kept, without consent of the owner ... or shall be aiding or assisting therein; and shall be convicted thereof by confession or oath of one witness, before one justice, in six months after the offence committed, he shall forfeit for every offence £20, half to the informer and half to the owner of the deer, by distress; for want of sufficient distress, to be committed to the house of correction for six months to hard labour, or to the common gaol for one year; and not to be discharged thence, till he hath given sureties for his good behaviour for a year next after his enlargement...

10. The next act is the 3 W. c.10 [An Act for the More Effectual Discovery and Punishment of Deerstealers] on which most of the convictions have been since that time; which (together with the alterations and additions made in and to the same by the 5 G. c.15 ...) is as followeth:

If any person shall unlawfully ... kill, wound, or take away, any red or fallow deer, in any forest ... and shall be convicted thereof, in 12 months after the offence, by confession or oath of one witness, before one justice where the offence shall be committed, or the party apprehended: every such person ... and in case any deer shall by such person be wounded, ... or killed, he shall ... for want of sufficient distress ... be imprisoned for a year, and set in the pillory an hour on some market day in the next adjoining town to the place where the offence was committed, by the chief officer of such market town, or his under officer.[9]

The acts are hereafter abbreviated to 13 Charles II and 3 W. & M. Both are relevant to events which occurred after July 1733, and are useful in determining the length of sentences which were imposed on offenders. For example, the Act 3 W. & M. and no other makes provision for offenders to be set in the pillory; we know therefore that John Fuller must have been convicted under that statute, and similarly in a later case where the only information we possess is that the offender was set in the pillory, we can assume that he was also sentenced to a year's imprisonment. Record of these summary convictions does not appear to have survived except in the forest keepers' claims to rewards which were passed to the Treasury Solicitor for his consideration. These do give some details, but are not always consistent in their coverage of events.

The surprising thing here is that although the authorities were dealing with an obviously violent crew, they only provided incentive for their capture. It was not until 1737, when the Act of 3 W. & M. was amended by 10 Geo. II, c.32, s.7–9, that the penalty of seven years transportation in cases of armed deerstealing was introduced to act as an additional deterrent. Deerstealing was a domestic offence which whilst it did not infringe civil laws was not judged in civil courts, but before Justices of the Peace who (in Essex at least) appear for the most part to have been senior forestry officials as well.

When one considers the savage punishments which were provided for comparatively innocuous offences tried before other courts, it can only be said of the authorities that they were, in respect of deerstealing of this magnitude, a little complacent in resting content on capture. For although the crime itself was a humble enough breach of the law, the manner in which it was committed and the period in which it continued unchecked were surely matters which might have been the proper consideration of a higher court.

But although the laws were no doubt inadequate, the authorities on this occasion were determined at least to put a temporary stop to the slaughter. By 18 July the Keepers had bagged four deerstealers, and on 20 July, in response to Chandos's letter at the beginning of that month, 'A General Council was held [at Hampton Court] and his Majesty ordered a proclamation to be issued promising a reward of fifty pounds for every deer-stealer that should be apprehended and convicted of destroying the deer in *any* of his Majesty's chases or forests.'[10]

On 8 August, the Keepers' claim for the reward was forwarded to the Treasury Solicitor,[11] and if one wonders at the rapidity with which they made themselves eligible it is only fair to reiterate the words of John Scrope, apparently quoting Tylney, '...without a good reward, people will not venture their lives in apprehending them.' On 11 August, John Fuller was captured a second time by Henry Thompson, Under Keeper of New Lodge Walk in Waltham Forest. He was taken before Richard Lestock, J.P., convicted of the June offence, and taken by Joseph Barrd, the constable, to Chelmsford gaol.[12]

III

Of the women in this account we have heard nothing as yet, but the first to come to our notice is Turpin's wife. James Smith, the man who brought about Turpin's denouement and was a principal witness at his trial, stated in evidence, 'I knew his father and all his relations, he married one of my father's maids.' The evidence of marriage has still to be discovered, but Turpin did not marry at Hempstead. Similarly, the evidence is negative in those places with which his wife's name has been traditionally associated.

There are two contemporary versions of this elusive young woman's name. In *Life of Richard Turpin,* by Richard Bayes and others in Essex, she is said to have been 'the daughter of one Palmer.' But in an 'Extract from a letter from York, dated March 2nd 1739', there appears the following passage:

> ... several more letters were intercepted ... and [he, Turpin] desires them [unspecified relatives] to persuade his cousin Betty Millington to do something for him, it being the last she may ever do. Now his wife's maiden name was Millington.[13]

Neither of these versions is corroborated elsewhere and of the two, Bayes' is the less reliable, this particular account being more given to invention than the other. The letter from York was unsigned, and without some knowledge about the author it is impossible to determine if he was in a position to know such details of Turpin's relations, but although apparently sent from York the letter does reflect a surprising familiarity with Turpin's domestic relationships, and on this evidence may well have been written by James Smith. Of the passage itself it can only be said that it contains a clear implication that his cousin was in fact his wife.

Turpin wrote the fatal letter which gave his identity away early in February 1739. James Smith did not make the actual identification until 23 February, and until that time Turpin did not know that his alias was a useless cloak to his real identity. It may be assumed therefore that he continued writing letters in the name of Palmer and if this was so he could hardly refer to his wife by her own name. The letter from York dated 2 March suggests that these other letters from Turpin were intercepted not long after the first. This may well have been if the authorities hoped to have written confirmation of Turpin's identity, but it is clear that they did not get it since only the first was exhibited as evidence, and that but briefly. The heavy emphasis of the 'something', 'being the last she may ever do', is significant of past favours more likely to have been obtained from a wife than a cousin, and the information 'Now his wife's maiden name was Millington,' is perhaps superfluous.

The other reason why preference should be given to Betty Millington rather than Hester Palmer (the Hester apparently being a Christian name invented by subsequent authors to go with the Palmer of Bayes' creation) is reflected in a vital piece of evidence which goes half way towards corroborating the Betty Millington claim, and which is itself corroborated elsewhere.

> Elizabeth, wife of Turpin the butcher, was committed to gaol on suspicion of being a dangerous rogue and of robbing upon the highway.

Elizabeth Turpin was committed in company with a man called Robert Nott, a fact which not only supports the claim to her name having been 'Betty' Millington, but also points to the landlord of the inn at Clay Hill near Enfield having been Turpin's grandfather. For the moment that is as much as can be said about Elizabeth Turpin. Her name does not appear frequently in this account, and not a great deal more is known about her. In the autumn of 1733 we can do little more than assume that she was helping mine host Turpin at the inn of which he may have been landlord at this time.

But the other woman we introduce at this point is one of the principal associates of the Gregory Gang, and it is probable that October 1733 was the month when she first became acquainted with at least one of them. Her name then, before she assumed several aliases, was Mary Brassier *or* Brazier, and it is probable that she lived at Southchurch, near Leigh in Essex, for this is where she first came to be noticed by the authorities.

On 1 October 1733 Mary Brazier went stealing. Since the items stolen were small and personal it is possible they were, for the most part, picked from pockets or sneak-thieved. Whatever the method, she relieved three people of certain possessions, and circumstances point to the felonies having been committed in some public place like a market.

Charles Graham, clerk, was the first to suffer. Mary stole from him a cambric handkerchief and a damask clout, worth two shillings, and tenpence respectively. Peter Morebeck was next, losing a diaper napkin (presumably of the patterned variety) and a lace handkerchief, worth 1s. and 5s. respectively. And from Ann Turford, widow, was taken a holland smock worth 5s. Stealing from one or other of these people proved to be her undoing because she was arrested and placed in Chelmsford gaol,[14] where four of the deerstealers were already confined. If she did not meet with them in the prison, there can be no doubt at all that she met them within days of their release, and that circumstance is by itself suggestive of previous acquaintance. Chelmsford gaol does not appear to have been much different from others of the period, and even if segregation was observed opportunity for the two sexes to meet no doubt existed or could be arranged. In fact, not so very long before the deerstealers were committed the gaoler, and his officers went in fear of their lives of the smugglers confined there, and admitted as much in a petition for assistance to prevent their escaping. It is important to establish how Mary

Brazier may have become one of the gang, because she was by no means a merely pretty bystander when its members turned to more violently criminal pursuits.

IV

On 24 October 1733 Henry Thompson's claim for rewards for twice catching John Fuller was referred to the Treasury Solicitor. Thompson was in fact claiming both the reward of £10 offered in 1731 and the £50 offered by advertisement and proclamation in June and July 1733. This was a substantial sum of money, and despite evidence of the deerstealers' behaviour when out in force some might think that Thompson was perhaps exaggerating a little when he stated that he 'did, at great hazard and peril of his life, apprehend John Fuller,' a solitary deerstealer.[15] Were these men really desperate individuals, so desperate they might kill if cornered? Two days after Thompson made this contention, it was proved in startling fashion on a busy London street.

V

On the 26th [October] one William Johnson, who had served his apprenticeship to a cooper in London, had the assurance, notwithstanding warrants being out against him for deer-stealing, to ride through the City about four o'clock in the afternoon with a sack full of venison before him; but being known by some persons in the streets, two men laid hold of him as he was passing through Budge Row; and they having pulled him from his horse, one Thomas Tanner, his companion, came to his rescue, whereupon a great struggle ensued, and at last the said Johnson got loose, left his horse, and betook himself to his heels, but was pursued with an outcry of his being a deer-stealer: Upon finding himself pursued he pulled out a long knife and pistol, and with the knife drawn in one hand, and the pistol cocked in the other, he ran as far as Hind Court in Thames Street, before any man dared to touch him; at last one James Tarman, a carman belonging to a dung wharf seized him by the collar, and refusing to quit his hold, Johnson fired, and shot him through the head; by this most dangerous weapon being made useless, and his pursuers more irritated, he was soon after seized, secured, and disarmed; and both he and his companion were committed to Newgate. The poor carman lived till next day about noon, and then expired; so that Johnson was charged in prison with murder as well as deer-stealing.[16]

Johnson was committed on the oath of John Griffin and others for firing a pistol at James Tarman, who was shot in the neck and died.[17] For this humble labourer the reward of £50 would have been a fortune. The lure of it lost him his life. It was a calculated incentive and there can no longer be any doubt that the deerstealers of Waltham Forest were desperate men who did not hesitate to give short shrift to those who dared to oppose them.

FOOTNOTES

1. P.R.O./S.P.36/29 f.281.
2. P.R.O./T.29/27 p.196.
3. P.R.O./T.27/25 p.171
4. P.R.O. /S.P.36/29 f.281
5. *London Gazette,* 19—23 June 1735.
6. P.R.O./S.P.36/29 f.281.
7. P.R.O./S.P.36/30 f.4.
8. P.R.O./T.53/37 pp.288—291
9. *Justice of the Peace and Parish Officer,* by Richard Burn, Clerk: one of his Majesty's Justices of the Peace for the County of Westmorland. 3rd Edition, 1756, p.311
10. *London Gazette,* No.7214 [my italics]
11. P.R.O./T.4/11 p.11 (IND. 4625)
12. P.R.O./T.53/37 pp.293—295.
13. *Political State,* Vol.LVII, pp.191—194, taken from *General Evening Post,* 8 March 1739.
14. P.R.O./Assizes 35/174/1, Essex, Winter 7 Geo.II 1733/4.
15. P.R.O./T.4/11 (IND. 4625), p.15.
16. *Political State,* Vol.XLVI, pp.456—457.
17. Guildhall, London Sessions, Gaol Delivery 5 December 1733.

CHAPTER THREE

I

IT DOES not follow that all the men of the company known subsequently as the Gregory Gang were deerstealers, and one who probably became associated with them by some other means was Herbert Haines. Haines was of pale complexion, about five feet seven inches tall, wore a brown wig, and was about twenty-two years of age in 1733. In December of that year he was described as a labourer, but during 1734 he was employed as a barber or perriwig maker, which appears to have been his trade. The one thing he may have had in common with the others was a familiarity with the East End of London, for Haines lived in Shoreditch.

In December 1733 Haines and a man called West Drake were suspected of stealing a quart silver tankard from the dwelling house of one John Sharrat of the Liberty of Norton Folgate in Shoreditch. Haines was arrested and committed by Anthony Chamberlain Esq. to Hick's Hall in St. John's Street. Drake was never caught.[1] On 5 December, Haines was removed from Hick's Hall to Newgate and from thence to the Old Bailey to stand trial at the General Sessions. He and Drake were indicted 'that [they] on the first of December 7 George II ... one silver tankard of the value of nine pounds of the goods and chattels of one John Sharrat [previously rendered *Sharrol* in the Calendar] in the dwelling house of him the said John did steal &c.'[2]

The witnesses were John Sharrat, James Winter and Randall Halmark, but Haines was acquitted. James Tarman's killer, who was tried on the same day, also at the Old Bailey, was not so lucky. William Johnson, described as a labourer, was indicted with murder. He pleaded not guilty, but was convicted and sentenced to be hanged. No mention was made of his deerstealing involvement.[3]

II

It would have been a cold, dank Waltham Forest in December 1733. The trees, some time since denuded, would have offered scant cover to any deerstealers prepared to brave the conditions and the keepers. But on 19 December five men, induced by circumstances we can only imagine, entered the forest, ostensibly to make off with some more of his Majesty's dwindling herd. They were met by an equal number of keepers and, as a result, spent Christmas in Chelmsford gaol. The keepers involved were William Mason Snr., William Mason Jnr., Thomas Mason, Thomas Heybourne and Henry Painter; the same five responsible for the July captures, except that then, they were assisted by Thomas Hide. One of these keepers subsequently had good cause to remember the date when the deerstealers were committed.

They were taken before the same Justices of the Peace who dealt with those caught in July, but in neither of these cases was the actual sentence described in the document which refers to both incidents. From subsequent events however it is clear that Field, Downham, Woodward and Rose served a year for the July offences, but since the source of information (covering September 1733–September 1734), which supplies evidence of one of their known associates having been pilloried, does not make any reference to them, it is to be assumed that they were sentenced to one year in the common gaol under the Act of 13 Charles II, which did not make provision for deerstealers to be pilloried.

Similar factors suggest that Philip Onyon, Edward Brook, John Pateman, George Hicks and John Croot, the five captured in December 1733, were convicted under the same Act and sentenced to the same term of imprisonment, but their names, except in connection with their capture, will not be met with again during this account. They may have been released in December 1734; what happened to them after that is not known, but they were not actively involved in the subsequent criminal activities of the other deerstealers.[4]

III

In the condemned hold of Newgate, William Johnson spent an even more miserable festive season, with the prospect of a bleaker new year to follow. At the London Sessions of 16 January 1734, he was described in the *Calendar of London Prisoners upon Orders* as 'William Johnson attainted last Sessions of felony and murder and received sentence of death,' annotated 'Executed'.[5] And having made Johnson an example of the extreme violence of which the

The Gregory Gang

deerstealers were capable, there would ordinarily be no great purpose in mentioning him further were it not for his name having been used subsequently as an alias by Samuel Gregory. This may of course have been coincidence, but Samuel Gregory was a deerstealer, and moreover was not the only member of the gang to adopt the name Johnson as an alias. It may be that his friends, insensitive to ill omens, chose to perpetuate his name in this manner.

IV

Having obtained the certificates of conviction of the deerstealers from the Justices of the Peace, the six Keepers of Waltham Forest sent their claim for the rewards to the Lords Commissioners of the Treasury. They in turn instructed their Secretary to forward the claim to the Treasury Solicitor, Nicholas Paxton, for his consideration, who in his turn returned a comprehensive report to the Commissioners on 14 February 1734.[6]

In this he referred to the certificates of conviction, the various advertisements and proclamations under which the rewards were offered, and concluded by recommending that if their Lordships thought fit the Keepers were entitled to the reward money, and should receive it in the following manner:

> By the 1731 proclamation a total of £50 was due to the three Masons, Heybourne *or* Hebborne, and Painter *or* Pater, being £10 each for the conviction of Onyon, Brook, Pateman, Hicks and Croot in December 1733.

> By the proclamation of 1733 a total of £200 was due to the same five, with Thomas Hide *or* Hyde, being £50 each in respect of Downham, Woodward, Field and Rose, convicted in July 1733.

V

Ten deerstealers had by this time been caught and imprisoned, but there may have been double that number engaged in such activities. Another of them was Jeremy Gregory. In November 1731 his gun was confiscated. In November 1732 a man was the victim of a shooting incident with which Jeremy's name was later associated. Between 19 December 1733 (after which the keepers claimed for the rewards upon conviction of all the other deerstealers to that date captured) and 6 March following (by which time Jeremiah Gregory stood indicted of another offence), William Mason Snr., Thomas Roades, John [Attreidge] and John Mugaredg 'did apprehend

Jeremiah Gregory at Hackney ... [They] ventured their lives in taking him ... he being a very desperate fellow [having] a pistol in his hand when [taken].[7]

A claim for the reward for his conviction was referred to Paxton for his consideration at a date *after* 6 March 1734,[8] and since Gregory stood indicted at and was included in the Gaol Delivery for Chelmsford of that date, it appears his capture must have occurred between 19 December 1733 and 6 March 1734, possibly in January 1734. These circumstances become clearer in the next passage.

VI

On 6 March 1734, Jeremiah Gregory and Joseph Rose stood indicted for shooting at one John (Henry in the indictment) Deakins in a dwelling house, and were ordered to remain until discharged. On the same day the Sheriff of Essex was served with a writ commanding him to seek out John Coster (also named in the indictment) of the parish of Chingford (where the shooting occurred) to answer the same charge.

From this it is clear that Gregory and Rose, both in Chelmsford gaol serving sentences of deerstealing, were brought up in March and indicted but not tried upon charges brought against them *since* they were committed in (?)January 1734 and July 1733 respectively. Coster being at large would not have affected a March trial because once indicted he could have been tried at any time once captured. The trial of Gregory and Rose was probably held over until they had completed the sentences imposed upon them for deerstealing. In Rose's case, if as has been assumed he was serving a year, he would have been released in July 1734. Jeremy Gregory was tried with him then, which suggests that he was convicted under the 13 Charles II Act and sentenced, perhaps in January, to six months hard labour; his release would then have coincided with Rose's, and there was no obstacle to their both standing trial in July, as indicted in March, upon the more serious charge. The March indictment upon which they were tried in July described their alleged offence as follows: 'Jeremiah Gregory, Joseph Rose and John Coster, labourers, on the 28th of November 1732, did shoot at Henry Deakins, (lately deceased) in a house at Chingford.'

The witnesses sworn in court were William Rogers, Henry Deakins, William Peirson and Thomas Hyde, the latter probably the Waltham Forest keeper of that name, previously mentioned. There seems good reason to suppose that as Henry Deakins appeared as a witness, the deceased's name was John Deakins *or* Deakin as stated in the March gaol delivery. This was not the only confusion arising from the charges being brought so long after the event. The six, being the year of the reign in the indictment, was an alteration, it no doubt having been originally written as seven, which would have dated the offence in the November of the previous year. This was not so as Rose for one was in Chelmsford gaol at that time.

So Gregory and Rose, both left with about the same time to serve, could only look forward to being tried for a much more serious offence when their sentences were completed.[9]

VII

At the same Assize at which Gregory and Rose were indicted, Mary Brazier stood trial upon two indictments for stealing various articles (previously described) from Charles Graham, Peter Morebeck and Ann Turford on 1 October 1733.[10] On the first count of stealing from Graham and Morebeck, the witnesses sworn were Margaret Morebeck and Priscilla Graham, and John Corbey respectively (the victims' names appeared first but these were struck through). On the second count Ann Turford, Priscilla Graham and John Gorbey (*sic*) were the witnesses. Mary was found not guilty on the second count but judgement was given on the first on the conviction of stealing a damask clout worth 10d. from Charles Graham. The *Gaol Delivery* recorded the judgement as follows: 'Mary Brazier (and others) convicted on several pleas must be openly whipped on their backs till their bodies are bloody.

VIII

On 29 April 1734 the Treasury Commissioners decided the claims for rewards for the capture of deerstealers and their conviction in July and December of the previous year. They allowed rewards totalling £200 under the terms of the 1733 proclamation, but were blunt in refusing others promised in the 1731 proclamation, which were for accomplices discovering their associates. The proclamation of 19 July 1733 however did make provision for persons other than accomplices, and if the apprehender brought about conviction for offences committed between 20 May 1733 and 29 September 1734, then he was entitled to the reward. This is why the keepers were successful in respect of this claim and not the other. The original claim might have shed some light on the reasons why Paxton made distinction between the cases, because his report does not. It can only be assumed that the offences for which Onion and his four friends were. convicted were committed before 20 May 1733. If this was so, then at the time of their capture in December they may well have been caught taking nothing more than an innocent ride through the forest.

On the same day the Commissioners made the same distinction in respect of Henry Thompson's claim for twice capturing John Fuller. Paxton had made his report on this case (although the claim was submitted some time before in October) at the same time as the others, therefore all were dealt with simultaneously at Treasury Chambers.[11]

The last claim made for rewards came from William Mason Snr. and Messrs. Roades, Attreidge and Mugaredg for the capture and conviction of Jeremy Gregory at Hackney. This claim was referred to Paxton on 20 June 1734, but so far as is known the Treasury Solicitor did not make a report, either at that time, or subsequently.[12]

IX

With eleven deerstealers in Chelmsford gaol, things were much quieter in Waltham Forest than they had been the previous summer. But towards the end of summer in 1734, Jeremy Gregory and Joseph Rose, having completed their sentences for deerstealing, were obliged to stand trial on the indictment which had been hanging over them since the previous March. On 31 July they were brought up at Chelmsford Assizes to answer the charge of shooting at Deakins. The writ to the Sheriff (dated March 6) was produced and endorsed: 'John Coster is not found in my Bailywick,' and the case proceeded against Gregory and Rose. The witnesses sworn were William Rogers, Henry Deakins, William Peirson and Tomas Hyde. The shooting was alleged to have occurred in November 1732 and contrary to appearances, Gregory and Rose *were* charged with the offence at the earliest opportunity after the event, viz. before the Grand Jury at the first Assize after two of them were taken into custody for other offences. If they had been convicted of deerstealing *before* July 1733, they would perhaps have been arraigned on the shooting charge at the Summer Assize of *that* year.

There were persons willing to testify against them, who did come forward once they had been caught. One of them ostensibly a relative of the deceased victim, another with the same name as and possibly the same Forest Keeper who has been mentioned previously. The names of the other two are not familiar, but there is no reason to suppose at this stage that they were anything other than law-abiding citizens seeking justice.

But at this same Assize something rather odd occurred, for the past was raked up again and another almost forgotten incident brought to light. Three weeks after the Deakins affair, John Boston had sustained a fatal injury when a bullet penetrated his skull as he was riding through Wanstead. At the

Coroner's inquest it was found that he languished nine hours before he died, and the jury brought in a verdict of 'killed or murdered by a person or persons unknown.' At the same Assize at which Gregory and Rose were tried for shooting at Deakins, a witness against them, William Rogers, appeared charged with killing Boston. The witnesses against Rogers were Jeremy Gregory, Mary Brazier, Abraham Woodward and Mary Bryant. Who the last named woman was we do not know, but the first three names look strange when ranged against a prosecution witness who was to testify against one of them.

Was there a conspiracy here to pervert the course of justice? There is no hint of this in the old parchment records, nothing but the formal wording of the indictment, 'William Rogers of Wanstead on the 16th of December 1732 did shoot and kill John Boston the bullet penetrating three inches into his skull he died instantly.'

The fact that the inquest jury found that he lingered nine hours before he expired is by the way, all that matters here is that Rogers was found not guilty and discharged.

The judgement against Gregory and Rose was the same as against Rogers, so how did they obtain an acquittal? Rogers is the key. He was named in March as a witness against the two deerstealers, the charge brought against him by them was not made until July. The reason for doing this must have been that they hoped to intimidate Rogers; and to do so there must have been some foundation to their charges. Not only did Gregory and the others have knowledge of the manner of Boston's death, they had some detailed knowledge which could be used to implicate Rogers. When this becomes apparent one wonders if Rogers in any way anticipated the countercharges which were brought against him, whether he in fact realised what he was getting into when he agreed to testify against Gregory and Rose.

Because the deceased's relative and a possible Keeper of Waltham Forest were fellow witnesses against the deerstealers, we have assumed that the charges arising from the Deakin's incident were straightforward, and that the testimony of all the witnesses would be valid, but it is possible that Rogers and his fellow witnesses had some axe to grind against Gregory and Rose, and that when those two were found to be in prison they took the opportunity to bring a really serious charge against them. There is a reasonable possibility that this did occur, but several years elapse before the evidence appears which suggests that it could have actually happened in such a way.

At the Assizes held at Chelmsford at Lent 1739 a man called William Rogers was tried on three indictments for shooting at or assaulting various Keepers or their servants on three occasions between 6 July and 10

September 1738. A man called Nimpous Fuller was also charged with Rogers on one of the assault indictments, but was acquitted. Rogers was sentenced to death for shooting at Samuel Mason. All the offences took place in Waltham Forest, apparently whilst Rogers was bent on stealing deer.

This is interesting information in that it relates to one William Rogers, a deerstealer with a tendency to violence when cornered; but is there anything else which might distinguish him from other men with similar inclinations? The Sheriff of Essex, some time after Rogers had been executed, craved allowance of the following expenses incurred when Rogers was convicted:

> ... for conveying William Rogers (and others) under a very strong guard to the place of execution and executing them pursuant to their sentence. A great number of guards and ancillaries being obliged to be had for fear of William Rogers being rescued he being a notorious deerstealer and against many of his gang being there £10.10s. 0d.

Nimpous Fuller was acquitted of complicity in the second indictment against Rogers, but the Sheriff's cravings for the same year in which the expenses for Rogers' execution appeared shows him to have been in trouble again. He was taken from Chelmsford to Waltham Abbey and stood in the pillory but to prevent any attempt at rescue, the Sheriff and twenty-five men were obliged to be present; the cost of the day's outing being £18 18s. 0d.

The expenses claimed were incurred during the year 29 September 1738 to 29 September 1739. Fuller was discharged at the Lent Assize 1739 and did not appear at all at the Summer Assize. From this it would appear that he was sentenced by another court, possibly by J.P.'s in circumstances similar to those in which the earlier deerstealers were tried.

It is clear that both Fuller and Rogers were regarded as dangerous men who possessed lawless friends capable of and willing to attempt to rescue them should the opportunity arise. That a small army of twenty-five men was needed to escort Fuller is a remarkable reflection of the authorities' fears on this score. There was in fact a precedent which may have inspired a certain amount of exaggerated caution in these two instances, brought about when one of the earlier deerstealers was rescued from the pillory. But how does this later evidence concerning Rogers and Fuller affect what happened at Chelmsford Assizes held in the summer of 1734?

There is one factor to consider. Were William Rogers, witness against Gregory and Rose, William Rogers indicted with the shooting of John Boston, and William Rogers the deerstealer one and the same person or three separate identities? It has been assumed that the first two in fact were because the deerstealers would not have volunteered evidence against William Rogers unless they had some good reason, and the only William Rogers who could

The Gregory Gang

have given them good reason was the one who was going to testify against them. So was this Rogers the deerstealer who was hung in 1739? A witness appearing for the Rogers who stood indicted in that year, said that he had known him between five and seven years and that he used to steal a deer now and then. So Rogers could have been a deerstealer from 1732 onwards, the year in which the two shooting incidents took place. He seems also to have had an itchy trigger finger, and it has already been observed that, without necessarily being guilty of shooting Boston, the Rogers who was indicted of the offence was vulnerable to the charge. Furthermore, Rogers, the leader, and Nimpous Fuller, were notorious deerstealers in a gang whose other members were thought to be capable of rescuing them from the gallows and the pillory respectively. And upon the indictment made against them at the Lent Assize 1739, these two appear to have achieved this respected status by July 1738, just three years after the earlier gang of deerstealers and robbers had been eliminated from the vicinity of Waltham Forest. And on the first and third indictments against Rogers at the same Assize, there appears the name of Henry Thompson, one of the Keepers of the forest. In 1731 and 1733 a Henry Thompson was Under Keeper of New Lodge Walk in Waltham Forest, and in those years he caught a deerstealer by name of John Fuller. Now Roger's chief associate was Nimpous Fuller, and although he was not necessarily related to John Fuller, there is every appearance here of Rogers and the latter Fuller being thorns in the flesh of the same Thompson who was previously aggravated by John Fuller. The evidence is circumstantial but even so it would be extremely difficult to prove that William Rogers the deerstealer hung in 1739 was *not* the same William Rogers who was involved with the other deerstealers at the Summer Assize in 1734. And if this was so, does the fact help to clarify the events of 1732 and 1734? It helps to make more sense of them than was possible before and also lends greater credibility to a theory which would otherwise have had no more substance than fiction.

In November 1732 William Rogers, in company with John and Henry Deakins, and William Pierson, was present in a house at Chingford when an argument arose between Jeremy Gregory, Joseph Rose and John Coster, and one of the Deakins men. A shot was fired at Deakins, a fact which caused considerable enmity and malice between the two parties.

Rogers, like Gregory and Rose, was a deerstealer, and if he and his friends were not rivals of these two before, they were after this incident had occurred. Three weeks later the two factions or certain members of each confronted each other at Wanstead, on the highway from Woodford to London. Further argument ensued and again a shot was fired, this time, possibly, by Rogers. The bullet however hit John Boston, a passing traveller, and gave him a head wound which was to prove fatal. The rival factions forgot their argument and went to his aid, but on finding the wound to be so serious panicked and ran away. Neither faction stood to gain anything by informing on the other at this time because they were both involved, and the incident was ignored until Gregory and Rose were imprisoned for deerstealing. In the meantime the rivalry was no doubt maintained, but even so the first shooting incident might not have been resurrected had not John Deakins died. Although there is no evidence of his death being the result of a wound inflicted during the shooting incident, this may well have been the case; and if this was so, then Henry Deakins may have felt some urge to prosecute those responsible. Having lived a year or eighteen months after the shooting there might have been some difficulty in proving he died as a direct result of it, in which case Henry Deakins could have had second thoughts about charging the three responsible with murder. But desiring some retribution and being convinced he would obtain as much on a conviction for shooting at a person on enclosed premises as he would on a conviction for murder, he preferred the shooting charge instead. William Peirson was recruited as a witness, and Thomas Hyde, although his testimony may well have been restricted to identification of the persons charged since, at least in the case of Rose, he was one of the last persons to see him before he was imprisoned for deerstealing. And it is in such circumstances that Rogers, so vulnerable to a countercharge, may have been persuaded, albeit unwillingly, to testify against Gregory and Rose.

Who else could have belonged to the Rogers' band? The five captured in December 1733, who had never been heard of previously and were never heard of again? It is possible, but it is more likely that they were less committed members of the Gregory faction. Not only were they captured by the same Keepers who captured Jeremy Gregory, Rose, Fielder and the others; but on the occasion of the anniversary of the committal of those five to prison, the Gregory gang chose to perform a savage act of reprisal on one of the Keepers. This may have been a coincidence but it is more significant of an association with Gregory than with Rogers.

It is impossible to expand further on the theme of a rivalry, but there is a final point concerning the Rogers and Gregory factions. The course of justice at the Summer Assize has every appearance of having been perverted although it is a moot point whether or not Gregory and Rose had much choice but to do what they did. What really matters here is the strength of their allegations that Rogers shot Boston, because although there no doubt was a second confrontation between the two factions, there remains a possibility that Gregory or one of his companions shot Boston, and that Rogers was accused of the offence because their own lives were in danger. One piece of evidence which supports this theory is the appearance of Mary Brazier as a witness against Rogers.

Until she was brought to Chelmsford in October 1733 there is no evidence that she had ever been in any other part of Essex except Southchurch. Here, a long way removed in time and distance from Wanstead in 1732, she apparently lived and stole, and remained until her arrest. This is the place (and there is corroboration of the fact) with which she was most familiar and to which her thoughts returned even after she had formed her association with Rose and adopted his name; although so far as is known she did not return to live there after her conviction in March 1734. Subsequent to that date her real name was usually qualified with the alias Rose. When caught and first convicted she was known only as Brazier. If she had been Rose's companion from the time of the Boston manslaughter until his arrest in July 1733, she would during that time have been domiciled in East London or some other part of it adjoining Waltham Forest in Essex. To have left the area and returned to Southchurch when Rose was imprisoned, only to be reunited with him at Chelmsford in October would seem to be an unlikely coincidence.

The facts suggest that Mary Brazier was not in or near Wanstead in December 1732, and therefore cannot have been a witness to the Boston shooting. So unless there was some other extraordinary reason for her giving testimony against Rogers, she committed perjury. There were four witnesses, and if it was necessary for her to perjure herself, the evidence of the other three would appear to be either inconclusive or suspect. On these grounds it seems clear there was a conspiracy to intimidate Rogers into persuading Deakins, Peirson and Hyde that unless Gregory and Rose went into court knowing they would be acquitted, he himself stood a good chance of being convicted of their countercharge. The conspiracy succeeded, the course of justice was perverted, and all the deerstealers involved in those two cases were released to follow their separate ways. The date was 31 July 1734, it was high summer and time for the deerstealers to take stock of the situation in Waltham Forest and consider their future.[13]

X

By the Autumn of 1734 the position of the villains was as follows:—

1. Samuel Gregory, a blacksmith, last heard of at Edgware in 1732, but now a deerstealer.

2. Thomas Rowden, a pewterer, acquitted of counterfeiting in 1733, but by now probably familiar with the deerstealers.
3. Jeremy Gregory, a convicted deerstealer, acquitted of shooting John Deakins and released from Chelmsford gaol in July 1734. Brother of Samuel Gregory, possibly younger than he.
4. Richard Turpin, butcher and more recently landlord of an inn. Friends and acquaintances in Hempstead have not seen him for some time. May have received venison from the deerstealers when working as a butcher, and might by now have joined them.
5. John Field, convicted deerstealer, probably released July 1734.
6. Abraham Downham, the same.
7. Robert Woodward, the same.
8. Joseph Rose, convicted deerstealer; tried with Jeremy Gregory on a charge of shooting at John Deakins, acquitted and released from gaol in July 1734.
9. John Fuller, twice convicted deerstealer. If serving a year upon his last conviction would have been due for release in August 1734. Not a known associate of any of the above, but may have been one of William Rogers', below.
10. William Rogers, deerstealer and witness against Jeremy Gregory and Joseph Rose. Tried and acquitted of a charge of killing John Boston. Probably a rival of the Gregory and Rose faction.
11. Mary Brazier, convicted of stealing and whipped in March 1734. Presumed to have met Joseph Rose in prison and become his companion subsequently. Believed to have given perjured evidence against William Rogers on the charge of shooting John Boston.
12. Herbert Haines, a barber or perriwig maker, acquitted of stealing a silver tankard in December 1733. By now keeps a Barber's shop in Hog Lane, Shoreditch; and has probably begun an affair with the wife of John Carroll, a tradesman whom he had formerly served as a journeyman.[14]
13. William Johnson, deerstealer. Convicted of murder and executed in January 1734. Possible carrier for Gregory gang.
14. West Drake, companion of Herbert Haines. Fled.
15. John Coster, companion of Jeremy Gregory and Rose. Fled.
16. John Gassey *alias* Gaskey, companion of Thomas Rowden. Fled.
17. William Falconer *or* Faulkener, companion of Thomas Rowden. Turned King's Evidence against Rowden and then went his own way. Is heard of subsequently.
18–22. Philip Onyon *or* Onion, Edward Brook, John Pateman, George Hicks and John Croot. All convicted deerstealers, probably due for release from Chelmsford gaol in December 1734.

Discounting the deceased Johnson, and Rogers (with whom we are not further concerned), exactly half of the remaining twenty persons were never heard of again. Fuller and Falconer were, but not in the particular context with which we are concerned. The other eight all became prominent members of the Essex or Gregory Gang. In the case of Drake, Coster and Gassey, all fled, their acquaintance appears to have been so fleeting and their flight so sudden, it may be presumed they did not return. Where Downham and Woodward and the last five deerstealers are concerned it is not possible to dismiss them so easily, and it may be that at least the first two resumed their association with the criminal element, if only briefly.

What of Samuel Gregory and Richard Turpin, both of officially unblemished records? Gregory is the more enigmatic figure. The one obvious physical characteristic which did distinguish him from his fellows was the scar upon his cheek, almost as good, when it came to writing about him, as a black patch over the left eye.

When and where did Gregory get this scar? According to an uncorroborated newspaper account[15], it resulted from a wound inflicted on him by a horse. The information suggests that the smithy where the accident occurred was in Buckinghamshire, and if the story is true, then it is conceivable that the accident happened before Gregory was employed at Edgware. By then he would have been about nineteen, and assuming that that was not his first job, then the likelihood is that the accident occurred when he was younger and less experienced. But even so the scar, one and a half inches long, would not have automatically qualified him as leader of the gang, and this is what Gregory is reputed to have been.

The *written* evidence supporting this reputation is inconclusive. He was a deerstealer but the evidence of the fact comes very late during the period when his associates were active and there is nothing to indicate whether or not they relied on his initiative in that sphere. When they became a robber gang and their names ultimately became common knowledge, the gang was still called 'the Essex Gang', or with various qualifications 'the gang that ...' When Gregory for a time survived the denouement which broke the gang, the newspaper space allotted him increased proportionately the longer he remained at large. But even so, categorical allusions to his leadership were still mingled with such references as 'the gang with Gregory', or 'one of the gang with Gregory and others', and it was not until finally he was captured, tried and executed that the definitives 'his gang' or 'Gregory's gang' became general.

The only official recognition of his leadership was given somewhat obscurely when another survivor was captured and described as 'one of Gregory's gang'. This was almost a year after his death and in Essex, but it does not really prove the point. One isolated official reference, at the right time, perhaps stemming from Whitehall, would have been worth all the subsequent newspaper attributes, but since his leadership was only acknowledged by degrees, one cannot from that method alone deduce the fact. However it must be admitted that whatever the description given to him, it was his name that assumed prominence over the others. Did Gregory himself admit leadership? One newspaper quotes him as admitting 'that he and his gang', but at the trials of his associates, and at his own trial, neither he nor they gave any hint of his having led them. Gregory in fact did at times infer that his role had been a humble one; but if he was leader, then on trial for his life, he is not likely to have admitted it himself.

Was there then a leader, or was Gregory's leadership a myth, made and gradually upheld by the newspapers of the day? Turpin in a brief confession stated that 'there was a gang of twenty one', a figure he by no means exaggerated on other evidence available. So could Samuel Gregory, a man of no more and possibly less than average intelligence have controlled such a number, or even dominated them, particularly when he would have been one of the youngest members of, and a comparative newcomer to the gang?

A clue to the answer is to be found in the number of Gregorys who were active members of the gang. Samuel and Jeremy have already been mentioned, but there was also Jasper, or, as he was more commonly identified by the press, Joseph Gregory. These three formed the gang's core and intially at least and, possibly before the robberies started, the rest were more than likely influenced by a brotherhood of Gregorys rather than any particular one of them. Oddly enough the single alleged admission of leadership made by Samuel was recorded after the other two were dead. But although no evidence exists which would prove which was the more dominant when they were all alive, there is however a combination of factors which indicates conclusively that Samuel was.

During December 1734 and January 1735 Jeremy could not have participated in any of the robberies because he was in prison. Jasper, however, although known to have been involved in some robberies, was certainly absent from the last three major ones, which were committed in February 1735. Samuel was involved at the beginning and the end and it can be assumed that he was not only a member of all the expeditions but that he led them as well. In fact on one occasion a robbery involved only four men, Samuel Gregory and three others; and none of the other three could have been leader of the gang. All things being equal at that time, and Turpin not having then acquired his later reputation, it only needs one positive indication of Gregory having actually led on one occasion for us to accept his prior claim. It is probable that by the time the reporters were sure of their facts about the leadership, it didn't really matter any more because the public no longer cared. But it should matter to us that there was some foundation to the fact that Samuel was the reporters' constant if uncertain choice of leader, because it has never before been proved. But then, until now, nobody had ever questioned this and many other facets of Turpin's career, and the robbery which proves Gregory's leadership of the gang has never before

The Gregory Gang

appeared in Turpin annals. So there is no valid reason to dispute Samuel's leadership; but having been led with such great flourish to extinction it could be said of his followers that they would have made a wiser choice in Turpin, who at least had the greater instinct for survival.

It is perhaps coincidental that facts about Turpin's and Gregory's early membership of the gang should be equally vague, and that subsequently the published facts about both their lives should have been equally confused. But having established Samuel Gregory's prior claim to fame at this particular time, we now turn to Turpin's part in the proceedings to date.

Having acted as distributor to the deerstealers when he was a butcher, it would not have been difficult for him to have resumed his acquaintance with them at latest during the Autumn of 1734. Since his last known employment was as the landlord of an inn, a post he either undertook when the first of the deerstealers was jailed in July 1733, or else when eleven of them were in prison and his supplies jeopardised in December of the same year, it is possible to suggest the extreme dates between which he could and probably did serve as an innkeeper.

Of the deerstealers with whom Turpin is definitely known to have associated, Field, Rose and Jeremy Gregory were in Chelmsford gaol until July 1734, and deerstealing generally suffered from lack of deerstealers between July 1733 and December 1734. Turpin as receiver would have been particularly affected until his associates were released in July 1734. He is not likely to have waited until then for the supplies upon which he had probably come greatly to rely, and although difficult to prove he may have decided to give up butchery when Field and Rose were taken in July 1733. His instinct for survival could have contributed to such a decision, especially when persons eager to have a share in rewards offered at that time might have been tempted to discover his involvement in deerstealing to the authorities. July 1733 to July 1734 appears to be the most likely period during which Turpin could have been an innkeeper, the last time he could have been considered in any respect whatsoever a law abiding citizen. And Turpin was not the only one who with the advent of Autumn had reached the point of no return. Deerstealing was not a felony, robbery with violence was.

XI

To quote Turpin's confession again, but in greater detail, he stated, 'There was a gang of twenty one at the House of James Parkinson of Susan Ferry near Waltham, the landlord of which was one ... '[16] Susan, like Souson, is another corruption of Sewardstone, and below Sewardstone Mill on the River

Lea there was a ferry situated about midway between Waltham Cross and Chingford.[17] For events which have already been described, and for those to follow, the ferry would have been a strategic point for all the gang's activities. It does also appear to demolish Bayes' story of Turpin's having stolen cattle from Mr. Giles of Plaistow and then fled from Sewardstone where he lived when the hides were discovered at Waltham Cross. If this had been true, he would hardly have dared return there afterwards, and if Turpin's word is reliable (and it was an offically recorded confession) Sewardstone was their rendezvous.

The lack of future in deerstealing, and a desire for revenge against the Keepers and the Establishment in general, probably led the deerstealers to begin criminal activities, but there is one other event which indicates that a change in policy was inevitable. At the end of December 1734, Colonel Martin Bladen, J.P., in a letter to Lord Tylney concerning outrages committed by the gang, stated also ' ... and perhaps the same [gang] took the deerstealer, not long since at noon day, out of the pillory at Epping, in defiance of the Law.'[18]

Bladen was correct in this assumption, but it was no ordinary deerstealer who was rescued from the pillory, it was their leader; the evidence is in the Sheriff's Cravings for allowance of expenses, 1733—34:

> For erecting a pillory at Epping being 16 miles distant from the county gaol and putting Samuel Gregory in the same pursuant to his sentence and for raising a posse and carrying him there with a very strong guard he being a notorious deerstealer £10.0s.0d.[19]

In his letter Bladen referred to two robberies committed in October in the same context as two committed in December, and made no chronological distinction between them other than mentioning the December pair first; but in referring to the pillory incident he described it as having occurred 'not long since ... ' It could not have happened after 29 September 1734 because the Sheriff was only claiming expenses to that date; but in the volume of Cravings,[20] there is no doubt that this entry reflects the last expense incurred by the Sheriff in that particular Exchequer year. Other efforts to date the rescue have not been successful, but it would seem, on the evidence available, that it most probably occurred in September.

The Statute 3 W. & M. was the only one which made provision for the pillorying of deerstealers, a punishment which was no doubt inflicted as a prelude to the year's imprisonment which accompanied it, when the crime for which the person had been convicted was still tolerably fresh in the public's mind. Epping was the place indicated in the statute as being, 'the next

The Gregory Gang

adjoining town to the place where the offence was committed,' so Waltham Forest is where the offence occurred. That after being set in the pillory for an hour on a market day he should then have to serve a year in prison, gives some point to his being rescued, but can we be sure that Gregory's being pilloried and Bladen's account of a rescue are related?

Gregory's was the only pillory expense in the Sheriff's claim for the year. Both the Craving and Bladen's letter may be linked by the approximation of dates deduced from both sources of information. But the proof exists in the fact that a pillory had to be built at Epping before they could put Gregory in it. Without this evidence one would have inferred from Bladen's letter that the pillory there was a permanent structure; since it wasn't and only one was built there in that year, the person sentenced to stand in it must have been Samuel Gregory. And given such a unique opportunity one cannot imagine others besides his brothers and their friends who would have wanted to or been able to have effected a successful rescue. By throwing down the gauntlet in this manner, in open defiance of the law, the gang now had no recourse but to put deerstealing behind them and turn to more profitable and dangerous avenues of crime.

Allowing but a few weeks for the hue and cry to fade away, they commenced their new type of activities at the end of October. And whereas before a certain figure has been content or contrived to remain in the background, there is now no doubt that one Richard Turpin has entered the limelight and become a permanent member of the Gregory Gang.

FOOTNOTES

1. Middlesex/MJ/SR 2605 Gaol Calendar, No.80.
2. Middlesex/MJ/SR 2606 Gaol Calendar, No.72 and Indictment No.62.
3. Guildhall/London Sessions for December 1733.
4. P.R.O./T.53/37 p.288.
5. Guildhall/London Sessions for January 1734.
6. P.R.O./T.53/37 pp.288–290.
7. P.R.O./T.1/277 No.56 (abbreviated and edited)
8. P.R.O./T.4/11 (IND. 4625), p.35.
9. P.R.O./Assizes 35/174/1, Essex, Winter 7 Geo.II 1733/4 (Gaol Delivery for 6 March); Assizes 35/174/17, Essex, Summer 8 Geo.II 1734 (Writ to Sheriff for Coster's apprehension, dated 6 March and Indictment. Both of these filed on the previous Assize roll, later filed at front of this one)
10. P.R.O./Assizes 35/174/1, Essex, Winter 7 Geo.II 1733/4.
11. P.R.O./T.53/37 pp.288–291; 293–295.
12. P.R.O./T.4/11 (IND. 4625), p.35; and T.1/277 No.56.
13. P.R.O./Assizes 35/174/17, Essex, Summer 8 Geo.II 1734, Indictments for shooting John Deakins and John Boston, and Gaol Delivery of 31 July: Assizes 35/179/1, Essex, Winter 12 Geo.II 1738/9, Indictments Nos.7, 20, and 21 against Rogers and Nimpous Fuller; T.90/147 (Sheriff's Cravings) pp.332–333 (Rogers), and p.333 (Fuller): alternative source E.368/725 Essex, Mich.13 Geo.II; *Political State*, Vol.LVII, 1739 Jan.–June, pp.433–436, Roger's trial.
14. P.R.O./T.53/39 p.271 and *Political State*, Vol.XLIX p.461 for Mrs. Carroll details.
15. *Old Whig*, 15 May 1735.
16. P.R.O./T.53/40 p.157.
17. *Chapman and Andres Survey of Essex*, 1772.
18. P.R.O./S.P.36/33 ff.163–164.
19. P.R.O./T.90/146 p.102: alternative source E.368/722 Essex, Mich. 8 Geo. II.
20. From the collection deposited with the Treasury Commission which investigated the Royal Courts of Justice, and distinct from the parchment Memoranda Rolls kept in the Lord Treasurer's Remembrancer's Office in the Exchequer.

BOOK TWO

THE GREGORY GANG

CHAPTER ONE

I

THE FIRST major robbery committed by the Gregory Gang occurred on 29 October 1734. Sunset on this particular day was at 4.37 p.m. and the movement of men and horses after that time would have been shrouded in darkness. It is deduced from subsequent robberies that this one was committed in the early evening, about seven or eight o'clock. The account is one of several which appeared in the same publication in January of the following year under the heading of 'Audacious Robberies'.

> A large gang of rogues have lately associated themselves together, and have committed some very audacious robberies in Essex and other places, some of which we shall give an account of. On the 29th of October, in the evening, three of them went into a chandler's shop, near the *Loggerheads* at Woodford Row, and called for a half pint of brandy; soon after two others came in, who were immediately followed by three more, all men: they had not been long in the shop when one of them pulled out a knife, and then they threatened the master of the house, his wife and daughter with immediate death, if either of them offered to make the least outcry: while some of them thus stood sentries in the shop, to prevent the family's making any noise, the rest rifled the house of everything of value they could easily carry off; but were so generous as to give back a suit of head cloths, of about £6 value on the daughter's entreaty to whom they belonged; there being a sack of meal in the shop, they emptied it on the floor, put all their plunder therein, and carried it clear off.[1]

The victim of this first robbery was Peter Split, chandler and grocer at Woodford. Most Turpin accounts post 1739 describe the man as being Mr. Strype of Watford, but Martin Bladen, J.P. in his letter of 27 December 1734, *q.v.*, refers to two robberies at Woodford (of which this was one); and on 8 February 1735 the Duke of Newcastle signed the reward advertisement, naming Split of Woodford, subsequently published in the newspapers on 13 February 1735. Mr. Strype emanates from Bayes' account, and in that immediately precedes a robbery which occurred in February of the following year; but though name, date and place were rendered incorrectly, he was accorded the distinction of being the first victim of the 'Essex Gang'.

The first person who was so unhappy as to be served by them was one Mr. Strype, an old man that keeps a chandler's shop at Watford (*sic*) from whom they took what little money he had scraped together, but did him no further mischief, so that he was in some measure content.

It was some months before descriptions of the men responsible for this and other robberies appeared. Bayes made no reference to the individuals who might have been involved, and none of the gang was ever tried for taking part in this particular crime. The identities of some of the eight men are hazarded as descriptions of each successive robbery are related. The evidence supporting such identifications is inevitably circumstantial, but one member of the gang is known to have frequented the vicinity of the crime within a few days of it having occurred. His name was Jasper Gregory, and his brother Samuel, as leader of the gang, is unlikely to have conducted operations from an inn remote from the scene of the crime. Two men nominated, and seemingly no other evidence, even slight, which would allow speculation about others. But evidence has survived which was not created until nearly four and a half years had passed by, and the incident had been forgotten by all except a few interested parties. One of them was Peter Split, and he had good reason to remember:

> There were enclosed [in a letter of 21 March 1739]
> [No.3] Information of Peter Splidt of Woodford in the county of Essex taken before John Goodere Esq one of his Majesty's Justices of the Peace for the said county, dated the 17th March 1738/9.[2]

The letter in which this information was enclosed was from the Duke of Newcastle to the Recorder of York, to the end that if Turpin was acquitted of the crime for which he stood indicted at York, he should remain in prison there to await removal to stand trial charged with this or other robberies. To what extent Split could have implicated Turpin in the robbery is not known, but since his evidence must have been relevant in some respect, the significance of the use to which it was put cannot be ignored. Thus Turpin may have been one of the eight men who robbed Peter Split, and to find him involved at the commencement of the gang's activities does perhaps suggest an even greater familiarity with the others than one might previously have been led to suspect.

II

Two nights later the second robbery occurred, also at Woodford, and the victims on this occasion were Richard Wooldridge, Furbisher of Small Arms in the Office of Ordnance in the Tower of London, and his wife Ann. His annual salary for the quarter ending 31 December 1734 was £80, and the *War Office Registers* entry in the quarterly lists for this period renders the name as R. Wolldridge;[3] other spellings do occur in the present account, but Wooldridge appears to be the appropriate version. *The Political State (ibid.)*, takes up the story following immediately on the heels of the Split account.

> Two nights after, about eleven of them, masked and armed, entered the house of Woolridge, at Woodford, a gentleman belonging to the Office of Ordnance in the Tower (the family being then in town, and none but a servant in the house) and plundered it of all the brass, pewter, the clock, window curtains, most of the beds and bedding, two fine fowling pieces, and many other things to the value of about £200, and after drinking, or destroying, all his rum, brandy, ale and other liquors, they loaded several horses with their booty, and carried it off.[4]

Two robberies so far, both at Woodford and both attributed to this gang. How can we be certain they were committed by the Gregory gang, and not isolated events involving persons unknown? As the robberies became more numerous, rewards were offered for the discovery of the persons responsible; these rewards were advertised either in respect of individual robberies or for several lumped together. For reasons which are not entirely clear the Woodford robberies were grouped with two others which occurred in January of the following year and the reward was not offered until February. There is no doubt at all that Wooldridge was a victim of the Gregory gang, and the others, if only by association, must be regarded in like manner. The evidence in this particular case is obtained from the details of committal of one Thomas Barnfield, the receiver into whose hands some or all of Wooldridge's property subsequently came. Barnfield was committed: 'On oath of Ann Wooldridge on a strong suspicion of being concerned with Rose, Gregory [? and others in] robberies in the county of Essex particularly breaking open the house of Richard Wooldridge.'[5]

Rose was Joseph Rose, and the Gregory referred to here is Samuel. But the reference to these two is a general one rather than particular, and should not be taken to mean that they, any more than Barnfield who was merely a receiver, were in fact present at Woodford. It would read more appropriately, 'of being concerned with the gang in robberies in Essex, particularly with breaking open the house of Richard Wooldridge.'

III

The next crime is part of the pattern which is being established, and suggests that Jasper Gregory can be associated with those robberies at Woodford. Jasper was a carman, or carter, who, if not at this time some few months later, was living in Old Gravel Lane, just off Radcliff Highway, between the Tower and Shadwell Basin.

The two shootings with which Jeremy Gregory may have had some involvement in 1732 were committed in the neighbourhood of Woodford, and Chingford which is adjacent; so there is already reason to suppose that the Gregory brothers were all familiar with the area.

On 16 November 1734, Jasper Gregory assaulted one George Cory and robbed him of fourpence on the King's Highway in the parish of Woodford. It was little more than two weeks since the robberies there, and the probability of his having been involved cannot be ignored. He was not tried for the assault until the following year, and if he was alone on that occasion, he rejoined his companions very soon afterwards.[6]

IV

One could speculate endlessly about those who took part in the Woodford robberies. The gang members were all tried for other offences and the corroborative evidence which might have existed had they been tried for the Woodford crimes therefore does not exist. Another reason is that the Bayes' account, which has formed the basis for much of the plagiarism which has been thrust down the throat of a gullible public by Turpin authors since it first appeared, lists only seven members of the Gregory gang and does not describe all the robberies.

Bayes dismisses Peter Split in a few lines as Mr. Strype, and Richard Wooldridge he mentions not at all. There are no alternative sources of information from which one might learn the names of those who were present at the two robberies at Woodford, and only for Turpin and Samuel Gregory has a case been made for their having taken part in either or both of those raids.

Four days after Jasper Gregory's assault on George Cory we are able to eliminate from the ranks of those who were active during December 1734 and January 1735, the names of two of the gang who might otherwise have been implicated during that period. In the Calendar of Middlesex Prisoners in Newgate from 16 October to 4 December 1734 is the following entry: 'No. 19 Jeremy Gregory and William Saunders committed by Samuel Tysson Esq., on oath of Robert Iles for assaulting and wounding him and for want of sureties. 20 November.'[7]

The committal was made on the same day as the assault occurred, and the two elected to be tried at the Middlesex General Sessions on 2 December. William Saunders may only have been one of several aliases of the person so called; the William was constant, but Saunders was also known as Saunderson, Bush and Schooling. The aliases employed by various members of the gang are an unusual feature of this account, but any reference made to them will normally be by the name by which they were most commonly known. Jeremy Gregory and Saunders were tried for assaulting Iles at St. John Hackney on 20 November.[8]

The names of the witnesses sworn in court were Robert Iles, Prudence Johnson and George Stretton. The judgement entered upon the indictment was (in both cases), 'Po se and (by his consent immediately) Jury &c. Guilty, fined 12d. to be estreated and committed to the house of Correction (Bridewell) there to labour six months.' A final reference to Jeremiah Gregory's imprisonment (from a newspaper report which appeared six months' later) would *appear* to have a link with the next recorded robbery by the gang:

> ... he [Samuel Gregory] declared he never committed any crime till about a fortnight before Christmas last, and then turned housebreaker to support his brother Jerry who was confined in gaol on suspicion of deerstealing, and joined with Fielder &c. ...[9]

But since, as just recorded, brother Jerry was convicted of assault and sentenced to hard labour, Samuel's extenuating circumstances (if indeed they were his and not invented by the press) show such a surprising lack of familiarity with his brother's activities, that the reliability of the rest of the statement must be suspect.

This is not to say that Samuel Gregory could not have made such a claim, for on the contrary, very little of what he did say *was* reliable. And this is all the more reason for regarding the claim that he did not turn housebreaker until a fortnight before Christmas, as a fiction. That the first robbery for which there is positive evidence for his having taken part (14 December 1734) should roughly coincide with that date is a result either of his or the newspaper report's contrivance. Samuel Gregory was criminally involved with Fielder and the rest (as he implied) from the moment they rescued him from the pillory at Epping, and however modest *he* might have been about his role in their subsequent activities, the inescapable fact which remains is that it was the most prominent one.

V

There have lately died in Epping Forest near 100 head of fallow deer, and in a very short time. They are supposed to be poisoned by some malicious, ill dealing people.[10]

Some unknown disease is the probable simple explanation for these mysterious November fatalities, and assuming the report was accurate insofar as the number of deer affected was concerned, it suggests that if during the gang's period of inactivity in November there were some faint hearted former colleagues with apprehensions about their future in organised crime, then this disease could have prevented their return to deerstealing and thereby denied them a choice.

VI

Already towards the end of November snow and sleet had fallen but it was to prove to be one of the *wettest* winters ever experienced in London and the areas surrounding. In December, for example, the rainfall was 7.8 inches, and during periods when the gang was inactive, adverse weather may have been the reason.

Apart from two individual acts which netted fourpence, and six months hard labour and a fine respectively, there had not been a robbery since those at Woodford, possibly because the gang members were a little overwhelmed by their early successes and suspicious of public and official reaction. We find however that the Woodford robberies aroused little interest and this is borne out in that although the next robbery was committed in nearby Chingford, the possible significance of this was overlooked by the press.

Only four members of the gang were present when the house of John Gladwin was broken into at about 7 p.m. on 14 December 1734. John Gladwin (or Gladden as his name sometimes appears) was a higler who lived at Chingford Green. In the same house lived John Shockley, and it would appear that they were both at home when Jasper and Samuel Gregory, John Jones and a young man called John Wheeler burst in and ransacked the premises. Proof of these identifications is to be found in (i) indictments naming Jasper and Samuel Gregory and John Jones, in (ii) a claim for a reward which names the same two and refers to but does not name two others, and in (iii) a retrospective newspaper account written at the time of the capture of one of them which names all four on the evidence of one of them.

The Gregory Gang

The two Gregory's and Wheeler have been described. Jones was born at Hackney and was about 25 years of age. A carpenter by trade he was about five ft. six in. high, fresh coloured but with a pockmarked face, and given to wearing a brown wig.

Gladwin and Shockley appear to have been of comparatively humble estate, but despite this they were stripped of all their possessions of value. An inventory of their losses is given below:

Of the Goods and Chattels of John Gladwin		£ s d
1 pair of Holland sheets	worth	1. 0.0.
1 hat		5.0.
1 peruke		15.0.
1 pair of worsted stockings		3.0.
1 pair of yarn stockings		2.0.
1 Holland shirt		10.0.
5 pewter dishes		1. 0.0.
12 pewter plates		12.0.
12 diaper napkins		10.0.
and one and a half guineas in gold coin of the realm.		

Of the Goods and Chattels of John Shockley	
1 Drugget coat	15.0.
1 cloth waistcoat	8.0.
1 dimity waistcoat	7.0.

Since this was only the third robbery committed by the gang it is a moot point whether or not these four men represented the most experienced members of that company. Samuel Gregory undoubtedly was the leader, Jasper would appear to have played a much more active role at this stage of their activities than he did subsequently. Wheeler was unquestionably involved in all those robberies which resulted in prosecutions, and like Samuel Gregory, was probably present at the earlier ones as well. About John Jones one cannot be certain because this is the only robbery in which he is *known* to have taken a part, but if we accept Jones' word for it, this was the only robbery he committed:

> He declared he never was concerned but in that single robbery in his life; and that drinking with [Samuel] Gregory, Rose and company they made him drunk, and when his reason was absent they drew him into that fact; that the next day after it he had such a horror at what he had done, that he run away, and continued in a distant country.[11]

Jones was alleged to have made this declaration after his conviction for his part in the above robbery, and insofar as he can have had no other defence we can accept that it was *his* story and not a reporter's invention; the truth of it however is open to question, particularly since his life depended on it. That it was his first and only robbery depends on how one views the inclusion of

Rose as a drinking companion, because Rose did not attend the robbery, and if Jones ran away he cannot have known Rose afterwards.

Future events suggest that part of Jones' story was true. The man who ultimately turned evidence against the rest of the gang (and who was probably present at the first two robberies) only implicated Jones in the Gladwin robbery, but once this was known to the authorities and Jones' description was published, there is some suggestion that a frightened Jones temporarily rejoined forces with a splinter group of the gang and was involved in some robberies with them. There is even some suggestion that the reunion was brought about a week or so *before* his description was published, when news of the betrayal was conveyed to those members of the gang who were not in a position to have obtained it first hand. So if one amends his statement to read, 'he never was concerned in more than one robbery to which there was a witness,' (a fact he knew full well when he made the statement), we are a little nearer the truth. If he went abroad some time between May and July 1735 this would be a little nearer again, and if during his drinking with Gregory and Rose and the rest he knew them to be wild fellows and was excited by tales of their experiences, we see him at least as a fool if he did not anticipate what a mess he might be getting himself into.

The Gladwin robbery was not a very ambitious venture, and the presence of Jones and the absence of Rose suggests that it was an unpremeditated crime, perhaps inspired by drink. It is more in keeping with the paltry offences of Jasper Gregory and Jeremy Gregory and William Saunders in November, and reflects very well the protracted spending of ill gotten gains from the end of October robberies. It was in fact the last wild fling before necessity obliged them to take crime more seriously again, and the enlisting of Jones may be seen as a spontaneous filling of the gap left through the irresponsibility of Jeremy Gregory and William Saunders.

Turpin, the three Gregory brothers, Fielder, Rose, Wheeler and Saunders all appear to have been members of the gang before Jones came on the scene, and although perhaps not all were present at both Woodford robberies, there were certainly enough in that number to have combined at one or the other. After the Gladwin robbery more names appear, two of which are known already; but even without them there *could* have been eight at the first robbery, a figure which was reported. None of the crimes so far described has involved any great show of violence, perhaps because the gang bore no personal animosity towards its victims. But 15 December brought snow and sleet, and with it temporary respite to Chingford and Woodford. By the following week the gang had moved from that area and were not to return for some time.[1 2]

VII

They moved to Barking, and on 19 December forced their way into the house of Ambrose Skinner. Although fully described in the newspapers of the day,[13] this robbery was dismissed in a few lines by Bayes as the Rippleside robbery where £700 was taken and Turpin remarked with an oath, 'Ay, this will do, if it would always be so ... ' Neither the date nor the name of the victim was given, and the people involved were described as, 'The old man, the old woman, the servant maid, and a son-in-law of "the old farmer's coming unluckily." ' Since, with the exception of the daughter-in-law, the other principals are reasonably identified, and Rippleside was adjacent to Barking, there is no doubt at all that Bayes was referring to the same event. With little variation the Rippleside version has been perpetuated in each successive edition of the *Newgate Calendar,* and every other account published since 1739. Fortunately, however, information of a much more detailed nature exists in other sources and from these it is possible to build up a surprisingly complete account of this crime.

The newspapers were inaccurate in some respects but as reliable as one might hope for or reasonably expect at that time. There is however nothing quite so impressive as eyewitness accounts, and of these we have four. They were given in the form of Informations to Martin Bladen, J.P. and were taken down by him on Christmas Day and 28 December 1734. Bladen was also M.P. for Aldborough Hatch, near Barkingside, and took a personal interest in this and other robberies committed in the vicinity. To avoid repetition the Informations have been translated into the first person and nothing but the relevant parts of each statement retained. Each of the informants swore upon the 'Holy Evangelists', and their statements are presented in the order in which they became involved in the events that affected them.

Ambrose Skinner Snr., aged 73, Farmer, of Longbridge in the Parish of Barking
On Thursday the nineteenth of December about the hour of seven in the evening as I was going to shut the door of the hall in my house which was then unlatched six armed men unknown to me with their faces muffled and disguised rushed in upon me with violence and presenting their carbines to my breast swore they, if I made any noise or resistance, would immediately put me to death or words to that effect. Whereupon I having at that time no other person in the house with me but a maidservant only thought it the safest way to submit to their pleasure and accordingly without any resistance

on my part the six armed men or some of them took off my garters and having therewith bound my hands compelled me to walk about the house with them from one room to another to discover where my money and effects lay, after which they took my purse and keys out of my pocket and therewith attempted to open all the chests and trunks belonging to me and my son and my daughter-in-law who dwell in the same house with me, but finding the keys did not answer their expectations they immediately broke open all the chests and trunks and took from thence and from my dwelling house whatever they pleased; that is to say, upwards of forty-seven pounds sterling in ready money which I had laid up to discharge the rent due to my landlord together with several pieces of plate, goods, linen and wearing apparel, amounting in the whole to three hundred pounds in value, according to the most moderate computation I can make thereof.

And the six armed men continued in my dwelling house, rifling the same, near the space of three hours and a half, after which having taken two horses out of my stable to enable them to carry off their spoil, they departed; and as I have since been credibly informed, were seen to pass with others in their company on foot and part on horseback through the town of Barking, and also through some of the turnpikes in the High Road from Epping to London. And I apprehend that unless some stop be put to these outrageous violences in such great bands and combinations, it will be impossible for any of his Majesty's good subjects in this neighbourhood to be secure either in their lives or fortunes.[14]

Elizabeth King, Spinster, aged 21 of Longbridge in the parish of Barking
My master and I being in the house, six persons armed and disguised entered and having bound my master and me and shut us up in an upper room ransacked the house, broke open a great number of chests and trunks and took from thence money, goods and plate to a very considerable value.[15]

Daniel Styles, aged 24 of Longbridge in the parish of Barking
Between seven and eight of the clock in the evening I and a young lad named Henry Spellar, who is likewise a servant to my master, returning home from our business found our master's house possessed by several armed men whose faces were muffled and disguised. These men immediately seized upon us and bound our hands and feet commanding us upon pain of death not to make any disturbance or stir from the place where they laid us down. The men having ransacked the house broke open many trunks and chests and took from thence all the money and plate and goods they thought proper, and after sometime went off with their booty taking two horses out of the

master's stable to enable them to carry it away. I cannot justly say of what number this band might consist but believe them to have seven or eight at least.[16]

Ambrose Skinner Jnr., aged 35, Farmer, of Longbridge in the parish of Barking
About the hour of eight in the evening my wife and I, returning to my father's house at Longbridge, found it possessed by several armed men, and upon my going to enter the door I was seized by some of them who presented their carbines to my breast and threatened to shoot me if I did not immediately surrender myself to them; and as there were many of them I thought it both dangerous and fruitless to resist. I therefore submitted myself to be bound and they set me down by my wife whom they had already bound and commanded me upon pain of death not to make any disturbance or stir out of the place where they set me down or to attempt to look at them.

And whilst I was bound they ransacked the house and took away from thence whatever they thought fit in money, plate and clothes, not leaving me nor my wife nor my father any other wearing apparel, either linen, silk or woollen, but those upon our backs.[17]

The sun set at 3.56 p.m. on 19 December, and, as on previous occasions, the gang assembled in pitch darkness before bursting in. Six men appear to have taken part in the actual crime, although Skinner Senior suggests that they were joined by others afterwards, and they were all inside the house. If there had been guards posted outside, the men inside would not have been disturbed as frequently as they were, and this leads to a most significant point. The old farmer was alone except for his maid and was in the process of latching the door when the gang rushed in. They did not, as the newspapers suggested, wait until everyone was accounted for before they commenced ransacking the house, but forced the old man to show them where everything was, and despite subsequent interruptions, continued to do so throughout the course of their stay. No noise from within the house alarmed the newcomers, they merely walked in unsuspectingly and were immediately secured almost as though each and every one of them had been expected. This is particularly noticeable in the case of Skinner's son and daughter-in-law, 'who had been out on horseback, visiting some of the neighbours in the country.' A woman suddenly arrives in riding habit, unaccompanied, and is secured and bound. No-one looks out, or goes out to stop her companion, they merely wait until he has stabled the horses and comes through the door of the house himself.

Another point to note is the absolute insistence upon silence, and the fact that each pair of victims appears to have been deposited in different parts of the house. No pair seems to have been aware of the existence at any time of others except themselves, and yet individually it is a little surprising that the maid overlooked the fact that her master was not immediately locked away with her in an upstairs room. One might have expected a guard to be set outside, just in case something untoward occurred to upset the plan, but no, the trap was set inside the house, as though no persons other than those who walked into it were expected. And odd too, that although there might at any time during the evening have been three able bodied men in the house, the gang should come when the only inhabitants were an old man and a maid, and when the door was conveniently open. The evidence is not very strong, but there are indications that even if the gang were not familiar with the daily habits of the family and its retainers, they had some good idea of their programme on that particular day. Another factor which might point towards there having been assistance given by some person within the household is that the name Elizabeth King reappears (7 May 1737) in incriminating circumstances. It may not have been the same person, and Ambrose Skinner's maid did testify against persons tried for the Longbridge robbery; but it cannot be said on the evidence of her information that she would have been able to have contributed very much towards a conviction of the men accused. She was sworn as a witness against one of the men indicted for stealing horses from the stable, and her knowledge of that incident would seem to have been negligible. But the most intriguing thing about Miss King is that Turpin not only met *her* at the Barking robbery, he knew the other Elizabeth King as well. Two women with the same name in the same story is one thing, but for the principal character in that story to have known one in a criminal context and to have robbed the other, is perhaps stretching the bounds of coincidence a little too far.

Upon the evidence of one of them we know that Richard Turpin, Thomas Rowden, Herbert Haines and John Wheeler were four of the six men in the house at Longbridge; but apart from Samuel Gregory it is not possible to suggest which of a number of others might have made up the half dozen. With each successive robbery however it becomes obvious that there were others who could be called upon to make up the number needed for any one operation. But on this particular occasion six men shared quite a considerable haul. From Ambrose Skinner Senior they took:

The Gregory Gang

		£ s d
1 Silver tankard	of the value of	5. 0.0.
1 Silver cup		2. 0.0.
1 Silver porringer		1. 0.0.
4 Silver spoons		2. 0.0.
4 Linen table cloths		10.0.
10 Linen napkins		10.0.
4 Linen shirts		10.0.
1 Perriwig		1. 0.0.
1 Hat		5.0.
1 Pair of shoes		2.0.
1 Cloth riding coat		10.0.
1 Hat		2.6.
1 Perriwig		•1. 0.0.
1 Cloth coat		1. 0.0.
1 Cloth waistcoat		10.0.
3 Shirts		7.6.
1 Muslin neckcloth		1.0.
2 Sacks		2.0.
	Total	£16.10.0.

From Ambrose Skinner Junior in the same house:

	£ s d
1 Silver watch	2. 0.0.
1 Pair of stays	1. 0.0.
3 Perriwigs	1.10.0.
1 Hat	5.0.
1 Silver snuff box	10.0.
1 Silver buckle	5.0.
2 Silver spoons	15.0.
2 Gold rings	1. 0.0.
1 Coral	10.0.
1 Callicoe night gown	5.0.
1 Burdett gown	10.0.
1 Turkey silkgown	1. 0.0.
1 Yellow lutestring gown and petticoat	2. 0.0.
1 Brocade gown and petticoat	2. 0.0.
2 Silk quilted petticoats	2. 0.0.
1 Velvet hood	1.10.0.
2 Alamode hoods	10.0.
2 Cloth coats	1. 0.0.
2 Cloth waistcoats	10.0.
2 Pairs of cloth breeches	10.0.
1 Pair of buckskin breeches	10.0.
6 Linen shirts	15.0.
6 Shifts	15.0.
2 Suits of laced headcloths	4. 0.0.
6 Linen aprons	6.0.
6 Pairs of ruffles	6.0.
2 Pairs of dimity pockets	2.0.
95 Gold guineas	99.15.0.
5 Shillings	5.0.
Total	£136. 4.0.

With goods and money worth £152 14s. 0d. to share between them the six men were no doubt well pleased with their night's work. And Herbert Haines took a gelding of a bay colour and a black mare from the stable as they left the scene of the crime. One newspaper stated that a horse marked A.S. was taken, so it was possibly this one of the two stolen which was identified and subsequently provided the proof that they were removed by Haines.[18]

We do not know who, nor how many were the willing helpers who met the gang after the robbery at Longbridge farm, but it must have been a curious cavalcade that passed through Barking, some on horseback with sacks of loot on the pommel, some jogging alongside on foot carrying their weapons, a coarse, rough crowd, joking and laughing, their merriment accompanied now and then by the snort of a horse or the clink of silver plate. On they went, in no great hurry lest the pedestrians be left behind, on through the turnpikes, unwashed fingers crushing a woman's finery, or gentlemen's perriwigs on their heads. It is not to difficult to conjure up the romance and adventure that surrounded these maurauding brigands. But behind them men and women lay bound on floors, their possessions gone; and although some of the goods were to be recovered, the gang had not yet finished with Ambrose Skinner Junior.

Also on 19 December, but in 1733, five deerstealers were locked up in Chelmsford gaol. The man mainly responsible was William Mason Senior, Keeper for Earl Tylney and living at Hainault Lodge in Waltham Forest. But although the gang visited him only two days after the Barking robbery, the coincidence of date should not be allowed to override all other considerations. There is no known link between the five deerstealers and those who were members of the Gregory gang, and they were in fact never heard of again. Rose, Fielder, and Jeremy Gregory (now in Bridewell) however, were all taken by Mason, so there was a grudge element present without recourse to the grievances of others. Even so the date is an intrusive factor, not easily dismissed, and it is impossible to ignore the five completely.

So on Saturday 21 December 1734, some time after the sun set at 3.57 p.m., the gang converged on Hainault Lodge. The forest was black, the wind swaying the trees, lashing men and horses with rain. Their passage was silent, hooves trampled sodden leaves and water ran from man to beast, from steaming flanks to forest floor. Thunder cracked, lightning illuminated horse and rider blue and white, trees black in silhouette; and for William Mason it was without doubt a very black Saturday.

FOOTNOTES

1. *Political State*, Vol.XLIX pp.24–27 (from *Read's Weekly Journal*. 9 Nov. 1734).
2. P.R.O./S.P.44/131 p.107.
3. P.R.O./W.O.54/92.
4. First published on 23 November 1734 in *Read's Weekly Journal*.
5. Middlesex MJ/SR 2634 Calendar. Entry No.3.
6. P.R.O./Assizes 35/175/1, Essex, Winter 8 Geo.II (1735). The first Indictment against Jasper Gregory.
7. Middlesex/MJ/SR 2626 Gaol Calendar.
8. Middlesex/MJ/SR 2625 Indictment No.6. Details of the fine estreated are also to be found in P.R.O./E.362/64, Middlesex Estreat of fines set at the General Sessions for 2 December 8 Geo.II, *m. 7 dorse.*
9. *London Evening Post*, 3 to 5 June 1735.
10. *Ibid.*, 30 November to 3 December 1734.
11. *Ibid.*, 1 to 3 April 1736.
12. *Ibid.*, 18 to 20 December 1735; P.R.O./T.53/38 p.406; P.R.O./Assizes 35/175/1, Essex, Winter 8 Geo.II (1735) Indictment No.2 against Jasper Gregory; Assizes 35/176/1, Essex, Winter 9 Geo.II (1736) Indictment No.12 against John Jones; and *London Gazette* no.7378 for the description of Jones.
13. *Political State*, Vol.XLIX pp.24–27 (from *London Journal*, 23 November 1734).
14. P.R.O./S.P.36/33 ff.170–171.
15. *Ibid.* ff.151–152.
16. *Ibid.* ff.153–154.
17. *Ibid.* ff.149–150.
18. Assizes 35/175/2, Essex, Summer 9 Geo.II (1735), Indictment No.1 (stealing of a gelding and mare), and Indictment No.3 (felony and burglary, Skinner).

CHAPTER TWO

I

About half an hour after five o'clock in the evening, no less than fifteen fellows, with their faces blacked, and well armed, came to the house of Mr. Mason, one of the Keepers of Epping Forest, at the old lodge there, and calling out Mason, his man opened the door, when a great number of them rushed in; upon hearing the noise, Mr. Mason snatched up a blunderbuss and presented it at them; but his wife stepped in between and prevented his firing, fearing they should all be murdered if he killed or hurt any of the rogues: upon this they immediately came up, knocked Mr. Mason down, cut him over the head, and bruised him so that he lay dangerously ill for some time; then they rifled the house, where, among other things, they found about 150 guineas in money, after which they packed up all the goods that could be easily carried away, loaded two horses with them, and broke those to pieces they could not carry off, such as tables, chairs, chests of drawers, etc. Though Mr. Mason was prevented from firing, yet his presenting the blunderbuss put them in such fright, that the servant who opened the door got through them, and ran directly to the stable, in order to mount one of his master's horses, and alarmed the country, but he found three of the rogues watching the stable door, who fired at him, upon which he ran another way; these three pursued him, and fired again at him, but the night being dark they missed him, and at last by turning round a hay stack he got clear off from them, and alarmed the country so fast, that by eight o'clock there were 50 men well armed got to his master's house; but it was too late, for the rogues knowing that the servant had escaped, and from thence judging that the country would be alarmed, had made all possible dispatch, and were gone off with their booty before any relief came up. That night they could get no account which way the rogues were gone, but by the description it appeared afterwards, that they turned through Stratford Turnpike towards London.[1]

BY 1739 this description had changed radically, and readers who had by then forgotten what they had read in the newspapers were presented with Bayes' version of the same incident:

Turpin, flushed with this success [the 'Rippleside' robbery], encouraged his companions to proceed in their villanies, to be revenged on several who had endeavoured to detect them. Among several others, Mason the Keeper upon Epping-Forest was pitched upon to feel the effect of their resentments; for upon consultation what they should do next, says Turpin, there's Wil. Mason has used two or three of us ill, and we'll be revenged on him; accordingly a time was fixed when they should go and attack his house; Turpin having shared so much money could not refrain from coming to London for pleasure, and by getting drunk, forgot the appointment with his companions, and never went near them; they waited for him a long time, but finding he did not come, they determined not to be baulked in their designs, and *Fielder* and *Rose* taking upon themselves to command in the expedition, they all set out to Mason's, having first bound themselves in an oath not to leave one whole piece of goods in the house. Accordingly having broke open the door, they beat and abused Mason in a most terrible manner, and when they had beat him as they thought enough, they kicked him under the dresser, and there left him; the old man was sitting by the fire, but upon declaring he knew none of them, when they asked him, they did not meddle with him. Mason's little girl in her fright got out of bed, and without any clothes ran into the hogsty, and there hid herself; they then went upstairs, and broke everything they could lay hands on, and at last espying a punch bowl, that stood a little out of the way, they broke that, and out dropped a hundred and twenty guineas, which they took after they had done as much mischief as they possibly could, and went away very well satisfied.

In this particular 'Life', it is not too difficult to distinguish between fact and fiction; in more recent accounts this is sometimes almost impossible. Many of the mid-nineteenth century chroniclers that followed Ainsworth were content to churn out cheap imitations of his imaginative and turbulent novel, *Rookwood,* but apart from the incident which he used to precipitate his fiction of the ride to York, Ainsworth cannot be accused of distorting the facts of Turpin's life. His romance, which merely included Turpin as a character, gave pleasure to innumerable people, but his successors not only distorted the facts, but incorporated the legend and other fictions as well, in their grotesque parodies of truth.

Thus a man like Charles G. Harper, a conscientious biographer concerned with authenticity, was led naively, perhaps unconsciously, into borrowing from such authors parts like the following, which also describes the Mason robbery:

> Rust, Rose and Fielder were the three concerned in the affair, and it clearly shows the spirit in which they entered upon it, when it is said that, before

starting, they bound themselves by oath not to leave anything in the house undamaged ... Fielder gained admission to the house by scaling the garden wall and breaking in at the back door, then admitting the other two by the back entrance. Mason was upstairs, sitting with his aged father in his bedroom, when the three suddenly burst in upon them, and, seizing them, bound them hand and foot. They asked the old man if he knew them: he said he did not, and they then carried him downstairs and laid him, helplessly tied up, under the kitchen dresser. Mason, the Keeper, had a sack forced over his head and tied round his waist; his little daughter, terrified at what she heard, slipping hurriedly out of bed and out of doors, and hiding in a pigsty.[2]

Harper's account continued with the systematic smashing up of the furniture and the finding of the guineas in the punchbowl, before the gang's departure and reunion with Turpin at the Bun-House in Rope Fields, at which place they shared their booty with him. In such manner is fiction perpetuated. However, these three versions are not given merely to illustrate anomalies; two of them contain elements of truth vital to the overall picture, and one of them names a man who might not have existed at all. But there were eyewitnesses to the event. As with the Skinner robbery, Col. Martin Bladen took it upon himself to enquire into the robberies, and on 25 and 26 December 1734 he took down the informations of the adult members of the household. As on the previous occasion the informants were sworn upon the Holy Evangelists, and their evidence is translated into the first person.

Jonathan Richards, aged 28, servant to William Mason at Hainault Lodge

On Saturday last the twenty-first of December about six in the evening some person knocking at the master's door, the master's daughter went to ask who it was and a person from without enquired whether Mr. Mason was at home. The child answering Yes, I immediately run to the door to see whom it was that wanted the master, and having a candle in my hand opened the same. Whereupon a certain person with his face blacked and disguised immediately discharged a gun at me and cried out to his companions, 'Come away for By God we have got him,' or words to that effect. Whereupon I forthwith returned into the house to give the master notice to be upon his guard, upon which he took down a gun, but the mistress and the child being both in the same room intermixed with the thieves, I apprehend the master could not discharge his gun for fear of killing them instead of the thieves, who soon knocked both him and the mistress down. Whereupon I endeavoured to make my escape with the intention of raising the whole neighbourhood in their defence. With great difficulty I got out through the roof of the garret by knocking off the tiles, and several shots were fired at me whilst I was getting off. In less than an hour I returned with several neighbours, the nearest being

The Gregory Gang

at a distance of a mile from the master's house. But before my return the thieves had ransacked the house and were gone off with their booty. And I verily believes that some or one of the persons concerned in this robbery had a personal enmity to the master for discharging his duty faithfully as a keeper of the forest.[3]

William Mason, aged 40, Keeper to the Earl Tylney at Hainault Lodge in Waltham Forest in the parish of Dagenham

Several armed persons with their faces disguised, some with black and some with white colouring, violently entered into my house, and one of them immediately shot at me. They afterwards beat and abused both me and my wife, and upon my endeavouring as I did to make my escape they discharged three more shots at me, one in the passage of the house and two more after I had got out of it. It was with great difficulty that I, my wife, and my daughter aged thirteen escaped with our lives, especially myself, they or some of them having threatened to murder me.

We having fled out of the house and no persons remaining there belonging to the family but a servant maid and my uncle, an ancient man, the armed men (as my uncle has since acquainted me) obliged him to shew them where they might get candles to enable them to search the house, and then having set a sentinel over him to prevent his giving them any disturbance, they ransacked the whole house, smashed several chimney glasses, great quantities of china, tables, corner cupboards, chests and glass windows, and took from the house £140 sterling in ready money, nine silver spoons, twelve guns and all or most of my wife's wearing apparel, all of which money and goods were taken away before we returned again to the house.

I cannot certainly tell what number this gang of robbers might consist of, but I am positive that I saw six of them myself, and believe they might be more. I apprehend that unless some stop be put to these outrageous violences in such bands and combinations, it will be impossible for any of his Majesty's good subjects in this neighbourhood to be secure either in their lives or their fortunes.[4]

Mary Mason, aged 34, wife of William Mason above
Mrs. Mason's version is substantially the same as her husband's.[5]

William Roades, aged 68, Mary Mason's uncle, living with the family
Unlike the Skinner robbery informations, these people were all in the house at the same time, and apart from Richards, the versions given by Mason's wife and uncle are almost identical in substance, and merely corroborate each

other. The only relevant detail added by Roades was that he thought there were five or six men and that there might have been more outside tending the horses.[6]

It is clear that they did not intend to kill Mason. One of the gang subsequently claimed that this had been their intention, but they could have done this without any difficulty; they were content to take their revenge in terrorising him and his family, and stealing, regardless of whether or not they needed them, all his possessions of any value. There is a curious little rider to the above episode: 'The firearms, which they took from [Mason] they brought as far as Cambridge Heath, near Hackney, and then threw them into a pond ... '[7]

Since there were no visible signs of pursuit when this occurred, and the gang afterwards passed through Stratford Turnpike towards London, it cannot be said that the guns were jettisoned in the course of flight from danger. Furthermore, other than the money, the total value of the guns was more than that of all the other stolen household possessions put together.[8]

		£ s d
1 Flowered satin gown	of the value	2. 0.0.
1 Yellow satin gown		2. 0.0.
1 Silk quilted petticoat		1. 0.0.
1 Camblett riding hood		1.10.0.
6 Silver tea spoons		15.0.
3 Large silver spoons		2. 0.0.
1 Silver chain		8.0.
1 Silver snuff box		1. 0.0.
6 Yards of yellow satin		10.0.
1 Velvet hood		1. 0.0.
1 Velvet scarf		2. 0.0.
1 Callico quilted petticoat		5.0.
10 Guns (Mason stated twelve)		20. 0.0.
8 Gold Portugal pieces		28.16.0.
70 Gold guineas		73.10.0.
20 Gold half guineas		10.10.0.
− Other money		30. 0.0.
	Total	£176.19.0.

And the men who took these things? Bayes related the tale that Turpin was so drunk he forgot the appointment. Whether or not he was in fact drunk it is not possible to say, but he was certainly not at Hainault. Again on the evidence of one of them, we know that Herbert Haines, Thomas Rowden and John Wheeler were there; but since with the addition of Turpin, the same men were present at the Skinner robbery, there is no reason why the informant amongst them should have left Turpin out if he was at the Mason robbery also. Bayes also named John Fielder and Joseph Rose, a statement corroborated in a report which describes the capture of Fielder, Rose and the man who turned evidence against them who, 'declared that they had been concerned with him in robbing Mr. Mason of Epping Forest.'[9] Of the known members of the Gregory Gang, this pair would have had more reason than any of the others to have wanted to have been in on this grudge robbery. Jeremy Gregory would also have had reason but at this time he was still in Bridewell. If one accepts that Samuel Gregory led the gang, possibly at the instigation of Fielder and Rose, then the number, excluding any assistants, who may have stayed with the horses outside, is made up. Fielder was an alias, for in his deerstealing days he was known as John Field.

Jonathan Richards was right when he stated that he, 'verily believed some or one of the gang had a personal enmity towards Mason for faithfully discharging his duty as Keeper of the forest', but did Mason himself think so? He can, for instance, hardly have overlooked the fact it was a year to the day since he caused five deerstealers to be put away. And yet although obvious to his servant, Mason made no reference to the revenge motive in his information, nor, apparently, did he convey his private thoughts in the matter to Martin Bladen, at least, not in any particular, because when Bladen reported to Earl Tylney he confined his observations on who might have been responsible to a general opinion which embraced both deerstealers and smugglers. Which is rather odd because the number of men who had real grievances against Mason were limited, and a number of other robberies might have been prevented had that information been given to the authorities. Were in fact any of the other deerstealers involved? The probable attendance of Fielder and Rose, and the date, are factors which cannot be ignored, and although they do not by themselves prove the existence of other men, there is nothing which would serve to dispel the shadows in the background.

The final point about this robbery is that in Harper's account of it, a man called Rust appears. In another account of a subsequent robbery this is expanded to Ned Rust. The name persists to this day, and yet, search high and low in records, in newspapers, in contemporary 'lives', there is no-one amongst Turpin's known associates who bears that name. Did he exist or was he imagined? Harper was not the first to introduce the name. In *Rookwood* there is a Bob Rust and in earlier and later nineteenth century chap-books, Ned Rust and other names frequently appear out of the blue. Some, plainly, are inventions; others are corruptions of known names, and some are corruptions of inventions. But of which category was Ned Rust?

On 8 October 1688 a Thomas Rust married Alice Turpin (relationship obscure) at Hempstead. The baptismal registers for that parish do not commence until 1693, but no children were born to this couple subsequently, although an Edward Rust was buried there 16 July 1692. On 8 May 1734, at nearby Newport Pond, there occurred an affray, and Edward Rust Jnr. was indicted with assault at Chelmsford in Michaelmas term of that year and ordered to appear before the King's Bench at Westminster, Hillary term 8 Geo. II (1735). There is unfortunately no record of the judgement in this case, so we cannot tell what happened to Edward Rust Jnr. in January or February of 1735.[10]

If this was not the Ned Rust of the chap-books, could he by a very remarkable coincidence have been one of Turpin's associates in his own right? It is doubtful if this question will ever be answered, for so far as is known, the name does not appear anywhere during the 70 years which elapsed between the Edward Rust Jnr. of legal record, and the Ned Rust who first appeared in a chap-book published c. 1808.

II

On Sunday 22 December, the night following the Mason robbery, ' ... the same gang were out again, and fourteen of them were seen to go down Three Coney Lane near the forest, threatening some houses thereabouts; but we don't yet hear they have done any more mischief.'[11] This account illustrates, perhaps better than any other, the intimidating appearance of this by now notorious gang. But Christmas was near and whereas the gang were content to rest throughout that period (particularly since the weather was rapidly deteriorating, with great storms on Christmas Eve and Christmas Day, snow and sleet 28 December and more storms the following day), the machinery of law and order was slowly beginning to grind. And for Martin Bladen, J.P., Christmas Day was a very busy one. William Mason brought Earl Tylney's instructions concerning the course of action he [Bladen] was to follow; and on the same day Bladen took the informations of Elizabeth King and Daniel Styles, the servants of Ambrose Skinner Snr., and of William Mason and his wife, and their servant Jonathan Richards.

On 26 December he took the statement of William Roades, Mason's uncle; and the next day he wrote the following long letter to Earl Tylney:

Albrohatch December the 27th 1734

I received your commands by *Mason* on Christmas Day; but I had already begun to enquire into the two extraordinary robberys, lately committed in our neighbourhood; and I send you enclosed several depositions concerning them.

I wish some Justice of the Peace had done the like for those two, which we heard of not long ago at *Woodford*. I am entirely of opinion, that unless his Majesty shall be graciously pleased, to interpose his authority, for the discovery of these outrageous practices, the common course of Law, will prove an insufficient barrier, for the lives and fortunes of his good subjects.

I would therefore humbly propose, that your Lordship should lay these depositions before one of the Secretaries of State, desiring him to move his Majesty to issue his Royal Proclamation, with promise of pardon and reward, to any of the persons concerned in these robberys, that shall discover his accomplices, or the receivers of the goods by them stolen; and as their numbers are great, the premium might be at the rate of fifty pounds per head, for every person discovered, and brought to condign punishment.

I am convinced the persons concerned in these robberys, are deerstealers or smugglers, or perhaps both; and therefore to make the temptation for the discovery still stronger, I would apprehend the pardon might extend to all offences committed before the time of discovery, except murder only.

It is certain the robbery at Skinners, and that at Masons were both committed by the same gang; in all probability the same persons were concerned in the two robberys at Woodford also, and perhaps the same took the deer stealer, not long since at noon day, out of the pillory at Epping, in defiance of the law.

The terror these robberys have struck into the country people especially the wealthy farmers, is incredible; and your Lordship cannot do an act of greater charity, than to endeavour to deliver them out of it ...[12]

Bladen was right in suggesting that the gang rescued the deerstealer from the pillory, but one wonders why, if he knew that Samuel Gregory was that person, he did not identify him in the letter. We cannot be certain, even had he done so, that the authorities would have acted upon the information; but the fact remains that by the time Gregory was betrayed and his name had become common knowledge, the gang had committed another seven robberies. It seems probable that Bladen did not know the rescued deerstealer's name, because not long before Gregory's denouement Bladen wrote another letter on the same subject, and Gregory's name was not mentioned in the reward notices advertised as a result of it.

The statements eventually reached their destination, and Tylney was not slow in seeing that they were put into the right hands. In less than a week, Bladen's suggestion of a proclamation reward had the Royal approval, and the hunt was up. In the meantime the goods for which there was a market were disposed of through receivers. Bladen knew of their existence and mentioned them in his letter. Two of them were eventually exposed, but there may well have been others. The possessions of Richard Wooldridge, one of the Woodford victims, passed into the hands of Thomas Barnfield, who found Wooldridge's feather bed too comfortable, or else too bulky an item of which to dispose. Whatever the reason we may be sure the feather bed was not continually on the move from one place to another, and as it was traced to Barnfield he no doubt received it not long after it was stolen.

The next part of this account concerns another Justice of the Peace for Essex, the proposed victim of the crime that never was.

III

This particular incident allows the maligned Bayes to redeem himself, for if it had not been for Bayes' *Life,* we might not have known that a crime was planned, and the attempt aborted. But although we only have his word for it that what happened occurred in just this way, the fact of its having been planned in the manner described is corroborated:

The gang had also formed a design to rob the house of justice Asher near Leigh in Essex, upon the information of the woman who kept company with Rose, and with that intention met at a public house near Leigh, and in the evening went to put their design in execution, but not rightly knowing the way into the house, they got to a side lane near it, waiting for an opportunity, and with that view tied their horses against some furze bushes, and concealing themselves under them, intending to have surprised somebody passing that way, and to have obliged them to have shewn them the way to the door; but whilst they were thus lying perdue there, they heard several persons riding along together, which happened to be some of the neighbouring farmers, who had been at the justice's, and over-hearing their discourse, supposed the justice had other company still remaining at his house, they did not think it advisable to attempt it at that time; therefore adjourned their design, which so far proved of advantage to them, that it prevented their being taken, which otherwise they could have hardly avoided, by reason they having been observed in the neighbourhood, were suspected to be smugglers, and information having been given to the custom-house, and other officers thereabouts: and a party of dragoons were out in search after them, whom they met, but not having anything with them, were suffered to pass; whereas if they had committed the robbery they intended, and been stopped by the soldiers, the goods upon search would have been found upon them, and though they might have been only stopped on suspicion of being smugglers they would thereby be discovered to have been housebreakers, and committed accordingly.

Since no newspaper report of this incident has been found we cannot say whether the above description came from such a source or not, and for evidence of the actual planning we have had to rely on an informer: 'Mary Johnson *alias* Brazier *alias* Rose charged on the oath of ... for persuading John

The Gregory Gang

Wheeler and several others to rob the house of George Asser Esq. at Sechurch in Essex.'[13]

Was this the origin of Bayes' story, subsequently embellished? Legends have sprung from less. But there is a strong suggestion in the existence of a charge, that this 'crime' had progressed beyond the planning stage.

Sechurch was Seachurch *alias* Southchurch near Leigh in Essex, nearly forty miles from London. Mary Brazier was convicted at Chelmsford in 1734 of stealing handkerchiefs there in 1733, and we have assumed that she was also living there at that time. Thus her knowledge of the district and her part in the planning of the crime cannot be disputed. Apart from Wheeler, Joseph Rose, who was living with Mary Brazier, and Samuel Gregory, the naming of other possible companions on this trip would be guesswork. We do not know how many went nor when it took place except that it was before 11 February 1735, the date on which the person who subsequently implicated Mary Brazier was himself captured.

Until the Mason robbery at Hainault, the gang's main activities had been confined to within a few miles of the Lea River valley area, a fact which supports Turpin's admission that they used to rendezvous at Sewardstone Ferry (at least until the end of 1734). Between 4 and 7 January, rewards for the Mason and Skinner robbers were posted but even without these, common sense would have made the gang cautious of appearing in the vicinity of Waltham Forest, where the incensed Mason and his fellow keepers would have been more than grateful for an opportunity to have met up with them again. For a gang which so far had shewn not only a great familiarity with, but a positive preference for Essex, it is difficult to imagine any of the other possibly unfamiliar counties having a great deal of appeal; but the next two robberies to occur which can be dated took place in Kent and Surrey respectively, a complete shift in the gang's area of operations. After this they appeared briefly somewhat to the north of the scene of their previous activities in Essex, before moving into Middlesex to meet with their inevitable fate. The only other robberies committed south of the River Thames which may be attributed to this gang occurred when the last few survivors were obliged to keep on the move. When taken together these facts indicate that crossing the river was something to be attempted only when urgent necessity demanded.

Apart from November 1734, the only other lull of any length between known robberies was that between the Mason one on 21 December 1734, and that which took place in Kent on 11 January 1735. Three weeks in the middle of a phase of robberies during which the next longest space of time allowed to elapse was seven days.

Towards the end of December the weather deteriorated rapidly. At the beginning of January there was heavy rain on the 4th, storms on the 6th and 8th, and heavy rain again on the 9th. Although evidence suggests that the gang were put off by bad weather, the Mason robbery and one other provide precedents for the gang being prepared to face it if they had to. Thus it is possible that the Seachurch robbery was planned in early January, when the gang preferred to remain in familiar Essex rather than look elsewhere. And certainly an abortive expedition in that county at that particular time would have been more than sufficient reason for them to *then* cross the river into Kent.

FOOTNOTES

1. *Political State*, Vol.XLIX p.27 (from *London Evening Post*, No.1107).
2. Harper. *Half Hours with the Highwaymen*, Vol.II pp.181–182. London. Chapman and Hall Ltd., 1908.
3. P.R.O./S.P.36/33 ff.155–156.
4. *Ibid.* ff.157–158.
5. *Ibid.* ff.159–160.
6. *Ibid.* ff.161–162.
7. *London Evening Post*, 18 to 20 February 1735.
8. P.R.O./Assizes 35/175/2, Essex, Summer 9 Geo.II (1735), Indictment No.2 (felony and burglary, Mason) the charge incorrectly rendering the date upon which the offence occurred as 22 December.
9. *Reid's Weekly Journal*, 15 February 1735.
10. P.R.O./K.B.11/32 No.10. Mich.8 Geo.II; K.B.21/34, and 36/72 Thursday next, and Monday next after 15 days of St.Hillary 8 Geo.II; K.B.28/131 and 132, Mich.8 Geo.II; K.B.29/394 Mich.8 Geo.II; and IND.6658, Hillary 8 Geo.II. All references to Essex.
11. *London Evening Post*, 21 to 24 December 1734.
12. P.R.O./S.P.36/33 ff.163–164.
13. Middlesex MJ/SR 2634, Prisoners upon Orders (edited entry).

CHAPTER THREE

I

APART FROM two or three men, it has not been possible to identify with any certainty those who took part in the Woodford robberies because no-one was charged with having participated in those crimes. This explanation should be qualified by adding that with one notable exception members of the gang were only indicted with having committed robberies at which the man who turned King's evidence was himself present. This does not mean that although other robberies were committed by them, the subsequent informer was not then present; on the contrary, for the gang members were tried *and convicted* of committing crimes in particular counties, and although there may have been evidence of crimes committed in other counties, the necessity for trying them at other courts, did not arise. This point is made now because none of the gang were ever charged with taking part in any of the next four robberies.

Richard Bayes' account of the first is substantially the same as that which appeared in a newspaper;[1] it also contains additional information at beginning and end which is of some relevance.

On Saturday the 11th of January 1735, at seven or eight o'clock in the evening, Turpin, Fielder, Walker and three others came to the door of Mr. Saunders, a wealthy farmer at Charlton in Kent, and knocked at the door, enquired if Mr. Saunders was at home, being answered he was, the door being opened, they all rushed in, went directly to the parlour, where Mr. Saunders, his wife, and some friends were at cards; desired them not to be frightened, for that they would not hurt their persons, if they sat still, and made no disturbance. The first thing they laid hands on was a silver snuff box which lay upon the table before them, and having secured the rest of the company, obliged Mr. Saunders to go about the house with them, and open his closets, and boxes, and scrutoire, from whence they took upwards of one hundred pounds in money, and all the plate in the house, a velvet hood, a mantle and other things. Whilst this was doing the servant maid got loose and ran up stairs, barred herself into one of the rooms, and called out at the window for assistances, in hopes of alarming the neighbourhood; but one of the rogues ran up stairs after her, and with a poker broke open the door; then brought her down again, bound her and all the rest of the family, then rifled the house of divers other things of value; and finding in their search some bottles of wine, a bottle of brandy and mince pies, they all sat down, drank a bottle of wine, ate a mince pie, and obliged the company to drink a dram of brandy each. And Mrs. Saunders fainting away with the fright, they got her a glass of water, and put some drops in it, and gave her, and were very careful to recover her from her fright. They stayed about two hours in the house, before they packed up their plunder, and marched off with it. But threatened them, that if they stirred within two hours, or advertised the marks of the mare they would murder them.

When they concerted this robbery, they met at the *George* at Woolwich, in order to go from thence to put their intentions in execution. And after they had effected their design, they crossed the water, and brought the goods to an empty house in Ratcliff Highway, where they divided their plunder.

The names at the beginning were added by Bayes, whereas the newspaper stated 'four men'. The last paragraph is additional to the newspaper report which ends with reference to the 'Marks of the Plate', which is more reasonable than those of a mare. But by Charles G. Harper's time (in *Half Hours with The Highwaymen),* Bayes' six had become Turpin, Ned Rust, *George* Gregory, Fielder, Rose and Wheeler, and Walker had disappeared altogether. If one substitutes Walker for the fictitious Ned Rust, one is left with as likely a half dozen as it is possible to select. One must include Samuel Gregory. Turpin's presence is uncorroborated, but it having been missed at the Mason robbery his assistance on this next occasion may well have been invited if he was to continue to justify his membership of the gang.

Humphrey Walker is a newcomer to this company. He was a lusty man, about 50 years of age, fresh coloured, a little marked with the smallpox, and given to wearing a light wig. The evidence which would involve him in the Charlton robbery is not so clear. The details given in records of committal were not always consistent, i.e. one of the gang was charged with having committed several robberies in Essex, Kent, Middlesex and Surrey, but those who may have been his companions on those occasions were not necessarily implicated in the context of their own records of committal. In the case of

Walker, committed specifically for robbery in Middlesex, there was also reference to Essex and Surrey, but not to Kent.[2]

There is however no evidence that Walker attended any robberies in Essex, although Bayes, in describing the next robbery south of the Thames, in Surrey, gives Walker such a part that it would be difficult to imagine it not having had some good foundation. Corroboration of Surrey and not Kent may well be due merely to inconsistency in the record that states Essex rather than Kent to be one of the counties in which Walker was active. One of the gang had some knowledge of Kent and Surrey, and a man who played no prominent role in Essex would possibly be the man most likely to possess it.

Who else crossed the river to Charlton? The details of Joseph Rose's committal are the same as for Walker. He too is charged with having robbed in Surrey, but not Kent. Yet Bayes named Fielder, and where Fielder went Rose was almost sure to be, in Waltham Forest or at Tyburn. And finally John Wheeler, who was named in his record of committal as the man having robbed in all four counties.[3] In the final paragraph of Bayes' account of the Saunder's robbery he states that they met at the *George Inn* in Woolwich and after the robbery 'crossed the water, and brought the goods to an empty house in Ratcliff Highway.'

Samuel Gregory used to lodge at his brother Jasper's house in Old Gravel Lane, off Radcliff Highway; Thomas Rowden came to stay there, towards the lower end of Shadwell church; and Turpin lived not far away, at Whitechapel, and at a later date even left his horse in Old Gravel Lane. We might even say that the robbery was planned at Jasper Gregory's house in Old Gravel Lane, that the majority of the gang set out from there and crossed the ferry at Woolwich, possibly meeting Humphrey Walker at the *George Inn* before proceeding, perhaps on foot (having left their horses on the north bank), the short distance to Charlton. And then back to Woolwich, across the ferry to their horses, and westward coming into the highway again to Old Gravel Lane.

Were Jasper Gregory and Rowden involved? It is certain that somebody would have been left to look after the horses. Rowden possibly, with Jasper waiting at home to ensure that it was safe for them to return there with the plunder.

II

Exactly one week later they visited Croydon in Surrey. The following account of it differs but slightly from the longer Bayes' version.

> Last Saturday the house of ... Sheldon, Esq. at Shirley at Croydon in Surrey, was entered by five rogues, masked and armed with two pair of pistols each, they knocked at the door and were let in by the servants, whom they bound, they afterwards robbed Mr. Sheldon and his lady of their money, jewels, laces &c. and plundered the house of their plate and what other moveables they could carry away in five sacks, which they filled, they returned Mr. Sheldon two guineas begging his pardon for what they had done and rode off with their booty. It is supposed, they are the same gang who committed the late robberies in Essex and Kent.[4]

The curious thing about this and the Charlton robberies is that whereas the newspapers felt able to commit themselves, albeit hesitantly, in attributing these robberies to the same gang, the authorities were not convinced until the following month. Evidence of this appears in a reward advertised during the second week of February. The reward was offered not only in respect of the two robberies immediately following that at Croydon, but for those two committed at Woodford as far back as in October of the previous year. Since rewards for the Gladwin and Mason and Skinner robberies were advertised separately, rewards were offered for robberies committed by the gang up to and including 1 February. The only exceptions being the two above mentioned in Kent and Surrey. And of those it could be said that they were lumped together with all others in the proclamation reward which named all the counties in which robberies occurred. This however did not appear until after the informer was captured, and the fact that Kent and Surrey were not officially recognised until that time does suggest that in January the authorities were not prepared to accept that the gang's activities might extend across the Thames. Bayes however was in no doubt, but his view was retrospective, and although unsupported now, looks to be remarkably authentic:

On Saturday the 18th of January last, Turpin, Fielder, Walker and two others, made an appointment to rob Mr. Sheldon's house near Croydon in Surrey, and for that purpose, agreed to meet at the *Half Moon Tavern* at Croydon, which they accordingly did in the evening about 6 o'clock, and about 7 [o'clock] went to Mr. Sheldon's. Walker having some knowledge of the house, going at the head of his companions into the yard, perceived a light in the stable, went thither, where they found the coachman dressing the horses, him they bound, and going from thence met Mr. Sheldon in the yard, whom they seized, and compelled him to shew them the way into the house; where, as soon as they entered, they bound Mr. Sheldon, and the rest of the family, and fell to plundering the house; and took from Mr. Sheldon eleven guineas, and several pieces of plate, jewels, and some other things of value, which they carried off with them; but before they left the place, they returned Mr. Sheldon two guineas of the money back again, asked pardon for what they had done, and bid him Good Night.

By the beginning of this century some accounts of this incident differ in one remarkable respect; the appointment at the *Half Moon* tavern *before* the robbery has become an impudent visit afterwards to have a quick one for the road paid for with one of Mr. Sheldon's guineas. The meeting before the robbery is more acceptable than this obvious transposition of events.

It rained on 18 January. This is a recorded fact. But about the identity of the robbers one can do no more than reiterate the arguments used to identify those who attended the Charlton robbery. In which case, to those named by Bayes, one must add Samuel Gregory, Joseph Rose, and John Wheeler, with the conditional elimination on this occasion of other assistance. About the Charlton affair it has been observed that having crossed the ferry at Woolwich the gang could have proceeded on foot, but this obviously could not have been the case at Croydon. Assuming that most of the gang came from Radcliff Highway again, one must also accept that on this occasion they were mounted and crossed London Bridge.

III

On the Thursday following (23 January) there occurred a robbery which has not been included in previous Turpin annals, and had it not been officially associated with other robberies attributed to the gang, there would have been nothing to distinguish it from other run of the mill felonies which received little or no recognition at that time. So far as we know only two persons were involved, and this in itself would have discouraged identification with the notorious company which roamed the countryside in greater numbers. Again, the event was so far removed from the last excursion, that if it had not happened in Essex it might not have been linked with the earlier robberies in that county:

> Last Thursday sevennight in the evening, two fellows came to the house of the Reverend Mr. Dyde, minister of Great Parnedon in Essex, and knocking at his door, the same was opened by a man servant, of whom they enquired for the Parson, and being told he was not at home, they cursed him, rushed in upon him, and cut him in several parts of the face in a barbarous manner, they then seized the maid servant, and bound her, during which time the poor fellow stole away and hid himself. Mr. Dyde, hearing the maid cry out, came downstairs with a piece charged in his hand, and would have fired at the rogues, but was afraid of killing the maid; upon which he went out of doors in order to get assistance, and

the rogues missing the man servant at the same time, and supposing they were both gone to alarm the neighbours, made off, carrying only a silver spoon along with them, but they left behind them a bundle of cords, a pistol charged with four balls, and a handwhip. Mr. Dyde has ever since had his house well guarded for fear of a second attack.[5]

This unsuccessful venture was linked with the two Woodford robberies and one which occurred on 1 February, in a reward advertisement which stemmed from Whitehall on 8 February. A report does exist which states that a member of the gang was captured on 25 January, but this has not been confirmed and there is nothing to indicate that the authorities had in their possession any reliable information whatsoever about the particular activities of the gang or its members until 11 February at the very earliest.

The source of information which linked these four robberies was Colonel Martin Bladen, who had already linked the Woodford crimes with those of Barking and Hainault, and who now saw fit to remind the authorities of the fact when two more occurred at Great Parndon and Loughton. It is impossible to say who the two fellows at Great Parndon might have been, except that this episode shews no evidence of leadership, and may be nothing more than a reflection of the November/December 1734 incidents, when individual members of the gang acted on their own initiative in committing isolated acts of robbery and assault. The important thing to note here is that the next robbery which can definitely be attributed to the gang *was* committed in this very vicinity a week later. It is difficult to question Bladen's theory that *all* the robberies were committed by the same gang when, the Great Parndon robbery apart, we know that he *was* right about all the others!

IV

The next robbery occurred at Loughton on 1 February 1735. Not far from Woodford and Chingford it was to be the gang's last full scale depredation in Essex. But first there is the matter of the report of the capture of one of the gang, which appeared in the same newspaper from which the above account of the robbery at the Rev. Mr. Dyde's house was taken:

> One of the gang of villains who have committed such robberies of late as are without example by rifling houses in Essex and Kent being taken last Saturday [25 January] in Southwark, was by Sir John Lade, Bart. commited to the New Jail there, since which Mr. Saunders and his wife, whom they robbed, have positively sworn against him, so that there are hopes, that his accomplices may be discovered.

Sir John Lade was a Surrey magistrate and Mr. Saunders and his wife are said to have made a positive identification. But Saunders lived at Charlton in Kent, and nobody was removed by Habeas Corpus from Surrey to Kent to stand trial at Maidstone Assizes in March, nor in fact was any of the gang indicted for the Charlton robbery.

A similarly worded report of the capture also appeared in another newspaper of the same date[6], but in a 1962 book, there appears a somewhat different report from an unknown source:

> By the middle of January, the law officers had good descriptions of at least some members of the gang, supplied by Mason, Saunders and Sheldon. A newspaper report at this time suggested that Sheldon had identified as one of the gang a man who had been arrested, but the report gives no clue as to the man's identity. It may have been that the magistrate who committed the anonymous felon to the New Prison felt that a little secrecy might help the law to lay others by the heels.[7]

Even rough descriptions of any of the gang were not forthcoming until 11 February, but even so this report relates to the same event reported in the newspapers. Sheldon did live in Surrey and is more likely to have identified a man captured in Surrey and committed by a Surrey magistrate; but he would not have been committed in the first instance to the New Prison which was in Middlesex.

The Assize roll for Winter 1734/5 Surrey is *Missing* from the Public Record Office class of South Eastern (Home) Circuit Indictments, but the man does not appear to have been brought to trial. If he had been he would have been indicted for felony at the Assizes at Kingston, and assuming that a positive identification had been made he would have been found guilty. In an account of the Assize Proceedings at Kingston,[8] eight capital convictions were listed, none of which was for the Sheldon robbery. This disallows acquittal, or the Bill not being found, or the captured man having died in prison prior to the commencement of prosecution proceedings. But if there was a man captured, and by reason of elimination it would have had to have been in Surrey, then these are the extreme possibilities which could account for there being no other evidence of his existence. For no-one was removed by Habeas Corpus to any of the other relevant counties besides Kent, not to Middlesex, nor Essex, nor to London. None of the gang stood trial in London because they did not commit any crimes there, but in Essex and Middlesex there exist fully corroborated accounts of every member of the gang who was captured or stood trial in those counties. Nor, in the event, were any of the payments of Blood Money, or other rewards for the capture and conviction of individual members of the gang given in respect of anyone captured in Surrey.

There was no follow up to the report of a capture in Southwark, which suggests that it was nothing more than the case of a man thought to be one of the gang being arrested, and of Saunders (or Sheldon) being called to make an identification which turned out to be negative. The arrest of a person helping the authorities with their enquiries is always news but his release of no import at all. The sequence of recent events should now be considered. The Sheldon robbery at Croydon on 18 January, the Reverend Mr. Dyde robbery at Great Parndon on 23 January and the Widow Shelley robbery at Loughton on 1 February (not yet described). The first of these was in Surrey, the last two in Essex. Assuming that the Great Parndon robbery *was* the precursor of the Loughton one, and that after the Croydon robbery the gang decided to resume operations, however temporarily, in Essex; then it is unlikely that any of the gang would have again crossed the river after 23 January, to be caught in Southwark on 25 January. But if one does not accept that the Great Parndon robbery was committed by any of the gang, and prefers instead to think that a week after the Croydon robbery they were still reconnoitring south of the Thames, then news (however unlikely) of an arrest of one of their number in Southwark on 25 January would have then given the gang added incentive to resume their activities north, and look to Loughton for their next inspiration.

V

Some mention has been made of a robbery at Loughton on 1 February, but on the same day the following incident occurred:

> Last Saturday [1 February] as a person who had been to see an acquaintance in Clerkenwell–Bridewell was letting out again, the man who opened the gate *was knocked down* and some of the prisoners made their escapes, but by the alarm and diligence of the Keeper, several others were prevented.[9]

The escape probably occurred in the afternoon, and there were loosed on society two members of the Gregory gang who had been serving six month sentences there (for assault) since 2 December 1734. Their names, Jeremiah Gregory and William Saunders *alias* Saunderson *alias* Schooling. The proof is in the Orders of Court of the Middlesex Sessions held at Hick's Hall in February 1735: 'Order that a committee of justices be appointed into the escapes of Jeremy Gregory and William Saunders, two prisoners, from the House of Correction.'[10]

How was the escape effected? Over a period of time the calendar of Middlesex Sessions provides some details. The Keeper of the prison, Peter

Creswell, was required to attend the committee concerning the escape and other matters. All manner of information about the prison was considered by the committee of justices, and from their report three facts emerge which contribute to what is known. First, a man named William Walker was employed as clerk of the House of Correction,[11] second, the report recommended that, 'the shed, leading into the outward court, over which the scaping (*sic*) prisoners got, ought to be raised',[12] and third, a woman, Mary Best, who had lived in the House of Correction for many years, was the turnkey of the prison.[13]

Upon certain information being given to the committee, Peter Creswell was ordered, 'for several reasons offered' (but unspecified), to immediately discharge Walker from his employ. It may be inferred that Walker was negligent, but how would the negligence of a clerk have assisted the escape? If he actually helped the escapers, why was he only discharged? Or was he discharged because it was subsequently discovered that he was related in some way to Humphrey Walker, one of the gang and, what is more, one who robbed in company with William Saunders, one of the escapers? Was he perhaps the victim of purely circumstantial evidence, possibly innocent? The only comment possible is that the committee of justices was nothing if not thorough in its examination of the many deficiencies which existed in the Bridewell at that time. Certainly in William Walker's case, he was found to be lacking in those qualities thought necessary to the position he held. Mary Best on the other hand, although considered not to be a fit person for the post of turnkey, and because 'for want of such a one, escapes may happen,' was recommended to be re-employed as matron, in place of one who had been so infrequent in her attendance of that duty, Keeper Creswell could not be persuaded to meet her claim for expenses.

Of the escapers, Saunders immediately rejoined the gang (though hardly on the same day), whilst Gregory, oddly enough, appears not to have done, at least not in a visibly active capacity. But whatever happened subsequently, their escape during the daylight hours of 1 February can have had no bearing on what happened after the sun went down at 4.55 p.m. For whereas those two were probably still on foot, their former associates were at that time on the point of setting out on horseback for Loughton.

VI

> On Saturday night last, about seven o'clock, five rogues entered the house of the Widow Shelley at Loughton in Essex, having pistols &c. and threatened to murder the old lady, if she would not tell them where her money lay, which she obstinately refusing for some time, they threatened to lay her across the fire, if

she did not instantly tell them, which she would not do. But her son being in the room, and threatened to be murdered, cried out, he would tell them, if they would not murder his mother, and did, whereupon they went upstairs, and took near £100, a silver tankard, and other plate, and all manner of household goods. They afterwards went into the cellar and drank several bottles of ale and wine, and broiled some meat, ate the relicts of a fillet of veal &c. While they were doing this, two of their gang went into Mr. Turkles, a farmer's, who rents one end of the widow's house, and robbed him of above £20 and then they all went off, taking two of the farmer's horses, to carry off their luggage, the horses were found on Sunday the following morning in Old Street, and stayed about three hours in the house.[14]

Treating the Mason robbery exceptionally as a crime of vengeance, the robbery of Mrs. Shelley marks the end of the gang's restraint towards its victims, and from now on there is a notable change for the worse. In their concern for the fainting Mrs. Saunders and their unusual charitableness towards Mr. Sheldon, the gang shewed surprising signs of humanity, but in less than two weeks this tolerance had begun to evaporate, and the subsequent violence resulted in loud and insistent demands for retribution. The reasons for this must be that the gang did not take kindly to being thwarted, and that the rendezvous for each robbery was usually at an inn.

The Great Parndon robbery, which has been tentatively attributed to the gang, was not a success; ignominious flight left a sourness at having been thwarted and a determination not to allow the same thing to happen again. Meeting at an inn before each robbery did not help. At the beginning of their activities the gang no doubt met in such a manner more for convenience than anything else; and an inn, however isolated, was an obvious rendezvous. Later however, with the knowledge that the odds against their remaining at large were inevitably shortening, they began to drink more. With a pint or two of ale they might have been in good humour, but with more their natural aggressiveness would have quickened into impatience and brutality. Taking these factors in combination, it is clear that Mrs. Shelley was lucky to have a son on hand who regarded material loss preferable to a roasted mother. The victims who came after the widow were less fortunate.

Who were the men who threatened Mrs. Shelley? Bayes when short on facts could be long on imagination, and from his account stems the still popular extravaganza of Mrs. Shelley being roasted by Turpin, usually accompanied by a lurid print of the same incident. Bayes placed the event between the Split robbery in October and the Skinner one in December 1734, unlike the subsequent crimes where he appears to have been in possession of the dates:

Their next attempt was upon a widow gentlewoman that lives at Loughton, which was a scheme of Turpin's; for he acquainted the gang that he knew of an old woman at Loughton, that he was sure had seven or eight hundred pounds by her, and D--n her, says he, 'tis as good as in our pockets as here, and we'll have it. Accordingly the time was fixed for the enterprise, and they all set out; when they got to Loughton, Wheeler (who upon those occasions never went into the house with them, but was placed as a scout at the door) 'twas agreed that he should knock at the door, which so soon as he had done Turpin and his companions all rushed in, and the first thing they did was to bind the old lady, her son, her man and maid; then Turpin began to examine her where her money and effects were hid, telling her at the same time that he knew she had money, and 'twas in vain to deny it, for have it they would; the old gentlewoman being very loth to part with her money, persisted in it that she had none, and would not declare anything more of the matter, upon which some of the crew were inclinable to believe her, and were sorry for their disappointment, but Turpin as strenuously insisting she had money as she that she had none, at last cried, 'G-d d--n your Blood, you Old B--h, if you won't tell us I'll set your bare A--se on the Grate.' She continued obstinate for all that, imagining that he only meant to threaten her, and so very fond she was of her darling gold, that she even suffered herself to be served as he had declared, and endured it for some time; till the anguish at last forced her to discover, which when she had done; they took her off the grate indeed, and robbed her of all they could find; some persons talk of a much larger sum, but 'tis certain they stole upwards of four hundred pounds.

Bayes made no reference to the unfortunate Turkle and the account generally is so bereft of facts as to illustrate clearly what a curious mixture of fact and fiction the Bayes' *Life of Richard Turpin* really was. In this instance the author/authors was or were content merely to give melodramatic treatment to what even by 1739 had become a local tradition.

The crime is said to have been conceived by Turpin, and of Wheeler we are advised that he never did more than stand watch outside at the door. Were either of them in fact there? John Wheeler, probably the youngest member of the gang, was a regular, if not the most regular (next to Samuel Gregory) participant in these robberies, so that it is difficult when evidence to the contrary is lacking to ignore any more or less contemporary account which includes him; especially that of an author who on the occasions he does name the robbers, names those about whom it is easier to make out a case for their attendance than to refute it. We cannot say that he was not at Loughton, but assuming that he was, it is possible to say with conviction that his role in the robbery would not have been that of a mere bystander. He commands a little

The Gregory Gang

more respect than that.

With Turpin there is slightly more to go on. A famous partnership, about which more will be heard, is that of Rowden the Pewterer and Turpin the Butcher. Not all the gang were captured in one fateful month, and of the survivors Turpin could have chosen any as his companion, but he elected to ride with Rowden, or vice-versa, and for either of them to have made this decision there must have been some (comparatively) long term respect for each other. So if on the one hand there exists an account of the Loughton robbery which names Turpin, and another which names Rowden as having been present, then even if one is cautious about accepting the evidence of the first, the existence of the other makes it easier to regard them both as being complementary. And of Rowden we have the following short account: 'One of the robberies which he committed in the said county [of Essex] was, in the house of the widow Shirely at Loughton which he robbed of a silver tankard, in which were 37 guineas; a silver cup, 3 silver spoons, and a pair of silver spurs.'[15]

This statement is taken from a long report of Rowden's capture, in which other reliable biographical details appear. There is no reason to doubt that Rowden was at Loughton, and that being so we may assume that Turpin was probably there as well.

Who was the odd man, Walker or one who had not, so far as is known, taken part for some time, *viz.* Jasper Gregory, John Jones and Herbert Haines? There is every appearance of Jasper Gregory's having assumed a less active role in these proceedings. Possibly that of caretaker of the stolen goods until an agent like Thomas Barnfield could be found for their disposal. Jones' description was not published until 22 February, following the gang's betrayal on 11 February, and until the earlier date fear is unlikely to have driven him to seek out again the only men he could trust, they by then being in like circumstances. Haines, the philandering barber with a shop in Shoreditch, not only appears to have had other things to think about, but the Loughton robbery is the last one in which he *could* have taken part before his description was published. There is no evidence to implicate him in this robbery, and when he could as easily have been in bed with his former employer's wife, it would be more charitable to take the romantic view and eliminate him in favour of the more recently active Humphrey Walker.

FOOTNOTES

1. *Country Journal,* 18 January 1735.
2. Middlesex/MJ/SR 2631, Calendar of Prisoners in Newgate, No.27.
3. Middlesex/MJ/SR/2630, Calendar of Prisoners in New Prison, No.46.
4. *Read's Weekly Journal,* 25 January 1735.
5. *Ibid.,* 1 February 1735.
6. *Universal Spectator and Weekly Journal,* No.CCCXXX.
7. *Knights of the High Toby,* Barrows, London, Peter Davies, 1962, p.117.
8. *Gentleman's Magazine,* March 1735.
9. *General Evening Post,* 1 to 4 February 1735 (words in italics additional in *London Evening Post*)
10. Calendar of Middlesex Sessions and Orders of Court, July 1732–December 1735, p.121.
11. *Ibid.* p.131.
12. *Ibid.* p.141.
13. *Ibid.* p.140.
14. *Read's Weekly Journal,* 8 February 1735.
15. *Political State,* Vol.LIV July–December 1737, p.145.

CHAPTER FOUR

I

THE GANG was entering the final phase of its activities; and it is necessary to establish the whereabouts, known or conjectural, of each member at the beginning of February 1735. The rendezvous for the early Essex robberies was Sewardstone, but from that time until about the beginning of February the gang members had lived in various places in and about London, *viz*. Richard Turpin at Whitechapel, not far from Thomas Rowden and Jasper Gregory; Thomas Rowden in Radcliff Highway, towards Shadwell Church; Jasper Gregory off Radcliff Highway, in Old Gravel Lane; Jeremy Gregory and William Saunders in the Clerkenwell Bridewell; Samuel Gregory with Jasper in Old Gravel Lane; and Herbert Haines at or near his barber's shop in Hog Lane, Shoreditch.

There now appears a curious distinction, for whereas the above (excluding Jeremy Gregory and Saunders) could be said to represent the East End of London, the remainder, for the most part, appear to represent what could be termed the West End. Joseph Rose and Mary Brazier in Dawes Street near the *Black Horse Inn* in the Broadway, Westminster; John Wheeler, apparently with them; Humphrey Walker, probably in Westminster; and John Fielder, near enough to Rose to meet him in the *Black Horse* on at least two occasions.

Finally, although not affecting the events of the first three weeks of February, there is reason to believe that John Jones may have lived at Hackney during the same period. He was born there and his family lived there, and after the rest of the gang had been captured or dispersed he eventually returned there.

A number of changes of address took place *before* 4 February. Turpin for one, moved from Whitechapel, and took up lodgings, near Millbank,

Westminster. Jeremy Gregory was never out of touch with his brothers and may have gone to Old Gravel Lane after his escape from the Bridewell with William Saunders who, although there is no direct evidence, may have joined Humphrey Walker in or about Westminster.

It is important to note the distinction between the East End and Westminster, because it is at this time that the attention becomes focused on the latter district. The emphasis to date has been more on the East End, and it can only have been accidental that Westminster became the backcloth against which the final scenes were enacted.

The source of the above information lies mainly in reward advertisements and printed proceedings of trials; the East End details being taken from the former and those for Westminster from the latter. But in the following passage there appear some other associates of whom we have heard nothing before:

> Turpin was now thirty [sic] years old ... During this period [January/February] he was living in a house in a court near Millbank, Westminster. It was also near here that Rust and Rose lived, together with another member of the gang named Fletcher. The last named was at that time living with the notorious Nan Turner of Golden Lane memory, who was a fugitive from justice, being wanted by the authorities for the murder of a fellow lodger of her own class, in one of the dens she frequented.[1]

The reappearance of Rust is no surprise, but what of the notorious Nan? Miss Turner may not have been quite so memorable a character as her description here suggests; she does not prove very easy to find in the Calendars and Chronicles and Registers, those crowded printed epitaphs of criminals long dead and for the most part for as long forgotten. Assuming that she did exist, that she was a contemporary of Turpin's, then there may have been some account of her which linked her name with him or his fellows, from which the nineteenth century chronicler drew his information. But it is unlikely in this case because these new characters appeared for the first time in the same chap-book in which Rust originated, an account remarkable for its invention if nothing else.[2] The fictions it created were however perpetuated in subsequent chap-books and eventually incorporated in more ambitious biographies of which the above is a more recent example. If the notorious Nan was eventually captured, and one had known the date of committal, it would have been possible to have said at least that she might have been in London in 1735; as it is her name does not otherwise appear with known members of the Gregory gang, and since the ubiquitous Rust is also present, it would seem more reasonable to relegate Nan Turner and the man called Fletcher to his company than to allow them into the known and proved company of the Gregory gang.

II

On 1 February 1735 two of the gang escaped from the Bridewell and others went to rob the Widow Shelley. On 2 and 3 February snow and sleet would have driven most people, including robbers, to seek the warmth of their firesides. It had been a generally mild winter, wetter than normal, so on those few occasions when the temperature did drop below 40°F., or low enough to produce snow, the contrast would have been quite marked and keenly felt. On 4 February the weather had cleared again and the scene is Earlsbury Farm, about a mile equidistant from Edgware and Stanmore in Middlesex. The household consisted of Joseph Lawrence Snr., Thomas Lawrence his son, Dorothy Street a maidservant, John Pate a manservant, and James Emmerton a shepherd lad. Not far away, on property belonging to the same farm, lived Joseph Lawrence Jnr., the farmer's other son. Both dwellings were completely isolated. At about 6 a.m., Thomas Lawrence left the farm on business, not intending to return until the evening.

At 2 p.m. the same day John Bowler, (otherwise referred to as Rowler *or* Rowletts), the landlord of the *Black Horse Inn* in the Broadway, Westminster, observed five men enter the premises. Their names were Samuel Gregory, Richard Turpin, John Wheeler, Joseph Rose and John Fielder. Bowler recognised Wheeler and Rose because they lodged in Dawes Street nearby and were regular customers, and Fielder who had been with them twice. He does not appear to have known Gregory or Turpin. Three horses belonging to Rose, Wheeler and Fielder stood in his stables, a sorrel, a brown and a bay; although another source of information suggests that only Wheeler's and Gregory's horses were stabled there on that day. Their meeting there was not accidental. Gregory had told them that several years before he had worked at Richard Taylor's smithy at Edgware and had shod horses at both houses at Earlsbury Farm. He knew that Farmer Lawrence paid all his employees very well and that he must therefore be very rich. With this advice the other four would have needed very little persuasion to accept Gregory's offer to shew them the way. The *Black Horse* was merely their rendezvous and they remained there but a short time before setting out.

Gregory, Rose and Wheeler went off first, and Fielder and Turpin overtook them on the road to Edgware. At about 4.15 p.m., on a hill on the London side of Edgware, they stopped at the *Nine Pin and Bowl* (which Wheeler knew as the *Bowl and Skittle*) to refresh themselves after their journey. Richard Wood was the proprietor who served them with two or three pots of ale during their stay, and who noticed as he was feeding their horses that in addition to a sorrel, a brown and a bay, one of the horses was black. He was also to remember the faces of Gregory and Wheeler, and Fielder who was tall and wore a blue coat. The five men did not stay more than three quarters of an hour, and at about a quarter to five they were on the road again. Fifteen minutes later the sun had set, and the sky was darkening when they made their next stop at the *Queen's Head Inn* at Stanmore. The landlord was Joseph Ironmonger, and it was about 6.15 p.m. when the gang came into his establishment and ordered bacon and eggs and beer for their supper. It was too dark for the landlord to notice the colour of their horses, but two other customers, Thomas Martin and Arthur Allen were able to confirm the landlord's statement that the five men stayed about an hour. It was by that time four or five minutes past seven o'clock and the riders turned their horses back towards London. This time however, they did not keep to the road, but turned instead towards Earlsbury Farm, tying up their horses about quarter of a mile from the house. It was quiet then and they were just about to start forward towards the house when they heard James Emmerton, the sheep boy, calling up the sheep; so they waited a little and then went forward again.

Having crept forward unobserved right up to the sheep house, Fielder vaulted over the half door and seized James Emmerton; then threatening him with a pistol not to make any noise, he tied the lad's hands together with his own garters. The others had by this time come into the sheep house and they asked Emmerton what servants there were in the house and he told them. They told the boy he would not be harmed and that they would give him some money if he would go to the farmhouse door and knock and then answer anyone who should ask who was there. His hands were unbound and he was led to the door, but he was so frightened he could do nothing and in the end Gregory himself knocked and called out for Mr. Lawrence.

John Pate unbolted the door and they all rushed in. Gregory, Rose and Wheeler had a pistol in each hand, but Turpin and Fielder probably had but one apiece. The room was lit by just two candles, and one of the gang swore at Pate, 'Damn your blood! How long have you lived here?' which must have been Gregory since he was the only one who had any knowledge of the household.

The night was quite cold, and in a room off the one they had first entered a log fire blazed in the hearth. They wasted no time warming their hands however and whilst the inhabitants were still in a state of shock, made them powerless to resist.

James Emmerton's hands were retied and sitting him on the floor they threw a tablecloth over his head. John Pate was similarly prevented from seeing what went on. Dorothy Street was in the back house churning butter when she heard all the noise in the parlour. Her immediate reaction was to snuff out her candle and stay quiet. She had not long before taken some of the scalding water from the kettle, replenishing it with cold. A number of things all seemed to happen at once. Whilst old Joseph Lawrence was being blindfolded with his neckcloth, others were taking James Emmerton into the room with the fire and removing the tablecloth from his head. They asked him what firearms there were in the house, and when he told them his master kept an old gun they found it and smashed it to pieces. John Pate had the cloth taken off him and his hands bound, and then he too joined Emmerton by the fire. Others meantime had discovered Dorothy Street cowering in the darkness in the scullery. She too was bound and by the time she was deposited in the room with the fire, Joseph Lawrence had been put there. Some of the gang swore at him and demanded his money, whilst others opened a cupboard and took out a bottle of elderberry wine from which they made everybody take two drinks. There was also some linen and plate in the cupboard, and this was removed to take away.

At this point in the proceedings, which with the wine had so far been quite a convivial affair, Joseph Lawrence's personal nightmare began. He was threatened with death if he did not reveal where his money was, and when he didn't, willing hands removed from his pockets a gold guinea, a thirty six shilling piece and about a pound in silver. Two buttons were snapped off his breeches in the process, and when they began to fall of their own accord, Turpin helped them on their way until they shackled the old man's ankles. To his lasting shame he lacked other means of preserving his modesty, but that was really the least of his worries.

He was forced upstairs and more money demanded of him, but he appears not to have told them anything. He could see nothing for he was blindfolded all the time, and his breeches dragged round his ankles. Apart from what was done to him, his only recollection of the gang was that when they came in they all had their capes up and one of them had a linen cloth over his face. But whilst they were upstairs ransacking the house, Wheeler was downstairs guarding the three servants. Closets were broken open and various articles taken, gold, silver, linen, plate, even the bed sheets were ripped off and the mattresses trodden all over in case money should have been hidden inside, and still they were not satisfied and Lawrence had to suffer further indignities. On coming downstairs Turpin dragged him into one of the rooms and whipped him about the buttocks with his hands until the old man was black and blue, then the others came and beat him over the head with their pistols, took him into the scullery and emptied the kettle of water (which Dorothy Street had partly refilled with cold water) over him and dragged him back into the parlour and made dire threats to induce him to tell them what other money was in the house. Their frustration at finding little cash when Gregory had told them Lawrence was a rich man appears to have made them act in a wholly malicious manner towards the farmer, and even then his torment was not complete, for he was forced to lay down near or sit on the fire. With blood running down his face from the head wounds inflicted by their pistols, his clothes soaked through with water and his buttocks burnt, Lawrence must have presented a pathetic figure, but Rose still thought fit to put the point of a case knife under his chin and threaten to cut his throat; whilst another placed a bill hook across his shins and swore to chop his legs if he did not reveal his fortune. But by then they were weary of trying to persuade him to reveal what else might be found in the ransacked house, and whilst Turpin, Rose and Fielder thought it might be fun to sport with the old man, Gregory left them and went into the room where the other prisoners lay bound, and guarded by Wheeler.

For Lawrence the experiences of the next ten minutes or quarter of an hour were to prove, if not as painful, then more humiliating than anything he had suffered before. The three mens' idea of sport was to pull the farmer around by his nose or, alternatively, the hair of his head. That his condition before this treatment began should not have aroused some sense of remorse or compassion in these men is perhaps the truest reflection of their characters that has been seen to date. As deerstealers their cruelty was shrouded by the forest until terrorism and murder revealed them as they were. Their preliminary robberies were committed in a harmless enough manner until revenge prompted the wanton violence and destruction committed in Mason's house in December 1734. And in January an almost charitable regard for their victims perhaps brought reciprocal indulgence from the public, if not their victims and those in authority who were beginning to appreciate just how dangerous a gang was responsible for a, by then, long and unsolved series of crimes. But February revealed them finally as desperate, brutal men without pity, men whose feeling towards the rest of humanity was one of contempt.

Whilst Fielder, Rose and Turpin were tormenting Lawrence, Samuel Gregory went into the room where James Emmerton, John Pate and Dorothy Street were being guarded by John Wheeler. Their hands were all bound, Wheeler had merely stood watch over them with pistols in each hand. Gregory, sullen and frustrated at not having found as much ready money as he had expected, surveyed the group and his eyes were drawn to Dorothy Street. She no doubt regarded him fearfully, particularly when he dragged her to her feet and demanded, 'Damn ye, shew me where your master's money

The Gregory Gang

is.' Miss Street, a maidservant, curtsied and replied, 'Sir, I do not know where it is.'

Gregory then said that she should go upstairs with them, and with Wheeler leading the way forced her in front of him up the stairs into Joseph Lawrence's room. One of the other three presumably stood guard in Wheeler's place, but in Wheeler's mind it is possible there was beginning to form some seed of doubt concerning Gregory's real motive for bringing Dorothy Street upstairs. There was some talk of ransacking Lawrence's room, which must surely already have been accomplished; and then, since Wheeler went to the foot of the garret stairs, a suggestion from Gregory that they should go up there instead. It seems clear that at this point there was no longer any doubt about Gregory's intentions, because whereas he swore that he would go up and forced or carried the girl up to the garret, Wheeler refused to accompany him and returned downstairs.

Once in the garret Gregory swore that he would lie with her. Dorothy Street protested that she was a young girl and a virgin. Her captor however bolted the door and swore that if she did not yield he would kill her. To emphasise the threat he threw her on the bed and proceeded to lay one pistol beside her and another on a chest near the bed. He told her he would shoot her if she cried out, then he threw up her petticoats and raped her. Dorothy Street's description leaves no doubt in the mind, and since, so far as is known, her hands were still tied, there can be no doubt that it was rape. 'He pulled up my coats and took out what he [had there] and [pushed it] into me. And he pushed as hard as ever he could for the Life and Soul of him.'

When Gregory had finished what he had probably had in mind to do for some time he asked Dorothy Street if she had been a virgin. She replied she had not lain with a man before, and he then allowed her to go downstairs. She was weeping when she arrived back on the ground floor, and Wheeler, who was possibly naïve, asked her, 'What is the matter, has anybody beaten you?' Her reply was, 'No, but one of your men has lain with me.'

The gang had by this time spent about an hour and a half in the house, and ordinarily there would have been nothing left for them to do except ensure they were not followed before they departed. On this occasion there was a complication, for despite their having ravaged the house to such a degree and maltreated Joseph Lawrence, who was over 70 years of age, they had failed to find anything of great value. Lawrence's son Joseph however, lived nearby and Gregory wanted to go and ransack those premises as well. This they would have done had it not been for one thing; Lawrence's other son, Thomas, was expected home, but it was not known at what time. There were only five in the gang on this occasion, insufficient number for Gregory to split the party, leaving some on guard at one house whilst they broke into the other, and yet too dangerous for them all to go to Joseph's house and have Thomas come home and find his father and servants bound on the floor, and then to raise the alarm before they had had good time to escape.

Gregory asked James Emmerton if Thomas would be home that night, and being told he would, they had some discussion about their best course of action. Gregory told Dorothy Street that they would rob the son's house, and eventually they took James Emmerton with them to shew them the way, having first threatened to kill him if, when they returned in half an hour, they found anyone had managed to loosen their bonds. The linen and plate were left behind whilst they were away, and the prisoners made no attempt to escape. Emmerton led them to the door of Joseph Lawrence the younger's house, but they all stayed outside wondering if Thomas might ride up at any moment. Joseph Lawrence knew nothing of their being outside his door and after about half or three quarters of an hour they returned to his father's house. Here they bound the shepherd boy hand and foot, and having made certain the others were also securely bound, brought them all into the parlour and laid them on their backs on the floor. The linen was put into sacks and the plate and other articles stuffed in the deep pockets of their greatcoats. Then they locked the door and threw the key away in the garden before trudging away in the darkness to find their horses.[3]

Bayes' account, presumably from a newspaper source, is basically the same as the above description, but with much less detail. The gang appear to have left Earlsbury farm at about 9 p.m. and a newspaper takes up the story from then on:

> The son [Thomas] who came home soon after they were gone called the boy to take his horse, but could make nobody hear, but at last the old man called out, and told him rogues had been there, and they were all bound and that the said rogues had said they would go rob his brother [Joseph], whereupon he rode and alarmed the town, went to his brother's, but they had not been there, they pursued them to the turnpike, and found they had been gone through for London about an hour.[4]

One would imagine Thomas paused long enough to release his father, and that he went to his brother's to see if all was well there before raising the alarm. Thomas probably went to Edgware to gather help for the chase, but by the time the pursuers reached the turnpike, the gang had passed through an hour before. Even so, Thomas Lawrence must have reached his father's house only five or ten minutes after the gang left.

The gang on their homeward journey, riding hard to escape pursuit, were probably a little soured by their disappointing haul, but Gregory was preoccupied with pleasanter thoughts. One of his companions on the long journey back to London described Gregory's state of mind: 'Gregory, as we were going home, told us, I believe twenty times, that he had lain with the maid in the garret; that be bolted the garret door, and laid a pistol on the bed while he lay with her.'

The gang arrived back in Westminster at about eleven o'clock that night; their day was almost finished, but the Lawrences were no doubt counting the cost of having played unwilling hosts to the Gregory Gang. In money and other articles it did not amount to very much, so it is conceivable that Joseph Lawrence had good reason for keeping quiet; and of the actual cash that was taken, almost all of it belonged to the son Thomas. It is not possible to distinguish exactly because there is a slight discrepancy between the total of the amounts stated in evidence to have been taken, and that which appeared in the inventory of their losses. The father said that there was taken from his pocket a guinea, a thirty six shilling piece, and about twenty shillings in silver; and from the closet upstairs (in cash) two guineas and ten shillings. Thomas Lawrence stated that he lost twenty pounds in money. The inventory of their combined losses was as follows:[5]

		£ s d
1 Silver cup	of the value of	2. 0.0.
4 Silver spoons		1. 0.0.
4 Gold rings		2. 0.0.
1 Pair of linen sheets		4.0.
12 Linen napkins		9.0.
1 Linen table cloth		5.0.
6 Towels		2.0.
6 Linen pillowbiers		3.0.
6 Linen handkerchiefs		3.0.
1 Dimity waistcoat		2.0.
15 Pieces of gold coin called guineas		15.15.0.
3 Foreign gold coins called Moydores		4. 1.0.
– and in loose money		1.10.0.
	Total	£27.14.0.

The total represented here is more than the sum actually shared by the five, for Mary Brazier, the receiver of the negotiable articles, was no more generous in her allowance than any other receiver, despite the fact that Joseph Rose, the man she lived with, was one of the gang. But it is as well to remember the amount of cash taken came to no more than £21 6s. 0d., because a belief to the contrary contributed to the gang's downfall.

The ill treatment of the old man and the rape of his maid were more than even a hardened public could stomach. It also brought about a most remarkable personal vendetta waged by Joseph Lawrence's sons. But it is still

4 February and in a number of Turpin accounts, there are descriptions of the Lawrence robbery which refer to the hiring of horses for the expedition to Edgware. These originated in a retrospective commentary on robberies committed by the gang which appeared in a newspaper over a week later: 'The robberies had hitherto been carried out almost entirely on foot with only the occasional use of a Hackney Coach, but now they aspired to appear on horseback, for which purpose they hired horses at the Old Leaping Bar, High Holborn, whence they set out about two in the afternoon, and they arrived at the *Queen's Head* at Stanmore about five.'[6] The only parts of this report which contain any validity at all are those which give the time of departure and which mention the fact that they called at the *Queen's Head* at Stanmore. The rest is spurious invention. Holborn Bars figure in this account, but at a later date and in an entirely different context. Our concern now is with what occurred after the gang had returned to Westminster at 11 o'clock in the evening of 4 February.

III

The following statements are taken from the trials of Gregory and Mary Brazier and from the testimony of the member of the gang who turned evidence against them. The testimony is given verbatim but where the personal pronoun might reveal the identity of the evidence, his name has been substituted.

From the testimony given at the trial of Mary Brazier.
After John Fielder and Joseph Rose, and the rest of us had robbed Joseph Lawrence, we carried the goods to Joseph Rose's lodging near the *Black Horse Inn* in Dawes Street, in the Broadway, Westminster. We laid the goods on the table and appraised them amongst ourselves. Joseph Rose agreed to take them at the price and to pay us our shares; and they were delivered to the prisoner [Mary Brazier]. We told her where and how we got them. Joseph Rose lay with the prisoner, John Wheeler lay at his back. In about two days she sold most of the goods and paid the money to him [Rose].

From the testimony given at the trial of Samuel Gregory
We came home about eleven, and next day we divided our booty. Rose gave us fifteen shillings for all the linen and he likewise bought of us the two handled silver cup, three gold rings, three silver spoons, but I can't say for how much; and Mrs. Rose made them off for him. He [Samuel Gregory] was with us when we divided the money, and had his part.

Also from testimony given at Gregory's trial we learn John Wheeler alleged that he received four pounds as his share, and Samuel Gregory was alleged to have told a man who visited him in prison that he received 25 shillings of the money taken. Gregory however made every effort to minimise his part in the robbery, and it is probable that his share was at least the same as that supposed to have been received by Wheeler, a sum roughly equivalent to a fifth share in the cash proceeds from the Lawrence robbery.

The statement that the division of booty took place the next day is almost certainly an error. Gregory, for at least another week, was still living with his brother Jasper on the other side of London and had some distance to travel before he reached home. Turpin and Fielder lived nearby, Rose and Wheeler together with Mary Brazier. It is unlikely that Gregory would have gone home and come back the next day, or that the others would have waited until then before they shared the spoils. Gregory did in fact come back three days later, but there is no reason to believe that he would have needed to have done so before then. Besides which, in the first statement, the inference is that the share-out was made before the three, at whose lodging it took place, retired to bed. This is the more logical sequence of events. In all these trial proceedings we depend on the ear of the shorthand writer employed to take down the evidence, and the person who edited his notes for publication. Courts were often noisy and furthermore, it is often clear from nonsensical testimony which appears in print that the true sense of the evidence has been lost somewhere in transition between the witness's mouth and the printed page. So the confusion caused by the inclusion of the word 'day' in the second statement need not necessarily be the fault of the witness; and if this word is deleted, the sense of this passage is then the same as that in the first statement.

There is a similar discrepancy between three versions of what is supposed to have actually been received by Mary Brazier. First there are the goods detailed in the second statement above, secondly the printed proceedings list the goods Mary Brazier was supposed to have received, and thirdly those goods detailed in the original indictment. The inventory of the latter was, 'the pair of linen sheets, nine of the twelve linen napkins, the linen table cloth, two of the six linen pillowbiers, the dimity waistcoat.'[7]

The printed account, in addition to these, gives a silver cup, four silver spoons and four gold rings; which apart from being one short on spoons and rings is the same as given in the first instance. From this it is clear that Mary Brazier was not indicted with having received all the linen, and it may be that although initially she did receive all the goods taken, she was only indicted with having received those articles which were still in her possession at the time of her capture.

IV

On 5 and 6 February Mary Brazier sold what items she could from the Lawrence haul and gave the money to Joseph Rose. He however had already paid the others the agreed price, and none of them can have received much more than five pounds apiece. Only a fraction of this sum came from the sale of goods to Rose, and since Mary Brazier could not have got more than the valuation given to them by Lawrence, the total she and Rose received would by comparison have been less than that received by the others; but by 7 February they all needed more. The Earlsbury five were now rejoined by William Saunders, who had escaped from the Bridewell only a week before, and by Humphrey Walker.

At 5 p m. on 7 February, these seven came to the *White Hart Inn* at the upper end of Drury Lane, where they lingered for some time drinking ale.

A few miles away at Dagot's Farm near St. Marylebone, Stephen Manning *or* Mannington was on the point of lighting the candle in his lanthorn; and in the adjacent stable Edward Jones was about to feed the horses. The master of the farm, William Francis, a near-sighted gentleman with some sense of humour and a liking for punch, was soon to make his way home on foot. Inside the farmhouse, Francis's wife, his daughter Sarah, and their maid Eleanor Williams enjoyed the comfort and safety of their home. They may even have talked of Sarah's sister, who, like her father, was also bothered by her eyes and wore a piece of gold with a hole in it, given to her by her father, hoping it would cure her complaint.

It was a comfortable household, a happy sentimental family; the mother possessed a gold ring with a posy inscribed, 'God did decree our unity'. Another ring, inscribed 'Love entire is my desire' was possibly a partner to the first, belonging to Mr. Francis. They were comparatively wealthy and as one of their treasured possessions was a silver picture of Charles I, washed with gold, it is possible they were of proud Royalist stock. They may have heard of the Lawrence robbery at Edgware a few days previously, but as the women of the household sat at the fire, they can hardly have dreamed that about two hours later they would be the victims of a similar outrage.

The seven, Fielder, Gregory, Rose, Saunders, Turpin, Walker and Wheeler, remained at the *White Hart* until half past six, and then they mounted their horses and rode to the farm in Marylebone Park. They arrived about 7 p.m. Turpin smeared his face with dirt before he and Saunders went into the cow house and bound Stephen Mannington the servant. Then having warned him

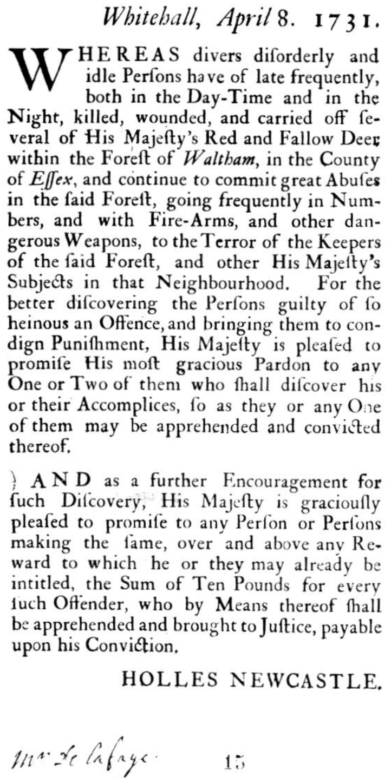

Whitehall, April 8. 1731.

WHEREAS divers disorderly and idle Persons have of late frequently, both in the Day-Time and in the Night, killed, wounded, and carried off several of His Majesty's Red and Fallow Deer within the Forest of *Waltham*, in the County of *Essex*, and continue to commit great Abuses in the said Forest, going frequently in Numbers, and with Fire-Arms, and other dangerous Weapons, to the Terror of the Keepers of the said Forest, and other His Majesty's Subjects in that Neighbourhood. For the better discovering the Persons guilty of so heinous an Offence, and bringing them to condign Punishment, His Majesty is pleased to promise His most gracious Pardon to any One or Two of them who shall discover his or their Accomplices, so as they or any One of them may be apprehended and convicted thereof.

AND as a further Encouragement for such Discovery, His Majesty is graciously pleased to promise to any Person or Persons making the same, over and above any Reward to which he or they may already be intitled, the Sum of Ten Pounds for every such Offender, who by Means thereof shall be apprehended and brought to Justice, payable upon his Conviction.

HOLLES NEWCASTLE.

Mr. de la Faye   15

Plate 1. Printed proclamation offering reward of £10 for the capture of deerstealers. *(Reproduced by courtesy of the Public Record Office. S.P. 36/23/15)*

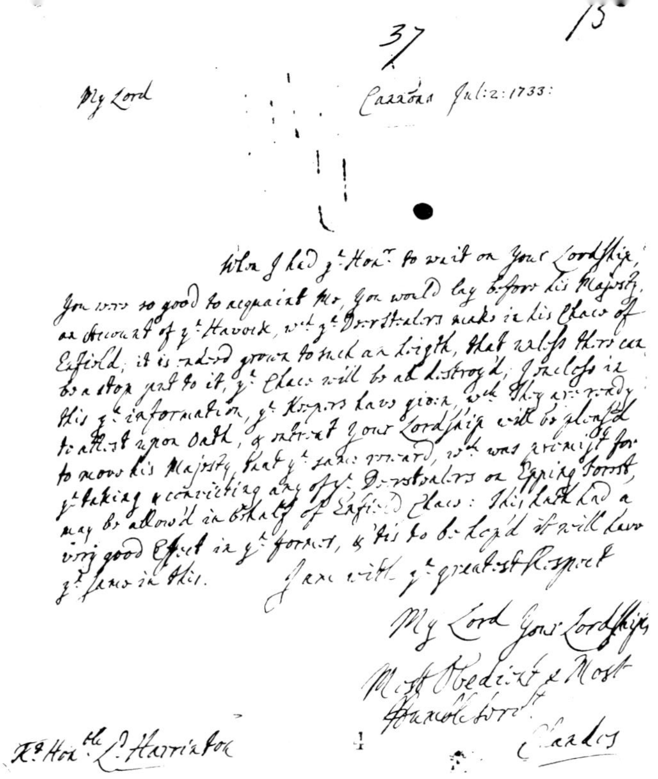

37   13

My Lord   Cannons Jul:2:1733:

When I had ye Honr to wait on Your Lordship, You were so good to acquaint me, You would lay before his Majesty an Account of ye Havock, wch ye Deerstealers make in his Chace of Enfield; it is indeed grown to such an heigth, that unless there can be a stop put to it, ye Chace will be al destroy'd; I enclose in this ye information, ye Keepers have given, wch they are ready to attest upon Oath, & intreat Your Lordship will be pleased to move his Majesty, that ye same reward, wch was promis'd for ye taking & convicting any of ye Deerstealers on Epping Forrest, may be allow'd in behalf of Enfield Chace: This hath had a very good Effect in ye forrest, & tis to be hop'd it will have ye same in this. I am with ye greatest Respect

My Lord Your Lordships

Most Obedient & Most Humble Servt

Chandos

Rt Honble Ld Harrington

Plate 2. Letter from the Duke of Chandos, asking for rewards in respect of the Enfield Chase deerstealers, on the same terms as those offered for Waltham Forest. *(Reproduced by courtesy of the Public Record Office. S.P. 36/30/4)*

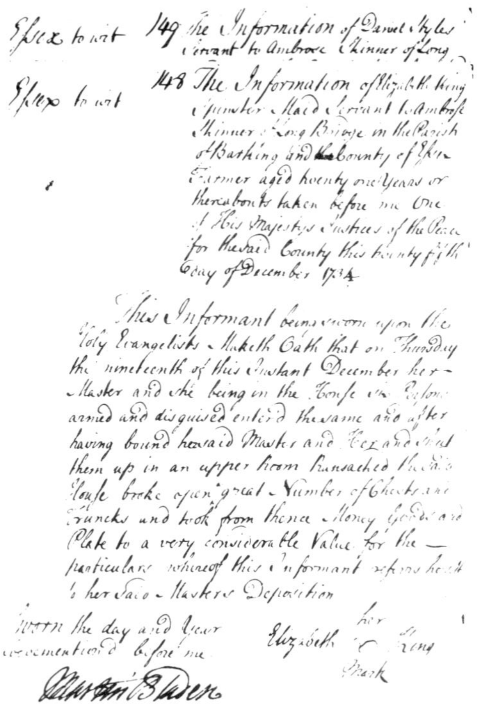

Essex to wit 149 the Information of Daniel Styles servant to Ambrose Skinner of Long

Essex to wit 148 The Information of Elizabeth King Spinster Maid Servant to Ambrose Skinner of Long Bridge in the Parish of Barking and the County of Essex Farmer aged twenty one Years or thereabouts taken before me One of His Majestys Justices of the Peace for the said County this twenty fifth day of December 1734

This Informant being sworn upon the Holy Evangelists Maketh Oath that on Thursday the nineteenth of this Instant December her Master and she being in the House ... armed and disguised entred the same and after having bound her said Master and Her and shut them up in an upper Room Ransacked the said House broke open great Number of Chests and Trunks and took from thence Money Goods and Plate to a very considerable Value for the particulars whereof this Informant refers herself to her said Masters Deposition

Sworn the day and Year abovementioned before me

Martin Bladen

Elizabeth her King mark

Plate 3. Information of Elizabeth King, servant to Ambrose Skinner, a victim of the gang.

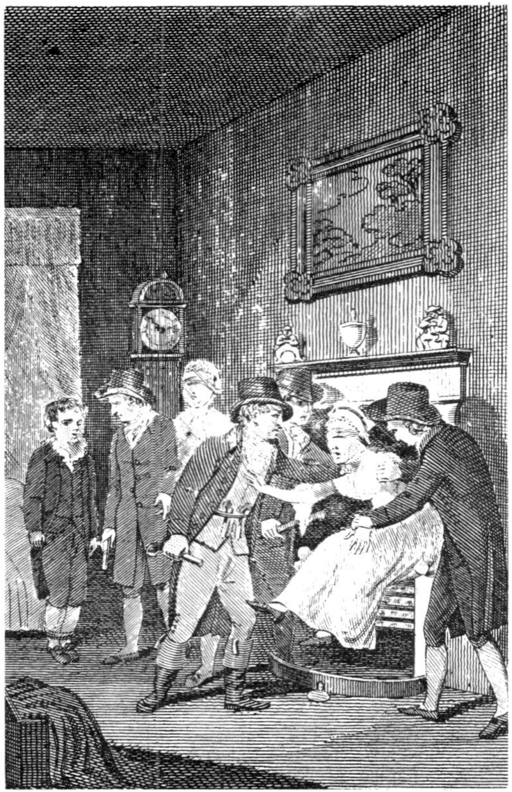

Plate 4. The Widow Shelley being roasted by the gang.
(Reproduced by courtesy of the

to be silent, they went next door into the stable and dealt with Edward Jones who was feeding the horses. They tied him up with his garters, then brought Mannington in from the cow house and laid him next to Jones and remained there, pistols in hands, standing guard over them.

The other five being satisfied that it was safe to move to the house, were about to do so when they heard someone approaching the gate. It was William Francis, and there was just enough light left for him to see three of them approach him before they clapped strong hands on his shoulders and around his neck and prevented him going any further. Francis thought they were having some sport with him and said, 'Methinks you are mighty funny, gentlemen,' but realised his mistake when they displayed their pistols. They bound him then and deposited him in the stable with the other two under the care of Saunders and Turpin.

Wheeler then led the way to the house and knocked on the door. Sarah Francis left her seat by the fire to open it, and then Wheeler came in with the others close behind him. They all had pistols in their hands and they bade her hold her tongue or they would shoot her. The maid, Eleanor Williams, cried out, 'Lord, Miss Sarah, what have you done?' This reaction provoked one of the gang into striking the maid, and another struck Sarah Francis. Mrs. Francis, confused by their entrance, was startled by this treatment of her daughter and maid and cried out, 'Lord, what is the matter?' Fielder (the evidence conflicts on the identification, for one witness named Rose; Fielder is probably correct) swore at her, 'Damn you for an old bitch, I'll stop your mouth presently,' and struck her over the head with the handle of his whip. Blood flowed down over her face and clothes but this did not stop Fielder tying her down in her chair. Gregory stood over her then to make sure she made no more noise, but the daughter and the maid were tied up and carried into the kitchen. Gregory then remained in the parlour whilst three or four of the others went upstairs and ransacked the house.[8] One newspaper was so accurate in reporting the dialogue which occurred, it would be as well to record other details from it which do not appear above. These commence at the point where Mr. Francis has been made prisoner:

> No harm, they said should come of him if he would but give his daughter a note by one of them, authorising her to pay bearer a hundred pounds in cash. Mr. Francis declared he could not do so, he had not anything like that amount in the house. Then knocking at the door of the house, and Miss Francis opening it, they rushed into the passage and secured her as well. The foremost men were particularly rude and violent, but one, remonstrated with them about this gross usage, and stopped it, only assuring her that it would be best if she remained quiet, and that if she made any resistance she would be treated even worse. Miss Francis and the maid were tied to the kitchen dresser, and one was deputed to watch them.[9]

It is not known which of the four besides Gregory remained on guard in the kitchen, but this news item suggests that one of them had some finer feelings left. The idea of obtaining £100 by a trick seems a little unlikely in the circumstances, mainly because such chicanery would not have required a force of seven men to accomplish it. Rather than dismiss this part of the report entirely however, it would be as well to observe that on this occasion the gang were unusually nervous, they were also more in need of cash than kind, and it is possible that they thought by this device to accomplish their purpose with the minimum of risk.

They had every reason to feel nervous. For such a large combination of men to operate for over three months with such frequency without one of them being identified let alone captured was remarkable. They had survived the Mason/Skinner reward advertisement, and had not been in any great danger since its publication, but with three robberies in the first week of February, they were indeed living dangerously. There was really no need for them to see the spate of reward advertisements which began to appear after the Francis robbery, nor for them to feel any premonitions about the future, because by this time there can be no doubt that they were not so much spurred on by immediate necessity as drunk with power, adventure, excitement, money and a compulsive dicing with death. Each successive ride was another tilt at the Tyburn tree, inevitably fatal and without redeeming virtue, and one must concede that Samuel Gregory was leading his gang by the shortest and quickest route to the gallows. This wasn't very intelligent, but since he ended up there himself there remains the question, what qualities did this man have which distinguished him from the rest?

In these days of comparatively sophisticated criminal leadership and organisation, one tends to forget that it was not so very long ago that the basic attribute required to lead lawless men was to be stronger than they were. Gregory, a farrier, probably possessed those qualities which inspired the traditional image of the English smithy, a brawny muscular figure in leathern apron, hammer thudding on anvil, great bulging forearms and a ham fist reputed to have been capable of felling an ox. If he was half such a man he would have commanded the respect of the others, finesse would have brought him a bloody nose and a thick ear.

Gregory claimed that his share of the Francis robbery proceeds was two guineas. At his trial he seemed to deliberately quote a low figure in an attempt to minimise his guilt in the Lawrence robbery, but when all the evidence against him for that robbery had been presented he acknowledged his part in the Francis one and stated this amount to have been his share. If this was so then Gregory was being duped by the others who went upstairs and

The Gregory Gang

stole in cash enough to have guaranteed about seven guineas per man. But that is something which may not be resolved, for although one member of the gang believed himself to have been cheated out of his proper share of the proceeds of various robberies, it was not Gregory. The certainty is that from Francis and his household the gang removed a most impressive collection of valuables.[10]

		£ s d
1 Silver tankard	of the value of	6. 0.0.
1 Gold watch		10. 0.0.
1 Gold chain		5. 0.0.
1 Gold seal		1. 0.0.
1 Silver picture of King Charles I washed with Gold		10.0.
1 Silver punch ladle		15.0.
1 Silver cup		12.0.
1 Pair of silver spurs		2. 0.0.
1 Coral for a child set in silver		10.0.
1 Mourning gold ring with a cypher		10.0.
1 Piece of gold with a hole in it		8.0.
1 Silver strainer		10.0.
1 Silver thimble		1.0.
1 Gold ring enamelled in blue with a stone in the middle and a diamond on each side and under it two angels holding up a crown with a cypher under the crown		2. 0.0.
1 Gold ring with a posy "God did decree our unity"		15.0.
1 Gold ring with a posy "Love entire is my desire"		10.0.
2 Plain gold rings		1. 0.0.
1 Gold ring with four diamonds and a stone in the middle		1.10.0.
1 Gold ring set with diamonds		1. 0.0.
1 Perriwig		2. 0.0.
6 Cambric handkerchiefs		10.0.
4 Linen shirts		1. 0.0.
1 Velvet hat		12.0.
2 Pistols		10.0.
37 Pieces of gold coin called guineas		38.17.0.
and in loose money		10. 0.0.
	Total	£88. 0.0.

As they emptied their sacks, each member of the gang must have felt some stirring of envy for those members of society who could own such property and whose standard of living would always be above theirs. People who did not have to steal and convert what they had stolen into money which itself would dwindle away to nothing like sand in an hour glass. Envy was perhaps the root cause of their rebellion against society. But whatever the reason, the rebellion was nearly over. There were very few grains of sand left, for the seed of destruction lay in their own midst and had been there from the beginning of their association as a robber gang. His name was John Wheeler, and when he was taken in company with two others four days later on 11 February, he then turned evidence against the rest of the gang.

Wheeler was directly responsible for the execution of seven men, the transportation of two men and one woman, and indirectly responsible for the deaths of two other men. Turpin was the instrument of his own downfall and is not included in the above statistics. But when one man causes the deaths of nine others, former friends to boot, there is good reason to inquire into the circumstances which brought about their end.

FOOTNOTES

1. *Immortal Turpin,* Arty Ash and Julius E. Day, 1948, Staples Press.
2. *Life and Trial of Richard Turpin,* A New Edition, with Additions, c. 1808.
3. Based on evidence submitted at the trials of John Fielder and Joseph Rose, and of Samuel Gregory. *Old Bailey Sessions Proceedings,* for March and May 1735, printed by J. Applebee.
4. *London Evening Post,* 4 to 6 February 1735.
5. Middlesex/MJ/SR 2631 Indictments Nos.14 and 15.
6. *Read's Weekly Journal,* 15 February 1735.
7. Middlesex/MJ/SR 2634, Indictment No.46.
8. Based on evidence submitted at the trial of John Fielder, Joseph Rose, William Saunders and Humphrey Walker. *Old Bailey Sessions Proceedings,* for March 1735, printed by J. Applebee.
9. *London Evening Post,* 18 to 20 February 1735.
10. Middlesex MJ/SR 2631 Indictments Nos.12 and 13.

BOOK THREE

JOHN WHEELER THE EVIDENCE, AND ARCHELAUS PULLEN, CONSTABLE

CHAPTER ONE

I

THE DAY following the Francis robbery there appeared a proclamation offering a reward for the discovery, etc. of criminals involved in four robberies:

Whitehall, February 8th 1734/5

> Whereas the dwelling houses of the several persons following vizt. of Peter Split at Woodford chandler and grocer, of ... Eldridge at Walthamstow, of Mrs. ... Shelley widow at Lawton, of the Revd. Mr. Dyde at Parnedon all in the county of Essex were lately forced into in the night time and robbed of money and other things to a considerable value; his Majesty for the better discovering and bringing to Justice the several persons concerned in the above-mentioned robberies, or either of them is pleased to promise his most gracious pardon to any one of the said persons who shall discover his accomplices or accomplice, in the said facts or either of them; so as he or they be apprehended and convicted thereof; and as a further encouragement his Majesty is also pleased to promise a reward of fifty pounds for every one of the criminals who shall be discovered and apprehended to be paid upon the conviction of the offender or offenders.
>
> Holles Newcastle[1]

This was published in the *London Gazette* of the same date, and subsequently in the daily and weekly newspapers, but why were these four robberies associated with each other, and what was the source of the information which led to them being identified as the work of one particular group of criminals? If there had been some substance to the report that one of the gang had been captured on 25 January, or some other person, perhaps on the fringe of the gang's activities, had secretly informed on them, one would have expected the proclamation to have been more specific about those responsible for the robberies, but lacking such details it is clear that the association of events was little more than inspired guesswork on the part of someone who convinced the authorities by his argument. The clue to this exists in the re-iteration of the two Woodford robberies, although that of Richard Wooldridge has suffered a little from the passage of time and become ' ... Eldridge at Walthamstow'.

Martin Bladen, J.P., had already suggested as far back as December 1734 that the Woodford robberies were committed by the gang responsible for the Mason and Skinner affairs, and proof of his having connected the Rev. Mr. Dyde and Mrs. Shelley appeared almost two years after his original suggestion. On 14 December 1736 he wrote to Lord Harrington about a case of intimidation, and prefaced his letter in the following manner:

> Albrohatch near Ilford in Essex
> 14th December 1736
>
> Your Lordship was troubled with an application from this neighbourhood, about two years ago, on account of some robberies, that had been committed by numbers of rogues in bodies; and his Majesty was pleased to order notice to be given in the *Gazette,* of his gracious intention of granting a pardon to any of them, that should discover his accomplices, together with a reward of fifty pounds each, for so many of them as should be convicted by such discovery. And though no formal information did ensue upon that notice, and consequently the Treasury was put to no expense by it, yet it certainly had a good effect, for there is reason to believe, that it created such a distrust amongst those miscreants, as broke the combination, for they were never known to rob in such numbers together afterwards, and almost all of them have since been hanged.[2]

Bladen was naïve in believing this particular notice was responsible for breaking the gang, but he was right about the one thing which distinguished it from all others published in connection with the activities of the Gregory Gang; no-one was ever tried for their part in these robberies, and without a conviction from charges arising from them, no-one ever had opportunity to claim this particular reward. On all other offers made, claims were put forward by a large number of people, and the total paid out in settlement by the Treasury was quite considerable. So only a few days before the above proclamation appeared in the *Gazette,* Bladen wrote to Harrington who acted on his letter. One thing is certain about the letter's date; it must have been after 1 February because that was the day when the Widow Shelley was robbed.

II

Less than three months before the date of Bladen's corroboratory letter, evidence was created which makes it difficult to appraise the appearance of the Split & Company advertisement with a completely open mind. For on 30 September 1736 Wheeler the Evidence was released from New Prison, and the Keeper of the prison claimed expenses for his board and lodging. The only unusual feature about this claim was the fact that it was inclusive from date 8 February 1735! Since substantial proof exists for Wheeler's not having been captured until 11 February 1735, this information raised a number of questions, particularly since Wheeler himself, when giving testimony at the trial of Mary Brazier, stated that she had taken his money and linen from a box at their former lodgings whilst he was in the Gatehouse at Westminster. Prison accounts for this period and this prison have not survived, so it is not possible to substantiate the Keeper's claim. But details of committal to the Gatehouse have, and it is certain Wheeler was *not* kept a prisoner there. His reference to the Gatehouse relates to his attendance on the Justice of the Peace there to inform against the rest of the gang. His belongings were found to be missing when search was made for Rose and Mary Brazier at the address Wheeler himself had given to the authorities. The Keeper's claim was subsequently allowed in full, but the evidence of Wheeler's capture on 11 February is otherwise so overwhelming one cannot do more than ignore this apparent contradiction; similarly, there is no evidence whatsoever that would support Wheeler's having collaborated with the authorities *before* 11 February.[3]

III

One newspaper, referring to Wheeler's capture in retrospect, declared that Wheeler was himself impeached by a member of the gang who had been captured a few days previously:

> Wheeler the housebreaker who was taken with two of his accomplices on Tuesday sevennight in King Street, Bloomsbury, was himself then impeached together with all the rest of the gang by a fellow who had been apprehended some days before and committed to Chelmsford Gaol, so that it is questioned whether he will be admitted to the advantage of an evidence, unless he obtains favour by some extraordinary discoveries. It is said the gang consists of no less than 50 persons.[4]

It is important to note that this was a retrospective view, which appeared on 22 February, for by this date it was common knowledge that one of the gang was in Chelmsford Gaol. The man was Jasper Gregory and although the actual date of his capture is not known, he was the only member of the gang committed to Chelmsford Gaol on or before the newspaper date. If, as was claimed, someone impeached Wheeler and the rest, it would have had to have been him.

This is an absurd notion from an irresponsible report. Samuel Gregory lived with Jasper at Old Gravel Lane, and although latterly Jasper does not appear to have travelled with the gang, having his brother living with him suggests an amicable relationship. A betrayal of this order seems unlikely in the circumstances.

But the main reason for disputing a betrayal by Jasper lies in the fact that it was Wheeler who did. Whether or not Jasper was committed before Wheeler is immaterial, because if he had impeached the gang before Wheeler did, there would have been no justifiable reason for preferring the latter's evidence. And no-one else besides Wheeler ever did give evidence against the others.

Could Jasper Gregory have been captured before Wheeler and the others, by some means other than as a direct result of Wheeler's betrayal? There is a very strong possibility that he was, because Jasper was the only member of the gang at whose trial Wheeler was not called upon to give evidence. But if Jasper was not captured as a result of Wheeler's information (which did in fact name him), he must have been recognised and identified as one of the men who had taken part in one of the robberies. The only evidence of this is contained in a Treasury warrant dated 25 June 1735, authorising the payment of Blood Money: 'John Harrison, Gent., Under Sheriff of Essex; Paid to John Gladwin and others for apprehending and convicting Jasper Gregory for felony and burglary, as by certificate dated 9th April 1735, &c. £40. 0. 0.'[6]

This is not entirely conclusive of John Gladwin, the victim of the Chingford robbery in the previous December, having effected his capture with or without the assistance of others. As with the payment of rewards offered by proclamation, the lists of persons to whom the money was distributed made no distinction between those making the arrest and those upon whose evidence the offender was convicted; but since in this case Gladwin and Shockley, the victims, were the only persons independent of the gang who could have possessed knowledge of Jasper's involvement, it is almost certain that he was captured as a result of his having been identified by one or the other of those two.

No claim for reward offered by proclamation was made in respect of Jasper's capture and conviction because the publication of the Gladwin reward advertisement postdated his capture. But when it did appear John Jones was named as the accomplice of Jasper, who was described as being in prison, and two others unnamed [*viz.* Samuel Gregory and John Wheeler], who appeared in the *accompanying* proclamation which named those either wanted or who had been captured in connection with robberies committed in *several* counties. Both proclamations emanated from Whitehall on 21 February, three days after Wheeler's officially dated information of 18 February. This document, no longer extant, was the result of all the evidence obtained from Wheeler at several examinations held during the week following his capture, and it was perhaps by this means that Jasper was identified as a member of the gang whilst he was in Chelmsford Gaol. The authorities had no reason to associate the Chingford robbery with the Essex gang before the week beginning 11 February, and it is possible that Wheeler knew Jasper had been captured and made the revelation himself.[6]

Once Wheeler was captured the newspapers, with varying degrees of accuracy, contained reports of the captures of all the rest of the gang and some who were not even members. But the capture of Jasper was not remarked upon at all, which suggests that until 11 February the newspapers like the authorities had no reason to connect the man committed to Chelmsford Gaol, 'some days before,' with the man everyone else was looking for. It should however be noted that what the authorities learned after the 11 February was not *officially* released by them until published in the *London Gazette* of 22 February.

IV

On Monday 10 February, following an account of the Francis robbery committed on 7 February, this oddity appeared in the press: 'These villains are called the Irish Clan, and have made it their practice to go in a body and rob several of the most noted farmhouses in Kent, Essex and Middlesex, and it is said they chiefly consist of haymakers.'[7]

It is particularly curious to find the counties in which the gang operated (with the exception of Surrey) named in this report. Until 11 February the information which would have enabled the press to associate the crimes committed in these counties with the same gang was not forthcoming, so this instance may have been as much guesswork as the reference to haymakers of the Irish Clan. But since most of the robberies committed by the gang were exceptional and similar in execution, it is perhaps not so remarkable that someone made a deduction linking most of the counties in which they were committed. That it appeared the day before the beginning of the week during which Wheeler told all must be regarded as a coincidence.

V

Tuesday 11 February 1735 was the beginning of the end for the Gregory

Gang, although none of them, particularly when they awoke that morning, can have had any intimation of impending disaster. If Jasper Gregory was in Chelmsford Gaol and they knew it, they clearly trusted him, because before midday three of them, Fielder, Saunders and Wheeler, and possibly others, were to meet in normal circumstances.

But even as the proclamation of 8 February was published the authorities in Whitehall were busily extracting information from statements made after the Lawrence robbery, and only a day or so before 11 February, an account of this event had been presented to the King, submitting that a proclamation be published promising a reward for the discovery of the persons responsible for the outrage. The King gave his assent and the proclamation was drafted and sent off to the office of the *London Gazette.* It appeared in the edition for 8 to 11 February.

In the *London Evening Post,* covering the same part of the week, there appeared the following short report:

> Mr. Lawrence, the farmer at Edgware–Bury who was robbed last week (as we mentioned) lies so ill, of the bruises &c. he received that it is questioned whether he will recover, the rogues, after he had told them where his money was, not finding so much as they expected, let his breeches down, and sat him bare on the fire, three several times, which burnt him prodigiously.

This roasting was not mentioned when he testified at the March trial; but it was curiously enough brought forward in evidence at the subsequent trial of Samuel Gregory in May. Even so it may have been some comfort to him that on the same day one newspaper reported his condition, the *Gazette* should include promise of reward for the discovery of the men responsible.

Not far from where Mr. Lawrence lay ill in bed, there lived another man who had good reason to remember the robbery at Edgware. His name was Richard Wood, the landlord of the *Ninepin and Bowl* at Edgware, and not only was his name to appear in connection with the capture of Wheeler and the others later that day, he was to some extent responsible for providing the descriptions which appeared in the *Gazette* that morning:[8]

A Description of the Men

1. A tall black man, with his own black hair; 2. A middle sized man with a large scar in his right cheek; 3. A middle sized man disfigured with the smallpox; 4. A middle sized man; 5. A fresh coloured lusty man, between 40 and 50 years of age.

A Description of the Horses

1. A large bay nag; 2. A little bay nag about 13 or 14 hands high; 3. A bay

nag about 14 hands high; 4. A large black nag; 5. A brown nag about 15 hands high.

The substance of the actual account of the robbery which precedes the descriptions in the *Gazette* has already been described in more detail in a previous chapter. The conditions of the proclamation, which promised a pardon, and £50 reward, were couched in the by now familiar terms which applied in such cases. The exception in this case was that the pardon clause did not apply to 'the person who ravished the maid servant.'

So for the first time since their operations began over three months before, there now appeared descriptions of five members of the gang. With the exception of the man with a scar, they were vague enough to allow the other four to walk the streets alone without much fear of being recognised; but if they were seen together there was a danger that they might be. Assuming that the proclamation was eventually drawn to their notice, there must have been a few misgivings about their immediate future.

Which descriptions fit which men? We know who the five men were who robbed Lawrence, but the only official descriptions we have of any of them are of Samuel Gregory and Turpin. Ash and Day however made a rashly misguided claim: 'Turpin is not clearly identifiable in the above description, but he was number four, since from the details given the others can be recognised.'[9] This was not substantiated in any way, but not only can we associate the men and descriptions, we can also add another description to those given previously, *viz.* Joseph Rose. The identifications are as follows: 1. Fielder—Two witnesses at his trial referred to him as the 'Tall man in blue'; 2. Gregory—From his scar; 3. Turpin—Disfigured by smallpox; 4. Wheeler—Who was described by one newspaper[10] as a young fellow and who therefore cannot have been the next; 5. Rose—A fresh coloured lusty man between 40 and 50 years of age.

But even if some of the five did read their descriptions on the morning of 11 February, none of them could have foreseen what was to happen before midday. Accounts of what happened vary so much that two are used here as a basis to find out what did actually occur. The first is retrospective from a periodical which drew for its material upon various newspapers, the second is from a newspaper which appeared the following day.

> 1. *These rogues providentially discovered.* In all the robberies, which have lately been committed by the numerous gang of rogues, we do not hear that they committed any rape, or behaved in any very cruel and barbarous manner, but at farmer Laurence's; and here we may observe a very remarkable interposition of providence; for that very robbery has been the occasion of most of the

gang's being apprehended, and the whole dispersed, which happened thus: On the 11th of last month [February], being that very day seven night on which the robbery was committed, Richard Wood, who keeps the *Nine Pin and Bowl* Alehouse at Edgware, at whose house the rogues had drunk as they went to Stanmore, coming to town, and passing along King Street, Bloomsbury, he saw some horses standing at an alehouse door, and knew them to be the horses belonging to the fellows who had drunk at his house the Tuesday before, and who, he suspected, were the persons that robbed his neighbour, Farmer Laurence: Upon this he called a constable, and getting some other assistants, they went into the alehouse, where the horses were standing, in which they found a woman drinking punch with three fellows, whom Mr. Wood immediately knew to be three of the five fellows that had been at his house, upon which the constable and his assistants laid hold of the company, and, after some resistance, they were secured, and five pistols taken from them. They were immediately taken before Justice Hind, in Great Ormond Street where they declared their names to be John Fielder, Joseph Rose *(sic)*, and John Wheeler, but obstinately denied their having been concerned in robbing Mr. Laurence, or any other robbery: however, the Justice most prudently signed their *Mitimus* to New Prison, on suspicion; and as they were carrying thither, Wheeler, as may be supposed, then began to foresee, that they would be discovered, and sufficient proofs found against them, before they could get out of jail, whereupon he told the constable, that if he would carry them back to the justice he would confess, and inform against the whole gang: accordingly they were carried back, and Wheeler made an ample confession of all the robberies they had committed, whereupon Fielder and Rose *(sic)* were committed to Newgate, and Wheeler to New Prison, and soon after several others of the gang were apprehended.[11]

2. Yesterday [11 February] about twelve a servant of Mr. Lawrence of Edgware going by at the *Punch Bowl* in King's Street, Bloomsbury, saw one of the villains ... and took three of them, the other two made their escape. The three were carried before Justice Hind in Ormond Street and their *Mittimus* made for Newgate. Whilst two of them were putting in a coach, the third, a young fellow, by the pressing of the crowd, was hindered for some time from being carried to the coach, and the Justice's lady expostulated with him how certain his death would be if he did not confess. He thereupon made a full confession of the whole gang, and that there were seven more not yet taken, upon which he was sent to New Prison in order to be an Evidence, and the other two carried to Newgate. Strict search is making after the rest.[12]

The weekly, or twice and thrice weekly newspapers all carried accounts similar in substance to the first described above, and one[13] contained some distorted elements of the second; but it is clear from almost all except the latter, that the reporters coming late to the scene experienced some difficulty in piecing together the events of the day. All of them however lack in certain vital respects which have been obtained from other sources.

A number of newspapers name Rose, but Saunders was the third man taken in this instance. Similarly *Reid's Weekly Journal* erred in stating that Wheeler was committed to the Compter, he was committed to New Prison.

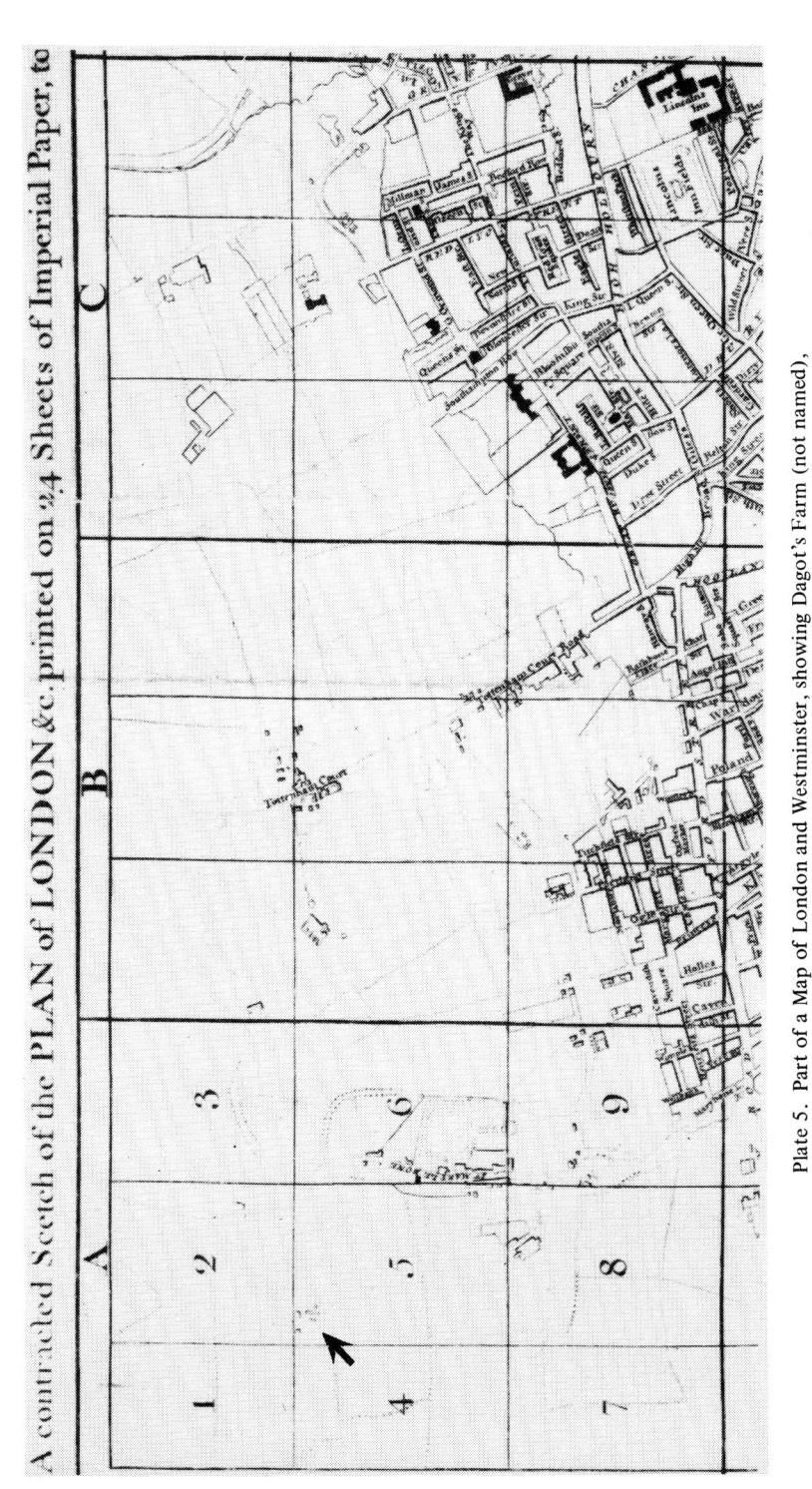

Plate 5. Part of a Map of London and Westminster, showing Dagot's Farm (not named), the scene of the Francis robbery. From the key to J. Roque's 'A Plan of the Cities of London and Westminster ...', 1746. 26 in. to the mile.

Plate 6. Newgate Prison in the 18th century.

Plate 7. New Prison, Clerkenwell in the 18th century.

The claim entered for their capture states specifically that it was effected 'at the *Punch House* in King Street, Bloomsbury,' and names Fielder, Saunders and Wheeler.[14] The two following entries of committal corroborate both the names of the persons and the places to which they were in fact committed: 'No. 46 John Wheeler committed [New Prison] 11th of February by Robt. Hind Esq. on his own confession of being concerned in several robberies in Middlesex, Essex, Kent and Surrey.'[15] 'No. 14 John Fielder and Wm. Schooling[16] committed [Newgate] by Robt. Hynde Junr. Esq. on the oath of Jno. Pates[17] for entering the house of Joseph Lawrence beating him and stealing thence &c. Date 11th February.'[18]

There is some divergence of opinion as to whether Richard Wood saw the horses, or Lawrence's servant saw one of the men in King Street. In the event this hardly matters, but since Jonathan Pates (servant to Lawrence) charged the prisoners there can be no doubt that he was the servant mentioned in the newspapers. For either of these two persons to have recognised horses or men must be regarded as something more than coincidence, and this is supported by testimony given at the trial of Fielder and Saunders:

Richard Wood
Coming to London, I saw the same horses standing at a door in King Street, Bloomsbury. I went in and saw Fielder and Wheeler there with others. Fielder and Wheeler made a great resistance when they were taken, and five pistols were found upon them.

John Pates
I was present when the prisoners were taken, they had several pistols and made a great resistance.

Thomas Lawrence
I was at the taking of the prisoners; I was forced to throw Fielder down before I could secure him.

A number of people clearly shared a vested interest in wanting these men captured, and had been pursuing their own enquiries. Vengeance may be attributed to Thomas Lawrence and Pates, and the capture appears to have been made as a direct result of their intensive search for the robbers and not by means of accidental recognition.

To the claims made by various persons to rewards promised for effecting the capture and conviction of the men responsible for the Lawrence robbery are annexed the awards made in respect of these claims; these list the persons to whom the money should be distributed, and although no distinction is made between persons capturing the robbers and those whose testimony enabled a conviction to be brought against them, it is possible to eliminate some and leave others whose involvement may have been limited to the actual capture. Where known, reasons for receiving share of reward are given: James Emmerton (trial witness), John Wheeler (evidence against his accomplices), Dorothy Street (trial witness), Richard Stevenson, James Powell, William Lindsey, John Davies, John Burt, John Herbert, Thomas Wyatt, George Liddiard, Thomas Wright, John Cookes, John Pate, (trial witness and at capture), Thomas Lawrence, (trial witness and at capture), Richard Woods, (trial witness and at capture), Thomas Taylor, Anthony Wood, Westby Parker, Joseph Lawrence [? Snr.] (trial witness).[19]

The awards were on an ascending scale from Emmerton, who received 12s. 6d., to Joseph Lawrence, who received £7 10s. 0d. Of the twenty persons named, thirteen do not appear elsewhere and the reason for their receiving a share of the reward is not known. The actual distribution was recommended by Mr. Baron Thomson, before whom the prisoners were tried, so to him at least their entitlement must have been clear. But since it is unlikely that Pates, Thomas Lawrence and R. Wood alone effected the capture of three armed criminals, some if not all the other thirteen must have in some way assisted them.

The assistance may have been limited to giving information which resulted in the robbers being traced to the *Punch House,* and since this service did not involve risk to the informers' lives, it would be reasonable to expect to find their names lower down the award scale. Conversely, one would expect to find those actively involved in the capture at the upper end, and of those Thomas Taylor, Anthony Wood and Westby Parker received as much as Pates, Lawrence and R. Wood, which three also testified at the trial. John Cookes received only 10s. 0d. less than those six, so he might also have had more than a spectator's role; but in the lower and middle orders where the awards were half or less than those received by Pates and the other five, it is hard to imagine the men named there having played much more than a supporting role. In various nineteenth century accounts there also appears an entirely fictitious Bob Berry, who, being an innocent bystander, received a dangerous cut on the arm, below the elbow. No such person is listed with those who did receive a share of the reward for the capture and conviction of Fielder, Saunders and Wheeler, and the hapless Berry can be traced only as far back as the 1808 *Life,* with 'additions', in which the elusive Rust and others of dubious origin first appear.

The final comment upon the capture comes, perhaps inevitably, from Bayes. Having dealt with the Lawrence and Francis robberies he describes the undated attempt to rob Justice Asher and then disposes of the Gregory Gang in the following passage:

These transactions alarmed the whole country, nobody thinking themselves safe; upon which Mr. Thompson, one of the King's Keepers, went to the Duke of Newcastle's office, and obtained his Majesty's promise of a reward of one hundred pounds for whoever should apprehend any of them; this made them lie a little more concealed; however, some of the keepers, and others, having intelligence that they were all regaling themselves at an alehouse in an alley in Westminster, they pursued them thither, and bursting open the door found Turpin, Fielder, Rose and Wheeler and two women; Fielder, Rose, and Wheeler, after a stout resistance were taken, but Turpin made his escape out of a window, and taking his horse rode away immediately; Wheeler made himself an evidence, and the other two were hanged in chains.

The gang was then broke, and Turpin quite left to himself ...

Apart from obvious anomalies like the obtaining of the reward and the part played by the keepers, our concern here lies mainly in establishing whether or not Turpin and others were present in addition to the three actually captured. The evidence is slight, and the three relevant items have already been quoted: 'they found a woman drinking punch with three fellows'; 'the other two made their escape'; 'I went in and saw Fielder and Wheeler there with others.'

A number of newspapers stated that a woman was present when the others were taken. This is not disputed. Similarly, from the number of reports which stated Rose to have been captured, there seems little doubt that he too was at the *Punch House*. And since Wheeler was the companion of Rose, we may identify the woman as Mary Brazier. If Rose's presence is disputed, it should be borne in mind that his name was not known at this time and that it must therefore have been mentioned by Wheeler at the arrest. But if two made an escape would Rose and Mary Brazier make up this number? Rose yes, Mary Brazier no, because the searchers were looking for men and Mary Brazier's role of receiver was not known. She could have stood aside from the general melee and merged with the spectators. If anyone escaped with Rose it is more likely to have been Turpin or Humphrey Walker rather than any of those who lodged in the East End of London.

Bayes' passage is so much a fiction based on vaguely remembered facts, his inclusion of Turpin would appear in this case to have been more wishful thinking. The most that one could say about Turpin in this instance is that he *was* able to disassociate himself from the company of others when danger threatened. Perhaps it was nothing but rare instinct, but it did enable him to survive longer than his less fortunate associates. It was the sort of situation from which Turpin would have escaped had he been there, but there is really nothing which would prove conclusively that he was.

The capture was made on the morning the reward advertisements appeared and assuming the searchers had been looking for the gang since 4 February, it is odd that they did not meet with success until that particular moment. If this was not coincidence, we must attribute to the searchers motives based upon expectations of reward for their efforts, which from the date and time of capture would suggest that they already knew where to find the robbers and were merely waiting for the rewards to be published before they pounced. It is appropriate to recall at this point the immediate results obtained with the increased rewards offered for the capture of the Epping deerstealers, and the observation made at that time, that people would not risk their lives tangling with desperate men unless there was sufficient incentive.

In assessing the reasons why John Wheeler betrayed his companions it is worthwhile establishing one thing first. He did so on the day he was captured, within an hour or so of being taken, without any coercion on the part of his captors, and despite his being on such familiar terms with his immediate companions Rose and Brazier that he was allowed to share their bed. Seven men were executed (this includes Walker who died a few hours before he was due to be hung, but who nonetheless was hung in chains), two men and one woman were transported and two others died as a result of his betrayal. Did Wheeler stop to consider, or realise what would be the price of saving his own miserable skin. He was described as a, 'young fellow', as young, possibly, as 15, and certainly not older than 17. He was without doubt the youngest member of the gang; in February 1735 Samuel Gregory was about 23, Herbert Haines about 24, John Jones about 25, Turpin was 30, Thomas Rowden about 30, Joseph Rose between 40 and 50, and Humphrey Walker nearer 50.

Wheeler's having been allowed to travel with them and take part in the robberies suggests that he associated with them prior to their criminal activities, possibly as a carrier to the deerstealers. Even so his graduation to crime appears to have been achieved without difficulty, and in attending as many robberies as any of them (with the possible exception of Samuel Gregory), it is clear that he was trusted by his companions. However, since he was living with the much older Rose, and Mary Brazier, it may be that he was still regarded by the others as the junior member of the gang, an attitude he may have resented somewhat since he must have considered himself their equal when it came to robbery.

From his testimony at the various trials of his fellows it appears that with the full power of authority behind him he did not lack in confidence in condemning them, and the parallel to this is that he must have been equally bold when the gang was all conquering and apparently invincible. It must have been a rude shock when this bubble abruptly burst in his face with first Thomas Lawrence and his assistants overpowering them, and then an unsmiling Robert Hind, J.P., ordering their committal, not to New Prison, but to Newgate. At this point it is not too difficult to imagine the scene and the state of Wheeler's mind.

He, John Wheeler, was to be cast into Newgate. Farmer Lawrence's servant had already sworn they were the men who took part in the robbery, so it would be only a matter of time before they were tried and hanged. His senses were numb but a gradually awakening fear spread from his bowels to bring perspiration to the palms of his hands and desperation to his mind. But Fielder and Saunders stood beside him, heads bloodied but unbowed, denying everything. When his turn came to answer the charge their eyes watched him and hardened at his hesitation, and though his resolution was so weak he would have confessed to his own part, he denied the fact also. Their eyes remained upon him, suspicious and intimidating, apprehensive when his voice faltered and he was unable to control his trembling limbs. And the eyes of his accusers seemed as brutal and unrelenting. Rose and his wife had escaped, but for how long? Even Saunders had been in Bridewell but eleven days ago, and now he was being returned, albeit unrecognised, to another prison. Yet just four days ago he and six others had drunk together before setting out for the farm at Marylebone, and it had all seemed so easy. Did it begin to go wrong when Samuel raped the girl at Farmer Lawrence's, was that when their luck began to run out? Hardly any money came from that raid, and although they got more at Marylebone there were more to share it and it seemed to be less. Then the rumour that Jasper was in the jail at Chelmsford and Samuel talking about trying to get him out and nobody keen. Would they try and rescue them and what would happen to his fifteen pounds in the box he left at Rose's lodgings, would it be safe?

This perhaps was Wheeler's state of mind as the three of them waited for the carriage to take them to Newgate, their hands and feet shackled and guards all around them. But since he was drinking with them that morning, it cannot have been until later that the small amount of money from the last shareout, resolved itself into doubts, real or imagined, about whether or not he had received a fair share at all. And if these doubts did not come of their own accord, they were certainly implanted by someone else:

Wheeler
We took away what money, linen and plate we could find [at Lawrence's]. I saw no more than three guineas and six shillings and sixpence and if they found any more they cheated me of my share. He [Gregory] was with us when we divided the money and had his part and perhaps more than I, for they cheated me in every respect; so that out of £60, I had but four.
FR/L,G/L

Wheeler
As for guineas I saw none, and if there were any [at Francis's] they sunk them upon me.   FSRW/F

Wheeler
When I was in the Gatehouse, she [Mary Brazier] broke open my box which was left in her room, and robbed me of my linen and fifteen pounds in money [presumably accumulated from various robberies].   MB/LF

Thomas Lawrence
When I visited him in prison Gregory said that he had twenty five shillings of the money that was taken.   G/L

Gregory
I own I was at that house [Francis's], and took the money and goods and had two guineas for my share.   G/F

Code:— Trial FR/L   Fielder and Rose for Lawrence robbery.
FSRW/F   Fielder, Saunders, Rose and Walker for Francis robbery.
G/F   Samuel Gregory for Francis robbery.
G/L   Samuel Gregory for Lawrence robbery.
MB/LF   Mary Brazier for receiving goods from both Francis and Lawrence robberies.

There is every reason to believe that Gregory understated the amounts received by him as his share of the proceeds from both robberies, and an interesting result is obtained if one divides the totals of *cash* actually taken on those occasions by the number of men who took part: **Francis** cash taken by seven men totalled £48 17s. 0d., **Lawrence** cash taken by five men totalled £21 6s. 0d. The seven men should each have received about seven pounds from the Francis robbery, and the five men four pounds from the Lawrence proceeds. Wheeler on his own admission did receive four pounds of the Lawrence money and on this occasion at least he did get his fair share. It is certain no-one in the gang told him that £60 was taken from Lawrence, and this figure can only have been suggested to him after his arrest, perhaps to persuade him to reveal some item of evidence he was reluctant to give. Similarly, that his belongings had been rifled may or may not have been true, since when Rose and Mary Brazier fled their lodgings they would in any event have taken removables with them. The irony here is that Wheeler must have given their address to the authorities, with instructions to recover his personal possessions. That they were removed was to be expected and Wheeler could hardly complain, nor could he expect them to be returned to him after he had betrayed the people who took them. Someone had already implanted the seed of suspicion in Wheeler's mind, and to be told that his possessions were gone would have served only to embitter him further.

The *Daily Post* version of the event is as concise as one could wish, and probably as accurate. This was excellent reporting by someone who was either on the spot or there not long afterwards to obtain a quick interview with Justice Hind or someone equally sensible of what had occurred. Its accuracy is underlined by the revelation, 'that there were seven more not yet taken,' a statement which could not have been nearer the truth because there remained at large at that moment the following men, Samuel Gregory, Thomas Rowden, Dick Turpin, Joseph Rose, Humphrey Walker, Herbert Haines and John Jones. Seven principals exactly, and a total which perhaps lends support to the possibility of Jasper Gregory's having already been taken. If therefore one accepts that the rest of the report is as accurate as the above, we have evidence of the circumstances conducive to Wheeler's confessing; namely that he should have become separated from the other two.

He had been beaten and kicked, put in chains, committed to Newgate and shewn the prospect of death. He was also young enough to appreciate that if it ended there, his life would be over before it had really begun. Perhaps he had always harboured some resentment against those who treated him as the junior member of the gang, and realised now that he was in a position to hold sway over them all. Perhaps he was fickle in allegiance, a young fellow vain enough to opt out of being a public enemy if the rewards for being a public hero were greater (it was doubtless pointed out to him that being eligible to claim a share in all the rewards which had been offered for the gang, he *might* ultimately not only escape with his life and freedom but more money than he had received from all the robberies in which he had taken part). But on the afternoon of 11 February, a threatening mob separating him from Fielder and Saunders in the coach, guards on either side trying to push and jostle him through the crowd, and a voice reminding him of his fate, fear won. The gang at this moment in time was possibly symbolised by the two in the coach, tawdry thieves like himself who were doomed to hang unmourned as felons on Tyburn gallows. They seemed far away, small white frightened faces peering at him from the coach windows over the heads of a jeering mob, and they would not be able to exact vengeance now if he chose the alternatives offered by the Justice's wife, his life and recognition as public benefactor. And there was a chance anyway, having seen his hesitation, that the other two would quietly dispose of him in Newgate if he said nothing now and accompanied them there. So he turned his back on a stunned Fielder and Saunders, and as the coach moved away on its journey to Newgate he was escorted back into Justice Hind's house to make his confession.

He gave testimony at the trials of all the gang members except Jasper Gregory, and, ultimately, Dick Turpin. During a period of what can only be termed protective custody of almost two years, subsistence of one shilling a day was claimed for his keep. As might have been expected he did claim and receive a share in a number of the rewards offered, and even after his release, he was sought and found and gave evidence against one of the gang who had contrived to evade capture by serving a short term of imprisonment under an assumed name. He became an honest citizen. We do not know that he suffered from remorse, and if as seems likely he eventually convinced himself that he had been cheated by his companions, it is doubtful that he did. For that reason alone he appears to us as perhaps the most abject figure in an altogether sorry saga of sordid deeds. The times were hard, the justice harder, but an awareness of this is not to condone the violent acts committed by these men on defenceless people. Wheeler was every bit as bad as the rest of them, but his betrayal of them is indefensible. If there is anything which can be said in his favour, it can only be that he was 'a young fellow'.

FOOTNOTES

1. P.R.O./S.P.44/128 p.345.
2. P.R.O./S.P.36/39 ff.338−339.
3. P.R.O./S.P.36/39 ff.145−146.
4. *London Evening Post,* 20 to 22 February 1735.
5. P.R.O./T.53/38 p.16.
6. *London Gazette,* No.7378 (proclamations of 21 February); and P.R.O./S.P.44/131, description of enclosures to letter on p.107 (for date of Wheeler's Information).
7. *Daily Journal,* No.4388.
8. *London Gazette* No.7375; and P.R.O./S.P.36/34 f.52 (date erroneously amended to 18th February) and f.80 (probably a copy of, or the original version of events submitted to the King.
9. *Immortal Turpin,* p.29.
10. *Daily Post,* No.87.
11. *Political State,* Vol.XLIX, Jan.−June 1735, p.242.
12. *Daily Post,* 12 February 1735.
13. *Universal Spectator and Weekly Journal,* No.CCCXXXII.
14. P.R.O./T.53/38, p.159.
15. Middlesex/MJ/SR 2630 (Calendar of Prisoners in New Prison).
16. Schooling was an alias of William Saunders.
17. Jonathan Pate *or* Pates was a servant to Mr. Lawrence.
18. Middlesex/MJ/SR 2631 (Calendar of Prisoners in Newgate).
19. P.R.O./T.53/38 p.160.

CHAPTER TWO

I

THE IMMEDIATE result of Wheeler's action was that those who were not taken with him fled from their usual haunts. A newspaper of Thursday 20 February described the taking of three more of the gang at a Mr. Lloyd's chandler's shop in Thieving Lane. The man who enquiries resulted in this capture was a constable, Archelaus Pullen, whose beat, if one can call it that, was in the vicinity of Tothill Street in the parish of St. Margaret, Westminster. The rider to this report is significant, 'They came to this new lodging but Friday last.'[1]

Friday 14 February, Wheeler taken on Tuesday 11 February, and since the persons referred to were Joseph Rose, Mary Brazier and Humphrey Walker, all of whom might have been present when Wheeler was taken at the *Punch House* in King Street, there is every possibility that the move to Thieving Lane on Friday may not have been their first. We do not know that anyone actually followed prisoners and escort to Ormond Street and learned of Wheeler's betrayal the same day, but those who escaped from the *Punch House* would not have waited for the weekend edition of the newspapers to find out what had happened to their companions.

Rose and his wife immediately removed from Dawes Street, off the Broadway in Westminster; they were joined, either then or when they moved a second time to Thieving Lane, by Humphrey Walker. Turpin, who had lodged at Millbank, but who knew Whitechapel intimately, elected to inform Gregory and the others in the East End of the capture of Wheeler and the other two, and possibly of their all having been betrayed. He did not return to the Westminster area, a fact which is deduced from subsequent events, but even so he was not one to linger at the scene of misfortune or with people associated with it. By the evening of 11 February, there can have been but one or two of the gang who had not been told of the *Punch House* incident. Their reaction to Turpin's news is predictable. On 22 February, there appeared descriptions of those of the gang still at large:[2] Samuel Gregory, 'lodged lately', Herbert Haines, 'kept a barber's shop', John Jones, 'lately resided'. Turpin himself did, 'lately lodge', but of Thomas Rowden nothing more was known except that he had, 'lately arrived'; which references, leaving aside Rowden, are all rather pointedly in the past tense, and the recent past at that. Rowden's would have been, had the authorities been able to establish with greater exactitude the location of the lodgings to which he had but recently come. We know where Rose and his wife and Walker ultimately settled, but wherever the other five went, they didn't stop for long, and this becomes clear within a very short time.

The only other individual reference to flight concerns an unnamed man not closely associated with the gang, but one who certainly feared he might be involved. At the trial, of Rose, Fielder, Saunders and Walker for the Francis robbery, Mr. Francis had this to say, 'We could not bring the man at the *White Hart* in Drury Lane, because he is run away'.

In context it is clear that Francis meant the landlord of the inn at which the gang met before setting out for Marylebone, and though he may have been implicated, it is possible that he was merely scared at the prospect of being called to give evidence at that trial, and at the thought of intimidation by those of the gang still at large. If this was true he may not have fled until such time as he learned he would be called as a witness, which date would have been more towards the end of February.

If there remain any doubts about the immediacy of Wheeler's betrayal *and* the flight of those still at large, these must be dispelled by two separately dated newspaper statements; that of 12 February which said, 'Strict search is making after the rest', and the one on 15 February anticipating by a full week the official pronouncement which described six of those still at large. Descriptions being available on 15 February confirms not only the completeness of Wheeler's betrayal, but the fact that the search had failed.

Having fled and temporarily evaded capture, what did the gang do then? When found, Rose and his companions were calmly drinking punch, but this was six days after the first disaster, time enough for the initial shock to have worn off. 13 February may not have been regarded as a particularly favourable date for doing anything, and on the next day, Rose and his wife and Walker were calm and sensible enough to move to new lodgings in Thieving Lane. That the other five were not cowering in fear and trembling in dark corners is illustrated in a remarkable manner by something which happened on the same day.

II

> On Friday night last, five men masked came to the house of Farmer Savage of Brockley in Kent, entered the same, and rifled the house of all the money and plate and took each of them a shirt, which they said they were in great want of. They stayed some time in the house, eating and drinking, and then went off with as much unconcern as common visitors.[3]

This account is not in other Turpin annals, and there is no tangible evidence which would prove that this robbery was committed by Gregory and the others, but there are three points of particular significance. Firstly the assurance of the robbers, obviously men of some experience at this type of crime, brazen and brimming with confidence. Secondly the place; Brockley now has been swallowed up by suburbia, but in the eighteenth century it was a small, scattered community just outside Lewisham and below Deptford and Greenwich, and within easy reach of London Bridge from the end of the Canterbury to London stretch of the Watling Street. It would have presented no more of a problem to the Gregory Gang than did those other excursions south of the River to Charlton and Croydon. The third point is the curious theft of five shirts, one for each man. In an era when personal hygiene was not considered to be of paramount importance, the stealing of shirts by men who were presumably wearing shirts already is something of a paradox. Even had the robbers been mere down and outs, cold, hungry and driven to desperation, the choice of shirts in February, would still seem odd. But there is a plausible explanation. Travelling men, living out, would have carried some food and a change of clothing with them. Turpin, when driven to living out in Epping Forest some two years later, carried clean shirts with him, and Gregory resorted to the same habit in similar circumstances. We know that Gregory, Turpin, Rowden, Jones and Haines fled their lodgings in the East End, and the events of the next few days suggest that they did not look for new ones. It cannot be proved, but the robbing of Farmer Savage has every appearance of being the prelude to a period when this same five chose to remain continually on the move, in the hope that by this means they would somehow contrive to evade capture. Including Jones as one of the five not only presumes the number represented by the newspaper to have been accurate, but that upon learning of the gang's betrayal, Jones could see no alternative but to rejoin those he could trust.

III

The following morning (15 February) the *Courant* scooped the other newspapers and published an article which anticipated the official pronouncement on the same subject by exactly a week. How the information was obtained, and why it was not picked up by other newspapers during the ensuing week is not known; why the *London Gazette* of 15 to 18 February did not contain the same information is not known; but in printing the report when it did, the *Courant* also gave two descriptions which, because the men to whom they related were captured before the next *Gazette* was published, were not included in *that* edition.

The most likely explanation of this scoop is that the information was leaked out; and other newspapers did not pick it up because the authorities were not ready to release the information (Wheeler's information did not become of official record until 18 February) and therefore suppressed it:

> The under-written persons are charged, by informations upon oath for committing the several robberies and burglaries lately in the neighbouring counties and towns to this city, for whom a reward of £50 each is advertised in the *Gazette*.
> John Wheeler in New Prison
> Joseph Rose a fresh coloured man, about five feet eight inches high, about forty years of age, a blacksmith
> Richard Turpin very much marked with the small pox, about five feet nine inches high, a butcher, about twenty six years of age
> John Fielder in Newgate
> Samuel Gregory a blacksmith, five feet seven inches high, a long scar on his right cheek, ravished the Maid of Joseph Lawrence the Elder of Earlsbury Farm in the Parish of Edgware in Middlesex.
> William Saunders alias Schoolin in Newgate
> Thomas Roden a little thin man, about thirty one or thirty two, a pewterer, wears a light natural wig.
> Herbert Hains a very pale man about twenty five years of age, wears a brown wig, about five feet seven inches high, a barber by trade.
> Humphrey Walker a lusty man about fifty, fresh coloured, a little marked with the small pox, wears a light wig.[4]

The addresses at which the men lived were not given by the *Courant*. They did appear in the subsequent *Gazette,* and it is possible that the *Courant* reporter was unable to obtain more information than he did. The descriptions, except in minor respects, tally with those which appeared in the *Gazette.* Similarly the descriptions of Gregory, Rose and Turpin tally with the outlines which appeared after the Lawrence robbery. But one significant piece of information is that Rose, like Gregory, was a blacksmith. Having this trade in common suggests that their acquaintance was of long standing and that it may even have been made before they turned to deerstealing.

As Jones was omitted from this list and even in the *Gazette* appeared separately in connection with the Gladwin robbery, it is now certain that this was the only robbery committed by him *before* Wheeler's arrest. For this reason it is conceivable that the *Courant,* assuming they possessed his name and description, did not consider the information to be germane to their report, any more than the *Gazette* did in theirs.

Appearing as it did just the once and in only one newspaper, the report may have escaped the notice of the gang, and as events of the same day illustrate, they may in any case have been too busy to bother about publicity. These events are reflected in two incidents which involved the two by now separate factions of the gang. The time at which these incidents occurred is not known, but they are assumed to have taken place on the evening of 15 February.

IV

At the Middlesex Sessions which ended at the Old Bailey on 1 March, John Fielder, Joseph Rose and Humphrey Walker were indicted with having stolen from Ambrose Skinner the Younger, in the Parish of St. Margaret, Westminster, the following goods:[5]

		£ s d
2 Silk gowns	of the value	6. 0.0.
2 Silk petticoats		2.10.0.
1 Silk quilted petticoat		10.0.
2 Suits of cambric headcloths laced		8. 0.0.
8 Muslin handkerchiefs		8.0.
6 Cambric handkerchiefs		10.0.
1 Linen shift		4.0.
1 Pair of leather breeches		10.0.
1 Velvet hood		10.0.
1 Silk hood		3.0.
2 Linen pockets		2.0.
		£19. 7.0.

This was the second time that Ambrose Skinner had suffered at the hands of this gang, a somewhat curious circumstance. At the previous robbery at his father's house in December, when Skinner lost considerably more goods than did his father, he and his wife were living with the old farmer at that time. In this latter instance however the bulk of the possessions taken belonged to a woman, and it is possible that the address in St. Margaret, Westminster was Skinner Junior's town house, and the occupier was, except for occasional visits by Skinner, his terrified wife. The gang are unlikely to have selected this house by chance, nor could they have done so expecting to find much by way of reward, for having three months before stripped the Skinners of practically all they possessed, there cannot have been much left or bought since. Which suggests that the purpose of this otherwise pointless exercise might have been intimidation.

Of the three men captured on 11 February, only Fielder and Saunders were likely to be indicted, and even if they were involved in the earlier Skinner robbery, there would be no guarantee that they would be indicted with that particular offence; and since they were captured by members of the Lawrence family and friends, there was a greater likelihood of their being tried for that offence rather than any other. And as this criterion must apply to the other robberies also, a campaign to dissuade former victims from testifying against those captured, hardly seems reasonable in the circumstances. But since the gang, or this part of it, knew that Thomas Lawrence and his friends were responsible for putting Wheeler and the others behind bars, this robbery may well have been committed to discourage other former victims from following their example. The only other possible reason is malice. Skinner and Lawrence were of a kind, and since it was either not convenient or the Lawrences were now considered to be too powerful adversaries, poor Skinner fell foul of their fit of pique. It is something of a mystery, as is the identity of one of the robbers.

When Fielder, Rose and Walker appeared at the Old Bailey, they were not tried for robbing Ambrose Skinner Junior because conviction had already been obtained against them upon two other indictments. Which is a pity because it would have been interesting to have seen whether or not the jury found for or against the defendant John Fielder who was in Newgate on the day Ambrose Skinner Junior and his wife were robbed! But if Fielder was not the third man, then who was? The authorities were restricted on this occasion by the fact that Wheeler was captured before the event took place. But if Skinner, his wife or some other person identified three men, then they were obviously wrong when it came to Fielder.

The accused were from Westminster and the crime was committed there, but Turpin, the only other man to lodge in that vicinity, is presumed to have left it some four days before. It was a small mean robbery, and the sole occupant of the house, possibly, was Mrs. Skinner. It was not a crime which would have required the inspiration of Samuel Gregory or reinforcements from the East End, and in the event it seems likely that that group was employed elsewhere the same evening. So if the third man was not Turpin, who could it have been? The alternative is, surprisingly, a woman.

Mary Brazier, Rose's 'wife', was not without some initiative. Her record shews that she was possessed of a certain enterprise in the subtle art of picking pockets, and she was, according to Wheeler, able to 'persuade' the rest of those hard men of the advantages in robbing Justice Asher near her home town of Southchurch. A pair of breeches, a hat and a mask, and by lanthorn light not many would know she was a woman. Perhaps she even knew that the contents of the house consisted mainly of woman's finery and was confident she could dispose of this perhaps with greater ease than she could other goods. When she and Rose and Walker were found huddled over their punch but two days later, it was not reported that a fourth party escaped. Mary Brazier was the third 'man', she and the other two were the rabbits of the gang, ensnared in Westminster and rooted to the spot where they must inevitably be caught. Turpin was that much wiser, and he and the other four had the sense to keep on the move and postpone their inevitable fate with varying degrees of success.

V

A newspaper which appeared the following Tuesday perhaps helps us to trace the other part of the gang's movements from Brockley. 'A few days since Mrs. St. John's house at Chinkford *(sic)* was robbed by three or four men of money, plate and linen of about £60 value. There was only one elderly man left to take care of the house whom they used barbarously.'[6]

Although undated there is a particular reason for ascribing this event to 15 February. Chingford was on the road to Epping and at least two of the gang were about 30 miles north of Chingford on the same road the next day. The day before they were at Brockley. This at least fits the theory of the gang keeping on the move, and that it was Gregory and his companions who robbed Mrs. St. John's house seems to be borne out by the treatment of the elderly caretaker. This is in accord with their use of Mr. Lawrence, and suggests that violence was again used to persuade someone to tell them where the money was kept. Two robberies on successive days? It should be remembered that they were on the run, and apart from keeping a watchful eye open for pursuit there was little else to occupy them at this time. From the events of the following day, and allowing for the accuracy of the report, Gregory, Haines, Turpin and Rowden would have been the four men, with Rowden eliminated if there were only three. From Chingford, about 8 or 9 p.m., they probably rode on towards Epping and remained in that vicinity overnight.

VI

The postscript to the events of 15 February is supplied by a man who was following closely on the heels of the gang, and constable Archelaus Pullen was certainly not far behind, as the next report well shews:

The Gregory Gang

> On Saturday night last Mr. Pulleyn, a constable near Tothill Fields, Westminster, seized two boxes full of wearing and household linen and other household goods, and another person has in his custody, two silver watches, all of which goods are supposed to have been stolen by the persons or some of them who committed the late notorious burglaries about London. By a mark upon a sack taken amongst the above goods, it seems to belong to Mr. Skinner one of the persons robbed.[7]

The inventory of goods stolen from Ambrose Skinner in December lists two sacks valued at 1s. 0d. each; similarly, a silver watch was stolen from his son in the same house, and this also may have been one of the two recovered.

The address at which the property was found is not given, but since Wheeler stated that Rose gave them 15s. 0d. for all the linen stolen from Farmer Lawrence, and the goods Mary Brazier was indicted with receiving consisted mainly of linen, it is likely that the goods were found at Rose's old lodgings at Dawes Street. They were seized on Saturday night, 15 February, which is not indicative of a search having been made at Dawes Street immediately after Wheeler's arrest. There are two explanations why this should be; first that they were *not* found at this address, second, that they were found there and left with a watch to apprehend the thieves should they return to collect the goods left behind. On Saturday, by which time it would have been clear that the goods had been abandoned, they would have been impounded.

VII

The next morning, Sunday, the company which had been at Chingford rode north from Epping. By the afternoon, Turpin and, if he was with them, Rowden, parted company with Gregory and Haines, probably on the understanding that they would all rendezvous again later that day or early the following morning. In the event it is probable that Gregory and Haines broke the arrangement and went looking for Turpin:

> They write from Debden near Saffron Waldon in Essex, that on Sunday last in the afternoon, Samuel Gregory the blacksmith, one of the rogues advertised in the *Gazette*, remarkable for the scar on his right cheek, with another pale fellow, supposed to be Herbert Haines, came into an alehouse in that parish, drank plentifully and ordered a shoulder of mutton to be roasted for their supper. In the meantime one Palmer an innkeeper of Thaxted happening to call at the said alehouse and seeing the rogues knew them to be the same that were in his house lately at the same time when several robberies were committed in the neighbourhood and perceiving they had pistols about them, the constable was acquainted with it and prevailed upon to go in order to apprehend them. About

seven at night he charged several of his assistants (all as wise as himself) who entered the room where the rogues were, without any weapon in their hands, very innocently, acquainted the rogues with their errand, upon which Gregory rising drew a pistol and cocked it, but it missing fire, was beat out of his hand and he thrust down. He soon rose and drew a dagger with which he wounded two slightly and two more as is supposed mortally. They then made their escape through a crowd of people leaving behind them a bundle in which were some shirts and stockings, powder and ball and a pistol loaded with a bullet and slug.[8]

It cannot be supposed that Gregory and Haines had come this far without the company of Turpin, because Debden, some little way off the road from Epping to Saffron Walden, was also en route to Hempstead. It was in fact roughly equidistant from Turpin's birthplace and Thaxted, the place where he may have been a butcher.

Turpin cannot have seen his family for some time and riding north from Epping and coming to Debden late in the afternoon, the company no doubt agreed that Turpin (with or without Rowden) should continue on to Hempstead whilst Gregory and Haines lingered at Debden; and ordering a shoulder of mutton to be roasted suggests that they intended to stay the night. Instead they left in a hurry, and they did not linger long in that vicinity because events of 17 February indicate that they were some distance away by the following night. The experience of Gregory and Haines no doubt precipitated such a move, and it is possible that they went to Hempstead from Debden before they *all* journeyed south. Some other aspects of the Debden account are deserving of comment. Although not conclusive of the fact that Gregory and the others were at Brockley on the Friday, it is interesting to note that there were in the abandoned bundle an unspecified number of shirts.

Some reports of this same event were still appearing in other newspapers as late as 1 March, and irrespective of when they were printed, the incident was still described as having occurred, 'on Sunday [or in some cases Saturday] last in the afternoon'. They are invariably, apart from the error of date, verbatim cribs of the above report, a press mannerism which makes the dating of certain events exceedingly difficult.

One biography suggests that the man named Palmer may have been a relative of Turpin's mother, and that his action in this episode may have been an attempt to ingratiate himself with the law to avoid charges of collusion. The evidence which suggests Turpin's mother was named Palmer has not been corroborated, and the authorities had quite enough to worry about without concerning themselves over matters about which they had no evidence. They had Wheeler and they wanted the rest of the gang, but it is doubtful if they wanted Turpin's improbable relative. The authors of this suggestion follow up the Debden report by accepting as fact a report of Gregory's capture which anticipated the event by about six weeks.[9]

VIII

At the subsequent trial of Mary Brazier for receiving goods stolen from Francis and Lawrence, she was indicted with receiving them on 16 February. This is not consistent with the facts and the only reasonable explanation of this date having been used in the charge is that it was the last full day upon which she was at liberty to receive, in whole or in part, or hold in her possession, the goods which it was alleged had been stolen. This theory is not entirely satisfactory however because although it seems clear that she did not receive all of the Francis possessions, and the actual day they came into her possession is not recorded, the goods taken from Lawrence were handed over to her immediately after the robbery. And since she was tried upon two separate indictments, the use of this date in both cases seems neither justified nor technically correct and permissible. It is a minor point, and although generally the date inserted in indictments was consistent with the date upon which the offence occurred, some inexplicable departures from the norm were occasionally made.

IX

The final event of 16 February illustrates the attention the authorities were prepared to give to particular details of Wheeler's evidence:

> John Wheeler has confessed all the particulars of the robbery of Mason the Keeper in Epping Forest and particularly that the firearms, which they took from him they brought as far as Cambridge Heath, nr. Hackney, and there threw them into a pond, which pond being searched on Sunday last (16th), several of the guns were found there.[10]

X

Turpin chroniclers lost all interest in his colleagues once those captured on 11 and 17 February 1735 had been dealt with by law. Some more recent chroniclers make passing reference to Haines and Rowden, but that to Samuel Gregory is usually confused, and there is none at all to Jones and the third Gregory brother Jeremy. Perhaps in accounts which do after all purport to be biographies of Turpin, this lack is to be expected; but in the proper criminal perspective in which Turpin's activities should be regarded it is perhaps the wider view of the gang itself which is more interesting and deserving of recognition in the history of crime. We move therefore from the certain and proved activities of the gang, largely corroborated by Wheeler's testimony, to a robbery of apparently uncertain instigation, but which like those at Brockley and Chingford (of recent date) coincides with the theoretical movements of the gang at this time. Thus although the next report concerns a robbery in Kent on 17 February, when the men with whom we have been concerned were last seen far to the north in Essex on the previous day, it is possible to shew some validity for its inclusion.

> On Monday night last between 8 and 9 o'clock, the house of Mr. Berry, a noted farmer at Gravesend, was robbed by five men who came to the stables to the man [there] armed with pistols &c. and asked him for his fellow servant, who told them he did not know where he was, upon which they seized him and carried by force into the dwelling house and afterwards bound and blindfolded him and then seized the master and treated him in like manner and also his wife, who upon being blindfolded, desired that they would use the children tenderly, being infants. They answered they would blindfold them with handkerchiefs only. Then two of the rogues went and plundered the house and left the rest as guards to watch over those bound, but not finding so much as they expected, they came down to Mrs. Berry, swearing there was more money in the house. But she answered not as she knew of, unless her husband had some unknown to her. Upon that they struck her over the face with a pistol, which cut her in a violent manner. Then they went to Mr. Berry and took the keys of his drawers out of his pocket, and, upon diligent search, they found a considerable sum of money amounting to about £160 which sum he had lately received. After they had secured the money and other things of value, they unbound the manservant, and left a guard over the rest that were bound, while they went with him to the stable, and commanded him to saddle three of the best horses, or they would immediately shoot him, which he did accordingly. After this they led him back into the house and there bound him a second time. At their going away they acquainted him that they would turn the horses loose about Greenwich or Deptford, which they accordingly did. But before they left Mrs. Berry begged to be unbound or otherwise they should all perish. They answered Damn you Madam, somebody will release you all in the morning and that is time enough.[11]

This particular report appears to be accurate enough in describing what occurred, but other reports differ in respect of certain details, e.g. 'Between six and seven o'clock, three men with their faces blacked broke into the house of Mr. Bury of Cliff in Kent. £20 in plate was left behind when they found between £40 and £50 in cash. Mr. Bury was advised that the horses would be left between Deptford and New Cross turnpikes.'[12]

Another account, longer, but in substance the same as the above appeared some time afterwards.[13] This stated that £150 in cash was taken, but the odd thing about this report is that it is *with* the Lawrence robbery under the title 'Robberies' and precedes by two pages the report under the heading of, 'These rogues providentially discovered', which described the taking of Wheeler. This association is almost certainly accidental, but the Berry robbery would not necessarily have been noticed had the reports not appeared together in this way.

Cliff was another isolated community, just east of Gravesend and on the edge of Cliff Marshes, the latter being a wide expanse of treacherous mud between Cliff and the Thames estuary. The method of entry, etc., is almost identical with that employed at the Francis robbery, even to the brutal treatment of the woman present. The disregard of plate when money was found is definitely in keeping with a desire for unencumbered progress from men on the move.

The most significant aspect of this robbery is in the taking of three horses, and then leaving them in the same area to which Brockley was adjacent. The apparent paradox in this story is the arrival of five men presumably on five horses (being a dead-end off the Watling Street, Cliff was not the place to arrive at on foot), and the subsequent borrowing of only three horses. One would have imagined this to be more consistent with the arrival, as one report stated, of three men. But *Read's* report, which has the appearance of being more familiar with what took place, states that two went to plunder the house whilst the rest stood as guards. Can this discrepancy be explained?

There is some doubt about Rowden's having accompanied Turpin to Hempstead on the previous day, and if one discounts his presence there would have been but three men at the Chingford robbery on Saturday, and afterwards on the ride north to Debden. There was no alternative but for Gregory and his companions to leave that area after the Debden escape, and rather than go east towards the coast, which limited their avenues of escape, or north or west into unfamiliar territory, they would have returned south towards London. London however was unsafe, and the alternative, as has been seen previously when desperate measures were necessary, was to continue south across the river. On this occasion however it would seem that Gregory, Haines and Turpin picked up Jones and Rowden on the way, and that having crossed the river via London Bridge, they then turned east towards Gravesend. Having committed the robbery at Cliff, nothing would have been more natural for the first three named to have borrowed fresh horses, and trailed the exhausted ones behind them.

By mid-week they were back around their old haunts in the vicinity of Woodford, so it is possible that after they returned from Gravesend they kept near to Epping Forest. There would have been little cover at that time of year, but they did have the advantage of being exceptionally familiar with the country. It is doubtful that they all five remained together all the time, and there has already been some indication of this insofar as Jones and, as now seems clear, Rowden, did not accompany the others to Debden. In ones and twos they were more likely to have found overnight refuge at least with friends outside the gang, and unless they met someone like Palmer, as they did at Debden, who recognised them as men having been in the neighbourhood where a robbery or robberies had been committed, there was nothing to prevent them putting up at inns; for apart from the one newspaper which published their names and descriptions on 15 February, these details were not in general circulation until 22 February.

XI

But on 17 February, by about the time the five would have arrived at London Bridge on the return journey from Gravesend, say between ten and twelve o'clock, their three former associates in Westminster were in dire trouble and desperate for assistance which in the event was not forthcoming. Why did Rose and his wife, and Humphrey Walker choose to remain in the Westminster area, their movements hampered by boxes of stolen goods in excess of those they had already abandoned? Why, like Turpin, did they not join Gregory and the rest? Age and loyalty were possible reasons, for Rose and Walker were much older than all the others, and unless Mary Brazier was an accomplished horsewoman there was really no question of her being able to accompany anyone in general flight. Assuming she couldn't ride, a resigned Rose may have decided to stay with her, but since his life was threatened some considerably stronger tie is indicated.

The continued presence of Walker is less easy to understand, unless as suggested his age (50) made him philosophic and he too lingered out of some sense of loyalty, or affection for the other two. But whatever these three had in common, it is certain that despite their local manoevrings in Westminster they were little more than sitting ducks to the men who were hunting them down:

> On Monday night about ten o'clock, Mr. Pulleyn a constable (having made diligent enquiry), went to a house in Thieving Lane alias Bow Street belonging to Mr. Lloyd. He recruited eight persons for the raid, amongst whom were two of Mr. Lawrence's sons. There were taken Joseph Rose, Humphrey Walker and Mary Brazier who were drinking punch. Two trunks of stolen articles were recovered and some at a house in nearby Duck Lane. There are sixteen warrants out for the rest of the gang.[14]

The concensus of newspaper opinion is that the capture was effected between 10 and 12 p.m. on Monday 17 February. Mr. Lloyd was a chandler, but the fact the three were drinking punch suggested to a number of newspapers that the premises functioned for the sale of strong liquor, it being described either as a brandy shop or a gin shop. They do not appear to have been seen by a magistrate that night, but remained in the Gatehouse, Westminster until the morning.

There is ample evidence which confirms the recovery of pistols, gold articles, rings and linen, but a surprising item is the inclusion of *tea* in another report of the capture.[15] This is an isolated reference, but so odd as to warrant some mention. One can hardly conceive its having been mentioned at all unless it was true, and if this was so it leaves us with the one link with smugglers known to exist outside Bayes' description of the gang's pre-deerstealing days, and Martin Bladen's possibly unfounded supposition concerning the identity of the Mason/Skinner robbers. Unfortunately it proves nothing, for Mary Brazier was a receiver, and coming from Southchurch on the Essex coast she could as easily have disposed of smuggled goods as stolen ones. It is an interesting point but one which at best leads only to fruitless speculation.

The house in Duck Lane is a mystery, unless this was Walker's address. His drinking with Rose and Mary Brazier suggests nothing more than a purely convivial evening and it is probable that he did lodge nearby.

Another newspaper stated that the three were taken upon John Wheeler's information.[16] Wheeler cannot have known where they were living on 17 February, but by this time he was being credited with every setback suffered by the gang. So far as is known the information he gave did not lead to any immediate arrest, but it did cause the gang to disperse and leave Rose and the other two trapped in Westminster. To that extent he was responsible, but the most damning information he was to give was in the evidence at their trials. Without it some of them might have been acquitted; with it none of them stood a chance.

The newspaper coverage of this second capture was not as extensive as one would have imagined it might have been; accounts of what actually occurred are very sketchy and give little more than the names of the protagonists. But it was as violent a confrontation, if not more so, than that which happened on 11 February.

Thomas Lawrence
I took Rose in Thieving Lane in Westminster, he made what resistance he could.[17]

Richard Bartram

These pistols I took from Rose ... And this, he held within a pistols length of my breast, and pulled the trigger, but I clapped my finger in between the hammer and the lock and so prevented his firing.[18]

Thomas Lawrence

Walker resisted, and had like to have shot a chairman, but was prevented by a Hackney Coachman.[19]

... Harrowfield (a coachman)

Walker had hold of his pistol and was pulling it out of his pocket, but it hung by something and he could not get it out, and so I came upon him and knocked him down.[20]

Rose and Walker both survived their trials, but there are indications that they may have suffered quite severe injuries when they were captured. Walker died in Newgate the night before he was to be executed, and Rose on the scaffold was described by one observer as 'being so sick he could scarce stand', but there is little to choose between them having been injured in the fight and having contracted gaol fever or some other such virulent disease prevelant in Newgate. The alternative is that being the eldest members of the gang they may not have had much resistance to injury or sickness, and the latter could easily have been accelerated by the former.

Who else was involved in the fight? The following persons received a share of the reward for the capture and conviction of Joseph Rose. Jonathan Watham, Francis Lewis, Mary Lloyd (? wife of chandler at Thieving Lane), Jane Westridge (? wife of man to whom goods were sold), John Wheeler (evidence against his accomplices), Richard Bartram (trial witness and at capture), Ralph Rogers, John Mitchell, Ralph Hughson, Henry Stowers, George Haverfield (trial witness and at capture), Thomas Lawrence (trial witness and at capture), Joseph Lawrence [Jnr.] (present at capture), John Pate (trial witness), Archelaus Pullen (constable present at capture and trial witness).[21]

Pullen, who received £10, was stated by the *London Evening Post* to have recruited eight men. Bartram, Rogers, Mitchell, Hughson, Stowers, Haverfield *or* Harrowfield, the two Lawrences and John Pate, nine in all, each received £3 15s. 0d., and the other awards being insignificant it would be reasonable to accept these nine as having played a major part in the taking of Rose, Walker and Mary Brazier. Pullen's award, or rather its amount compared with the others, confirms that it was by his diligence the remnants of the gang were traced to Thieving Lane. Not much is known about the pre Bow Street Runners era, but that so many criminals convicted of serious crimes were caught in those days, must have been due in part at least to the zeal of men like Pullen.[22]

XII

As a final comment upon this chapter and a preface to the next, nothing could be more fitting than the following item of evidence:

Second enclosure to a letter of 21 March 1738/9
Information of John Wheeler for burglaries in the said county [Essex] taken upon oath the 18 day of February 1734 [/5] before Nathaniel Blackerby Esq. against Joseph Rose, Humphrey Walker, John Fielder, Wm. Saunders, Jasper Gregory, Richard Turpin, Thomas Bowden [*recte* Rowden], Herbert Haines, John Jones, Samuel Gregory, Mary Johnson *alias* Rose *alias* Brazier.[23]

FOOTNOTES

1. *London Evening Post*, 18 to 20 February 1735.
2. *London Gazette*, No.7378.
3. *London Daily Post and General Advertiser*, 19 February 1735.
4. *Daily Courant*, 15 February 1735.
5. Middlesex/MJ/SR 2631 Indictment No.53.
6. *Daily Journal*, 18 February 1735.
7. *London Evening Post*, 15 to 18 February 1735.
8. *Daily Post*, 21 February 1735.
9. Ash and Day, *Immortal Turpin*, pp.34–35.
10. *London Evening Post*, 18 to 20 February 1735.
11. *Read's Weekly Journal*, 22 February 1735.
12. *Grub Street Journal*, No.269.
13. *Political State*, Vol.XLIX, p.240.
14. *London Evening Post*, 18 to 20 February 1735 (abbreviated).
15. *Daily Courant*, 19 February 1735.
16. *London Daily Post and General Advertiser*, 19 February 1735.
17. Trial of Fielder and Rose for Lawrence robbery.
18. Trial of Fielder, Rose, Saunders and Walker for Francis robbery.
19. *Ibid.*
20. *Ibid.*
21. P.R.O./T.53/38 p.195.
22. Pullen was a constable in the parish of St. Margaret's, Westminster, and although nothing more is known about him than this, it is almost certain that his enquiries were influenced to some extent by Thomas de Veil, the Westminster and Middlesex magistrate who did his own detective work, and moved to offices in Bow Street in 1739. Perhaps the most significant thing about de Veil and his methods is that he was succeeded at that address by Henry Fielding in 1746, and that it was Fielding who was responsible for the formation of the Bow Street Runners. But although there was no organised force as such in 1735, the parish constables were responsible to magistrates and even though we do not know that de Veil the Westminster magistrate personally directed Pullen he doubtless influenced the course his enquiries about the Gregory gang should take.
23. P.R.O./S.P.44/131 p.107.

CHAPTER THREE

I

WHAT HAPPENED on Tuesday 18 February? The newspapers of the next day all refer briefly to 'yesterday's examination', but do not describe it in great detail.

The three prisoners taken to the Gatehouse, Westminster on the night of 17 February, were not at this time committed because they had not then appeared before a magistrate. On 18 February, they were examined by Nathaniel Blackerby, J.P., and to confound any evasions or alibis which they might have hastily contrived, Miss Sarah Francis, daughter of William Francis of Marylebone, was also present.

The *Daily Courant,* in the edition for 19 February, although having described Rose and Walker in *their* wanted list of 15 February, were not now prepared to commit themselves very strongly on this same subject. The persons captured were named, but the article finished somewhat cautiously. 'They are supposed to be the persons concerned with Wheeler ... ', an attitude which supports to some extent the theory that in publishing descriptions of the men before the *Gazette* they had thereby incurred the displeasure of the Establishment.

Little more is known of what happened at the examination, but something may be deduced from testimony given at the trial of Fielder, Rose, Saunders and Walker for the Francis robbery:

Keeper of the Gate House
These two bullets, and this piece of gold with a hole in it I took from Walker in the Gate House.

Sarah Francis

This [the piece of holed gold] is my father's. My sister used to wear it for her eyes.[1]

Keeper

This medal was taken from Rose's wife, and these two rings I took from Rose himself ... One of them is a brass ring.

Eleanor Williams (the maid)

That brass ring is mine; I lost it when they robbed the house.

Sarah Francis

And this other stone ring with the posey is my mother's.

Constable [Pullen]

This cup was found at Walker's lodgings.

Sarah Francis

This is my father's punch cup.

We may imagine Justice Blackerby displaying the stolen property which had been recovered, and asking the three to account for it. With Sarah Francis identifying a piece of gold with a hole in it, they no doubt despaired of giving very satisfactory answers, and what should be considered is that at some time during the day they were either taken before Wheeler, or he brought to them, and identified. There is no report of this having actually occurred, but it does happen on so many other occasions it almost certainly did on this. There was, in any event, no doubt in Justice Blackerby's mind, and he returned them to their cells in the Gatehouse, to be formally committed the following day: 'No. 46 Mary Johnson *or* Brazier *or* Rose committed [Gatehouse] 19 February by Nathaniel Blackerby Esq. on oath as accessory to several burglaries in Middlesex, Essex and Surrey in receiving stolen goods knowing them to have been stolen. For examination.'[2,3] 'No.27 Joseph Rose and Humphrey Walker committed [Newgate] by Nathan. Blackerby Esq. charged on oath with forcibly entering the house of William Francis and stealing thence about £50 in money and several other things of value and for several robberies in Essex and Surrey. Date 19th February.'[4]

The gang was gradually being whittled away; Mary Brazier remained in the Gatehouse for further questioning, and Rose and Walker were escorted across London to Newgate to join Fielder and Saunders. In New Prison, Clerkenwell, however, it was visiting day:

> On Wednesday last, Mason the Keeper in Epping Forest went to see Wheeler in New Prison ... Wheeler confessed the whole, and that their design was to have murdered him, for a grudge they bore him, for several times pursuing them and preventing their stealing deer (for they are all noted deerstealers) and that occasioned them shooting after him, when he escaped.[5]

Wheeler was really blackening the characters of his former associates for, as has been previously stated, the gang had plenty of opportunity to kill Mason had that in fact been their intention. The reason for Mason's visit is not known, but it was not unusual for victims to make such calls. Mason was very keen to capture Gregory, who was rescued from the pillory at Epping, and it may be that he hoped to obtain some information from Wheeler which might lead to his whereabouts.

II

Mason would probably have been better served had he remained at home, for the gang had by this time returned to the forest and one of their old haunts in particular: 'The Essex gang are not yet dispersed, for the latter end of last week several fellows armed attempted a gentleman's house at Woodford, Essex, but the inhabitants of the town took the alarm and drove the rogues off without their being able to accomplish their design.'[6]

This is by no means a certain identification but it probably was Gregory and some of his companions. Eventually the remainder of the gang split up into even smaller units of ones and twos, but this does not appear to have occurred before the end of the month. They did not attempt any more robberies in London and Westminster for some considerable time, and it is extremely doubtful that they even ventured near. With each day that passed by, more avenues of escape were cut, and until the end of the month they kept very much under cover, probably in and about Epping Forest, which in those days covered a very wide area indeed.

The date of the attempted robbery at Woodford is not stated, but the latter end of the week may be taken to have been between Thursday 20 and Saturday 22 February. But in Westminster on Thursday night the search was still on:

> On Thursday night a countryman was seized in bed at the *Blue Boar's Head* in King Street, Westminster, on suspicion of being an accomplice in the gang of housebreakers; when they first searched him, there was only a sum to the amount of about 40s. found upon him, but by examining more narrowly, they discovered 26 guineas concealed in a handkerchief in his shirt sleeves. He was yesterday (21st) carried before several of his Majesty's Justices of the Peace, and confronted with Wheeler the Evidence, but was not known by him. We hear he is to be re-examined this day (22nd).[7]

There is no record of any other member of the gang having been committed on or about this date, and since Wheeler did not know him it may be safely assumed that this man was not connected with the gang. But on the Friday there appeared another report guaranteed to discourage the gang from making any appearance in public places: 'Orders are sent to all the sea ports to stop all suspicious persons, least any of these notorious robbers should escape. Search warrants are out against the whole gang.'[8]

One suspects that this may have been a little bit of sensationalism, for although there is a 1735 parallel in the case of Henry Rogers, wanted for murder in Cornwall, in which instructions were sent to the Admiralty for all merchant shipping to be stopped and searched if it was thought he might be on board, no such similar order appears to have been given in respect of members of the Gregory gang. This is not to say that copies of the proclamation signed in Whitehall on 21 February, which gave descriptions of those members of the gang still at large, were not sent as a matter of routine to the Custom House for circulation to all the ports between Harwich and Dover.

III

On Thursday Wheeler had set his signature to an information which had taken a week to complete, and which was to have long and far reaching effects. On Friday the relevant parts of this document were translated into proclamation form and the final draft sent to the *Gazette* office. On Saturday 22 February the details which had been anticipated by the *Daily Courant* on 15 February, finally, and with official sanction, appeared in print. They did not this time include descriptions of Rose and Walker who had been captured in the meantime:

Whitehall February 21st.

> Whereas it has been represented to the King, that John Jones, a carpenter by trade, about five and a half feet high, fresh coloured, pock holes in his face and wears a brown wig, aged about twenty five years of age and born at Hackney in Middlesex, where he lately resided, was concerned (with Jasper Gregory, now in Chelmsford Gaol and two others) in entering the house of Mr. Gladwin at Chinkford *(sic)* Green ... and robbing the same in December last, his Majesty for the better discovering and bringing the said John Jones to Justice is pleased to promise a reward of £50 to any person or persons who shall discover the said criminal, so as he may be apprehended and convicted thereof, to be paid upon such conviction.

> The persons undermentioned are charged upon oath for committing several robberies in Essex, Middlesex, Surrey and Kent, and are not yet taken, for each of

the Gregory Gang 141

whom a reward of fifty pounds is advertised in the *Gazettes* of the 4th and 7th of January last past and on the 8th and 11th of this instant February.

Samuel Gregory, lodged lately at Joseph Gregory's his brother's a carman in Old Gravel Lane, Radcliff. He is about five feet seven inches high, has a scar about an inch and a half long on his right cheek, is fresh coloured wears a brown wig and about 23 years old is a smith or farrier by trade.

Thomas Rowden lately arrived at Radcliff Highway, towards the lower end of Shadwell Church, is a little man, well set, fresh coloured and full faced, has small pockholes in his face, wears a blue grey coat and a light wig, a pewterer by trade, aged about 30 years.

Herbert Haines, a barber or perriwig maker by trade kept a barber's shop in Hog Lane in Shoreditch he is about five feet seven inches high, of a pale complexion, wears a brown wig and a brick coloured cloth coat, aged about 24 years.

Richard Turpin, a butcher by trade, is a tall fresh coloured man, very much marked with the small pox, about 26 years of age, about five feet nine inches high, lived some time ago in Whitechapel and did lately lodge somewhere about Millbank, Westminster, wears a blue grey coat and a light natural wig.

The following persons are in custody viz. John Wheeler in New Prison; Joseph Rose, Humphrey Walker, John Fielder and William Saunders, *alias* Saunderson, *alias* Schoolin, in Newgate; Joseph [*recte* Jasper] in Chelmsford Gaol; Mary Johnson, *alias* Brazier, *alias* Rose, committed to the Gate-House Westminster as being accessory in receiving the goods knowing them to be stolen.[9]

An abbreviated version of the above appeared in an official copy, but Turpin is the only person described. It mentions, by name only, some of the others, and renders Haines' Christian name as, 'Robert'. It is endorsed, 'Copied from the *Gazette* of 22 February 1734/5' but its preoccupation with Turpin suggests that it was copied in 1737 to supplement details of his appearance given in another description of him published at that time. The descriptions of Gregory, Rowden, Haines and Turpin, and the list of those in custody, also appears in *Immortal Turpin*.[11] In the list the name of John Fielder is rendered, 'John Palmer', an alias which Turpin employed in later years, and is not known to have used during this period.

A final comment about the text of the above proclamation concerns the reference to the reward offered in the *Gazette* of 8 February. This offered reward in connection with the Woodford and other robberies committed by persons unknown, and by making reference to it in this latter proclamation, the authorities had at last accepted that those robberies had also been committed by this same gang. This had not been previously acknowledged, and that it was at this stage can only have been through Wheeler's evidence. Although this implies that Wheeler had knowledge of these robberies it does not *prove* that he was present at them, and it can only be reiterated that prosecutions were not initiated in those four cases. Wheeler's information is no longer extant; this is unfortunate in more ways than one for it would without doubt have been as much a revelation to us as it was to the authorities in February 1735.

IV

The only members of the gang who can have felt any sense of security were those in prison, and on Sunday 23 February one of those was transferred to the place where if a prisoner did escape he achieved some lasting fame: 'On Sunday Mary Rose the wife of Joseph Rose now in Newgate was brought from the Gatehouse to the said gaol by a warrant from Justice Blackerby, on suspicion of having been concerned in several robberies with her said husband, and then receiving several goods knowing them to have been stolen.'[12]

The case against Mary Brazier was not so straightforward as that against the men, for although with Wheeler's evidence against her, her part as receiver of the stolen property was clear, the authorities were anxious to establish the extent of her involvement in the actual robberies. Thus when her husband Rose went to his trial, she remained behind: 'No. 35 Mary Johnson *als* Brazier *als* Rose committed [Newgate] by Nathaniel Blackerby Esq. for being accessory to several felonies. Date Feb. 23d. *To remain*'[13]

V

There is in the Middlesex Sessions records an undated reference to Wheeler, 'John Wheeler referred to Mr. Robt. Hind the Younger', but this may be taken to have occurred after 18 and before 26 February.[14]

This entry appears under New Prison and Hind was the magistrate who had committed Wheeler. Having obtained his information the next service required of him by the authorities would have been to aid the prosecution in the preparation of their case. There was in fact something less than a week until the trial, and although the extent to which Hind would have been personally involved in the preparation of the case for the Crown is not known, it is possible that Wheeler was at this point removed to his care, to remain in his custody for the duration of the Sessions.

VI

At some point during the next week or so the authorities either obtained definite evidence, or were led to believe, that an attempt would be made to

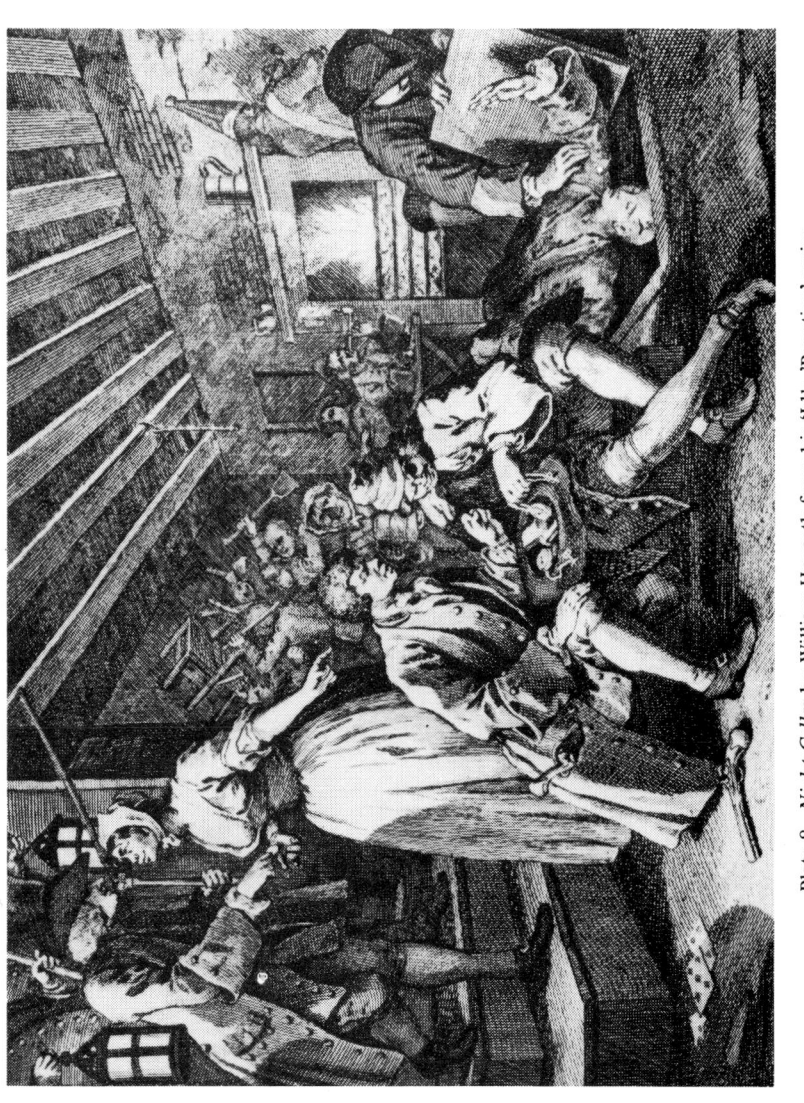

Plate 8. *Night Cellar* by William Hogarth from his 'Idle 'Prentice' series. The scene depicts a thieves' kitchen with the Watch entering to arrest the apprentice who is sharing the spoils of robbery.

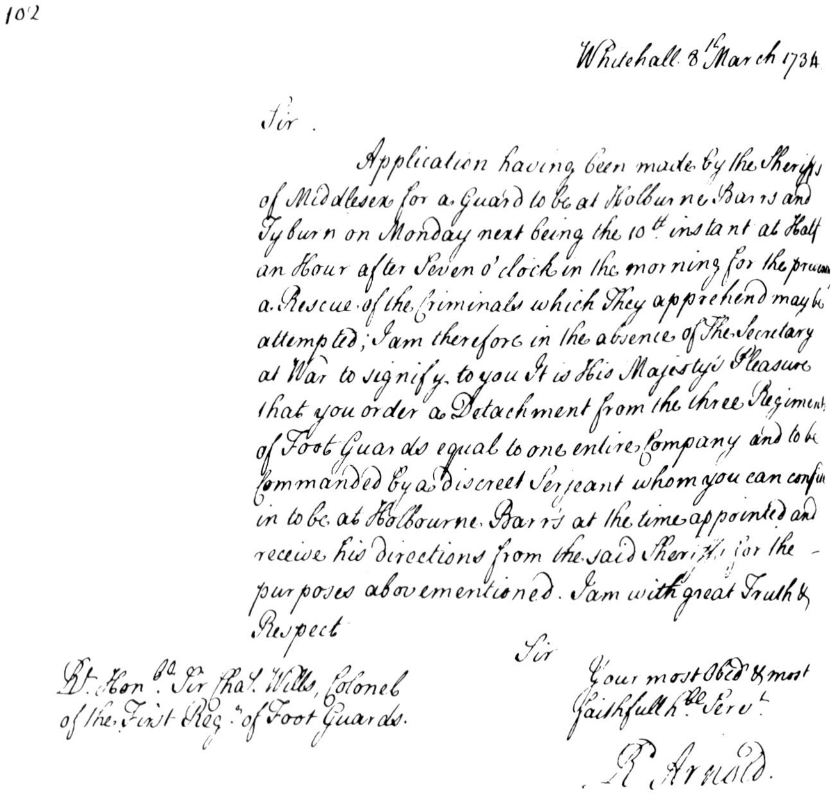

Whitehall 8th March 1734

Sir.

Application having been made by the Sheriffs of Middlesex for a Guard to be at Holbourne Barrs and Tyburn on Monday next being the 10th instant at Half an Hour after Seven o'clock in the morning for the preventing a Rescue of the Criminals which They apprehend may be attempted; I am therefore in the absence of The Secretary at War to signify to you It is His Majesty's Pleasure that you order a Detachment from the three Regiments of Foot Guards equal to one entire Company and to be commanded by a discreet Serjeant whom you can confide in to be at Holbourne Barrs at the time appointed and receive his directions from the said Sheriffs for the purposes abovementioned. I am with great Truth & Respect

Rt. Honble. Sir Chas. Wills, Colonel of the First Regt. of Foot Guards.

Sir

Your most Obedt & most faithfull hble. Servt.

R. Arnold.

Plate 9. Letter requesting military escort to Tyburn for members of the gang being executed.
(Reproduced by courtesy of the Public Record Office. W.O. 4/33 p.102)

The Gregory Gang
143

rescue Fielder, Rose, Saunders and Walker, but not from Newgate. It would be after their trial when they were removed from Newgate to be executed at Tyburn, and extravagant precautions were in fact taken to prevent it happening.

A precedent existed in the rescue of Gregory himself from the pillory at Epping, but although it was common knowledge that the gang had previously been deerstealers, it should not be presupposed that the circumstances of Gregory's rescue ever received much more than local publicity at the time it occurred. For having built a pillory and raised a posse to carry Gregory to Epping to stand him in it, it seems unlikely that the guard would have then been removed which suggests that he was rescued despite the precautions taken. To avoid embarrassment it is possible that this incident was treated as a purely domestic affair, but when four of the gang were convicted and sentenced to death it was considered politic to mention what had happened previously. This would perhaps have made the Sheriffs of Middlesex a little apprehensive about their ability to conduct the executions under normal conditions, a state of mind which may or may not have existed independently of the following newspaper report:

> The beginning of this week [Monday 24 February][15] three fellows of indifferent character were stopped at Thaxted in Essex and are now in custody for counterfeiting the hands of a Justice of the Peace and a constable to a warrant for raising hue and cry after the aforesaid gang, by virtue of which they demanded the use of a horse of a butcher at Leytonstone, but he denying it them, they had the impudence to threaten to indict him at the next Quarter Sessions, and then went on for Thaxted, where the cheat being discovered they were secured. Its thought their design was to ride clear off with the horses they might have procured under this sham pretence. It seems one of them is brother in law to Joseph Rose, now in Newgate on the information of Wheeler.[16]

There is no reference to men being charged for this offence in either Assize or Quarter Sessions records, and although they might have appeared at the Petty Sessions for the Dunmow Division of Essex, records do not exist for this period. The attempt to obtain horses could only mean one thing, that they were needed for Rose and the others should the attempted rescue at Tyburn be successful. Anyone reading this account at the time, particularly the Sheriffs of Middlesex, would have noted the reference to Rose's brother-in-law and interpreted what had occurred in exactly the same way. Because one attempt failed, the authorities could only anticipate that the gang would be driven to using even more desperate methods in their efforts to secure the freedom of their associates, but it is very likely that when this attempt did fail they abandoned the rescue plan altogether. Any movement was becoming increasingly difficult and a new hazard in travelling by regular routes is well illustrated by a passing comment in a newspaper: 'We hear that names and descriptions of the gang of robbers impeached by Wheeler are posted on all the turnpikes about London; and such strict search is made after them, that it is thought they cannot escape.'[17] This was an optimistic view as the survivors were not exposing themselves unnecessarily. They, or anyone remotely connected with them, even those who were unfortunate enough to bear any resemblance to them, were liable to become the hunted the moment suspicions were aroused. All things are possible in such circumstances, but it is perhaps a little surprising to find a moment of pure farce:

> On Tuesday last (25th) one Arnold was taken at Chelmsford in Essex, being in the information as one of the Essex gang; he was flying from a hue and cry which was in close pursuit of him, and endeavoured to go over Chelmsford Bridge when a waggon was upon it, by which means his mare was jammed in betwixt it and a post so that he could not stir, and he was taken with great ease. He was carried on Thursday before Justice Pratt at Stratford and after an examination was committed to the care of the constable there, in order (as is supposed) for his being removed by Habeas Corpus to Newgate. There was another with him who was thought to belong to the same gang, but he had the good fortune to overshoot the waggon and make his escape.[18]

There was a man named Arnold in Chelmsford gaol at this time, but he had already been there some years and cannot have been the same. As to his being removed to Newgate, there is no record of a man by that name being committed, either at this time or subsequently. Records for the Petty Sessions of the Becontree Division of Essex, at which he might have appeared, do not exist. Nor does he appear in the list of names previously stated to have been given in Wheeler's information. It is possible that he did have some connection with the gang, but it is equally possible that he was merely a man with a guilty conscience. Similar considerations must affect the next report, which purports to be of some greater significance than the last:

> On Wednesday last (26th), a countryman going to Moulsham near Chelmsford in Essex saw at an alehouse, Samuel Gregory (one of those who robbed Farmer Lawrence at Earlsbury Farm, near Edgware, and who ravished the maid) whom he knew, whereupon without taking any notice he went and got proper assistance well armed, came to the house and there seized him, chained and handcuffed him, he was well dressed and had about fourscore pounds about him, and on Thursday morning being handcuffed and put on a horse and his legs chained under the horse's belly and padlocked he was conducted under proper guard, to Justice Pratt's at Stratford, in Westham in Essex, who granted Warrants out against him, and others, where, after an examination, he was committed, and it's thought will be brought to Newgate to be tried this Sessions.[19]

This was not Samuel Gregory, which accounts for his not being removed to Newgate, and although the real Gregory was not executed until June, Ash and

Day in *Immortal Turpin* did not regard this time lag as being of any moment. Unfortunately for them they failed to observe a slight inconsistency in that in their next report of Gregory he languished in Winchester gaol. He was in all probability many miles from Moulsham on 26 February, but on the same day the public's interest was also beginning to revive in those less fortunate members of the gang who *had* surrendered their freedom.

VII

The Middlesex General Sessions, at which Rose, Fielder, Saunders and Walker were tried, lasted from 26 February to 1 March 1735. The court adjourned each day until eight o'clock the following morning. The venue was the Justice Hall in the Old Bailey, 'in the suburbs of the City of London'. The Grand Jury found each of the presentments against the accused to be a True Bill, which meant that they should go for trial before the twelve man Petty Jury.

Many of the details contained in the indictments, such as inventories of goods stolen, etc., have already been abstracted and presented out of context in some other form, and for this reason and the fact that the phrasing of each indictment is repetitive, only a brief resumé of each is given below.[20] One other detail which is omitted here is the parish of which the accused is usually described as having been late; this does not relate to his place of birth or residence but presumes his presence in the parish in which it is alleged he committed a crime.

Indictment No. 12
John Field *als* Fielder, William Bush *als* Saunders *als* Saunderson *als* Schooling, Humphrey Walker and Joseph Rose, for burglary in the house of William Francis.

Indictment No. 13
The same four for robbery on the same Francis.

Indictment No. 14
John Field *als* Fielder and Joseph Rose, for burglary in the house of Joseph Lawrence the Elder.

Indictment No. 15
The same two for robbery on the same Lawrence.

Indictment No. 53
John Field *als* Fielder, Joseph Rose and Humphrey Walker, for burglary in the house of Ambrose Skinner the Younger.

It should be noted that Samuel Gregory and Richard Turpin were also named in Indictments 12 to 15, and that Gregory was tried on these subsequently. This did not involve any duplication of the parchment record since when his turn came the date of conviction and nature of the judgement were merely entered upon the above. Each indictment was endorsed not only with the finding of the Grand Jury, but also the names of the witnesses to appear in court. The witnesses on Indictments 12 and 13 were William Francis, John Wheeler, Sarah Francis, Edward Jones and Stephen Mannington. Those on Indictments 13 and 14 were John Wheeler, Thomas Lawrence and James Emmerton. None appeared on Indictment 53 because in the event nobody was called to give evidence upon that indictment.

The stage was set for the appearance of Fielder, Rose, Saunders and Walker at the Old Bailey, but even then one newspaper could not refrain from indulging in a little bit of sham theatricality in the wings:

> We have a surprising account from Essex, that one of the unhappy sufferers by the gang infesting that county had been impeached of smuggling and obliged to give £3000 security for his appearance the next assize at Chelmsford, but this is supposed to be a contrivance of some of that gang, in order to stifle his evidence against their accomplices.[21]

FOOTNOTES

1. The identification of this item on 18 February is confirmed in *Hooker's Weekly Miscellany*, for 22 February 1735.
2. Westminster/Gatehouse/Bundle 1/10, 9 April 1735.
3. Entered in the left hand margin is, 'Newgate'.
4. Middlesex/MJ/SR 2631 (Calendar of Middlesex Prisoners in Newgate).
5. *London Evening Post*, 20 to 22 February 1735.
6. *Country Journal*, 1 March 1735.
7. *London Evening Post*, 20 to 22 February 1735.
8. *Daily Post*, 21 February 1735.
9. *London Gazette*, 18 to 22 February 1735.
10. P.R.O./SP.36/34 f.63.
11. *Immortal Turpin*, by Ash and Day, pp.32–33.
12. *London Evening Post*, 22 to 25 February 1735.
13. Middlesex/MJ/SR 2631 (Calendar of Middlesex Prisoners in Newgate).
14. Middlesex/MJ/SB 925.
15. This report comes after one relating to 'Wednesday last' (26 February) and precedes one relating to 'Tuesday last' (25 February). It is assumed the distinction, 'The beginning of this week' can only relate to Monday 24 February.
16. *Reid's Weekly Journal*, 1 March 1735.
17. *London Evening Post*, 22 to 25 February 1735.
18. *Reid's Weekly Journal*, 1 March 1735.
19. *Ibid.*
20. Middlesex/MJ/SR 2631, Indictments Nos.12–15 and 53.
21. *General Evening Post*, 25 to 27 February 1735.

BOOK FOUR

THE OLD BAILEY TRIALS AND A REMARKABLE COINCIDENCE

CHAPTER ONE

I

SOME TESTIMONY has already been taken out of the context of the trials and used elsewhere to make up deficiencies in details available from regular sources, but it would be wrong if for that reason the trial proceedings were not reproduced in their entirety in this account, for insofar as they relate to members of the Gregory gang this is where they belong.[1]

To facilitate future reference, the statements of witnesses &c. are numbered consecutively:

John Field *alias* Fielder and Joseph Rose were indicted with Richard Turpin and Samuel Gregory not then taken, for breaking the house of Joseph Lawrence, the Elder, and stealing a silver cup, four silver spoons, four gold rings, a pair of sheets, twelve napkins, a table cloth, six towels, six pillowbiers, six handkerchiefs, a waistcoat, fifteen guineas, three moidores, and 30s. Feb.4 in the night.

They were a second time indicted for assaulting Joseph Lawrence, the Elder, in his house, putting him in fear, and taking from him the goods and money above mentioned.

1. Richard Wood

I know Fielder the tall man in blue: he and the Evidence Wheeler, and three more were drinking at my house the *Nine Pin and Bowl* at Edgware the day my neighbour Lawrence was robbed. His house is about a mile from mine. They came at a quarter past four in the afternoon and stayed till five. Their horses stood the while in my yard and I gave them some hay. They went away together. Coming to London, I saw the same horses standing at a door in King Street, Bloomsbury. I went in and saw Fielder and Wheeler there with others. Fielder and Wheeler made a great resistance when they were taken, and five pistols were found upon them.

2. John Wheeler

On Tuesday the fourth of this month about two in the afternoon, the prisoners and I and Richard Turpin and Samuel Gregory, went from the *Black Horse* in the Broadway in Westminster to the *Nine Pin and Bowl* at Edgware, where we stayed near an hour, and then went to the *Queen's Head* at Stanmore, and stayed about an hour and a half, and went from thence to Lawrence's house at eight or between eight or nine at night. Fielder got over a hatch into the sheep yard, and took the sheep boy and bound his hands and brought him to the door and bid him speak when we knocked, but the boy was frightened and could not, so Gregory knocked, and called Mr. Lawrence. A servant opened the door and we all rushed in with pistols in our hands. We bound the old gentleman and his man and maid. Turpin pulled the old man's breeches down and dragged him into another room, and beat him to make him discover where his money was. Gregory took the maid up into the garret and lay with her there, as he afterwards told us. We took away what money, linen, and plate we could find. I saw no more than three guineas and 6s. 6d. and if they found any more they cheated me of my share. We left them bound in the parlour, locked the door, and threw the key into the garden.

3. John Bowler

I keep the *Black Horse* in the Broadway, Westminster. Wheeler and Rose had been several times backwards and forwards at my house, for they lodged hard by, and Fielder had been there twice. Their horses stood at my stables, one was a sorrel, one a brown, and one a bay.

4. Richard Wood

They had such coloured horses when they came to my house at Edgware, and one that was black.

5. Bowler

They and two more came again to my house on the fourth of this month, and rode away together about two in the afternoon.

6. Joseph Ironmonger

I keep the *Queen's Head Inn* at Stanmore. The prisoners and Wheeler and two more came to my house at a quarter past six that Tuesday night Mr. Lawrence was robbed. My house is about a mile from his. They stayed about an hour, and went away together. It was dark, and I did not take notice of their horses.

7.
This was confirmed by Thomas Martin and Arthur Allen.

8. **James Emmerton**, the prosecutor's boy.
That man in blue (Fielder) came into the sheep house, and holding out a pistol, said, he would shoot me if I offered to cry out. There were four more with him. He took off my garter and tied my hands. They asked me what servants my master kept, and I told them. They said they would not hurt me, but they would knock at the door, and I should answer, and they would give me some money. So one of them knocked, and my fellow servant opened the door, and they all rushed in with pistols. I went in and sat down, and they threw a table cloth over my face ... I don't know him in the great coat (Rose) but I remember the Evidence (Wheeler) was there. In a little time they took the cloth off my face and carried me into another room, and asked what fire arms my master kept. I told them there was an old gun, so they took the gun and broke it. Rose took a knife and made an offer to cut my master's throat.

9. **Court**
How can you tell it was Rose when you do not know his person?

10. **Boy**
I saw such an offer made by one of the men, and heard that man's name was Rose.

11. **John Pate**, servant to the Prosecutor.
Between seven and eight at night some body knocked; I unbolted the door; the two prisoners, Wheeler and three more came in with pistols in their hands, and said, *D... your Blood! How long have you lived here?* We had two candles in the room, and I saw their faces plainly. They put a cloth over my eyes, but in five or six minutes they took it off, tied my hands before me, and carried me into the room where the boy was, and sat me down by the fire. My master was tied and hoodwinked at the same time ... They opened a closet, took out a bottle of Elder wine and made us drink twice. They took out some linen and plate. I was present when the prisoners were taken, they had several pistols and made a great resistance.

12. Joseph Lawrence

Between seven and eight at night when I had just paid some workmen, and my boy was putting up the sheep, I heard some body knock at the door and call Mr. Lawrence! My man opened the door, and in rushed five men with pistols. I can swear positively that Fielder, the tall man in blue was one of them. They swore at me and demanded my money: They took off my neckcloth and tied it over my eyes. They broke down my breeches, and took out my pocket a guinea, a six and thirty shilling Portugal piece, and between ten and twenty shillings in silver. They said they must have more, and they would make me shew them where the rest of my money was.

They drove me up stairs with my breeches down, and coming to a closet they broke it open, though they had got the key of it, and took out two guineas, ten shillings, a silver cup, thirteen silver spoons, two gold rings, and what else they could find. They took all my linen, not only table cloths, napkins and shirts, but the sheets off the beds, and then they trod the beds about to try if there was any money in them. They carried me down again, and whipped me with their bare hands as hard as they could strike; so that I was black the next day. They broke my head with their pistols. They carried me into the kitchen, and took a kettle of water off the fire and threw upon me. The maid had just taken out some of the scalding water and put some cold in, so that it did me no harm. Then they hauled me back again, and swore they would rip me up and burn me alive if I did not tell them where the rest of my money was. One of them put a bill to my legs, and swore he'd chop them off. One of them held a knife under my chin, and threatened to cut my throat. Some pulled me by the nose, and some dragged me about by the hair of the head. My breeches were down, and I was blind folded all the while.

13. Dorothy Street

I was in the back house a churning butter, and hearing a great noise I put out my candle. They rushed in upon me, and tied my hands. The Evidence Wheeler, and both the prisoners were there. They put me into the room where my master was. They rifled the house of what they could find, and one of them made me go up, and swore I should shew him where my master's money was; I said I did not know. But he carried me into the garret, where he bolted the door, and threw me upon the bed. He had two pistols, he laid one upon the chest, and one upon the bed, and swearing he would shoot me, if I offered to cry out, he lay with me by violence ... He afterwards told me they would go to my master's son's house, and rob him.

14. The Boy again
They asked me if my master's son would come home that night, and I told them, Yes ... Then they said they were going to the next house, and would return in half an hour: and if they found any body loose they would kill me ... Afterwards they made me go with them to the door of the house, but when they came there they did not go in.

15. Thomas Lawrence
I went out at six in the morning, and when I came back at night, my chest was broken open and all my linen and twenty pounds in money was lost. I was at the taking of the prisoners; I was forced to throw Fielder down before I could secure him. I took Rose in Thieving Lane, in Westminster, he made what resistance he could.

16. Mr. Pullen
Some of the goods were taken in Duck Lane, and some in Thieving Lane. We found Rose in a room in Thieving Lane, drinking a bowl of punch with a woman that is, or goes for his wife, and one Walker.

17.
Some of the linen found in Rose's custody, was produced in Court, and proved to be the Prosecutor's.

18. Fielder
I know nothing of what you are talking about.

19. Rose
Nor I neither.

20.
The Jury found them guilty of both indictments.

John Field, Joseph Rose, Humphrey Walker and William Bush *alias* Saunders *alias* Schooling, with Richard Turpin and Samuel Gregory (not yet taken) were indicted for breaking and entering the house of William Francis, and stealing a silver tankard, a gold watch, and chain, and seal, a silver picture of King Charles I washed with gold, a silver punch ladle, a silver strainer, a silver cup, a pair of silver spurs, a coral set in silver, a mourning gold ring with a cypher, a gold ring enamelled blue, with a stone in the middle, a diamond on each side, and two angels holding a crown, a gold ring set with diamonds, a gold ring set with a stone and four diamonds, two gold rings with posies, a wig, six handkerchiefs, four shirts, a velvet hat, two pistols, a piece of gold with a hole in it, thirty seven guineas, and ten pounds in silver, Feb. 7 in the night.

They were again indicted for assaulting William Francis, in his house, putting him in fear, and taking from him the goods and money aforesaid.

1. John Wheeler

The prisoners and I and Richard Turpin and Samuel Gregory, met at the *White Hart Inn* the upper end of Drury Lane, about five in the evening. We stayed till half an hour past six, and then went to the Prosecutor's house at Marybone *(sic)* Park; we came there between seven and eight. We went first into the cow house, where we found a servant [Stephen Manning(ton)] and bound him, and carried him to the stable, where we found another servant [Edward Jones] whom we likewise bound. The Prosecutor happening to come home, we seized upon him at the gate and carried him into the stable and bound him as we had done his men. We left Bush and Turpin to stand over them with pistols, and then I and the four others went to the door of the house and knocked: the maid opened it, we pushed in and bound her and the daughter.

The old gentlewoman crying out, Fielder broke her head, and set her in a chair; and Gregory stood over her to keep her quiet. We searched the house, and took a silver punch ladle, cup and strainer, a gold watch with a chain and seal, and a picture, four rings, two shirts, two pair of stockings, and a great many other goods, ten pound all but eighteen pence in silver. As for guineas I saw none, and if there were any they sunk them upon me. When we had got all ready to go off; we threatened the family that if they made any noise we would come back to them, and so we left them all bound and went away.

2. Mr. Francis

I lost thirty seven guineas, and ten pound in silver besides plate and other goods ... They met with me just as I was going in at the gate. Three of them came up and clamped me over the head. I thought they were upon some game, and said, *Methinks you are mighty funny, Gentleman.* Upon that they presented their pistols and carried me into the stable, where they bound me with my men. My eyes are bad, and I can't swear to their persons.

3. Sarah Francis, the daughter.

About seven o'clock some body knocked, and I opened the door. Wheeler entered first, and the rest followed with pistols, and bid me hold my tongue or they would shoot me. One of them struck me. They bound me and the maid and set us in the kitchen, and then went up stairs and rifled the house ... I know none of them but Wheeler.

4. **Eleanor Williams**, the maid.

We were sitting at the fire: They knocked, and we opened the door. They cocked their pistols at us, and pushed manfully to enter, and so they got in. *Lord, Miss Sarah,* says I, *What have you done?* Upon which one of them gave me a knock, and another struck her. My old mistress cried out, *Lord, What is the matter! D... ye for an old Bitch,* says one of them, and I think it was he in the great coat (Rose), *I'll stop your mouth presently,* and then he broke her head, and tied her down in a chair, all in her blood.

5. **Stephen Manning[ton]**

I was in the cow house with a candle and lanthorn, two fellows came in and bound me, Bush was one of them, but I don't know the other, for his face was smutted. They carried me into the stable and stood sentry over me.

6. **Edward Jones**

I was in the stable feeding the horses, two fellows laid hold on me. One of them had his face all dirty, and he untied my garter and bound me. The other was Bush. They brought Manning[ton] to me, and they both stood over us with pistols an hour and a half or more.

7. **Keeper of the Gate House**

These two bullets, and this piece of gold with a hole in it I took from Walker in the Gate House.

8. **Sarah Francis**

This is my father's. My sister used to wear it for her eyes.

9. **Keeper**

This medal was taken from Rose's wife, and these two rings I took from Rose himself ... one of them is a brass ring.

10. **Eleanor Williams**

That brass ring is mine, I lost it when they robbed the house.

11. **Sarah Francis**

And this other stone ring with the posey is my mother's.

12. **Constable**
This cup was found at Walker's lodgings.

13. **Sarah Francis**
This is my father's punch cup.

14. **Richard Bartram**
These pistols I took from Rose ... And this, he held within a pistol's length of my breast, and pulled the trigger, but I clapped my finger in between the hammer and the lock and so prevented his firing.

15. **Thomas Lawrence**
Walker resisted, and had like to have shot a chairman, but was prevented by a Hackney coachman.

16. **[George] Harrowfield**, a coachman.
Walker had hold of his pistol and was pulling it out of his pocket, but it hung by something and he could not get it out, and so I came upon him and knocked him down.

17. **John Rowler,** the inn keeper, at the *Black Horse* in the Broadway.
I do not know Bush nor Walker, but the others have been several times at my house.

18. **Mr. Francis**
We could not bring the man at the *White Hart* in Drury Lane, because he is run away.

19.
About fifteen pistols, with bullets, a bullet mould, and several powder horns which had been taken from the prisoners and Wheeler, were produced in Court.

20. **Fielder**
I know nothing of the matter.

21. **Rose**
Nor I.

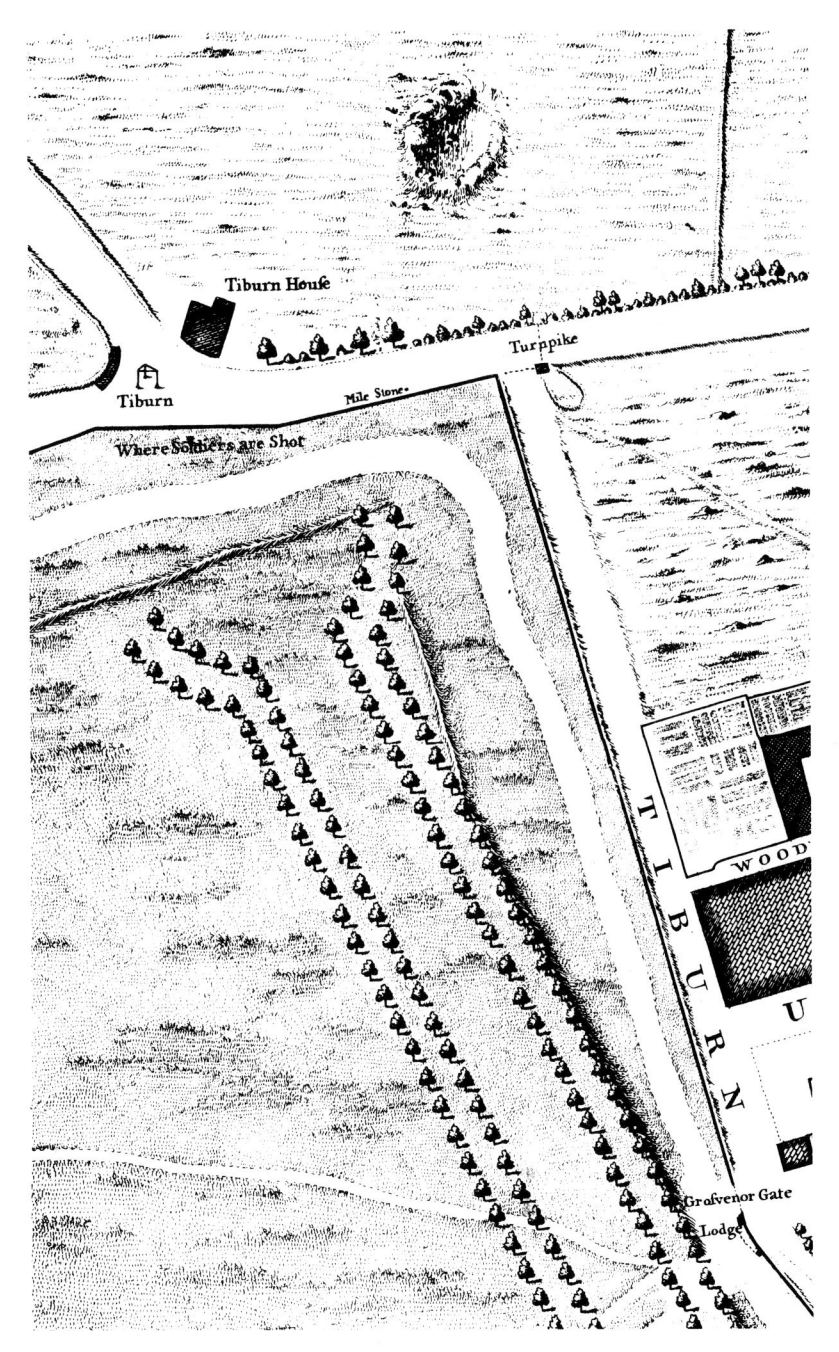

Plate 10. The site of the Tyburn gallows, 'where soldiers are shot'.
From J. Rocque's 'A Plan of the Cities of London and Westminster...', 1746,
26 in. to the mile.

Plate 11. *Cock Match* by William Hogarth.

22. **Walker**
   Nor I.

23. **Bush**
   Nor I.

24.
   The Jury found them all guilty of both indictments. Death.

There was another indictment against Field, Walker, and Rose, for robbing Ambrose Skinner, in the parish of St. Margaret's Westminster, of linen and other apparel, Feb. 15. But the Court thought it unnecessary to try them for this, after they have been convicted of the former.

Judgement in respect of the above two cases was noted on the first indictment in each case. Thus, although found guilty on both counts, that in the Lawrence trial was written upon No. 14 for burglary; and at the Francis trial upon No. 12, for the same: 'Put themselves upon their country. Jury said Guilty. No goods. To be hanged by their necks until dead.'[2]

The accused, although not represented by any defence counsel, appear to have had as fair a trial as they could have expected at that time; but what does seem very clear is that without Wheeler's testimony the prosecution may have been hard put to satisfy the court upon the witnesses' identification of each member of the gang. The claim of John Pate(q.v. Lawrence/11), 'We had two candles in the room, and I saw their faces plainly.' must in view of subsequent events, be hotly disputed.

II

On the evening of the day they gave their testimony at the Sessions, Joseph Lawrence, his son Thomas, and Richard Wood, the landlord of the *Nine Pin and Bowl* inn at Edgware, made their way home, satisfied no doubt that they had seen justice done. It is probable that they were accompanied by John Pate, James Emmerton and Dorothy Street, who were also at the trial. Jospeh Lawrence the Younger did not give evidence, but it is possible that he was a spectator at the trial and was in the company which returned from London. In any event they all returned home safely, but some time afterwards it transpired that they might have passed very near to danger:

> 1. Young Mr. Lawrence of Edgware has been to see Gregory who now owns himself to be the person who robbed Farmer Lawrence. He declared to Young Lawrence that he and his gang way-layed him, his father and the man at the *Ninepin* alehouse in order to have hanged them up, as they were returning from giving evidence against their companions Rose, Fielder, Walker and Saunders, but missed them.[3]
>
> 2. He [Gregory, to a witness independent of the Lawrence group] then confessed the robbery of Farmer Lawrence, and his lying with the maid (though not directly as sworn) and how he waylaid the farmer's son, &c. coming home from the trial of his companions.[4]

Was this mere bravado, as with Wheeler's claim that they had intended to murder Mason, or did Gregory and others actually wait in ambush at Edgware? One would have imagined that if they felt bitterness towards anyone, it would have been in Wheeler's direction; but then, if it had not been for Lawrence, Pate, Wood and others, Wheeler would not have been captured, and he in any case was well beyond reach. So they could indeed have laid in wait, and missed them in the dark; on the other hand upon seeing the party numbered more than their own, their resolution may have failed. If there is evidence of anything in this non incident, it is that Gregory and the others that remained had by now given up their former associates as lost; which is a little ironic because it would appear to have been but a day or so after the convictions were obtained that the Sheriffs of Middlesex became apprehensive of a rescue attempt being made at Tyburn.

III

The actual date of the letter from the Sheriffs of Middlesex is not known, except that it was written between 2 and 7 March 1735. From the official reaction to this letter (of which there is record) we may assume that it was couched in roughly the following terms:

> It has been reported to us that ... by which means we apprehend that an attempt may be made to rescue their accomplices upon the road from Newgate to Tyburn, which will be less crowded than the place of execution and allow them **all** to escape unimpeded in the midst of a general confusion. To prevent such attempt being made we submit that proper guard should accompany the prisoners along the route and remain until they have been executed. This desperate gang has already made one rescue of their number from the pillory at Epping in September last, and in this case it is supposed they may make even greater effort to save their associates. Therefore we humbly submit that these facts be represented to his Majesty and that your Lordship may move him to allow a detachment of Foot Guards to meet with us at Holburne Barrs and march as escort to Tyburn, the time appointed being half an hour after seven o'clock on Monday next, the 10th day of this present March.[5]

To obtain prompt action, and since the Secretary of State was also Lord Lieutenant of Middlesex and Westminster, the letter may well have been sent to the Duke of Newcastle. A few words of recommendation during one of his daily audiences with the King and the matter would have been settled. Then, in the absence of the then Secretary at War,[6] the necessary directions would have been speedily conveyed to Richard Arnold, the Deputy Secretary at War, into whose hands they came either on 7 or early on 8 March 1735. But some few days before this date, and certainly before 5 March, a remarkable precedent was established.

IV

This concerned a man named John Lyndon who was identified as being Samuel Gregory, imprisoned, identified by two of Gregory's victims, and removed by Habeas Corpus to Newgate, a set of circumstances which even to the prison to which he was taken upon first being arrested were identical to those in which the real Gregory found himself some few weeks later:

> The account he gives of himself is thus; that he was born at Wolverhampton in Staffordshire, is a locksmith by trade, that his father is an organist at the seat of a certain noble peer in that county, and that he worked in town at his trade, with a locksmith near Hockley in the Hole. But having a frolic to go in the country, he entered himself a soldier, and going a recruiting with a Serjeant and a Corporal, and some others, he was seized at Basingstoke for Gregory, and carried before the Mayor there, who, upon examination, discharged him. After which he was a second time seized, at a place called Sutton, and being carried before a Justice was committed to Winchester Gaol.[7]

Lyndon was taken to London on 5 March, but to enable some estimate of the date when he was arrested to be made, another report must be taken into consideration: 'Two of the servants of Mr. Lawrence [John Pate and James Emmerton] having been at Winchester Gaol have sworn that the person there in custody is the man that ravished the maid.'[8]

From this it is possible to calculate that upon the day following Lyndon's imprisonment a messenger rode to London to inform the authorities there, and that the same day it was arranged that the two witnesses should accompany him upon the return journey the following day. Having identified him the witnesses would either have returned to London the next day or waited to accompany the party removing Lyndon from Winchester to Newgate. Assuming that the Habeas Corpus was granted without delay, this journey would probably have been made either upon the day following the identification by the witnesses or the day after that. Which suggests that Lyndon was arrested on either 1 or 2 March, or allowing for unforseen delays, the last two days of February. The conviction that Lyndon was Gregory is illustrated by the extraordinary precautions taken to prevent his escape:[9]

> **Southampton**   Robt. Graham Esq. late Sheriff of the county aforesaid for the year ending Michaelmas 1735 craves an allowance of the sums following.
>
> Paid for removing John Lyndon otherwise Samuel Gregory by Habeas Corpus from Winton to Newgate in London being upwards of 60 miles and a very strong guard being so commanded by the Right Honble. Sir Edmund Probyn Knight, Sir John Comyns Knight which guard consisted of eight men.
> £16. 0. 0d. [sum allowed]   £25. 12s. 6d.

The Gaol Delivery for the County of Southampton for 5 March 1734/5 merely records, 'John Lyndon to be removed by Heas Corps &C. Co. Mx.'[10] But his arrival in London on the same day aroused greater interest: 'Before the Keeper of Winchester jail brought John Lyndon (said to be Samuel Gregory) to Newgate last Tuesday,* he carried him to New Prison, to confront him with Wheeler the Evidence, who declared, that he was not Gregory, nor did he remember ever to have seen him before.'[11] Wheeler of course cannot have been in any doubt, but of John Pate's trial claim, 'I saw their faces plainly', it can only be said that the, 'two candles in the room', did not burn very brightly. The authorities however were not immediately satisfied with Wheeler's disclaimer, nor prepared to take any chances upon his having suffered a change of heart: 'No. 12 Jno. Lyndon *alias* Samuel Gregory brought by Ha.Cor. from Winchester committed on oath of Jno. Pates and Jas. Emerson for entering the house of Joseph Lawrence robbing and ravishing the maid servant. Date 5th March.'[12]

> * Although Lyndon was brought to London on 5 March, the above report from a newspaper of 22 March stated that he was brought to Newgate 'last Tuesday', a discrepancy which can be explained. The practice of newspapers appropriating material from other newspapers has been a vexed point in the course of research into the activities of Turpin and his associates, mainly because the 'borrowed' reports were rarely edited, and the date when an event was first reported was not subsequently translated in time. The error in this particular instance is easily rectified because the date is corroborated elsewhere, but in other cases where the dating of a report is suspect, it is not always possible, unless the original report is located in one of a considerable number of other newspapers, to say on which day a particular event did occur. Care has been taken in this account to arrive at the correct date, and each report treated with caution, but there is still no guarantee that in one or two cases errors may have escaped notice. For the most part however, where there is any doubt, some reference is made to it in the text.

V

If the authorities were disappointed in their discovery that they had not, after all, captured Gregory, they were able to content themselves with one of the little fish. They already had one receiver safely tucked away, and on 7 March they managed to bag another:

> On Friday night last (7th) one Barnfield was committed to Newgate by Justice Dennet on suspicion of his being one of the Essex gang. Several goods belonging to Mr. Wooldridge, a gentleman of that county whose house had been entered and robbed in the same manner as several others formerly mentioned, being found upon him, and of which goods he could make no satisfactory account before the Justices.[13]

Not a great deal is known of Barnfield because although two people entered into recognisances to prosecute him he did not live long enough for them to keep their promises. The second recognisance was entered into on 11 March and one assumes he was still alive at that date, but on which day he died between then and 16 April, the terminal date of the *Calendar of Prisoners in Newgate* which states simply that he was, 'dead', is not known. Nor, unlike Walker, is there anything known about him which would suggest the reason for his death; it could have been anything from gaol fever to heart failure. What we do know about him is that he did in all probability receive certain goods stolen by the gang in 1734. The fact that they were still in his possession when he was taken suggests that he possibly had some difficulty in disposing of them and at some point, perhaps December 1734, became reluctant to accept any more goods from the gang and ended the association. This would explain to some extent why Rose and his wife became the receivers for the goods stolen in the latter stage of the gang's existence. We do know however that suspicion did not fall on Barnfield alone:

> No. 3 Thomas Barnfield committed by Robert Dennet Esq. on oath of Ann Wooldridge and William Wood on a strong suspicion of being concerned with Rose, Gregory [? and others in] robberies in the county of Essex particularly breaking open the house of Richard Wooldridge and stealing thence several goods part being found [...]
> No. 4 Ann Barnfield committed by Nathaniel Blackerby Esq. charged on oath with harbouring felons and receiving goods from [? them][14]

There were marginal annotations made in each case, (No. 3) 'Dead' and (No. 4) 'Del.d', meaning delivered. Ann Barnfield was probably Thomas Barnfield's wife, and it is presumed she was released because it was not possible to substantiate the charges brought against her; but from the quantity of goods found in Barnfield's possession it is unlikely that his wife can have had no knowledge of how he came by them. The fact that two magistrates were responsible for the individual committals, suggests that these occurred on separate days, but since in both the above cases there was deterioration at the edges of the parchment where the date would have appeared, this cannot be proved.

Richard Wooldridge appeared on the day after Barnfield's committal, to enter into his recognisance to prosecute; the other victim who was prepared to enter into similar agreement did not appear until a few days later:

> Richard Wooldridge of the Tower of London gentleman. doth acknowledge to owe our Lord the King the sum of £40 UPON CONDITION that he doth promise to appear at the next General Quarter Sessions of the Peace to be held for the County of Middlesex at Hick's Hall in St. John's Street and prefer to the Grand Jury there a Bill of Indictment against Thomas Barnfield for receiving several household goods, that is to say, a feather bed and several pieces of brass and pewter the property of the said Richard Wooldridge knowing them to be stolen and if the said bill be found and returned to be a true bill there to appear at the next session of Oyer and Terminer held for the said County of Middlesex at Justice Hall in the Old Bailey then and there to prosecute the law with effect against the said Thomas Barnfield upon the said indictment that then &c. Taken and acknowledged the 8th March 1734/5 before me Robert Dennet.
> Dead in Newgate so returned in the Calendar.[15]

VI

Saturday 8 March was a busy day for a number of people who were connected in one way or another with members of the gang, and significantly enough much of the work done on that day was in preparation for Monday 10 March when the execution of the four condemned members of the gang was scheduled to take place.

Whitehall 8 March 1734/5

Sir,

Application having been made by the Sheriffs of Middlesex for a guard to be at Holburne Barrs and Tyburn on Monday next being the 10th instant at half an hour after seven o'clock in the morning for the preventing a rescue of the criminals which they apprehend may be attempted: I am therefore in the absence of the Secretary of War to signify to you it is his Majesty's pleasure that you order a detachment from the three Regiments of Foot Guards equal to one entire company and to be commanded by a discreet Serjeant whom you can confide in to be at Holbourne Barr's at the time appointed and receive his directions from the said Sheriffs for the purposes abovementioned. I am [&c.]

Rt. Hon. Sir Chas. Wills,
Colonel of the First
Regiment of Foot Guards.

Rd. Arnold[16]

Also on Saturday, because the spectacle would no doubt have brought strong protests from the local inhabitants if it had been done on Sunday, four rather forbidding structures were erected at Edgware. These were the gibbets, and apart from the carpentry and sinking of the holes in which to stand them, there was also the plating with iron to prevent their being cut down by sympathisers or inhabitants who objected to the smell when the wind blew in their direction.[17]

The criminals themselves were probably measured for their suits of chains a day or so after conviction.

The only other point of interest to be linked with Saturday 8 March was the appearance in one of the newspapers of a report concerning the possible whereabouts of Gregory and the rest: 'At East Sheen in Surrey a gentleman saw four suspicious men coming torwards his house, they went on to a nearby alehouse and inquired for a Mr. King of Ham Farm, but being forewarned and having dogs they were driven off on approaching the place. One with a great scar was supposed to be [Samuel] Gregory.'[18]

This incident probably occurred only a day or two before the report was made. East Sheen is just below Mortlake, and in an area which the gang is not known to have frequented previously. The number of men, the visit to the alehouse, the farm as their objective, and the man with a scar all point to Gregory and three companions. East Sheen was some way from their known areas of activity, but so too were Southchurch and Gravesend, and it is perhaps significant that Rowden and Turpin returned to that area when they became highwaymen. The fourth man was probably Haines who, to judge from subsequent events would appear to have stayed with Gregory almost until the end. Certainly, the gang had not shewn itself for some time, but it was perhaps for this reason that they were obliged to venture out now, and in daylight. In this case revealing their identities was of no great consequence when there was little chance of them being ambushed in a place where no-one can have anticipated their coming. And when there was some sign of resistance they wisely did what any wanted men would have done, they rode away.

VII

In Newgate, amid filth and suffering and unimaginable wretchedness, on Sunday 9 March 1735, a man lay dying. There was no incentive for him to live because if he did, they would, if he still breathed, throw him in the cart for Tyburn and hang him with his fellows. His name was Humphrey Walker.

FOOTNOTES

1. *Old Bailey Sessions:* Printed Proceedings for 1735.
2. Middlesex/MJ/SR 2631.
3. *Old Whig,* 8 May 1735.
4.   *Ibid.,* 15 May 1735.
5. Deduced from P.R.O./W.O.4/33 p.102 and previous history.
6. Sir William Strickland, Bart. He died 1 September 1735, but since he had previously been succeeded in his office by Sir William Yonge on 9 May, and Arnold was his acting Deputy until that date, it is presumed that he was absent by reason of an illness from which he did not recover. This is to some extent supported by the announcement, on 10 March 1735, of his resignation.
7. *Read's Weekly Journal,* 22 March 1735.
8. *Hooker's Weekly Miscellany,* 15 March 1735.
9. P.R.O./T.90/147 p.6.
10. P.R.O./Assizes 23/6.
11. *Read's Weekly Journal,* 22 March 1735.
12. Middlesex/MJ/SR 2634 (Calendar of Middlesex Prisoners in Newgate).
13. *General Evening Post,* 8 to 11 March 1735.
14. Middlesex MJ/SR 2634 (Calendar of Middlesex Prisoners in Newgate from 26 February to 16 April 1735).
15. Middlesex MJ/SR 2633, Middlesex General Quarter Sessions for April 8 Geo.II, Recognisance XXXIII.
16. P.R.O./W.O.4/33 p.102.
17. That this barbaric practice was objected to by people unfortunate enough to have a gibbet contiguous to their dwellings, is well illustrated by the complaint and petition of the inhabitants of St. George the Martyr, Southwark. *See* P.R.O./S.P.36/17/156–158.
18. *Country Journal,* 8 March 1735.

CHAPTER TWO

I

HUMPHREY WALKER died about 3 a.m. in the morning of 10 March.[1] His body appears to have been left in Newgate until Wednesday, when it was removed.

At about 7 a.m. Fielder, Rose and Saunders, in company with ten others who were to die that morning, left Newgate under strong guard and were met at Holborn Bars by the company of foot guards. Most newspapers stated that there were about fifty soldiers present, but if Sir Charles Wills carried out his instructions to the letter there would have been eighty men lined up, this being the strength of a foot guard company in 1735. It is assumed that they marched either side of the cart in which Fielder, Rose and Saunders were conveyed to Tyburn; none of the other poor wretches could boast associates whose reputation called for extra precautions being taken to prevent their rescue. Tyburn was situated near where Marble Arch stands today, and allowing for the usual exchange between topsman and victims, and the more popular exchanges between victims and crowd, it is unlikely that the executions commenced much before 9 a.m.

Eventually the cart carrying Fielder, Rose and Saunders was drawn up beneath the gallows. The reporter for the *Old Whig,* covering the executions for the first edition of that newspaper, observed that, 'Rose was so sick he could scarce stand', and once the ropes had been placed around their necks, another reporter wrote, 'The executioner allowed the cart to be drawn away before the caps had been placed over their heads.' So they met their end, a grisly spectacle enough but not for them the ultimate degradation; the gibbets at Edgware stood waiting to receive their bodies.

One of the other ten executed was William Falconer, condemned upon his conviction for stealing a glass showcase.[2] Falconer had been a counterfeiting associate of Thomas Rowden in 1732. When charged with that crime, Falconer gave evidence against Rowden, who was nevertheless acquitted. Obviously they went their separate ways after that episode, but it is curious to find Falconer in the same circumstances as Rowden's later companions.[3]

II

On the same day at Chelmsford in Essex, Jasper Gregory appeared at the Assizes charged upon two indictments:[4] No. 1 That on 16 November 1734 he assaulted George Cory upon the King's highway at Woodford, and stole from him the sum of fourpence. No. 2 That on 14 December 1734 he [in company with John Jones, Samuel Gregory and John Wheeler] burgled the house of John Gladwin at Chingford, and stole goods, etc. from him, and from John Shockley living in the same house.

The witnesses were Daniel Eyres, Philip Tongue and George Bosgrave upon the first indictment; and John Gladwin, John Shockley, Mary Theed, Philip Tongue and George Bosgrave upon the second. Jasper was found guilty on both counts and judgement was recorded on the second, 'No chattels. To be hanged &c.'. Gregory had three weeks to wait until his execution, and some time before that date, probably as soon as the Assize ended, his brother Samuel received word of the conviction. It was this news and the events which followed which brought about the end of the Gregory gang.

III

On Tuesday 11 March, Ambrose Skinner Junior entered his recognisance to prosecute Thomas Barnfield for receiving: 'Ambrose Skinner Junr. of Barking farmer ... against Thomas Barnfield for receiving several pieces of plate knowing them to be stolen ... Taken and acknowledged the 11th March 1734/5 before Robert Dennet.'[5]

We know that at some time after this agreement was made, Barnfield the receiver died, but what might not be so clear in this particular instance is the appearance of the younger Skinner, whose own house was burgled in February. However the fact that he would have prosecuted Barnfield for receiving plate indicates that he was preferring charges on behalf of his father and himself who were robbed in December 1734. In the inventory of goods stolen from Barking a number of *silver* articles were included in respect of both father and son, but none were mentioned in the inventory of goods removed from the house in St. Margaret's Westminster. But even if Skinner did not have the satisfaction of prosecuting the receiver, he did at least recover some of the most valuable goods stolen.

IV

By Wednesday 12 March the body of Humphrey Walker must have been becoming objectionable, and a somewhat tardy decision was made to remove it: 'Yesterday the body of Humphrey Walker who died in the cells in Newgate on Monday morning last was carried from thence in a cart, in order to be hanged in chains with the rest of the gang near Edgware.'[6]

It is assumed that the bodies of Fielder, Rose and Saunders were taken to Edgware on the same day that they were executed, and the only reasonable explanation for Walker's body being left behind is that it was forgotten, or else there was some argument about the ethics of gibbeting the body of a man who had not been executed. But whatever the reason for the delay in Walker's case, the whole ugly business was not conducted without very considerable expense.[7]

> **London** Micajah Perry Esq. and Sir John Salter Knight Sheriffs of the City of London and county of Middlesex [Cravings for the year] September 29, 1734 to September 29, 1735.
> 1. Paid for the special execution of Fielder, Rose, Saunders and Walker; guards and attendance. £7. 0s. 0d. 2. paid for making and putting up gibbetts in Edgeware Road and for hanging up the said 4 persons in chains thereon. £16. 10s. 0d. 3. for 4 suits of chains for the said Fielder, Rose, Saunders and Walker and plating the gibbetts. £25. 0s. 0d.

Take away a probable 1s. a day allowance for the 81 foot guards from the £7 and we find that it cost £2 19s. 0d. to hang the three men; a sum of £41 10s. 0d. spent on exhibiting four bodies as a deterrent to other lawbreakers, must therefore be regarded as something of a luxury.

V

We do not have record that Gregory and the rest were seen at Edgware, but the executions appear to have had a sobering effect upon them; the next reported sighting was not made until the end of that month:

> On Sunday last (March 30th) three highwaymen, supposed to be Gregory and two of his gang, attacked on Epping Forest the Earl of Suffolk's servant, and took from him a fine horse worth £80. The servant alarmed the country and pursued and overtook the three fellows, and accordingly shot the Earl of Suffolk's fine horse which Gregory rode upon. Whereupon he jumped up behind one of his

companions, and rode to Little Wash [not identified], where the horse threw them, and the three highwaymen clapped themselves back to back, and stood on their defence, and the country people finding them so resolute, let them escape.[8]

This is one newspaper which when making retrospective quotes was careful to qualify the original date. Which is particularly useful in this case because the significance of the report might have been overlooked had it been accepted that the report referred to an incident which occurred on 6 April; for on Monday morning of 31 March, Jasper Gregory was due to be executed at Chelmsford.

Henry Howard, Earl of Suffolk, was Recorder of Saffron Walden from 1735–1745, but the reason for stealing a horse would appear to have been that one of the men lacked a mount, and although previously there is no evidence to suggest that the gang at any time had difficulty in obtaining horses (except on the occasion when they failed to do so by false pretences) things were rather different for them at this point in time. If one of their horses cast a shoe, they could do little more but turn the animal loose because they could hardly show their faces at a smithy, and Gregory could do nothing without a forge. So stealing was the last resort. On this occasion they failed, and if any attempt to rescue Jasper had been intended, it was thwarted by the Earl of Suffolk's servant's aim.

There is little doubt that this was Gregory and two companions and that it was he who had lost his own mount, for within a week he was more successful in his efforts to obtain another. But he had not been so successful in keeping together what was left of his once numerous gang, as this latest disaster illustrates.

The last report of the gang, which appeared on 8 March stated that there were four. Gregory, Rowden and Turpin, with Haines preferred as the fourth man. Jones was never a regular member of the gang, but there is a case for a reluctant reunion following Wheeler's betrayal. But even allowing that Jones did resume his acquaintanceship with the gang for a short time, it is certain to have been broken off again soon after the Old Bailey convictions. So who were the two with Gregory on 30 March?

As Jasper, Jeremy and Samuel Gregory were brothers, it is unlikely that the last two would have remained unaffected by the fate in store for Jasper on 31 March. Jeremy has not been heard of since he escaped from the Bridewell. His fellow escaper, Saunders, resumed his acquaintance with the gang (and was hanged for his pains) but Jeremy, so far as is known, did not; nor did Wheeler name him in his Information. By 7 April however he had become Samuel's only companion.

This points to a *reunion* with Samuel when Jasper brought about a family crisis by getting himself condemned. It is unthinkable that on the eve of his execution, efforts were being made to obtain a horse which were unconnected with thoughts of rescue. But with Samuel Gregory on foot, or at best a passenger, an attempted rescue was out of the question. Whose loyalty could Samuel command in what after all was a family affair? Who would be prepared to take a greater risk in rescuing one man, than they would have been prepared to take to rescue four who were virtually constant companions? The logical answer is Jeremy Gregory. He and Samuel were two of the men in Epping on 30 March, two of the men who stood, 'clapped back to back, upon their defence' at Little Wash. But who was the third man?

Had it not been for the reappearance of Jeremy the answer would have been Rowden or Turpin, for Haines, in less than a fortnight, was displaying a romantic attitude to survival which might not appear consistent with the desperate measures of a rescue attempt from the scaffold. But by 7 April, all the survivors had gone their separate ways anyway, so one must look for some other common factor which would link one man with another.

Rowden and Turpin were cool in times of crisis, the execution of Jasper Gregory was not the end of the world for them, nor did it drive them to desperate measures such as those adopted by Jeremy and Samuel Gregory and Haines for they, once Jasper was dead, felt obliged to flee the country. Rowden and Turpin remained in London and its surrounds and travelled the roads together as highwaymen. Whether or not they broke away from Samuel Gregory on or before 30 March cannot be determined, but it is certain they would not have been prepared to risk their necks on such a foolhardy rescue attempt as was proposed. To rescue four from Tyburn may have appealed to them, but not one from Chelmsford. Herbert Haines, the romantic barber, is the probable albeit unlikely third man in Epping, whose loyalty to Gregory remained constant to the end.

A postscript to the reappearance of Jeremy Gregory is contained in a retrospective reference to him in an authorisation for reward to be paid for his capture, ' ... Jeremy Gregory a notorious Highwayman ... '[9] Certainly he and Samuel tried to obtain money by such means, but there is no evidence that either of them had ever done so before.

VI

March 1735 ended with the execution at Chelmsford of Jasper Gregory, and as at Tyburn precautions were taken to ensure that nothing went amiss:[10]

Essex Thomas Ambrose Esq. Sheriff for year ending Mich. 9 Geo. II.
1. For guarding and keeping Jasper Gregory and three others condemned to be hanged from the time of their conviction till their execution being three weeks. £1. 10s. 0d ,[£1. 10s. 0d. allowed]. 2. For conveying them under a strong guard to the place of execution and for executing them there. £10. 0s. 0d. [£7. 0s. 0d. allowed].

Of Rowden the pewterer and Turpin the butcher there was no sign at this time, but there is however one curious fact which might indicate that even though there were differences of opinion over making an attempt to rescue Jasper, they remained on amicable terms with Gregory.

Gregory, in company with brother Jeremy, left London on 4 April. His last known whereabouts were without the city walls, in the parish of St. George, Middlesex *alias* St. George in the East. Some few weeks later, the next occasion on which Turpin was reported as having been seen, he and two companions, who may have been Rowden and Jones, were at an alehouse in Whitechapel. The centre of Whitechapel is at the City end of Commercial Road, and between that end of Commercial Road and the London Docks lay the parish of St. George. To the East of the docks was Old Gravel Lane where Gregory had lodged when Jasper had his home there. This is not evidence that they were all in that vicinity at the same time, but insofar as they had returned to their old haunts and were there within a comparatively short time of each other, there remains the possibility that they were in touch with each other up to and including the time Gregory left London. There would have been no point in remaining together as a band because Samuel and Jeremy Gregory, and Herbert Haines, were now making their own plans for leaving the country, and not as it transpired, together.

Haines adopted the alias of Joseph Butler and intrigued with Mrs. Carroll, the wife of his former employer, to flee the country together and go to Holland. Samuel Gregory adopted the alias of William Johnson (possibly in memory of the deerstealer of that name who was executed in 1734), and looked about him for a reliable mount to steal. Jeremy Gregory took the name ..... Lisle, and waited for Samuel to obtain a horse; once that was accomplished, they would try to get off for Boulogne from one of the south coast ports. The only obstacle so far as they were concerned was their lack of negotiable assets; the money taken from all the robberies was almost gone, the goods upon which they might have capitalised had all been retrieved by the authorities. But Samuel Gregory was a marked man, he could no nothing to hide the scar on his face, and his companions had therefore gradually come to realise they stood a better chance of surviving if they went their own way. It was understandable, but it left him with no choice but to try and get out of

The Gregory Gang

the country. That he and Jeremy lingered at all near London is entirely attributable to the fact Samuel needed a horse. There was one in the parish of St. George, Middlesex, which Samuel would steal on 4 April, but late on 31 March he and his brother were no doubt more concerned with mourning the passing of Jasper.

VII

On the same evening, another Jasper suffered at the hands of a gang such as Samuel's, and the latter's was mentioned in passing:

> **Resolution of Mr. Hale of Peckham.**
> Though the gang who had made themselves terrible all round the country, for entering and robbing houses, was dispersed, and most of them hanged, as formerly mentioned, yet three other fellows had a mind, it seems to imitate them; and on the last day of March came about eight o'clock at night to the house of Jasper Hale, of Peckham.[11]

There was a possibility that this crime might have been committed by Gregory himself, but research showed that an equally colourful character called Black Jack John James was responsible. The Gregory gang was finished, nothing but stories of its exploits, and its reputation remained, and for a few days longer two of the three Gregory brothers.

VIII

It is appropriate at this point to mention a source of information which has *not* been used in this account. In the *Gentleman's Magazine,* a monthly publication, there used to appear a list of books and other printed material such as pamphlets which had been published since the previous month. Thus in, 'A Register of Books for March 1735', there was included the following work: '13. The Ordinary of Newgate's account of 13 malefactors executed at Tyburn the 10th, and of the pirate executed at Execution Dock the 14th, in 3 parts, per 6d. each, printed for J. Applebee.'

Although this account did exist, efforts to find a copy have not been successful. Any number of accounts by the Ordinary of Newgate do survive, usually filed with the Printed Proceedings of Trials at the Old Bailey for the relevant session, but this particular edition has not so far been traced in London libraries and repositories. Which is a pity, because this document no doubt had some considerable bearing on the shaping of contemporary Turpin literature, and on one work in particular, *The Life of Richard Turpin, being taken from Richard Bayes, at the Green Man on Epping Forest, and Others in Essex, 1739.* Some of Bayes' account was fiction, some was based on contemporary newspapers and printed proceedings of the trials of Turpin's associates, but other parts of his story were neither fiction nor drawn from any known extant contemporary account of Turpin and his companions.[12] But upon examination of the Ordinary of Newgate's accounts of other malefactors, it could be said that they do contain material of the type which appears in Bayes' *Life*. Even so the men executed on 10 March 1735 would no doubt have still been represented as little more than commonplace rogues, and Turpin, since he remained at large, would have been lucky to have been mentioned in passing. Bayes' assignment of leadership to Turpin was merely a device to glamourise the villain of his piece, but it would still have been interesting to have compared it with what the Ordinary had to say.

FOOTNOTES

1. *London Magazine,* 1735, p.158.
2. January Sessions, 1735.
3. The counterfeiting episode has already been described in an earlier chapter, but reference to Falconer's trial and execution appears in the *Gentleman's Magazine,* 1735, p.162: and details of his previous record are given in the *General Evening Post.* No. 201.
4. P.R.O./Assizes 35/175/1 Winter 8 Geo.II (1735), Felony File for Essex.
5. Middlesex MJ/SR 2633, Middlesex General Quarter Sessions for April 8 Geo.II, 1735 (abbreviated) Recognisance XXXIIII.
6. *General Evening Post,* 11 to 13 March 1735.
7. P.R.O./T.90/147 p.59.
8. *Old Whig,* 10 April 1735.
9. P.R.O./T.52/39 p.44.
10. P.R.O./T.90/147 p.63.
11. *Political State,* Vol.XLIX, 1735 Jan.–June, p.461.
12. e.g. Justice Asher.

CHAPTER THREE

I

'ON 4 April 1735, in the parish of St. George, Middlesex, Samuel Gregory stole a bay gelding worth £20 from Thomas Humphrey.'[1] At his trial this particular charge was dealt with very quickly: '**Court** What do you say as to stealing the horse? **Prisoner** I am guilty of that too.'[2] So Samuel Gregory had at last obtained a mount and there was nothing more to detain Jeremy and himself in London. From the events of the next few days it is clear that they crossed the river the same day and headed south. For Jeremy there was to be no return. Samuel Gregory describes what they did from 4 to 6 April.

> Me and Jeremy went to Brighthelmstone, and Shoreham, but no vessel was then going off, and we had not money enough to hire one and pay for the full passage to Bullogne. We then went to Southampton, and would have gone off to Guernsey, but had not enough money to pay our passage. We therefore intended to make up the sum by robbery, and as soon as we had got it would have gone off, being well satisfied we could not stay in England with safety.[3]

On Monday 7 April the two brothers were almost half-way back to London again in their quest for a suitable victim, and a few miles from Guildford before they were successful.

> On Monday Sir John Osborne was robbed on Milford Heath, Nr. Godalming [Godliman *sic*], of a gold watch, and a considerable booty by two highwaymen, one of them was supposed to be the infamous Gregory. The same villains afterwards attempted to rob Mr. Spooner, who keeps the *Red Lion* at Guildford, but refusing to deliver his money, fled. They fired a ball after him, but happily missed him. These two highwaymen were well mounted one on a bay [Samuel], the other [Jeremy] on a dun.[4]

There is no doubt that the two brothers were the men involved in this robbery, but apart from a tentative identification of Samuel, no-one had any

The Gregory Gang

idea who the other man was until some days later. This particular report of the robbery is however very brief and for an account of the method employed we must turn to another newspaper.

> When Sir John Osborne was attacked last Monday upon Milford Heath, between Godalmin in Surrey, and Liphook in Hampshire, he pressed so much to have his watch returned, as what he valued, and promised to send a sum of money equivalent to it to any place they should appoint, to which one of the highwaymen agreed, but the other swore he would not trust his life in the hands of any person. One of the men rode with Sir John, and talked to him some time before they robbed him, and Sir John liked his horse, and bid him money for him, the other was in a different road, and crossed into the road to the man, who was before Sir John and after speaking a few words, clapped a pistol to his breast, and told him if he offered to stir, he would immediately shoot him, on which signal the other threw himself upon Sir John's pistols and then robbed him.
> Afterwards they attacked Mr. Spooner, master of the *Red Lion* at Guildford, who rode away from them, then they attacked a man who was with him, and took from him what money he had and so made off.[5]

The man who rode with Sir John Osborne was Samuel Gregory, and since the substance of their conversation formed the basis of our introduction to the blacksmith it is appropriate to recall what passed between them now.

> So then Gregory confessed he was the person that robbed him [Osborne] and said he knew him at the same time he did it, and referred to some discourse that passed between them and asked Sir John, if he was not once in Buckinghamshire at a gentleman's, and sent his horse to the smiths to be shoe'd and that the horse kicked the smith's man? Sir John replied yes; then says Gregory that was me, and this is the scar on my cheek.[6]

The *Old Whig's* coverage of the last days of the brothers Gregory was quite extensive, and leaving out the parts already quoted from the 15 May edition, the remainder, which is quite remarkable reportage, is given herewith.

> The following is a particular account of the taking of Gregory, and his confession to Sir John Osborne in Winchester Gaol. A day or two after Sir John Osborne was robbed, the two Gregorys went to a cock match near Petersfield, and there betted, and as Samuel Gregory was reaching to a person across the pit, his greatcoat flew open, and several people saw a pistol stuck in his belt; this presently was whispered about, and they made off; Next day, the robbery being much talked on, and the men described, enquiry was made after them which way they went &c., and they were traced to an alehouse at Rake near Petersfield, so about five o'clock two young fellows, one armed with a pair of pistols and a hanger, the other with a gun and a hanger, and two old fellows, one with a sort of scythe, and the other with a pistol and a sword, went to this alehouse, and hearing they were above in bed, went up stairs, broke open their chamber door, and took them before they scarce knew of their design; upon this and the Gregorys protesting their innocence, and declaring how willing they were to go before a Justice, to clear themselves, the country fellows suffered them quietly to put on their clothes, and dress themselves, which as soon as they had done, Samuel

Gregory stamped with his foot, and they both instantly went to the bedhead and took from under the pillow a brace of pistols each; Samuel fired one pistol, and wounded one of the fellows, then he with the gun fired and missed, then Samuel Gregory closed in and got one of the young fellows down, and was just going to murder him when the other young fellow with his hanger cut at Samuel Gregory and cut off the tip of his nose and part of his cheek, and one of the old fellows, at the same time shot the other Gregory in the thigh, so that he fell down, and Samuel Gregory was immediately seized too, though with some difficulty and it is thought that if Gregory's brother had not had that shot in his thigh they would have got away, for till then the battle ran in their favour. After they were seized, being carried before a Justice of the Peace and giving a very indifferent account of themselves, they were committed to Winchester Gaol on suspicion. Soon after their coming in, the Gaoler unloaded Gregory's pistol that was not discharged, and found the ball was rammed in with a bit of paper whereon was a direction to Gregory. This confirmed his suspicion, and he wrote word of it to town. And some little time after they had been in Gaol, Gregory's brother died of his wounds and Sir John Osborne came to the Gaol to see Gregory and was pretty positive to him, but very positive as to his watch found upon him. So then Gregory confessed ... the robbery of Farmer Lawrence, and his lying with the maid (though not directly as sworn) and how he waylaid the farmer's son, &c. coming home from the trial of his companions, and said he expected to be hanged, but desired to be used civilly whilst he lived, and only desired that he might not be hung in chains, or anatomised, and said his design of coming into that country[7] was to get off by sea. That he and his companion had been at Brighthelmstone ...

Some elements of this story are not, despite the swashbuckling description, very clear, and particularly so in respect of the date when these events are supposed to have occurred. Similarly, although the next account of the same proceedings does clarify the matter of the date, it does leave open to speculation the exact location of the capture, and how it was effected.

Gregory apprehended. On the 8th of last month, two men on horseback came and took up their lodgings at the *Flying Bull* near Hinehead in Hampshire, and Sir John Osborne having been robbed some days before by two highwaymen, whose description suited with these two, the landlord suspected they were the two; however he behaved very civilly towards them that night; but as soon as they were gone to bed, he acquainted his neighbours with his suspicion about his guests, and a great number of country people having got together, they surrounded the house early in the morning: the two fellows got up very early, and were coming down stairs, but, finding themselves beset, they retreated to their room, secured their door, and resolved to stand a siege: This confirmed the landlord and his assistants in their opinion, whereupon they began their attack; the two fellows fired several pistols, and wounded one of the countrymen in the groin; but this was so far from terrifying, or abating the courage of the honest brave fellows, who had laid siege to the place, but they renewed the attack with more vigour, and at last broke into the room: The two rogues still persisted in their defence, and both gave and received several wounds, but being at last overpowered, they were disarmed and secured; and Sir John Osborne's watch, with some other things having been found in their custody, they were immediately carried before a Justice, and committed to the county jail. They called themselves Johnson and Lisle, but one of them was suspected to be Gregory, and both supposed to be of that gang who robbed

Farmer Lawrence, and so many other country houses in Middlesex and Essex. The fellow supposed to be Gregory, had a scar upon each cheek, but one of them appeared to have been lately made, and was supposed to have been made on purpose, to evade the description that was given of him in the *Gazette*.[8]

And one final abbreviated report from another newspaper. 'On Tuesday at the *Flying Bull* at Hinehead, Gregory who had his nose quite cut from his face in the skirmish [was captured with a companion]. The other is thought (by his description) to be Turpin.'[9]

There is much conflicting evidence in all these accounts and for the purpose of comparison, reference to them will be made by using the initials of each publication, *viz.* O.W. *(Old Whig)*, P.S. *(Political State)*, and R.W.J. *(Read's Weekly Journal)*.

Sir John Osborne was robbed on 7 April on Milford Heath, south west of Godalming. By the following day they were some 18 miles further south west at a cock match near Petersfield (O.W.). After this they went to an inn and retired for the night. Some of the men whose suspicions had been aroused at the cock match happened to call at the same inn that same evening. If they were really making enquiries (O.W.) they would hardly have waited until the next day, and it is more than likely that in conversation with the landlord of the inn, the robbery of Sir John Osborne was casually introduced into the conversation and a description of the men at the cock match bandied about. From the description the landlord recognised his guests, and plans were accordingly laid to take them at dawn. Five o'clock (O.W.) and very early in the morning (P.S.) are consistent with dawn, and the two *were* in bed at five o'clock.

Samuel and Jeremy were obliged to play the role of highwaymen by force of circumstances. They had obtained money from Sir John Osborne and, possibly, from Mr. Spooner's companion. Having reached Petersfield from Milford Heath suggests that they were satisfied with their haul and were retracing their steps to the coast, but a chance to capitalise on what they had stolen would have appealed to Samuel, especially when they intended going to a strange country where they would need some ready money. Some idle reference to a cock match by a drinking companion could easily have diverted them from their destination, and by the time they had left it, it would have been too late to continue their journey that day. They were still able to afford a night's board and lodging, and it is unlikely that they would have ridden nearly two thirds of the distance *back* towards Milford Heath to look for it. Although the *Flying Bull* at Hindhead is mentioned (P.S. *and* R.W.J.), it seems much more feasible that they should have remained near Petersfield in order to continue their journey, possibly to Portsmouth, the following morning. The alehouse at Rake, about four miles north east of Petersfield is an eminently reasonable choice because if, as seems probable, the cock match was held between those two points, the brothers would have been more likely to have selected the isolated inn rather than one in the town of Petersfield itself. And so, believing themselves to be safe and but a day or so from escape across the Channel, they slept at Rake, but with pistols under their bolsters just in case. They rose early in order to be on their way back to the coast, and came downstairs to be greeted by a demand to surrender themselves, from the armed and waiting countrymen (P.S.). To have opened fire on the unsuspecting pair without knowing they were going to be met with any resistance would have been rash; to have opened fire without knowing for certain who they were would have been madness. When the brothers retreated to their room and barricaded the door the countrymen were sure. There was probably an exchange of shots through the door before the locals burst in when the Gregory's were reloading. Once inside, there was a furious battle which was resolved only when Jeremy Gregory was shot in the thigh. Samuel, his pistols useless, could only flail them about him like clubs, but even they were of little use in close quarter combat. Eventually he fell to the floor struggling with one of the men and managed to gain the upperhand until a blow across the face from a short sword wielded by one of the others caused him to submit, his nose half gone and his face covered with blood. For the fight in the bedroom the O.W. version is the more detailed, and the reconstruction of the struggle has been *based* upon it. The suggestion of how Samuel Gregory came to be scarred on both cheeks (P.S.) reflects a certain unfamiliarity both with the manner by which these wounds are most likely to have been caused and the circumstances in which they occurred.

The two wounded men were removed to Winchester Castle and there, on a date unknown, Jeremy died. This is confirmed in the text of an *ex gratia* payment of a reward, made despite the fact he died before he could be brought to trial (for highway robbery), to the persons responsible for his capture.[10]

At some time not long after they were committed, it is stated that the jailer discovered Samuel's undischarged pistol ball to be rammed in with a piece of paper with Gregory's name on it. The O.W. account suggests that he did only fire one piece, but although this is not consistent with the battle royal described in the same report, the number of pistols fired is perhaps irrelevant. What does seem unreasonable is the idea of his having rammed a piece of paper with his name on it into his pistol, and that particular pistol having been the one which remained undischarged during the ensuing struggle. The convenient discovery of the same piece of paper by the jailer seems almost an anticlimax.

In trying to present an as accurate as possible a picture of what happened at the inn at Rake, no reference has been made, other than that actually reported, to the men responsible for the capture; but at this point it is convenient to introduce the others involved. The source of information is that which has been used previously; the claims for rewards for apprehending and convicting various members of the gang. In this case the person captured was Samuel Gregory, but the settlement thereof differs from those encountered before, in that it was only in respect of actual discovery and capture, and in no way involved the participation of claimants in the conviction of Gregory at his subsequent trial. They in this case had no part in the advertised reward, but did receive from the Sheriff of Middlesex a share in the Blood Money paid in respect of the capture *and* conviction. The seven men named in the reward were as follows 'Richard Cooper the Younger, Thomas Cragg, William Goddard, Henry Challen, John Cooper, Richard Cooper the Elder, John Hickman.'[11]

The first man named was awarded £20 of the £50 reward, but as the others each received £5, it would seem obvious that *they* were regarded as having taken equal risk in the venture. In both the O.W. and P.S. accounts of the capture, the wounding of one man (on the side of law and order) is treated exceptionally, and the latter version goes so far as to record that he was shot in the groin. It would be reasonable to assume that this was Richard Cooper the Younger, and that he received £20 for his pain and loss of earnings, and possibly permanent disability.

II

Appropriate to this period, and under the heading, *'House of Correction (Bridewell)',* the following appears in a Middlesex Sessions Book: 'John Wheeler to be ref[erred] to Mr. Norris.'[12]

Insofar as the Keeper of the New Prison, Clerkenwell, subsequently claimed expenses for playing host to Wheeler, this particular reference to his being in the Clerkenwell *Bridewell,* which was adjacent to the prison, is something of a puzzle. A similarly undated reference to Wheeler occurred in February 1735, and in that case also he was referred to a Justice of the Peace. This particular item is attributable to April 1735, and since on the former occasion it was assumed Wheeler was required for examination in connection with the preparation of the prosecution's case against the other members of the gang, it may tentatively be supposed that he was required for similar reasons consequent upon the advice received of Samuel Gregory's being in

Winchester Castle.

Wheeler was not, technically, a prisoner. Although manifestly a criminal he was not a convicted felon; he was the chief prosecution witness against all members of the gang, several of whom were still at large. His confinement, whatever the legal terms of reference at that time may have been, can only be described as, 'protective custody', and since this undoubtedly was the condition of his confinement, his name did not normally appear on prison calendars, nor did it recur at the times of gaol deliveries in lists of prisoners upon orders. Such references to him as do exist are isolated as in the instances quoted above. At no other time does the name John Wheeler appear under Clerkenwell Bridewell, and the reason for his being there, even temporarily, is purely conjectural.

III

The Gregory brothers were taken on 9 April, but not until the following month was there another reported sighting of Turpin. The first report identifying him and Rowden as highwaymen did not appear until early July, too long a time for them to have remained inactive. So far as is known they did not commit any more robberies at isolated farmhouses, and it would be reasonable to assume that the decision to go on the road was made sooner rather than later, particularly since their funds would by this time have been running low. Since the Gregory brothers were obliged to turn to highway robbery for the same reason, it is probable that the London survivors were forced to do so at about the same time, *viz.* the first week of April. And when Samuel and Jeremy left London it would appear that Turpin remained in Whitechapel, an area he knew well. Rowden certainly was one of his two sighted companions, and since they were all three very much in the same predicament, Jones seems to be the only choice for the third man. But having made a case for a trio of highwaymen, what evidence is there to support not only their existence, but their being active on or about the date suggested?

> Last Thursday [10 April] Mrs. Pyecroft, wife of a noted brewer in the Minories, returning from Plaistow in Essex was attacked by three highwaymen near Mile End about eight o'clock, who clapping a pistol to her breast and demanding her money, she pulled out her purse in order to give them part of what was in it, but they desiring her not to trifle with them, she delivered it, upon which they bade her not to be afraid, that she should not be attacked any more, and accompanied her a considerable way, then bid her goodnight.[13]

Plaistow is due east of Mile End, and Whitechapel is roughly south west of

The Gregory Gang

Mile End and adjacent to it. It is implied that the foolish woman was travelling alone, but even so it took three highwaymen, who must have been desperate for money, to empty her purse. That they were so calm as to accompany her on her homeward journey does however suggest two things, one, that they saw no need for urgent flight and, two, that the poor woman happened to be travelling the road they had to follow if they too were to get to Whitechapel by the most convenient route. Three was about the least common number of highwaymen to band together. One or two was customary and three not unknown, but because the individual net gain might be small if shared amongst three, it was unusual for that number to band together for such a purpose.

The three, quoted in the report, may well have been Turpin, Rowden and Jones; but it is not possible over a period of two years to determine which of all highway robberies committed were those done by Turpin, with or without companions. He was reported to have been the culprit on a considerable number of occasions, in as many different places throughout the length and breadth of the land. It is certain that not all these robberies can be attributed to him. Similarly there were an even greater number of robberies committed, and reported, where no attempt was made to identify the person responsible, and in some of these Turpin must undoubtedly have been involved.

FOOTNOTES

1. Middlesex/MJ/SR 2636 Indictment No.11.
2. *Old Bailey Sessions:* Printed Proceedings for 1735.
3. *Old Whig,* 15 May 1735 (Gregory's confession, edited and translated to first person).
4. *Ibid.,* 10 April 1735.
5. *Reid's Weekly Journal,* 12 April 1735.
6. *Old Whig,* 15 May 1735.
7. Country used in this fashion meant no more than the district or part of the countryside which was germane to the text; its relationship to county, both in spelling and meaning is no more than accidental, for in whatever part of the country one is, one is bound to be in a county. Nor, in the extreme, should it be mistaken for the country or nation proper.
8. *Political State,* Vol.XLIX, Jan.–June 1735, p.462.
9. *Reid's Weekly Journal,* 12 April 1735.
10. P.R.O./T.52/39 p.44.
11. P.R.O./T.53/38 p.197.
12. Middlesex/MJ/SB 927.
13. *London Evening Post,* 12 to 15 April 1735.

CHAPTER FOUR

I

ON 12 April 1735 there remained at large only four of the gang; they were Haines, Jones, Rowden and Turpin. Three were in custody; Wheeler the Evidence in New Prison (or temporarily in the Clerkenwell Bridewell), Mary Brazier *alias* Rose in Newgate, and Samuel Gregory in Winchester Castle. Five were dead if not buried; Fielder, Jasper Gregory, Rose, Saunders and Walker. Thomas Barnfield the receiver would be dead by 16 April, if indeed he was not dead already; and the same may be said of Jeremy Gregory whose death was not reported until towards the end of April.

The reason for calling the roll on 12 April is quite absurd; it was the day upon which John Carrol found out that his wife had 'eloped' with Herbert Haines.

The newspaper accounts of what occurred afterwards are as reasonable as might be expected, but for descriptions of personal involvement we turn again to the claim for the reward promised for Haines' capture. There is a surprising amount of detail preserved in the Treasury Solicitor's submission of the claim to the Lords Commissioners of his Majesty's Treasury, and this was obtained from the original petition for the reward, and sworn affidavits by other persons concerned:[1]

The Petition of Henry Palmer
On the 12th of April 1735 John Carrol told me that his wife had eloped from him and was gone on board the *Chandos* (Chandois *sic*) sloop to one Herbert Haines, whom I have known many years. And having read in the *Gazette* of his crimes I immediately took boat to go on board the sloop to apprehend him, but was informed the ship went for Gravesend that tide, whereupon I took a pair of oars and followed the ship to that place where I was told the

ship was cleared and ready to sail. I immediately went on board and desired of the Chief Mate to have a sight of passengers (which he after a great deal of scruple granted), and there saw Haines in company with Carrol's wife, he having shipped himself for Holland under the name of Joseph Butler. I immediately and without any warrant secured him, and with the assistance of the sailors brought him on shore to Gravesend where I kept him in custody all night until the tide served next morning for London. During that time not only Haines but likewise Carrol (who accompanied me) and his wife told me that I should have £50 to permit him to escape, but I brought him to London at my own expense and carried him before Sir Richard Brocas who committed him to Newgate upon my producing to him the *Gazette* setting forth a description of his person.

The Affidavit of John Carrol
My wife being eloped from me and being informed that she was gone away with Herbert Haines and that he was concealed on board some ship in the river, I desired the assistance of Henry Palmer to go in quest of them, and for company's sake we took with us James Freeland. And having got intimation that my wife and Haines were that tide fallen down for Gravesend, Palmer hired a pair of oars and went in pursuit of them, and having a suspicion that they were on board of a sloop bound for Holland Palmer and I went on board the sloop (leaving Freeland on shore at Gravesend) where by the contrivance and good management of Palmer, Haines and my wife (who were concealed under feigned names) were discovered and taken and by him brought on shore. Freeland was no further concerned in discovering and apprehending Haines.

The Affidavit of James Freeland
Me and Henry Palmer received information that Haines was at Gravesend and went and found him there, and having secured him without any other assistance we brought him to London and carried him before a magistrate who committed him to Newgate.

Sunday 13 April was not Herbert Haines' lucky day, and by the time it was over the philandering barber was no doubt wishing he had never set eyes on Mrs. Carrol. He had after all achieved his purpose and obtained passage without being recognised, but now, because of her, he was back on shore instead of being well on the way to Holland and freedom. But some aspects of Haines's capture are not clear, particularly the actual dates upon which he was captured and committed. Reading the account as it stands one might think that all the action occurred on Saturday night and Sunday morning, and that Haines finally came to rest in Newgate sometime on Sunday, having spent the night in custody at Gravesend. One might also think that he was committed by Sir Richard Brocas, but with regard to both points, and without the original statements necessarily being in error, there is some confusion.

Those newspaper accounts which mention the fact are in agreement that Haines was taken on Saturday night; they are similarly agreed that he was not committed until Monday, and that the person committing him was Brocas. But the following record, whilst confirming the date of committal, names another magistrate as being responsible for those proceedings. 'No. 50 Herbert Haines charged in custody by Nat: Blackerby Esq. Charged on oath with being concerned in several robberies in the county. 14 April.'[2]

It is obvious that Carrol was being cuckolded long before his wife 'eloped', and it is conceivable that her liaison with Haines began when he worked for Carrol as a journeyman. The affair may even have been the reason for Haines leaving his employ; but later, when Haines became a barber, it was resumed. Carrol must have known this, but was either bullied into submission by Haines or was afraid that he would lose his wife if he made too much fuss about it. In any event, even when it became known that Haines belonged to the Gregory gang, Carrol did nothing, and it was only when they actually went off together that his hand was reluctantly forced. There is no doubt that his role in the pursuit and capture of Haines was a passive one, he received no share in the reward for his capture and Palmer's account of his attempt to bribe him suggests that he may not even have instigated the pursuit downriver, but merely mentioned it to Palmer (who also knew Haines) either to engage his sympathy or enlist his aid to get his wife back. The last thing Carrol wanted was for Haines to be brought back as well, in or out of custody. But when he did tell Palmer that his wife was believed to be with Haines on board a ship in the Thames, he had not reckoned with Palmer's greed.

James Freeland, the man recruited to accompany Palmer and Carrol, is modest about his part in the proceedings, and it is unfortunate that his account is the shortest when Palmer's is so self indulgent and Carrol's is so self effacing. Palmer could not have cared less about Carrol's wife, but when he heard Haines was on board the *Chandos,* he took the shortest route to the mooring, with Carrol and a possibly uncommitted Freeland in tow. The time all this occurred was probably between 8 and 9 p.m. on Saturday 12 April, for when the mooring was reached the *Chandos* had sailed with the tide, and the tidal prediction for London Bridge on that date has been calculated as having been 19.20 hours. Sailing on the ebb the master of the *Chandos* probably cast off about 7.30 p.m., and was some way down river when the three men appeared at the dock side. It was not so long afterwards however because they were still able to hire a pair of oars prepared to row them the 21 miles to Gravesend. The time this journey would have taken *on the falling tide,* and with favourable conditions, has been estimated as five hours plus. From the estimated time of arrival of the pursuers at the mooring, this would mean that the party arrived at Gravesend between 1 and 2 a.m. on 13 April. Once there they had to find the *Chandos,* which took more time, and when they (or two or three of them) did get on board they found that it had been there long enough to be cleared by the customs and was ready to sail. With some greater assistance from Freeland than was alleged by Palmer, Haines was taken; and prisoner and escort stayed *all* night at Gravesend.

Palmer states that their intention was to wait for the morning tide, but insofar as they were either too tired, or they (Palmer and Freeland) were afraid Haines might escape in the dark, or they were too late to take advantage of the tide which would have borne them upriver from Gravesend at about 2 a.m., the statement is wrong because the next tide which would have carried them with it from Gravesend to London did not occur until about 2.15 p.m. on 13 April. High water at London Bridge on the morning of that day is predicted as having been 07.44 hours, and until about two p.m. the tide would have been ebbing towards Gravesend. But although this fact contradicts Palmer's morning tide, it does make our assessment of subsequent events a little easier. Fortified by both breakfast and lunch the party returned, possibly a little slower this time because with two extra passengers the boat would have been lower in the water. By the time Haines was brought before Sir Richard Brocas it could have been 9 p.m. or later.

But was it in fact Brocas, and not Blackerby, to whom the strange party came? The clue to what happened was written in the margin against the Haines entry in the *Calendar of Middlesex* prisoners, *supra,* a clue which even an ultra violet lamp could not reveal entirely; [? Orders (*or*) ? Order] Made [? from] London'. The only words positively legible being 'made' and 'London', and such marginal entries being often either cryptic or abbreviated, it would be futile to try and recall the exact wording used, but the sense of the direction, as will be seen, was probably something like, 'Orders made from London'. For the equivalent London Sessions roll contains the following entry: 'No. 30 Herbert Haines committed [Newgate] by Sir Richard Brocas on oath of Jn.º Carroll for being concerned with Jn.º Wheeler and others in several robberies in Middlesex Surrey Essex and Kent as appears by the information of the said Wheeler. Date 14 April'[3] Again there is an indistinct marginal entry which as well as may be determined with the assistance of a lamp can be taken to read, '... to be sent [to] the Several Counties the first the Assizes [,] begin at first.'

It is now possible to determine the sequence of events from the time the Gravesend party reached London. The Haines entry on the Middlesex Calendar is the *first* of a number of entries written in darker ink than those which were made previously, and without exception those following Haines (No. 50) relate to persons brought to Newgate from other prisons such as the Gatehouse, Westminster. Haines, in a sense, must be regarded as belonging to this same group, for although he did not change prisons he did change his status from that of London prisoner to Middlesex prisoner. He had not committed any crime in London for which he could be indicted in London, and therefore, in theory, he had to be 'removed' to Middlesex.

Arriving somewhere near London Bridge from Gravesend, it would have been more convenient for the captors to look out a London magistrate than one for Middlesex and Westminster, and so, somewhat late in the evening of the 13 April, they eventually came to Sir Richard Brocas.

That would appear to be a reasonable chronology of events, but when a report of 15 April states that Haines was *committed* by Brocas, 'yesterday about noon,'[4] the night of 13 and morning of 14 April are still not accounted for. So what happened in that time? Haines did not have to be committed to ensure his overnight stay in Newgate. Mary Brazier, Rose and Walker were examined for two days in the Gatehouse before Mary Brazier was committed there, and the two men to Newgate. In Haines' case Brocas had to be convinced of the identity alleged by his captors, a fact perhaps not at first borne out by Mrs. Carrol. For although Henry Palmer apparently had the *Gazette* description in his possession, he might have had difficulty persuading Brocas that a man, 'about five feet seven inches high, of a pale complexion, wearing a brown wig,' was in fact Haines, especially if Mrs. Carrol maintained that he was Joseph Butler. But persuaded Brocas must have been because Mrs. Carrol was released, and her husband (who received no part of the reward, and whom Palmer alleged tried to bribe him into releasing Haines) swore to the fact that Butler was Haines. Some part of either the night or morning may also have been employed in taking Haines to New Prison to be identified by Wheeler. Thus satisfied, Brocas could then have formally committed the wanted man into Newgate as a *London* prisoner, and by that time it was possibly, 'about noon,' on Monday 14 April. Blackerby no doubt was then advised of what had occurred and travelled to Newgate to formally charge Haines into custody as a *Middlesex* prisoner in the same prison.

II

Two days before, on 12 April, there was more news of Jeremy Gregory *alias* Lisle, and Samuel Gregory *alias* William Johnson, recently committed prisoners to Winchester gaol. 'The persons apprehended on Wednesday morning at an inn near Hine Head, were one Johnson and one Lisle, a wine cooper of this town ... Lisle was shot in the thigh and had his bone shattered to pieces; at length they were seized, and after their wounds were dressed ... committed to Winchester Gaol.'[5]

This is the only description of Jeremy Gregory which tells us anything whatsoever about him. It is not corroborated, and he may or may not have been a wine cooper of London Town, but even if he supplied this information at the same time he told observers he was called Lisle, there is no reason to suppose he had reason for inventing a trade as well as a name.[6]

It is rare to hear of compassion for men such as Samuel Gregory and his brother. In fact it is so unusual one wonders, perhaps a little cynically, whether or not their captors were more concerned about preserving them for justice than their personal health. Jeremy died anyway before he could be brought to trial, but who can say but that with a wound like his he might not have died sooner without attention. And Samuel wasn't exactly unscathed with half his nose missing. But then again, even in those days, it perhaps just wasn't done to let a man bleed to death.

III

Also on Saturday night there occurred the second highway robbery which may be attributed to Turpin and his two companions, evidence yet again of their early activities as highwaymen. 'Last Saturday night Sir Caesar Child, Bart, was attacked upon Epping Forest by three highwaymen, who fired at the coachman without bidding him stand, and shot off the tip of his nose ... They robbed him of £25.'[7]

There was more to the incident than that of course, some curious dialogue for instance, which went as follows: 'Have you got his money?' 'Yes.' 'Damn him, shoot him.' 'No we wont.' And some argument with an irate coachman, who warned them that they would have to deal with him. It was a somehow indecisive end to the proceedings, because without being impressed by the coachman's threat, they eventually retired into the forest and disappeared, leaving Sir Caesar the poorer by £25 and the coachman minus the tip of his nose.[8]

The dialogue shews one of the men to have been in a belligerent mood, but does not suggest who the men were. And although they were three in number, and the incident did occur on familiar ground, this is hardly conclusive evidence that they were Turpin, Rowden and Jones. But if *they* had seen the newspapers on 12 April, which contained reports of Gregory's capture and disfigurement, and his companion's terrible wound, the news could have inspired a defiant gesture against authority, an expedition into the forest to tax someone, anyone wealthy enough to be identified with the establishment. Sir Caesar Child of Wivenhoe in Essex was their accidental choice of victim. It was a coincidence that the coachman, like Samuel Gregory, should lose the tip of his nose.

IV

At the Old Bailey Sessions which commenced on 16 April, one who was not a member of the gang was set free: '... the sham Gregory, who was discharged at the Sessions at the Old Bailey last week.'[9] So John Lyndon survived his experience, and no doubt lived to tell the tale many a time over a pint of ale. But in looking down a list of others who were less fortunate than he, we come to a person whose fate might easily have been obscured by the events which followed her commitment. '**Middlesex Prisoners Upon Orders** Ind[icted] No. 66. Mary Johnson otherwise Brazier otherwise Rose. Committed for being accessory to several felonies was ordered to remain since charged by Thomas Robe Esq. on oath of John Wheeler for persuading him and several others to rob the house of Geo. Asser Esq. at Sechurch in Essex.'[10]

The abortive robbery at Southchurch has already been described, but although Mary Brazier was indicted at these sessions, it was not upon the charge described above. There were in fact two indictments for receiving, filed on the sessions roll quoted in footnote. The first indictment (No. 45) named the persons convicted of the robbery of Mr. Francis of Marylebone and described again in full detail the goods stolen. The second indictment followed the same form in respect of the Farmer Lawrence robbery, but in both cases this preamble was followed by the usual terms of reference which stated the charge, abbreviated as follows:

Indictment No.45
Mary Johnson otherwise Brazier otherwise Rose widow afterwards to wit on the sixteenth day of February at the parish of St. Margaret Westminster the said silver picture of King Charles the first washed with gold, the said mourning ring with a cypher, two of the said four linen shirts and the said velvet hat parcel of the said goods did receive and have, knowing the goods [to have been] stolen.

The bill was found to be a True Bill and there were sworn to appear in court; John Wheeler (the evidence), William Francis (the prosecutor), Sarah Francis (his daughter), Thomas Dowell (this entry struck through in the record), Archelaus Pullen (the arresting constable), Mary Lloyd (? wife of the chandler at Thieving Lane), Charles Westridge (Gunner at the Tower of London), and Alice Gardner (identity unknown).

Mary Brazier, 'put herself upon her country' but having been tried and convicted on the other indictment she was not tried on this one. The form and wording of Indictment No. 46 were exactly the same as rendered above, except that being concerned with goods stolen from Lawrence these were described as follows: 'the said pair of linen sheets, nine of the twelve linen napkins, the linen table cloth, two of the six linen pillowbiers, the said dimitty waistcoat.' John Wheeler, Thomas Lawrence, Archelaus Pullen, Richard Mitchell and Mary Lloyd were the persons sworn in court, and although the plea was the same as above, the judgement was 'Jury say guilty—no goods—to be transported for fourteen years'.

The indictments describe Mary Brazier as a widow. When tried at Chelmsford in 1734 she was stated to be a spinster and although there is no record of a marriage to Joseph Rose, there have been numerous references to her having been his wife. To describe herself thus after his execution suggests that she was in fact his common law wife.

The date upon which it was alleged the goods were actually received, *viz.* 16 February, was not the date upon which the offence occurred. The trial proceedings, or such part of them as appears to have been recorded, are quite short:

Mary Johnson *alias* Brazier *alias* Rose *alias* Cox *alias* Head, was indicted for receiving a silver cup, four silver spoons, four gold rings, a pair of sheets, nine napkins, two pillowbiers, one table cloth, the goods of Joseph Lawrence, February 16, knowing the same to have been stolen; and for stealing which, John Fielder and Joseph Rose were convicted last Sessions.

She was a second time indicted for receiving two gold rings, with mottos, a mourning gold ring with a cypher, a silver picture of King Charles I, washed with gold, and a velvet hat, the goods of William Francis, February 16, knowing the same to have been stolen; and of stealing which John Fielder, William Bush, Humphrey Walker, and Joseph Rose were convicted last Sessions.

John Wheeler

After John Fielder and Joseph Rose, and the rest of us had robbed Joseph

Lawrence, we carried the goods to Joseph Rose's lodging near the *Black Horse Inn* in Dawes Street, in the Broadway, Westminster. We laid the goods on the table and appraised them among ourselves. Joseph Rose agreed to take them at the price and to pay us our shares: And then they were delivered to the prisoner. We told her where and how we got them. Joseph Rose lay with the prisoner, I lay at his back. In about two days she sold most of the goods, and paid the money to him ... When I was in the Gatehouse, she broke open my box which was left in her room, and robbed me of my linen and fifteen pounds in money.

It further appeared that some of the Prosecutor's goods were found at a chandler's shop in Thieving Lane, where they had been left by the prisoner, with orders to deliver them to Charles Westridge, a gunner, belonging to the Tower. These goods being produced in court, were sworn to by the prosecutor. Guilty.[11]

The addition of the two aliases, Cox and Head, is intriguing. There appears to have been no official recognition of these names having been used by the accused, and no reference to them has been found elsewhere. But it is conceivable that on the odd occasion, when disposing of stolen goods, Mary Brazier did use these names, and that the fact was made known in the testimony given at the trial.

It is unlikely that at these sessions Wheeler was the only person called upon to give testimony. Although principal witness for the prosectuion the conviction would hardly have been obtained upon his evidence alone, but it was by his testimony that the prosecution were able to prove Mary Brazier knew that the goods were stolen. The absence of other evidence indicates that this trial was not regarded as being so important as those of other members of the gang, and therefore did not warrant the same detailed coverage.

The reference to the goods found at the chandler's shop in Thieving Lane implies that they belonged to the prosecutor Joseph Lawrence: but this is wrong because the person to whom they were to be sent, Charles Westridge,[12] was sworn upon the Francis indictment. Mary Brazier was not tried on this count (a fact not mentioned in the printed proceedings), but Francis did identify his property in court; it is this brief exchange which the court reporter failed to distinguish from the rest.

FOOTNOTES

1. P.R.O./T.53/39 pp.271–272 (edited and translated into first person).
2. Middlesex/MJ/SR 2634 (Calendar of Middlesex Prisoners in Newgate).
3. Guildhall/London Sessions of Gaol Delivery 16 April 1735. (Calendar of London Prisoners in Newgate).
4. *General Evening Post*, 15 April 1735.
5. *London Evening Post*, 10 to 12 April 1735.
6. William Johnson, the deerstealer executed early in 1734 upon his conviction for murder, was apprenticed to a cooper in London.
7. *London Evening Post*, 15 to 17 April 1735.
8. The point about the coachman's nose has some relevance to this account, for in *Dick Turpin* by Henry Downes Miles, p.202, there is a puzzling reference to the proclamation published on 8 February 1735 which promised rewards for the discovery of the persons who robbed Peter Split and others. The puzzle arises from the fact that, "Sir Caesar Child who had his nose shot off" is stated to have been included within the terms of the proclamation. This is a gross error compounded by a footnote reference to pp.282 and 391 of the *London Magazine* of 1735, an examination of which does nothing to clarify the point made. Miles' book was a novel after the style of *Rookwood*, but one which had Turpin as the central character and a motley assortment of real and imaginary companions. It was not a work of reference, but again like *Rookwood*, additional and often superfluous information was given in footnote form. It is mentioned here only because Child has been mentioned in a Turpin context, not to sway the case for their being connected in this instance.
9. *London Evening Post*, 19 to 22 April 1735.
10. Middlesex/MJ/SR/2634.
11. *Old Bailey Sessions*, Printed Proceedings for April 1735.
12. P.R.O./W.O.54/204. Charles Westridge was a Matrosse (an apprentice gunner) in one of two Marching Companies of Artillery belonging to the department of Military Ordnance. He was paid one shilling per day.

CHAPTER FIVE

I

INEVITABLY, WITH only three members left at large, the almost day to day reporting of the Gregory gang must cease. From the time of the April Sessions to the May Sessions when Samuel Gregory was brought up for trial, the intervals between events of any significance grew longer; but whereas any event in the past would have been related to the activities of the Gregory gang, we are now entering a new phase where more and more they involved a surviving member of the same gang and a succession of different companions. The man who came into the limelight was of course Richard Turpin, but before he could really claim to have stolen the headlines (which in those days did not exist), he had to wait some little time for the removal of Samuel Gregory from the scene; although after the John Lyndon travesty, the newspapers were a little reluctant to commit themselves about the identity of the men imprisoned in Winchester Gaol. 'There is some reason to believe, that the person now in Winchester Gaol and lately taken near Petersfield as a highwayman, is Gregory ... so persons are sent down to see him, though from that Gaol was brought before the sham Gregory, who was discharged at the Sessions at the Old Bailey last week.'[1] 'The person lately taken at Rake near Petersfield, with the supposed Gregory, having had his thigh broke in the fight when taken, is since died in Winchester Gaol.'[2]

The identity of the persons sent to Winchester is not known; it may have been Emmerton and Pate again, but since on the previous occasion they identified John Lyndon as Gregory, some doubt must have remained about their being able to identify Gregory himself, even when everyone else was more or less certain. Whoever was sent, the Sheriff of Southampton was no doubt anxious not to incur further unnecessary expense in removing the second supposed Gregory to London, only to find when he arrived that he was someone else. In the event, there was no doubt about Gregory's identity, and within three weeks a warrant of Habeas Corpus had been made out for his removal to Newgate.

Since the news of Jeremy Gregory's death was not reported in the London press until 29 April, he may have lingered anything between a week and a fortnight after his committal, but insofar as he was implicated in the robbery of Sir John Osborne, he would, even if he had recovered from the wound, have been convicted upon that charge and hung. Samuel however, before his removal to London, had one final visitor. 'Young Mr. Lawrence of Edgware is returned from Winchester Gaol where he has been to see Gregory who now owns himself to be the person who robbed Farmer Lawrence. He declared to young Lawrence that he and his gang waylaid him.'[3]

Allowing for the time factor in reporting, there is no reason why the report of persons going and the later one of Lawrence's return, should be confused and regarded as the same party going and coming back, because in both cases the source of news was not Winchester, but London, and the information could have been obtained on those days it appeared in the respective newspapers. Thus there is a considerable gap between the two reports, one which is not accounted for by the time it would have taken to reach Winchester and return. The persons originally sent down were probably in some doubt about the identity of the person they saw, Gregory's facial injuries having altered his appearance, and Thomas Lawrence, although not familiar with Gregory's face, may have gone to satisfy himself by means of conversation with the man, that he was the one they were after; Gregory, who said, 'he expected to be hanged, but desired to be used civilly whilst he lived,' no doubt felt that he could speak more freely with the man who had hunted down his accomplices than anybody else.

The date when Gregory confessed should be clarified. A fuller version of the above *Old Whig*, 8 May, report of his having declared he waylaid Lawrence after the Old Bailey trial, appeared in the *Old Whig*, 15 May edition. In this, no mention of Lawrence's visit was made and Gregory's statement (amplified) was tacked on the end of a long account of the capture and subsequent events, thus giving it the appearance of having been made immediately after the committal on 9 April, when in fact it wasn't made until the beginning of May. This is confirmed by the reluctance of editors to commit themselves over the identity of the Winchester prisoner throughout the month of April. In the second week of May, Gregory was brought to London, but three days before this event, there was a brief flurry of activity in Whitechapel.

II

On Saturday night [10 May] last Turpin the butcher a companion with Gregory in robbing Farmer Lawrence near Edgware was with two men more at an alehouse in Whitechapel. A countryman who knew Turpin who was there at the same time, went secretly to see for a constable, but before he could get one they went off, and left half a guinea upon the table in such haste, that they would not stay for their change.[4]

The anonymous countryman who knew the man who escaped is a figure who turns up fairly frequently in this account, but there were three men present in the alehouse, who left in something of a hurry. They could have been Turpin, Rowden and Jones, for if Turpin saw someone he knew, was aware that the man recognised him, and then saw that same man leave shortly afterwards, he would not have waited to find out if the man had informed on him or not. The particular significance of this incident is that it appears to have been the last when the surviving three men were together. By July, Jones had either deserted Turpin and Rowden, or been abandoned by them, which is perhaps one reason why they survived longer.

III

On Tuesday 13 May 1735 Samuel Gregory was brought to London:

1. Tuesday in the afternoon the notorious Samuel Gregory was brought by Habeas Corpus to Newgate from Winchester Gaol, being handcuffed and chained under a horse's belly, with seven or eight persons well armed to guard him; the Keeper of Winchester Gaol took him to New Prison to Wheeler the Evidence, who declared as soon as he saw him that he was the man, nor does Gregory himself disown it.[5]
2. ... and on the 13th of last month [May] Samuel was brought up to town, where he was first carried to New Prison, and confronted with Wheeler, who, though his face was very much disfigured, swore directly that he was the man concerned in robbing Farmer Lawrence's house at Edgware, and in a great many other robberies, whereupon he was carried to Newgate and confined in one of the cells there.[6]

The number of men who escorted him is more accurately recorded in the County of Southampton's Sheriff's craving for allowance of expenses for the journey, and this number may be taken to have included the Keeper of Winchester Gaol: 'For removing Samuel Gregory otherwise William Johnson from Winton to Newgate in London under a very strong guard which guard consisted of ten men all well armed ... £30 8s. 0d. [£20. 0s. 0d. allowed]'[7]

The last word upon this event is to be found in Newgate: 'No. 26 Saml.

Gregory otherwise Wm. Johnson brought from Winchester by Habeas Corpus standing indicted of felony &c. Date 9 April'[8] It was usual for the last date to be that on which the prisoner was committed into the receiving prison, but in this case there seems no other explanation but that the date upon which Gregory was committed at Winchester was appended in the Middlesex Calendar. And so Gregory arrived in London in good time for the May sessions. He was placed in a cell set apart from the other prisoners, who at that date still included his old friend Herbert Haines. Gregory however hardly had time to settle down in his new surroundings before the visitors began to arrive:

Thomas Lawrence

I went to see him in Newgate on the fourteenth of this month, and he owned to me, that he shewed the others the way to our house, for he thought we had got a great deal of money. "Why did you think so?" says I. "Because you paid everybody very well," says he [having knowledge of the fact through having worked there some several years previously], "and therefore I thought you must be very rich." He told me too that he lay with the maid, and that he had twenty five shillings of the money that was taken.

Archelaus Pullen

The day after the prisoner came to town, I went to see him in Newgate. He told me he lay with the girl; but that she was either as willing as he, or else she was afraid; for he said he had two pistols and laid them down by her. He confessed likewise that he was concerned in the robbery.[9]

From his conversations with Lawrence and the constable, it is obvious Gregory had no illusions left about the outcome of his trial, and was prepared to be quite frank about his past villainy. Hardly a noble figure, he appears nevertheless to have possessed a certain swagger, and despite his circumstances from the time of his capture to his execution, he does not appear to have lost any of his bravado.

IV

A few days later, on 18 May, Herbert Haines was sent to Chelmsford. Why at this particular time is not known because the Summer Assize for Essex was not until July, and the only possibly significant point about his departure from Newgate is that it was remarkably soon after Gregory's arrival: 'Herbert Haines, one of the gang with Gregory was removed by Habeas Corpus, on the

The Gregory Gang

18th of last month [May], to Chelmsford jail, in order to be tried at the next Assizes, for several robberies committed in the county of Essex ... Wheeler having nothing to allege against him as to any robberies committed in the county of Middlesex.'[10]

For the date of the removal from Newgate to Chelmsford we have to rely on the date given by the newspapers because the fact is not mentioned elsewhere. The list of Middlesex Prisoners upon Orders, which is written below the Calendar in which Samuel Gregory's name appears as described above,[11] has been badly eaten away by decay, and although this is where one would have expected to have found reference to the order for Haines' removal to Essex, it is not on that part which survives. Similarly the Essex Assize roll for the summer term, although containing reference to Haines, makes no mention of the manner of his arrival from Newgate. But we do have record of the romantic barber's last but one journey:

> **London** Micajah Perry Esq. and Sir John Salter Knight sheriffs of the City of London and county of Middlesex. [crave allowance &c.] September 29, 1734 to September 29, 1735. **Middlesex Summer Assizes** For conducting Robert [*recte* Herbert] Haines to the county of Essex charged with felony and burglary for five men and five horses hire three days and for horsemeat &c. £9. 0s. 0d. for two writs of Habeas Corpus £1. 4s. 0d.[12]

Haines had two months to wait for his trial, but when the escort which had taken him to Chelmsford arrived back in London, there was less than a week left for Samuel Gregory to wait for his.

V

There were six indictments against Samuel Gregory, recognisances to prosecute had been entered into by Dorothy Street, on the charge of rape, and by Thomas Humphrey *or* Humphries, on the charge of stealing a bay gelding; the other four were Crown prosecutions, for burglary and robbery in the house of Joseph Lawrence, and for burglary and robbery in the house of William Francis.

On the last four counts the indictments stood from the Sessions which had ended on 1 March, Gregory (and Turpin) having been named in them together with those who had stood trial at that time and been convicted. When the judgements were noted at the previous Sessions, blanks were left for Gregory and Turpin, and in respect of Gregory these blanks were filled in at the time of the May Sessions. Turpin was never brought to trial in Middlesex so the blanks against his name were not filled in.[13] The other two indictments were, firstly, for stealing a bay gelding worth £20 from Thomas Humphrey on 4 April 1735 in the parish of St. George, Middlesex,[14] and secondly for the rape of Dorothy Street:

> Middlesex Samuel Gregory late of the parish of Edgware in the county of Middlesex Labourer not having God before his eyes but being moved and seduced by the Instigation of the Devil on the fourth day of February in the Eighth year of the reign of our Sovereign Lord George the Second King of Great Britain &c. with force and arms at the parish aforesaid in the county aforesaid in and upon one Dorothy Street spinster feloniously did make an assault on her and against her will feloniously did ravish and carnally know.[15]

The single witness upon the first indictment was Thomas Humphrey. The witnesses sworn upon the second indictment were John Wheeler, Thomas Lawrence and Archelaus Pullen. The appearance of constable Pullen is perhaps surprising in connection with this charge, but it does transpire that he was able to supply material evidence.

The jury were sworn at the Delivery of the King's Gaol of Newgate taken for the County of Middlesex at Justice Hall in the Old Bailey on Thursday 22 May 1735. On the following day Samuel Gregory appeared before the court, but before he was brought in a slight formality was observed: 'Gregory having declared a particular enmity and malice against Wheeler the Evidence, it was apprehended he would have concealed a pistol to have shot him, but before he was carried into court he was searched, and nothing found.'[16]

Gregory would no doubt have been quite content had he been allowed opportunity to get near Wheeler with his bare hands, but he wasn't and it is perhaps unfortunate that in our record of these trials, such expressions of 'Enmity and Malice' that were undoubtedly directed at Wheeler, have been omitted.

Although Jones, Rowden and Turpin were still at large, this trial was the climax to nearly four months of endeavour on the part of those on the side of law and order to rid themselves of a particularly dangerous and violent gang of criminals; and for them to have succeeded without the assistance of an organised police force is quite remarkable.[17]

Samuel Gregory, was indicted first for breaking and entering the house of Joseph Lawrence, the Elder, at Edgware, and stealing a silver cup, four silver spoons, four gold rings, a pair of sheets, twelve napkins, a table cloth, six towels, six pillowbiers, six handkerchiefs, a dimity waistcoat, fifteen guineas, three moidores and thirty shillings. Feb. 4 about the hour of nine in the night.

2d. For assaulting the said Joseph Lawrence in his house, putting him in fear, and taking from him the goods and money mentioned in the first indictment.
3d. For assaulting, ravishing, and against her will, carnally knowing Dorothy Street, spinster, Feb. 4.
4th. For stealing a bay gelding, value 20 1. the property of Thomas Humphries, in the parish of St. George, in Middlesex.
5th. For breaking and entering the house of William Francis, in the parish of St. Mary la Bonne, and stealing a large quantity of goods, and money, Feb. 7 about the hour of nine in the night.
6th. For assaulting the said William Francis, putting him in fear, and taking from him the said goods and money, Feb. 7.

First, Second, and Third Indictments.

1. **Joseph Lawrence, the Elder.**
On the fourth of February last, about nine at night, my house at Edgware was broke open. Somebody came to the door and called me by my name. My servant, John Peats, unbolted the door, and presently five men rushed in with ten pistols, each of the men having one in each hand. I cannot say positively that the prisoner was one of them, but there was a man among them pretty much like him. They swore they'd kill me, if I did not give them my money. They took out of my pocket a guinea, a six and thirty shilling piece, and between ten and twenty shillings in silver. They broke the two buttons off my breeches and let them down. They took me upstairs, and said they wanted more money. They broke open a closet door there, and took out two guineas, ten shillings, a silver cup with two handles, four gold rings, and three silver spoons ... they had taken another silver spoon below stairs ... still they wanted more, and swore they would kill me if I did not tell them where the rest of my money was.
My breeches being down, they set my bare backside on the fire. I was not burnt indeed, but sorely scalded. They took a case knife, and threatened to rip me up, and brought a bill to chop my legs off to make me confess. They carried me into a back room where the maid was beating up butter, they took the kettle off the fire with two pails of water in it, and throwing me down, they threw the water all over me, but it happened not to be quite scalding hot. My son had in the house between twenty and thirty pounds which was all lost ... They took my sheets, table cloths, napkins, and all the best linen I had ... They broke my head with their pistols, so that the blood run down and matted my hair, and swore that I should not live till morning if I did not

discover where my money was ... One of them had a linen cloth over his face, and they had pulled up the capes of their coats ... At their first coming in, they broke a fowling piece which they found in my room, and before they went, they said they'd go and serve my son Joseph just as they had served me, and bid my boy shew them the way to his house; but I having another son who was not come home, they were afraid to venture after they had stayed three quarters of an hour for his coming. They then tied my hands and legs, and the hands and legs of my man and maid and boy, and so leaving us lying upon our backs, they locked the door and went away ... They took from my house in money and goods to the value of about sixty pounds.

2. John Wheeler

The prisoner and I, and Joseph Rose and John Fielder, and Richard Turpin went on the fourth of February to John Rowlets at the *Black Horse Inn* in the Broad Way, Westminster, where my horse and Gregory's stood. The prisoner told us he had worked at Edgware, and had shod this farmer (the Prosecutor's) horses, and that he was worth a good deal of money, and it was by his advice that we went thither. The prisoner and I, and Rose, went out first; Turpin and Fielder followed, and overtook us on the road; we drank two or three pots at the *Bowl and Skettle* on the hill on this side of Edgware. Thence we went to the *Queen's Head* at Stanmore, where we drank beer, and eat bacon and eggs for supper. We set out again between six and seven. I believe it wanted but a small matter of seven, and so rode into the farmer (Lawrence's) grounds, as I suppose they were, and tied up our horses within a quarter of a mile of his house. Hearing the boy calling up the sheep, we stayed a little and then went forward, and Fielder jumped over a sort of a half door and seized the boy and tied his hands, and bid him go to his master's door and knock, and answer to any body that asked who was there. He knocked, a servant man opened the door; I and Rose and the prisoner had two pistols each, but I think that Turpin and Fielder had but one a-piece. We all rushed in; we bound the boy again (for we had unbound him) and then we bound the man and the maid.

I stood over them, while the others carried up the old man to make him shew them the house. All the money that I saw was three guineas, two half crowns and eighteen pence. The prisoner came down to the maid, and said, "Damn ye, shew me where your master's money is." She made him a curtsy, and said, she did not know. But he made her go up stairs with him: And when she came down, she cried: I asked her if anybody had beat her; she answered, "No, but one of your men has lain with me."

3. **Court**
   Did she say by force?

4. **Wheeler**
   I did not hear her say so. We put the linen in sacks ... the plate I believe they put in their pockets .. and carried all to our horses. We came home about eleven, and next day we divided our booty. Rose gave us fifteen shillings for all the linen, and he likewise bought of us the two handled silver cup, three gold rings, three silver spoons, but I can't say now for how much; and Mrs. Rose made them off for him. The prisoner, as we were going home, told us, I believe twenty times, that he had lain with the maid in the garret.

5. **Court**
   Did he say by force?

6. **Wheeler**
   He said, he bolted the garret door, and laid a pistol on the bed while he lay with her.

7. **Prisoner**
   I don't deny that I was with them at the Prosecutor's house, but I had nothing that came from thence, for they were taken that day seven night.

8. **Wheeler**
   He was with us when we divided the money, and had his part, and perhaps more than I, for they cheated me in every respect; so that out of sixty pounds, I had but four.

9. **Prisoner**
   I ought to have had my share of whatever was taken—though I cannot say that anything was taken, for I went no farther than just within the door where I stood to watch.

10. **Court**
    But when they went away, did you see no sacks carried out?

11. **Prisoner**
    Not to my knowledge.

12. Dorothy Street

I was in the back house when the rogues came in; there was five in all, and I am sure the prisoner was one of them. They *Rankshatteld* (Ransacked) the house. I did not see them take the goods, for I and the man and the boy were tied in the parlour. But then the prisoner came and said, I should go up stairs with them. Wheeler went foremost, and the prisoner took me up after him into my master's room, and they said, they'd *Rankshattle* in that room. Wheeler went to the foot of the garret stairs and would go no farther; but the prisoner swore that *he* would go up, and he forced me up with him into the garret, and there he swore he would lie with me. I told him I was a young girl, and knew nothing of the matter; but he bolted the garret door, and swore if I would not yield, he would kill me; and he threw me on the bed, and laid one pistol upon the bed, and another on a chest, just by, and forced me.

13. Court

How did he force you? Were you dressed or undressed?

14. Dorothy Street

I was dressed. He pulled up my coats and took out what he ... and ... into me. And he pushed as hard as ever he could for the life and soul of him.

15. Court

Did you perceive ...?

16. Dorothy Street

Yes; and then he asked me if ever I was lain with before? and I said, No. And then he let me go down; and I cried, and one of them said, "What's the matter?" and I said, "One of your men has lain with me."

17. Richard Wood

I keep the *Nine Pin and Bowl* on this side Edgware. On the fourth of February last, the prisoner and Wheeler and three more came to my house and drank together. They stayed about three quarters of an hour, and went away a quarter before five; but did not say whither they were going.

18. Joseph Ironmonger

I keep the *Queen's Head* at Stanmore. On the fourth day of February, five men came to my house; Wheeler was one of them, and I believe the prisoner was another. They stayed a little above an hour, and went away at four or five minutes past seven. They turned towards London, which is the way to Farmer Lawrence's house.

19. Thomas Lawrence

I was not at home when my father's house was robbed. But about three or four years ago, the prisoner worked for Richard Taylor, a smith at Edgware; and shod my father's horses ... I went to see him in Newgate on the fourteenth of this month, and he owned to me, that he shewed the others the way to our house, for he thought we had got a great deal of money. "Why did you think so?" says I, "Because you paid everybody very well," says he, "and therefore I thought you must be very rich." He told me too that he lay with the maid, and that he had twenty five shillings of the money that was taken.

20. Richard Taylor

He lived with me six months at Edgware, and he shod farmer Lawrence's horses at both houses.

21. Archelaus Pullen

The day after the prisoner came to town, I went to see him in Newgate. He told me he lay with the girl; but that she was either as willing as he, or else she was afraid; for he said he had two pistols and laid them down by her. He confessed likewise that he was concerned in the robbery.

22. Prisoner

I have no witnesses, nor one friend in the world, and so I must leave it to the Court.

Then the witnesses against the prisoner for breaking and entering the house of William Francis, and stealing the goods and money, and for assaulting and robbing the said William Francis, were called and appeared.

23. Prisoner

I'll give the Court and the Jury no further trouble. I own I was at that house, and took the money and goods, and had two guineas for my share.

24. Court

What do you say as to stealing the horse?

25. Prisoner

I am guilty of that too ... My Lord, there are two gold watches in the custody of Sir Simeon Steward, a Justice of the Peace in Hampshire, ought they not to be brought into Court?

26. **Court**
Are they part of the goods for which you are indicted?

27. **Prisoner**
No; one was Sir John Osbaston's watch; it had a gold case. The other was a little watch with a shagreen case.

28. **Court**
Then they are not before this Court, and we can make no order about them.

29. **Prisoner**
Besides, they took my silver buckles (which cost me 18s.) out of my shoes, and took away all my linen, in Winchester Gaol.

The Jury found the prisoner guilty of all the six indictments. **Death.**

The judgement was recorded on the Lawrence burglary indictment,[18] upon which charge Fielder and Rose had been convicted some time before; but the conviction obtained was a foregone conclusion, and Gregory would himself no doubt have been surprised had he been acquitted of even one of the charges brought against him. Justice was here seen being done a second time, because Gregory's known companions had already been convicted upon four out of the six charges; but under English law, even though Gregory was a condemned man before he entered the dock, the formality of the trial conviction was required to hang him. And although conviction upon one count would have been enough, let alone another five, proceeding with those other charges was a necessary formality. In view of the editorial opinion contained in one newspaper (and official reaction to it) this might seem surprising.

> As the rewards for taking Gregory and others are only paid on conviction, the bold country fellows will be deprived of the reward for apprehending Gregory's brother with him, because he died in Winchester Gaol before conviction, yet it is hoped for encouraging the apprehending of robbers, that the country will pay the reward themselves, or by their application procure it to be paid the same as if he had been tried and convicted, for it is the same benefit to the country whether a robber be killed in apprehending or execution.[19]

This opinion presumed guilt and conviction, and in the final comment dispensed with the necessity for trial altogether. Jeremy Gregory was not named in any of the proclamations which offered rewards for the apprehension and conviction of members of the gang, so that the reward the country fellows would have been denied by his dying must be regarded as that commonly termed 'Blood Money'. A conviction was the condition of payment of an advertised reward, settlement of any claim in that respect could not be made without the judges' certificate of conviction; and although claims were sometimes submitted despite the conditional clause, the Treasury Solicitor could be relied upon to decide entitlement before making his recommendations to the Lords Commissioners of His Majesty's Treasury. Similar conditions existed in the system of 'Blood Money' reward payments, but here settlement was made out of Sheriff's coffers. So although in cases like Samuel Gregory's, the trial and conviction might seem a formality, it was (all legal obligations aside) a necessary one where the people queuing up to collect rewards were concerned. Except, as it eventually transpired, in the case of Jeremy Gregory, for here the Establishment appear to have bowed to public opinion in authorising the payment of £60 to the persons who captured him, 'in reward for their service'.

There is little else one can say about the trial, but Gregory's testimony, from line 23 to the end, suggests that he found the whole business rather tiresome. And his final recrimination shews also that he had lost none of the bravado which aggravated and confounded his captors and other observers. The majority of his companions, including his two brothers, were dead, but far from filling Gregory with feelings of guilt, the fact only succeeded in making him feel bitter towards the person whom he felt was responsible, Wheeler the Evidence. But although Wheeler did betray them all, an act it is difficult to condone despite the company, he was only indirectly responsible for what happened; for Gregory, in recruiting so young a member to the gang, was responsible for implanting the seed of destruction in their midst. But Gregory led them to their deaths, and if anyone was the betrayer it was he, for with or without Wheeler, the end was inevitable. So when, subsequently, certain sections of the press condemned his scandalous behaviour at his execution, they were to some extent justified, for to them, Gregory's greatest crime against society was that he died unrepentant.

VI

There was, in the event, some week or so left until the execution for Gregory to think about what had happened since his associates released him from the pillory at Epping; and at the Gaol Delivery of Middlesex Prisoners in Newgate, taken the day before Gregory stood in the dock at the Old Bailey, one such associate was listed as being, 'On Orders.' 'Accessory. No. 16 Mary

Johnson *als* Rose *als* Brazier Convicted last sessions [with others] of several felonies and petty larcenies to be transported &c.'[20]

It was however another six months before Mary Brazier left the foul atmosphere of Newgate on the way to what may or may not have been a better life, for it was not until some months later that sufficient numbers of transportees had accumulated for their passage to the Colonies in America to be contracted, and not until December that they sailed. In the meantime there was the date of Gregory's execution to be fixed: 'And on the 30th [May], at a General Council held at Kensington, Mr. Serjeant Urling made report of ... six malefactors, condemned at the last Sessions, when her Majesty [Caroline, acting as Regent] was pleased to reprieve ... and to order the [others including Samuel Gregory] for execution on the Wednesday thereafter [4th June].'[21] The execution took place as scheduled, and although there were still three others still at large, Samuel Gregory was the last to be hanged for taking part in crimes committed by the gang.

> Yesterday morning between nine and ten o'clock, Sutton and Gregory in one cart, and Hughes and Lewis in another, were carried under a strong guard to Tyburn; Lewis for the murder of his aunt, appeared quite sick and stupified, so could give little attention at the gallows to the prayers; Hughes, for the murder of his mother, seemed very penitent; Sutton appeared not much concerned, but just before he was turned off shed a few tears, and made a speech to the spectators; his brother George Sutton was in the cart with him, to whom he spoke in private, and kissed him; but Gregory behaved in a bold, impudent, senseless manner, talking during the prayers to the people in the cart, and looking about him at the mob, who in a scandalous manner threw dirt; he did not shew the least concern; or once change countenance; he declared he never committed any crime till about a fortnight before Christmas last, and then turned housebreaker to support his brother Jerry (who died in Winchester Gaol of his wounds) who was then confined in gaol on suspicion of deerstealing, and joined with Fielder &c. he also pretended that his other brother, executed at Chelmsford, died wrongfully.
>
> After the execution, Sutton was delivered to his friends by a warrant, obtained from the Sheriffs for that purpose; Lewis was likewise delivered to his friends, and Hughes, the soldier, to the surgeons; but Gregory was carried and hanged on the same gibbet with two of his companions in Edgware Road, over against Hendon Lane End.[22]

So Gregory was not granted his recorded wish that his body should not be hung on the gibbet, but the statement made in the final paragraph about this particular indignity should perhaps be clarified. Fielder, Rose and Saunders were gibbetted at Edgware immediately after their execution in March, and Walker joined them some few days later when the Keeper of Newgate was asked what should be done with his body. Even had two of those four corpses completely disappeared by June, the evidence of the Sheriff's Cravings, 1734—35,[23] does not suggest that Gregory's replaced them: 'Paid for the special execution of Samuel Gregory and hanging him up in chains, guards and attendance, £5. 5s. 0d., for making and putting up a gibbett in Edgware Road and for hanging the said Gregory up in chains thereon, £8. 5s. 0d., for a suit of chains for the said Gregory and plating the tree, £6. 5s. 0d.' A final comment on Gregory's demeanour is supplied in the following account:

> On the fourth day of last month the four malefactors condemned at the sessions mentioned in our last, were executed at Tyburn, to wit, Gregory ... [who], during the whole time he was in Newgate, after his condemnation, and at the time of his execution, shewed he had no regard for religion, and as little sense of the crimes he had been guilty of; and what was still more extraordinary, it appeared, that his obstinacy did not proceed from a mad despair, or from being always intoxicated with strong liquors; for when he was carried to the gallows he appeared to be quite sober, and more tranquil than is usually observed in persons just going to submit to fate.[24]

A fitting epitaph, based on the above, would have been, 'He was sober and tranquil at his death, and about 23 years of age', but the authorities contented themselves with one terse statement: 'No. 4. Saml. Gregory. attainted last sessions of several felonies and received sentence of death.' The marginal annotation against Gregory's name was simply, 'executed'.[25]

FOOTNOTES

1. *London Evening Post*, 19 to 22 April 1735.
2. *Ibid.*, 26 to 29 April 1735.
3. *The Old Whig*, 8 May 1735.
4. *Ibid.*, 15 May 1735.
5. *London Evening Post*, 13 to 15 May 1735.
6. *Political State*, Vol.XLIX, Jan.–June 1735, p.566.
7. P.R.O./T.90/147 p.6.
8. Middlesex/MJ/SR 2636 (Calendar of Middlesex Prisoners in Newgate from 16 April to 22 May 1735).
9. *Old Bailey Sessions.* Printed Proceedings for May 1735.
10. *Political State*, Vol.XLIX, Jan.–June 1735, p.569; and (for last sentence only) *London Evening Post*, 17 to 20 May 1735.
11. Middlesex/MJ/SR 2636.
12. P.R.O./T.90/147 p.60.
13. Middlesex/MJ/SR 2631 Indictments Nos.12–15; Middlesex/MJ/GBB 314 p.130 for note of Recognisances entered into and subsequent appearance of the parties concerned at the trial.
14. Middlesex/MJ/SR 2636 Indictment No.11 (abbreviated).
15. *Ibid.*, 2636 Indictment No.19 (abbreviated).
16. *London Evening Post*, 22 to 24 May 1735.
17. *Old Bailey Sessions:* Printed Proceedings for May 1735.
18. Middlesex/MJ/SR 2631 No.14.
19. *London Evening Post*, 22 to 24 May 1735.
20. Middlesex/MJ/SR 2636.
21. *Political State*, Vol.XLIX, Jan.–June 1735, p.569.
22. *London Evening Post*, 3 to 5 June 1735.
23. P.R.O./T.90/147 p.59.
24. *Political State*, Vol.L, July–Dec.1735, p.8.
25. Middlesex/MJ/SR 2639 (Middlesex Prisoners Upon Orders).

BOOK FIVE

T U R P I N (part the first)

CHAPTER ONE

I

ON 10 and 12 April, there occurred robberies north of the river at Mile End and in Epping Forest, which we have attributed to Turpin, Rowden and Jones. On 10 May possibly the same three were seen at an alehouse in Whitechapel, but thereafter Turpin and Rowden travelled alone. It is not known where they were or what they were doing during the rest of May and the month of June, but there is no doubt at all that for some months after the beginning of July they rode together in those sparsely populated areas south of the Thames.

They were not the only highwaymen operating at that time and their activity before July may be deduced from the following urgent activity on the part of the authorities.

Whitehall July 3d. 1735.
Sir
    Her Majesty being extremely concerned at the frequent robberies and other outrages that have been committed of late in and about the Cities of London and Westminster and the neighbouring parts to the great damage and terror of his Majesty's subjects; and the Queen being determined to have the Laws put in execution, for the preventing in the most effectual manner such practices for the future; I am commanded to signify to you Her Majesty's pleasure that you should prepare the draught of a proclamation to be laid before her Majesty in Council on Wednesday next July 8th [*recte* 9th] for Her Majesty's approbation and signature; enforcing the several laws now in being for preventing the same; and renewing the offer of the rewards to such persons, as shall be concerned in the apprehending and legally convicting any highwaymen or street robbers in or near the cities of London and Westminster and strictly requiring all magistrates and other of his Majesty's subjects to be diligent in enforcing the execution of the laws; with such other clauses as have been usual; upon the like occasions, or as you shall think the most proper for this purpose. I am &c.
Mr. Attorney General   Holles Newcastle[1]

Caroline was acting as Regent at this time as King George II was in Hanover again. 3 July was also the day upon which Peter Creswell, Keeper of the House of Correction at Clerkenwell, had been ordered to appear before the Court of General Quarter Sessions for Middlesex concerning the escape of William Saunders and Jeremy Gregory from the Bridewell.[2] This however did not concern the Attorney General, and he, with some alacrity, pressed on with his brief from the Duke of Newcastle.

To emphasise the immediacy of the problem of highway robbery and like crimes, Charles G. Harper, in commenting upon an area apparently notorious for such proceedings, pointed shrewdly to a particular instance which he quoted from a newspaper.

> How well-named was "Thieves' Corner" we may perhaps judge from a brief and matter-of-fact account (as though it were but an ordinary occurence, demanding little notice) of a Reverend Mr. Amey, "a country clergyman who lodges at the *Star Inn,* in the Strand," being robbed two nights earlier than the foregoing robbery [committed by Turpin and Rowden on 10 July] "two miles this side of Richmond in Surrey, of his silver watch, four guineas, and some silver by two highwaymen, well-mounted and well-dressed. The rogues turned his horse loose and went off towards Richmond."[3]

Having described the subsequent robbery which occurred between Barnes Common and Wandsworth, Harper did not speculate about the identity of the two men who robbed the Reverend Amey on 8 July, 'two miles this side of Richmond'. To a reporter on a London newspaper, 'This side of Richmond' would have been towards London, and 'two miles', would locate the place where the robbery occurred somewhere between Barnes Common and Wandsworth. When highwaymen rob in the same vicinity within the space of two days, and in the same manner, the same pair were involved on both occasions.

But the Attorney General had drafted the Proclamation by 9 July, and although even when it was published it amounted to little more than a gesture (there being no other effective means of coping with the problem), it may have served to satisfy the general public and past and future victims of highway robbery, etc. that it was recognised that a problem did exist. The proclamation was read before the Queen and Privy Council at the Court at Kensington on 9 July:

> This day the following Proclamation was read at the Board and approved Vizt. By the Queens most Excellent Majesty Guardian of the Realm of Great Britain .... A Proclamation for putting in execution the Laws made against persons guilty of any murder or robbery in any street, highway, road, passage, field or open place, in the cities of London or Westminster, or within five miles of the same, and for discovering and apprehending such offenders ... Reward £100.   Caroline R.C.R.[4]

On the day following the meeting at Kensington, Turpin and Rowden were for the first time identified by the press as the highwaymen concerned in a particular robbery.

> Last Thursday night about eight o'clock Mr. Vane of Richmond and Mr. James Bradford of the Borough of Southwark, going from thence to Richmond were attacked between Wandsworth and Barns Common by two highwaymen supposed to be Turpin the butcher and Rowden the pewterer, the remaining two of Gregory's gang who robbed them of their money and c., dismounted them, made them pull off their horses' bridles, then turning them adrift they rode off towards Roehampton where a gentleman was robbed, as is supposed, by the same highwaymen, of a watch, and about £3. 4s. in money.[5]

Four days later, in the same vicinity, they came upon another victim. 'Last Monday, Mr. Omar of Southwark, meeting between Barnes Common and Wandsworth, Turpin the butcher with another person, clapped spurs to his horse, but they coming up with him, obliged him to dismount, and Turpin suspecting that he knew him, would have shot him, but was prevented by the other, who pulled the pistol out of his hand.'[6]

It is curious that on two occasions the victims should have come from Southwark, a place with which Rowden was familiar in his early counterfeiting days, and it does suggest that in choosing this area of operations, Turpin may have been influenced by Rowden's knowledge. A puzzling feature is Turpin's apparent willingness to have shot Mr. Omar. Turpin and Rowden were both wanted men, and the mere fact of recognition would have affected them little except perhaps to draw attention to their being highwaymen, a fact which had by now already been reported. They were in no danger, and Omar could as easily have recognised Rowden, who had after all lived in Southwark.

The following morning the proclamation was published,[7] and on subsequent days, in abbreviated form and with more emphasis on the reward, it appeared in the popular press. There had been several rewards offered which still applied in the case of Turpin and/or Rowden's capture and conviction, and to these there was now added another £100 to whomsoever cared to risk his life in fulfilling the conditions which were required to be met before a claim could be made.

II

One could say of crime in London and its surrounds during this period of the 18th century that it was inevitable that someone like Henry Fielding should see the need for an ambitious experiment like the Bow Street Runners; but that was a somewhat visionary enterprise and Fielding did not take up residence at that address until 1746. So although in 1735 the means of preserving Law and Order were becoming increasingly inadequate, the authorities were unable to do much more to rectify the state of affairs than increase rewards in times of crisis.

There were watchmen, and parish constables like Archelaus Pullen, but their existence did not prevent crime any more than did the increasingly ineffective *deterrent* of savage sentences, and it was a rare occasion in those days that a crime was discovered *before* it was attempted. At this point, if a person was detected in the act, or if he was known or identified and seen subsequently, or was suspected, legislation existed whereby a constable or other nominated person could pursue that person by raising Hue and Cry after him.

There were two Acts governing this procedure, both a little out of date, being the Statutes of 13 Edward I, commonly called *The Statute of Hue and Cry*, and 27 Elizabeth I, entitled *An Act for the Following of Hue and Cry*.

In the Session of Parliament which ended on 15 May 1735 an *Act for the Amendment of the Laws relating to Actions on the Statute of Hue and Cry* (Stat. 8 Geo. II, c.16) was passed which referred to the previous Acts as being, 'both attended with many and great inconveniences to subjects'. But the main purpose of this Amending Act was supposedly to facilitate the means whereby victims of highway robbery, etc. might (after 24 June 1735) lay claim on the Hundred of the County where the crime had occurred for the value of the money and/or articles stolen.

The Act refers to such losses as being, 'commonly very inconsiderable', but such were the conditions and sureties a victim was required to fulfil and enter into, it is doubtful if many people would have gone to the trouble of sueing the authority concerned.[8] In addition, although the person apprehending the robber was entitled to £10 reward payable out of assessed taxes, the local authority was not liable to any charge if the robber remained at large 40 days after the crime was committed. One small concession to the victim was made; for whereas on former occasions a witness to the crime was disallowed if he lived in the county where the crime occurred, the victim was now able to call upon such a witness to the fact that the crime had taken place in that county.

Such were the curious laws held in contempt by Turpin and the like in 1735, and if one recalls just how poor an incentive was the £10 reward offered for the capture of deerstealers, we begin to understand why in order to capture and convict criminals guilty of more serious and violent crimes it was necessary to offer additional incentive in the form of Blood Money (paid out by Sheriffs), and Proclamation Rewards (paid out by the Treasury). There are instances, particularly in the case, some years previously, of

The Gregory Gang

Jonathan Wild, where the Blood Money system was flagrantly abused; but in fairness to those who were concerned with the preservation of law and order and the administration of justice, however primitive their efforts might seem now, the larger incentives provided do appear to have inspired a surprisingly effective 'do it yourself detection service', one of the major enterprises of which was to dispose of the Gregory gang. Had the system not worked, Herbert Haines would have been in Holland instead of Chelmsford Gaol.

III

Haines' trial was on 20 July 1735 and he stood charged upon three indictments. The principal witness against him on all three counts was John Wheeler, and some few days before the trial Thomas Cavannagh, the Keeper of New Prison, delivered Wheeler into the custody of the Sheriff of Middlesex so that he could be sent to Chelmsford. It is interesting to note that although hardly any of the gang remained, the Sheriff still considered it necessary for five men to escort 'The Evidence' to the Assizes. 'Essex. [First indictment] Herbert Haines labourer on the 19th day of December 1734 at Barking one gelding of a bay colour of the price of five pounds and one black mare of the price of five pounds of the goods and chattels of one Ambrose Skinner did steal take and lead away.'[9]

The witnesses were Ambrose Skinner the Younger, Elizabeth King, John Wheeler and George Walten. The second and third indictments against Haines were for burglary in the houses of William Mason and Ambrose Skinner the Elder respectively. The inventories of the money and goods stolen have been given previously, it is therefore possible to summarise these indictments as follows.

> No. 2 The Mason robbery on 21 December 1734. For burglary and stealing money and goods to the total value of £176. 6s. 0d. Persons indicted, Herbert Haines and Thomas Rowden, the latter not being tried with Haines on this charge.[10]
> No. 3 The Skinner robbery on 19 December 1734. For burglary and stealing goods to the value of £16. 10s. 0d. from Ambrose Skinner the Elder, and £136 4s. 0d. from Ambrose Skinner the Younger. Persons indicted, Herbert Haines, Thomas Rowden and Richard Turpin, the last two named not being tried with Haines on this charge.[11]

The witnesses sworn on the second indictment were William Mason, Mary Mason, Jonathan Richards, John Wheeler, Archelaus Pullen, Thomas Lawrence, George Walten, Henry Palmer and James Freeland, the last two named being the persons responsible for Haines' capture. Those on the third indictment were Ambrose Skinner the Younger, Elizabeth King, John

Wheeler, Daniel Stiles, Archelaus Pullen and Thomas Lawrence.

Haines was convicted of the Mason felony and burglary and sentenced to be hanged, but it is curious to note that although found guilty on those charges, he was found *Not Guilty* of the burglary and *Guilty* of the felony in the case of Skinner. As the first indictment (which also relates to the Skinner robbery) charged Haines with stealing the horses, there is a definite suggestion here of Haines having remained in the stables throughout the robbery, and not having taken part in the forcible entry of the house.

This is as fair an assessment as can be made of the circumstances involving Haines at Barking, but it still does not explain why Elizabeth King was sworn as witness on the charge of stealing two horses. She stated that she was locked away in an upstairs room with Ambrose Skinner the Elder (an experience to which the old man made no claims to having shared), and therefore cannot have been aware of what went on outside. She could, although bound, have perhaps reached a window, but even so it was dark and she could have seen nothing. The only time she could have seen Haines would have been if he *had* taken part in the forcible entry, and even then the men who entered had their faces, 'muffled and disguised.' But since Turpin was at the Skinner robbery and knew an Elizabeth King who appears to have been related to Matthew King, who was one of Turpin's subsequent accomplices, it was perhaps convenient that she was locked away where she could see nothing of what went on. Even so, her testimony would have been no more assistance to Haines than it was to the prosecution. 'At the Assizes for Chelmsford the notorious Herbert Haines was convicted of several robberies in [Essex], and was accordingly ordered to be hanged, and his body to be hung in chains.'[12]

It would appear Haines was destined to suffer the same indignity accorded his fellows at Edgware, but the appointment with the hangman was not scheduled until 8 August and before that date Haines' mistress Mrs. Carroll was allowed to visit him. Immediately after the trial however, John Wheeler was taken back to New Prison. The sheriffs of London and Middlesex were put to considerable expense for the round trip and craved allowances as follows: 'For conducting John Wheeler to the County of Essex to give evidence against Herbert Haines for felony and burglary and reconducting him for five men and five horses six days for horsemeat &c. £18 0s. 0d. For two writs of Habeas Corpus £1 4s. 0d.'[13] The exact date when Mrs. Carroll visited Haines is not known, but since in the report of her visit his execution is assumed, there is no doubt that it was made after his trial and not before. 'Whilst he was in gaol his mistress came to see him, a homely creature and much older than he; she said or pretended she was with child, and told him, she should not long survive him, but die inch by inch, and soon follow

The Gregory Gang

him, and hoped that they should be happy again, as formerly: By this, one would think she imagined the same gross pleasures to be in the other world as in this.'[14]

But another newspaper was more concerned about Wheeler's future. 'Tomorrow Herbert Haines is to be executed and hanged in chains in Essex. Wheeler the Evidence against him and the rest of the Gang will be kept in custody till Turpin the Butcher and Rowden the Pewterer, two others, of the gang who now rob on the highway are apprehended.'[15] This report turned out to be accurate for Wheeler was to remain in custody for at least another year, but when it was written, it is clear that the authorities were optimistic that Turpin and Rowden would be apprehended in the near future. In the event their optimism was misplaced, but with Haines' execution to remind them of previous swift success, it was not the time for thinking they might be thwarted.

> Country News—Chelmsford, Saturday 9 Aug. Yesterday Herbert Haines, the barber, one of Gregory's gang and ... walked in their shrouds from the gaol at the bridge to the gallows; at the *Black Boy,* a man in a laced hat gave Haines a glass of wine, as he walked by, and Haines desired him *to take care of what he told him* and whispered to him; then the gentleman in the laced hat drank to him, and told him, he hoped he would be happy before night, which occasioned in the town an ill suspicion against the man. Haines has behaved very well ever since he has been in our gaol, in a sedate, grave manner, never once being heard to swear, and went calmly to the gallows, and behaved there like a man, decent, but not impudent.[16]

One is bound to wonder at the identity of the man at the *Black Boy* inn, but he is only mentioned here to dispel any idea that he might have been Turpin, who was also given to wearing a laced hat. Turpin did no doubt mourn the passing of Haines, but he was not a person to risk his skin for sentimental reasons. If the person was known to Haines, as seems to be indicated by his singling out of Haines to offer him wine, then the message that passed between them was probably a harmless instruction concerning the welfare of Mrs. Carroll. More than that we can only imagine, but so detailed is the account of this incident one might almost think the man might have been the author himself.

'On the 8th the notorious Herbert Haines was hanged, and afterwards hung in chains, pursuant to his sentence.'[17] This final report would seem to be superfluous, but since like other newspapers it maintains that Haines was hung in chains (a matter not mentioned in the Country News from Chelmsford) it is of some small import. What actually happened to Haines' body may possibly be determined by the following.

'For guarding and keeping Herbert Haines and three others condemned to be hanged from the time of their conviction till their execution being fifteen days [and] for executing them £11 0s. 0d.' Chains and gibbets were costly items, as the expenses claimed for those used at Edgware shew, so the Sheriff of Essex would hardly have overlooked them in *his* claim if they had in fact been employed in Haines' case.[18] The probable explanation for the reports of Haines being gibbeted is that it was generally assumed that he would be served in like manner to his former companions.

One might have assumed that since they claimed for the expenses involved, the sheriffs were responsible for directing that particularly notorious criminals should be gibbeted, but this may not have been so; in both the *Political State* accounts above (though apparently not valid in Haines' case) there is clear indication that gibbeting was carried out, *pursuant to sentence*. This is not corroborated in judgements recorded on indictments or in judgements recorded in trial proceedings (at least not on or in any encountered in the present context), but this is not to say that such directions did not emanate from the court in which conviction was obtained. In Richard Burn's, *The Justice of the Peace and Parish Officer,* 1756, there is no indication of what might have been the procedure in the cases dealt with in this account, *but,* in cases upon indictments for *Murder* it would appear that the judge before whom a person was convicted could direct that the body of the executed person should be either given to the surgeons or gibbeted. On the basis of this evidence and references made in the contemporary newspapers, it would seem probable that the judge was the authority in each case where instructions were given for members of the Gregory gang to be gibbeted, but perhaps not surprisingly it does not appear to have been a direction given to much publicity.

FOOTNOTES

1. P.R.O./S.P.44/128 pp.392–393.
2. Middlesex Sessions Books and Orders of Court, Cal. July 1732–Dec. 1735, p.128.
3. *Half Hours with the Highwaymen*, pp.196–197.
4. P.R.O./P.C.2/93 pp.194–196 (preamble only).
5. *London Evening Post*, 10 to 12 July 1735.
6. *Ibid.*, Thursday 17 to Saturday 19 July 1735. (N.B. in Harper's *Half Hours with the Highwaymen*, p.197 and Ash and Day's *Immortal Turpin*, p.38, this report is quoted from the *Grub Street Journal*, of 24 July, and commences, "Monday ...", thus giving the erroneous impression that the event occurred on Monday 21 July, instead of the week before.)
7. *London Gazette*, 15 July 1735.
8. The first reported claim under this Statute appeared in a newspaper of January 1736.
9. P.R.O./Assizes 35/175/2, Essex, Felony File Summer 9 Geo.II (Indictment No.1) (abbreviated).
10. *Ibid.*
11. *Ibid.*
12. *Political State*, Vol.L, July to Dec. 1735, p.130.
13. P.R.O./T.90/147 p.60.
14. *London Evening Post*, 12 to 14 August 1735.
15. *London Daily Post*, 7 August 1735.
16. *London Evening Post*, 12 to 14 August 1735.
17. *Political State*, Vol.L, July to Dec. 1735, p.252.
18. P.R.O./T.90/147 p.64.

CHAPTER TWO

I

BEFORE THE Proclamation of 15 July, which offered £100 reward for the capture and conviction of highwaymen, Turpin and Rowden conducted their activities in those wide areas of heath and common then to be found south of the Thames. They did not however immediately move elsewhere, and remained instead in the neighbourhood of Barnes Common. To what extent the authorities made any positive effort to capture this particular pair we do not know, but even with Haines gone, there were still reminders of the gang to which they had belonged.

> These are in his Majesty's name to authorize and direct you ...to issue and pay ... unto William Richards gent. or to his assignes, the sum of £60 without account, to be by him paid over to the several persons concerned in apprehending Jeremy Gregory a notorious highwayman in such manner and in such proportions as John Lord Viscount Lymington shall direct, in reward for their service, and in consideration that the said Jeremy Gregory died of the wounds he received in resisting the said persons, before he could be brought to his trial, so that they were not entitled to the reward that would have been payable to them had he been convicted of the crimes for which he was committed to Gaol. And for so doing this shall be your warrant. Given at his Majesty's Palace at Kensington the 14 day of August 1735. By her Majesty's Command.
> R. Walpole, Sundon [Wm. Lord Sundon], Cholmondeley [Visc. Malpas].[1]

The persons amongst whom the £60 was distributed would almost certainly have been the same who received shares in the reward for the capture and conviction of *Samuel* Gregory.

In a similar context was the Report of the Committee appointed to inquire into the escape of Jeremy Gregory and William Saunders from the Clerkenwell Bridewell on 1 February 1735 which issued from Hicks Hall in August.[2]

II

Turpin and Rowden now entered a period of intense activity the commencement of which coincided with the appearance of newspaper reports of Haines' execution. 'Last Saturday two gentlemen in a coach and six, with three on horseback, were robbed on Barnes Common by two highwaymen.'[3] This was the area in which Turpin was last reported to have been seen, and the robbery may be taken to have occurred on 16 August. The next report names him in connection with a robbery which occurred south of Barnes Common. 'Turpin and Rowden on Sunday, August 16th [*recte* 17th] robbed several gentlemen on horseback and in their coaches, in the district of the Portsmouth Road, between Putney and Kingston Hill.'[4]

There seems to be no doubt at all that at this date Turpin's constant companion was Rowden, but although their association ended in the following year (a fact of which the newspapers were unaware) his name was still linked with Turpin for some time afterwards. For the moment however they rode together and on the following Wednesday (20 August) appear to have crossed the river. 'On Wednesday last as Mr. Godfrey, a gentleman of considerable fortune at Egham in Surrey, was coming over Hounslow Heath to town, he was robbed by two highwaymen, of about six guineas and his pocket book, it's supposed to be Turpin the Butcher and Rowden the Pewterer, two of Gregory's gang that are robbing there, *as well as* in Surrey.'[5] This episode is entirely feasible for they would have experienced no difficulty in reaching Hounslow Heath across the river from the area where they were reported as having been seen previously, and at this time there was really nothing to restrict their mobility, a state of affairs which the public now sought to rectify. 'The inhabitants of Putney, Roehampton, Barnes &c. in the county of Surrey, are determined to raise money by subscription, for a fund to be deposited for the encouragement of such as should take, or cause to be taken, any persons who have or shall commit robberies on the highway.'[6]

Since Turpin and Rowden appear to have forsaken Barnes Common *before* the intention was published, there is reason to suppose they heard rumour of it and thought it prudent to move elsewhere. But this need not have been the only reason; their names were appearing with some frequency in the press and particularly in connection with robberies in the Barnes Common area, and this fact alone could have been sufficient reason for them to quit the district where their faces were becoming increasingly familiar. Of the two reasons the first is possibly most convincing, for the two survivors of the Gregory gang had good cause to remember the efficiency of the Lawrence 'vigilantes', and although to some extent contemptuous of the authorities' efforts to catch them, they would hardly have ignored a whisper that local inhabitants were intent on organising their capture. The report did not make specific reference to Turpin and Rowden, but since they had initiated and inspired highway robbery in the area during this period, there is little doubt that these were the two the locals were most anxious to apprehend.

A curious point about the idea of raising a fund by subscription is that it would hardly have improved on the £100 reward offered in July 'for apprehending highwaymen in London and Westminster or within five miles of the same'. But the reason is immediately apparent when one sees that Barnes and vicinity are somewhat further than five miles from Charing Cross.

This point might seem to be of purely academic interest, that is until one hears that Turpin and Rowden were believed to have moved to Blackheath, a place which would also have been just outside the area defined by the July proclamation, and plagued that district for several weeks. It now becomes clear that Turpin and Rowden not only chose, as one might expect, to operate in sparsely populated areas, but areas which were outside that in which they could anticipate there might be positive attempts made to take them. The reference to their activities on Blackheath appeared in October.

'We hear for about six weeks past, Blackheath has been so infested by two highwaymen supposed to be Rowden and Turpin that it is dangerous for travellers to pass.'[7] This estimate of the period of their Blackheath activity seems to be fairly accurate, appearing as it did during the second week of October; for after the Hounslow Heath robbery of 20 August, there are no further reports of robberies in the vicinity of Barnes Common which could reasonably be attributed to them.

The next positive identification of Turpin suggests that the news of his and Rowden's Blackheath activities was only brought to the notice of the press some week or so after they had again moved elsewhere. For by 2 October they had ridden northwards and were again some distance more than five miles from London. 'On Thursday morning last between nine and ten o'clock, one Farmer Forde, coming from Hertford to London was attacked on Northaw Common by Turpin the Butcher, with whom the farmer had been formerly acquainted.'[8] In 1948 the same incident was represented as having occurred in 1736;[9] but, apart from this slight anachronism, we find that although the preamble is the same as the above, a fuller report appeared in another newspaper. Thus, substituting a comma after 'acquainted', there follows:

... and making some slight resistance Turpin pulled off his hat, as a signal to another of his gang, supposed to be Rowden, who was about 200 yards off upon the scout, to join him, when they dismounted the farmer, and robbed him of 41. 3s. and some halfpence, and turned his horse loose, after which they were going to bind him, but two gentlemen on horseback appearing, they left the farmer and gave them the meeting, and robbed them of their money and a silver watch. Turpin changed his hat with one of the gentlemen, and afterwards obliged them to dismount, pulled their saddles and bridles off, and turned their horses loose. They made off towards Enfield Chase, were both well mounted and dressed, and used the gentlemen with good language and civility.[10]

Assuming that the farmer did know Turpin (it is a curious feature of Turpin's career that he was on a number of occasions either seen by or robbing people who knew him), why should he (and Rowden) now be found at Northaw, beyond Potters Bar, in Hertfordshire? Northaw is some way from Hempstead, and although it would be easy to say that Turpin and Rowden were on their way back from there, it is however difficult to reconcile the ever cautious Turpin with the risk involved in visiting his home; and although he did do so some years later, it was not at a time when he was known to be active near London. But Northaw is only a short distance from Enfield Chase, to which Clay Hill near Enfield is adjacent. Turpin's grandfather may have lived at Clay Hill and allowed Turpin the running of his public house when Turpin's business as a butcher failed. Admittedly the evidence to support this theory is slight, but there may have been good reason for Turpin's visit to Northaw. In 1737, Turpin's wife and a man called Nott (the same name as Turpin's supposed grandfather) met with Turpin, and there is a distinct possibility that Elizabeth Turpin was living with her own family at Clay Hill in September 1735, rather than with Turpin's at Hempstead.

But it was not long before Turpin and Rowden were back south of the Thames, and on 9 October, they were seen near the city centre going in that direction. 'On Thursday last Turpin and Rowden had the impudence to ride through the City at noonday and in Watling Street they were known by two or three porters who had not the courage to attack them, they were indifferently mounted and went towards the Bridge, so it is thought are gone the Tonbridge Road.'[11] The pair were travelling east towards London Bridge, but why it was thought they would take the Tonbridge Road cannot be imagined for they could as easily have decided to have gone to Canterbury, Brighton or Portsmouth. They were in fact thinking of Barnes Common again, and unless they lingered in Rowden's old stamping ground of Southwark, that is undoubtedly where they were headed.

On the day the Watling Street porters were gaping in some awe up at these two hardened criminals, an illustrious contemporary was giving some thought to their former leader Samuel Gregory. *'Letter [from] Horace Walpole to*

Thomas Grey *[9 Oct. 1735]* in style of Joseph Addison. From Arc (Bow) we travelled through a very pleasant country to Epino (Epping) ... We were here shown at a distance, the thickets rendered so famous by the robberies of Gregorio (Gregory, a noted highwayman).'[12] Walpole being a visiting dignitary it is probable that one thicket would have done as well as the rest, but the point is that Gregory had achieved some local notoriety which still lingered after his death. Turpin and Rowden for their part may have begun to realise that to enjoy notoriety during one's lifetime was not an achievement to be recommended, for, although they committed some few more robberies south of the Thames, the day was fast approaching when to all intents and purposes they disappeared from the face of the earth.

On 30 October two robberies occurred which were, by implication committed by Turpin and Rowden. The account below is an abbreviated and edited version of the report.

> On Thursday last Squire Thomas Durham Esq. was with his wife and daughter in a coach travelling from London to Richmond. About four in the afternoon as they were crossing Barnes Common they were attacked by two highwaymen who took a diamond ring and four pounds and then rode off towards Richmond.
> About half an hour later two well dressed highwaymen robbed a farmer called James Bone on Wimbledon Common. They took from him ten shillings and sixpence, turned his horse loose and then rode off towards Kingston. They are thought to be the same two that robbed Squire Durham and committed the great number of robberies of late on Barnes, Wimbledon and Putney Commons.[13]

The latter reference to robberies on the various commons is unlikely to relate to those which occurred before Turpin and Rowden moved from Barnes to Blackheath late in August, and probably related to robberies *not* reported which occurred between the second and last week in October. The reporting of robberies was not always consistent and probably, particularly when large numbers came to the notice of the press, a selection was made which depended on circumstances, personalities involved and worthwhile descriptions of the attackers. Otherwise, as in the case of Blackheath and the above, a general reference was made to robberies which occurred over a longish period of time in one particular area. Such differentiation becomes apparent in the next report.

> Tuesday [4 November] at four in the afternoon, Mr. Tebb a Grocer, opposite the *George Inn*, in Little Drury Lane, was robbed by two highwaymen just by the gibbet on Putney Heath, they made him dismount and searched all his pockets, and took from him 71. 5s. and then made off. One of them had the impudence to tell him he was Turpin, and bid him remember how civilly he had used him.[14]

Another account of the same incident describes there being two men hung in chains on the gibbet,[15] which some men might have found a grim reminder of what they might expect to happen to them if caught.

FOOTNOTES

1. P.R.O./T.52/39 p.44.
2. Calendar of Middlesex Sessions Books and Orders of Court, July 1732–December 1735, p.140.
3. *London Evening Post*, 16 to 19 August 1735.
4. *Grub Street Journal*, 21 August 1735.
5. *London Evening Post*, 21 to 23 August 1735 *(my italics)*.
6. *Ibid.*, 30 August to 2 September 1735.
7. *Ibid.*, 9 to 11 October 1735.
8. *Ibid.*, 2 to 4 October 1735.
9. *Immortal Turpin*, by Ash and Day, pp.44–45.
10. *Ipswich Gazette*, 4 to 11 October 1735.
11. *London Evening Post*, 9 to 11 October 1735.
12. *Letters of Horace Walpole*. Toynbee 1903. Vol.I p.6 (This letter is also reproduced in *Correspondence of Gray, Walpole, West and Ashton*. Toynbee. Vol.I, p.40).
13. *London Evening Post*, 1 November 1735.
14. *Country Journal*, 8 November 1735.
15. *London Evening Post*.

CHAPTER THREE

I

NONE OF the highway robberies committed by Turpin and Rowden took place at any great distance from London, and for the most part they were just beyond the limit defined in the July proclamation. But on 5 December 1735, if the report is to be relied on, they were seen much further away. 'Turpin the notorious highwayman, with another person, was seen last Friday sevennight, at Worthy within a mile of Winchester. They stopped at a blacksmith's, and had both their horses shoe'd, and pretended to be in a mighty hurry to get to Winchester; but were observed to wheel off towards London Road. They had several pistols and hangers under their great coats.'[1]

There is no known reason why Turpin and Rowden should have forsaken London and its surrounds *before* 5 December, and in doing so ventured so far afield. They did in fact remain in the area at times when it was exceptionally dangerous for them to do so. But the report suggests, if anything, that they were now in the process of returning to or at least travelling in the direction of London, and that they had been away. But would they have gone to Winchester at the beginning of December? Samuel and Jeremy Gregory went to Hampshire to obtain passage overseas, and Turpin and Rowden could have had the same idea in mind were it but for one thing, the event which could have motivated flight, the capture of John Jones, did not occur until mid December 1735.

II

At the Old Bailey in April 1735 Mary Brazier, or, as she was known to the gang, Mrs. Rose, was convicted of receiving and sentenced to be transported to the colonies in America for a term of fourteen years. In December of the same year she was still in Newgate (with numerous other convicts in similar plight) awaiting passage on the transport. There were three main reasons for this exceptional delay, firstly the time it took a transport to reach its destination (nearly three months), secondly the number of prisoners in London, Middlesex *and* the Home Counties who during the time since the Lent Sessions had been sentenced to transportation and had to await removal from Newgate, and thirdly delays in contractual arrangements with the shipping agents. For some years an East India Company merchant by name Jonathan Forward appears to have had a virtual monopoly on the transportation of prisoners to the American Colonies; but Forward carried other cargo besides convicts and the reason why Mary Brazier had to wait so long appears to have been that he just didn't have enough ships to handle both. By January however he had solved that problem and was able to clear Newgate of all those awaiting passage.

'A True list of all the prisoners taken from Newgate for the City of London and the County of Middlesex and shipped on board the *John*, John Griffin Commander for Maryland which were shipped by Mr. Jon.[a] Forward of London merchant December the 9th 1735,' [listed], 'No. 48 Mary Johnson otherwise Rose otherwise Brassier.'[2] There were fifty prisoners on the *John,* and we may obtain some idea of what it was like to leave Newgate for America from an account of one or two other ships which sailed in January. 'Yesterday morning about four o'clock 140 felons from Newgate were put on a covered lighter at Black Fryars, which fell down with them to the new transport ship lately purchased by Merchant Forward of the East India Company, now lying below the Red House ... 18 were likewise put on board from the New Gaol in Southwark.'[3]

From similar reports it is clear that the journey from Newgate to Black Friars was usually by wagon, with privileged prisoners being allowed to travel separately in a chaise, and subsequently on board ship in separate quarters; but since being privileged was a distinction only acquired by the possession of money we may assume that Mary Brazier travelled without those special comforts.

III

From the evidence which we have concerning John Jones' part in the activities of the Gregory gang, it has been deduced that until Wheeler was arrested in February 1735, Jones was rightly implicated in just the one robbery at Chingford. There is however some reason to think that he was the third man who appeared briefly with Turpin and Rowden when they first embarked on a career of highway robbery. It was not long though before he again lost his nerve and on or about 10 May, 1735. 'He run away, and continued in a distant country till almost starved, being destitute of friends, and returning to Hackney to see his family, was taken and committed to Newgate.'[4]

The suggestion in the above report is that Jones had been abroad, for although as has previously been observed the contemporary use of the word 'country' could on occasion be ambiguous, the phrase 'a distant country' cannot be said to be descriptive of an English province. Furthermore, although he could have been as destitute of friends in England as abroad, he is less likely to have come to the point of starvation in the country where he could at worst have obtained some employment, and at no particular risk, in the carpentry trade to which he had been apprenticed. In December he returned to England and made his way to Hackney. He is unlikely to have met Turpin or Rowden for although they may have known of his intention of going abroad, they can have had no intimation of his return. The first they can have had was when the reports of his capture appeared in the newspapers; but since there is some slight confusion about when the capture and subsequent events actually occurred, the newspaper references do not come first in the sequence which follows:

The annexed affidavit of Dison Green
In November [*recte* December] last having information that John Jones was at an house in Hackney he went to one Francis Francis and having got a warrant to apprehend Jones they gave it to Nicholas Graves a constable and all of them went and knocked at the door of the house where Jones was which being opened they rushed in and Dison Green going into the yard and seeing Jones there went to lay hold of him but Jones struck at him and after some struggle Green took him prisoner when the other[s] came to his assistance (they having been in other parts of the house to look for the criminal). And then they carried him before Henry Norris and Saml. Tyson Esquires, two of his Majesty's Justices of the Peace who committed him to Newgate.[5]

The same newspaper which reported the sighting of Turpin and Rowden near Winchester also described the capture of Jones and his having been taken before Norris on Tuesday, 16 December. The record of committal differs.

'No. 1 Jno. Jones committed by Henry Norris Esq. and charged on oath of John Wheeler with breaking open the house of Jno. Gladden in the county of Essex and stealing thence several [faded] Date 17th [Dec.]'[6] The newspaper which reported the capture as having taken place on Tuesday had altered the date by the time its Saturday edition came out.

The Gregory Gang

> On Thursday [18 December] about ten o'clock in the morning John Jones who was committed to Newgate on Monday night was brought before Nathaniel Blackerby Esq. one of his Majesty's Justices of the Peace for Middlesex &c. when John Wheeler the Evidence against the Essex gang charged him upon oath that he, Jones, Samuel and Jasper Gregory and the informant about a year ago did in the night time enter the house of John Gladden, a higler on Chinkford Green and took from thence one guinea and a half, wearing apparel and pewter which they divided among them and for which he will be tried the next Assizes at Chelmsford.[7]

The weekend edition of the *London Evening Post* stated that Jones was captured on Monday *night,* which is consistent with the midweek edition of the same paper stating that he was captured and committed on Tuesday. The Calendar in which the record of commitment appears stated that he was committed by Norris, and charged on oath by Wheeler (a separate event) on Wednesday; but the weekend paper which earlier had reported Jones being committed on Tuesday, now stated that the formal charge (dated Wednesday in Calendar, the same as the commitment) took place on Thursday. Now insofar as the Calendar links the formal charging of Jones with his commitment, it is clear that these two episodes took place, regardless of date, on the same day, so any single reference to either process may be taken to mean both. In which case, since the Thursday newspaper had already stated the commitment to have taken place on Tuesday (consistent with a Monday night capture), it follows the charge was also made on Tuesday. The Calendar date of Wednesday 17th is wrong, it should have been the 16th, and the Thursday reference in the Saturday newspaper should have been Tuesday, the same as it was in the Thursday edition.

Jones was captured late Monday night or early Tuesday morning and committed to Newgate by Henry Norris, J.P. A few hours later he appeared before Nathaniel Blackerby, J.P., who of all the Middlesex magistrates was most familiar with the background to his being wanted by the authorities. He was then formally charged upon the oath of Wheeler, who had no doubt been sent for at Blackerby's instigation as soon as word of Jones' capture was sent to him by Norris. There would have been no point in waiting until Thursday to charge him.

The mere fact of Jones' having lost his freedom would have been sufficient to worry Turpin and Rowden. For in December they could not have known *how* Jones was captured, and would no doubt have wondered whether it had been brought about by accident or design. Chance was a contingency they had to accept every day, but if the authorities were systematically tracking down the last survivors of the Gregory gang, then they would have to think twice about remaining in or near London.

At the beginning of July 1736 Rowden was in Stroud in Gloucestershire following his old trade of counterfeiting. This suggests that he had been in that area long enough to have forsaken highway robbery some time before.

It seems probable that immediately after Jones was captured Turpin and Rowden decided it was unsafe for two wanted men like themselves to continue in each others company. They split up before Christmas 1735 and Rowden, if he had not already done so, adopted the alias of Daniel Crisp and gradually made his way to Gloucestershire.

Turpin apparently went to Holland and lingered there for several months if not a year. Since the authorities appear to have been conviced of Turpin's absence from this country, there is at least some argument for his having gone abroad, which is far from being the case for his having remained in England.

IV

January 1735 and an inevitable lull in which we gain some insight into one aspect of the contemporary scene as Hogarth saw it, but did not record until some few years later; for in, 'A Report to the General Sessions of the Peace for the County of Middlesex by the Gentlemen appointed to enquire into the number of Gin shops within [the area covered by] the Weekly Bill [of Mortality] and parts adjacent in the said County'[8] it was stated that there were at least 7,044 houses, etc. (a ratio of one in six) retailing 'spiritous liquors'.

Although Hogarth was a contemporary of Turpin's, he had only a passing interest in recording the likeness of condemned persons; and lacking a contemporary portrait of Turpin it is a matter of some slight regret that Hogarth did not go to York in March 1739 as he did to Newgate in March 1733 when he produced the striking portrait of Sarah Malcolm the murderess. But in the *Rake's Progress* series of engravings which were published after the Copyright Act was passed in June 1735, the 'Scene in a Gaming House' does at least have as one of its characters a disgruntled highwayman who has lost all his money, sitting next to the similarly unfortunate Rake. The Tyburn execution (of the Idle Apprentice), and the skeleton of James MacLean the highwayman as background to the 'Anatomy Lesson of the President of the Royal College of Physicians', are both from a later period, but interesting commentaries on scenes to which one has become accustomed in this account.

V

The following reference to Turpin has a place here by default; its authenticity is highly suspect and the date attributed to it anachronistic. The authors of *Immortal Turpin* cut short Turpin's association with Rowden immediately after the robbery of Mr. Tebb by the gibbet on Putney Heath, and in its relation to newspaper reports this was as an appropriate point to separate them as any other, but the reason given is not in accordance with the facts.

Having worked the riverside areas and the South of London until these districts were becoming too warm for comfort, they decided that it was time to part company, and the next news of Turpin indicates that he is back again in Essex and preying singlehanded on unwary wayfarers. By keeping to the North of the county he was able to show himself with less fear of recognition. His chief hunting-ground was now the Cambridge road, but here he was trespassing on ground that was already being covered by other knights of the road.

It was in February, in the early spring of 1736, that this was rather forcibly brought home to him.[9]

There follows the famous meeting with Tom King, but although Ash and Day quite rightly pointed out that King's name was not Tom, they still failed to identify him correctly because they confused him with his brother. Turpin was actively associated for a short time with a highwayman called *Matthew* King, whom he had possibly known as far back as 1734, but the meeting with him as described in the account from which Ash and Day obtained their information, is every bit as much a fiction as the legendary Ride to York; and what is more, his *active* association with Matthew King cannot have commenced *before* February 1737.

The Turpin/King confrontation appeared originally in the Bayes' *Life* and it is appropriate to recall his material here.

The gang was then broke, and Turpin quite left to himself, and notwithstanding he met with so many booties, yet his extravagance had pretty well drained his pockets; he took a resolution to be concerned in no other gang, but to go his own bottom, and with this view he set forwards towards Cambridge, which he thought would be the best way, as he was not known in that county.

But before he reached his journey's end, the following odd encounter got his best companion, as he hath often declared. King the Highwayman, who had been towards Cambridge upon the same account, was coming back to London. Turpin seeing him well mounted, and appear like a gentleman, thought that was the time to recruit his pockets, and accordingly bids King stand, who keeping him in discourse some time, and dallying with him, Turpin swore, if he did not deliver immediately he would shoot him through the head; upon which King fell a laughing, and said, 'What! Dog eat Dog? Come, come, Brother Turpin, if you don't know me, I know you, and should be glad of your company.' After mutual assurances of fidelity to each other, and that nothing should part them but death, they agreed to go together upon some exploit, and met with a small booty that very day, after which they continued together, committing divers robberies, for near three years, till King was shot.

King being very well known about the country, as Turpin likewise was, insomuch that as no house would entertain them, they then formed the design of making their cave, and to that purpose pitched upon a place enclosed with a large thicket, situate between Loughton Road and King's-Oak Road, here they made a place large enough to receive them and their horses; and while they lay quite concealed themselves, could see through several holes made on purpose, what passengers went by in either road, and as they thought proper would issue out and rob them, in such a bold daring manner, and so frequently, that it was not safe for anyone to travel that road, and the very higglers were obliged to go armed. In this cave they lived, ate, drank, and lay; Turpin's wife supplied them with victuals, and frequently stayed there all night.

From the Forest, King and he once took a ride to Bungay in Suffolk, where Turpin having seen two young market-women receive money for corn, would rob them; King dissuaded him from it, telling him they were two pretty girls, and he would not be concerned in it. Turpin swore he would rob them, and accordingly did, against the consent of King, which occasioned a dispute between them.

At their return to their cave, they robbed a gentleman of London, one Mr. Bradele, at Fair-Maid-Bottom, who was taking an airing in his chariot, with his two children; King first attacked him; but he being a gentleman of spirit, was offering to make resistance, thinking there had been but one; upon which King called Turpin by the nick-name of *Jack,* and bid him hold the horses heads; they took first his money, which he then readily parted with, but insisted upon not giving his watch, which he said he would not part with; but the child, in a fright, persuaded his father to let them have it; they further insisting upon an old mourning ring of small value, which Mr. Bradele humourously told them, that it was not worth eighteen pence to them, but he prized it very much; King insisted upon having it off, which when he had, he returned to him, saying, they were more of gentlemen than to take anything a gentleman valued so much. Mr. Bradele asked him, If, as he had given him his ring, he would let him purchase his watch? Upon which King said to Turpin, "Jack, here seems to be a good honest fellow, shall we let him have the watch?" "Ay", said Turpin, "do just as you will," ... and then Mr. Bradele enquiring what would be the price, King told him, "Six guineas, we never sell one for more, if it be worth six and thirty," upon which Mr. Bradele promised not to discover them; and said, he would leave the money at the *Dial* in Birchin Lane; when Turpin cried out, "Ay, but King, insist upon no question asked." It was about that time Turpin shot Mr. Thompson's man.

The incident referred to in the last sentence occurred in May 1737, but none of the others have been identified with any known robberies. The whole of this passage seems implausible, and may only have been inserted to link the section on the Gregory gang and that with which Richard Bayes himself had some personal albeit confused recollection, *viz.* February to May 1737.

The Turpin caution to King 'insist upon no questions asked,' used at that time to be an obligatory rider to any advertisement inviting the return of goods lost or stolen to an inn or other place where a reward would be paid, and *No questions asked* is very much in the same humourous vein as the idea of Turpin robbing King.

Ash and Day did not take *their* accounts of the meeting with King, the robbing of the Bungay market women,[10] and the Mr. Bradele hold up,[11] from Bayes' version, because in certain respects, particularly in the latter incident, other details have been added; it is not suggested that they added these details themselves, merely that they obtained them from one of many authors who used and embellished Bayes' material to add colour to a drab period in the Turpin story. Ash and Day implied that the three incidents occurred in February 1736, September 1736 and post April 1737 respectively, but this distribution in time is purely arbitrary and of even less significance than the stories themselves.

The one thing which did occur in February 1736 which is relevant was brought about by the man who caused Turpin and Rowden to disappear. 'No. 18 John Jones committed for a felony and a burglary in the county of Essex was ordered to be sent to the said county.'[12]

VI

Jones was to appear at the Lent Assizes for Essex which began at Chelmsford on 10 March, and provision had already been made for a former associate of his to be there as well:

> John Wheeler to be delivered by the Keeper of New Prison to the custody of the Sheriff of Middlesex to be sent to the county of Essex by Warrant of Habeas Corpus to give evidence at the next Assizes to be held for the county against John Jones for felony and burglary and after he has given his evidence as aforesaid then to be redelivered by the said Sheriff of Middlesex to the said Keeper of New Prison who is hereby requested to receive the body of the said John Wheeler to keep him in his custody until he should be delivered by due course of law.[13]

And so that neither Jones nor Wheeler should be kept waiting for the trial to begin, there was an early start to their journey on the same day that the Assizes began.

> Yesterday morning between five and six o'clock John Jones, late a carpenter at Hackney, who was committed to Newgate some time ago, for a robbery at Chingford *and other robberies in Essex, with Gregory and his gang,* was carried in a chaise to Chelmsford in order to be tried there. Wheeler the Evidence against [him] went on horseback; and all under a strong guard.[14]

A better idea of how strong the guard was, and the expense incurred is obtained from the Cravings for Allowances by the Sheriff of Middlesex, for the year ending Michaelmas 1736. 'For conducting John Jones to the county of Essex charged with felony and burglary for five men and five horses hire three days for horsemeat &c. £9. 0s. 0d. For two writs of Habeas Corpus £1. 4s. 0d. For conducting John Wheeler to the county of Essex to give evidence against John Jones and reconducting him. For five men and five horses hire five days for horsemeat mansmeat &c. £15. 0s. 0d. For a writ of Habeas Corpus and Testificandum 12s. 0d.'[15] And that Jones was expected is shewn on the Felony File for Essex, under, *Names of the Prisoners.* 'John Jones one of Gregory's gang to be brought from Newgate the 10th of March instant charged with burglary and felony on the oath of John Wheeler.'

Jones was indicted with burglary in the house of John Gladwin at Chingford and with stealing from Gladwin and John Shockley goods and money to the total of £6 7s. 0d. These have been detailed previously and are identical to those in the indictment against Jasper Gregory who was convicted on the same charge at the previous Lent Assizes for Essex. The persons sworn in court and listed (in different order) on the back of the indictment were John Gladwin, John Wheeler, Mary Theed, John Mashin, Nicholas Graves, Francis Frances and Dison Green. The last three were responsible for Jones' capture, Mary Theed appeared at Jasper Gregory's trial, but John Mashin is not known.

Jones was found guilty on the charge of felony, but only to the value of 45 shillings, which presumably was the sum he admitted to having received as his share; on the burglary charge he was found not guilty, which indicates that the jury were inclined to believe his story that he was induced to take part in the robbery when he was drunk. The judgement however remained the same as if he had been convicted on both indictments; he was sentenced to be hanged, and it was recorded on the same file at the Gaol Delivery that, 'John Jones was attainted for stealing above forty shillings in a dwelling house.'[16] The marginal annotation against this entry was,. 'Reprieved in order for transportation', but in the next item of news from Chelmsford, the issue was

The Gregory Gang

confused by a report of his execution:

> Letters from Chelmsford mention that [four persons] were reprieved for transportation for fourteen years, and that only one was executed, viz. John Jones one of Gregory's Gang, for a felony and burglary at Chinkford; he behaved mighty well while under condemnation, and declared he never was concerned but in that single robbery in his life; and that drinking with Gregory, Rose and company they made him drunk, and when his reason was absent they drew him into that fact; that the next day after it he had such a horror at what he had done, that he run away, and continued in a distant country till almost starved, being destitute of friends, and returning to Hackney to see his family, was taken and committed to Newgate for that fact, and from thence removed to Chelmsford, and convicted on Wheeler's evidence; he forgave everybody, and seemed mighty sincere and penitent.[17]

Jones was not executed because he, along with the others referred to above, was recommended, 'as a proper object of her Majesty's Mercy on condition of transportation', by the Judge before whom he was tried, and although the recommendation was not approved for some months, he did remain in Chelmsford gaol until the reprieve was confirmed, and *was* transported subsequently. In that respect at least the letter writer was wrong, but from the fact Jones was found not guilty of burglary one can only assume that he told much the same story in court; this, together with a sincere and penitent manner would perhaps have swayed the judge in making his decision to recommend Jones for mercy.

If the judge was one who read his Bible, he could hardly have had much choice in the matter, for a more remarkable parallel to the parable of the Prodigal Son would be very hard to find. But if Jones did flee the country in December 1734 and not return until December 1735, and during that time was, as he claimed, destitute of friends, he contrived to stave off starvation for a remarkable length of time, particularly if one considers that he fled with but 45 shillings from the robbery which filled him with such horror. Judges were never swayed by *un*repentant criminals, and although we perhaps do Jones an injustice, there does seem some basis for supposing that he was not quite so innocent as he claimed to be. He would appear to have parted company with Turpin and Rowden some time between May and July 1735.

VII

By May 1736 Mary Brazier would have arrived in America, Jones was kicking his heels in Chelmsford gaol, Rowden was counterfeiting in Gloucestershire, Wheeler was back in New Prison in Clerkenwell, and Turpin, lacking any evidence to the contrary, might as well have been in Holland as anywhere else. One is inclined to forget that at Edgware there still hung in

238   Dick Turpin and

chains what was left of Samuel Gregory, Joseph Rose, John Fielder and Humphrey Walker. It would have been a grisly enough scene then, and one which hardly bears thinking about now, but in the Merry Month of May 1736 something happened on the gibbet at Edgware which may be regarded as the most macabre or most redeeming event to have touched that site before or since:

> Last Sunday a countryman viewing the bodies which hang in chains near Edgware perceived a tom-tit pitch upon Gregory's head, and upon a narrow view thought he saw a nest, upon which he borrowed a ladder, and under his ear, among some rags which were wrapped about his neck, found a nest with several young ones, which he sold at a good price, being esteemed very great curiosities by the *Virtuosi* of that country.[18]

Also in May a man under sentence of death escaped from Newgate. His name was Daniel Malden, and it was not long before he was recaptured and returned to Newgate to begin the dreadful wait all over again. Special precautions were taken to ensure that he did not try to cheat the hangman again, but early on the morning of 14 June he did escape a second time, and marking the date well we follow his progress from Newgate, via Enfield and Yarmouth, to Holland, because that is where Turpin had probably been for some months.

The Gregory Gang

FOOTNOTES

1. *London Evening Post,* 16 to 18 December 1735.
2. P.R.O./T.53/38 p.255.
3. *London Evening Post,* 24 to 27 January 1736.
4. *Ibid.,* 1 to 3 April 1736.
5. P.R.O./T.53/38 p.406.
6. Middlesex MJ/SR 2650 (Calendar of Middlesex Prisoners in Newgate, 10 December 1735 to 15 January 1736).
7. *London Evening Post,* 18 to 20 December 1735.
8. *Ibid.,* 20 to 22 January 1736.
9. *Immortal Turpin,* by Ash and Day, pp.40–41.
10. *Ibid.,* p.42.
11. *Ibid.,* p.50.
12. Middlesex/MJ/SR 2652, Calendar of Newgate Prisoners, 9 Geo.II Feb. 25 (Middlesex Prisoners Upon Orders).
13. Middlesex/MJ/GDB 314/216, March 1736.
14. *London Evening Post,* 9 to 11 March 1736 (*my italics*).
15. P.R.O./T.90/147 pp.100 and 101 respectively.
16. P.R.O./Assizes 35/176/1, Essex, Felony File Winter 9 Geo.II (1735/6), Gaol Calendar, Gaol Delivery, and Indictment No.12.
17. *London Evening Post,* 1 to 3 April 1736.
18. *Ibid.,* 18 to 20 May 1736.

CHAPTER FOUR

I

Daniel Malden, an ex sailor and petty criminal under sentence of death, may have met Turpin in England, but there is no evidence of such a meeting. He could have been a chance acquaintance, but it is doubtful, and the fact that Malden went to Great Yarmouth *via* Enfield (near which town Elizabeth Turpin may have been living) on his escape route to Holland can only be regarded as coincidence.

Malden escaped from Newgate on 14 June 1736. It is feasible since he got away early that morning, that he could have reached Enfield by nightfall; but even assuming he left there the following day we can have little idea how long it took him to reach Great Yarmouth which is over a hundred miles away, and a minimum of three days seems reasonable in the circumstances. This suggests that he could not have arrived at Great Yarmouth *before* 18 June, at which date he fell ill, and was obliged to remain there for a month. On or about 18 July he obtained passage to Holland and allowing some few days for the voyage he is unlikely to have landed there much before 25 July. At the beginning of July however there were two reports concerning Rowden and Turpin respectively.

> ... he [Rowden] became acquainted with the evidence Wheeler and his gang, and committed several robberies with them, until they were taken up upon Wheeler's information; whereupon he immediately went into the country, and took up his old trade again of making bad half crowns and shillings; and in putting off one of these bad shillings at a baker's at Stroud in Gloucestershire, he was detected by the baker's wife, who happening to see him two or three days afterwards, told her husband that was the man she took the bad shilling of; whereupon the baker immediately seized him, and, in a struggle, Rowden dropped a purse in which was a quantity of the same pieces, which he had put off to the baker's wife; upon this he was carried before a Justice of the Peace, who committed him to Gloucester jail by the name of Daniel Crisp.[1]

The Gregory Gang

As will be seen by the date of the report, Rowden's true identity was not discovered until almost a year had elapsed, and until this occurred no-one, least of all the authorities, can have had any idea where Rowden might have been.

The report is wrong on two points: Wheeler did not, as is implied, lead the gang, and Rowden did not immediately go into the country. The gang was led by Gregory, and Rowden remained with Turpin, near London until December 1735.

The date when these events occurred is determined from the following entries in the *Process Book of Indictments* for Gloucester Summer Assizes 1736. '1st Ind. Daniel Crispe labourer for unlawfully paying away a counterfeit shilling knowing it to be so to Ann Dobbs widow as good money the 2nd day of July [1736] at Stroud. Ann Dobbs pros[ecutrix]. 2nd Ind. For the like offence to Elizabeth the wife of Thomas Davis the same day year and place. Thomas Davis pros[ecutor]'[2]

On 2 July then, Rowden, armed with a purse full of counterfeit shillings, went shopping in Stroud and gave one shilling to Ann Dobbs, widow, and another to Elizabeth the wife of Thomas Davis the baker. On 4 or 5 July he was recognised by the baker's wife and committed to Gloucester jail to await his being brought up at the Summer Assize. Daniel Crisp *was* the alias of Thomas Rowden, and with the aid of hindsight we have the advantage of the authorities in knowing exactly where he was from 4 or 5 July 1736 onwards.

Leaving Rowden in Gloucester we come next to a report which purports to shew where Turpin was at that time. 'We hear that Turpin the butcher, who was one of the noted Gregory's Gang, has been seen lately at Rotterdam.'[3]

This report, appearing out of the blue, suggests that there may indeed have been word from Holland which alleged a Turpin sighting there. It was uncorroborated and no attempt was made to expand on the theme, which would no doubt have been the case had the idea been a newspaper contrivance. If Turpin was in fact seen in Holland, then allowing time for the news to reach London the sighting would have occurred at the end of June, at which time Daniel Malden was still at Great Yarmouth. As soon as Malden was well he obtained passage and sailed for Flushing, arriving there, as has been estimated, on or about 25 July. 'While I was at Flushing, I saw two merchants that live at Hoxton, drinking together at the sign of the *Three Dutch Skaters,* I went into the house to them, and while I was there, in came Turpin and Rowden. I drank with them, and they persuaded me to enter into Foreign Service, but I refused, telling them, I did not care to serve any other nation than my own.'[4]

We know that by the time Malden reached Flushing, Rowden was in Gloucester jail and that he had probably been in the county for some time. We know also that there had already been a report of Turpin being seen in Holland. So if the story *was* Malden's he obviously did not see Rowden, in which case it is unlikely that he saw Turpin.

The implausibility of Turpin's acting as a recruiting agent (*see* notes to footnote 4), or an inn in Holland being called the 'Three *Dutch* Skaters', also indicates that Malden's story was a fiction, but Malden's fiction rather than the Ordinary of Newgate's, whose powers of imagination are unlikely to have been so strong. If stories of Turpin being in Holland were circulating in Flushing (which is possible since they appeared in a London newspaper before Malden got there), Malden could have heard them and used them to bolster up his own story of patriotic denial. For in turning down an invitation to join a foreign service, a condemned man might hope to obtain some reprieve when recaptured, especially if he could introduce some well known personalities to make the account seem credible. In the event Malden was recaptured, but although his pretence to patriotism did not save him, there is irony in the fact that his story appears to have been believed. This however is a facet of Malden/Turpin history which should be examined in its proper place, and for the moment we leave Malden at Flushing, possibly at an inn the sign of which depicted skaters, listening to two merchants from Hoxton telling him that Turpin had been seen at Rotterdam.

II

Assuming Turpin to have been in Holland (but discounting Malden's claim), the life of the man whose capture was the reason for Turpin's fleeing this country, still hung in the balance. On 26 July however John Jones' fate was resolved:

Whitehall 26th July, 1736.
Gentlemen,
The following persons having been tried and convicted at the last Assizes held for the Home Circuit, of the several crimes hereafter specified, vizt ... John Jones, attainted, at Chelmsford in Essex, the 10th day of March last, for stealing above forty shillings in a dwelling house ... And the respective Judges, before whom the persons were tried, having by certificate under their hands, recommended them to the Queen, as proper objects of her Majesty's mercy, on condition of transportation for the several terms of years mentioned in the said certificates. I am commanded to signify to you her Majesty's pleasure, that you give the necessary orders for transportation of ... [and] John Jones, for seven years ... to some of his Majesty's Colonies or Plantations in America, pursuant to the Act of Parliament in that behalf. I am &c.
Justice of Assize for the Home Circuit.   Harrington.[5]

The Gregory Gang

There is no possibility, as stated in the report from Chelmsford, that he was the only one of those convicted at the March Assize who suffered execution.[6] And if further proof is needed on this point we need only to look to the 1736 Summer Assize roll for Essex, wherein John Jones is described briefly as, 'convict'.

III

On or about 21 August 1736, or so several newspapers would have us believe, Turpin returned from Holland *via* the Ostend Packet Boat; the newspapers in which this report appeared did not come out until 25 September, and the events which immediately ante dated the news of Turpin's return seem to have inspired such a report rather than justified it. Assuming Turpin was in Holland there is no reason to suppose that he did return to England in August, or for some months afterwards.

IV

The Summer Assize for Gloucester did not end until 3 September, and some days before when the Oxford Circuit judge heard the charges against Daniel Crisp, he had no idea that the man who stood in the dock was Turpin's notorious companion Rowden.

> **Gloucester** Daniel Crispe labourer being a person of evil name and fame and dishonest conversation on the second of July [1736] at Stroud one piece of false money made of base metals counterfeited to the likeness and similitude of a piece of good lawful and current money and coin of the Realm called a shilling did utter and pay to Elizabeth the wife of Thomas Davis as a shilling (he knowing the said piece to have been false and counterfeit) to the great damage of Thomas Davis.[7]

The second indictment was the same except that the person to whom the shilling was paid was named as being Ann Dobbs. The witnesses sworn in court were, on the first indictment, Elizabeth Davis, Thomas Davis, Edward Watkins, John Rogers, Dorcas Poulton; and on the second indictment, Ann Dobbs, Richard Arundell and Giles Bishop. Of the persons sworn on the second indictment, Richard Arundell was the person who apprehended Crisp, and Giles Bishop was the constable into whose custody Arundell charged him.[8]

The jury found him guilty in each case. He was fined 20 shillings on the first count and committed to gaol until he paid the fine, *but* on the back of the second indictment (to which reference was made on the front of both) was entered 'his further judgement'. 'To be publicly whipped two several market days till his body be bloody at Gloucester and one at the Market Town of Stroud and fined 20 shillings and committed to gaol for one year without bail or mainprize unless he give sufficient security before a Justice of the Peace for the County for his good behaviour for three years himself in forty pounds and his two sureties in twenty pounds each.'[9]

The *Gaol Book* for the Oxford Circuit amplifies the first part of the further judgement insofar as it gives the date when the first whipping should take place, there is no reference to the second. 'To be publicly whipped in the Open Market at Gloucester until his body be bloody the 11th September 1736.'[10]

Both the *Gaol Book* and *Process Book* entries are confused over the amount paid in fine, it having been taken to have applied in each case and totalled to make 40 shillings. This does not appear to have been so, and a fine of 20 shillings is borne out by the newspaper report which reached London. 'Country News. *Gloucester Sept. 4* Our Assizes did not end till yesterday ... Daniel Crisp, for uttering false money, knowing it to be so, to be whipped twice, viz. at Gloucester and Stroud, to pay a fine of 20s. and to remain in gaol for one year.'[11]

Considering he could, if correctly identified, have been tried on a capital indictment in Essex, Rowden no doubt thought himself, despite two painful episodes, lucky to be alive with his assumed identity still intact and a year in which to cultivate it to perfection. He was also lucky there was no evidence upon which the authorities might have proceeded against him on a charge of counterfeiting, for if convicted of that offence he would have been liable to a direr punishment than that which he received. It was not, as events turned out, the last time fate was to smile on Thomas Rowden *alias* Daniel Crisp.

V

During the second week of September 1736 Daniel Malden returned to the country where he faced almost certain death. 'Last Monday morning [13 September] a messenger from Canterbury brought advice to Newgate of the capture of Daniel Malden.'[12]

The news of Malden's recapture heralded a period of speculation about the past and present whereabouts of Richard Turpin, and in a provincial newspaper which appeared a week *after* the above report came the first account of Turpin in England to be published for nine months. It ante dated by one day the report of his return from Holland five weeks earlier, the London newspapers including *that* item on 25 September. Thus we are led to believe that Turpin and a companion were at Clapham on 17 September.

The Gregory Gang

> Turpin was seen last Friday morning drinking at a Public House in Clapham. The person who knew him immediately told the landlord, but before they could contrive how to secure him, he and his companion mounted their horses, threw down a shilling instead of sixpence for two pots of beer, and made off towards Wandsworth. He was mounted on a fine gelding and his companion on a dark bay horse. Turpin was dressed in a red waistcoat and a brown coat.[13]

The remarkable thing about this incident is that although it was supposed to have occurred at Clapham, no reference to it appears to have found its way into *London* newspapers; but the form of the report is in fact almost identical to that which described the flight from a Whitechapel alehouse on 10 May 1735. In *Immortal Turpin* the companion is again made out to be King, and the account is followed by reference to the undated Bungay in Suffolk robbery which originated in Bayes' account, as shown below.

> From the forest, King and he once took a ride to Bungay in Suffolk, where Turpin having seen two young market-women receive 13 or 14l. for corn, would rob them; King dissuaded him from it, telling him they were two pretty girls, and he would not be concerned in it. Turpin swore he would rob them, and accordingly did, against the consent of King, which occasioned a dispute between them.[14]

This and similar episodes involving King were fictions created to introduce some interest during quiet periods of Turpin's career. The newspapers in September 1736 no doubt acted from similar motives when Malden returned from Holland and Turpin rumours were suddenly rife. This translation of rumour into print is best illustrated by the following passage.

> Tuesday morning about nine o'clock a gentleman with his lady and son in a coach and six were attacked by two highwaymen, well mounted (supposed to be Turpin and his companion) on Barnes Common and robbed of their watches and money to the value of 40l. and made off through the fields.
> We hear that Turpin has been in Holland, from whence he returned about five weeks ago in the Ostend Packet Boat. It is said that Daniel Malden knew him there and that Turpin endeavoured to prevail with Malden to go into Foreign Service, and see England no more.[15]

The venue was Barnes Common again, the area in which Turpin and Rowden were last known to have operated (in 1735), but the really interesting point about the robbery is that in order to justify Turpin's existence in England the newspaper has had to bring him back from Holland; but insofar as the Ostend Packet Boat story was published verbatim in other newspapers of the same date, there is some suggestion either of 'agency distribution' or 'syndication'. It is significant that the recruiting aspect of Malden's story which subsequently formed part of the Ordinary of Newgate's account (not published until 2 November, nor, supposedly, put on record until 21 October) should first appear on 25 September, a week after news of Malden's capture reached London, and after he had had time to tell his story to interested parties.

Malden's return inspired reports that Turpin had been in Holland, Turpin had returned to England, Turpin was active again about London; but the effect these had on the authorities could hardly have been more surprising, for on 29 September 1736, John Wheeler the Evidence was released from the New Prison in Clerkenwell, freed from the protective custody which had kept him there since 11 February 1735. The newspapers had very little to say about his release and restricted their observations to a minimum. Thus Wheeler was discharged, 'Wednesday about noon,'[16] is a typical comment. On the following day the Keeper of New Prison Clerkenwell filed a claim for the expenses incurred in keeping Wheeler in his custody.

> To the Right Honourable the Lord Harrington, his Majesty's Principal Secretary of State.
>
> Sheweth
> That John Wheeler was committed to the said prison the eighth of February 1734/5 and remained there 'till the 30th September 1736, in order to give evidence against Samuel Gregory, John Fielder, Humphrey Walker, Thomas [*recte* Joseph] Rose, William Saunders, Jasper Gregory, John Jones and Herbert Haines, who have all been executed for several notorious burglaries and robberies committed by them in company with the said evidence, and against whom there were proclamations issued.
> That the said Wheeler being very poor and having nothing to subsist on your memorialist allowed him one shilling a day for his support, besides having been at other expenses in coach hire several times attending the Justice at Westminster, who took the said Wheeler's information, and at the Old Bailey amounting to thirty one pounds and eleven shillings as appears by the bill annexed and therefore humbly prays your Lordship to order the payment thereof to him.
> And your memorialist shall ever pray.
> Thos: Cavenaghs bill keeper of the New Prison at Clerkenwell for the maintainance of John Wheeler the Evidence at one shilling per day from the 8th day of February 1734/5 to the 30th day of September 1736 both days inclusive being in all 601 days.
>
> | | |
> |---|---|
> | For his boarding and lodging | £30 1. 0. |
> | For expenses & coach hires to be further examined | 1 10. 0. |
> | | £31 11. 0. |
>
> The humble Memorial of Thomas Cavannagh Keeper of the New Prison Clerkenwell. 30 Sept. 1736.[17]

There is incontrovertible evidence that Wheeler was taken on 11 February 1735 whereas the expenses claimed were from 8 February *inclusive,* and although apparently released on Wednesday, Cavanagh claimed to Thursday *inclusive.* His list of people against whom Wheeler gave evidence contains a

The Gregory Gang

number of inaccuracies; Rose's name is wrong, Walker died and was not executed, Wheeler did not attend Jasper Gregory's trial, Jones was transported, Mary Brazier (against whom Wheeler did give evidence) was left off the list.

Wheeler was not as poor as Cavanagh made out. He obtained £7 10s. 0d. from proclamation rewards, plus a share in £280 paid out in Blood Money. If he received only ten per cent of the Blood Money, the total reward money paid out to him whilst he was in New Prison would have amounted to more than the total expense claimed by Cavanagh for a period of 601 days. Cavanagh knew about rewards (at a later date he succeeded in obtaining a share of some himself), and unless the money was withheld from Wheeler until his discharge, he should have had some money to subsist on. But even so, Cavanagh was no doubt obliged to keep Wheeler at a standard above that of ordinary prisoners, and these were therefore legitimate expenses.

If as Cavanagh claimed Wheeler left on 30 September, Cavanagh, the man in charge of the prison, made time to account the expense of Wheeler's long stay on the same day that Wheeler left, an impatient act to say the least, especially since his claim took nearly three years to be settled. Cavanagh was not dishonest, he was greedy, and greed made him careless, and it was lucky perhaps for him that it took so long for the claim to be settled, for by June 1739, not one of the gang remained alive in England, and all their days, let alone Wheeler's extra four, were for the most part forgotten.

No reason for Wheeler's release appears to have survived as a record of that time, but it is surely more than coincidence that his discharge should have followed so closely the return and recapture of Daniel Malden, and his story of meeting Turpin and Rowden in Holland. Reports and speculation about Turpin's whereabouts came to an end when Malden was executed, and apart from one isolated report in October do not extend beyond the relevant post Malden recapture period in September. Not even the Ordinary of Newgate's account of Malden's escapes, published after Malden's demise, was able to revive the spark of Turpin interest which had flared briefly and as suddenly died.

Wheeler was a very special person, allowed subsistence in prison and closely guarded on those few occasions he left it. Witness for the Crown and obliged to remain in protective custody until all members of the Gregory gang had been disposed of by law or other means, his last public appearance had been in March, six months before; so why, when so far as the authorities were aware both Turpin and Rowden were still at large, was a decision made to release Wheeler at this particular time? One theory is that the authorities believed Turpin and Rowden to be in England and released Wheeler in the hope he would lure the others into a trap. Two things confound this theory, one, insufficient publicity was given to his release, and two, no watch was kept on Wheeler subsequent to his release from New Prison, a fact observed in the passage, 'Mr. Cavanagh the Keeper of New Prison Clerkenwell was at some trouble to find out Wheeler the witness,'[18] which described a call upon Wheeler's services in 1737.

The important thing about Wheeler was not so much his willingness to testify against any member of the Gregory gang, but his ability to identify them, and the case of John Lyndon is a case in point. Wheeler's evidence was always secondary to his being able to identify the person captured, and since after his discharge no effort was made to keep in touch with him let alone watch him, there must have been some valid reason for letting him go.

Prior to Malden's return, the last reported sighting of Turpin and Rowden in England, positive or otherwise, was in December 1735, nine months previously. Before that, although there was a long interval of time between the captures of Haines and Jones, hardly a week went by without there being some reference to the activities of Turpin and Rowden, a fact which justified the keeping of Wheeler in New Prison throughout that period. With the capture of Jones, the authorities were obliged to keep Wheeler at least until he testified against Jones in March 1736, but since between Jones' capture and trial nothing was heard of the two highwaymen, one would imagine once the trial was over that the authorities were already beginning to wonder how much longer they would need to keep Wheeler in 'protective custody'.

By September nothing more had been heard of Turpin and Rowden, except one report at the beginning of July that Turpin had been seen in Holland, so when Malden's story of having seen both Turpin and Rowden came to the notice of the authorities, it must inevitably have aroused more than passing interest. Obviously the reports of Turpin being back in England and near London cannot have found much favour in Whitehall, but were the reports of his being in Holland preferred? Apparently so, although there does not appear to have been sufficient time between Malden's recapture and Wheeler's release for the authorities to have instigated some investigation in Holland to satisfy themselves that Malden's story was true.

From the time the Flushing recruiting story first appeared to the time it was incorporated in the Ordinary of Newgate's account of Malden's escapes, the details of his meeting with Turpin and Rowden did not change, and since it shewed him in a favourable light there was no reason why Malden should have changed it all the time he stood to gain a reprieve. When he knew he was still going to be hanged it would have been pointless for him to have changed it, and at his execution he was able to derive some satisfaction from the knowledge that he had been believed. For this appears to have been what happened, Malden was questioned, he stuck to his story, and since the elements of the story satisfied the authorities not only that Turpin and Rowden were in Holland but that they would stay there, this resolved the problem of what to do with Wheeler and they believed what they wanted to believe.

Rowden managed to disappear for 18 months in this country (including 11 spent in prison under an assumed name), Turpin, in his last two years, disappeared for 20 months (including four in prison under an assumed name), and during both those periods nobody had the slightest idea where the two men in question were, except that in Turpin's case he did on one occasion give away the fact that he was in this country somewhere. But the fact that we have some knowledge of Turpin's later disappearance, and to some lesser extent Rowden's only one, is related to their culminating in denouement and publicity about their immediate pasts, and there is no such parallel for the disappearance here under discussion. However, if one accepts that the post Malden references are suspect, then there is no case for Turpin being in England, and both before and some time after Malden there were uncorroborated reports of his being in Rotterdam. The total Low Countries reports of any kind is four, two Rotterdam, one Flushing and one Ostend, no further apart than some of the distances Turpin used to cover in England. He could not have been both here and there, and it is significant that although the authorities had a vested interest in Turpin, neither the press nor the public were particularly interested in his whereabouts at the beginning of July 1736, when the first report of his having been seen in Rotterdam suddenly appeared.

VI

From September to November 1736 there was an increase in highway robberies in the vicinity of Finchley Common, and as with other open spaces around London, Turpin traditions still linger. Ash and Day made reference to such activities, following an October 1736 newspaper report,[19] but at no point during his career was Turpin active in Finchley, and contemporary reports linking him with the area, even on isolated occasions, are virtually unknown. The series of robberies reported in newspapers from September to November 1736 eventually came to an end with the capture of a man called Cocky Wager, who was aided in those attacks by a man named Bonner.

Another Turpin tradition, without reference to which no account of Turpin seems to be complete, is that of his stolen kiss from Mrs. Fountayne.

Marylebone Gardens It is said that Dick Turpin once publicly kissed in the gardens a beauty of the time related to Dr. Fountayne. The lady expostulated, but Turpin exclaimed, "Be not alarmed, Madam, you can now boast that you have been kissed by Dick Turpin. Good morning." '[20]
A year later, she had become the 'Wife or Sister in Law of a Dean of the Established Church,' and was taking the air when Turpin 'kissed her before company and all the quality'; the relation of Dr. Fountayne had become Mrs. Fountayne.[21] Ash and Day, apparently borrowing from Walford's text,[22] used Mrs. Fountayne as padding between 1736 and 1737, but strictly speaking the next author after Walford should be Thomas Seccombe, in 1902. 'At Marylebone Gardens, in 1737, so Dr. Fountayne was informed by one of the principals in the adventure, Dick Turpin once kissed a youthful beauty and reigning toast of the day.'[23] And finally in 1927. 'It was in Marylebone Gardens that Dick Turpin stole a kiss from Mrs. Fountayne, wife of the Marylebone schoolmaster, and comforted her by telling her she had been kissed by the notorious Dick Turpin.'[24]

It is significant that the story does not appear before the late nineteenth century; not that this should be taken to mean that it is a fiction, but that this was when it was first noted and used as Turpin material. There was a Dr. Fountayne, 1747–1802, who was Dean of York, who could conceivably, as Seccombe suggested, have heard of the incident from the surviving principal in the affair; but how far Seccombe differs from Wroth and Walford in having used original material, it is difficult to say, as he does not give his source. Seccombe made use of a great diversity of Turpin material and was usually obliging enough to quote his sources. For that reason, possibly, his short account of Turpin, plus a useful but basic bibliography, was found suitable for inclusion in the *Dictionary of National Biography,* although the *Essex Review* articles of January and April 1902 are probably of much more use. In the D.N.B. he quotes both Wroth and Walford, so it is possible he used one or the other of these as his Mrs. Fountayne source. Seccombe shewed little discernment in his choice of material, a fact well illustrated by the fact he dates *his* meeting with *Tom* King, February 1735; so really there is no reliable source for the Mrs. Fountayne incident at all. It was very likely a joke, the act of a young blade, if indeed it ever happened at all. Turpin appears to have been a somewhat dour character, not romantic or given to humour and somewhat mean of nature. One can imagine him stealing almost anything except a kiss.

VII

The last post Malden report of Turpin in England, completely isolated from any others in time, came in mid October 1736. 'Last Saturday, Turpin was seen to ride through Edgware (Edgworth *sic*) towards Harrow on the Hill, mounted on a strong bay horse, he called to one Moreland, a drover, a little beyond Edgworth, and asked him how he did, but did not attempt to rob him.'[25]

Given the practice of London newspapers in their use of the word 'last', one would assume this alleged sighting to have occurred on 16 October, but since Friday to Friday editions, as in this instance, were an uncommon span, one cannot be certain. The story appears to have originated from the cattle drover Moreland, who would no doubt have been delighted if a highwayman had robbed him. Perhaps he longed for the excitement of 1735 when farmer Lawrence was robbed and they afterwards hung the rogues on the rustic gibbet, but rather than speculate what his motive might have been for spreading the tale which eventually reached a provincial newspaper, it would be better to recall that even the Edgware victims were notoriously inept when it came to identifying the men who took part in that robbery. Besides, Turpin was in Holland at this time.

On 21 October, Daniel Malden told the Ordinary of Newgate all about his escapes and extraordinary adventures, and with his execution early in November died the briefly resurrected interest in Turpin. Not long after this the Finchley highwayman Cocky Wager was taken, and by December 1736 unusual criminal activity in or near London had virtually ceased. On 14 December however, Martin Bladen was reminded of past events and still felt strongly enough about them to comment upon them in a long letter to Baron Harrington, the purpose of which was to plead the case of a Widow Langford, who was being intimidated by a gang of roughs. Most of the letter is of no relevance to this account, but those parts which reflect the impressions formed by Bladen's previous experiences are reproduced below.

Albrohatch near Ilford in Essex.
14th December 1736.

My Lord,
   Your Lordship was troubled with an application from this neighbourhood, about two years ago, on account of some robberies, that had been committed by numbers of rogues in bodies; and his Majesty was pleased to order notice to be given in the *Gazette*, of his gracious intention of granting a pardon to any of them, that should discover his accomplices, together with a reward of fifty pounds each, for so many of them, as should be convicted by such discovery. And though no formal information did ensue upon that notice, and consequently the

Treasury was put to no expense by it, yet it certainly had a good effect, for there is reason to believe, that it created such a distrust amongst those miscreants, as broke the combination, for they were never known to rob in such numbers together afterwards, and almost all of them have since been hanged.

It is the misfortune of people who dwell upon the skirts of a forest near London, to be more liable to alarms of this kind, than in other situations ... I have made the best inquiry I can concerning these fellows, and do believe their proper occupation may have been that of smuggling or deer stealing, which are natural nurserys for the breeding of robbers and housebreakers; for these kind of people originally set out with a full persuasion, that the King has no property; by an easy gradation they soon come to believe that nobody else has any; and when they are disappointed in the forest, raise contributions on the neighbourhood. They are certainly the most dangerous kind of thieves, because they generally travel in very large gangs.[26]

The reward notice was the proclamation published in the *Gazette* on 8 February 1735 in respect of the Split, Wooldridge, Widow Shelley and Reverend Mr. Dyde robberies. Bladen was right insofar as there were no proceedings in respect of any of these robberies, but he was wrong in thinking it had any effect on the gang. Fielder, Saunders and Wheeler were taken on 11 February as a result of the independent enquiries of members of the Lawrence family and others who, if they were not motivated by it, claimed the reward published in the *next* edition of the *Gazette* which appeared after the above.

Bladen's description of the Rogues' Progress is as true as our evidence has led us to believe, except that the gang's disappointment in the forest was due more to the incentive given to indolent Keepers by increased rewards, rather than unsuccessful hunting. The gang however did bring the law down upon itself when its members became hardened criminals without much regard for person or property. Yet a lot of them were young, and the deerstealing exploits which started it all could have begun harmlessly enough with the idea not so much of the King having no property, but rather that he and other privileged members of society had more than was reasonable or decent when there were so many who had none.

VIII

The capture of John Jones heralded the period of Turpin's absence, the transportation of John Jones marks the end of the blank year of 1736 and in effect makes way for Turpin's return to the English scene.

Essex William Dawtrey, Esq. Sheriff of the said county, for the year ending Mich. 10 Geo.II 1736 [Craves] for guarding and keeping ... John Jones ... condemned to be hanged but reprieved for transportation from the 10th day of

March to the 20th of December following being 40 weeks at 2.6. a week each [*Total* £25 0s. 0d.] For conveying ... John Jones ... the transports being 11 in number from Chelmsford to Blackwall being above 20 miles from whence they were transported the 20th December last guards and attendance. [*Total* £20 0s. 0d.][27]

The second item in the Craving brings us to Blackwall, and Jones' embarkation on board the transport for the Colonies. 'A True list of all the prisoners taken from the counties of Hertford, Essex ... and shipped on board the *Dorsetshire*. Wm. Loney Commander for Virginia which were shipped by Mr. Jonathan Forward of London, Merchant Dec. 25th 1736. No. 14 [Essex convicts] John Jones.'[28]

Jones left Chelmsford on 20 December for Blackwall, and on Christmas Day he was shipped on board the *Dorsetshire*. There is no record of this ship's arrival in America, and this is the last we hear of Jones. Wheeler was now a free man, 1736 was past, and in January 1737 the newspapers printed domestic and foreign news, and, if there wasn't much of that, obituaries. From February onwards it was just like old times.

FOOTNOTES

1. *Political State,* Vol.LIV, July–December 1737, p.145 (August).
2. P.R.O./Assizes 4/19 (N.B. the 2nd indictment was actually the first).
3. *London Evening Post,* 1 to 3 July 1736.
4. *A Genuine Account of the Two Surprising Escapes of Daniel Malden taken from his own Mouth in the Old Condemned Hold in Newgate – October 21st 1736,* in the Ordinary of Newgate's account of Malefactors executed at Tyburn 2nd of November 1736. J. Applebee. 1736. 6d. *N.B.* If there was one activity which British exiles could engage in on the continent which was *guaranteed* to arouse the interest of the authorities at home, it was that of recruiting men already serving with the British Army, deserters from it, and other miscreants and adventurers, into service with another power. Turpin was not in a position to draw attention to himself in this way, besides which the office of recruiting agent called for a degree of familiarity with domestic and foreign service and recruiting background which Turpin just did not possess.
5. P.R.O./S.P.44/83.
6. On rare occasions when no-one was capitally convicted (as opposed to being convicted and having the sentence commuted to transportation) that particular session was called a 'Maiden Assize' (for definition see *Cunningham's Law Directory,* 1783) and the judge awarded a pair of white gloves.
7. P.R.O./Assizes 5/56.
8. P.R.O./T.53/39, p.325.
9. P.R.O./Assizes 5/56.
10. P.R.O./Assizes 2/11.
11. *London Evening Post,* 7 to 9 September 1736.
12. *Ibid.,* 16 to 18 September 1736.
13. *Ipswich Gazette,* 17 to 24 September 1736.
14. *Life of Richard Turpin,* by Richard Bayes and Others in Essex, p.15.
15. *Country Journal* or *Craftsman,* by Caleb D'Anvers, 25 September 1736.
16. *London Evening Post,* 30 September to 2 October 1736.
17. P.R.O./S.P.36/39 ff.145–146.
18. P.R.O./T.53/39 p.326.
19. *Immortal Turpin,* p.45.
20. *London Pleasure Gardens of the 18th Century,* by Warwick Wroth, F.S.A., of the British Museum, MacMillan, 1896, p.100.
21. *Old and New London,* Walford, 1897. Vol.IV, p.435.
22. *Immortal Turpin,* p.46.
23. *Essex Review,* No.42, Vol.XI, p.65. April 1902, Thomas Seccombe.
24. *London.* George H. Cunningham. 1927. p.189.
25. *Ipswich Gazette,* 15 to 22 October 1736.

26. P.R.O./S.P.36/39 ff.338–339.
27. P.R.O./T.90/147 pp.111 and 112. There appears to have been some carry over of the account for the year 1735 to 1736 insofar as in the case of Jones and his companions the expenses were taken up to December 1736, but being unable to anticipate the date of transportation this was no doubt allowed to clear business commenced much earlier in the year. The main point to be observed in the above is that prisoners were a liability upon the county only up to the date of conviction or other court direction which required them to remain in custody. Thereafter any expense incurred in their maintenance or execution, etc. was included with the Sheriff's Craving for administrative expenses incurred in the execution of his office, which money he was obliged to pay out of his own pocket. This is more clearly illustrated in other entries where the office changed hands during the Exchequer year and both Sheriffs entered claims for the parts of the year they had been in office.
28. P.R.O./T.53/38 p.458.

CHAPTER FIVE

I

THE NEXT two items of news appear to cancel each other out, but a look at the facts shews them to be not quite so straightforward as they appear.

> About the same time [Thursday, 10 February] the following paragraph appeared in one of the papers. "Account of Turpin the butcher's being in Holland". A letter from Turpin the butcher was delivered at a public house in Southwark on Monday last, dated at Rotterdam, and directed to two of his companions. By the contents thereof it seems, that he had quarelled with them at an alehouse near Wandsworth, about the division of a booty of £50, he taking £30 himself; which so enraged them, that they threatened his life; whereupon, making an excuse to go out, he mounted his horse and rode off before they perceived what he was about. The letter has been delivered to a magistrate, and there being a direction of the abode of his companions, diligent search is making after them.[1]

Also on 10 February (but not reported until the weekend) there occurred the following, 'On Thursday last were committed to Hertford Gaol, Elizabeth the wife of Turpin the butcher; Hannah Elcombe her pretended maid, and one Robert Nott, who said he had formerly been huntsman to Mr. Harvey of Chigwell; they had been all night in company with Turpin at Puckeridge, but Turpin got his horse and made his escape towards Cambridge.'[2]

There is ample corroboration of the second report, and of Turpin being in England from this time until his capture in 1738; but the really significant aspect of these two accounts is that Turpin was at Puckeridge in Hertfordshire on the night of 9/10 February, less than three days after a letter supposedly written by him at Rotterdam was received in Southwark. Turpin could have followed the letter from Rotterdam, or even come over on the same boat with it, but in the event it will be seen that we are not so much concerned with this letter, but with another which has not survived.

To find out why there must have been another letter we need to establish the reason why Turpin and the others were at Puckeridge. 'Hertford Gaol Calendar Elizabeth Turpin, Robert Nott, Hannah Elcome Committed the 10th February 1736/7 by Thomas Rolt Esq. on a violent suspicion of being dangerous rogues and of robbing upon the highway.'[3]

Richard Bayes described how after Turpin's meeting with King they lived in a cave in Epping Forest, and how, 'Turpin's wife supplied them with victuals, and frequently stayed there all night.'[4] Ash and Day describe this idyllic episode as having occurred, 'about March 1737'.[5] But with no reason to suspect that Turpin's wife was ever committed to gaol, one would not have looked for evidence of the fact, and its discovery was the result of an attempt to verify one of the apparently less imaginative episodes in Bayes' account.

It was about that time Turpin shot Mr. Thompson's man [actually May 1737] ... This man's death obliged Turpin to make off precipitately; so he went farther into the country, in search of King, and sent his wife a letter to meet him at a public house in Hertford, who accordingly went, with two of Squire H....s's servants; she waited for him about half an hour, and when he came to the house, he asked for her by a fictitious name, left on purpose, found she was there, and going to her through the kitchen, saw a butcher to whom he owed five pounds; the butcher taking him aside, "Come Dick," says he, "I know you have money now, if you'd pay me, it would be of great service." Turpin replied, his wife was in the next room, and she had money, and he would get some off her and pay him presently. The butcher apprised two or three then present who it was, and that he would get his five pounds first, and then take him; but Turpin, instead of going to his wife, jumped out of the next window, took horse, and went away immediately without seeing her, while the butcher waited some time in expectation of his having the five pounds.

From hence he went to King, and one Potter, whom they had then lately taken along with them ...

There followed an incident which occurred on 30 April 1737, but the Hertford escape is not otherwise dated. Reports in May newspapers however (following the murder referred to above) suggested that Turpin had been captured and taken to, amongst other prisons, Hertford Gaol. It seemed possible that there was a connection between the undated Bayes' item and the newspaper reports (in actual fact there was none, the May reports were merely rumours), and a search in the Lent and Summer Assize felony files for Hertford soon revealed the above and related evidence of the taking of Elizabeth Turpin and her two companions.

Bayes' story could easily have had its origins in the Puckeridge incident, especially since it was after that event that Turpin did take up with Matthew King and a man called Stephen Potter. But the one thing common to both accounts which would seem positively to indicate that they were versions of the same affair, is the reference to Robert Nott, formerly huntsman to Mr. Harvey of Chigwell, and Squire H....s's servants. It seems possible that Squire H. was in fact Mr. Harvey, but if there was any doubt about this, it must surely be dispelled by the description in both accounts of two people accompanying Elizabeth Turpin to a rendezvous in Hertfordshire. One could be dogmatic about the newspaper report giving Puckeridge and Bayes giving Hertford, but the same could be said of the latter setting the scene at a public house and the newspaper not mentioning a dwelling of any sort; for if the four were to stay anywhere overnight, where else but at an inn? The main difficulty with regard to Bayes' version is to what extent one can rely on the entirely uncorroborated inclusion of the butcher, a somewhat bizarre confrontation considering Turpin's former trade; it is when we return to establishing why the company of four were at Puckeridge that this begins to take on the semblance of yet another Bayes fable loosely based on fact or hearsay.

Puckeridge in Hertfordshire lies roughly halfway between Enfield (near which we have assumed Turpin's wife was living) and Royston, and it is at this point that the road northward from Enfield is now joined by the main east to west road from Harwich. The modern road appears to have closely followed the route of the old, running right across Essex from Harwich *via* Colchester, Braintree, Great Dunmow to the Essex/Hertfordshire border at Hockeril not far from Bishop's Stortford; and although it did not then reach Puckeridge, it would only have been a matter of riding a few miles through country lanes *via* Much Hadham and Standon if one wanted to get to their rendezvous.

Elizabeth Turpin and her companions were committed on suspicion of being dangerous rogues and of robbing on the highway. The idea is not feasible, and since all three were eventually released it is clear there was no substance to such suspicions. By keeping them in custody however it would soon become apparent whether or not Turpin might be drawn by the fate of his wife. To keep them at all was not possible without some charge, and the legal invention of suspicion was sufficient until the advent of the Assize forced the admission that there was no evidence upon which to bring indictments against them.

The Puckeridge meeting itself was a reunion upon Turpin's return to England via Harwich from Holland, and clearly, as Bayes stated, Elizabeth Turpin was acting on Turpin's *written* instructions; but with regard to when and where they would meet he can only have told her to be at a rendezvous which she would understand to be Puckeridge on a certain date. But by some means, probably by the interception, accidental or otherwise, of a letter from Holland at the distributing post office for Clay Hill near Enfield, the authorities learned of the arrangements and rerouted the letter. It would then have been a simple matter to follow Elizabeth and her companions to the rendezvous, but the man with such a peculiar instinct for survival again eluded them, even when drawn into an ambush.

Turpin, even had he anticipated his letter being intercepted and been on his guard must have been demoralised by this turn of events, and it was almost two months before he was again heard of anywhere in the Home Counties. There is some evidence which suggests that some part or all of the weeks following the Puckeridge catastrophe were spent in the county of Leicestershire, but for the moment, there is still the matter of the *Rotterdam* letter to be dealt with.

The Puckeridge fracas occurred three days (or more) after the supposed Turpin letter from Rotterdam was received at Southwark. It would have been a really incredible coincidence if for the first time in over a year positive evidence of Turpin's being in England had come to hand such a short time after the letter he posted in Holland was intercepted in Southwark, and another coincidence lies in the fact that an authentic Turpin letter leading the authorities to the Puckeridge rendezvous *was* intercepted with results comparable to those described in the Southwark letter.

It is so odd that two Turpin letters should arrive in this country, apparently simultaneously, and for the one not reported to be genuine and the one reported to be of doubtful authenticity, that one wonders if they could, despite their dissimilarity, be the same. Rumour of the authentic rendezvous letter could have come to the newspapers, who then fabricated their own version for publication. This is perhaps borne out by the incredible gullibility of Turpin's companions and the suggestion that he signed the letter with his own name, neither of which circumstances can have had much basis in fact. Turpin, even in writing to his wife, would (as he did later) have used an alias, but a letter sent under an assumed name to an address in Southwark would have meant little to anyone, whether it came from Holland or Hull. If the theory of a fabricated letter is not accepted then there is no other likely explanation possible within the context of the argument for Turpin being in Holland, and this in the final Puckeridge analysis appears now to be stronger than ever. It would otherwise, as stated, have been a really remarkable coincidence.

II

Turpin disappeared after the Puckeridge escape and was not heard of again until the end of March 1737, but it appears that he joined forces with two other highwaymen, Matthew King and Stephen Potter, and that they were for some time in Leicestershire. It is not known how Turpin came to meet Potter, unless he was an associate of King's, but there is a possibility that Turpin was already acquainted with King.

Nearly all the evidence of the relationship of these three men comes from documentary sources relating to events which occurred immediately after the owner of a racehorse called Whitestockings was robbed on 30 April. Turpin and Matthew King and others were involved in an ambush at Whitechapel during which King was shot and taken prisoner. Potter was taken a few days later and so too was a woman by name Elizabeth King. From the circumstances of her arrest there is no doubt that she was an associate if not a close relative of Matthew King's, which fact recalls the other Elizabeth King, previously mentioned.

In December 1734, Elizabeth King, aged 21, was servant to Ambrose Skinner, when his house was robbed by the Gregory Gang. Turpin was also present on that occasion. Miss King subsequently gave evidence at the trial of Haines, but there is some doubt that she would have been able to have contributed much towards his conviction since throughout the robbery she was locked in an upper room of the house. The most significant aspect of that robbery is that although there might have been three able bodied men in the house at any time during the evening, the gang attacked when the door was unlatched and the only persons at home were the 73-year old farmer and his maid. The evidence is purely circumstantial, but there is some reason to believe that the gang were informed of the movements of every member of the household by someone who lived there. It could have been Elizabeth King and although the point cannot be proved it is strange that Turpin should meet both of the women known by that name.

In May 1737 Matthew King was 25, the Elizabeth King servant to Skinner would by then have been 23 or 24, and could have been his sister. The closer relationship of wife is more likely to have been mentioned in the evidence in which her name appears, if indeed there was a relationship with Matthew King and the two women were one and the same. It is a nice point, and inconclusive, but on it hinges Turpin's knowledge of Matthew King before 10 February 1737. The only factor which lends support to this argument is that Turpin, having just returned from a year or more in Holland, would have hesitated about striking up new friendships and is much more likely to have

The Gregory Gang

looked to those he knew to be reliable. There cannot have been that many from pre-December 1735 days, and it is therefore reasonable that the brother of a girl who assisted the gang in one of its robberies might be one of them.

The Leicestershire evidence was given by Matthew King, who having been mortally wounded in the Whitechapel ambush was perhaps susceptible to the idea that Turpin had deserted him. 'Stephen Potter committed on the oath of Matthew King for being concerned with him and Richard Turpin in several robberies in the counties of Leicester and Essex.' The Essex robberies occurred in April, so if the three were in Leicestershire it can only have been in February and/or March 1737, and since Matthew King was dying when he made his statement there would have been no point to his saying they were there if it was not a fact. There are several curious Turpin traditions which are associated with Leicester and have survived until recent times, but these are either connected with ancient hostelries or else are so absurd as to preclude comment. Of greater interest is an item used by Thomas Seccombe.

> Thus in *A Collection of Diverting Songs* (1817), to the burden of "When a robbing he doth go, doth go," we find a true ballad with the following commencement:
>
>> Of all the famous robbers,
>>   That doth in England dwell;
>> The noted Richard Turpin,
>>   Doth all the rest excel.
>>
>> He is a butcher of his trade,
>>   And lived in Stanford town;
>> And did eight men near Leicester rob,
>>   As it is full well known.
>
> That Richard had attained a certain bubble reputation from the ballad's mouth is perhaps true, but this claim to a pre-eminence among robbers cannot in any way be substantiated. His fame was in fact restricted to the crime loving classes, nor could it well have been otherwise, for apart from the ride-to-York episode, (which was not as yet connected with his name) there was nothing to give distinction to his story or differentiate it from that of the ruck of highwaymen.[6]

There are few criminals who in their lifetime can have been so notorious for such a span of years (1735–1739), and Seccombe may now be seen to have been wrong, not only in his estimation of Turpin's reputation, but about other things as well.

The ballad, two verses of which appear above, was originally written before the end of 1737 and possibly in the summer of that year; it differs only in the refrain and may be seen to have been directly inspired by events of that particular year. To that extent, since there do not appear to have been any newspaper reports of Turpin having been in Leicestershire, the reference to the county town must be a reflection of some local London rumour inspired by Matthew King's confession. Thus the 1817 ballad may be seen to be not a later fiction, but perpetuation of a contemporary fiction based on contemporary fact.

The Stanford where it is alleged the eight men were robbed may have been intended to represent that Stanford on the border of Leicestershire and Northamptonshire, but the story, being nothing more than that, cannot be regarded as corroboration of a Turpin visit to Leicester. He was there, for some weeks perhaps, in company with Matthew King and Stephen Potter, and he may well have been there still when the Assize for Hertford began at the end of February.

III

The Gaol Delivery for Hertford was held on 28 February 1737, and the fate of the three persons committed on 10 February was decided at that time. The two women were a little more fortunate than their male companion.

> **Hertford Gaol Delivery** 28th February 10 Geo.II
> Elizabeth Turpin [and] Hannah Elcome are delivered by proclamation and must be discharged paying their fees. Robert Nott charged upon suspicion of robbery on the highway must remain in gaol until he shall find sufficient sureties before Thomas Rolt Esq. one of his Majesty's Justices of the Peace for [Hertford] for his personal appearance at the next assizes.[7]

There was clearly no case against the women, and since Nott was released at the next Assize there cannot have been much of one against him; in fact if he had been able to find bail he would have been released with the women, a somewhat unusual course if the authorities had any good reason to believe he had been actively involved with Turpin. Obviously they didn't, but there must have been some slight doubt left for it to be necessary for him to appear at the next Assize; unless in the interim they thought they would capture Turpin and thereby implicate Nott or *vice-versa*. The offer of bail might appear generous, but we do not know at what figure it was set, and there is the possibility that it was deliberately prohibitive. We cannot know for certain the reasons why Nott was held until July, but if the authorities wished to hold him despite the lack of evidence, then the legal gesture of allowing bail would to some extent have solved their problem, because the onus would then have been on Nott to find the money if he wanted to leave. But from other evidence it would appear clear that the reluctance to release Nott *was* connected with the hope that Turpin would be captured by July.

> **Essex.** *to the Sheriff of Essex* greeting. We command you that you omit not for any liberty in your Bailywick but that you take *Thomas Rowden late of Dagenham labourer Richard Turpin late of Barking labourer Thomas Rowden late of the same ...* if they shall be found in your Bailywick and then safely keep so that you have their bodies before our Justices appointed to deliver our Gaol of [Essex] at the next Session of Gaol Delivery to be held for [Essex] to answer to us concerning certain felonies whereof they stand indicted and have you then there this Writ Witness Sir William Thompson Knight at Chelmsford the second day of March [1737].[8]

Although initially served in March, the writ was returned into court at the Summer Assize. It was a common form of order from the Clerk of Assize (in this case Michell) to the Sheriff, found on most files where wanted persons were still at large, but it is significant, their names not having appeared on previous writs, that Turpin and Rowden should appear on this one. Clearly there would have been no point in giving the Sheriff of Essex such orders in 1735, when, after it was known that Turpin and Rowden had taken part in the Essex robberies, they spent most of their time in Kent or Surrey; and in 1736 Turpin was in Holland, whilst for the second half of that year Rowden was in Gloucester Gaol. This last fact was still unknown to the authorities, but following the Puckeridge incident they did not waste much opportunity in reminding the Sheriff of Turpin's part in the Skinner robbery and Rowden's part in that *and* the Mason robbery, upon which indictments their names still stood. Rowden was not at Puckeridge, which confirms that the opinion that he and Turpin were in Holland *was* held in general favour until Turpin returned on 10 February. But in Gloucester at the Gaol Delivery for the Lent Assizes, it was remarked of Daniel Crispe that he was, 'To remain according to his sentence.'[9]

IV

Turpin was not heard of again until the end of March and one assumes that for part of that time he was with Matthew King and Stephen Potter in Leicestershire. On 29 March however, it was suggested that he was on his own. 'On Tuesday morning about two o'clock several higglers were robbed between Enfield Wash and Waltham Cross by Turpin the noted highwayman who was seen to count the money at the turnpike, amounting to 4 1. with which he rode clean off.'[10]

For Turpin to act on his own was unusual. He had not done so before, and such was the personal risk involved in individual exploits there is some doubt that he would have at this time. Once Matthew King and Potter had been captured, his circumstances became such that for a time he had no real alternative to robbing on his own, but until they were captured there is every reason to believe that he acted in concert with one or both of them. This is borne out by subsequent reports, dated between mid-April and the end of that month, which all bear testimony to the fact that Turpin was riding with at least one companion. The next report however is much more credible, and indicates that two if not all three of the Leicester company had returned home. 'Last week the Hon. Mr. George Shirley was robbed on Epping Forest by Turpin and his companion, of 6 guineas, as he was returning from Newmarket; and its thought we shall hear more of their robberies of gentlemen going to the second meeting of Newmarket.'[11]

In all the robberies reported during the next week or so Turpin is never described as having more than one companion, whereas Matthew King's testimony states that in Essex as well as Leicester, the three of them acted together. That the newspapers were no more reliable in getting their facts right at this time than they had been during the period of the Gregory gang's activities, is illustrated at the end of April when Turpin is credited with having committed a robbery single handed when he, King and Potter are *known* to have taken part. The 'Last Week' is taken to mean that which ended on Saturday, 16 April, on which particular day, the highwaymen were out in the forest again.

> On Saturday last as a Gentleman of Wittam [in other versions rendered correctly as West Ham], and others in a coach, were going to Epping to dinner on the forest, the famous Turpin and a new companion of his, came up and attacked the coach, in order to rob it; the Gent had a carbine in the coach loaded with slugs, and seeing them coming, got it ready, and presented it at Turpin on stopping the coach, but it flashed in the pan; upon which says Turpin G... D.... *you, you have missed me, but I wont you,* and shot into the coach at him, but the ball missed him, passing between him and a lady in the coach; and they then rode off towards Ongar, and dined afterwards that day at Hare Street, and robbed in the evening several passengers of the forest between Loughton and Rumford, who knew him; he has not robbed on that road for some time before.[12]

This report appeared in the edition of the *London Evening Post* which came out before the one from which the previous report was taken, and therefore the reference to the 'new companion' is quite valid. Although the identity of the man who was seen was not known, we do know with hindsight that this was the first appreciation of Matthew King and/or Stephen Potter's association with Turpin, and in *Turpin's Confession,* a pamphlet which appeared after Turpin's execution, an incident was described which may have had its origin in the one above. '... some time after he returned to the forest again and attempted to rob Captain Thompson and his lady in an open chaise but the Captain firing a carbine at him, which missed and fired a pistol after the Captain which went through the chaise between him and his lady without

The Gregory Gang

any further damage, than tearing the left sleeve of his coat, the Captain driving hard, and being just in sight of a town, Turpin thought it not proper to pursue him any further.'[13] In the *Confession* chronology this occurred post May 1737, but since there is no resemblance between Turpin's actual confession and the pamphlet version, it would be unrealistic to describe the latter as being anything more than a concoction of reports, like the one above, culled from newspapers published a year or so before.

The latter part of the report of events of 16 April names a number of places which form a triangle with points at Chipping Ongar, Loughton and Romford, all within or adjacent to the Forest as it was then defined. Of a number of Hare Streets in the home counties, the one referred to is identified as that which is near Romford. In the same area on 22 April, yet another victim suffered at their hands. 'On Friday last William Hucks, Esq., Member of Parliament for Wallingford, was attacked by Turpin and his companion on Epping Forest; in his coach and four horses; they took about eleven guineas from Mr. Hucks.'[14]

But the next two reports not only suggest that Turpin and his companion/s have moved somewhere else, their chronology is somewhat confusing when compared with the above.

> 1. The famous Turpin who rides in an open gold lace hat, and his companion (who sometimes passes for his man) in a plain gold lace hat, were last week [16–23 April] at Bedford, and have since [same week] been seen at Market Street and Colney; and last Saturday [23 April] they lay at a house near Whetstone, where Turpin left his dun horse, and took away next morning [24 April] a gray mare of the landlord's in his room, and went off; and its supposed have changed their road to rob.[15]

> 2. Thursday last [28 April] Turpin the highwayman was seen at Cunnington, a village not far from St. Ives, waiting, as is supposed, for some booty from the graziers or butchers on the road to that market, but missing his aim, he came towards London.[16]

Matthew King stated that he, Turpin and Potter were concerned with robberies in Essex and Leicester, but if the Bedford, Markyate Street, Colney, Whetstone and Conington sightings were reliable, then Turpin (either on his own or with others) was also in Bedfordshire, Hertfordshire, Middlesex and Huntingdonshire, and did from 16 to 30 April travel nearly two hundred miles without doing much more mischief than exchange his mount.

On 16 and 22 April, Turpin was with one or two companions in Epping Forest, and on 30 April, he, Matthew King and Stephen Potter were definitely at Leytonstone, on the edge of the forest. It is not necessary to offer complicated explanations involving time, distance and problematical overlapping journeys merely to reach a conclusion that although Turpin, moved by some motiveless, aimless impulse could have passed through all those places, he could more reasonably have been in Epping Forest throughout all that period. Turpin was back in England, Turpin was news, and as a result Turpin was everywhere.

FOOTNOTES

1. *Political State*, Vol.LIII, January to June 1737, p.255.
2. *Daily Post*, 12 February 1737, and *London Evening Post* of same date.
3. P.R.O./Assizes 35/177/3, Hertford Felony File, Winter 10, Geo.II.
4. *Life of Richard Turpin*, p.15.
5. *Immortal Turpin*, p.48.
6. *Essex Review*, No.42, April 1902 Vol.XI, pp.67–69.
7. P.R.O./Assizes 35/177/3, Hertford Felony File, Winter 10, Geo.II 1736/7.
8. P.R.O./Assizes 35/177/2, Essex Felony File, Summer 11, Geo.II 1737.
9. P.R.O./Assizes 2/11 Gaol Book.
10. *Reid's Weekly Journal*, 2 April 1737.
11. *London Evening Post*, 21 to 23 April 1737.
12. *Ibid.*, 19 to 21 April 1737.
13. *Turpin's Confession.*
14. *London Evening Post*, 23 to 26 April 1737.
15. *Ibid.*, 28 to 30 April 1737.
16. *Political State*, Vol.LIII, 1737 January to June, p.552; the date from *London Evening Post*, 30 April to 3 May 1737.

CHAPTER SIX

I

ON 29 April 1737, Turpin, depending on the source of information, stole a horse either from Hare Street near Romford, or from Plaistow Marshes; but from descriptions of events of the following few days it is clear that the horse was stolen by Matthew King. It was described as 'an indifferent horse from Hare Street,'[1] or alternatively, 'the horse from Plaistow Marshes; and the saddle from one Arrowsmith.'[2]

Bayes stated that immediately before a robbery committed on the following day, the Plaistow horse began to tire, but although the figure of Bayes looms large in this chapter, he does not enable us to decide which was the horse Matthew King took in exchange for his own on 29 April. Neither horse appears to have been in very good condition, and compared with the one met with the next evening, even the average beast would have hung its head in humility. One inclines, since Bayes was writing two years after the event, to accept the indifferent horse from Hare Street as the one stolen by Matthew King, after which, on 30 April, he rejoined forces with Richard Turpin and Stephen Potter, and towards the evening of that day rode with them in the direction of the *Green Man* inn at Leytonstone. Richard Bayes was the landlord. From another direction Joseph Major, owner of the racehorse Whitestockings, was also approaching the inn, and although in various reports of the incident his ownership of the horse is the only relationship mentioned, it is certain that he was actually riding, possibly exercising it, when he was suddenly confronted by one of the highwaymen. Being so close to the *Green Man,* the attack was unexpected and he was taken completely by surprise.

The newspapers relate that the robbery which ensued was committed by Turpin, without any other assistance; but in subsequent reports of a connected incident, retrospective references to the robbery made it clear that others were involved. Bayes was in no doubt that it was the three named above, a fact corroborated elsewhere, but about what happened afterwards he appears to have been as confused as everybody else.

It is unlikely that the three men were together when Mr. Major was robbed, for Turpin would not otherwise have been credited with a single handed robbery; there is also some suggestion that Mr. Major was unable to identify Potter when the latter was taken. It was either Matthew King on his own or with Turpin that stopped Mr. Major some forty yards from the inn, or as Bayes put it, 'and although they were so near the houses, ventured to rob him'. They took from him, 'a mare, a knife, a horse whip and seven or eight pounds in gold and silver.'[3] Matthew King in fact exchanged his own horse for Whitestockings, and his saddle as well, and afterwards rode with Turpin and Potter back to Whitechapel. Mr. Major however was disturbed at his loss and went to the *Green Man* to complain:

Mr. Major got to the *Green Man*, and acquainted Mr. Bayes of it, who immediately said, "I dare swear it is Turpin has done it, or one of that crew, and I'll endeavour to get intelligence of your horse; this that they have left you is stolen, and I would have you advertise it." This was accordingly done, and the horse proved to have been stolen from Plaistow Marshes; and the saddle which he had kept, was stolen from one Arrowsmith.

This anyway was Bayes' recollection of the conversation when he put it in writing in 1739; but what happened to the three highwaymen, when they returned to Whitechapel that night, and afterwards? We know that Matthew King gave the authorities information about their activities, and one of the reports which appeared after he had done so contains elements which are corroborated elsewhere 'This King had made several discoveries, particularly that he, Turpin and Stephen Potter robbed Mr. Major of seven guineas and his mare, which mare he put up at the *Red Lyon* at Whitechapel ... that Turpin's horse then stood in Old Gravel Lane ...'[4]

Since Jasper and Samuel Gregory had previously lived in Old Gravel Lane, Turpin was certainly familiar with that address and there might still in 1737 have been sympathetic friends or relatives of the Gregory brothers who lived there and would have been prepared to put up Turpin's horse in a back-yard. It is suggested that Turpin lodged at Well Close Square, somewhat nearer the centre of Whitechapel and not far from Red Lion Street. He was there the night Matthew King was captured, and since this information appears to have emanated from the wounded highwayman, it is reasonable to suppose that Turpin *was* staying there on Saturday 30 April.

Matthew King did leave Whitestockings at the *Red Lion*, and Potter probably left his horse there as well. '... a bay gelding starr and snipp [white mark on forehead and nose] with saddle spots curled tail, and a sorrel mare bald face with saddle spots curled tail and her two hinder feet white which were out to grass in the name of Matthew Plear ... are suspected to be stolen and belonging to a gang of highwaymen.'[5] The description, 'her two hinder feet white' is distinctive enough to identify the horse as Whitestockings, Matthew Plear can hardly be other than Matthew King's alias, and the gang of highwaymen Turpin, Potter and Matthew King.

Where Matthew King lived is not known, but Potter probably went to an address in Farmer Street, which like part of Well Close Square was also in the parish of St. George Middlesex and therefore not far from where the horses had been left.

On Sunday 1 May there was no sign of the highwaymen, but the industrious Bayes had either been making his own enquiries about Whitestockings or else offered payment for information of the horse's whereabouts, for by late Sunday night he appears to have known where it was. One newspaper however was still living in the past, and in a report which located Turpin at Conington on 28 April and the *Green Man* on 30 April, rounded off the item with an echo from 1735. 'It's Rowden (the pewterer that was) which robs with Turpin, who was also concerned with Gregory and that gang; and they the only two remaining of the Essex gang, except Wheeler the Evidence, who being pardoned works honestly, and they two were seen yesterday on Finchley Common, riding towards London.'[6]

Rowden was secure in Gloucester gaol and content to remain so, but since the time had not come for Matthew King to give the names of his associates, no-one was in a position to dispute the naming of Rowden as Turpin's companion. Neither Turpin nor Potter nor Matthew King were anywhere near Finchley Common on Monday 2 May 1737, for it was on that day that they tried to retrieve the horses from the *Red Lion*.

When and where and by whom the attempt was made has been a matter of some speculation ever since it happened, for being dark at the time, the newspaper reports were conflicting and a clear picture has never been obtained. The confusion was aggravated by Bayes' own melodramatic version of the incident rendered two years later.

This robbery was committed on Saturday night, and on Monday following, Mr. Bayes received intelligence, that such a horse as Mr. Major had lost, was left at the *Red Lion* Inn at Whitechapel; he accordingly went thither, and found it to be the same; and then resolved to wait till somebody came to fetch it; nobody came at the time it was left for; but about eleven o'clock at night, King's brother (as it afterwards proved) came for the horse, upon which they seized him immediately, and taking him into the house, he said, he bought it, and could produce proof of it. But Mr. Bayes looking on the whip in his hand, found the button half broke off, and the name *Major* upon it, seemed a confirmation of the thing; they charged a constable with him; but he seeming frightened, and they declaring, that they did not believe but that the horse was for somebody else, and if he would tell them where they waited, he should be released; he told them, there was a lusty man in a white duffle coat waiting for it in Red Lion Street. Mr. Bayes immediately went out, and finding him as directed, perceived that it was King, and coming round upon him, attacked him; King immediately drew a pistol, which he clapped to Mr. Bayes' breast; but it luckily flashed in the pan; upon which King struggling to get out his other, it had twisted round his pocket and he could not. Turpin, who was waiting not far off on horseback, hearing a skirmish, came up, when King cried out, "Dick, shoot him, or we are taken by G.d," at which instant Turpin fired his pistol, and it missed Mr. Bayes, and shot King in two places, who cried out, "Dick, you have killed me," which Turpin hearing, he rode away as hard as he could. King fell at the shot, though he lived a week after and gave Turpin the character of a coward; telling Mr. Bayes that if he had a mind to take him, he knew that he might then be found at a noted house by Hackney Marsh and that when he rode away, he had three brace of pistols about him, and a carbine slung. Upon enquiry, it has been found, that Turpin did actually go directly to the house which King mentioned, and made use of something like the following expressions to the man; "..... What shall I do? Where shall I go; d..n that Dick Bayes, I'll be the death of him; for I have lost the best fellow-man I ever had in my life; I shot poor King in endeavouring to kill that dog." The same resolution of revenge he retained to the last, though without means of effecting it.[7]

Bayes never did identify Matthew King, either because he didn't know his Christian name or because by the time he wrote about him he had forgotten, and similarly Matthew King's brother was not identified. The newspapers however, without exception, all referred to him as Robert King, and nearly all of them described the incident as having occurred about four o'clock or just before dawn on Tuesday 3 May. This is perhaps consistent with events occurring after Bayes' eleven o'clock on Monday 2 May, but in this instance, more than in any other, it is wiser not to rely too much on what the papers (or Bayes) said. The reconstruction (below) of what probably did occur is based for the most part on information drawn from other sources.

II

It must have been obvious to the three highwaymen that the horse they had stolen on Saturday night was no ordinary horse, and the caution employed when they came to retrieve it was brought about either because they suspected an attempt might have been made to trace it, or because one of them had heard enquiries were being made about it and they were not sure if it had been traced or not. It had been traced, to the *Red Lion* in Red Lion Street, Whitechapel, Richard Holdworth, Prop. Richard Bayes was there, probably because he had initiated enquiries in the Whitechapel area with which Turpin was known to be familiar, and been told of the discovery.

Word was also sent to Mr. Major, residing near St. Sepulcher's, who no doubt came as quickly as he could to identify the horse. The time was probably late on Sunday evening. Two other people who may have been present then or during the next few hours were John Sherman of St. Mary's, Whitechapel, a sadler; and Robert Savages of Red Lion Street.

Joseph Major had no difficulty in identifying his horse, but the question was what to do next. It was late at night and since the ostler had expected Whitestockings and another horse to be collected earlier in the evening, they could only hope that the highwaymen, whoever they were, would need the horses before long. The ostler was instructed to inform the party if anyone came, and the company settled to their vigil.

Not far away, Potter had left Farmer Street and Turpin had gone from Well Close Square, both making their way on foot to Matthew King's address somewhere in Whitechapel. Also present were Matthew's brother John, and Elizabeth King, who was possibly their sister. They discussed what to do about the horses, about which, it had been heard, enquiries were being made. It was decided that the safest course would be to go to the *Red Lion* at a time when they would be least expected, in the small hours of the morning, not long before dawn; and as an extra precaution John would go to the stable and say he had been sent. John King, a younger and less experienced member of the King family, was reluctant, but was eventually persuaded that it was quite safe and that he had nothing to fear, particularly since his brother would be just around the corner with Potter and Turpin if anything went wrong. Turpin agreed to this arrangement only because they depended on their mounts and they would be exposed to even greater risk if they tried to steal other mounts when they were themselves on foot. A little apprehensively he walked to Old Gravel Lane and returned to Matthew King's lodgings on his own horse; then not long before sun up he, on his horse, and Potter and the two King brothers on foot, made their way towards the *Red Lion.*

For safety, Turpin and Potter remained a short distance from Red Lion Street, in Gloucester Street in Goodman's Fields, whilst Matthew King went with John King as far as Red Lion Street itself and waited there a few yards from the inn whilst John went through into the stables to enquire about the horses. It was very dark, with but a few lights burning and most of these coming from the *Red Lion*. John King disappeared into the shadows and eventually found the ostler who said he could have the horses if he liked to wait whilst he went and got the key. When he came back he was accompanied by a number of grim faced men who took John King into the inn, one of them with a hand over his mouth to prevent him from crying out. They were red faced, serious and menacing, and there was a constable with them. When he told them the horses were his one of them snatched the whip Matthew had handed to him and shewed him the name *Major* on the butt. They said then that he had stolen Mr. Major's horse if not the other and that he should be given into the custody of the constable and charged. John felt sick then, and the man who owned the horse they called Whitestockings said he was but a lad and that he thought that someone else had sent him and that if he told them where the other man might be found he should be released. So he admitted there was a man and then was silent when they asked if he was waiting outside in the street. Whereupon one of the men grasped his arm tightly whilst the others produced pistols and sticks and went quietly out of the side door.

It was perhaps unfortunate for Matthew King that he was the only man in sight and since it was dark it didn't matter much if his appearance tallied with the description given by his brother John. He only had time to pull out a pistol and fire off a warning shot before they were almost upon him. There seemed to be three or four, one with a lantern by the light of which he could see pistols glinting; there was no time to run, and as he struggled to get the other pistol from his pocket the hammer caught in the lining. There were shouts and the sound of horses hooves not far off and the lantern light leaping and the faces of men in the darkness, and then as he brought the pistol free an urgent shout of warning and a loud blast very near and a great blow which exploded in his chest and smashed him reeling against the wall of a house off which he bounced on to the cobbles to roll into the filthy runnel. There was no breath in his body and he lay flat on his back with his arms outstretched, eyes wide and flickering stupidly in the lantern's light, not seeing the faces above him, and when he breathed there was a sound he did not recognise and a wetness at his mouth and an exclamation from one of the faces, and somewhere a very long way away but very close to his ear the uncertain drumming of a horse's hooves as its rider reined it in. There were more shouts then and the light swivelled away from him and a name was called and footsteps ran, but the hooves outpaced them all before he knew the terrible pain in his chest and he became unconscious.

They carried him into the *Red Lion* where a boy saw him and wept and a constable conferred with his bearers before going out with the lantern. And not far away as windows opened and heads searched for the lost sounds of the disturbance, a man on a horse bent down from his saddle and spoke to a man waiting. They went their separate ways, Potter on foot back to Farmer Street, and Turpin on horseback back to Old Gravel Lane before returning to Well Close Square. By first light there was no sign of what had happened outside the *Red Lion*. It was now the morning of Monday 2 May 1737, and those who had been involved in the incident in Red Lion Street were assembled before the magistrate Richard Ricards to provide him with the details of what had occurred.

III

To give some better idea of the general confusion surrounding this famous incident, two newspaper reports, obviously originating from the same pen, are compared below.

> 1. On Tuesday morning two highwaymen were taken in the following manner. One of them named Matthew King, left on Saturday night last at the *Red Lion* Inn in Whitechapel a bay mare, that they had exchanged with a gentleman on Saturday last on Epping Forest after they had robbed him. The gentleman going into the inn, saw the ostler watering the said mare and enquired who had left her and being informed the persons would call the same morning, they waited their coming and about four o'clock Matthew King came for the mare and being stopped confessed that his brother Robert King was in Gloucester Street in Goodman's Fields on foot with Turpin on horseback, where being taken, Turpin fired, shot King in his left breast and rode off. The two brothers were carried before Justice Ricketts, Robert was committed to the New Prison and Matthew to Bridewell. There were found upon Robert King a brace of pistols and a bag of bullets.[8]
> 2. On Tuesday, May 3rd early in the morning two highwaymen were taken in the following manner; one of them, named Matthew King, left on *Sunday* night before at the *Red Lion* Inn in Whitechapel, a bay mare, ... Matthew King came for the mare, and being stopped confessed that his brother, Robert King, was in Gloucester, Street in Goodman's Fields on foot, with Turpin on horseback, where King being taken, *one Bayes fired,* shot King in his left breast and rode off ...

The latter report did not appear until June, but the marked difference in specific details was the result of fairly common practice in editing original material, and between the two editions there were other newspapers which had already corrected the impression that Turpin had shot King. The point being that although Bayes claimed Turpin shot Matthew King, the newspapers which had initially supported the story subsequently retracted and laid the responsibility on Bayes.

We return to Justice Ricards on the morning of 2 May, and what was recorded in his presence is almost as good as an eyewitness account insofar as it establishes who was taken and when.

> **Middlesex** Be it remembered that the 2nd day of May in the year of our Lord 1737 Joseph Major of St. Sepulcers in the county of London gent. Richard Bayes of Low Layton in the county of Essex Innholder John Sherman of St. Mary's Whitechapel in the county of Middlesex Sadler Richard Holdworth of Red Lion Street in the county of Middlesex Innholder and Robert Savages of the same aforesaid and c. came before me one of his Majesty's Justices of the Peace for the said county of Middlesex and acknowledged themselves to be indebted to our Sovereign Lord the King (that is to say) the said Joseph Major in the sum of £40 and [the others above named] in the sum of £20 each of good and lawful money of Great Britain if default shall be made in the conditions underwritten.
>
> The condition of this recognisance is such that if [they] do personally appear at the next General Sessions of the peace to be held for the said county and then and there prosecute the Law with effect and give their evidence on his Majesty's behalf upon a Bill of Indictment to be examined to the Grand Jury against Matthew King and John King for being concerned with two other persons not yet taken in stopping one Joseph Major on the King's Highway and feloniously taking from him a mare a knife a horse whip and seven or eight pounds in gold and silver the property of the said Joseph Major and in case the Bill be found and returned by the Grand Jury to be a True Bill then if you the said ... do appear at the now next Session of Gaol Delivery at Newgate to be held for the said county and then and there prosecute and give evidence against the said Matthew King and John King upon the said Indictment then the recognisance to be void or else to remain in full force. Taken and acknowledged the day and year above written before me Richard Ricards.[10]

The recognisance was annotated, 'Oct 10th 1737 respited by the Court until &c.' because no proceedings were taken against the persons named. This document, and the one which follows, establish the date on which the *Red Lion* incident occurred, because the evidence was heard during the daytime on Monday 2 May, and Matthew King was similarly committed on that day. '30 Mathew King committed [New Prison] 2nd May by Richard Ricards Esq on oath of Joseph Major for being concerned with two other persons not yet taken in stopping him on the King's highway on Saturday night last ... further examination'[11] The right hand margin of this entry records that the prisoner was, at a later date 'dead', but it is clear that on 2 May, before the 'further examination', his companions were not known by name on 2 May. However, the Robert of the newspapers was in fact Matthew whereas the Matthew was John, but what did happen to John King? He was not committed, that much is certain, but he was for some time helping the authorities with their enquiries: *'House of Correction* [Bridewell] John King referred to Mr. Ricards'[12] There is no further trace of him in the Middlesex Sessions records. He was neither committed nor proceeded against, and lacking evidence to the contrary it must be presumed that there was no reason to hold him and that he was released. But with regard to the recognisance which named him, we do know a little more about two of the people who entered into sureties of £20. These are Richard Holdworth and Richard Bayes.

The first named has by implication been identified as the landlord of the *Red Lion,* and the following entry in the *Wine Licences Revenue* records for 1737 to 1738 proves the point. 'St. Mary W^{t}Chappell, Richard Holdsworth'[13] These records only list landlords licenced to sell wine, and although neither Turpin, nor his grandfather Nott, nor even Richard Bayes appear to have sold wine, their absence from this record does not cancel out any suggestion that they sold other forms of refreshment. Bayes however, whatever it was he sold, may not have done it so well as others of the same trade. 'Richard Bayes late of Layton Stone in the parish of Low Layton in the county of Essex Victualler & Chapman ... Certificate of Conformity allowed.'[14]

This issue of a certificate meant that Bayes had conformed himself to the several statutes made concerning bankrupts. The previous entry related to an 'Innholder, Victualler and Chapman', so from Victualler and Chapman when the Gregory gang roamed Epping, to Innholder when Turpin rode with Matthew King was a not unreasonable progression. We do not know how Bayes' financial affairs stood in May 1737, but he did try very hard to obtain a share in the outstanding rewards for Turpin, and in whatever Blood Money might have been forthcoming from the capture and conviction of any of the three highwaymen. As it transpired, he was cheated by fate of anything he might have gained from the Whitestockings affair, and thereafter had to wait until Turpin's death before he was able to capitalise on his personal interest in that elusive adversary.

Why then did Bayes deny having shot Matthew King? There are two reasons for this, one that if King was told he had been shot by Turpin and abandoned it would have confirmed his suspicion that Turpin and Potter had left him in the lurch and made him more ready to give them away, which he did. From the very seriousness of the wound he received, Matthew King must have known he was unlikely to survive and stand trial, so giving information about Potter and Turpin was hardly necessary unless he was convinced of what in the circumstances appeared to be their disloyalty. Turpin, being the only man on horseback, could probably have created great confusion in the ranks of the ambushers if he had galloped through them, and it is the ease with which Matthew King was taken which suggests that his plight was apparent when (and if) Turpin arrived on the scene. Potter on foot could have contributed little, and it is an indication of his absence from Red Lion Street itself that he wasn't taken with Matthew King.

Bayes was anxious that no-one should escape their trap, and when Matthew King was observed to be armed it would have been a foolish man who took the chance of the pistol misfiring, as Bayes claimed he did, or waited for the intervention of a shot by Turpin to prevent King pulling out another pistol. Bayes shot King, when King either fired or misfired or was trying to fire; Turpin did what came naturally to him in times of crisis, he fled. By blaming Turpin, Bayes not only finally convinced Matthew King of Turpin's treachery, he also indemnified himself again reprisal from friends or relatives of King. Reprisal from Turpin was of less concern because in a few days Turpin became the most wanted man in England and it could not be anticipated that he would remain at large much longer. There are several instances of the newspapers and Bayes favouring the idea of Turpin being revenged on Bayes and Wheeler, and it may be that the newspapers and Bayes influenced each other in this respect even if there was no active participation in giving the idea publicity. In any event, having shot Matthew King, Bayes appears to have been torn between his desire for glory and the need to hide, and depending upon from which direction he was threatened most was his version of the Whitechapel shooting at any given time.

IV

Matthew King had confessed his involvement with Potter and Turpin by 4 May, and also given other useful information. Since the authorities were unable to name his associates on Monday 2 May, but had acted on his information by the Wednesday, it would seem that he had sufficiently recovered by Tuesday to tell them what they wished to know.

> Matthew King the highwayman, now in New Prison, who was shot by Bayes at the *Green Man* on his making resistance when apprehended near Whitechapel, lies very ill, he was not shot by Turpin by accident, and mentioned in some papers, for Turpin rode off and left him when he was taken. This King has made several discoveries, particulary that he, Turpin and Stephen Potter, now in Newgate, robbed Mr. Major of seven guineas and his mare, which mare he put up at the *Red Lyon* at Whitechapel, and was the occasion of his being taken, that Turpin's horse then stood in Old Gravel Lane and he had discovered several of Turpin's haunts, so its thought he will soon be taken.[15]

Turpin was not soon taken, although he twice came perilously near to being captured during that same week. There is no doubt that the first escape was the result of Matthew King's information. Earlier on 3 May, Turpin was mentioned in what turned out to be a curiously prophetic context, for although the newspaper report which referred to Turpin concerned another man, the same circumstances attended Turpin almost two years later and at the same place. 'An account is come from York of the apprehending of Toby Goodall, and of his commitment to the Castle of York, to which place he was very numerously attended, and where great numbers of people flock daily to see him, he having been for some years a very notorious highwayman, and as terrible in those parts as Turpin has been in Essex.'[16]

That the newspapers during the first two weeks of May should have been confused over how and when the Whitechapel incident occurred is possibly due in part to their receiving information about Turpin's Tuesday night/ Wednesday morning escape and being obliged to bring the two episodes together in the same edition, e.g. the *London Evening Post* described the *Red Lion* fracas as having occurred on Tuesday morning about *four o'clock,* and then continued with the following. 'The same night late, information was given, that Turpin would lie that night at a house near Well Close Square, and yesterday morning three men beset the house very early, but being discovered by a woman, she called out to Turpin, who was in bed, and gave him warning of his danger, by which he found means to escape over the houses.'[17] From the date of this edition it is clear that Turpin escaped on the morning of Wednesday 4 May, although following on the previous item the first sentence implies that the information was given the same night on which the capture of Matthew King was made. Since *he* was taken not long before dawn (on Monday morning, not Tuesday) there could have been no point in Turpin going to bed, nor time for anyone to find him there the same night. The 'yesterday morning' reference in the edition of Thursday 5 May does however help to restore perspective to the chronology of these events.

Matthew King was captured on Monday morning, but was not fit to make a statement during that day. On Tuesday he was restored sufficiently to give his information. From New Prison the addresses of Turpin *and* Potter were sent to the appropriate officials who organised parties to go and search the premises concerned, *viz.* Turpin at Well Close Square and Potter at Farmer Street. The parties came to those addresses early on Wednesday morning, Stephen Potter was captured and Turpin escaped to make his way to Epping Forest via Old Gravel Lane where he was obliged to go to collect his horse.

Things were going very badly for Turpin; his friend Matthew King had been shot and captured and his Well Close Square hide-out discovered. By Wednesday evening, having taken refuge in the forest, he was in a very jittery

The Gregory Gang

state indeed. We do not know that he knew of Potter's capture earlier that day, but it is possible that having fled *his* lodgings he called on Potter's only to learn that he had been taken not long before. He was on his own once more, demoralised and desperate, and weary with being continually on the run. Stephen Potter however, without realising how fortunate he would be, was on his way to Newgate at about the same time Turpin was riding furiously for the cover of the forest. 'No. 3 Stephen Potter committed by Rd. Ricards Esq., on the oath of Mathew King for being concerned with him and Richard Turpin in several robberies in the counties [of Leicester and] Essex Date [4 May] To [be sent] to Essex and Leicester.'[18] The date in this document is corroborated in the next.

> **Middlesex** Be it remembered that the 4th Day of May 1737 Margaret the wife of John Grant in Farmer Street in the parish of St. George Middlesex came before me one of his Majesty's Justices of the Peace for [Middlesex] and acknowledged herself bound on pain of imprisonment if default shall be made in the conditions underwritten.
>
> The Condition of this Recognisance is such that if she the said Margaret do personally appear at the next General Sessions of the Peace for [Middlesex] and prosecute with effect and give her evidence on his Majesty's behalf upon a Bill of Indictment to be examined to the Grand Jury against Stephen Potter charged upon the information of Matthew King taken in writing on oath for being concerned with him the said Stephen Potter and Richard Turpin not yet taken for stopping one Joseph Major ...[19]

It is clear from this that by 4 May John King had been exonerated of any part in the robbery of the previous Saturday, but our main interest in this document is the appearance of Margaret Grant. Her evidence can have had little to do with what happened outside the *Green Man* or the *Red Lion*, and therefore about the only useful purpose she might serve would be to identify Potter. This she would probably have been required to do because Joseph Major could not. In the event the successful prosecution of Potter depended on Matthew King living to give evidence against him, and since he died and the authorities eventually were obliged to drop the charges against Potter, it can only be inferred that Major's evidence was unsupported by the vital identification of the man concerned. In which case Margaret Grant's independent identification, and Matthew King's posthumous evidence were of no use in the prosecuting of Potter. His imprisonment continued for some time but he did eventually go free, much to the chagrin of Richard Bayes who was thwarted by one man dying, one being released and one remaining at large, thus denying him any opportunity to claim a reward for his efforts to bring them to justice.

Margaret Grant's evidence was subordinate to Matthew King's and Joseph Major's, and without the former, it was of no use at all. Highwaymen being of nomadic habit a person living in the house where one lodged would have been able to identify the man and that would have been about all; but it would have established Potter's identity without there having been the need to disturb the ailing Matthew King, and from this point of view Mrs. Grant's testimony was important. Being Potter's landlady is about the only reasonable explanation of there being any connection between them in the first week of May 1737.

V

The night of 4/5 May 1737 was a turning point in Turpin's life, for by the morning he had added murder to his long list of crimes.

> On Wednesday night last a servant to Mr. Thompson one of the Keepers on Epping Forest (who lives at Fair Maid Bottom) saw the famous Turpin on the forest, and suspecting he was going to steal some particular horse in that neighbourhood, went to a house at King's Oak and borrowed a gun, and charged it, and said he would go and take Turpin, who was not far off, and accordingly went with the gun after him; but approaching him with his gun too near (apprehending, its supposed, he had only pistols) Turpin saw him, and immediately discharged a carbine at him loaded with slugs, and shot him into the belly dead on the spot, and he now lies at Forest Oak: Turpin rode away and quitted his horse, which was on Thursday night in the pound at Waltham Abbey. The same day all that part of the country was up in arms in pursuit of him, but its supposed he is gone northwards. If the laws were more severe on the harbourers of known highwaymen, this desperate fellow could not have escaped so long.
>
> We hear that a Royal Proclamation, with a reward of £200, will be issued for the apprehending and taking of Turpin, the famous robber and murderer.[20]

The servant's name was Thomas Morris, but in other accounts of the same incident, it would appear that he had a companion.

> On Thursday the fifth, a man belonging to Mr. Thompson, one of the Keepers of Epping Forest, having intelligence that Turpin lay hid in a certain place in the Forest, got a higgler to go with him to assist in the taking of that arch rogue, who they at last met with. Mr. Thompson's man seized him by the collar, and told him he was his prisoner; upon which Turpin pulled a pistol out of his pocket, and shot the man dead on the spot; the higgler, being very much surprised, ran away (though he had a gun in his hand) and acquainted several gentlemen that were coming by from hunting with what had happened, who made narrow search for him in that part of the forest, and in a thicket found a cavern, wherein was a bed of hay, part of a loaf, part of a bottle of wine, and three clean shirts, which is supposed to be one of his places of concealment, but could not find Turpin himself.[21]

Bayes, with eloquence and invention, had no need to mention ham, but he did anyway.

It was about that time Turpin shot Mr. Thomson's man in the following manner: the reward for apprehending him had set several on to attempt it; among the rest, this fellow would needs go in company with a higgler; Turpin was unarmed, standing alone; and, not knowing the man, took him for one poaching for hares, and told him, he would get no hares near that thicket; "No", says the fellow, "But I have got a Turpin," and presented his piece at him, commanding him to surrender; Turpin stood talking with him, and creeping up to his cave, laid hold of his carbine, and shot him dead, at which the higgler made off. This man's death obliged Turpin to make off precipitately; so he went farther into the country in search of King. [Here follows the Hertford butcher confrontation, the *Green Man* robbery and the Whitechapel incident]. After this he still kept about the forest, till he was harrassed almost to death; for he had lost his place of safety, the cave, which was discovered upon his shooting the keeper's man; and when they found his cave, there was in it two shirts in a bag, two pair of stockings, part of a bottle of wine, and some ham; so that being drove from thence, he skulked about the woods, and was once very near being taken, when Mr. Ives, the King's huntsman, took out two dry footed hounds to find him out; but he perceiving them coming, goes up in a tree, and seeing them go underneath him, was then so terrified at it, that he took a resolution of going away that instant for Yorkshire.[22]

We are again confronted with an incident about which there were many conflicting reports, and the only indisputable fact which did emerge from these was that Richard Turpin shot and killed Thomas Morris, a servant to Henry Thomson, one of the Keepers of Epping Forest. A proclamation named him as the murderer and offered a large reward for his capture, and since such promises were not made lightly, one assumes that the authorities went into the matter a little more deeply than the newspapers and established to their satisfaction that Turpin had in fact been responsible.

Fair Maid Bottom, now more modestly Fairmead Bottom, is some little way south of King's Oak at High Beech, but the chances of two men setting out to find Turpin in the forest without having any idea where he was is preposterous, particularly since he had only just arrived there and nobody can have anticipated his presence. So Morris's accidental sighting is probably true, and it was about dusk when Turpin was observed. The circumstances did not favour Morris's returning home to inform the Keeper and he chose instead to borrow a gun. The people from whom he borrowed it either did not believe that he had seen Turpin or else were not prepared to accompany him without other support, and a higgler, conveniently to hand, was recruited as an eyewitness to murder. Morris approached the cave with the higgler crouched nervously at his back, but as soon as they were exposed at the entrance to the cave Turpin fired and Morris fell with a shot in his stomach.

The higgler fled, and if, as seems indicated, the shooting occurred in the evening rather than at night, it is possible that he met with, 'several gentlemen that were coming by from hunting.' It is this version of what happened after the shooting which probably inspired Bayes to write about the hounds, and Turpin being obliged to hide up a tree, a story which has been perpetuated for over 200 years. We do not know that Turpin ever told anyone that he hid up a tree (how else might the story have been obtained?), but the story does serve to prompt the questions, what happened to his horse, and, if one was in the pound at Waltham Abbey, how was the owner identified?

In *The History of Clerkenwell*,[2,3] there appears a short account and an illustration of a portmanteau inscribed R.TVRPIN. The author infers that Turpin knew the place where it was found but does not commit himself further; but would the man who did not hesitate to rob other people of their property have bothered to mark his own, and then left it by accident or design for it to be found in the second half of the nineteenth century? It was coincidence that it should eventually turn up at an inn, but the reference points to the incredibility of Turpin riding a horse which bore some means of readily identifying him as its owner.

The existence of a pound at Waltham Abbey, quite close to where the shooting must have occurred, suggests that it was not unusual for stray horses to be found in that vicinity. If one was found loose that night or the following day, there probably wasn't one person in Waltham Abbey who did not associate it with the hunted highwayman, but does a man who was just committed murder immediately abandon his one means of eluding his pursuers? It is possible that either the horse went lame or the story of the higgler's meeting the hunting party was true, and the horse was deliberately abandoned to send those following in the wrong direction. In the latter case the horse would eventually have been stopped and the murder/higgler/murderer's horse chain of circumstantial evidence pointing to Turpin would have been complete.

Bayes would have us believe that after the Whitechapel incident Turpin said, 'What shall I do, where shall I go?' but if ever there was a moment when this wretchedly unglamourous character was reduced to proclaiming his desperation, it must surely have been after he had shot Thomas Morris. The newspaper was no doubt quite right in adducing his long survival to, 'Harbourers of known Highwaymen', but whereas there were still some people who might have been willing to hide Turpin the highwayman out of loyalty or for a price, there would not have been many left who would have done it for Turpin the murderer, especially as the *London Evening Post* intimated (with surprising accuracy so soon after the event) that a reward of £200 would be placed on his head. The publication of the reward was delayed because for the next month or so the newspapers were full of reports that he had been captured.

Turpin must have anticipated greater incentives would be offered for his capture, and this factor made it even more difficult for him to solve the immediate problem of where to go when that part of Epping Forest was no longer safe. He could move to another part of the forest and contend with the Keepers or he could take his chance on returning to the crowded streets and alleys of East London where he stood as good a chance of remaining at large for a short time as he might have done in much less comfort in Epping. He can have had no illusions about his future at that time, but he needed somewhere to collect himself and think of his best course of action, and the indications are that he decided the lesser of two evils to be London.

VI

The Coroner's inquest on Morris was held at Waltham Abbey on 6 May 1737, and had the formal record which described the manner of death survived it would have been a unique document in the annals of Turpin history. Unfortunately it was removed from the Assize roll, on which it was the practice to file such documents (normally in association with other records such as indictments, which would have been created had proceedings been taken in the same connection), and never restored. There are however two contemporary references to the record and these are contained in a copy of a letter written to York, 'I send you herewith the Coroner's Inquest for the county of Essex taken in May 1738 [*recte* 1737] by which you will see that Richard Turpin ... stands charged with murder,' and a description of enclosures to the same, 'The Coroner's Inquest for the county of Essex, taken at Waltham on the 6th day of May 1738 [*recte* 1737]'[24]

This and other documents were being sent to the Recorder of York by the Duke of Newcastle, as evidence that Turpin would be required to face other charges in the event he was acquitted of those brought against him at York. It is not known what happened to them after they were delivered into the custody of the Recorder in March 1739.

VII

Morris's murder released a flood of Turpin reports which did not abate for some time, but the ones with which we are immediately concerned are those which relate to incidents which occurred from the time of the murder up to and including Saturday 7 May.

> On Friday last [6 May], at eleven o'clock in the morning, Turpin robbed two coaches on Epping and last Saturday [7 May] he robbed a gentleman upon Buckworth's Hill upon Epping Forest, of his money and a mare, and then told the gentleman that he desired to kill but two people, and then he did not care if he was taken. Its surprising when we have so many soldiers idling about in almost every town that parties can't be sent to patrol and surround him, or at least guard those that help to pay them.[25]

The second report, from the next but one edition of the same paper, probably refers to the same incidents. 'Turpin, formerly a butcher, but having since by his own merits and excellencies raised himself on horseback continues to levy illegal war on the good people of England without distinction. After he had left the man dead in Epping Forest, he attacked some ladies in a coach and six, then a gentleman on horseback, and got good booty.'[26] The latter passage was written to serve as an introduction to a general account of Turpin's activities covering a period of about one week; it was not intended to give news, merely remind and renew interest, and it serves to bring us to 7 May, where our main interest lies.

> **Gaol Calendar** [torn, but for New Prison, May 1737]
> No. 43 Elizabeth King committed the 7th May by Richard Farmer Esq., on oath of Benj. Chandler for coming to the house of his father and demanding a bay gelding star and snip with saddle spots curled tail, and a sorrel mare bald face with saddle spots curled tail and her two hinder feet white which were out to grass in the name of Mathew Plear which by information taken before Richard Ricard Esq. one of his Majesty's Justices of the Peace for the county of Middlesex are suspected to be stolen and belonging to a gang of highwaymen. Further examination.[27]

The 'further examination' of Elizabeth King does not appear to have aided the authorities in establishing a case against her; she was not indicted and the only other reference to her is appropriately brief: '*New Prison* p Eliz. King $\overline{dd}$'[28] The abbreviation, '$\overline{dd}$', means 'delivered', in this case at the General Session of Gaol Delivery on 24 May. So as far as the authorities were concerned it would appear that her only offence was to have acted in the same way as John King, in the capacity of messenger to some other person or persons not named in the records.

The Gregory Gang

If, as in one case reported, Turpin did lose his horse, any subsequent theft of a horse would have been attributed to Turpin. In this connection there is the robbery of a mare at Buckhurst Hill on 7 May, and Elizabeth King's demanding stolen horses from Benjamin Chandler's father, also on 7 May; but whether mounted or on foot one cannot imagine Turpin being at Buckhurst Hill three days after he had committed murder less than three miles away. He could, even had he travelled on foot, have been in Whitechapel before dawn on the morning after the murder, and the greater distance he could put between himself and the body in the shortest possible time must surely have been the most urgent thought in his mind, regardless of which direction he took. Temporarily at least, Turpin must have foresaken highway robbery, and we can ignore the reports of his being in Epping on 6 May and at Buckhurst Hill the next day; he had after all just murdered a man and exposing himself for the sake of a few pounds would not have been worth the risk involved when the hue and cry was running high. He was not a footpad, he was a highwayman, and since country movement is restricted without transport, he came to London again where there was probably greater opportunity for stealing a horse with saddle. Thus, inevitably, there is at this point an implied link with Elizabeth King's unexplained action of 7 May. It has been assumed that the horses were still at the *Red Lion* on 7 May, a fact not proved; nor for that matter has it been proved that Elizabeth King went there because although there cannot be any doubt of her connection with the King family and the two highwaymen Potter and Turpin, we know only that she went to the house of Benjamin Chandler's father and demanded two horses. But although the landlord of the *Red Lion* was Richard Holdworth, the horses were out to grass, left by Matthew Plear. Matthew Plear was Matthew King and if the horses had been moved from the *Red Lion,* perhaps for reasons of legal custody pending prosecution, then they would have ceased at the new address to have been left by Matthew Plear, and Elizabeth King would not have known where they had gone. It is largely irrelevant where the horses were on 7 May; we are concerned with where Elizabeth King believed them to be, and that can only have been at the *Red Lion*.

Given the abnormal circumstances which existed in the first week of May 1737, there can be no normal explanation for Elizabeth King's action, especially when the attempt to retrieve the horses was bound to fail. Turpin however was a very desperate man, and it is just conceivable that since neither he nor Elizabeth King could have known much of what happened at the *Red Lion* or afterwards, he persuaded her to go there and lay some claim to ownership. It was his one hope of obtaining a mount without exposing himself to personal risk, and when wanted for murder this would have been the last thing he would have cared to do. As things turned out, Elizabeth King was sent to the same prison as Matthew King, and Turpin was obliged to make his own way in what had become a very hostile England.

We do not know that Elizabeth and Matthew King came together in New Prison, it is possible they did, but if such a prospect had been the motive for her contriving to be taken into custody, the implied relationship between them would be man and wife. It would be surprising if given all the other information in the entry of committal this had not been stated if it was a fact; and even more surprising if some report of it had not reached the newspapers. As it is no report of Elizabeth King's brief part in the proceedings of the first week of May appears to have reached the press, and had it not been for her committal her existence might not have been suspected. Her name alone under New Prison would have meant nothing, it is the details in the Gaol Calendar which make her such an intriguing figure.

VIII

Turpin was so constantly reported during the weeks following the Morris murder that the effect was like an explosion in the columns of domestic news; it was perhaps inevitable then that his fragments were seen everywhere, but no-one knew where he might be found in one piece. It is therefore almost impossible to give a precise account of his movements for about a month after the events of the first week of May. In one respect however we have the advantage over the press of that time, for we know that he was giving serious thought to his future and on the verge of making a momentous decision which would change his life completely. Turpin saw the necessity, not only of removing from the vicinity of London, but of giving up completely his role of highwayman.

When he did leave for points north he never again joined forces with anyone else, a fact which suggests not so much that he could not trust others of criminal bent, but that he was no longer prepared to enter into the sort of working relationship which in his experience had almost always turned out to be an unfortunate liaison ending in disaster for his companions and near disaster for himself. He did not give up crime, but took up quieter pursuits like horsestealing, which although not devoid of an element of risk did not bring him into contact with the people from whom he stole. He shunned publicity and in assuming the guise of horse dealer was not only able to move

		Brought Over	
9	0	Paid for removing John Willis from Winton to the new Goal in the County of Surry being upwards of Sixty Miles and Conveyed with a Strong Guard	11 5 0
16	0	Paid for Removing John Jordan otherwise Samuel Gregory by Habeas Corpus from Winton to Newgate in London being upwards of Sixty Miles and a very Strong Guard being so Commanded by the Right Hon:ble Ordinand Bretyn Knight & Sr John Eveyn Knight which Guard Consisted of Eight Men	26 12 6
		Paid for removing Samuel Gregory otherwise William Johnson from Winton to Newgate in London under a very Strong Guard which Guard Consisted of ten Men all well Armed the said Gregory being one of the Essex Gang and he that Robbed Farmer Lawrences house at Edgware and ravished the Servant Maid	30 8 0
0	0	Paid for Dyetting and Guarding Amos Brown otherwise John Gardener & &c at Prizes held at the Castle of Winton on the 5 day of March 1734 to the	3 10 0

Plate 12. Sheriff's craving of allowances of expenses for the removal to London from Winchester of both Samuel Gregory and the man mistakenly thought to be him, who was later released. (Reproduced by courtesy of the Public Record Office. T.90/147 p.6)

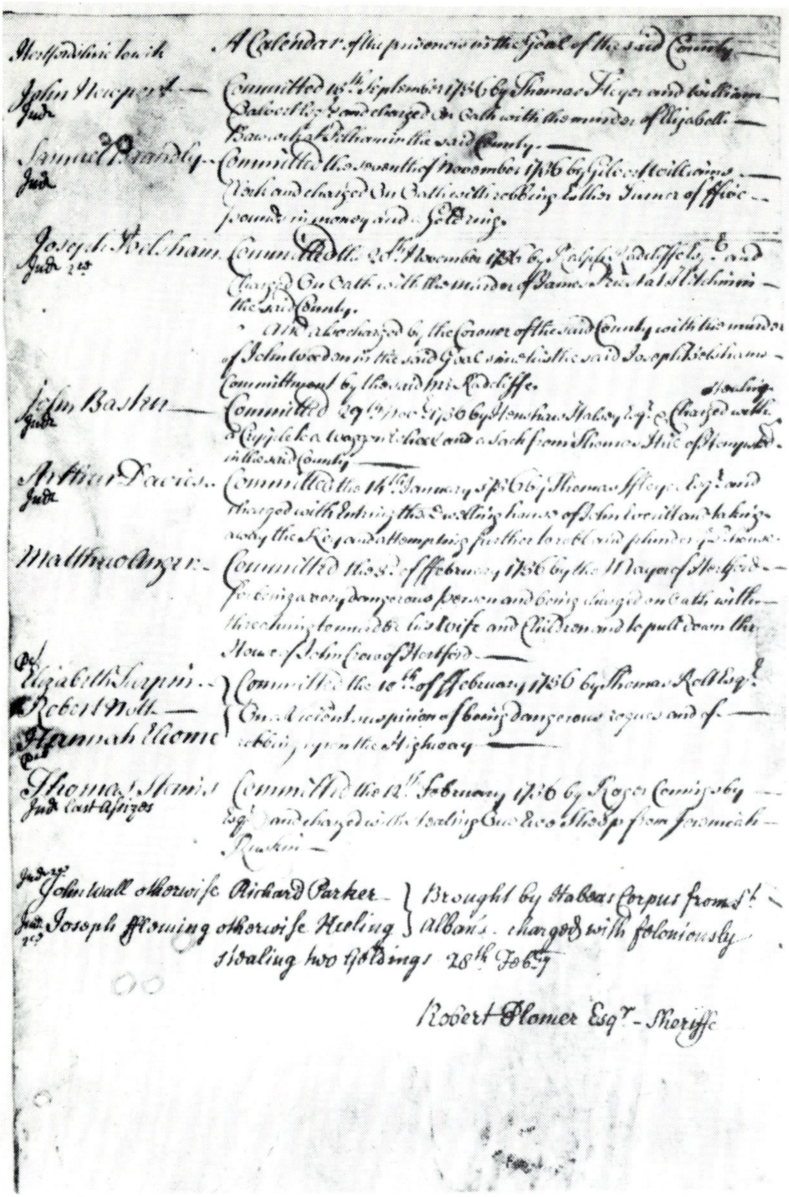

Plate 13. Entry on the Assize Roll of the capture of Turpin's wife and her companions.
(Reproduced by courtesy of the Public Record Office. Assizes 35/177)
Hertford fel/file Winter 10 Geo. II 1736/7)

about freely without causing suspicion but was accepted as a legitimate and respectable trader by those with whom he became acquainted. It was, for Turpin, what amounted to a change of character, and in that sense was better than a disguise.

At least one contemporary source suggests that Turpin did not remove northwards until *after* the proclamation, promising £200 for his capture in connection with the murder of Morris, was published; but what would then have been a panic flight is not consistent with the carefully planned strategy he put into operation when he arrived in Yorkshire. This could not have been formulated overnight, nor in a state of agitation, and since Turpin must have anticipated a really big reward being offered for his capture, he would not have waited for it to be published before making his move. The public were anticipating a big reward as well, and they were not only expecting it, the newspapers had advised them there would be one. The authorities, with calculated meanness, delayed publishing the reward for as long as they dared or thought he would be or had been taken; but once the figure of £200 had been mentioned in the press, it would have been very surprising if Turpin had been taken before the prophecy became reality.

£200 was an enormous sum to the majority of people in those days, but rather than try to express what it might be worth today it is more to the point to reiterate the fact that it was the Establishment's incentive in lieu of other means of catching the criminal, and not as it virtually is today, an additional incentive provided by other interested parties concerned. One could say that with every pound offered as a reward in 1737, you created a policeman or policemen where none existed before, and since they might all be in plain clothes Turpin exposed himself to ever increasing risk with every day he remained in or near London after the murder of Morris. He could not know when the reward would be published, and although he imagined it would be soon, he similarly cannot have known that it would be delayed so long. We can only assume that once given a breathing space and time to collect his thoughts and make his plans, Turpin journeyed northwards as soon as was conveniently possible, and eventually crossed the Humber into Yorkshire. It seems very unlikely that he was at all familiar with that part of the country to which he came, and for this reason it must be assumed that he settled where he did because the place seemed particularly suited to his needs. But to get anywhere at all he needed a horse and having failed on 7 May and being still desperate to obtain one, it must also be assumed that he was more successful within the next few days.

IX

The report which follows does nothing to establish Turpin's whereabouts but it does contain some extremely valid editorial comment and reference to an openly defiant Turpin.

> On Tuesday [10 May] a single highwayman robbed four coaches and several passengers at different times on Hounslow Heath and they gave out it was Turpin, but that fellow having done so much mischief of late [he] runs in everybody's head. The people about Epping Forest say he will never be taken till a proclamation is published offering a reward for the apprehending of him and give the reason, that as he had declared he will never be taken alive but he will kill, or be killed, and it will be dangerous to attempt it, and if they should take him he'll be tried for the murder of Thompson's man and if convicted of that, the persons that apprehend him will then be entitled to no reward unless there's a proclamation, which makes them backward in endeavouring to take him.[29]

Turpin's alleged claim that he would not be taken alive has a certain affinity with his declared intention of wishing to kill but two people. The impression gained from these recorded statements is that Turpin was so familiar a figure he might almost have been a tourist attraction. On the exchange of a sum of money he would make a speech, the money being recoverable on sale of the speech to any newspaper. It required little imagination to suggest that he would be taken dead or alive, but quoting Turpin on the subject gave it added interest. Most of the reports in this vein make obvious points, but the observation about his being in everybody's mind is very pertinent. There must have been a number of criminals who took advantage of the fact that following the Morris murder the public would attribute almost any highway robbery to Turpin, whereas in the circumstances it was most unlikely that he himself would be abroad. The newspapers however were only too ready to accept that he was out and about, and were prepared to publish not only the most bizarre reports, but some extremely unnewsworthy items as well. One of the latter variety, appearing in the midst of a resumé of his reported activities covering several days, is worthy of some closer attention. 'This week we hear, he marched his forces into Middlesex, and passing an Exciseman in his way near Barnet he said only, "Goodmorrow Brother." '[30]

Barnet is close to Enfield Chase on the edge of which used to lay Clayhill near Enfield. When his wife was captured in February, Turpin went to Leicestershire with Potter and Matthew King, and even assuming he obtained news of her release, he had no opportunity to visit her subsequently. His experience at Puckeridge would have made him think twice about making another attempt, that is until after he had murdered Morris. Murderers on the run do not have many friends, and one of the few places where they can hope to find any sympathy whatsoever is at home or where members of the family are to be found. The authorities appear to have been in some confusion as to where his home was (the subsequent draft and published proclamation giving his place of birth as Thaxted), but Turpin was not to know of their mistake and probably avoided Hempstead like the plague.

It has been suggested that his wife stayed with her family at Clayhill, and being situated on the edge of Enfield Chase, its approaches afforded a considerable amount of cover which might have encouraged Turpin to risk a cautious visit. There is not much else to be said of the reported sighting near Barnet except that if it was Turpin his behaviour was at least consistent with a man who does not wish to draw attention to himself. But this report is curious, for unless the Exciseman was very sure that the person who passed him was Turpin, there was not much point in reporting or relating the incident at all. It is perhaps germane to this little episode to draw attention to a curious knowledge which one 'Exciseman' did have of Turpin, and the following abbreviated testimony is taken from his trial in March 1739:

Counsel
Did you not teach him at school?

James Smith
Yes I did, but he was only learning to make letters ...

Counsel
Do you know anything more about him?

James Smith
I think he might be about eleven or twelve years old, when I went to the Excise, and he worked with his father, who was a butcher.

Counsel
Was he ever set up in the butcher trade?

James Smith
Yes I know he was.

Counsel
How long might he live in that way?

James Smith
I cannot tell he lived at [due to noise in court taken to be Boxhill or some such name] in Essex.

Counsel
Did you afterwards see him?

James Smith
Yes ... six miles from thence.

This is not the place to discuss Smith's relationship with Turpin, but it is sufficient to shew that he did know him and that he was what could be termed an Exciseman. Boxhill has been identified as Buckhurst Hill, about six miles from Clayhill. Smith lived at Hempstead and we do not know where he was employed, but since Excisemen were required to travel about pursuing their investigations into smuggling, there remains a tenuous but inconclusive link here between Turpin at Barnet and James Smith who worked for the Excise and was perhaps familiar with Clayhill and its vicinity. But leaving aside the identity of the man Turpin met, it is feasible that he attempted to contact his wife during the week 8 to 14 May, and that he was seen at Barnet.

A final point concerning this area and time comes where Ash and Day draw similar conclusions about a traditional Turpin hiding place, Camlet Moat, on Enfield Chase, it being, 'not far from members of his own family, for his wife at this time occupied a small cottage at Hornchurch in Essex, which is still in existence.'[31] Across country, Hornchurch is about 16 miles from Clayhill, mentioned by the authors as being *near* the Camlet Moat hiding place, and although it was perhaps convenient for Turpin to reach his wife at Clayhill, using the Chase as cover, the same could not be said of Hornchurch.

From Clayhill Turpin could go north or west (as Rowden had done), but south, from the recollection of what had happened to Jeremy and Samuel Gregory, was not a particularly suitable choice. Lincolnshire or Yorkshire however both possessed ports if he did at some future stage feel inclined to risk the passage to Holland again; and he could perhaps still, without traversing the breadth of the country, visit home.

Turpin is not likely to have been familiar with Yorkshire before he went there in 1737, and from his background there is nothing which would indicate that he could have ever been to Lincolnshire before. But he appears to have travelled through that county before being attracted to a remote village the other side of the Humber, its only direct access from the south being by ferry. To reach Lincolnshire he no doubt passed through Cambridgeshire, and if he followed a fairly nor nor east course he may have gone through Cambridge itself. His progress was deliberate and slow for his primary aim was to avoid drawing attention to himself, but the further from

London he could get without being recognised, the shorter the distance he might eventually be obliged to travel. If he did pass through Cambridge he probably approached it from Hertford, and in all the reports which concern him at this time it is remarkable how many relate to that city.

On 10 May, it was reported that Matthew King was very ill,[32] but from this day onwards for a week or more, rumours of Turpin having been captured flew thick and fast.

> We hear that Turpin the notorious highwayman and murderer, after having committed several robberies on or about Epping Forest was luckily discovered by a higgler woman belonging to Bishop's Stortford, to whom he had given a bumper of brandy, and made her drink Turpin's health; after some conversation, and just before they parted, he told her he was the man, upon which she immediately gave information of him, and described him and his horse, he was pursued five or six miles and then taken, and committed to Hertford Gaol.[33]

The following, although somewhat confused in its presentation, appears to have some connection with the same report.

> We heard an account on Thursday night from Hertford that Turpin the famous highwayman was not taken, but on Tuesday last a person was taken up in the said town on suspicion of being Turpin, but set at liberty the same day.
> On Wednesday last he appeared about the Forest; but it is imagined he has changed his road, or lies concealed: The reports of him being taken was first raised by some relation of his, in order, as it is imagined, for him to escape the more easily.[34]

And the next edition of the same paper celebrated its denials and imaginative explanatory retractions of the reported capture with a report which served to reassure those of its readers to whom any news of Turpin was better than none. 'On Friday last [13 May] Turpin the highwayman attacked a gentleman on the Hertford Road; but the gentleman having a better horse than Turpin outrode him, and saved a great quantity of money he had about him.'[35] Other newspapers of the same period in May mixed up all the Turpin ingredients obtained from previous reports, added the spices of confusion and contradiction, stirred well and served afresh. 'It is reported that Turpin the noted highwayman for many years the terror of Essex roads was taken and committed, as some say, to Chelmsford, and others to Watford Gaol. The country was raised when he least expected it, so that he could not keep his vow of murdering two certain persons, nor that of never being taken alive.'[36] The weekly newspapers had their way with this mess of pottage, and as with all Turpin reports over the years, even when they were stone cold, there were still some journals prepared to print them again.

Ash and Day stated, 'there is certainly evidence [and] records show' to prove their point about Turpin being in Hertfordshire at that time; there was even an inn, where he stayed under an assumed name ('I am Dick Turpin but I am staying here under an assumed name'), and Bayes' Hertford butcher to clinch the non-argument, but the sum total of their evidence was no more than that which the newspapers of the time were able to summon.[37]

Turpin may have passed through Hertfordshire about this time, and the press reported that he either had or had not been captured there, or was active there; but so far as may be established the contemporary fancy was not based on any fact. Yet that same 'fancy' has been arrived at merely by drawing a conjectural line from point A to point B, and suggesting that Turpin had probably travelled that far along it by the end of the second week in May. His leisurely progress during the next three weeks took him through Cambridgeshire and Lincolnshire to Yorkshire, arriving there, as one man recalled, on or about 6 June 1737.

X

Turpin had perhaps given up Matthew King for dead on the morning of 2 May, but his companion lingered on seriously ill for longer than anyone might have anticipated; he died of his chest wound on 19 May. 'Thursday morning King (one of the persons concerned with Turpin in several robberies) died in the New Prison Clerkenwell of wounds he had received when taken.'[38] We have a remarkable description of events connected with his death and occurring immediately afterwards.

> Report of the Committee appointed to inquire concerning prisoners dying in the New Prison and House of Correction at Clerkenwell.
> ... At a subsequent meeting the same witness [Mr. Cavenagh, Keeper of the New Prison] informed the Committee of the death of one other prisoner. Matthew King, one of Turpin's gang, who being shot in the breast before he could be taken, was committed to New Prison, and the coroner having a jury with him hard by the prison, enquiring into the death of another person, the beadle apprising the coroner that the said King was then just dead, the coroner and jury came to the prison, but neither the coroner nor jury had then any fee or reward, as he remembers or believes.[39]

Two days later Matthew King was buried. '**St. James Clerkenwell** 1737 May 21 Mathew King, New Prison, shot. Age 25'[40] And on the same day, in Whitehall, there was drafted the proclamation, giving a description of Turpin and offering an as then unspecified reward for his capture (the sum left blank in the draft), intended for publication in the *Gazette*. That it was not published for more than a month was probably due to the various reports of Turpin having been captured. Such an event, had it occurred before the reward was published, would have saved the Treasury a sum of (as it transpired) £200. Turpin was by this time probably passing through Cambridgeshire, and it is a moot point in which he was least interested, the sum to be offered in reward for his capture or several gentlemen in their coaches and chaises at Holloway and the back lanes of Islington. There, in any event, is where most newspapers reported him to have been active on 22 May and making one of his oft quoted speeches. This had been reproduced on numerous occasions, with, depending on the particular newspaper version used, curious emphasis on the slang term used for the money being demanded, but there is nothing which would reconcile the idea of his being in Holloway/Islington (or anywhere else in London) on 22 May with the fact of his being at Brough in Yorkshire on or about 6 June. The relevant item is shewn below.

> (May 22, 1737) The noted highwayman Richard Turpin, the butcher, who lately killed a man who endeavoured to take him in Epping Forest robbed several persons in their coaches and chaises at Holloway and the back lanes of Islington. One of the gentlemen signified to him that he had reigned for a long time; Turpin replied "It is no matter for that, I am not afraid of being taken by you; therefore don't stand hesitating, but give me the *cole*."[41]

XI

It is perhaps fitting to close this chapter with another London report of Turpin which places him there on a date nearest to that upon which it is said he arrived at Brough; the report is given in such fine detail that although in similar vein to many others which appeared previously, there is no doubt in this case that the incident described actually occurred. But the date of the incident conveniently illustrates how other highwaymen were not only willing to take on the identity of Turpin, but to act out the role as well.

> Further account of Turpin's exploits. June 5. As Mr. Loan of Bristol, and another Quaker, were coming to London to the General Meeting, a man rode up to them on Hounslow Heath with a pistol cocked, but did not demand anything of them, and desired they would not be afraid, for he would not hurt them; they answered, they must be under apprehensions while his pistol was in that position, upon which he put it on a half cock, and told them his name was Turpin, and rode some time in company with them; coming near some of the fellows hanging in chains, he pointed to one of them, and said, That would be his fate, they said, if he thought so, they wondered he would pursue it; he replied, He could not help it, for he could trust nobody, nor make his escape; besides he would never rest till he was revenged of the man who took his companion; and if he could kill him, he did not care what became of himself afterwards. Just as he had said those words, he espied a gentleman with laced clothes on horseback, and pointing to him, cried, You get your money easily, I must speak with you, and taking his leave in a complaisant manner, rode full trot after the gentleman, and they saw no more of him.[42]

FOOTNOTES

1. *London Evening Post*, 30 April to 3 May 1737.
2. *Life of Richard Turpin*, by Richard Bayes & Co., p.17.
3. Middlesex/MJ/SR 2676, the Recognisance of Margaret Grant.
4. *London Evening Post*, 7 to 10 May 1737.
5. Middlesex/MJ/SR 2676. Gaol Calendar, entry No.43.
6. *London Evening Post*, 30 April to 3 May 1737.
7. *Life of Richard Turpin*, Bayes, pp.17–18.
8. *Country Journal*, 7 May 1737.
9. *Political State*, Vol.LIII, January to June 1737, p.553 *(my italics)*
10. Middlesex/MJ/SR 2676 (filed on the roll).
11. *Ibid.*, (heading of Calendar badly torn).
12. Middlesex/MJ/SB 944 General Sessions, 24 May 1737.
13. P.R.O./A.O.3/1229 p.108.
14. P.R.O./B.6/1 p.7, No.86 September 25, 1734.
15. *London Evening Post*, 7 to 10 May 1737.
16. *Ibid.*, 30 April to 3 May 1737.
17. *Ibid.*, Tuesday 3 to Thursday 5 May 1737.
18. Middlesex/MJ/SR 2677, Calendar of Middlesex Prisoners in Newgate, (bracketed sections read with ultra violet lamp).
19. Middlesex/MJ/SR 2676 (filed on the roll), abbreviated, the form the same as given in the previous recognisance, of 2 May.
20. *London Evening Post*, Thursday 5 to Saturday 7 May 1737.
21. *Political State*, Vol.LIII, January to June 1737, p.554.
22. *Life of Richard Turpin*, Bayes, pp.16 and 18.
23. *History of Clerkenwell*, by W.J. Pinks, with additions by E.J. Wood, 2nd edition, 1881, p.164.
24. P.R.O./S.P. 44/131 p.107 (the second part written above the first).
25. *London Evening Post*, 7 to 10 May 1737.
26. *Ibid.*, 12 to 14 May 1737.
27. Middlesex/MJ/SR 2676 (Left hand margin torn off and what remains up to entries is badly crumpled).
28. Middlesex/MJ/SR 944 General Sessions for 24 May 1737.
29. *Reid's Weekly Journal*, 14 May 1737.
30. *London Evening Post*, 12 to 14 May 1737.
31. *Immortal Turpin*, p.68.
32. *London Evening Post.*
33. *Ibid.*, 10 to 12 May 1737.
34. *Ibid.*, 12 to 14 May 1737 (relating to 10 to 12 May).
35. *Ibid.*, 14 to 17 May 1737.
36. *London Daily Post*, 11 to 14 May 1737.
37. *Immortal Turpin*, pp.60–61.

The Gregory Gang

38. *Reid's Weekly Journal*, 21 May 1737.
39. Calendar of Middlesex Sessions Books and Orders of Court, January 1739 to December 1741, p.138.
40. Harleian Society Publications: Register Series 1894: *Registers of Burials for St. James Clerkenwell.*
41. Islington Central Library newspaper cutting YL 635; also in *London Magazine*, Sunday 22 May 1737, and substantially the same form in *History and Topography of the Parish of St. Mary, Islington*. S. Lewis Junr. 1842, p.280 n.5.
42. *Political State*, Vol.LIV, July to December 1737, p.28.

BOOK SIX

TURPIN (part the second)

CHAPTER ONE

I

IN OCTOBER 1738, Richard Turpin *alias* John Palmer was arrested for threatening to shoot a labourer named John Robinson, the man having reprimanded him for shooting a fowl belonging to Francis Hall, a cowherd. In connection with this incident, the landlord of the inn where Turpin had stayed at Brough in Elloughton, volunteered the following information which establishes the approximate date when Turpin arrived in Yorkshire in 1737.

East Riding of the County of Yorks

The Information of William Harris of Brough in the East Riding of the County of York innkeeper taken upon oath before us three of his Majesty's Justices of the Peace for the said Riding the third day of October 1738.

This Informant said that on or about Trinity Monday was twelve months one John Palmer came to [his] house at Brough and boarded with [him] four or five months and during that time went from [his] house over the water into the county of Lincoln at divers times and returned to [his] house at Brough with several horses at a time which he sold and disposed of to divers persons in the county of York and this Informant inquiring of the said John Palmer the place of his abode he told [him] that he lived at Long Sutton with his father and that his sister kept his father's house there and the reason [for] leaving his father was for debt and was feared of being arrested by Bailiffs and said that if they once caught him they would kill him and this Informant answered and said it would be very hard to kill a man for debt and that he went unarmed but Palmer then told [him] if he would go over the water with him he would shew him such a pair of pistols as he never saw in his life and that he did not fear the Bailiffs for in plain terms I am everything or words to that effect and further this Informant said that at the same time Palmer told him that if he would go over with him says Palmer "twenty pounds is as easily got as two pence" he then had laid upon the table to pay for a pint of ale and then said drink about not catch me not have me but before they do catch me a great deal of blood shall be spilt.

Will. Harris

Taken and sworn the day and year first above written [before] Geo: Crowle, Hugh Bethell, Marm: Constable[1]

The date when Turpin arrived at Brough was, on or about 6 June 1737, and until about October he had a room at the inn of William Harris. A Justice of the Peace who was subsequently active in making inquiries about John Palmer, and who wrote an account of his activities when his real identity became known, referred to this inn as the *Ferry House* at Brough.

In the latter part of the information Turpin, perhaps with some ale inside him already, appears as a braggart, and finally makes a statement which is virtually identical with that reported in the newspapers in May 1737. At the time when Harris gave this information he can have had no idea that Palmer was in fact Turpin, and the words must be regarded as authentic. This does not however affect the argument made before; that Turpin, in or about London in May, having just murdered Morris, was not in a position to be vainglorious about that act or about what he would do if anyone tried to catch him, and more important, he was not in a position to advertise his identity to anyone. At Brough the circumstances were different, the catchers were disguised as bailiffs, and the threat was a common enough one to be made or be said to be made by a desperate man trying to evade justice.

In Brough, in Yorkshire, far from the dangers from which he had fled, Turpin felt his confidence return; he drank freely, allowed his tongue to run too loose for comfort, and announced to the perhaps surprisingly naïve publican, 'I am everything'.

William Harris appears to have had a good memory for one who doubtless had to deal with many people at the *Ferry House,* but he would have been obliged to take more notice of the stranger who boarded with him for five months. But how reliable should he be regarded in respect of the all important date of Trinity Monday, or how moveable was Harris's Moveable Feast?

So far as the Calendar was concerned, it had to be 6 June 1737, but Harris said, 'on or about' that date. His recollection was that Turpin had come to Brough 16 months before he made his statement, there was no doubt in his mind about which of the dates affected by Easter could be connected with that arrival, and if he was in any doubt its proximity to the beginning of a particular month would surely have corrected his impression. Perhaps he was not so precise about the duration of Turpin's stay, but whereas Turpin came and went on a number of occasions and the covering period could have become confused in Harris's mind, the date of first arrival was a singular event easier to relate to a particular date. And in 1737 such Moveable Feasts were regarded as being of greater significance (and thereby more memorable occasions) than they are today.

II

> Last Monday sevennight a young man returning from Birmingham to Lincoln, was robbed upon Eggington Heath four miles from Derby, by a highwayman, who took from him £4. 14s. and his watch, the latter of which, with the 14s. he returned to him again. He lay at the *King's Head* in Derby that night, and gave out that it was done by the noted Turpin.[2]

Derby is not so very far north of Leicester, to which place Turpin went with Matthew King and Stephen Potter; and since he was familiar with the road north, at least as far as Leicester, the possibility of his having gone that way to Brough should be considered.

The date on which the incident occurred may be taken as 6 June, a reasonable date since Turpin could still have reached Brough within a few days, but whereas bearing north eastwards on a route from Cambridge, he would *inevitably* have come to the Lincolnshire landing stage of the Brough ferry when he reached the Humber, the same cannot be said if he had decided to travel east or north east from Derby. Brough was not Turpin's intended destination, he was brought to it by the accident of the Humber riverline appearing in his path; and the chances of his going anywhere near the Humber on an unknown course from Derby would have been extremely remote.

The *Daily Gazette* article was based purely on the fancy of a young man, who oddly enough, came from Lincoln. To what extent the same newspaper's reporters could be relied on to distort even known facts is well illustrated in the following short report. 'Mr. Stephens who keeps the *Sign of the Oak* on Epping Forest is made Keeper of the said Forest in the room of the late keeper (presumably Thompson), who was shot some time ago by Turpin the highwayman.'[3] After all the publicity given to that particular murder, it is incredible that anyone should have confused the master with his unfortunate servant.

III

But at about the same time that one person's identity was being confused, another's was being firmly established; or, as Turpin concealed his identity and disappeared, Rowden the Pewterer shewed his hand, so to speak, and was revealed.

> ... he was carried before a Justice of the Peace, who committed him to Gloucester Jail by the name of Daniel Crisp; he was tried at the Assizes held for the City and County of Gloucester and convicted; he was sentenced to be imprisoned for two years [*recte* one year], and fined 20 marks, and if he had stayed till the 22nd of October next, his two years had been expired [so far as can be established he could have anticipated being released during the first week of

September 1737]. He was discovered to be Rowden after the following manner, viz.

    A man going to Gloucester jail to see a friend who was a prisoner there, this prisoner and Rowden were drinking together, and in talk Rowden asked the man, if he did not know such a person, that lived in such a place; Yes, says the man, very well, I am intimately acquainted with him; then pray sir, says Rowden, be so kind as to tell him, that one Daniel Crisp gives his kind services to him. Some few days after, he meets the very man in Gloucester town, on a Market Day, and acquainted him that he had been to see a friend in Gloucester jail, and there was one Daniel Crisp a prisoner in the same jail, confined for putting off bad money, who desired kindly to be remembered to him; the man did not know any such person as Daniel Crisp, but says he, I know one Rowden very well, that used to put off bad money, and I suppose it must be him; no, replied the countryman, he says his name is Daniel Crisp, and he knows you very well. The countryman upon this goes to the jail, and asked one of the prisoners, if there was any such person as one Daniel Crisp, confined there for putting off bad money; Yes, says he, that is the man yonder you see playing at fives; (a game so called) the man immediately knew him to be Rowden, and took no notice, but got a horse and came to London, and applied himself to a Magistrate, that one Rowden, who was concerned with Gregory and his gang, was actually a prisoner in Gloucester jail, by the name of Daniel Crisp, whereupon the Magistrate informed him, he must go down and make oath of this before one of his Majesty's Justices of the Peace for that county, and then he should have a Habeas Corpus granted to the Keeper of the said jail. The countryman followed directions, and Rowden was accordingly brought up to town on Monday evening last, in order to go to Chelmsford, to take his trial for robberies committed in the county of Essex.[4]

The date of Rowden's removal from Gloucester was in July and should not be confused with that of his discovery in the previous month; so far as can be established this must have occurred not more than a week *before* 23 June, by which date news of the revelation had reached London.

    The Treasury claim, representing the petitions of several persons interested in the reward for Rowden's discovery and conviction, is extraordinarily long but contributes little to what we know about the circumstances of the denouement. That which is relevant to the actual discovery is given in the following short extract. 'Thomas Bailis saw the said Rowden in Gloucester Gaol, who went there by the name of Daniel Crisp, and was the first person that discovered him in the said Gaol to be Thomas Rowden.'[5]

    Bailis had at some time known Rowden and that he used to be a counterfeiter, but he did not know him as Daniel Crisp, which suggests that Rowden had not seen him in Gloucester since he had parted from Turpin. Rowden did however know that he lived somewhere in that vicinity, ergo the probability was that he, Rowden, had been to Gloucester before. Rowden, from 1732, when suspicion was aroused that he was counterfeiting in Southwark, to the time he and Turpin went their separate ways, appears to have been an associate of the deerstealing faction (in their various guises) and is unlikely to have visited Gloucester at any time during that period.

Plate 14. Turpin in his cave in Epping Forest, where he fled from London in May 1737.
(Reproduced by courtesy of the British Museum B.M.010854 aa 1 frontis (1739))

Plate 15. Turpin shooting Thomas Morris outside his cave. Morris was the servant of one of the keepers and was killed while attempting to capture Turpin.
(Reproduced by courtesy of the British Museum. B.M.1131 e (3) facing p.110 (1768))

Plate 16. Map of the East Riding of Yorkshire to the Humber and part of Lincolnshire, showing Brough and Welton areas where Turpin stayed. From a map of 1772 by T. Jefferys. (Reproduced by courtesy of the Public Record Office Library.)

Therefore the conclusion must be that Rowden, who would have been aged between 25 and 27 in 1732, did on some previous occasion counterfeit money in Gloucester and know Thomas Bailis. Whatever their relationship on that occasion, it failed to inspire any sense of loyalty in Bailis in June 1737, and apparently having associated Rowden with being Turpin's companion and one of the last survivors of the Gregory gang, there was always the thought of the reward to spur him on if sentiment made him undecided about what to do. There is no doubt that Rowden's description would have been published in Gloucester, for one of the duties which fell to the Sheriff of each county was the distribution of Royal Proclamations, and those which offered rewards would have attracted more public notice than those concerned with mundane matters of Government.

Between the uninformative Treasury claim and the detailed account of how the denouement came about, there is possibly some room for doubt that it did actually happen in this way; yet there is such a curious parallel with the discovery of Turpin's real identity one can only observe that it could have happened as described. The hesitation in accepting it as fact perhaps derives from the absence in the Treasury claim of the man who is said to have conveyed the message to Bailis, although there is some fine distinction here which may have prevented him being admitted to the claim: 'Bailis was the first person that *discovered him* in the said Gaol *to be Thomas Rowden.*' This cannot be denied and although perhaps hard on the man who passed the message it does at least explain why he was not considered for a share in the reward.

A person's willingness to bring about the capture and conviction of a criminal must have been determined to some extent by his own personal circumstances, and although perhaps something of a paradox it would be true to say that if Bailis had been poor and in desperate need of money, he might not have divulged his knowledge that Rowden was masquerading as Crisp. For even taking into consideration an anticipated share in the reward, Bailis could easily (as Richard Bayes in all probability would have done had he not been recompensed through publicity and a vested interest in Turpin's biography) have ended up out of pocket.

He was in fact, 'at great expense in going and coming from Gloucester ... and going to Essex and Kent to bring the prosecutors to town', and since he was not reimbursed for over a year with his share in the reward, it seems clear that he could afford to indulge his Judas streak to the limit. Loss of time similarly does not appear to have worried him, and being something of a celebrity he did perhaps quite enjoy his travels and the stay in London, to the extent that he was not unwilling to recount the manner of Rowden's unmasking on an offer from the most enterprising newspaper reporter. And in this Bailis would have been fortunate because although in June the public's interest in Rowden was pale in comparison with Turpin, a story which not only explained his disappearance but his discovery as well did at least make him worthy of equal publicity and serve to restore him for a time to the columns of domestic news. But until Bailis reached London, the newspapers only had ears for news of Rowden's former companion, and although they were not to know that he had found refuge in Yorkshire, some of them might at least have compared notes and considered just how ubiquitous a number of their reports made him appear to be.

> Last week the famous Turpin met Sir Charles Turner one of the members of Lynn, upon Epping Forest, as he was returning into Norfolk, and saluted him after this manner, "Sir Charles Turner, I am Turpin, and do not design to offer you any incivility or rob you of anything. In a little time I shall come to the gallows, and hope that when I have occasion, you will do me your best service."[6]

This is a ludicrous tale, and the public were either becoming weary of such reports or beginning to wonder which they might believe, especially when as in the case of the next report Turpin was alleged to be in a place some way removed from Epping and at roughly the same time. 'Advice is brought to town from Coventry, that the noted highway robber Turpin is taken near that place and committed to the gaol there.'[7] A few days later the same newspaper received the news about Rowden, but feeling uneasy about the lack of any follow up story from Coventry, they used the Gloucester news to preface a retraction of the Turpin capture report. 'Information was received last Thursday that Rowden was in Gloucester Gaol [abbreviated]. There's not confirmation of the taking of Turpin at or near Coventry, and its supposed he is still lurking about Epping Forest.'[8] But at least the reporter was sensible enough to restore him to one of his known haunts, rather than venture any other theory.

The next entry describes in greater detail how the news of Rowden came to London.

> On the 23rd June, an information was given by Mr. Peters, Keeper of Gloucester jail, to Nathaniel Blackerby, Esq., one of his Majesty's Justices of the Peace for the City and Liberty of Westminster, as also an affidavit made by another person, that Thomas Rowden, who belonged to that notorious knot of thieves called Gregory's gang, was in Gloucester jail; and we hear that he was tried and convicted at the last Assizes there, by the name of Daniel Crisp, for uttering counterfeit money, and the time for which he was imprisoned for the said offence was almost expired; but the person who made the aforesaid affidavit, accidentally went to the jail and knew him, whereupon he was detained. Mr. Blackerby bound the informant over to appear against him, and a Habeas Corpus was granted for removing him from thence to Newgate, in order to take his trial at the next sessions at the Old Bailey.[9]

Bailis was the 'other person' who made the affidavit, the contents of which no doubt were almost the same as the detailed account of Rowden's denouement, previously ascribed to Bailis. The name of the Keeper of Gloucester jail was Benjamin Heming *or* Henning, and this fact and details of what occurred when he and Bailis came before the Justices, and what happened subsequently, are correctly defined in the following commentary on affidavits made by them and one other person.

> And by the affidavit of Thomas Bailis sworn before Nathaniel Blackerby Esq. ... hereunto annexed it appears that he ... was the first person that discovered him in the said gaol to be Thomas Rowden upon which he was removed to Chelmsford where he was convicted for robbing the house of Ambrose Skinner, and that he has been at great expense in going and coming from Gloucester where the said Rowden was apprehended and going to Essex and Kent to bring the prosecutors to town besides loss of time and hindrance of business in going to Chelmsford to which place he was bound in recognisance to appear upon the trial of the said Thomas Rowden.
>
> And by the affidavit of Benjamin Heming Keeper of the county gaol of Gloucester and Thomas Cavenagh Keeper of New Prison Clerkenwell sworn before J. Pulson Esq. one of his Majesty's Justices of the Peace for the county of Middlesex, it appears that ... Benjamin Heming by attending in London, where he was bound over to appear at Chelmsford aforesaid at the said Assizes, and in taking out the Habeas Corpus for removal of the said Rowden from Gloucester to Chelmsford, and attending at the said Assizes, and horsehire it cost him 10 1. or thereabouts, and it thereby further appears that the said Thomas Cavenagh the latter end of June last [1737] received an order from Justice Blackerby to find out Wheeler (who was evidence against the whole gang) and to bring him before him, and by the like order kept him in custody above a month and bore all his expenses and carried him down to Chelmsford to give evidence against the said Rowden all which expenses he believes amounted to 10 1. or thereabouts.[10]

By 23 June the formalities required to bring Rowden to London had been observed, and a few days later all the necessary arrangements made, including those for the all important confrontation with Wheeler, to ensure his safe custody until such time as he would be required to stand his trial at Chelmsford. A number of problems relating to Turpin's companions were resolved at Chelmsford and Hertford in July, but in the meantime the authorities had not forgotten Turpin himself and the outstanding matter of Morris's murder.

IV

The proclamation offering a reward for the capture of Turpin in connection with the murder of Morris had been drafted on 21 May, but because of the possibility of his being captured without the necessity of additional incentive, the publication of the proclamation was put off, apparently indefinitely. On 25 June however, despite reports and denials of his capture in the same week, the authorities in Whitehall must have concluded that nobody had the foggiest idea where he was, or if they had, they would not reveal the fact until the reward was offered. It was ironic that when Turpin was captured and convicted of another offence, the Crown was obliged to make settlement in excess of the £200 eventually offered in respect of the murder of Morris.

Whitehall, June 25, 1737

> Whereas it has been represented to the King, that Richard Turpin did, on Wednesday the fourth day of May last, barbarously murder Thomas Morris, servant to Henry Tomson, one of the Keepers of Epping Forest; and that the said Richard Turpin hath, at divers times, committed several notorious felonies and robberies in and near the said forest, and other places near the Cities of London and Westminster; His Majesty, for the better discovering and bringing the said Richard Turpin to Justice, is pleased to promise his most gracious pardon to any one of the accomplices of the said Richard Turpin, who shall discover him, so that he may be apprehended and convicted of any of the said offences. And as a further encouragement, his Majesty is pleased to promise a reward of two hundred pounds to any person or persons who shall discover the said criminal, so as he may be apprehended and convicted as aforesaid, to be paid upon such conviction, over and above all other rewards to which the said person or persons may otherwise be entitled.
>
> Holles Newcastle
>
> The said Richard Turpin was born at Thacksted in the county of Essex, is about thirty years of age, by trade a butcher, about five feet nine inches high, of a brown complexion, very much marked with the small pox, his cheek bones broad, his face thinner towards the bottom, his visage short, pretty upright, and broad about the shoulders.[11]

In 1739, after Turpin was identified at York Castle, the *Political State* reproduced a letter sent to one of the London newspapers, of which the following is a short extract. 'It seems that about the time that the reward for taking him came out, which was June 25th, 1737, instead of going beyond sea (as was reported) he only crossed the Humber, and boarded at a public house at Brough Ferry for some time.' The implication in the above is that instead of fleeing the country when the reward was published, Turpin went to Brough instead. In actual fact the author of the letter cheated a little to suit the story, because it is clear from the rest of the letter that he was very familiar with some of the things said by Turpin which had been previously quoted by William Harris of the *Ferry House* at Brough. It is likely therefore that the author *had* learned about Turpin having come to Brough on or about Trinity Monday 1737, but found it convenient not to mention it in his letter.

£200 was a lot of money, to be earned legally; and in times when people were prepared to commit all manner of crimes to earn a lot less, it would have been impossible for Turpin to have remained long in London or its vicinity and gone unnoticed. But there were comparatively few reports of his having been seen, none which described or denied his having been taken, and none even which turned out to be cases of mistaken identity; which is surprising despite the fact Turpin had been in Yorkshire for some time, for one might have expected the rumours to fly thick and fast. Perhaps at long last, now that everyone realised the game must be played seriously, anyone that had any ideas at all about his whereabouts was keeping them to himself, with the result that the reality of his disappearance killed the rumours of his continued presence. Only one post proclamation report is worthy of any regard. 'We hear that Turpin is still harbouring about Epping Forest; that he was seen a few days ago near Harwich, and its supposed was hovering about the coasts to get off; but those that saw him near the sea side he knew, and he rode directly towards the London Road, for fear, as it is thought, the town would be raised upon him. The reward of £200 it is hoped will soon take him.'[12]

There were of course a number of people who did know him, and as became apparent in 1739, some of them were only too anxious to claim a share in the reward. It is therefore absurd to suppose that if there were people who knew him to be near London in 1737, not one was prepared to come forward *then* and say where he was. It wasn't possible because he *was* by then at Brough, and the people who would have liked to have claimed the reward in 1737 were therefore frustrated.

The idea of his having been seen near Harwich was a good one, but all that can really be said about it, it appearing so soon after the proclamation was published, is that it was a fairly predictable report in the circumstances. A less responsible idea, completely without foundation and promoted purely as a vehicle to deliver sensational bits of Turpin fact and fiction to a less discerning public than that which read the newspapers, concerned his escape to Ireland, and was published some time not long after the June proclamation appeared.

V

The first published work which may have included references to Turpin's activities was the previously mentioned *The Ordinary of Newgate's Account of the 13 Malefactors executed at Tyburn the 10th [March 1735]*, printed for J. Applebee. No copy of this has been traced, but insofar as the persons executed included a number of Turpin's companions, such description of Turpin as may have been made would not have distinguished him from other members of the Gregory gang of which he was then a member. By June 1737 he had achieved considerable personal notoriety by reason of his exploits as a highwayman; by the same date his career as a highwayman was at an end, and for these reasons it would be true to say that the following publication was probably the only account of Turpin *the Highwayman* written during his own lifetime, and as such is conceivably the most important and significant public reflection of his contemporary notoriety that one is likely to find.

News News; great and wonderful news from London in an Uproar or a Hue and Cry after the great Turpin, with his escape into Ireland.[13]

Here you have the comical humors of Mr. Turpin, his going to the *White Lyon* in Westchester, and ordering a dinner, he pays his reckoning honourably, takes post for Parkgate, in order for Ireland: Notwithstanding his Majesty had given orders at all sea ports, that none should go over sea without being examined; but Turpin by his policy cheated both King and Country, telling the captain of the pacquetboat, that he was his Grace the Duke of Richmond's steward, and was going to Ireland with a letter from his Grace to the Lord Lieutenant, the Duke of Devonshire; so he believed him, took him on board, and landed him safe in Ireland.

It is worth note, that on the 2nd of the last month, Mr. Turpin went to the *Bird in Hand* in Huntingdon, and called for a bottle of wine; at that instant the parson of that parish happened to be in the same house, and seeing Turpin observed him to be the person described in the newspapers, so sent for a constable to apprehend him; before he came, Turpin, having a guilty conscience, which needs no accuser, was getting off, but the constable catching hold of him, Turpin discharged a pistol, which did not explode, but only singed his wig; the constable imagining himself killed, cried out, *by G-d, I'm dead,* and the parson hearing the shot, and the constable declare he was dead, took to his heels, but had the misfortune to stumble against a stone, which, through fear made him befoul his breeches. In this confusion Turpin made his escape.

A description of Turpin, a notorious highwayman, and the following notice were published in the *Gazette,* June 25.

[here followed the advertisement and description published in the *London Gazette, No. 7613.*]

Of all the rogues that ever graced Tyburn (whether *Whitney, Nevison, the Golden Farmer,* or *Hind*) none ever came up to the famous TURPIN and his companions, and who had the good fortune to reign so long in their villainies, as to become a terror to gentlemen and others that are obliged to travel through the whole Kingdom, for fear of falling into the hands of such rogues, who take a pleasure in robbing, assaulting and murdering all such as resist their villainous attempt. But as the knot is at present broke, they apprehending and taking two of them, and Turpin with great difficulty escaped, it is to be hoped it will put a stop to the progress of their robberies for the future.

On Wednesday the 4th March last, the two Kings, Brothers; and Turpin their accomplice, drinking at an inn in Red Lion Street, White-Chapel, were apprehended and taken by Mr. Bayes, Keeper of the *Green Man* in Epping Forest. Turpin was seized by Bays, but had his heels struck up by Turpin, and received a shot or two without much damage, and he made his escape without a horse, but the other two was seized by Bays, as they were going to take horse, and were committed to New Prison. One of them, viz. Matthew King, had decided to be admitted evidence against his brother, but is in a weak condition by an accidental shot from Turpin when they were taken, the bullet lodging in his shoulder. Turpin lay the next night at a house in Wek [*recte* Well] Close Square, of which information was given, and the house beset early next morning, but this being discovered by a woman of the house, who called to Turpin who was in the bed, gave him warning of his danger, and he made his escape out the house. He has since robbed a gentleman within 40 yards of the *Green Man* on Epping Forest of seven guineas, and finding the gentleman's beast better than his own, he exchanged with him, leaving in lieu of a good mare, a bad horse stolen the night before. Turpin lying some weeks ago at the *Bell* in Stilton, rode the next morning up to Yaxton, a little town about two or three miles from thence, and put up at a public-house there, which it was presently alarmed in the town, that Turpin was there; upon which the constable and his posse came and beset the house, but Turpin gaining the meaning of their attendance there, made out at the window, and got across his horse, just as the constable came up to him; on which he pulled a pistol and fired it over the constable's head, which so frightened him that he fell down, and cried out *Dead by G-d*, at which all the attendants ran out, and gave Turpin an opportunity to get off.

Turpin lately saluted a gentleman in the following manner; *Good-morrow Sir, do not you hear talk of one Turpin a robber? O Lord Sir, I heard an account of him in the public newspapers.* Turpin replied, *Sir I have a small matter of money at me, and am very much afraid of being robbed, but for security I have put it in my boot tops, Sir,* says the Gentleman, *that is a very good place.*

Place! well Sir, my money is all carried in the cape of my coat. Riding about two miles further, *Sir,* says Turpin, *Pray Sir, what might be your business or calling? Sir,* says the gentleman, *I am a lawyer.* Then says Turpin, *if you are a lawyer, I am a cutter, and must cut the cape of that coat of yours before we go any further.*

[here followed an edited version of the Thomas Morris murder as reported in the *London Evening Post* of 5 to 7 May 1737]

[here followed the last few lines of a similar account which described the finding of a cave after the murder: the relevant item appeared in the *Political State,* Vol.LIII, January to June 1737, p.554]

[here followed a version of the Holloway and back lanes of Islington report, 22 May 1737, various sources.]

On Wednesday following Turpin robbed several coaches and persons alone not far from the powder mills on Hounslow Heath, particularly a gentleman and his lady, who live in Cork Street, Burlington Gardens, and were coming to town from whom he took upwards of 30 guineas. Since then the said Turpin, we are told, dined at a tavern with some gentlemen of Ailesbury, and leaving the room soon after dinner went out ordered his horse out, and told the landlord he had left the reckoning in the room; and rode off. As soon as the landlord perceived he had bilked him, and told the gentlemen in the room, one of them offered him his horse if he would pursue him, which he accordingly did; and after riding about three miles overtook him, and warmly upbraided him with his ungrateful treatment, in going away without paying for his dinner &c. Turpin desired him not to be in a passion, and told him he apprehended he had some Yellow Boys in his pocket, which he should take care to ease him of; and accordingly he put a pistol to his breast and robbed him of ten guineas, and then seemed pleased with the landlord's horse, making an exchange with him, and desired he would give his service to the gentlemen with whom he dined, and tell them his name was Turpin, and rode directly off.

And now it is generally supposed he sailed for Ireland, from whence it is thought that we shall soon hear more of his villainies.

>   Of all the famous robbers
>   That does in England dwell,
>   The noted Richard Turpin
>   does all the rest excell;
>   Tho' to Ireland he did go, go, go &c.

The Gregory Gang

He is a butcher by his trade
    and lived in Stanford town
And eight men did at Leicester rob
    as it is full well known;
Now to Ireland he is gone, gone, gone &c.

He only taketh from the rich
    what they well can spare;
And after he hath served himself,
    he gives the poor a share,
Tho' to Ireland he is gone, gone, gone &c.

He met with a poor tenant
    upon a certain day;
Whose landlord would seize on his goods
    'cause his rents he could not pay.
Tho' to Ireland he is gone, gone, gone &c.

Then Turpin he does lend him
    directly fifty pounds
That when the landlord called for's rent
    he might pay the money down;
Now to Ireland he is gone, gone, gone &c.

The landlord came and got his rent
    but was met upon the day
By Turpin who did take it all
    and then run quite away
Now to Ireland he is gone, gone, gone &c.

The very next that he did meet
    at the highway side
Was a gentleman and lady fine
    who in a coach did ride:
But to Ireland he is gone, gone, gone &c.

He soon made the gentleman
    deliver all his money
But madam she did put her watch
    into her hairy c---y
Tho' to Ireland he is gone, gone, gone &c.

> But Turpin quickly found it out
>   which made the lady cry
> Because he handled her twat
>   and stroked her plump soft thigh
> But to Ireland he is gone, gone, gone &c.
>
> Then he killed the Keeper's man
>   on Epping Forest wide
> For which if ever he is caught
>   he must to Tyburn ride;
> Tho' to Ireland he is gone, gone, gone &c.
>
> But if ever he returns again
>   unto the English shore
> They'll hang him up on Tyburn Tree
>   where he can rob no more;
> Tho' to Ireland he is gone, gone, gone &c.

From its contents and the fact that the last two verses of the ballad anticipate Turpin's capture there can be no disputing the date attributed to this pamphlet. It is a curious work, undeniably coarse, and crudely unimaginative in that for the most part it is made up of a random selection of newspaper reports concerning events which occurred during May and June 1737; the chronology is slightly erratic, and in some of the incidents (some previously described) it is unlikely that Turpin was involved, but being flavoured with a little fact, a little fiction and a slighty bawdy song, it probably made a quick sale in the market for which it was intended. For having not long returned from obscurity and in rapid succession been involved in a number of sensational incidents, popular interest in Turpin the Highwayman was probably at a peak which may only have been surpassed at the time of his trial, and posthumously during the 19th century. What is interesting however is that this really unpretentious pamphlet contained the bare bones of fact and fiction essential to legend, and with the passage of time, instead of crumbling away, the bones were fleshed to such an extent that Ainsworth needed only to window dress the figure within the framework of a successful novel to make Turpin's immortality secure.

   Some closer examination of the pamphlet is quite revealing. The description of the passage to Ireland is pure fiction, possibly of the pamphlet compiler's own invention, but although the next story about the parson has clearly been embellished the inclusion of a date suggests that it may have had some basis in an unidentified newspaper report. The comparison with [John] Nevison is quite remarkable because although for some long time it has been generally supposed that Turpin's 'Ride to York' had its origins in one attributed to this 17th century highwayman, proof of the connection has only been obtained during the writing of this present account.

The garbled version of the Whitechapel incident is particularly misleading insofar as it is presented before the *Green Man* robbery which precipitated those events.

The Yaxton affair would again appear to have its roots in fiction, and is not very far removed from the Huntingdon parson tale which also has a constable given to sudden intimations of mortality.

Turpin's confrontation with the lawyer did not end with the robbery, for this piece of scintillating dialogue eventually became a ballad. That the dialogue wasn't inspired by an existing ballad may be clearly demonstrated.

> On Hounslow Heath, as I rode o'er,
> I spied a lawyer riding before.
> "Kind sir," said I, "ain't you afraid?"
> Of Turpin, that mischievous blade?"
>   O rare Turpin, hero! O rare Turpin, O!
> Says Turpin, "He'll ne'er find me out;
> I've hid my money in my boot."
> "Oh," says the lawyer, "there's none can find
> My gold, for it's stitched in my cape behind."
> As they rode down by the Powder Mill,
> Turpin commands him to stand still.
> "For my mare she wants a saddle cloth.
> Said he, "Your cape I must cut off."[14]

Another such version, reproduced by Ash and Day,[15] ends significantly enough with lines which clearly indicate its post April 1739 date:

> ' Now Turpin is caught, and tried and cast,
> And for a game cock must die at last,
> One hundred pounds when he did die,
> He left Jack Ketch for a legacy.

The clue to the progression from 1737 dialogue to 1739 ballad is to be found in the ballad's location of the meeting on Hounslow Heath, and the subsequent robbery near the Powder Mill. The Heath and the Mill, although not mentioned in the 1737 dialogue, are described on the next page of the pamphlet in which the dialogue appeared, as being the 'powder mills on Hounslow Heath', where the lady and gentleman from Cork Street were robbed. It would be surprising if the 1739 lawyer ballad received its location inspiration from some other source. The Powder Mill robbery story originated in a newspaper report,[16] not previously described in this account because at the date of the robbery Turpin would appear to have been in Yorkshire.

The ballad refrain was put in merely to popularise the idea of Turpin having gone to Ireland, and in 1817, by which time it was on record that he had gone somewhere else, the refrain had become 'When a robbing he doth go, doth go,' which is how Thomas Seccombe found it in *A Collection of Diverting Songs,* published in that year. The Leicester robbery has already been discussed, the Leicester tradition having originated with Matthew King's confession that he, Turpin and Stephen Potter had been active in the county *before* becoming involved in the events which culminated in the Whitechapel fiasco.

The *Robin Hood* tradition of verse three is something else again, and possibly because it had absolutely no foundation in fact did not achieve any general or permanent recognition;[17] similarly the location of Madam's watch has not been given too much publicity. The prediction that he would be hanged at Tyburn must be regarded as ironic, for although in the event he *was* executed at Tyburn, it was not in London but at York.

FOOTNOTES

1. Beverley QSF/Mich.1738/D.7 (repetitive terms edited out).
2. *Daily Gazette,* 14 June 1737.
3. *Ibid.,* 17 June 1737.
4. *Political State,* Vol.LIV, July to December 1737, p.145.
5. P.R.O./T.53/39 p.325.
6. *Kentish Post,* 22 to 25 June 1737.
7. *London Evening Post,* 18 to 21 June 1737.
8. *Ibid.,* 23 to 25 June 1737.
9. *Political State,* Vol.LIV, July to December 1737, p.63.
10. P.R.O./T.53/39 p.325.
11. *London Gazette,* 25 to 28 June 1737; and P.R.O./S.P.36/41 f.22 (for 21 May draft).
12. *London Evening Post,* 2 to 5 July 1737.
13. Brit. Mus./C.136 bb.2 (dated in General Catalogue as being 1737)– (purchased by the Trustees of the British Museum, 15 April 1962).
14. 'O Rare Turpin,' a 1739 ballad, this version that which appeared in G.S. Maxwell's *Highwayman's Heath,* New Edition 1949, p.196. Other versions are Brit. Mus./11621 h.12 and C.116 h.2 (44).
15. *Immortal Turpin,* p.129.
16. *General Evening Post,* 11 June 1737.
17. At least, not in England. However, in the Information of Thomas Seals taken on 5 July 1816, concerning the activities of Bushrangers in Van Diemen's Land, we see how effectively the idea was transported. 'They said that if I would be a friend to them, they would reward me well, and that there would be no danger in what they would give me for they were fully determined to be like TURPIN to rob from the rich to give to the poor.'P.R.O./C.O. 201/89 f.128 v. Item advised by Mr. D.S.Jones.

CHAPTER TWO

I

IN JULY 1737, leaving Turpin ferrying to and fro across the Humber, we hear news of three of his former associates, the first of which is Stephen Potter. 'No. 103 Stephen Potter Committed for several felonies and robberies in the counties of Leicester and Essex to be sent &c.'[1] The marginal entry against Potter's name in the previous entry of committal makes plain the intention of sending him to Chelmsford first, where he would be charged with robbing Mr. Major; for although committed to Newgate, with witnesses entering into their recognisances in Middlesex, the crime was committed in Essex.[2]

II

At the July Assizes for Hertford however, Robert Nott, the man taken with Elizabeth Turpin and Hannah Elcombe at Puckeridge in February, was to be given his freedom. A certain formality had to be observed before this was done, and the *Gaol Calendar* for the Summer term 1737 summarised the conditions upon which Nott had remained in the gaol, previously laid down at the February Gaol Delivery: 'Robt. Nott remains in gaol until security is given before Thomas Rolt Esq. for his appearance at the next Assizes.' The reason for making this statement in July served merely to explain his presence in the gaol, in the absence of any charges. Technically he had been held on suspicion of highway robbery, but it must have become clear long before the Summer Assize that there would be no hope of substantiating charges, and his release on 18 July must have been inevitable.[3] The final reference to Nott was made in the Sheriff's Cravings for expenses for the year ending Michaelmas 1737. 'for diet and guarding of Robert Nott (ordered to remain in gaol on a suspicion of robbing on the highway) from the 28th Feb. 1737 to the 18th of July 1737 being 20 weeks at 2.6. a week. £2. 10s. 0d.'[4] Mercy seasoned Justice in July 1737, for Robert Nott was only the first of Turpin's three companions who were to taste it in that month and appreciate its milder flavour.

III

On 18 July Rowden arrived in London en route for Chelmsford, but since the journey from London to Chelmsford was begun *and* completed on 20 July and the journey from Gloucester to Chelmsford took eight days, he must have been escorted from Gloucester on 13 July.

> On Monday the 18th [July] about seven o'clock in the evening, Rowden, one of the late Gregory's gang, was brought by a Habeas Corpus from Gloucester jail into Newgate, and was immediately put into the Old Condemned Hold for security. On Wednesday morning between five and six o'clock he was taken from thence and put on horseback, with his legs chained under the horse's belly, a proper guard attending him to Chelmsford, in order to take his trial for robberies which he committed in the county of Essex, in company with Rose, Fielder, Walker, Turpin and the Evidence Wheeler, who went down the same day, to be an evidence against him.[5]

On the same day that Rowden continued his broken journey from Gloucester to Chelmsford, and set out early in the morning from Newgate, Stephen Potter was also being removed from Newgate to Chelmsford. The probability is that he went in a chaise with a party which travelled somewhat faster than Rowden's.

The Gaol Calendar for the Essex Midsummer Assizes 1737 states that Stephen Potter was brought the 20th of July by Habeas Corpus from Newgate and charged with being concerned with Richard Turpin in robbing Joseph Major on the highway.' The Gaol Delivery for 20 July recorded that he was to be delivered by proclamation upon payment of his fees, and that 'Daniel Crisp *alias* Thomas Rowden [was] brought from Gloucester gaol by Habeas Corpus.'[6]

It cannot be assumed, because the various recognisances entered into to prosecute Potter related to appearance before the Middlesex Grand Jury, that no witnesses were present when he appeared at Chelmsford. The decision to change the venue for his appearance would no doubt have been conveyed to them and their attendance requested. With Matthew King dead and Turpin gone, the testimony of Joseph Major was insufficient to convince the jury that there was a case against Potter. This reliance upon the live testimony of Matthew King is further indicated by the fact that even though the Essex

Jury would not proceed against Potter, there was still no instruction for him to be sent to Leicester.

Rowden however was not to escape so lightly, but since for the time being the journeying of both Potter and Rowden had come to an end, some note should be made of the expenses claimed for bringing them to Chelmsford. The **Gloucestershire** Sheriff claimed £14 0s. 0d. 'For conveying Daniel Crispe *alias* Thomas Rowden a felon from the Castle of Gloucester to the county gaol of Essex being 8 days men horsehire and expenses,' and the Sheriff of **Middlesex** craved £10 4s. 0d. 'For conducting Stephen Potter to the county of Essex, charged with robbing a man on the highway for 5 men and 5 horses hire 3 days for horsemeat mans meat care panis &c. @ 12s. a day each man and horse, [and] 2 writs of Habeas Corpus'[7]

IV

During the days of the Gregory gang Rowden appears to have been a fairly regular member, and there is evidence that he was actively involved in the robberies of Skinner, Mason and Widow Shelley. No charges were ever brought in respect of the Widow Shelley robbery, but as Rowden's name was entered on the Skinner and Mason indictments, it might have been expected that he would be charged on both those counts. From the evidence in the Assize records and elsewhere however, it would appear that he was tried for the Skinner robbery and that the Mason charges were not proceeded with.

There is some slight element of doubt as to exactly what did happen at the trial because from the Mason indictment it would appear that Rowden did get as far as making the usual plea, and 'Puts himself' is entered on the document. Normally, if he had been tried, the judgement would have been written in after this, and even if having been tried on two counts the sentence was spelt out on the other indictment, there should have been some formal reference to it such as, 'judgement on another indictment'. The probable explanation is that, as in the case of the second Skinner robbery where the accused were also being tried on other counts and entered pleas in each case, a form of annotation which appeared on that indictment should have been written on this, *viz.* 'Not tried on this being convicted on another indictment.' So on Wednesday 20 July 1737 it happened that the first charge to be brought against Rowden was of robbing Ambrose Skinner Senior and Junior, and since he was convicted on that particular charge, it was also the last.

Rowden was charged with burglary and felony in the house of Ambrose Skinner, committed on 19 December 1734, in that he did break and enter and steal goods and money to the value of £16 10s. 0d. from Ambrose

Skinner the Elder, and £136 4s. 0d. from Ambrose Skinner the Younger. And the judgement was, 'Guilty of the felony only to value as in the indictment. No chattels. To be hanged.'[8]

Apart from Wheeler, Thomas Bailis, and the Keeper of Gloucester Gaol, all of whom were obliged to attend his trial, it cannot be said with any certainty which other witnesses were present. The persons whose names were endorsed on the indictment were those who attended the trial of Herbert Haines, and apart from Ambrose Skinner the Younger, it is unlikely that there would have been much point in any of the others being called. Thomas Bailis spoke of, 'going to Essex and Kent to bring the prosecutors to town,' but apart from the elder and younger Skinners (one of whom presumably had removed to Kent) and Wheeler, it cannot be imagined who else's evidence would have contributed towards Rowden's conviction.

The judge however recommended Rowden for mercy on condition of transportation but as Haines was tried on the same count and hung, why was Rowden treated so leniently? Haines was unlucky, for although like Rowden he was found not guilty of the burglary of Skinner's house, he *was* (unlike Rowden) also tried for the Mason robbery and found guilty. Thus having been found guilty of some involvement in both crimes there was little chance of *his* being recommended for mercy. There was also a third indictment against Haines, but the other two were in themselves more than enough to seal his fate.

It is, on the face of it, unlikely that Rowden's acquittal of the burglary made the judge decide in his favour; Rowden was a rogue, the jury knew it and the judge knew it, and despite the fact Rowden was only being tried for the one crime, it is still surprising the sentence was not allowed to stand, either by the judge, or the higher authorities who considered his recommendation. And since Rowden was not tried for the Mason robbery, one is bound to wonder how hard the authorities were trying to bring Rowden to the gallows, if at all.

Rowden had not been allowed to complete the term of imprisonment he had been serving upon his conviction at Gloucester. Had he been capitally convicted of a crime committed during his absence after an escape from Gloucester Gaol, then he would no doubt have been hanged; but the crime was committed long before he was convicted at Gloucester and it is this fact which probably saved Rowden from the gallows. The Crown would doubtless have been well satisfied to see Rowden dead and buried, but since it had prior claim to a prisoner completing an earlier sentence, it was presumably impossible to reconcile the two claims on Rowden's person. It is also conceivable that in considering the legal admissibility of hanging Rowden when the Gloucester sentence was completed the Crown found itself baffled by not having a precedent it could follow. In any event it appears that the authorities found it convenient to be merciful towards Rowden, and for this reason he must have considered his counterfeit shillings well spent.

The final irony in Rowden's case was provided by a somewhat dull clerk who copied the judgement, written between the lines of the text of the indictment, into the *Gaol Delivery Book*. '**Indictment No. 3** Richard Turpin late of the parish of Barking in the said County labourer &c. 20th July 1737 puts &c. Guilty felony only. To be hanged.'[9] For such is the insertion of the judgement in the indictment that it appears above both Turpin (who was never tried for this offence) *and* Rowden; perhaps it was wishful thinking that brought about this incredible error, if error it was and not the work of someone with a wilful sense of humour. A similar misrepresentation is used to conclude this present section on Rowden the Pewterer. 'Thursday [28 July], Rowden the Highwayman, one of Gregory's Gang who was tried at Chelmsford Assizes and cast for transportation was brought back to Newgate with his legs chained under a horse's belly, and it's thought will be tried at the Old Bailey for robberies committed in Middlesex.'[10]

Ash and Day, commenting on this report, cut short Rowden's life by a few years, '... and although Rowden the Pewterer at one time looked like cheating the gallows, fate decreed otherwise.'[11] Rowden *was* transported in 1738, but the newspaper report is interesting in that although inaccurate (Rowden remained at Chelmsford until he was transported), it does reflect the anticipation of other charges which were not, in the event, forthcoming. This lends some support to the argument that the leniency shewn to Rowden was unusual, and that both public and press no doubt expected that he would have been treated in the same manner as most of the hard core members of the Gregory gang.

V

The daily Domestic news of those days (particularly in the case of London newspapers) did not amount to very much compared with what we might read today, for the size of the average newspaper was never much more than four pages of which two were filled with advertisements and related matter; Court and Foreign news might fill the first page (reports from Foreign correspondents were always lengthy), with two or three items of Country News if there was room, and page two might just be filled with Domestic news of every conceivable variety. Thus in comparison with today's news a four or five line report on Turpin would have been the equivalent of a fairly meaty article, and certainly useful as a space filler in the fight to keep the circulation going. So although we know that Turpin on such and such a day in July or August 1737 was at Brough in Yorkshire, or some unspecified place in Lincolnshire, and the reports of him in London newspapers are hardly relevant to his new activities, we cannot ignore the fact that he was news, a stimulant to those who found his career exciting and who wondered where he might next appear and when, if ever, he would be caught. The first such report is somewhat retrospective, and relates to the beginning of July.

> ... an Owl, that had strayed from some house in the neighbourhood, was caught in the Butcher Row and carried to the *Swan* Ale House [Bromley]. It was immediately reported that the noted Mr. Turpin was taken, which occasioned such a concourse of people out of curiosity to see him, that several persons gave threepence for admittance into the house for the poor innocent bird to hoot at them.[12]

> On Monday morning [25 July] about nine o'clock Turpin was seen by several gentlemen who knew him, at Tottenham High Cross mounted on a grey mare, with a boy behind him as a servant, on a brown horse, with a black velvet cap and silver tassel, and rode through the town without being molested.[13]

The absurdity of the 'Owl' story is matched by the Tottenham High Cross report which would have us believe in a Turpin progress hardly becoming to a man with £200 on his head, but apart from stories which may have emanated from practical jokers and idle mischief makers, publicity seekers and sensation mongers, there was one occasion at least when politics appear to have inspired the writing of a letter which only purported to be about his remaining at large.

> [From] *Common Sense*, July 30th 1737, No. 26
> "The Nation excited against a great Robber.
> Public Spirit was every Foundation of the Roman Greatness, when every private Person places his first Concern and Interest in the Safety, Welfare and Honour of the Public.
> I thank God I was born in a Country that has formerly emulated the Romans in their Public Spirit, as is evident from their Conquests abroad and Struggles for liberty at home. But this noble Principal, though not utterly lost, I cannot think at present so active as it ought to be in a Nation so jealous of her Liberty.
> My Suspicion is grounded on a later Instance. I mean the flagrant, undisturbed Success of the infamous Turpin, who hath robbed in a Manner, scarce ever known before, for several years, and is grown so insolent and impudent as to threaten particular Persons, and become openly dangerous to the Lives as well as Fortunes of the People of England.
> That a Fellow, who is known to be a Thief by the whole Kingdom, shall for a long time continue to rob us, and not only so, but to make jest of us, shall defy the Laws and laugh at Justice, argues a want of Public Spirit, which should make every particular Member sensible of the Public Calamity and ambitious of the

> Honour of extirpating such a notorious Robber from the Society, since he owes his long Successes to no other Cause than his immoderate Impudence and the Sloth and pusillanimity of those who ought to bring him to Justice."
>
> Editor's note: If this writer really means Turpin the Highwayman it is a matter of wonder he did not think of applying our idle Soldiery for the security of the roads, as is done by the wise Government in China.[14]

The following month, under the heading, 'Weekly Essays in August,'[15] some reference was made to this letter in another, similarly taken from an earlier newspaper:

> From the *Daily Gazetteer*, No. 662
> 'Extract of a Letter from a Whig in Town to a Whig in the Country.'
> "... Had they wrote only against the Ministry, we could have borne it, though I could never yet hear a Reason why a Minister of State (See *Common Sense*, July 30.) should be compared to Turpin; and all Men of Honour called upon to unite in his Destruction or knock him over the Head as a Wild Beast.
> This is the New-Whig-Way of writing against the Ministry..."

One of William Harrison Ainsworth's more pertinently useful footnotes,[16] has his fictional character Mr. Coates as the author of the first letter, and describes it as a, 'diatribe against Sir Robert Walpole.' The details certainly are supported by Turpin's criminal activities and his remaining at large, but the use of capitals emphasises a concern for more high minded matters than the capture of a highwayman, and there is no doubt from the Editor's comment and the subsequent observations that this *was* an attack on a minister, Walpole being the most likely victim at that time.

The next report however was of greater interest to the general public, it reviving the vengeance theme against a person rarely named, but whom everyone assumed to be Richard Bayes. 'On Sunday morning about two o'clock the house of Mr. Bayes, The *Green Man* on Epping Forest was attempted to be broken open, but the maid being up and the rogues seeing a light made off. They are supposed to be some of Turpin's gang, who endeavoured to get in and it's thought with intent to murder the said Mr. Bayes. Turpin having often declared his intention as such.'[17] Bayes' ill fated attempt to emulate Jonathan Wild had possibly left him frustrated and it may be that he needed to restore his image of a man who had risked life and limb to capture Turpin and his associates, with no reward for his pains other than the fear of retribution being exacted upon him at any time.

By the following week the newspapers were prepared to accept any crumb of news, however unlikely. 'They write from Manchester in Lancashire that Turpin the highwayman was seen at the races there, likewise at the hazard table. He had a boy with him in a black cap and a green plush coat who went out of town together in the sight of many people, both well mounted.'[18] But less than a week had passed by before the newspapers were ready to capitulate by resigning their interest in Turpin, resorting finally to the story which received favour on the occasion of his previous disappearance. 'We are well assured that Turpin has found means to get out of the Kingdom, under pretence of being a gentleman in debt, and that he gave a considerable sum for his passage.'[19]

VI

According to William Harris, the landlord of the *Ferry House* at Brough, Turpin lodged there four or five months from 6 June 1737, and it may be assumed that he left the inn (he did on occasion return to Brough itself) during September or October 1737. His known movements from the time he arrived at Brough until the date of his capture are summarised below.

1737	June	Lodging at Brough)	Throughout this period he crossed to and fro between Brough and Lincolnshire where he stole horses.
	July	Lodging at Brough)	
	Aug.	Lodging at Brough)	
	Sept.	Lodging at Brough)	
	Oct.	In transit, possibly establishing a Yorkshire base at either Welton or North Cave, both near Brough, and a Lincolnshire base at Long Sutton on The Wash, not far from King's Lynn, and within easy reach of Cambridgeshire and Norfolk.	
	Nov.	These particular nine months can be roughly equated with the, "about three quarters of a year" a Long Sutton J.P. stated Turpin *alias* Palmer to have lived there. During these months Turpin stole horses from the vicinity of Long Sutton and took them to either Welton or North Cave near Brough where he disposed of them, presumably before returning to Long Sutton.	
	Dec.		
1738	Jan.		
	Feb.		
	Mar.		
	Apr.		
	May		
	June		
	July		
	Aug.	The sequence of events for this month reveals Turpin's sideline of sheepstealing, for which he was arrested; he escaped from custody at Long Sutton and returned to Welton with three horses stolen en route. During all the time be stayed at Welton he was known to a Richard Grassby who observed that he lived like a gentleman; and	

Sept. his Yorkshire biographer, Clerk of the Peace Mr. Robert Appleton, stated subsequently that, "he very often went out hunting and shooting with several gentlemen in the neighbourhood."

Sept. At the end of this month Turpin sold two of the horses he brought back with him in August (a mare and a foal) to a Captain in Brigadier Harrison's Regiment of Foot who was on leave from the regiment stationed at Bristol.

Oct. Turpin, having threatened to shoot a man, was arrested, and being unable to supply sureties for his good behaviour was committed to the House of Correction at Beverley. He never again obtained his freedom.

The above diary does not include one apparently exceptional visit to his family at Hempstead, which occurred during the summer of 1738, but for the year June 1737 to June 1738, during which Turpin was constantly on the move between Lincolnshire and Yorkshire, nothing more is known than has been related.

When Turpin first came to Brough he chose to lodge at an inn, a reasonable thing for a stranger to do and not one to arouse much suspicion. It was a temporary expedient, allowing Turpin time to settle down and look around, and for the local inhabitants to come to accept his comings and goings without question. We may assume however, from what appear to have been successful expeditions into Lincolnshire, that Turpin was gradually acquiring money sufficient for him to live in style, and by September 1737 he was probably able to lease or buy accommodation which provided him with the privacy more suited to his adopted profession and new found social position. The evidence which exists does not enable one to say whether he favoured North Cave more than Welton as his new Yorkshire habitat, but there is in Welton's being adjacent to Brough (and the ferry) the same element of convenience which brought him to Brough a few months earlier. His acquaintance Richard Grassby, who appears to have known him all the time he was in Yorkshire, regarded him as living at Welton. North Cave is some four miles from Brough, further north from the Humber, and insofar as Turpin would have been concerned of no particular strategic value as a place to live. North Cave is but a short way from South Cave *alias* Market Cave, the market town in that vicinity, and it is conceivable that, again as a matter of convenience, Turpin may have moved his horses there on nights before market days, in order to find buyers before the ready money was all exchanged. One could speculate further about North Cave, but apart from the market day theory and the possibility of his having stayed there on occasion with local acquaintances, there does not appear to be much which could have attracted him there on the semi permanent basis he enjoyed at Brough, and which he undoubtedly found at Welton from October 1737. But having established himself there why did he also find it necessary to do the same at Long Sutton?

With winter approaching he cannot have looked forward to roaming the countryside, but apart from necessity his particular choice of Long Sutton as a southern winter base may have been governed by familiarity.

It has been suggested that Turpin's flight to Brough involved him in passing through Cambridge, and that the reason he settled at Brough was because en route north he found the Humber in his path and a natural progress across the ferry more or less made the decision for him. Cambridge is about 40 miles due south from Long Sutton, and travelling north from Cambridge Turpin could easily have passed through it on his journey to Brough. He may even then have considered the advantages it possessed, but rejected the idea because it was too near London at a time when he needed to be further away. But upon reconsidering its advantages in October 1737, it is possible he found it to be a much more attractive proposition than before.

It offered immediate access to Cambridgeshire and Norfolk, it was near the coast and particularly the comparatively unobtrusive port of King's Lynn, and it also put the whole length of the county of Lincolnshire between the area from which horses would disappear and their ultimate destination in another county. It also served to bring him nearer to his home county of Essex. From Turpin's point of view, it would have been difficult for him to have found a more suitable place for the purposes for which it was required.

And until the end of June in the following year Turpin continued undisturbed and unsuspected, quietly plying his trade between the points he had well chosen. By that time he was, as one contemporary street ballad subsequently described him, 'the last of all the gang.'

VII

The newspapers seem to have been content to accept that Turpin was out of the country, for during the year following October 1737 it was unusual for him to be mentioned at all; in the meantime they had found a new hobby horse to ride, and their columns were filled with a considerable number of cases in which people had contravened the recent Act governing the retail of spiritous liquors. Gin shops were the cause of all the trouble, and since so many people sold gin and so many more drank it, the effect of the act may in some ways be compared with the atmosphere created during the more recently familiar Prohibition era in the United States of America. Thus with the prisons bulging with those who had contravened the Act, and the newspapers providing exceptional coverage to the proceedings of informers and committals and so forth, Turpin might have had some difficulty in finding himself an inch of column space, even had he ridden up to the portals of Newgate and surrendered himself. Certainly by the time sanity and sobriety had been restored most people had to all intents and purposes forgotten about the man who had figured so prominently in the newspapers of the previous year. In January of 1738 however, we have evidence of three people on whom his name and fame apparently made some more lasting impression.

> Be it known to all ye Goodselves That here do come to drink of my Good Beer or to those that do Here Come to Tarry and for to rest their Goodselves and Horses for the night, that the Clothes Here Set once were belonged to Dick Turpin the famous Highway Robber. He on the eve of January 12th 1738 Did'st put up at this Goodly inn as often he did but alack he was sudden surprised by Runners and did have at quick to go Just as he was with only his horse leaving behind his other chatels in my care.[20]

This notice, together with other relics of bygone days which once belonged to the landlord of the *Three Tuns* in Cambridge, was found by the authors Ash and Day in a small museum attached to a curio shop in Trumpington Street, Cambridge. Cambridge is not very far south from Long Sutton, and on a route to Enfield or places in Essex, but if at any time Turpin had been obliged to flee from an inn wearing only a nightshirt, one would have expected such an event to have been given some newspaper coverage. No such news item has been found. Allowing for certain eccentricities of language and/or local dialect, the wording of the document reflects an odd combination of literate and illiterate composition with a few 'Olde English' words and phrases thrown in for good measure, as though at some later period another landlord thought it would be a good advertisement to have such an exhibit, and composed this explanatory note in what he imagined would appear suitably archaic language. This theory is supported by the use of the word 'Runners' in a police context; in 1738 there were the parish constables and the watchmen, but runners, as a descriptive of law enforcement officers, is a term which did not come into use until law enforcement itself was conducted on a much more organised basis. The choice of date, 12 January 1738, was surely arbitrary, for although Turpin could have passed through Cambridge at that time, his known activities suggest that he did not.

Of greater significance is the report of a man who thought to achieve some brief notoriety by using Turpin's name. 'And on Monday last one John Ashwood, a strolling vagabond and a dangerous fellow was committed to [his Majesty's Gaol for the Eastern Division of the County of Kent] by Basil Dixwell, Bart., for cursing his Majesty King George in a most scandalous vile manner, and abusing other people then present. He affects to be called Turpin.'[21] It was perhaps an incident of small importance, but occurring on 30 January 1738, it provides us with opportunity to reflect on an almost unnoticed event. 'Last week died at Hackney the noted Wheeler, who was an evidence against Gregory and others of the Essex Gang all executed [or transported] except Turpin.'[22]

All we know of Wheeler is that he was a 'young fellow', but since there was no inquest, he must be assumed to have died of natural causes. It is remarkable that working honestly after his release he was fit enough to travel to Chelmsford and give evidence against Rowden in July of the previous year. But, with the passing of a mere six months he was dead, and we do not need to look further for an epitaph than the entry below.

St. John at Hackney (burial Register) 30 January 1737/8
John Wheeler (the evidence against some fellows hanged)[23]

VIII

With Wheeler's passing there remained of the original Gregory gang just Rowden and Turpin in England. In America, if they still lived, were Mary Brazier and John Jones, and Rowden was destined to go there as well. At some later date Turpin probably heard of Wheeler's death, and perhaps too of Rowden being transported, so there must have been times when he thought of his past and the tumultuous events in which he had been involved; again during his enforced Yorkshire/Lincolnshire exile, there were undoubtedly moments when he was aware of what it meant to be the last of all the gang, and alone.

Perhaps too, in February 1738, Thomas Rowden reflected on his good fortune, and thought about the future, and wondered where his elusive former companion might be hiding. And certainly, he must have wondered too what it would be like in America.

Whitehall. 10 February 1737/8

My Lord and Sir,
The following persons having been tried and attainted, at the last Summer Assizes held for the Home Circuit, of the several crimes hereafter specified, vizt: Thomas Rowden ... at Chelmsford in Essex, the 20th day of July, for stealing above forty shillings in a dwelling house ... And the respective Judges before whom the said persons were tried, having by certificate under their hands, recommended them to the King, as fit objects of mercy on condition of transportation for the term of fourteen years, I am commanded to signify his Majesty's pleasure to you, that you do give the necessary orders for the transportation of the said Thomas Rowden [to] his Majesty's Colonies and Plantations in America, for the said term of fourteen years.
Justices of Assize Home Circuit.   Harrington[24]

Rowden remained at Chelmsford until June 1738. Turpin in the meantime continued with his journeying to and fro between Long Sutton and Welton, but it would seem that he was becoming restless and bored with this routine and feeling weary of keeping up the pretence of being a law abiding citizen. Horsestealing was after all a clandestine trade, and although comparatively safe, it must nonetheless have been frustrating for a criminal who had long enjoyed the limelight to masquerade indefinitely as an honest fellow and be regarded as such by his Yorkshire acquaintances. And being obliged to spend so much time in a manner completely alien to his character, and rarely being able to relax in company, he was by June 1738, no doubt beginning to feel the strain, and perhaps drank more to compensate for all the things he missed most in that unnatural existence. In any event, there are some indications that his instinct for survival was becoming a little dull around the edges, for from this time on he made a number of serious errors of judgement, any one of which could have ended in disaster. The change may be said to have coincided with Rowden's departure from England.

Essex Robert Trist Esq. Sheriff of the said county for year ending Mich. 11 Geo. II, 1737.

for guarding and keeping ... Thomas Rowden ... condemned at the Summer Assizes but reprieved and ordered to be transported from the 22nd July 1737 to the 29th day of January 1737/8 when the said Sheriff was discharged from his office being 28 weeks at 2.6 a week each

£14. 0s. 0d. [sum allowed]   £14. 0s. 0d.

Hugh Smith Esq. Sheriff of the said county for year ending Mich. 12 Geo. II, 1738

for guarding and keeping Thomas Rowden ... convicted of felony and ordered for transportation from the 29th January 1737/8 When the said Sheriff was sworn in to the 6th day of June 1738 when they were transported at 2.6 per week each being 18 weeks

£9. 0s. 0d. [sum allowed]   £9. 10s. 0d.

for conveying Thomas Rowden ... under a strong guard from Chelmsford to Blackwall where they were transported.

[charge on the county]   £10. 0s. 0d.[25]

Rowden was almost a year in Chelmsford prison before he was transported. Then on 6 June 1738, he was removed with several others to London and taken on board the transport at Blackwall. Three days later they set sail for America. 'A true list of all the prisoners ... shipped on board the *Forward*, John Magier Commander for Virginia which were shipped by Mr. Jonathan Forward. June 9th 1738. No. 16 [Essex convicts] Thomas Rowden.'[26] The *Forward* arrived at Port South on the Potomac on 30 August 1738.[27]

It is of some interest to note what happened to some of the people Turpin had known and met up to June 1738. **Died** John Wheeler. **Died in Prison** Thomas Barnfield, Jeremy Gregory, Matthew King and Humphrey Walker. **Discharged** Anne Barnfield, Hannah Elcombe, Elizabeth and John King, Robert Nott, Stephen Potter and Elizabeth Turpin. **Executed** John Fielder, Jasper and Samuel Gregory, Herbert Haines, Joseph Rose and William Saunders. **Murdered** Thomas Morris. **Transported** Mary Brazier, John Jones and Thomas Rowden.

And then there was one.

FOOTNOTES

1. Middlesex/MJ/SR 2680 (Calendar of Prisoners in Newgate 26 May to 6 July 1737–Middlesex prisoners upon Orders).
2. Middlesex/MJ/SR 2677.
3. P.R.O./Assizes 35/177/4, Felony file for Herts. (Gaol Delivery and Calendar, Summer 11 Geo.II (1737).
4. P.R.O./T.90/147 p.150.
5. *Political State*, Vol.LIV, July to December 1737, p.145.
6. P.R.O./Assizes 35/177/2, Felony file, Essex, Summer 11 Geo.II (1737).
7. P.R.O./T.90/147 pp.193 and 197 respectively for Gloucester and Middlesex.
8. P.R.O./Assizes 35/175/2, Felony file, Essex, Summer 9, Geo.II (1735), Indictment No.3.
9. P.R.O./Assizes 31/1 f.15.
10. *Country Journal*, 30 July 1737.
11. *Immortal Turpin*, p.69.
12. *General Evening Post*, 7 July 1737.
13. *Ibid.*, 28 July 1737.
14. *Gentleman's Magazine*, Vol.VII, 1737 July, p.438.
15. *Ibid.*, p.499.
16. *Rookwood*, Cap.IX.
17. *London Evening Post*, 6 to 9 August 1737.
18. *Daily Gazette*, 15 August 1737.
19. *General Evening Post*, 20 August 1737.
20. *Immortal Turpin*, p.85.
21. *London Evening Post*, 2 to 4 February 1738.
22. *Ibid.*, 4 to 7 February 1738.
23. Guildhall Library MS 480/2., Registers, Vol.4, Burials.
24. P.R.O./S.P.44/83 pp.222–223.
25. P.R.O./T.90/147 pp.188 and 261 for the respective Cravings.
26. P.R.O./T.53/39 p.249.
27. P.R.O./C.O.5/144/5 f.12.

CHAPTER THREE

I

PINCHBECK IN Lincolnshire is about 12 miles from Long Sutton, and in 1738 the vicar of Pinchbeck was Thomas Townsend. Charles Townsend was probably his son, a young man ordained deacon by the Bishop of Lincoln on 18 December 1737; his title to ordination was 'cure of Pinchbeck, Lincs.' and as curate he no doubt assisted his father, the vicar, until he succeeded him in that office. These details are sufficient to establish that a man described as 'Charles Townshend, Clerk in Lincolnshire', was in July 1738 the curate of Pinchbeck, Lincolnshire, and that he lived not very far from the base from which Turpin conducted his horsestealing activities.[1]

Our main interest in Charles Townshend is that until about July 1737 he had in his possession 'a brown bay gelding'. Turpin stole the horse, and this is the one known occasion when he departed from his usual routine of trekking back to Yorkshire and ran south instead. The only reason he can have had for doing this is that the boredom and loneliness became too much for him and he was unable to resist the temptation to visit his home at the *Blue Bell* in Hempstead. How long he stayed (and it could not have been more than a few hours in the middle of the night) we cannot tell, but when he did leave, probably before dawn on the last occasion he was to see his father or any other member of his family, he left Charles Townshend's horse behind. Not long afterwards, some neighbour observed that his father had acquired a horse, and in a village as small as Hempstead this was not likely to go unnoticed. Not everyone in Hempstead was so friendly towards the Turpin family as to allow the unexplained acquisition of a horse to pass by without some reference being made to the father's notorious son. And at that point there were a number of people whose curiosity about the horse's origin increased proportionately upon recollection of the £200 reward offered for the capture and conviction of the son. So without mentioning their interest to John Turpin, some of his good neighbours instigated inquiries which eventually extended into the neighbouring counties; the method of inquiry probably involved the distribution of handbills headed, 'FOUND, a brown bay Gelding,' which would have had a further detailed description of the horse and the name of the person to contact in case of the owner's recognising his beast. This method would at least satisfactorily explain how Charles Townshend's horse was eventually found to be in John Turpin's possession, for which fact he was committed to Chelmsford gaol on 12 September 1738. It does appear to be the only explanation, for although by October Charles Townshend of Pinchbeck knew who had stolen his horse, and Mr. Delamare, J.P. of Long Sutton, knew that John Palmer, suspected of horsestealing in that vicinity, was in custody at Beverley in Yorkshire, it was not until February of the following year that Palmer's true identity was exposed; so it is clear that the horse was not traced *to* Hempstead because Townshend or someone else suspected that it had been stolen by Turpin.

In the normal course of events Turpin would have taken the horse back to Welton in Yorkshire, but none of the following suggestions satisfactorily explains why he took it to Hempstead instead. '[the horse], he pleads, was left with him by his son, to pay for diet and lodging'[2] 'Turpin confessed he bought the said gelding of his son Richard Turpin.'[3] 'And it is imagined ... they [Turpin and his father] used to meet and exchange.'[4]

Turpin's family were the only people with whom he could be himself, who despite the crimes of robbery and murder would not betray him to the authorities for the reward they might obtain. This is not to say his actions were condoned by them, merely that despite what he was, he was nonetheless John Turpin's son, who had brought them disgrace and little else, but still a son, a member of the family whom they could not send to his death. They may or may not have understood him or how he had become the most wanted man in England, they may or may not by this time have welcomed him with open arms, but the ties were still recognised; and if as seems likely, this visit was the first contact he had had with his family for over a year, then it was something of an occasion when despite considerable risk he came back to the place of his birth and upbringing. Turpin must have been aware of the disgrace he had brought upon his family, murder was not an easy thing to forgive even in a son, and it is conceivable that the horse was brought home, ostensibly as a gift, perhaps as some mean attempt at expiation, or merely as a peace offering to smooth over the awkwardness of unexpected reconciliation. Perhaps Turpin convinced his father this was one occasion when he had come by the horse legally, evidence of a new way of life as a legitimate trader in horses; perhaps by now his father had realised that he could not believe his son in anything but accepted the story as being easier than the lie. And in September 1738, when he was himself charged with stealing the horse left with him by his son, he may have found it less painful to say that he had bought the horse, rather than that he had accepted it as evidence of that son having put his life of crime behind him. Turpin appears to have learned of his father's fate but events which occurred between the time of his father's committal and his own rule out the possibility of his having found out on *another* visit to Hempstead, which suggests that he gave a name and address to his family by which he could be reached in Yorkshire if ever the need arose.

July 1738 is the only logical date for the Hempstead visit, after which Turpin went back to Long Sutton.

II

Upon Turpin's return he appears to have temporarily abandoned his role of horse trader and taken up sheep stealing, and this in itself was an irresponsible manoeuvre out of character with the man who had used some intelligence in creating a new one. In becoming a sheepstealer he immediately tied himself to and was identifiable with one particular locality, and lost his mobility into the bargain. For with sheep being much more difficult to handle and transport he would have been obliged to deal in small numbers and be restricted to very local markets and traders.

Assuming he did learn, possibly at Hempstead, that he was the last member of the gang, then there must finally have been brought home to him the absolute futility of his own position. In realising this the idea of more frequent contact with his family may have been conceived; but horse trading would no longer have provided him with the cover he needed, because to dispose of stolen horses south of Long Sutton was a much more dangerous proposition than taking them to Welton. Thus to establish himself more or less permanently at Long Sutton he somewhat irrationally decided on a course of action which was potentially even more dangerous. Allowing that his visit to Hempstead and leaving a stolen horse there was his first serious error of judgement, the sheepstealing episode at Long Sutton must be regarded as his second.

There are two sources of information which can be regarded as germane to this short period, Richard Turpin himself and a magistrate at Long Sutton. When Turpin was arrested at Beverley, he was examined by three Justices of the Peace for the East Riding of Yorkshire; and Robert Appleton, Clerk of the Peace who was involved in these proceedings, subsequently wrote an account of Turpin in Yorkshire and it is from his short work that Turpin's statement is taken.

> Who then said, 'He had about two years lived at Long-Sutton in Lincolnshire, and was by trade a butcher; that his father then lived at Long-Sutton, and his sister kept his father's house there; but he having contracted a great many debts, for sheep that proved rotten, so that he was not able to pay for them, he therefore was obliged to abscond, and come and live in Yorkshire'

This may be compared with the information of William Harris, landlord of the *Ferry House* at Brough, apparently taken the day before the Beverley examination. 'John Palmer told this informant that he lived at Long Sutton with his father and that his sister kept his father's house there and the reason of the said John Palmer's leaving his father was for debt and was feared of being arrested.'[5] The story about having got into debt over sheep was a very relevant reflection of recent events.

> The said John Palmer had lived there [Long Sutton] about three quarters of a year, and was accused before him of sheep stealing; whereupon he issued out his warrant against Palmer; who was thereupon apprehended, but made his escape from the constable; and soon after such his escape, Mr. Delamere had several informations lodged before him against the said Palmer, for suspicion of horsestealing.[6]

It would appear from this that various people in the vicinity of Long Sutton may have had their suspicions of Palmer confirmed by his being arrested for sheep stealing and escaping from custody. Charles Townshend of Pinchbeck did not lodge an information, because if he had done so, and learned subsequently that his horse had been taken by Turpin, it is inconceivable that Mr. Delamere did not hear of it also. Since Townshend knew in September and Mr. Delamere was writing to Appleton in October, we can only suppose that he remained unaware of what had occurred at Pinchbeck.

The exact period of Turpin's sheepstealing activities is difficult to define, but since he is unlikely to have conducted them simultaneously with horsestealing/trading, a few weeks following the Hempstead visit in July is the most likely. His arrest, as nearly as can be determined, must have been at the beginning of the third week in August, and delaying his inevitable fate by several months he somehow contrived to escape. He did not stay for longer than was necessary near Long Sutton, and set off more or less immediately for the only place which he knew to be safe, Welton in Yorkshire. There was only one obstacle to his getting there, he lacked a horse. We know that he did not have a horse when he escaped from the constable because the last of those which he stole subsequently was the one on which he was riding when

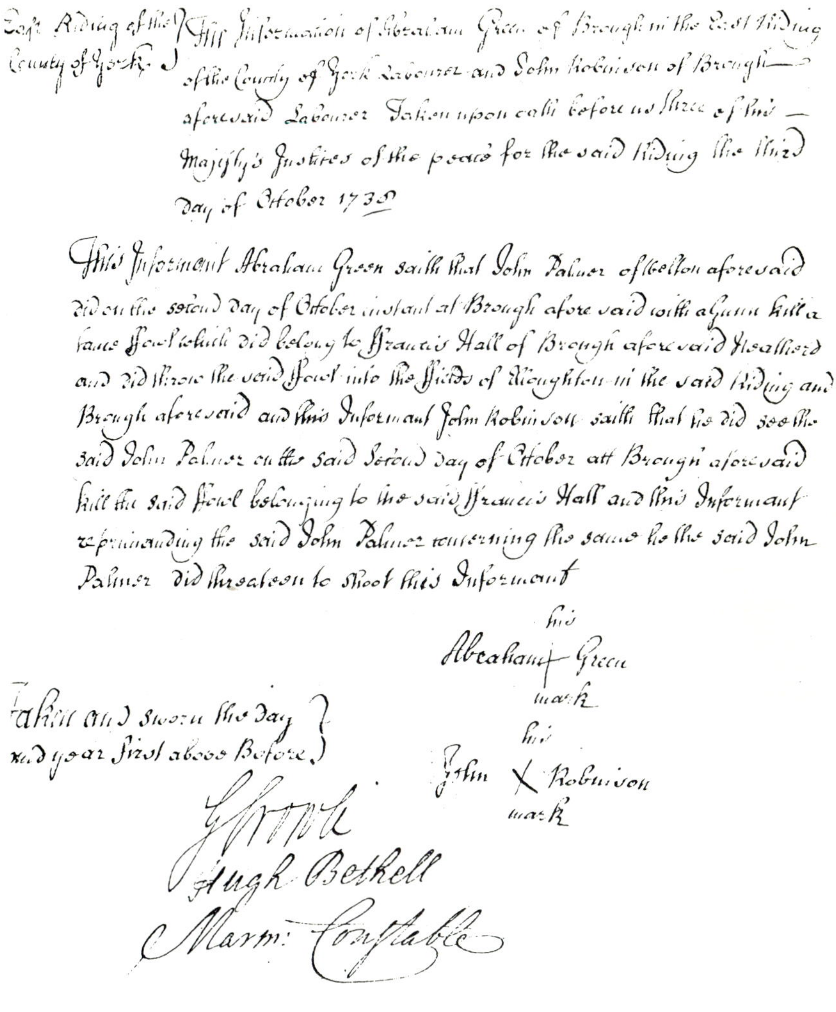

East Riding of the } The Information of Abraham Green of Brough in the East Riding
County of York. } of the County of York Labourer and John Robinson of Brough
aforesaid Labourer Taken upon oath before us three of His
Majesty's Justices of the peace for the said Riding the third
day of October 1738

This Informant Abraham Green saith That John Palmer of Welton aforesaid did on the second day of October instant at Brough aforesaid with a Gunn kill a tame ffowl which did belong to ffrancis Hall of Brough aforesaid ffealtherd and did throw the said ffowl into the ffields of Elloughton in the said Riding and Brough aforesaid and this Informant John Robinson saith That he did see the said John Palmer on the said second day of October att Brough aforesaid kill the said ffowl belonging to the said ffrancis Hall and this Informant reprimanding the said John Palmer concerning the same he the said John Palmer did threaten to shoot this Informant

Taken and sworn the Day }
and year first above Before }

                     his
           Abraham + Green
                    mark

               his
      John X Robinson
             mark

G Roo[?]
Hugh Bethell
Marm: Constable

Plate 17. Information against Turpin *alias* John Palmer bearing witness to the shooting of a fowl. One of the two Brough informations. Turpin was arrested for this offence and never again regained his freedom.
(Reproduced by courtesy of the East Riding of Yorkshire Record Office. Bev. QSF. Mich. 1738 D. 7 and 8)

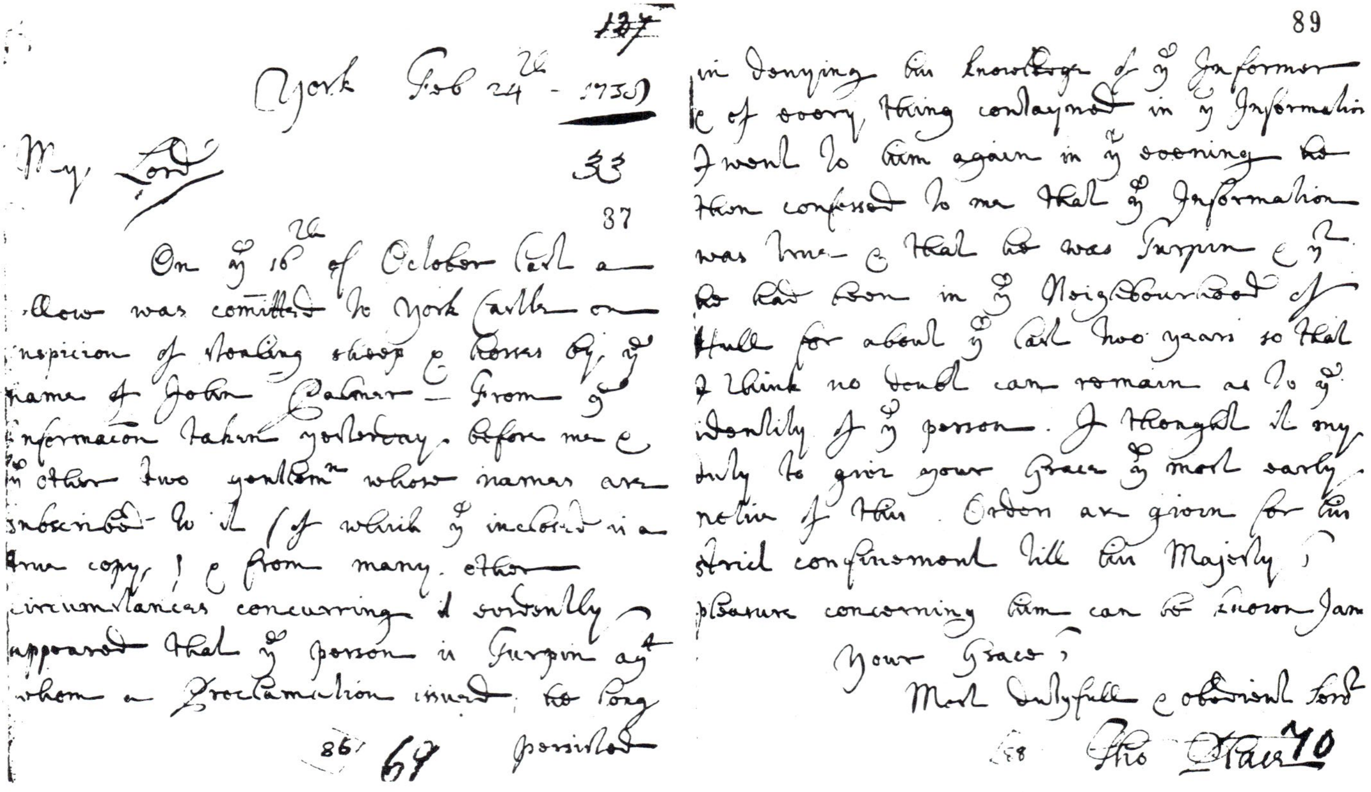

Plate 18. Letter from the Recorder of York advising the Secretary of State of Turpin's having been identified by one James Smith. *(Reproduced by courtesy of the Public Record Office. S.P. 36/47/86 and 88)*

eventually taken into custody at Beverley. From this it is possible to establish that having escaped from Long Sutton, he was somewhere between there and Heckington in Lincolnshire on the day that Thomas Creasy of Heckington last saw on Heckington Common his mare and her foal and a gelding; the date was Wednesday 16 August 1738, and by the following day all three had disappeared.

III

Stealing Thomas Creasy's horses was Turpin's third error of judgement, and the seriousness of it is determined by the fact that all our knowledge of what happened to these horses then and subsequently is contained in the testimony given at Turpin's trial for stealing them. The trial proceedings were published ten days after Turpin's execution, printed in a small volume which contained other Turpinalia. The British Museum edition is identified as the *Trial of Richard Turpin,* not to be confused with the fourth edition of the same which also contains the 'Life' by Richard Bayes, and which is identified as the *Life and Trial of Richard Turpin.* The pirate edition, *General History of the Life of Richard Turpin &c.,* published in 1739 before the fourth edition, contains a condensed version of the trial. The relevant part of the first edition, advertised in the *York Courant* of 17 April 1739 and published by Ward and Chandler of York, was described as: 'The Whole TRIAL of the notorious Highwayman RICHARD TURPIN, at York Assizes, on the 22nd Day of March, 1739, before the Honourable Sir WILLIAM CHAPPLE, Kt., Judge of Assize, and one of his Majesty's Justices of the Court of King's Bench. Taken down in Court, by Mr. Thomas Kyll, Professor of Short-Hand.'[7]

It should be stated that Kyll's record of the trial proceedings is not perfect; it contains ambiguities and errors and omissions, one of the latter being explained in the text as being due to the noise in court, but at the same time it is probably more complete and reliable than the Old Bailey proceedings which have appeared previously in this account. Thomas Seccombe added a footnote to Kyll's name. 'Both Thomas Gent in his *Life* (1832) p.185 and Robert Davies in his York Press (1868) p.244, speak poorly of Kyll, so we are not to rely upon his report as absolutely trustworthy.'[8] Gent, a printer of some repute, wrote his *Life* in 1746 (it being subsequently discovered and published in 1832), and it would appear that being charged with the authorship of Kyll's *Trial,* he fell into a passion. Davies, an antiquary and lawyer of somewhat later date, in his *A Memoir of the York Press,* merely observed of this entry that Gent referred to Kyll, 'disrespectfully'. This somewhat academic commentary does not appear to have had much to do with Kyll's ability to take down shorthand notes, and since he styled himself a professor, we must accept that he was sufficiently skilled to make his living from it. Some commentary on the adequacy of the Old Bailey trials coverage has been made already, and apart from reiterating that Kyll's reporting of Turpin's trial was probably a great improvement on those, it need only be said that the one other record of the proceedings is an allegedly pirated version which appeared in the same year.

Thomas Creasy was certain that he discovered his loss on a Thursday, '18 or 19 August', and that he had seen them last on Heckington Common the day before. Thursday was in fact 17 August in 1738 and Turpin therefore was approaching Heckington on foot on 16 August, having just escaped from the Long Sutton constable. It may have been the same day or the day before, the distance being just over 20 miles, but being accustomed to riding wherever he went he was no doubt somewhat footsore when he saw three horses grazing on the common, a gelding, a mare and a foal. Perhaps if he had merely stolen the gelding to make good his escape, it might not have been traced, but the loss of all three not only made Creasy determined to find them, but, since there was a foal, his task was made easier. George Goodyear, apparently a neighbour, had also seen the horses during August, and although he thought he saw them somewhat later in the month, Creasy's more precise recollection of the date must be preferred. It would appear to have been late afternoon or early evening on Wednesday 16 August when Turpin removed the horses, riding the gelding, because his own testimony provides us with a very good idea of what happened next.

Turpin's story was that he was going up to Lincolnshire (this is assumed to mean that he was travelling northwards through Lincolnshire) to see John Whitehead who kept an alehouse about a mile from Heckington. He stopped there for a drink, and the mare and foal (and by inference from his testimony upon the second indictment, the gelding also) were tethered outside the door. Whitehead had been to a fair and bought them, and wanted to sell them again. This occurred in August. Turpin inquired how much Whitehead wanted and gave him seven guineas for the mare and colt, and Whitehead gave him back half a crown. He stayed the night at the alehouse and left the next morning, visiting all the markets. The most interesting point about this story is that before telling it (at the trial), Turpin had elicited from Creasy that he also knew John Whitehead.

There is no doubt that Turpin did steal all three horses, but there is ample evidence that if required to answer potentially embarrassing questions, he resorted to twisting the truth to suit his own purposes. It is conceivable that on his regular trips between Long Sutton and Welton, Turpin did on occasion stop at John Whitehead's alehouse and was familiar with the landlord; it is unlikely that a mere passing acquaintance with him inspired the story Turpin told at his trial. This would appear to have been a distortion of what did actually occur.

Having come to Heckington Common somewhat late in the day and found three horses there, Turpin was unable to resist the temptation to take them all. He no doubt remembered Whitehead's alehouse and, convinced that the horses would not be missed before the morning and that he could leave early, decided to rest the night there. During conversation with Whitehead, the landlord probably observed that his neighbour Creasy had some horses like those Turpin was leading. Turpin bluffed his way out of this by explaining that he had bought them at a fair and paid seven guineas for them. It is possible that he finally dispelled the landlord's suspicions by asking if he might stay for the night, which the landlord would hardly have expected him to do if he had just stolen his neighbour's horses. In the morning Turpin departed, but he had a good start by the time Creasy discovered his loss and hired men and horses to ride 40 miles around Heckington to find out if they had been seen. There was no immediate response to his inquiry, nor to the loss being advertised in all the market towns in that vicinity, and Turpin eventually arrived at Welton, where Richard Grassby saw the mare in his possession. Grassby knew Turpin fairly well (for Turpin had on several occasions offered to sell him horses) and observed that he lived like a gentleman. All three horses technically remained in Turpin's possession (he appears to have employed a man to walk them) until he sold the mare and foal about the end of September 1738. He may well have tried to sell the mare and foal at markets en route to Welton, but not before he had put some distance between Heckington and himself, and for this reason it can be assumed that he had reached Welton by about 21 August.

From the events which occurred at Long Sutton before Turpin's arrest it appeared that he was prepared to abandon Welton and horsestealing for other activities but within a short space of time he was obliged to reinstate himself there and shew himself as a trader in horses once more. Unfortunately however, he did not find it easy to dispose of the mare and foal acquired at Heckington, not because he did not try but because he appears to have been reluctant to separate the two. Obviously his existence did not entirely depend on their sale, but it would not have been his policy to hold on to stolen horses when the longer he had them the greater the risk that they might be traced to him. But regardless of this particular problem, he would have been obliged to give some serious thought to what he would do in the future. The

Hempstead visit and forsaking horse trading for sheepstealing indicate some existing restlessness, but now he really only had a choice of two courses; one was to remain at Welton under his cover of horse trader and look for another situation like Long Sutton, the other was to take to the road again, a habit he had not by any means forgotten. 'Palmer then told [William Harris] if he would go over the water with him he would shew him such a pair of pistols as he never saw in his life and that if he would go over with him says the said Palmer twenty pounds is as easily got as two pence.'[9]

But on 12 September 1738 something happened which Turpin had not foreseen, his father was arrested for stealing Charles Townshend's horse. 'The names of the several prisoners confined in Chelmsford Gaol [as at 5th March 1739] **John Turpin** Committed 12th September 1738 by Thomas Warford Esq. and charged by James Stott for stealing a brown bay gelding, the property of Charles Townshend Clerk in the County of Lincoln, and the said Turpin confessed he bought the said gelding of his son Richard Turpin.'[10] But this 1739 information was anticipated by at least one newspaper in the same month that the event occurred. 'A few days since, the father of the noted Turpin was committed to Chelmsford Gaol, for having in his possession a horse supposed to be stolen out of Lincolnshire, which, he pleads, was left with him by his son, to pay for diet and lodging.'[11] At a time when Richard Turpin had nearly recovered from his recent escape, he was suddenly shocked to hear that his father was committed for stealing the horse which he had himself stolen. From this point on he would appear to have virtually ceased to care about what happened to himself, or was so insensible to what was going on around that this was the impression he gave.

How Turpin came by this news, whilst still remaining at Welton, has been determined by bringing together evidence from a number of sources, including a statement made by Turpin himself, and the only conclusion possible is that the news was sent by letter. The chain of evidence is as follows. 'A small time since a letter came with the York Post Stamp, directed for one Pomp. Revinal, to be left at the *Blue Bell* in Hempstead, near Saffron-Walden in Essex. It seems this Pomp. Rivinal married Turpin's sister, and since the old man is confined, they manage the house for him. Revinal refused taking it, saying, he had no correspondent at York.'[12] Turpin's sister was Dorothy, and the *Blue Bell* is generally referred to as the *Bell*. The author of the letter (of which the above passage is but a small part) was someone who although writing from York appears to have had some knowledge of the Turpin family which he was unlikely to have obtained from anywhere else except Hempstead, and of the two Hempstead witnesses present at the trial who had previously gone to York to identify Turpin, James Smith was without doubt the more literate of the two. Turpin himself appears to have been aware that his sister and brother-in-law had been managing the inn *since* John Turpin's committal. 'John Palmer told [William Harris] that he lived at Long Sutton with his father and that his sister kept his father's house there.[13] Harris gave his information on 3 October 1738 after Turpin had been arrested for threatening to shoot John Robinson, and it has already been illustrated that although Turpin's stories contained discernable elements of truth, he distorted them to suit his purpose. All Turpin did when he told Harris about his father was transfer a known set of circumstances from Hempstead to Long Sutton. Harris's recollection of what Turpin told him was in the main so clear as to indicate that he had been listening to Turpin on a recent occasion rather than when Turpin stayed with him at Brough. This is borne out by the fact that when the magistrates examined Turpin on 4 October that part of his statement which referred to his father and sister was exactly the same: 'His father then lived at Long Sutton, and his Sister kept his father's house there.' It cannot be supposed that the second version was taken from the first because the man who recorded the latter was Robert Appleton, the Clerk of the Peace to whom the magistrates went after the examination and instructed to write to Long Sutton to establish the facts.

Thus it would appear that Turpin must have had knowledge of his father's committal, but if the author of the York letter merely *assumed* Pomp. and Dorothy Rivernall had been looking after the house in John Turpin's absence, it could be argued that they had been living there some time before and that Turpin could have obtained such knowledge on the occasion of the July visit.

This is not feasible for the following reasons: Rivernall knew the letter from York was from Turpin. Even if he didn't know he was in Yorkshire, he might have guessed, but more significantly, at the point where he, a member of the family, failed to recognise the handwriting, someone else not connected with the family claimed that *he* did. It was not a malicious rejection, merely the action of a man married to a Turpin, who wanted nothing more to do with the affairs of the black sheep of the family. His lack of familiarity with Turpin may be inferred from the fact his marriage to Dorothy Turpin did not take place at Hempstead, and that they presumably, when not looking after the house there, lived somewhere else. If Turpin *had* seen Rivernall in July, his hostility would have been apparent then, and he would not (despite the validity of writing to someone who did not possess the name Turpin) have written to him subsequently when his circumstances became desperate. So far as Turpin knew he could trust his brother-in-law and rely on him, if he had not thought so, he would surely have written to his sister at the same address or, with less directness, some other member of his or his wife's family. Certainly in July 1738 Turpin can have had no idea that his brother-in-law would let him down in an emergency, and from this fact alone it would seem unlikely that he and Dorothy were present in the house when Turpin visited it at that time. To his knowledge they were then living elsewhere and it is the fact that he wrote to Rivernall at his father's address rather than any other which reveals that he did acquire the knowledge subsequently. The story he told William Harris at Brough was not an imaginary situation related at some unknown point during their acquaintanceship, it was information recently acquired which disturbed Turpin sufficiently for him to be unable to refrain from mentioning it. It was news which came by letter addressed to John Palmer at Welton, and when Turpin wrote to Rivernall he not only signed himself thus but took pains to ensure that the name of the sender appeared on the outside of the letter as well. Rivernall betrayed Turpin by default, a reaction Turpin could not have anticipated if he had known his sister and brother-in-law were living at the *Blue Bell* before John Turpin was taken to Chelmsford.

We have gone to some lengths to establish that Turpin did learn of his father's arrest, purely because the statement in the letter from York is not corroborated elsewhere. It is however an important point and the supporting argument also serves to introduce and clarify other events which occurred not long afterwards.

IV

By the last week of September, with the Heckington horses still unsold, Turpin's resources must have been running very low, and if he had not sold them when he did he would have had no immediate alternative but to return to those tried and true methods of making money which had brought him notoriety. His revealing conversation with William Harris at the *Ferry House* in Brough almost certainly took place not long before the sale was effected, for Turpin not only offered to show him 'such a pair of pistols as he never saw in his life' and told him, 'I am everything', but also confided to him that 'twenty pounds is as easily got as two pence'. Turpin then laid money on the table for a pint of ale, and drank to not being caught before a great deal of blood had been spilt.

It is a curious dialogue which reveals that Turpin was in his cups almost to the point of proclaiming his identity, and that he was perhaps resigned to becoming a highwayman once more with an end which now appeared to be more and more inevitable. But it was not to be, for if there is one thing which is clear about his last few weeks it is that he had lost his spirit, his interest in the future, and become a morose, dull figure for whom nothing would go right and who no longer had the incentive to do anything about it. It is a far cry from the romantic figure of legend, but having travelled with him from the time he was a butcher, stepping precariously from one disaster to another, separated from all those for whom he had any feeling, the survivor of all his associates and his identity forfeited, it is hardly surprising that a misfortune not his own but of his own making should bring him low; for with his father arrested, Turpin perhaps saw himself as he was, a man who although responsible for bringing his father to a predicament the outcome of which was far from certain, was unable even then to do the honourable thing and give himself up and confess to that particular crime. Instead he remained at Welton, wallowing in self pity, aware at last that he was a coward. It was a state he remained in for some time, because at the point where desperation obliged him to write to his brother-in-law for help, his father was still in prison, a fact which probably made all the difference, at the time when it mattered most, between indifference which might hae been swayed by family loyalty, and contempt.

Thus, towards the end of September, Turpin could well have given himself away or become so desperate for money as to commit some stupid and unplanned robbery which would have achieved the same end. But he proceeded instead to provide the silk for a web of circumstantial evidence which, although having nothing at all to do with the reason for his arrest, eventually made it certain that he would never again go free.

Captain George Dawson of Brigadier General Harrison's Regiment at Bristol, appears to have been on leave at Ferriby, about two miles from Welton, from about the end of September 1738 to the beginning of the second week in October. A few days before 2 October he bought Thomas Creasy's mare and foal from Turpin, and his story, albeit (as taken down) a little confusing, gives us some idea of how the transaction was effected.

I was one morning riding to Welton, and met a man leading his mare and foal. I asked him if that was his mare and foal. He told me, No, but they belonged to one Palmer, I asked him if he would dispose of the foal? He said, Palmer was coming up the street, I turned about and saw Palmer, who told me it was his mare and foal, and that they were bred in Lincolnshire, I asked, if he would dispose of the foal? He said, he would rather sell the mare with her, I replied, I had no occasion for the mare, only the foal, and asked the price of the foal, he said, Three guineas, I told him it was too much to ask for the foal, and offered him two guineas, and said I would not give him more, upon which I went about my business, and afterwards I observed the prisoner coming up a hill with the mare and foal, and, as I was going along, a country man said, Sir, you have been about bargaining, and offered two guineas for the foal, you see him come back again, and, if you please, I fancy you may have it, I said, let him come to my house, and I will pay him the two guineas, so about three o'clock in the afternoon he came with the mare and foal, and I had them both put in a stable, I went to pay the prisoner Palmer.

Nobody brought the mare and foal to me but himself, I went, and paid him for the foal two guineas and then he told me, I might buy the mare, for she was worth money, I told him I had no occasion for the mare, but the prisoner being a little pressing about it, I told him I had a horse of no great value, and if he would change, or let me have the mare to nurse the foal, I would rather do it. He did not like the first proposal, but I told him, I would not take the mare except he would have the horse, so I gave him four guineas, but being obliged to go to my regiment, I left the place soon after.

I think about October I went away and gave Richard Grassby the care of the mare and he had the liberty to work her.

Grassby subsequently confirmed that Captain Dawson received both the mare and the foal, which indicates that although Dawson refused to pay three guineas for the foal and didn't want the mare, he eventually took both and gave Turpin four guineas and another horse. But although the story is muddled, we do know that Turpin disposed of the stolen property and was restored in pocket. The unfortunate aspect of the transaction for Turpin was that although having made a profit of four pounds and a horse, the mare and foal had been so long in his possession a number of people were familiar with their descriptions and unlikely to forget them in a hurry. Eventually he might have heard that enquiries were being made about them and quietly left the scene on Thomas Creasy's gelding, but by the time Creasy did pick up the Yorkshire scent it was too late for Turpin to do anything about it at all, for by then he was in York Castle, *suspected* of being a highwayman or a horsestealer. The sequence of events which brought him there began on 2 October 1738, a day which for Turpin began like a number of others when he joined company with some of his local acquaintances and went out shooting.

FOOTNOTES

1. *Alumni Cantabrigienses,* Part I, Vol.IV, by J. and J.A. Venn, p.258; and Lincoln/Ordinations/Register No.38, p.340.
2. *Worcester Journal,* 29 September 1738.
3. P.R.O./Assizes 35/179/1, Essex Felony file, Winter 12, Geo.II, 1738/9 (Gaol Calendar).
4. *Political State,* Vol.LVII, January–June 1739, pp.191–194 (letter).
5. Beverley/QSF/Mich.1738/D.7.
6. Robert Appleton's account of the letter he received from Mr. Delamere, Justice of the Peace at Long Sutton.
7. Brit. Mus/518 f.41 (Book reference, the f. not a folio)
8. *Essex Review,* April 1902, p.69.
9. Information of William Harris, Landlord of the *Ferry House* at Brough.
10. P.R.O./Assizes 35/179/1, Essex, Felony file, Winter 12 Geo.II, 1738/9.
11. *Worcester Journal,* 29 September 1738.
12. 'Extract of a letter from York, dated March 2nd 1739' from the *General Evening Post,* Thursday 8 March 1739.
13. Beverley(QSF/Mich.1738/D.7, information of William Harris.

CHAPTER FOUR

I

MR. ROBERT Appleton, Clerk of the Peace for the East Riding, gave an account of what happened on 2 October, but whilst perhaps reasonably clear about what took place he somehow contrived to confuse those who had been involved.

He very often went out hunting and shooting with several gentleman in the neighbourhood; and in the beginning of October last, as he was returning from shooting, he saw one of his landlord's cocks in the town street which he shot and killed; and one Hall, his neighbour, seeing him shoot the cock, said to him, "Mr. Palmer, you have done wrong in shooting your landlord's cock". Whereupon Palmer said to him, "If he would only stay whilst he had charged his piece, he would shoot him too."

Whereas the two men who were actually present at the incident would appear to have been in a better position to know.

> East Riding of the) The Information of Abraham Green of Brough in the
> County of York) East Riding of the County of York labourer and John
> Robinson of Brough aforesaid labourer taken upon
> oath before us [G. Crowle, Hugh Bethell, Marm:
> Constable] three of his Majesty's Justices of the Peace
> for the said Riding the third day of October 1738.
>
> This informant Abraham Green said that John Palmer of Welton did on the second day of October instant at Brough with a gun kill a tame fowl which did belong to Francis Hall of Brough neatherd and did throw the fowl into the fields of Elloughton [at] Brough and this informant John Robinson said that he did see John Palmer on the second day of October at Brough kill the said fowl belonging to Francis Hall and [he] reprimanding John Palmer concerning the same John Palmer did threaten to shoot this informant.[1]

Appleton mentions neither Green nor Robinson, and instead gives them (as witnesses) the single identity of Hall, who was the owner of the fowl. It is difficult to understand how someone who appears to have had access to the correct information could have become so confused about what did occur, but with the facts to hand it is better to continue that part of Appleton's narrative which is relative to this particular incident.

Mr. Hall hearing him say so [Palmer had just threatened to shoot him], went and told the landlord what Palmer had done and said; thereupon the landlord immediately went with the said Hall to Mr. [George] Crowle, and got his warrant for apprehending the said Palmer, by virtue of which warrant he was next day taken up and carried to the General Quarter Sessions, then held at Beverley, where he was examined by George Crowle, Hugh Bethel and Marmaduke Constable, Esqrs., three of his Majesty's Justices of the Peace for the East Riding of Yorkshire, and they demanding sureties for his good behaviour, and he refusing to find sureties, was by them committed to the House of Correction.

Green and Robinson both saw Turpin shoot a fowl belonging to Hall, and Robinson reprimanded Turpin and was threatened by him. This is as recorded in the informations of the two witnesses. We do not know who made the complaint against Turpin because technically there were two injured parties, Hall, and Robinson who had been threatened; but if we are to place any reliance upon Appleton's account we might assume that Robinson told Hall what had occurred, and that Hall subsequently went to Mr. Crowle (accompanied by Robinson) and filed a complaint concerning the loss of his fowl.

Hall was a cowherd, but Appleton describes the owner of the fowl as being Turpin's landlord. The only known landlord with whom Turpin lodged or boarded was William Harris of the *Ferry House* at Brough, and after that time he probably rented accommodation at Welton. But even allowing that he was a tenant, it is difficult to see how Green and Robinson (both labourers), or Hall (a cowherd), could any of them have been his landlord when they would almost certainly have been tenants, and probably poor ones, themselves. It is just possible that the incident occurred outside an inn at Welton and that 'landlord' in this sense was intended to mean the landlord of that inn.

Shooting the fowl was a piece of bloody mindedness probably brought on by an unsuccessful morning's shooting which had aggravated his mood of futility and failure. It was an irresponsible act, but one which might even then have been settled amicably had he not compounded the offence with threats.

But being not only a stranger but an associate of the gentry was not in Turpin's favour, for the cowherd and labourer who made the complaint would have been unlikely to have acted in the same way had one of their own more influential local gentry been involved.

So far as can be established Hall and Robinson must have travelled to Beverley on 2 October and, on the same day persuaded George Crowle to issue a warrant for Turpin's arrest. This passed to Carey Gill the Constable at Welton, who, if Appleton is to be believed, arrested Turpin and took him to Beverley on 3 October (Carey Gill, in his trial evidence, said it was 6 October, but it could not have been as late as that). On 3 October the willingness of the local inhabitants to reveal their suspicions about Turpin was clearly illustrated, for not only were Green and Robinson on hand to give their account of the proceedings of the day before, but William Harris of the *Ferry House* was suddenly available to describe Turpin's drunken and suspicious disclosures. Hall, having presumably filed his complaint but not being a witness to the offence which inspired it, appears to have retired from the scene; but Messrs. Crowle, Bethell and Constable, having obtained the informations of Green, Robinson and Harris, and Turpin having failed to satisfy either their questions or their demand for sureties, ordered his committal to the House of Correction at Beverley. Turpin's progress to Beverley, to appear before the magistrates, appears to have been uneventful.

'**Carey Gill**—He was taken up by me for shooting a cock, upon which I carried him to Beverley Petty Sessions. He rode upon his own horse, and I along with him. He rode upon a horse which he called his own.'

The horse was Creasy's gelding from Heckington, and upon arriving at Beverley it was stabled at the *Blue Bell* in that town. The author of the letter from York, previously quoted, whilst appearing familiar with details of Turpin's Essex background, was something less than accurate about the actual circumstances which secured his arrest, but he did have this to say about the journey. 'He was carried next day, and suffered to ride his own horse, and was very jocose till he came near Beverley, but then seemed a little daunted.'

The author of this had done some research because he was writing before the trial took place, and it is clear from what follows that he was familiar with the contents of Harris's information. The general impression created by the complete letter is that it was either, as suggested, written by James Smith who combined his own knowledge with that obtained from people who to a greater or lesser degree were familiar with the facts of the Yorkshire events, or by someone who similarly obtained stories from the same people and one or both of the Hempstead witnesses. Thus depending on the author's source of information, we have a mixture of fact and fiction, of which the journey to Beverley has the appearance of being a more reliable item.

That Turpin could escape in similar circumstances has been illustrated, but here there is not even a hint that he made an attempt. Turpin was still at Welton on 3 October, a fact which indicates that he was not expecting arrest and considered the incident of the day before to be of no more than trifling significance. Certainly he was unaware of the lack of esteem in which he was held by the local inhabitants, and it is conceivable that his immediate reaction to Carey Gill's arrival at his door was one of complete surprise. There is no evidence to suggest that Gill secured his prisoner, whom he allowed to ride his own horse. At some point on the journey to Beverley one might think that Turpin would have become apprehensive of what might happen if he allowed himself to be taken into custody and tried to escape, but he didn't and we are left with three explanations for his lack of initiative; Gill was a man of formidable strength, Turpin thought the reasons for the arrest were so trivial he could bluff his way out of trouble, or he was so demoralised that he was no longer able to summon up sufficient confidence to make the effort. If he had wanted to escape Turpin would not have been deterred by Gill, and even if the constable had been armed, a horseman of Turpin's experience would not have been unduly daunted by the fact. Bluff was not a factor to be relied upon, and since Turpin does not appear to have been particularly anxious to maintain his pose at Welton, it is unlikely that he would have attempted to preserve his freedom by such subtle means. He should under *normal* circumstances have tried to escape, but although he subsequently became aware of his desperate plight and tried to do something about it, he was too weary of running to do anything about it at the time when he had the greatest opportunity.

At that moment it is possible that he was resigned to his fate and considering how capture would restore his identity and allow him the luxury of a London or Essex trial midst a blaze of publicity. Certainly his testimony at the York trial reveals that the idea did eventually cross his mind. But on 3 October 1738 this most notorious villain still clung to his anonymity and rode with the constable to Beverley. Turpin is remembered as a highwayman, and here was a highwayman who had come to the end of a long road, a fact which is well defined by that last telling phrase, 'but then [he] seemed a little daunted'. He was probably even more so when the three Justices of the Peace made out the order for his committal.

> To the Master, or Keeper, of the House of Correction in Beverley; Whereas it appears to us, upon the informations of divers credible persons, that John Palmer, of Welton, in the East-Riding of the county of York, is a very dangerous person, and we having required sureties for his good behaviour until the next General

Quarter Sessions of the Peace to be held for the East-Riding of the county of York, which he the said John Palmer hath refused to find; these are therefore to command you, to receive into your custody the body of the said John Palmer, and him safely keep, until he shall be discharged by due course of law; and hereof fail not at your peril. Given under our hands and seals the third day of October 1738.

It is presumed (purely from Appleton's account, there being no other evidence) that Turpin was delivered to the House of Correction on the same day that the order was made, *viz.* 3 October. Thereafter, until 16 October, we must rely mainly upon Appleton and the trial proceedings, for details of what occurred up to and including that date. The period is chiefly remarkable for the manner in which some of Turpin's more recent errors of judgement and lack of imagination combined to make his position much more serious than he could on 3 October have anticipated it might be.

The Gentlemen having taken several informations from persons of Brough and Welton, about Palmer's frequently going into Lincolnshire, and usually returning with plenty of money, and several horses, which he sold or exchanged in Yorkshire, had just reason to suspect, that he was either a highwayman or horse-stealer; and being desirous to do their country justice, and fearful to oppress the innocent, the next day went to the said John Palmer, and examined him again, touching where he had lived, and to what business he was brought up? Who then said, He had about two years before lived at Long Sutton in Lincolnshire, and was by trade a butcher; that his father then lived at Long Sutton, and his sister kept his father's house there; but he having contracted a great many debts, for sheep that proved rotten, so that he was not able to pay for them, he therefore was obliged to abscond, and come and live in Yorkshire. The Justices upon this confession, thought it the properest way to send a messenger into Lincolnshire, to enquire into the truth of this matter, and Mr. Robert Appleton, Clerk of the Peace for the said Riding, then wrote a letter to Long Sutton, signifying the whole affair; which letter was sent by a special messenger, and given to one Mr. Delamere, a Justice of the Peace, who lived there; and Mr. Appleton received a letter from him in answer thereto, with this account, That the said John Palmer had lived there about three quarters of a year, and was accused before him of sheep-stealing; whereupon he issued out his warrant against Palmer; who was thereupon apprehended, but made his escape from the constable; and soon after such his escape, Mr. Delamere had several informations lodged before him against the said Palmer, for suspicion of horse-stealing: and that Palmer's father did not live at Long Sutton, neither did he know where he lived, therefore desired Palmer might be secured, and he would make further inquiry about the horses so stolen, and he would bind over some persons to prosecute him at the next Assizes. Upon the receipt of Mr. Delamere's letter, Mr. Appleton immediately sent a messenger to Mr. Crowle, who came to Beverley next morning, and finding Palmer to be so great a villain, did not think it safe for him to stay any longer in Beverley House of Correction, so Mr. Appleton required him again to find sureties for his appearance at the next Assizes; and for want thereof he made his commitment to York Castle, which Mr. Crowle and Captain Appleyard then signed, and he was that morning, *viz.* 16th October 1738, sent away from the House of Correction to York Castle, handcuffed and under the guard of George Smith and Joshua Milner, who were directed by Mr. Appleton to conduct him safe to York Castle, and did it accordingly.

In general, and in the absence of other information about this period, one must accept this account of why Turpin was removed to York Castle; but there are some few points which require comment. If, after the exchange of correspondence, Turpin was regarded as a dangerous rogue, Mr. Appleton is unlikely to have asked him to find sureties for his appearance at the next Assizes, and since Mr. Crowle thought it unsafe for him to stay at Beverley and signed the commitment which resulted in a handcuffed Turpin being removed under guard, it cannot be imagined that he was allowed any option in the matter. The co-signatory to the commitment, Captain Appleyard, has not been identified, but George Crowle is the same Justice of the Peace previously mentioned, and Member of Parliament for Kingston-upon-Hull.

Mr. Delamere's undertaking to make inquiries about stolen horses does not *appear* to have borne any fruit; certainly Thomas Creasy and Charles Townshend would seem to have traced theirs without his assistance, but even if he had found someone to bind over to the *Lincoln* Assizes following, his efforts would have been invalidated because Palmer was tried at York.

Whilst Turpin was in Beverley House of Correction, there occurred two things of which he had no knowledge, but which had possibly contrasting effects on his immediate future.

> Likewise the same afternoon [8 October], Counsellor St. John and his lady going over Banstead Downs in their chariot, were attacked by a single highwayman, well mounted, on a black gelding, who robbed them of two gold watches, eight guineas, and some silver. The person who committed this robbery had a great scar across his face, and answered pretty exactly to the description given of the famous Turpin.[2]

In the description of the man responsible for this robbery, someone obviously confused Turpin with his former associate Samuel Gregory, but why Turpin should have been resurrected by the London press at all at this point in time cannot be explained unless by association with the reports of his father's committal. It is not known how widespread was this brief revival of rumour, but it does shew that the Pinchbeck/Townshend/Turpin and Long Sutton/ Palmer and Heckington/Creasy/Palmer episodes were not regarded as having any connection; nor had they anything to do with the manner in which in 1739 Palmer was discovered to be Turpin.

In the vicinity of Long Sutton the authorities were looking for an escaped horse and sheep stealer, a search which would not necessarily have been influenced by a report of Turpin stealing one horse from Pinchbeck, when he was to them an almost legendary highwayman. The London authorities on the other hand were still looking for a notorious highwayman and murderer, and the fact that he had stolen a horse in Lincoln and brought it to Hempstead would mean nothing more to them than that he had been away from his old haunts and had now returned south. They would have had no knowledge at all of sundry small crimes committed in the vicinity of Long Sutton and eventually attributed to a man called Palmer, and therefore never did have opportunity of associating the one set of circumstances with the others. So in this respect the above newspaper report, if it aroused any interest at all, would have served to enhance the idea that Turpin was still in the south and may even have delayed his denouement by several months.

The other thing which occurred whilst he was at Beverley had a very definite adverse affect on his future, for it involved the mare and foal stolen from Thomas Creasy at Heckington.

Counsel
Had you the mare of Captain Dawson?

Richard Grassby
Yes, I had the mare and foal.

Counsel
Did he give you leave to work her?

Richard Grassby
Yes.

Counsel
About what time did you work her?

Richard Grassby
About October the twelfth I think.

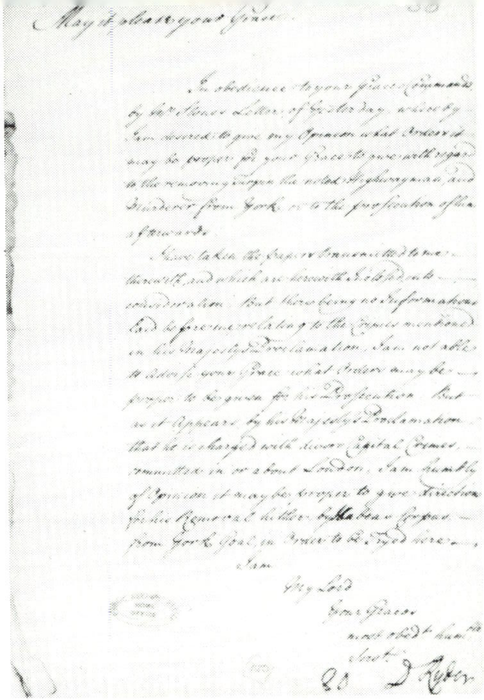

Plate 20. Sir Dudley Ryder.
(Reproduced by courtesy of the British Museum. B.M. 10859 a. 13 Frontis)

Plate 19. The Attorney General's opinion (signed 28 Feb. 1739) that Turpin should be brought South from York and tried. A few days later, George Crowle, M.P. for Hull, contrived to get Sir Dudley Ryder to change his mind, and the trial was held in York.
(Reproduced by courtesy of the Public Record Office. S.P. 36/47/100)

Plate 21. York Castle in 1750. From a plan of the city.
(Reproduced by courtesy of the Public Record Office. MPE 392)

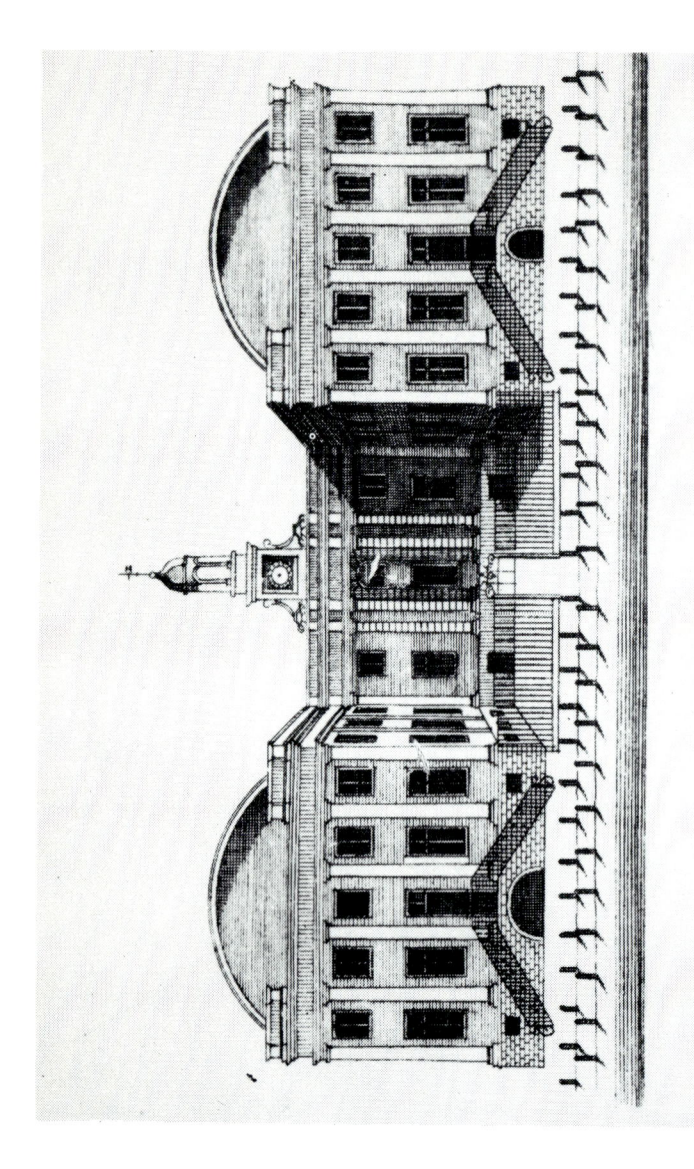

Counsel
   Did you work her?

Richard Grassby
   Yes I did, for I had a close belonging to the Captain.

The close referred to above appears from other testimony to have been at Ferriby, not far from Welton, and it was unfortunate for Turpin, particularly after his insistence on selling the mare and foal together, that they remained together in that vicinity when Captain Dawson returned to Bristol. If he had sold them together at Market Cave and they had been removed some distance from Welton, or if he had sold them individually not long after he had stolen them, they would neither have been so easily remembered nor so conveniently to hand when men from Lincolnshire arrived at Brough.

II

Appleton is the only man who gives an approximate date to the tracing and subsequent identification of Creasy's horses:

About a month after Palmer was sent from Beverley House of Correction to York Castle, two persons came out of Lincolnshire, and challenged a mare and foal which Palmer had sold to a Captain Dawson of Ferraby, and also the horse which Palmer rode on when he came to Beverley, to be stolen from them off Hickington Fenn in Lincolnshire.

Not even the trial testimony makes any reference to date (although the question was asked), and we must be content with the probability that Appleton no doubt rounded up the weeks involved and that perhaps three weeks or so after Grassby began to work the mare at Ferriby, at the beginning of November 1738, the following sequence of events was initiated. The account given below is condensed from the trial proceedings:

Thomas Creasy
   I heard of the mare and foal when one John Baxter, a neighbour of mine, told me he had been at Pocklington Fair in Yorkshire, and that laying all night at Brough he happened to hear of a man that had been taken up and sent to the House of Correction at Beverley for shooting a game cock, who had such a mare and foal as mine. Upon which information I came to Ferraby near Beverley and put up my horse at Richard Grassby's and began to enquire

of him about my mare and foal. He told me there was such a like mare and foal in their neighbourhood and from the description he gave of them, I thought them to be mine. So then I told him, I was come to enquire about such a mare and foal, and that his description agreed with mine. This all happened before I saw them, when I came to Ferraby after my neighbour had come home. The mare was black, blind of the near eye, with a little white on the near fore foot, and on the near hind foot just above the hoof; she was scratched or creased on both the hind feet and the near fore feet with 'I's, and marks resembling that letter burnt on the near shoulder, she also had a star on the forehead. I did breed her myself and keep her till she was ten years old. The foal was black. I saw them at Richard Grassby's stable door when they fetched them out to me, and I knew them both. I got them back later. I found my black gelding at the *Blue Bell* at Beverley after Richard Grassby had told me he was there. I had described a black gelding with a little star on the forehead and carrying a good tail. I went with the landlord and he shewed me the gelding and it was mine. I also shewed him to Carey Gill the constable at Welton and later recovered him by the Justice's order.

The Justice who was informed of these events and who gave the order which enabled Creasy to recover his possessions appears to have been George Crowle. Creasy returned to Heckington. Turpin remained in York Castle for although committed on suspicion only there was now ample evidence upon which to bring charges against him. His name, so he said and so everyone believed, was John Palmer. He was now held, and presumably charged, with horse stealing, and although at Long Sutton in Lincoln there were the matters of sheep stealing and escaping from custody to answer to, horse stealing was the more serious offence. As there was no doubt that he did, 'steal take and lead away' a gelding, a mare and a foal from Heckington in Lincolnshire, Turpin (assuming that he was told of the horses being traced and identified in a manner which indicated his involvement) might have anticipated being removed by *Habeas Corpus* from York to Lincoln, but there is no evidence at all that such removal was ever intended; and certainly when it was discovered that Palmer was Turpin, the Yorkshire authorities were prepared to go to some lengths to prevent his being removed anywhere.

So Turpin remained at York throughout the winter of 1738/1739, without communication with the outside world, and from November 1738 onwards without any prospect of being released. And with the advent of the New Year it became clear to him that he would be tried at the York Assizes in March 1739, under the name of John Palmer. It is perhaps some reflection of his apathy from the time of his arrest that he did not become aware of or begin to care about his desperate straits until it was much too late for anyone to help him. Had he been able to provide sureties in October 1738, before the evidence of the theft of Creasy's horses had been secured, he might well have been released; but at the end of January 1739, when he finally thought of doing something about his predicament, his position could only be regarded as hopeless. From the case of another horse stealer, of no notoriety whatsoever, tried at the same Assize, it is clear that even had John Palmer preserved his real identity the trial would still have been a mere formality to be observed before the execution.

III

On 1 February 1739, at which time Turpin would have clearly welcomed an opportunity to escape from York Castle, there were a number of felons in his home county of Essex who were planning a mass break out from Chelmsford gaol; but motivated either by his sense of duty as a good citizen or consideration of his own appearance before the Grand Jury, Turpin's father appears to have thwarted their intention by revealing the plan to the Keeper. 'Last Thursday fortnight, the felons confined in Chelmsford Gaol, attempted to break out, having got all things in great forwardness, for their design, when Mr. Emmerson the Keeper, was informed thereof by Turpin (father of the notorious robber of that name) who happened not to be of the party.'[3] There is no reason to suppose that John Turpin was anything other than a good and honest citizen, who may have viewed a prison escape with some seriousness, and a sense of responsibility towards his fellow citizens; but as he was committed to prison (and remained there) despite his account of how Charles Townshend's horse was obtained, he may not have felt one hundred per cent confident of the outcome of his appearance before the Grand Jury. He could hardly have chosen a more impressive method of convincing them of his innocence had he given up his own son, which greater example of good citizenry he had significantly failed to make, despite the knowledge that his son was in the extreme a murderer.

It was a point in John Turpin's favour, but it did nothing to help his son who, knowing only that his father was still in Chelmsford gaol, was obliged to wonder who else of the family would feel sympathetic if he wrote under his alias and informed them that Richard Turpin was in York Castle awaiting trial.

FOOTNOTES

1. Beverley/QSF/Mich.1738/D.8 (repetition edited out).
2. *Political State,* Vol.LVI, July to December 1738, p.297.
3. *Kentish Post or Canterbury News Letter,* Wednesday 14 to Saturday 17 February 1739.

CHAPTER FIVE

I

EARLY IN February 1739, John Palmer *alias* Richard Turpin wrote a letter to his brother-in-law Pomp[r.] Rivernall[1] at Hempstead. The one indisputable fact about the letter is that it was sent as stated above; the statement, 'His necessity in Gaol forced him to get a fellow prisoner to write the letter which he signed',[2] may be disregarded. One might imagine that the purpose of the letter was to solicit aid, but do we know its content? It may well be that we do not, for although this particular letter is one of four Turpin family letters published after his death, two purporting to have been written by Richard Turpin and two by his father, their authenticity is suspect. They may be described as follows:

1. Palmer to Pomp[r.] Rivernall at Hempstead, 6 February 1739.
2. Richard Turpin to his father John Turpin (released from Chelmsford Gaol), 24 March 1739.
3. John Turpin to John Turpin Jnr., 29 March 1739.
4. John Turpin to Richard Turpin, 29 March 1739.

No. 4 was published first, in the *Trial of Richard Turpin,* and presumably appeared in the second and third editions of this book. Nos. 1–3 were published afterwards in the 'pirate' work, *General History of the Life of Richard Turpin.* One of the most intriguing factors about this collection of letters is that No. 2 would appear to have precipitated both Nos. 3 *and* 4, despite the fact that No. 4 was published first and Nos. 2 and 3 and much earlier No. 1 were brought into print later by another publisher; but possibly even more intriguing is the fact that Nos. 3 and 4, written by the same person on the same day, should appear in different publications.

There was nothing unusual in correspondence like this appearing in print once the criminal to whom it related had been dealt with, nor was it unusual for unscrupulous publishers to print letters composed in their own offices. What we need to establish is whether or not any of these letters were genuine and therefore acquired legitimately by either publisher, or whether some or all of them were forged by one or both publishers. Turpin's trial was held between the date of the first and the last three letters, but they have no bearing on events which occurred after the trial.

1. York, Feb.6, 1738 [/9]
Dear Brother,
   I am sorry to acquaint you that I am now under confinement in York Castle, for horsestealing. If I could procure any evidences from London to give me a character, that would go a great way towards my being acquitted. I had not been long in this county before my being apprehended, so that it would pass off the readier. For heaven's sake, dear brother, do not neglect me; you will know what I mean when I say,

I am, your's, John Palmer.

2. York Castle 24th March 1739.
Dear and Honoured Father,
   The witness I called to my character was William Thompson, Esq; Mr. Whitehead and Mr. Gill, who not being so kind to appear as I expected, I have the misfortune to acquaint you, that I was convicted the day before yesterday at the Assizes, and am to suffer the 7th of April next for horse stealing, if you have any love remaining for your once dear son, I hope either you or my brother will go to Colonel Watson or Madam Peck, and if possible prevail on them to intercede for me, that I may get it off for transportation, I have no other hopes left but these and this is my last petition.

From your unfortunate son Richard Turpin.

3. John Turpin to John Turpin Jnr. Hempstead March 29th 1739
Dear Son,
   I have received letters from your brother Richard, the 27th instant, dated March 24th, and he is to suffer the 7th of April, which is on Saturday sevennight at York, on the suspicion of stealing a horse, or else a mare, his evidences not appearing according to promise. And now his last petitions are, that I or you would go to Colonel Watson in order to obtain transportation. Though he hath been remiss in many things, yet let your bowels of compassion yearn towards him. I would have you as abovementioned, and be as quick as possible. We are all at present in health, but deeply concerned to acquaint you in this, from your dear father,

John Turpin.

4. March 29, 1739
Dear Child,
   I received your letter this instant, with a great deal of grief; according to your request, I have writ to your brother John, and Madam Peck, to make what

intercession can be made to Col. Watson to obtain transportation for your misfortune; which had I £100 I would freely part with it to do you good; in the mean time my prayers for you; and for God's sake, give your whole mind to beg God to pardon your many transgressions, which the thief upon the cross received pardon for at the last hour, though a very great offender. The Lord be your comfort, and receive you into his eternal Kingdom.

I am your distressed, yet loving father, John Turpin

Hemsted.

All our loves to you, who are in much grief to subscribe ourselves your distressed brother and sister with relations.

Taking letter No. 4 first, it being the first to appear in print, one is immediately struck, as with all the letters, by the standard of grammar and the composition; for compared with contemporary journalese, the writing in these letters is very good. Colonel Watson has not been identified, but Madam Peck may have been either the wife of John Peck (a J.P. for Essex in 1739) or more likely of William Peck, a J.P. in the same year, but probably, a few years earlier, Sheriff of Essex. The preference for this Peck is that he was associated with Little Sampford, a short distance from Hempstead and therefore a man whose wife may have been known to the Turpin family. There is some evidence that Turpin did have a brother John but nothing else is known about him; the significant point about this reference to him is that even if the letter were forged, the forger would be unlikely to have mentioned a brother of that name if one did not exist.

A father who having been asked for help completely demolished the son's faint hopes by commending him to his Maker, would have been as much comfort to Turpin as the postscript which, assuming it was added by the couple in residence a few weeks earlier (*viz.* his sister Dorothy and brother in law Pomp[r.] Rivernall), would have served only to enrage him. There is some doubt that John Turpin would have written such a letter, for there was hardly time for an exchange of letters between him and his son John and Madam Peck asking them to make intercession with a third party, Colonel Watson. There was a need for positive action, for rallying the family around to contribute perhaps not £100 but as much as they were able to afford. Even as the black sheep of the family, Turpin could expect that much, but although admittedly he would have been a trifle optimistic in hoping to obtain transportation, there was no reason why a man in his position should not have tried. But if he did write to his father asking for help, the method by which (the letter suggests) his father went about obtaining it was the slowest he could have chosen.

This tardiness is even more apparent in letter No. 3. Turpin writes on 24 March, the letter is received on 27 March and the 'Dear and Honoured Father' does nothing until 29 March; he does however urge his son John to act 'as quick as possible'. This is not really credible, and any doubt which attaches to letter No. 3 must, since they were published together, attach to letters Nos. 1 and 2 also. These all appeared in the alleged 'pirate' *Life,* and it would be true to say that there is nothing in the context of any of them which could not have been obtained either from the letter and the trial proceedings published under the title of *Trial of Richard Turpin,* and printed in April 1739.

All three letters reveal flaws which support the theory that they were forged. Letter No. 1, by which it was claimed Turpin's identity was revealed, served no purpose because it failed to supply the date of the trial or the names of any persons of influence from whom the family might have obtained assistance. The request for evidences from London to attest to character had a precedent in a much earlier description of the letter's contents, published in London on 8 March. Letter No. 2 is addressed to a father long *dishonoured* by his notorious son, the names of witnesses not appearing were called at the trial, and the rest could have been construed from letter No. 4. Letter No. 3 suggests a certain disinterest on the part of Turpin's father, supplies the date of execution, and repeats the sad tale of the witnesses who failed to appear. The remainder is based on letter No. 2. All the letters are predictable in their content in that they contain nothing which the circumstances did not permit, each was based on information obtainable elsewhere, each contains the right amount of sentiment, and each (regardless of supposed author) contains a common denominator in the words, 'to acquaint you'. The criterion on which to base judgement on these letters is hardly the fact that the originals do not exist, for there is no doubt that Turpin 'relics' which did once exist have disappeared without trace. Somewhere there may be a document, or a poster advertising a reward for his capture, which lies buried and forgotten, waiting to be discovered, but the same could be said of anything connected with anyone famous or infamous, and the only relevant comment that could be made about these letters is that it is unlikely that they ever existed at all other than in amended draft form, soon and very conveniently destroyed.

By labelling *all* four published letters *forged,* it might be inferred by association that the Kyll's trial account was suspect, and that the alleged 'pirate' work was in fact pirated from Kyll's compendium. But Kyll's version of the trial, although containing errors, should not for any reason be regarded as a work of fiction. Similarly the 'pirate' version of the trial should not be condemned merely because it appears with letters which were undoubtedly forged. We do not know the date when Turpin wrote the fateful letter to Hempstead, other than that it must necessarily have been about the first or second week of February 1739, but we do know *something* about its content, and about the content of other letters which he *did* write.

The *other* letter from York, possibly written by James Smith, the man who 'knew all Turpin's relations', was dated 2 March, three weeks before the trial, eight days after James Smith had identified Turpin in York Castle, and one week after the Recorder of York had written to the Duke of Newcastle advising him of what had transpired. Thus within a very short time of Turpin's being positively identified, a letter was written (and subsequently published in London in the *General Evening Post,* of 8 March 1739) which contained a resumé of his activities in Yorkshire, the circumstances of his being captured, an account of the fatal letter and some indication of its contents, descriptions of his background and members of his family, the method of his being discovered, and commentary on his activities in York Castle after he was identified up to and including 24 February and possibly for some few days subsequently. All of which points conclusively to the letter from York on 2 March, being written by someone with personal knowledge of Turpin's background and an acquired knowledge of what had happened to him in Yorkshire. It could not have originated in London, for there would have been neither the facilities nor the time to present all the information in the form in which it appeared in print as 'Extract of a letter from York, dated March 2nd 1739'. The account it gave of *Turpin's* letters is as follows.

A small time since, a letter came with the York Post Stamp, directed for one Pomp. Rivinal, to be left at the *Blue Bell* in Hempstead, near Saffron Walden in Essex. It seems this Pomp.Rivinal married Turpin's sister, and since the old man is confined, they manage the house for him. Revinal refused taking it, saying, he had no correspondent at York, which being observed by one Mr. Smith (who lives at Hempstead, and taught Turpin to write) he acquainted a Justice of the Peace with this, and he sent to Saffron Walden and took the letter, which was dated from York Castle, wherein he complains he was in for a horse and a mare, and desires them to come down, and bring ten pounds &c.... Upon this several more letters were intercepted, in which he heavily complains of hardships, and presses them by all means to bring ten guineas and two witnesses, and then he don't fear but he shall come off; and desires them to persuade his cousin Betty Millington to do something for him, it being the last she may ever do. Now his wife's maiden name was Millington. Upon these circumstances being laid together, and the handwriting being thought to be Turpin's, the gentleman of Essex having had an account from the Governor of York Castle to whom they had wrote, that there was one Palmer that answered the description they had sent, they resolved to dispatch Mr.Smith into Yorkshire, who knew him perfectly well, and taught him to write.

The name of Turpin's wife has been discussed at length in an earlier chapter, and there is no reason to suppose that her name was not Millington. One might in fact have expected such letters to have been produced at the trial, but since proof of Turpin's identity rested on personal identification, written evidence was of much less importance. The requests for money are in keeping with Turpin's character, also the presumption that anyone would have been willing to perjure themselves to save his skin.* Neither money nor witnesses would have helped his case even had he, as he anticipated, been tried in the name of John Palmer. He did not have any constructive ideas about how his family might help him for there was nothing they could do without revealing him to be Turpin, and it must have been frustrating to discover his alias was as much a liability to him in those circumstances as his real name would have been. He was clutching at straws, hoping that something would save him, but the gesture was futile because the wretched letter was never read by the person for whom it was intended.

It was sent, according to the above account, to the *Blue Bell* in Hempstead. This reference to the Turpin homestead predates all others, and the plain *Bell* which appears in every Turpin biography written since would appear to have been inspired by testimony given by Edward Saward of Hempstead at the trial three weeks later. Saward thrice referred to the *Bell* as the public house kept by John Turpin, where Turpin was born and bred, but Saward, twice reprimanded by the court for the manner in which he gave his evidence, may not have been too concerned about the full name of the public house which was probably referred to locally as the *Bell*. The name is perhaps of minor importance, but lacking other evidence, the earlier reference to the *Blue Bell* is perhaps the more reliable source of information on this point.

The letter was refused by Rivernall, probably because he knew it was from Turpin and did not wish to have anything further to do with him. The excuse that he 'had no correspondent at York' was feeble, for mere curiosity should have prompted him to pay the postage and find out who it was at York who knew Pompadour Rivernall of Hempstead in Essex. Unlike the present day, when an unlimited number of organisations, etc. appear to have access to our letterboxes, the people who might write to you in 1739 were invariably those who knew you, or addressed you on official business. In any event Rivernall would not pay the postage and the letter possibly rested in the Post Office at Hempstead. The evidence on this point is not clear, for the letter was eventually retrieved from the Post Office at Saffron Walden which is five miles away.

* This idea was used in the letter, published after the trial, which purported to be the original from Turpin to his brother-in-law.

There was a Country Postmaster installed at Hempstead, but Saffron Walden being the nearest large town, the Post Office there may have been the place to which dead letters were sent from the village offices in the vicinity. James Smith would appear to have seen it at Hempstead:

Counsel
As you lived there [Hempstead], why did you come down here, to this place?

James Smith
Happening to be at the post office, where I saw a letter directed to Turpin's brother-in-law who, as I was informed would not loose the letter and pay postage, upon that account taking particular notice thereof, I thought at first I remembered the superscription and concluded it to be the handwriting of the prisoner, Turpin, whereupon I carried the letter before a magistrate who broke the same open (the letter was superscribed John Palmer) I found it sent from York Castle, I had several of Dick Turpin's bills and knew his hand.

Counsel
Are you sure this is his letter? (a letter produced in Court)

James Smith
Yes I am sure that is his letter.

Counsel
Was that the cause of your coming down?

James Smith
Yes.

Counsel
How happened you to take notice of the letter?

James Smith
Seeing the York stamp.

Smith just happened to see the letter at the Post Office, because it just happened to be lying around for him to see. The Postmaster just happened to mention that Rivernall would not accept it, and on reflection Smith thought the name Palmer sounded familiar. Since Smith could not have known this was Turpin's alias the only association it could have had would have been with the maiden name of Turpin's mother, and if this was known to Smith the question of his being able to recognise Turpin's handwriting after an interval of about six years is largely irrelevant. Smith was at some pains to establish that he had good reason to act as he did, but we may be sure that he only became convinced that he recognised the handwriting after he and the Postmaster had discussed the possible significance of Rivernall's refusing to accept the letter in the first place.

They were merely prompted by the curiosity which Rivernall appeared to lack, and supplied the answer to the question Rivernall should have asked, *viz*. not, 'who do I know at York?' but, 'who at York knows me?' That Smith may not have been so familiar with Turpin's hand is borne out by the information he made when he identified Turpin at York, a month before the trial. The information also describes the sequence of events which led to the opening of the letter, but in a manner which is curiously reminiscent of the description of the same events in the letter written one week later by the gentleman at York.

> Castle of Yorks   information of James Smith of Hempstead in Essex taken upon oath before George Nelthorpe John Adams and Thomas Place Esquires this 23d. day of February 1738 [/9]
>
> This informant said upon oath before us. That he saw a letter directed to one Pomp^r. Rivernall of Hempstead in Essex with the York post stamp upon it and Rivernall refusing to take the letter in [he] acquainted one Thomas Stubbing of Bumpstead Helion in the County of Essex Esquire, who sent to Saffron Walden Post Office and paid the postage. And this informant upon perusing the said letter had a suspicion that it was Turpin's handwriting, and four of his Majesty's Justices of the Peace in the County of Essex desired [him] to go to York Castle to see whether it was the said Turpin or not who says and declares before us that the person now shewn to [him] is Richard Turpin and no other person. And [he] is the better able to know Turpin by being bred and born in the same town with him and [Turpin] also went to school with [him] and hath constantly for several years since been in company with him till within these three or four years, and further said that Pomp^r. Rivernall married one Dorothy Turpin, Richard Turpin's own sister.
>
> James Smith[3]

James Smith, with the assistance of Thomas Stubbing, the Justice of the Peace from Bumpstead Helion, recovered the letter from Saffron Walden Post Office, opened it and read the contents. Stubbing also would appear to have been convinced of the writer's identity and as a result took counsel with three of his colleagues, about the course of action it would be best to adopt in the circumstances. The suggestion that they submitted a description of Turpin to the Governor of York Castle and inquired if it fitted that of the prisoner

Palmer is consistent with the precaution they might have taken not to send someone to York on a fool's errand; with the result that when James Smith was dispatched to York there was probably very little doubt in their minds that they would discover Palmer to be Turpin. The consideration given to the letter, the exchange of correspondence and the arrangements required to be made for Smith's journey would have taken some little time, and possibly a day or so before he set out for York, some word of the general suspicion of what might be found there had leaked out and reached the press. 'By some letters lately intercepted at Hempstead in Essex there are strong reasons to believe that Turpin the highwayman is confined in York gaol for robbery on the highway committed near that city.'[4] This first report is the only one to refer to more than the one letter, and although clearly the reporter knew nothing of how Turpin might have come to be at York, the fact that he did beat others to the story of intercepted correspondence suggests that in that respect he may have been quoting a reliable source; he could not have known the circumstances of committal because no-one outside Yorkshire (other than Thomas Creasy and his associates) did know. As it was the first letter which mattered, it is not surprising that if there were any others they did not receive the same publicity; but this reference does give support to the description (in *'Extract of a Letter from York'*) of other letters, even though it emanated from York ten days later.

James Smith came to York Castle on 23 February 1739, probably bearing credentials from the Essex J.P.'s; and on another occasion, the date of which is unknown, another resident of Hempstead came to York and identified Turpin and subsequently gave evidence at his trial. Positive identification was a matter of considerable concern to the authorities because it was such a long time since anyone who knew Turpin and was prepared to state as much had seen him; and, since John Wheeler had been dead for over a year, the more of his close pre-criminal days associates who could be found to identify him the better.

Counsel
  When you came to the Castle, did you challenge him or know him?

James Smith
  Yes I did, upon the first view of him, and pointed him out from amongst all the rest of the other prisoners.

It would appear from the 'letter from York' that identification was achieved by fair process, that Turpin may have been 'walking in the open yard amongst the felons', and that 'as soon as he [James Smith] saw him, he immediately declared and made oath before the Recorder and the Justices of the Peace, that he was the famous Richard Turpin. At first he denied it; but at night confessed it was true he was the man'. Just how well-informed the writer of the letter was on these points is illustrated by the Recorder of York's letter of the following day.

> York February 24th 1738 [/9]
> My Lord,
> On the 16th of October last a fellow was committed to York Castle on suspicion of stealing sheep and horses by the name of John Palmer. From the information taken yesterday before me and the other two gentlemen whose names are subscribed to it (of which the enclosed is a true copy) and from many other circumstances concurring it suddenly appeared that the person is Turpin against whom a proclamation issued; he long persisted in denying his knowledge of the informer and of every thing contained in the information. I went to him again in the evening he then confessed to me that the information was true and that he was Turpin and that he had been in the neighbourhood of Hull for about the last two years so that I think no doubt can remain as to the identity of the person. I thought it my duty to give your Grace the most early notice of this. Orders are given for his strict confinement till his Majesty's pleasure concerning him can be known I am [&c.]
> [Duke of Newcastle]
> Tho. Place[5]

II

The letter from Turpin, if not serving the purpose he had intended, had more than satisfied the authorities, and it is ironic that the man who had eluded them for so long should not only place himself in their hands, but eventually even provide them with the evidence by which they were able to identify him. In the days which followed, the news of Smith's errand to York spread from Essex, and rumour and speculation (nobody being quite able to believe what they heard) arising from what occurred when he arrived there gradually percolated southwards. 'A proper person has been sent to York Castle, to see whether a fellow lately committed there for robbery on the highway near that city, be the famous Turpin or not.'[6] A week later the same journal printed an account which emanated from York on 25 February.

> A man has been committed to our castle for horse stealing who, by means of a letter written by a prisoner here, which fell into honest hands near London, is suspected to be the notorious robber Turpin. And accordingly a person coming down from London, in order to make a proper discovery whether it was he or not, it is this day verily believed that it is he. He has been examined this morning before two or three Justices, and confronted by his countryman, who, they say, knows him very well, and affirms that he is Turpin, and he has been seen by an abundance of gentlemen, as well as by many of the inferior sort, this afternoon, and several persons were present at his examination, who are all of opinion that he is the man.

And on 27 February, even the residents of York were privileged to learn of the notorious highwayman's being discovered in their midst:

> In October last a man was committed to our Castle, under the name of Smith [amended in manuscript to Palmer], by Capt. Appleyard and George Crowle, Esq., Member of Parliament for Hull, on suspicion of horse-stealing and sheep-stealing in that neighbourhood, where he had lodged a considerable time. Last week a person came hither from Essex, by order of some Justices of the Peace for that County, to enquire whether he was the notorious highwayman Turpin or not, a suspicion thereof being raised by an intercepted letter wrote from hence. The messenger being examined before several Justices of Peace for this county, has positively sworn that he is Turpin; and his examination has been transmitted to the Duke of Newcastle, Secretary of State. By the account he gives of himself, and by a comparison of his person with the description in the *Gazette*, the belief of his being the man so generally prevails, that several wagers of ten guineas to one have been laid upon it; but whether he really is so or not, must be left to time to discover. The description in the *Gazette* of June 25th, 1737, is as follows ...[7]

Place's letter and enclosure were received in London by 27 February at the latest, and Newcastle, thinking primarily of Turpin's removal from York and his subsequent prosecution, instructed Andrew Stone, the Under Secretary of State for the Southern Province, to obtain the Attorney General's opinion on what should be done. Stone wrote to Sir Dudley Ryder on 27 February, enclosing Place's letter and enclosure (since detached) and Ryder replied to Newcastle the next day:

> 28th February 1738 [/9]
> May it please your Grace,
> In obedience to your Grace's commands, by Mr. Stone's letter, of yesterday, whereby I am desired to give my opinion what orders it may be proper for your Grace to give, with regard to the removing Turpin, the noted highwayman, and murderer, from York, or to the prosecution of him afterwards.
> I have taken the papers transmitted to me therewith, and which are herewith enclosed, into consideration, but there being no informations laid before me relating to the crimes mentioned in his Majesty's proclamation, I am not able to advise your Grace what orders may be proper to be given for his prosecution: but as it appears, by his Majesty's proclamation, that he is charged with divers capital crimes, committed in or about London, I am humbly of opinion it may be proper to give directions for his removal hither by Habeas Corpus, from York gaol, in order to be tried here [&c.]
> D. Ryder[8]

No time had been wasted in London, but even though, on the following day, Newcastle replied to Place *without* giving directions for Turpin's removal (presumably because he had not by then seen Ryder's letter), and merely indicated that instructions would follow as soon as possible, the authorities at York had moved even more quickly than those in London, and acted on their own initiative.

Up until 1 March 1739 the apparent venue for Turpin's trial may have been in some doubt; certainly it had not been decided in London, and at the date when Place wrote to the Duke of Newcastle there had hardly been time for much thought to have been given to it at York. Yet by 1 March, there does not appear to have been much doubt in the minds of certain influential people that Turpin should be tried there and nowhere else. Turpin however had resigned himself to his fate from the moment he confessed his identity to Thomas Place. The author of the 'letter from York' perhaps allowed himself a little licence.

He has endeavoured to escape, and with two more felons has laid a plot to murder the turnkey and porter, and so have rode off with the Governor's mare, but it was discovered and prevented. A great concourse of people flock to see him, and they all give him money. He seems very sure that nobody is alive that can hurt him, and told the gentleman with whom he used to hunt, that he hoped to have another day's sport with him yet. And that if he had thought they would have made such a rout with him he would have owned it before. He makes no scruple of owning his name is Turpin, and that his father lived at Hempstead, and has inquired after particular servants that lived with gentlemen of that neighbourhood, with whom he was acquainted. He is put every night into the condemned Hold, which is a very strong place; and it is expected he will soon be removed by Habeas Corpus into the southern parts.

Turpin had had over four months in which to plan an escape, and one feels that if he had ever had any idea of doing so he would have made the attempt before his security became a matter of some concern and he was put, as Place advised Newcastle, in 'strict confinement'. The above letter suggests that he was deposited in the Condemned Hold only at night, but even if this was so, we may be sure that he was very closely watched during the daytime.

The picture of Turpin enjoying all the attention is much more realistic; the centre of attraction, money in his pocket, drink for the asking, boasting, laughing and joking, and laying wagers, and the nights quiet by comparison with the day and the noisy endless stream of visitors, the brash coarse 'inferior sort', and the perhaps slightly more hearty, slightly less mannered than London, country gentlemen, with which latter breed of Englishmen Turpin had identified himself.

Small wonder he wished he had revealed his identity sooner, had he known they would have made such a fuss over him when they knew. It was his moment, and for a short time there were some compensations in at last being able to acknowledge his name. Perhaps if he had not murdered Thomas Morris

The Gregory Gang

he might not have gone to Yorkshire and there would have been a similar end in another place, perhaps at the end of February even Turpin was not sure that the end would be at York, but there can have been little doubt in his mind that he had at last come almost to the end of the highwayman's road.

By the first week of March it would appear that it was known that Edward Saward would be a witness at the trial, and this suggests that his visit must have been within a day or two of Smith's. If Saward made written deposition of *his* identification of Turpin, then the record has not survived, it no doubt having gone the same way as a number of related papers associated with the trial, some of which may be assumed to have existed and others which by reference are known to have existed. One record which has survived provides us with evidence of Saward's pre trial visit. 'Mr. [George] Crowle... takes notice of the expenses of two persons that went *twice* from Essex to York about the conviction of the said offender [Turpin]'[9] Smith and Saward were the only two Essex/Hempstead witnesses at the trial, Smith's visits to identify and give testimony against Turpin account for his two journeys to York, and the only reason Saward would have had for making another besides the one he made to give testimony would have been to similarly make identification of his former townsman. This process of elimination would not have been necessary had there not been a mistake in the Kyll's record of the trial proceedings which attributed part of Saward's testimony to James Smith:

Counsel
Now look at the prisoner, is this Richard Turpin?

Saward
Yes, Dick Turpin, the son of John Turpin who keeps the *Bell* at Hempstead.

Turpin denied he knew Edward Saward but he seemed at last to own Smith.

Counsel to Mr. Smith
When you spoke to him in the Castle did you know him?

Smith
Yes, I did, and he did confess to know me and said unto me two or three times, 'Let us bung our eyes in drink' and I drank with him, which is that Richard Turpin.

The 'pirate' version put in another way.

Saward

I know the prisoner at the bar to be Dick Turpin, the son of John Turpin, who keeps the *Bell* at Hempstead. When I spoke to him in the Castle, I knew him again, and he confessed he knew me, and said to me two or three times, Let us bung our eyes in drink, and I drank with him.

Turpin denied that he knew this Edw. Saward but seemed at last to own that he had some knowledge of Smith.

We know that following Smith's identification of Turpin, Turpin did not admit his identity until the evening of the same day, when he confessed the same to Thomas Place. Since it was through Smith's intervention that Turpin was discovered to be at York, it can hardly be imagined that Turpin would have felt very friendly towards his betrayer. On the other hand Turpin cannot have felt any animus towards Saward, who was twice reproved at the trial over the manner in which he gave his testimony, and who on one of those occasions was advised by the judge to speak seriously. If anyone drank with Turpin it was Saward, who in any event appeared to have had the closer former relationship with the Turpin family.

In confirmation of this is the fact that Smith had already testified to having seen Turpin at the Castle and identified him there. The note which suggests that Turpin denied Saward and acknowledged Smith whom he had previously denied, is common to both versions, but since the question of the validity of this note is reflected in the question of the 'pirate' version's authenticity, it is more convenient to leave it for the moment. What is clear is that there was no reason to recall Smith, and the 'pirate' version was correct in attributing all this testimony to Saward.

FOOTNOTES

1. The Christian name not established but possibly Pompadour; the surname spelling is that which appears in James Smith's information.
2. *Reid's Weekly Journal,* 31 March 1739.
3. P.R.O./S.P.36/47 f.87 (enclosure to Thomas Place's letter of 24 February 1739, repetition edited out).
4. *London and Country Journal,* 20 February 1739.
5. P.R.O./S.P.36/47 f.86 and 88. (Smith's Information is f.87).
6. *Ipswich Journal,* 24 February 1739.
7. *York Courant,* 27 February 1739.
8. P.R.O./S.P.36/47 f.100.
9. P.R.O./T.53/40 p.158 *(my italics)*

CHAPTER SIX

I

THE AUTHORS Ash and Day refer to 1 March 1739 as the date when the Grand Jury found each of the charges against Turpin to be a 'True Bill'.[1] In the event, the next stage would have been the returning of the bills into court to become the indictments on which Turpin was tried before the Petty Jury. Unfortunately, had the Grand Jury deliberated on 1 March, the Petty Jury would have been kept waiting three weeks because Turpin was not tried until 22 March.

It was the custom for the Grand Jury to consider bills after the opening of the Assize, which in this case did not begin until 19 March; and Ash and Day in attributing this function to 1 March were possibly misled by the fact that both Turpin indictments state this date to be the day when the offences specified were committed. Turpin however was in prison on 1 March, and since the offences took place in the previous year one imagines this would have been as good a reason as any for vitiating the indictments. 'No indictment can be good, without precisely shewing a certain day of the material facts alleged in it ... However, it is certain, that if an indictment lay the offence on an uncertain or impossible day, as where it lays it on a future day ... it is void.'[2] On this interpretation alone the indictments might appear to contain an 'impossible day' and therefore be void, but another authority is less dogmatic.

> But though the day or year be mistaken in the indictment of felony ... yet if the offence were committed in the same county, though at another time, the offender ought to be found guilty; but then it may be requisite, if any escheat or forfeiture of land be conceived in the case, for the petit jury to find the true time of the offence committed, and therefore it is best in the indictments to set down the times as truly as can be, though it be not of absolute necessity to the defendant's conviction.[3]

Both interpretations would appear to have been valid in 1739 (*Hawkins* is quoted in the first instance as the text is somewhat more lucid than in *Hale*), but how one might have been applied in preference to the other is difficult to understand. Clearly however, since Turpin was indicted for felony, one interpretation enabled the Court to convict him. A similar point about the indictments is that although Turpin stole the horses from Heckington in Lincolnshire, he was charged with having stolen them from Welton in Yorkshire. And on this point the danger of a layman committing himself on a subject with which he is not familiar becomes painfully apparent. 'No indictment can be good, without expressly shewing some place wherein the offence was committed, which must appear to have been within the jurisdiction of the court.'[4] This would seem to be relevant to the case in point, but in *Blackstone* (1778) there are a few significant lines which stem from *Hale*, and give an explicit and even more relevant interpretation of the law which applied in this case.

> If A. steal the horse of B. and afterwards deliver it to C. who was no party to the first stealing, and C. rode away with it *animo furundi*, yet C. is no felon to B. because though the horse was stolen from B. yet it was stolen by A. and not by C. for C. *non cepit* neither is he a felon to A. for he had it by his delivery ... and that is the reason, that if A. steal the goods of B. in the county of C. and carry them into the county of D., A. may be indicted for larcency in the county of D. for the continuance of the asportation is a new caption.[5]

Most of the points relating to the date and place where the offences occurred, and the legal admissibility of stating them to have been committed on 1 March at Welton, have been covered, but with regard to the date, it should perhaps be observed that in the Kyll's record of the trial proceedings, a short preamble to the giving of testimony states that Turpin was indicted for stealing 'on *or before* the first day of this Instant March' (my italics). It is possible that in the arraignment there was some such slight departure from the wording in the indictment which made more sense when the charges came to be read out in court, but since the other indictments on this particular felony file, in stating a variety of specific dates, shew Turpin's to be exceptional in this respect, it still seems odd that even if the date was not known when the bills were drawn up, 'on or before' was not used to prevent the absurdity of 'on'.

One thing however is clear and that is whatever the reason for putting the date 1 March in the bills, they had by that date been conceived in the form in which they were then or subsequently written; for certainly by the beginning of March and possibly by the end of February, at least one responsible official in authority in the county of York was not only convinced that convictions could be obtained on such charges, but was resolved by one means or another to ensure that they would be. In London however, the Duke of Newcastle was unaware that anyone might anticipate his directions in the matter.

II

Whitehall, March 1st 1738/9

Sir,

I have received the favour of your letter of the 24th of last month, giving an account of Turpin, the highwayman, being confined in York Gaol. I shall immediately take the opinion of his Majesty's Attorney General, in what manner it may be proper to proceed upon the occasion, with which I will acquaint you, as soon as possible; In the mean time, you will take the most effectual care, that the prisoner may be kept in the safest custody, and that all necessary precautions be used to prevent any possibility of his making his escape. I am &c.

Holles Newcastle.[6]

Thos. Place Esq., Recorder of York.

Newcastle's letter probably arrived on 2 March; it contained nothing except a rather superfluous instruction about Turpin's safe keeping, and as Newcastle stated that he would take steps to obtain Ryder's opinion when he had in fact taken that initiative two days earlier, it can only be assumed that he was being tactful in the absence of a reply. Clearly he was not aware that a reply had been made, but one might ask why he didn't wait until the opinion was available; again it can only be assumed that he considered some acknowledgement of Place's letter was called for. Why then is there no evidence of another letter following closely on the heels of that of 1 March?

Ryder's letter of 28 February is in the class of *State Papers Domestic* for the reign of George II, comprising original correspondence and other papers in loose form (once bound but subsequently rearranged on a number of occasions), a collection which is by no means complete. It could be said to reflect very general aspects of central government, but although in this sense the papers are of a miscellaneous nature, and are arranged chronologically and not under subject heads, one type of record which appears in the class is that which relates to criminal administration. The Home Office had not at that time come into being, but this type of record is at a later date to be found in the group of records of that department. Thus we have Ryder's letter (and its by now dispersed enclosures) in one collection, but that in which Newcastle's letter appears is the *Entry Books* class of correspondence, etc. related to various headings, the particular one under which the volume in which this letter was found being, *Secretaries of State*. The distinction between the two classes or categories is simple, the former in general reflects incoming original correspondence which has survived, the latter is a series of that outgoing correspondence which was considered to be sufficiently important to have record. From this it is possible to suggest that Newcastle, when he did receive Ryder's opinion, did not transmit instructions to York that Turpin should be removed to London, for if he had done so his letter would have been recorded in the *Entry Book*. So having advised Place that he would acquaint him with the Attorney General's opinion as soon as possible, why in fact did he not do so? The answer may be deduced from the following evidence.

> ... he [George Crowle, M.P. for Kingston-upon-Hull and one of the J.P.'s who signed Palmer's committal to York Castle] likewise got leave from the Secretary at War for an Officer in General Harrison's Regiment whose evidence was very material to be a witness upon the trial and he travelled from Bristol to York. Mr. Crowle observes further that upon the first discovery of Turpin's being in York Gaol, it was the Attorney General's opinion that he should be brought up here [London] to be tried which would have been a great expense to the Crown, and then doubtful whether he would have been convicted here, but upon the assurances that Mr. Crowle gave the Attorney General that there was sufficient proof against him at York he gave up his opinion and consented to his trial there, by which means a very large sum of money was saved to the Crown.[7]

This evidence from the Treasury Solicitor's long submission on the post trial claim for rewards for Turpin's capture and conviction, gives us no idea *when* Crowle was so actively involved in manoeuvring for a York trial, to which end the complementary letters below are much more revealing.

1. Whitehall 6th March 1738/9

Sir,
   I am directed by Sir William Yonge to signify to you it is his Majesty's pleasure, that you do immediately upon receipt hereof repair to York, there to attend the Assizes when Turpin the famous highwayman is to be tried for horse-stealing, representation having been made that your evidence will be very material, you having bought a horse of him, which has been challenged since. I am [&c.]

Rd. Arnold[8]

Captain Dawson

2. Whitehall 6th March 1738/9

Sir,
   I am directed by Sir William Yonge to signify to you it is his Majesty's pleasure, that you permit Captain George Dawson of the Regiment under your command to set out for York in order to attend the Assizes there, when Turpin the famous highwayman is to take his trial for horse stealing; representation having been made that the said captain may be a material evidence against him, having bought a horse of the said Turpin, which has been since challenged. By this post I write to the said Captain upon the same subject. I am [&c.]

Rd. Arnold[9]

Officer Commanding in Chief
Brigadier Harrison's Regiment at Bristol.

It is clear from the evidence shewn above that although Place, by 2 March at the earliest, did not not know the Attorney General's opinion, Crowle had not only learnt of it and persuaded him to change his mind, but also had had some successful representation made to the Secretary at War some time *before* 6 March; and since Sir Dudley Ryder didn't have an opinion until 28 February, it is also clear that Crowle did not learn and accomplish what he did by an exchange of correspondence involving the three eminent persons of Newcastle, Ryder and Yonge, because there wasn't time for the interchange of all the necessary letters to have been effected.

Another thing which is clear is that Newcastle, although writing to York on 1 March, must have read Ryder's letter to him by 2 March, and since he did not at that point write another letter to York giving instructions for Turpin to be brought to London, he must also on 2 March have been advised by Ryder that he had no objection to the trial being held at York. Crowle knew of Ryder's opinion, expressed in writing on 28 February, but could not have learnt of its contents unless either Newcastle or Ryder told him in person, which means that he presented himself either to Newcastle at his office in the Cockpit or to Ryder at his office in Whitehall, on 2 March, and on that day made the argument which enabled the venue for Turpin's trial to be at York.

At this point there appears an obvious discrepancy in policy as evidenced in Place's letter of 24 February in which he awaits instructions from Newcastle, and Crowle's persuasions of 2 March in London. Place, although he subsequently led the prosecution for the Crown at the trial, was clearly not committed to having it at York, but Crowle, only six days later, moved heaven and earth to obtain the necessary permission for it to be held there, a fact which might suggest some conflict of opinion. This was not so because Place, since Crowle was not available for consultation, was acting on his own initiative in writing to Newcastle on 24 February.

It is not known for certain, but it is entirely probable that George Crowle, M.P. for Kingston-upon-Hull had been in London since 1 February 1739, on which day the 5th Session of the 8th Parliament of England in the reign of George the Second was opened. If he was in London throughout February he might have read in the *London and Country Journal* of 20 February that a person was to be sent to York to identify a prisoner there suspected to be Turpin. He may at this point have written to Place asking to be kept informed of developments, and on 24 February or possibly a day or two later Place may have written to him giving him a full account of all the factors involved, *including* some brief reference to his having written to Newcastle asking for instructions upon how to proceed. It is possible also that by the end of

February, by which time Place had not received any communication from Newcastle, that Place (who would probably have felt some apprehension about sending a reminder to the Secretary of State) wrote another letter to Crowle suggesting he made some discreet inquiries about what was to be done with Turpin, and that in view of the impending March Assize there was some particular urgency in obtaining an answer. If Crowle did receive such a letter from Place late on 1 or early on 2 March, it would explain why he made it his business to obtain audience either with Newcastle or Ryder or both of them on 2 March. The question of why Crowle undertook to change the Attorney General's mind about where the trial venue should be (at a time when it does not appear to have occurred to the Recorder that it *should* be held in that city), provides an answer which is something of a revelation.

One might have supposed that George Crowle, in manoeuvring for a York trial, hoped to reserve all recognition for catching and disposing of the notorious Turpin for the county which he represented in Parliament, an understandable attitude and one which cannot be wholly dismissed from his thinking in the matter. But nepotism was the deciding factor in Crowle making the timely intervention which prevented Newcastle sending instruction to York for Turpin's removal to London; for the idea which germinated in George Crowle's mind when it was confirmed the prisoner at York was Turpin, was that his younger brother Richard, an Attorney in the Inner Temple, should be one of the members of the prosecution at the trial. If the trial had been in London or at Chelmsford, Richard Crowle would not have been considered for what was undoubtedly a privilege, but brother George, no doubt possessing considerable influence in the county and some useful connections in town, felt confident that if he could arrange for the trial to be held at York it would be a comparatively simple matter to arrange for Richard to assist the prosecution.

Kyll's record of the trial describes the junior counsel as being Richard Crowle of the Inner Temple. George Crowle, of Springhead in the parish of Cottingham in the county of York, was re-elected M.P. for Kingston-upon-Hull in May 1738, and also in May 1741. Richard Crowle, Esq., *of the Inner Temple* was elected M.P. for the same place in April 1754. The Institute of Historical Research, quoting as their source the *Charities of Hull* (Hull Central Reference Library), were able to shew that Richard appeared as younger brother to George in the Crowle pedigree. Richard was not a young man (he was admitted to the Inner Temple before 1720), but George's patronage in obtaining him a share in the prosecution brief at Turpin's trial may have resulted in his being nominated for the post of Reader in 1740, the year following the trial.

The Attorney General's main concern on 2 March was with evidence, and since George Crowle, in his capacity as one of the J.P.'s who had committed Turpin, was no doubt in possession of the relevant facts concerning the circumstances of Thomas Creasy's visit to Yorkshire, he had some advantage over Ryder in that whereas Ryder could only have had some woolly recollection of the crimes with which Turpin had some years before been charged in London and the Home Counties, he, Crowle, had the facts about Turpin's easily proven horse stealing activities at his fingertips. There was every reason why George Crowle should have felt confident about obtaining a conviction at York, and no reason why Ryder should not have been moved by his arguments, albeit he was moved in a remarkably short space of time. One could say that he had changed his mind almost before he had made it up, so how was George Crowle able to accomplish as much as he did in so short a space of time?

The time factor is quite important here, because allowing that Crowle did make his point on 2 March, even the small detail of a witness travelling from Bristol to York had been settled by 6 March. It was a rushed business, the haste no doubt precipitated by Crowle's reminder that the York Assize, if the trial was to be held there, began on 19 March; but even for an M.P. he would appear to have gained a signal success in achieving what he did. The explanation of how he did this probably lies in Arnold's letter wherein Turpin is credited with being 'famous', for Turpin had for so long been a thorn in the seat of Government, Crowle needed only to mention his name to obtain audience with the people who mattered most. At the same time it might seem surprising that Ryder surrendered Turpin to York at a time when one would have imagined there to be a greater interest and argument for trying him in London. But Crowle had appeared at an opportune moment, before any official word that Turpin would be tried in London had reached the newspapers and public, and Ryder did not have to think of the consequences of a public retraction. Thus the disposing of Turpin remained at that time a routine matter, and had not taken on the trappings of a show trial which advance publicity would have ensured. The matter of cost, as argued in the subsequent claim, was a secondary consideration, for Turpin would still have had to have appeared with the rank and file criminals (as indeed he did at York) at the General Sessions held at the Old Bailey, or failing that venue, at the Chelmsford Assize; and in terms of additional expense to the Crown the cost would have been negligible.

Ryder admittedly changed his mind, but only about the venue, for he did not qualify his first (written) opinion that Turpin should be brought south with the possibility of obtaining conviction. But when faced with Crowle's evidence which would be available at York, Ryder came to the conclusion that it was, 'doubtful whether he would have been convicted here'.

With Wheeler dead it might have been difficult proving Turpin's complicity in any of the Gregory gang crimes. Evidence which would have proved his guilt in individual acts of highway robbery was probably non existent, and of the charge of the murder of Thomas Morris committed two years before and at night it could be said that there might have been some difficulty in proving the fact even had Turpin been taken within a few days of the murder having occurred. From all these circumstances, it would appear that it was convenient for Ryder to change his mind, and persuade Newcastle to allow the trial to be held at York. What we do not know is why only a few days after Crowle wrote or returned to York with the news that Turpin could be tried at the Assize there, Newcastle was suddenly beset with doubts about the wisdom of his decision.

III

It was during the period of Crowle's London manoeuvrings that the fate of Turpin's father, confined since September 1738, was resolved.

> On * * * * a Bill of Indictment was preferred to the Grand Jury at Chelmsford against John Turpin, the unhappy father of Richard Turpin the noted highwayman, when the old man's general good character and innocency of the fact laid to his charge, plainly appearing to the satisfaction of the Grand Jury, of which Sir Caesar Child, Bart. was Foreman, the Bill was returned Ignoramus.[10]

It is of some interest to note that the foreman of the Grand Jury has already appeared in this account; on 12 April 1735, Sir Caesar was attacked and robbed in Epping Forest by three men who would appear to have been Turpin, Rowden and Jones. No reference to Turpin was made in the newspaper reports of the incident, but it may have occurred to Child subsequently that he had been a victim of the then soon to be famous highwayman. In any event now that it was almost common knowledge that Turpin Junior was confined at York, there must have been some comment amongst the members of the Grand Jury upon the irony of the situation whereby they were required to consider to what extent the sins of Richard Turpin were responsible for the predicament of his father. And it is clear that they found John Turpin the victim of circumstances over which he could not, nor could he have been expected to have had, any control. On the roll of the Gaol Delivery for Essex held at Chelmsford on 5 March 1739 it was recorded that John Turpin was 'delivered by proclamation' and that he was to be discharged upon payment of his fees.[1][1]

A final comment upon the events of this Assize is appropriate insofar as it concerns deerstealers. In March 1739 William Rogers was sentenced to death upon charges arising from his deerstealing activities. Rogers would appear to have been the same Rogers who testified against Jeremy Gregory and Joseph Rose, and who was himself testified against by them, during the extraordinary proceedings which involved rival deerstealing factions making a mockery of justice at the Summer Assize at Chelmsford in 1734.

Nimpous Fuller, an associate of Roger's, was acquitted of complicity on one of the charges against Rogers, but ended up in the pillory in 1739. John Fuller, who was possibly the same Fuller twice convicted of deerstealing in former years, and perhaps a relation of Nimpous Fuller, was discharged by proclamation, the Grand Jury not finding a case against him on charges of stealing silver spoons.

Rogers and his associates are mentioned here because they were rivals of the deerstealers who formed the Gregory gang, and ultimately, in the deerstealing sphere, their successors. They roamed those vast expanses of what was Waltham Forest, and are glimpsed but occasionally, touching the fringes of this account and disappearing again like shadows. They are like the incredible number of other people briefly mentioned but inexplicably interwoven with the thread of one man's not very glorious life, so much so that it was perhaps inevitable that the exploits of Turpin, but a short time a highwayman, lingered down the years to become an intangible and distorted memory, a thrilling moonlit ghost ripe for exploitation as a legend. Which, when all the other names were forgotten, is what he became.

By the time the Grand Jury at Chelmsford had returned John Turpin's bill marked *Ignoramus,* Mr. George Crowle, by his activities in London, had ensured that York would have a permanent place in that legend.

IV

By 6 March, the day on which the Deputy Secretary at War wrote the two letters which enabled Captain Dawson to travel to York, the newspapers were beginning to get their teeth into Turpin; but although reflecting a concensus of opinion that the man at York *was* Turpin, and shewing some other basis in fact, much of what was written owed a lot to invention.

> We are assured of a certainty, that a person committed to York Castle, and supposed to be the noted Turpin, is really Turpin, in relation to the taking of whom we have received the following particulars. That for about eighteen months last past he lurked about in the neighbourhood of Beverley in Yorkshire, where he passed for a farmer's son, of or near Spalding in Lincolnshire, from whence he

absconded on account of debt, but being charged with robbing hen roosts and stealing poultry he was committed to the house of correction at Beverley and during his confinement there for that offence the worthy and judicious magistrate who committed him sent to Spalding to make enquiry if any such person inhabited or was known there, as he pretended upon his examination, the whole proved an imposition, and during his confinement he was charged with horsestealing, whereupon he was removed from Beverley to York Castle. The prisoner wrote a letter to one in Essex who married his sister, which letter not being received a person in that county seeing the superscription and knowing it to be the handwriting of Turpin, acquainted a Justice of the Peace therewith, who despatched the said person to York to see the prisoner who proved to be the real Turpin. And we are further assured, that the prisoner has since confessed himself to be Turpin. We cannot help observing upon the occasion, that each of the magistrates before mentioned have acted with great prudence and assiduity in discharge of their trust, and deserve the thanks of their country for bringing so notorious and dangerous a rogue to his due punishment.[12]

The reference to Spalding is valid only because it comes within the area of Turpin's activities in Lincolnshire, but neither on 6 March nor at any time before the trial, was there a report which related the fact that the horses crucial to the charges against Turpin had been stolen in Lincolnshire.

The relevant points in the York letter published in the *General Evening Post* of 8 March have already been discussed, but in the manner of presentation, it is interesting to note the caption to the same letter when it was reproduced in the *Political State,* for March 1739 (published after the trial). 'Entertaining account of the apprehending the infamous highwayman and murderer Turpin. The public having been for some time amused with an account of the famous highwayman Turpin's being taken, the fact was at last put out of doubt by the following letter from York.' The York letter concluded with the expectation that Turpin would, 'soon be removed by Habeas Corpus into the southern parts', a fond idea eagerly subscribed to by other newspapers who took their anticipation a step further. 'Turpin is on the road from York for Chelmsford in order to be tried there, but its thought he'll scarce arrive there in time to be tried this Assizes.'[13]

The two Justices travelling the Home Circuit for the Lent Assizes had reached Maidstone by 14 March, which fact lays bare the absurdity of this report, dated 13 March; but also on 14 March, a report appeared which flatly contradicted that of the previous day. 'By letters from York we have an account, that the famous Turpin (committed to the Castle there for horse stealing, &c. by the name of Palmer) will not be removed by Habeas Corpus but will be tried at the Assizes there for horse stealing &c.'[14] The public, reading these accounts at the time, would not have known what to think, but in retrospect, it is possible to see that the last report was confirmation of what Crowle had achieved in London. The Assize at York was less than a week away and nothing would now stay the trial, whatever the newspapers might have to say on the subject. But the Duke of Newcastle however had not been idle.

V

Although on the days up to and including 17 March the press was in conflict about the trial venue, Newcastle had known since 2 March that it would be at York. And since he knew, his approval, in the first instance at least, has been inferred. It may also be inferred that it was by means of his personal representation to the Secretary at War that Captain Dawson's leave of absence was obtained. Thus until 7 March he would appear to have had no second thoughts about the trial being at York. But a week or so later he initiated the collation of evidence relating to crimes with which Turpin had been charged in the past, the same charges upon which the Attorney General had opined that it would be 'doubtful whether he would have been convicted here', for the specific purpose of sending the evidence to York to prevent Turpin's being discharged if he was acquitted. Since it would have been sufficient to have sent copies of two Royal proclamations implicating Turpin for robbery and murder, Newcastle's action may be seen to have considerably exceeded what was required of him by way of a purely formal precaution. Thus by 17 March Newcastle had gone some way towards compiling a dossier of evidence of Turpin's crimes, but by reason of its date the most significant document in that dossier is the one he obtained on that day. 'Information of Peter Splidt of Woodford in the county of Essex taken before John Goodere Esq. one of his Majesty's Justices of the Peace for the said county, dated the 17th March 1738/9.'[15]

Peter Splidt (*sic*) of Woodford was robbed by the Gregory Gang on 29 October 1734 and one might ask why, of all the gang's victims, Newcastle should have looked to this particular one? In respect of the activities of any member of the gang, Newcastle would have been obliged to look to a basic source of information on the subject, *viz.* John Wheeler's information dated 18 February 1735, which document Newcastle also saw fit to send to York, from whence it would appear not to have been returned. It is unlikely that Turpin could have been implicated in the Split robbery unless on Wheeler's evidence, and assuming therefore that Wheeler did state that Turpin was present, the one thing which then distinguishes Split from other victims is that being the first victim of the gang, Newcastle would in all probability have found his name first mentioned in Wheeler's information.

What value then would this information have been, in any subsequent proceedings against Turpin in Essex? On the basis of existing evidence it could only be said that it would have been of negligible value, particularly so without Wheeler's personal testimony to prove its substance. The advertisement offering a reward in respect of the Split and other robberies was published on 8 February 1735, three days before Wheeler was captured; it gave no descriptions of the men responsible and even allowing Turpin's participation, his description was not published (officially) until 22 February, four months after the Split robbery. Even if Split, upon reading Turpin's description, considered it to be that of one of the men who had robbed him, he did not see Turpin on any subsequent occasion, and in his information taken four years later could hardly have contributed anything new. Turpin's name still stood on the indictments for robbing Francis, Lawrence and Skinner, and if evidence implicating him in robbery was all that was needed, Newcastle had more than enough information concerning those crimes lodged in his own State Paper Office.

Apart from obtaining the Split item and Wheeler's information, Newcastle also sent to Essex for the Coroner's Inquest on the body of Thomas Morris; and when he did write to York the day before the trial, these were the three items he enclosed in his letter as evidence to prevent discharge in the event of *acquittal*. But the idea that Newcastle believed there could be an *acquittal* is quite preposterous in that it presumes an ignorance of both charges and evidence which is inconceivable, for even if he had not been provided with background details (e.g. the fact that the horses were stolen in Lincolnshire) there was nothing, if he subsequently had doubts about certain points, to prevent his asking Ryder or some other legal expert to explain and thereby dispel them. So why so very late in the day did he act as he did?

George Crowle negotiated for a York trial when it was still possible for Ryder to change his opinion, and within a very short time a decision was made which could not subsequently be rescinded without a certain loss of face and embarrassment on all sides. But there was one person who may have felt slighted about not being consulted over where the trial was to be held, and who in an annoyed state would perhaps have shewn some irrational concern when he learned then it was to be left in the hands of country bumpkins. The man who would have brooked no argument in the matter and expressed a desire that something should be done to preserve him from embarrassment was King George the Second himself, and his prompting is to be seen in Newcastle's diplomacy of neither mentioning his Majesty, nor sending nor mentioning that the crimes with which Turpin was charged were listed in Royal proclamations. Instead, in going through the motions of presenting evidence upon which Turpin would be tried if discharged, Newcastle deliberately exposed himself to the ridicule with which he must have known his letter would be greeted.

It is perhaps difficult to conceive that the King did not learn of all the events concerning Crowle's visit until after the trial venue had been decided and it was too late to change it, but despite Newcastle's regular audiences with the King (at this particular time at St. James's Palace), it is clear that up to and including 6 March, and perhaps for a week or more afterwards, *no-one* had suffered qualms about allowing the trial to be held there. To the public, to Crowle, to various officials at York, Turpin was no doubt of some *absorbing* interest, but there is no real reason why he should have been so to Newcastle, nor of more than academic interest to Ryder. There was more pressing business, more immediate matters of state, and to the Secretary of State it is quite probable that quibbling about where the wretched fellow was to be tried, amounted to nothing more than an irritation and a bore, so why bother the King with it? Apparently his Majesty did hear of it, perhaps through court gossip, with the result which we have seen. It was all very tedious, and Newcastle perhaps shuddered to think what the reaction at York would be; but something, no more than a gesture would have to be made, and then perhaps with the Royal Pleasure satisfied and the fellow Turpin tried and hung, they might all get some peace again in Whitehall.

VI

Two days after Peter Split gave his information the Assize opened at York. It was four years, almost to the day, since Turpin had been named in indictments upon which his associates had been convicted and hung, four long and very eventful years full of incident and violence.

When Turpin was committed to Beverley House of Correction, and afterwards removed to York Castle, his then known identity was recorded simply as being, John Palmer. This was in October 1738. By 19 March his real identity was known, but the authorities were less confident about Palmer than they had been previously, and in the Bill of Indictment preferred to the Grand Jury after the Assize had opened, the prisoner was identified as John Palmer *alias* Pawmer *alias* Richard Turpin.

In Line 193 of the trial testimony which appears in the next chapter, Turpin himself is recorded as having said, 'I changed my name to my mother's which was Palmer.' How then do we account for the late introduction of 'Pawmer'? There are three main sources of information from which the answer may be obtained, one and two are different versions of the previously quoted 'letter from York', and the third source is the Hempstead parish registers.

A. A small time since a letter came with the York Post stamp, directed for one Pomp. Revinal ... which letter was signed John Palmer, which they say is Turpin's mother's maiden name, and which he used to go by. Now Paumer and the Yorkshire way of pronouncing Palmer are very near, they always leaving out the L.[16]

B. A small time since a letter came with the York Post Stamp, directed for one Pomp. Revinal ... which letter was signed *John Parmen,* which they say is Turpin's mother's maiden name, and which he used to go by. Now *Parmen* and the Yorkshire way of pronouncing Palmer are very near, they always leaving out the L.[17]

Despite protracted efforts to trace it in this country and the United States of America, the original issue of the *General Evening Post* in which the letter first appeared has not been found. *Immortal Turpin* was published in 1948, but documentary and newspaper sources were not quoted; in this particular case the absence of the original is unfortunate because in all other respects, except the spelling of Turpin's alias, the two letters are identical.

In trying to establish which is the authentic version it should be remembered that we are contending with a dialect rendered phonetically, and that the author of the letter, probably James Smith of Hempstead, was at some pains to illustrate how differently spelt names could be related through similarities in Essex and Yorkshire pronunciation. Version A is the least straightforward and requires careful appraisal.

The first official recognition of a name other than Palmer appears in the Bills of Indictment. This variant, as spelt in all *official* records, was Pawmer, and the appearance of Paumer in a letter dated 2 March does have some validity. This is however considerably diminished by the following factors, firstly, the name Paumer does not appear elsewhere in the letter and, secondly, the author concludes his letter by anticipating Turpin's removal by Habeas Corpus into the southern parts. Despite the letter being described as an extract, it remains a long one, and although previous reference to Paumer could have been made, it is odd that it should have been edited out when there remained subsequent argument which depended on its staying in; as it is the unheralded appearance of Paumer is of no relevance whatsoever.

Of greater significance however is that through being unaware that the trial would be held at York, the author could hardly have been in a position to know about the distinction which would be made between Palmer and Pawmer when the Bills of Indictments were drawn up. How then came about the marked change in Version B?

By definition the *Political State* was a monthly digest which relied to some great extent on newspapers as a source of information, and there can be no doubt that Version B was taken from the *General Evening Post* of 8 March. Since Parmen appears in the place of both Palmer and Paumer a printing error seems unlikely, but how else explain the difference and the apparent contradiction in a copy which makes more sense than the original? The answer possibly lies in the fact that whereas Version B is a true copy obtained but two or three weeks after the letter was printed in the *General Evening Post,* the original Version A was amended in 1948 by the authors of *Immortal Turpin.* This is, without having had sight of the *General Evening Post* itself, a strong claim, but not an irresponsible one. If Parmen was the spelling used in the original letter, its significance would not have been apparent to the authors without a vital piece of complementary evidence which they clearly did not possess; this exists in the Hempstead parish registers in a marriage entry 1695.

Hempstead Marriages[18]
Johannes Turpin & Elizabeth [*struck through and* Mary *inserted above*] Parminter. Martii 25, 1695.

Parminter, also spelt Parmenter, is a very positive link with Parmen. Turpin accounts vie with each other in according the name Palmer either to his mother or to the girl he married, but there has never been produced a shred of documentary evidence to shew that either Turpin or his father married a girl of that name. In the case of the son, the most reliable information suggests that he married Elizabeth (known as Betty) Millington, but could the entry above really be the record of marriage of his father? The villages around Hempstead abounded with Turpins, but it is quite probable that we need look no further than the Hempstead parish registers, and in support of one point, a marriage and baptismal register for Thaxted. The following six entries of baptism are from the same register in which the above marriage appears.

Hempstead Baptisms.

1696	Thomas filius Johannis Turpin & Elizabeth	Martii 29
1698	Johannes filius Johannes Turpin & Magarita	April 28
1700	Christopher filius Joannes Turpin & Maria	[? Feb.] 28
1702	Maria filia Johannes Turpin & Maria ux	Aprilis 28
1705	Richardus filius Johannis & Maria Turpin bapt.	Sept. 21
1708	Dorothea filia Johannes & Maria Turpin bapt.	Feb. 10

There is some strong case for these six children being the offspring of John Turpin and Elizabeth Mary Parminter. The obvious objection to the argument is that although the father's Christian name is constant that of the mother is not, but this is no great obstacle to establishing relationship.

There is but this one Turpin marriage immediately preceding the sequence of births between 1696 and 1708, similarly these are the only Turpin births during the same period. For genealogical purposes the sequence of marriage *and* births reflects a natural progression in time and same place which is the ideal for proving ancestry.

The wife in all probability was called Mary Elizabeth the second name (written first in the register) being superfluous for the record. Having been entered in error it was no doubt amended soon afterwards, but it is conceivable that Elizabeth was the name by which she was known at the time of marriage *and* immediately afterwards at the time when Thomas was born. Turpin's association with Thaxted provides further support for Thomas having been the first child of this marriage.

Thaxted Parish Register[19]
Thomas Turpin & Martha Jud, married 25th of March 1726
Thomas son of Thomas and Martha Turpin baptised 15th of May 1726.
John son of Thomas and Martha Turpin baptised 27th of August 1727.

Thomas would have been 30 when this timely wedding took place and to have named the first son after himself and the second son after his father would have been normal practice. Which brings us to the John born at Hempstead.

Although the published letter from Turpin Senior to his son John is no doubt spurious, there would have been no point in the author having used the name John if it was not known that a son of that name existed. The name Margarita gives us pause to consider was this *the* John, but it is somewhat unlikely that an out of town John and Magarita suddenly arrive in Hempstead to deposit a child by name John in the middle of John and Mary Elizabeth's irresistible proliferating, and that *they* went somewhere else to have *their* John. Magarita is either another error, this time for Maria, or Mary/Maria was known as Margaret at this time. From this time on the names of husband and wife are constant, John and Mary, which is where we started, and it cannot be disputed that the third of the last four children born to them was the villain of this piece, or that Christopher and the two girls were his brother and sisters. We *know* that Turpin had a sister Dorothy whose husband rejected the letter from York Castle. Mary appears to have married Cesar Hasler on 24 August 1725. Christopher is never heard of again nor has search been made for him.

These few details are all that are relevant in Turpin genealogy and all that are necessary to prove with reasonable certainty that Mary Elizabeth Parminter (or Parmenter) was Richard Turpin's mother. It follows that the name under which he masqueraded *was* Parmen, and *not* Palmer, and that it was because the Yorkshire officials were unable to recognise the Essex dialect that the confusion has remained to this day. He did not have two aliases, Palmer and Pawmer, but just the one Parmen derived from his mother's maiden name (as he admitted in court) of Parminter/Parmenter.

The fateful letter, produced in court, is described in brackets within James Smith's testimony (line 121) as having been superscribed John Palmer. When committed at Beverley the magistrates no doubt asked Turpin his name and accepted it as Palmer, but with the letter in their possession it is possible that upon making out the bill of indictment the York officials were unable to reconcile the name on the letter with the Palmer previously accepted. Pawmer could in such circumstances be the compromise which resolved the difficulty of both verbal and written interpretation.

The latter theory, not only suggests that James Smith could have recognised the hand but that being able to read the name as Parmen there was no doubt in his mind that Turpin had written it; similarly the theory further emphasises either deliberate rejection or lack of curiosity on the part of Pomp. Rivernall.

The final point to be made with regard to Turpin's choice of alias reflects his previously observed habit of creating fiction on a basis of fact. In John Parmen he acknowledged both his father and his mother. In finding this name in the *General Evening Post,* the authors Ash and Day were faced with an unknown quantity and although a footnote to this effect would have been preferable, their conclusion that it was a printing error which needed but slight amendment was perhaps inevitable in the circumstances. Further proof that it was amended exists in the use of *Paumer* rather than *Pawmer.*

In the preparation of indictments and in the recording of the result of the trial and in all other official references to the subject made before or after the trial, the aliases used by Turpin are stated to be and spelt, Palmer *alias* Pawmer. The spelling Paumer does not appear until after the trial in the printed Kyll's version of the trial proceedings. In *Immortal Turpin,* the first page of Kyll's trial, the printed version of which reads, 'John Palmer, alias Paumer, alias Richard Turpin, was indicted', was rewritten, 'The Trial of John Palmer, alias Paumer, alias Richard Turpin, as the Indictments state.'[20] The indictments do not state 'Paumer', they state 'Pawmer', and it was from Kyll that Ash and Day obtained the name they substituted for Parmen in the *General Evening Post* letter.

VI

There would be no point in substituting Parmen for Palmer or Pawmer in what follows in this account, nor in what has been written previously, but returning to 19 March 1739, the day on which the York Assizes opened, it is appropriate to observe that having failed to get Turpin's alias right, the person who prepared the bill of indictment (in this case Henry Simon, the Clerk of the Assize) entered his real name as an alias. The reason for this is that although there was little doubt that the prisoner was Richard Turpin, it remained to be proved at the trial that he was in fact so named. Thus on the morning of Monday 19 March the two Bills of Indictment against Turpin waited upon the opening of the Assize and the swearing in of the Grand Jury to whom they would be presented.

First Bill of Indictment
Yorkshire To witt. The Jurors for our Lord the King upon their oath present that *John Palmer otherwise Pawmer otherwise Richard Turpin* late of the Castle of York in the county of York labourer on the first day of March in the twelfth year of the reign of our Sovereign Lord George the Second now King of Great Britain &c. with force and arms at the parish of Welton in the county aforesaid one mare of a black colour of the price of three pounds and one filley foal of a black ball colour of the price of twenty shillings of the goods and chattels of one Thomas Creasy then and there being found did then and there feloniously steal take and lead away against the peace of our said Lord the King his Crown and Dignity.[21]

Second Bill of Indictment
Yorkshire To witt. The Jurors for our Lord the King upon their oath present that *John Palmer otherwise Pawmer otherwise Richard Turpin* late of the Castle of York in the County of York labourer on the first day of March in the twelfth year of the reign of our Sovereign Lord George the Second now King of Great Britain &c. at the parish of Welton in the County aforesaid one gelding of a black colour of the price of three pounds of the goods and chattels of one Thomas Creasy then and there being found did then and there feloniously steal take and lead away against the peace of our sovereign Lord the King his Crown and Dignity.[22]

The Commissions appointing the judges having been read, the Grand Jury would then have been sworn and charged before retiring to consider the bills of indictments against those persons named in the Gaol Delivery. The preamble, and list of the Grand Jury which appear below were recorded in the *Minute Book* for the *North East Circuit*.

Yorkshire to witt The Delivery of the Gaol of our Sovereign Lord the King of his County of York held at the Castle of York in and for the County aforesaid on Monday the nineteenth day of March in the twelfth year of the reign of our Lord George the Second now King of Great Britain &c. before Sir Wm. Lee Knight

Lord Chief Justice of his Majesty's Court of King's Bench and Sir William Chapple Knight one of the Justices of his Majesty's said Court of King's Bench Justices of our said Lord the King assigned to deliver his Gaol there of the prisoners therein being &c.

The Grand Jury
Sir Robert Hildyard of Wynestead Bart. ...
Bryan Cooke of Wheatley; William Wrightson of Cusworth; Thomas Yarbrough of Campsall, John Twisleton of Rawcliffe; John Cooks of Warnsworth; Alexander Cooke of Ripon; Francis Foljambe of Aldworke; Godfrey Wentworth of Woolley; Thomas Fountain of Melton; William Dixon of Loversall; Henry Thompson of Kirkby Hall; Anthony Eyre of Adwick; Haworth Currer of Kildwick; Thos. Edmunds of Worsbrough; Geo. Montgomery of North Cave; Henry Beaumont of Whitley; Mordecai Cutts of Thorne; Edw.[d] Forster of the same; Mark Braithwaite of Deighton; Roger Portington of Barnby Dun; Henry Brown of Skelbrooke; Anthony Hall of Wombwell; Esqs.[23]

The exact day-to-day sequence of events at this Assize is not known because, although it opened on the Monday, Turpin was not tried until Thursday, on which morning the Petty Jury was sworn. This interval of days is probably accounted for, for the most part, by the 43 civil causes heard by Sir William Lee,[24] but apart from observing that the found indictments would no doubt have been returned into court to enable Sir William Chapple to take over from Lee without delay, it is difficult to say exactly when the Grand Jury started and finished its deliberations upon the bills.

Ultimately, however, the two indictments against Turpin were returned into court, the first was endorsed 'A True Bill' and signed by the Foreman of the Grand Jury, Sir Robert Hildyard; it bore also the names of the witnesses who would be called on the first count, Thomas Creasy, Carey Gill, George Dawson, Esq., George Goodyear, James Smith, Edward Sawood and Richard Grassby. With the exception of Dawson and Grassby, who were not called to give evidence on the second count, the witnesses named on the second indictment were the same. The Assize began on the Monday, but on Tuesday, in London, the rumour-mongers were still leading the public astray. 'It is now said that the person in York Castle, who has made such a noise in all the papers, is not the real Turpin.'[25]

It would really have made little difference to a person what his name was when there was substantial evidence that he was guilty of horse stealing, and without benefit of a defence counsel to do his thinking for him there was not much Turpin could do in the circumstances. Throughout the trial he maintained that he had not had time to prepare a proper defence because he had been led to believe that he would be removed elsewhere to be tried; he further claimed that he had sent a subpoena, and a letter by special messenger, presumably into Lincolnshire, to summon witnesses for his defence. A messenger did return from some errand on his behalf, apparently arriving back in York on the morning of the trial itself, and it is probable that he did not set out on his journey until 19 or 20 March, after the Assize had begun. Whether or not by these devices (knowing all the time that there was no-one who would be prepared to speak in his defence) he hoped to bamboozle the jury into thinking there might be some grain of truth in his version of how he came by the horses, it is not possible to say with certainty, but since bluff and playing on the sympathy of the jury was his only defence, it is possible that these manoeuvrings were but an empty gesture by which he hoped to deceive. In any event, on the eve of the trial, he can really have had few illusions about what the outcome would be.

The one person who did have doubts appears to have been the King, and it was on the day before the trial, a somewhat late hour when one considers the purpose of the gesture, that Newcastle committed the royal doubts to paper. Since Newcastle obtained Split's information on 17 March (the result no doubt of a request made some days before and probably at the same time as the search for the other evidence was initiated), one wonders if the interval of four days before a letter was written and dispatched might be some indication of Newcastle's enthusiasm for the project. Some such attitude may be deduced from the fact that Wheeler's information would have been to hand in the State Paper Office, and the inquest of Morris should have been quickly obtained by the sending of a special messenger to Chelmsford. Unless some other circumstance intervened, Newcastle's not writing until 21 March does suggest a certain lethargy emphasised by the fact that although he would have known the date when the Assize opened, he could hardly have known it would be another three days before Turpin came before the court. Thus it is possible to see that Newcastle's letter arriving on the day (presumably the morning) of the trial was purely fortuitous when for all his knowledge of the progress of the Assize it might just as easily have been over.

Whitehall. March 21st 1738/9

Recorder of York
Sir,
    I send you herewith the Coroner's Inquest for the County of Essex taken in May 1738 [*recte* 1737] by which you will see that Richard Turpin now a prisoner in the county gaol at York, stands charged with murder.
    I also enclose several informations relating to other felonies, committed by the said Turpin. And I am to desire that you would lay them before the Judge of Assize, when Turpin is tried; to the end, that in case he should be acquitted at the present Assizes at York, of the felony for which he is to be there tried; he may not be discharged upon such acquittal; but be continued under close confinement in the Goal at York till he shall be removed in order to take his trial for the facts mentioned in the enclosed inquest and informations. I am &c.

Holles Newcastle

There were enclosed:

The Coroner's Inquest for the county of Essex, taken at Waltham on the 6th May 1738 [recte 1737]
Information of John Wheeler for burglaries in the said county taken upon oath the 18 day of February 1734 [/5] before Nathaniel Blackerby Esq. against Joseph Rose, Humphrey Walker, John Fielder, Wm. Saunders, Jasper Gregory, Richard Turpin, Thomas Bowden [recte Rowden], Herbert Haines, John Jones, Samuel Gregory, Mary Johnson als Rose als Brazier.
Information of Peter Splidt of Woodford in the county of Essex taken before John Goodere Esq one of his Majesty's Justices of the Peace for the said county, dated the 17th March 1738/9

21 March 1738/9.[26]

So as Newcastle's courier galloped through the night from London to York, Turpin remained secure in his cell; it was a cold night and he may well have lain awake shivering waiting for the bleak dawn of Thursday 22 March 1739.

VIII

We do not know at what hour the fourth day of the Assize began, but it would be safe to assume it was not too late (the daily proceedings of the Old Bailey Sessions usually began at 8 a.m. at that time of year), otherwise the judges would have had no respite between one Assize and the next on their circuit.

The Grand Jury having completed its deliberations, and the indictments which were to be proceeded with having been returned into court, it was now the turn of the Petty Jury to be sworn.

Thursday morn[ing] the names of the Jury twixt the King and Prisoners

William Calvert	Robt. Wiggin	Robert Thompson
Saml. Waddington	Wm. Wade	William Frank
Wm. Popplewell	Thos. Simpson	James Boyes
John Lambert	Geo. Smeaton	Thos. Clarke[27]

The first case was one of horse stealing, not a particularly good omen for Turpin when the accused, John Stead, was found guilty, and Turpin found himself next in the dock being arraigned before the same jury ·and the no doubt awesome figure of Sir William Chapple, Justice of the Court of King's Bench.

Turpin 'put himself on his country'. There was no defence counsel. It was perhaps between nine and ten o'clock when Turpin was called, and Newcastle's courier, if he had not already arrived was rapidly approaching

York Castle. 'On Thursday last a messenger arrived here from the Secretary of State's office with the Coroners Inquest for the County of Essex, taken on the body of Mr. Thompson's servant killed in Epping Forest; and an account of the several robberies committed by the said Turpin; with a view as it is supposed of removing him to Chelmsford, if he had not been capitally convicted here.'[28]

The fact and the purpose of the messenger's journey to York does not appear to have been advertised in London, but the story, albeit slightly inaccurate, did not take long to surface in a number of London newspapers, of which the following is a fairly representative example. 'From the same place (York) we hear, that the day before he was convicted for horse stealing an express arrived there from the Duke of Newcastle's office to the Recorder of that City, directing that Turpin if he was not capitally convicted upon the indictments preferred against him, should be kept with the greatest care in hold till further orders from the Attorney General.'[29]

Since the courier set out on 21 March, the statement in the *York Courant* that he arrived on 22 March is preferred, not so much because the journey couldn't have been accomplished in one day but because an observer at York is more likely to have known when he did arrive than a reporter in London acting on second hand information. The latter report presumes an interest on the part of the Attorney General which is not reflected in Newcastle's letter, but the error was really of little consequence when there was to be no going back for Turpin, and his last journey was to be a short one from gaol to gallows.

FOOTNOTES

1. *Immortal Turpin*, p.103.
2. *Pleas of the Crown*, Hawkins, 1762, Book II p.235.
3. *Historia Placitorum Coronae, The History of the Pleas of the Crown*, by Sir Matthew Hale Knt., sometime Lord Chief Justice of the Court of King's Bench, Vol.II p.179. Printed in 1736.
4. *Pleas of the Crown*, Hawkins, 1762, Book II p.236.
5. *Hale*, Vol.I pp.507–508.
6. P.R.O./S.P.44/131 p.102.
7. P.R.O./T.53/40 p.158.
8. P.R.O./W.O.4/35 f.31.
9. *Ibid.*
10. *Ipswich Journal*, 17 March 1739 (incorrect date deleted).
11. P.R.O./Assizes 35/179/1, Essex, Felony file, Winter 12 Geo.II 1738/9.
12. *London and Country Journal*, 6 March 1739.
13. *Ibid.*, 13 March 1739.
14. *Universal Spectator and Weekly Journal*, 17 March 1739 (but first appearing in *Kentish Post and Canterbury News* of 14 March).
15. P.R.O./S.P.44/31 p.107.
16. 'Extract of a Letter from York, dated March 2nd, 1739' from the *General Evening Post* of 8 March 1739, as reproduced in *Immortal Turpin*, by Ash & Day, pp.99–101.
17. 'Letter from York–to Mr. J.A.', as reproduced in *Political State* for March 1739, pp.191–194.
18. Essex/D/P 314/1/1.
19. Essex/D/P 16/1/3.
20. *Immortal Turpin*, p.106.
21. P.R.O./Assizes 44/54 (part). (On permanent exhibition in the Public Record Office Museum, Floor Case N, No.6).
22. P.R.O./Assizes 44/54 (part). (In a broken incomplete file of loose indictments for the York Lent Assize).
23. P.R.O./Assizes 41/3 (part). (There are also two other rough minute books in this box with similar information).
24. P.R.O./Assizes 43/7 Circuit Account Book.
25. *London and Country Journal*, 20 March 1739.
26. P.R.O./S.P.44/131 p.107.
27. P.R.O./Assizes 41/3, Minute Book for the North East Circuit.
28. *York Courant*, 27 March 1739.
29. *Universal Spectator & Weekly Journal*, 31 March 1739.

CHAPTER SEVEN

I

IT WAS ironic that Turpin, whose life had for so many years depended on his possessing a speedy horse, and whose legend as a highwayman went foot in stirrup with a nobler creature than himself, should come to be tried for the comparatively pedestrian crime of stealing horses, an innocuous pursuit he was obliged to take up during his semi-retirement in provincial exile. It is doubtful however if anyone present in court that day was aware of the irony in Turpin's predicament, not the judge, nor the jury, nor the prosecuting counsel, nor the spectators, nor Turpin himself; for without exception they can only have been conscious of one thing, that the prisoner who stood in the dock was the most notorious criminal in England. And this one significant fact would surely have removed anyone's preconceived notions about the possibility of an acquittal. When it became known *who* Palmer was, there were wagers at York which allowed for error in the identification, but although there were still unfounded rumours being mooted abroad that the prisoner was not Turpin, we do not hear of any wagers being exchanged upon the outcome of the trial. And Thomas Kyll the shorthand writer was waiting with pen poised in anticipation of making a considerable sum of money out of the conviction.

> The Whole TRIAL of the notorious Highwayman RICHARD TURPIN, at York Assizes, on the 22nd day of March, 1739, before the Honourable Sir WILLIAM CHAPPLE, Kt. Judge of Assize, and one of his Majesty's Justices of the Court of King's Bench.
> Taken down in COURT, By Mr. Thomas Kyll, Professor of Short-Hand.

Since all other details have been described elsewhere, only the testimony is shewn here. Reference hereafter will be to the numbered lines of testimony given in evidence.

The Trial of John Palmer, alias Paumer, alias Richard Turpin

The Counsel for the King, Thomas Place Esq., Recorder of the City of York and Richard Crowle Esq., of the Inner Temple having opened the nature of the indictment proceeded to the examination of witnesses as follows:

Thomas Creasy (the owner of the mare)

1. **Counsel**
   Where do you live?
2. **Creasy**
   At Heckington in the county of Lincoln.
3. **Counsel**
   Pray, Sir, had you a mare and a foal?
4. **Creasy**
   Yes.
5. **Counsel**
   Where did they go, or feed?
6. **Creasy**
   Upon Heckington Common.
7. **Counsel**
   When did you first miss them?
8. **Creasy**
   Upon a Thursday morning I was enquiring for them and they could not be found.
9. **Counsel**
   What day of the month do you think it might happen?
10. **Creasy**
    Upon the eighteenth or nineteenth day of August.
11. **Counsel**
    What month?
12. **Creasy**
    The month of August.
13. **Counsel**
    You say you missed them on Thursday the eighteenth or nineteenth of August last? Pray then Sir, when did you see them last?
14. **Creasy**
    The next day before I lost them.
15. **Counsel**
    When you missed your mare and foal what did you do in order to get intelligence about them?

16. **Creasy**
    I hired men and horses and rode forty miles round and about us to hear of them, and got them cry'd in all the Market Towns about us.
17. **Counsel**
    How long was it before you knew of the mare and foal, or who told you of them?
18. **Creasy**
    One, John Baxter, a neighbour of mine told me, he had been at Pocklington Fair in Yorkshire and laying all night at Brough he happened to hear of a man that had been taken up and sent to the House of Correction at Beverley for shooting a game cock, who had such a mare and foal as mine. Upon which information I came to Ferraby near Beverley and put up my horse at Richard Grassby's and began to enquire of him about my mare and foal. Who told me there was such a like mare and foal in their neighbourhood which I thought by the description he gave me, to be mine, so then I told him, I was come to enquire about such a mare and foal.
19. **Counsel**
    Did you know the marks of the mare and foal, as he described them to you?
20. **Creasy**
    Yes, I did, and told him these marks agreed with my mare and foal, before I did see them.
21. **Counsel**
    Was it when your neighbour came home you made the enquiry?
22. **Creasy**
    Yes it was, and by the information of his, I went to Ferraby, and gave the landlord and people an account of their marks.
23. **Counsel**
    Describe their marks.
24. **Creasy**
    She was a black mare, blind of the near eye, having a little white on the near fore foot, and also the near hind foot, a little above the hoof, and scratched (creased) on both the hind feet, and the near fore feet with I's, or marks resembling that letter, burnt on the near shoulder, and a star on the forehead.
25. **Counsel**
    How long did you have her?
26. **Creasy**
    I did breed her myself, and kept her till she was ten years old.

27. **Counsel**
    Did you give this account to Richard Grassby, before he showed you her?
28. **Creasy**
    Yes I did.
29. **Court**
    Had the foal any marks?
30. **Creasy**
    Yes, it was a black-ball.
31. **Counsel**
    Where did you see her?
32. **Creasy**
    At the stable door, they fetched her out to me and I knew her.
33. **Court**
    From all these marks are you very positive the mare and foal was yours?
34. **Creasy**
    Yes, I am sure they were mine.
35. **Counsel**
    Did you receive them at that time?
36. **Creasy**
    No. I did not get them then.
37. **Court**
    Are you sure the mare and foal were yours?
38. **Creasy**
    Yes, indeed I am.
39. **Counsel**
    When you came to Ferraby did you tell these marks, or the description of them, and to whom?
40. **Creasy**
    Yes, indeed, I told them to Richard Grassby the landlord.
41. **Court to Prisoner**
    Have you any questions to ask this witness? You have heard what he had to say against you.
42. **Prisoner**
    I cannot say anything, for I have not any witnesses come this day, as I have expected, therefore beg of your Lordship to put off my trial until another day.
43. **Court**
    We cannot put off this affair, if you had spoke, and desired a reasonable

time before the jury was sworn and charged, it might have been granted you. Now you are too late, the Jury cannot be discharged. You have liberty allowed you to ask any questions of the witness.

44. **Prisoner**
This witness is wrong, because on the eighteenth of August I was here in York Castle.

45. **Counsel**
No Sir, you were not here the eighteenth of August.

Mr. Griffith the Gaoler being called informed the Court that it was October before Palmer was committed prisoner to the Castle.

46. **Prisoner**
I never did see this man (Thomas Creasy) in my life.

47. **Prisoner**
(to Creasy) Do you know one Whitehead?

48. **Creasy**
Yes.

49. **Prisoner**
He's the man I bought the mare and foal of.

Captain Dawson called—Second Witness.

50. **Court**
Pray Sir, inform us what you know of this affair.

51. **Dawson**
I was one morning riding to Welton, and met a man leading his mare and foal. I asked him if that was his mare and foal. He told me, No, but they belonged to one Palmer, I asked him if he would dispose of the foal? He said, Palmer was coming up the street, I turned about and saw Palmer, who told me it was his mare and foal, and that they were bred in Lincolnshire, I asked, if he would dispose of the foal? He said, he would rather sell the mare with her, I replied, I had no occasion for the mare, only the foal, and asked the price of the foal, he said, three guineas, I told him it was too much to ask for the foal, and offered him two guineas, and said I would not give him more, upon which I went about my business, and afterwards I observed the prisoner coming up a hill with the mare and foal, and, as I was going along, a country man said, Sir, you have been about bargaining, and offered two guineas for the foal, you see him come back again, and, if you please, I fancy you

may have it, I said, let him come to my house, and I will pay him the two guineas, so about three o'clock in the afternoon he came with the mare and foal, and I had them both put in a stable, I went to pay the prisoner Palmer.

52. **Counsel**
Pray who was it that brought the mare and foal to your house?

53. **Dawson**
Nobody brought the mare and foal to me but himself, I went, and paid him for the foal two guineas and then he told me, I might buy the mare, for she was worth money, I told him I had no occasion for the mare, but the prisoner being a little pressing about it I told him I had a horse of no great value, and if he would change, or let me have the mare to nurse the foal, I would rather do it. He did not like the first proposal, but I told him, I would not take the mare except he would have the horse, so I gave him four guineas, but being obliged to go to my regiment, I left the place soon after.

54. **Counsel**
When did you leave the country?

55. **Dawson**
Soon after, I think about October I went away and gave Richard Grassby the care of the mare and he had the liberty to work her.

56. **Court**
Have you anything to say as to what the Captain has said against you?

57. **Prisoner**
Nothing at all.

Richard Grassby—Third Witness

58. **Court**
What have you to say about the mare?

59. **Grassby**
I had leave to work her.

60. **Court**
How long have you known the prisoner?

61. **Grassby**
I have seen him several times since, and I think, I have known him about two years.

62. **Counsel**
What manner of visible living had he?

63. **Grassby**
    He had no settled way of living, that I know of at all, though a dealer, yet he was a stranger, and lived like a gentleman.
64. **Counsel**
    Had you the mare of Captain Dawson?
65. **Grassby**
    Yes, I had the mare and foal.
66. **Counsel**
    Did he give you leave to work her?
67. **Grassby**
    Yes.
68. **Counsel**
    About what time did you work her?
69. **Grassby**
    About October the twelfth I think.
70. **Counsel**
    Did you work her?
71. **Grassby**
    Yes I did, for I had a close belonging to the Captain.
72. **Counsel**
    Was the mare challenged when you had her.
73. **Grassby**
    Yes, she was, I had been drawing with her, and Thomas Creasy came to me, and gave me an account very fully of all her marks before he saw her.
74. **Court**
    Then when he saw her, was that the very mare and foal?
75. **Grassby**
    Yes, the very same.
76. **Counsel**
    Do you remember this man? (the prisoner)
77. **Grassby**
    Yes, for he offered to sell me horses.
78. **Counsel**
    What do you know further about Palmer?
79. **Grassby**
    He was about two years at Welton.
80. **Counsel**
    Did you know him then?

81. **Grassby**
   Yes, he was reckoned a stranger.
82. **Counsel**
   In what manner of way used he support himself or, how did he live?
83. **Grassby**
   He lived like a gentleman.
84. **Counsel**
   What time was it you saw the mare?
85. **Grassby**
   I saw the mare about August in his possession.
86. **Court to the Prisoner**
   Will you ask this witness any question?
87. **Prisoner**
   No, I have nothing to say.
88. **Court**
   Can you be positive that Palmer offered this mare for sale?
89. **Grassby**
   Yes, indeed, I can, I am positive this is the man (looking at Palmer).

George Goodyear called—Fourth Witness.

90. **Court**
   Do you know of a mare and foal lost where you live?
91. **Goodyear**
   Yes, very well.
92. **Counsel**
   Do you know about what time this mare and foal were lost?
93. **Goodyear**
   Yes, I know, and I remember the time they were missing, it was towards the latter end of August.
94. **Counsel**
   When did you see the mare?
95. **Goodyear**
   In August.
96. **Counsel**
   Have you seen the mare again?
97. **Goodyear**
   Yes.
98. **Counsel**
   Was it the same you saw before?

99. **Goodyear**
    Yes.
100. **Counsel**
    Are you perfectly sure?
101. **Goodyear**
    Yes, I am perfectly sure.
102. **Court to Prisoner**
    Would you ask this witness any questions?
103. **Prisoner**
    None.

The Court ordered Richard Grassby to be called in again.

104. **Court to Grassby**
    When did you see this mare?
105. **Grassby**
    In August.

Then Mr. James Smith and Mr. Edward Saward, who came from Essex by order of the Justices of that county, were called to prove this Palmer to be Richard Turpin, the noted highwayman.

106. **Court to Mr. James Smith**
    Do you know the prisoner, Palmer at the bar? Look at him, and tell what you know about him.
107. **Smith**
    Yes, I knew him at Hempstead in Essex where he was born, I knew him when he was a child.
108. **Counsel**
    What is his name?
109. **Smith**
    Richard Turpin, I knew his father and all his relations, he married one of my father's maids.
110. **Counsel**
    What, was you with him frequently?
111. **Smith**
    Yes.
112. **Counsel**
    When did you see him last?
113. **Smith**
    It is about five years since I saw him.

114. **Counsel**
Have you any particular marks to show this is the man?
115. **Smith**
This is the very man.
116. **Counsel**
Did you not teach him at school?
117. **Smith**
Yes I did, but he was only learning to make letters, and I believe, he was three quarters of a year with me.
118. **Counsel**
Do you think this is he?
119. **Smith**
Yes this is the man.
120. **Counsel**
As you lived there, why did you come down here, to this place?
121. **Smith**
Happening to be at the post office, where I saw a letter directed to Turpin's brother-in-law who, as I was informed would not loose the letter and pay postage, upon that account taking particular notice thereof, I thought at first I remembered the superscription and concluded it to be the handwriting of the prisoner, Turpin, whereupon I carried the letter before a Magistrate who broke the same open (the letter was superscribed John Palmer) I found it sent from York Castle, I had several of Dick Turpin's bills and knew his hand.
122. **Counsel**
Are you sure this is his letter? (a letter produced in Court).
123. **Smith**
Yes I am sure that is his letter.
124. **Counsel**
Was that the cause of your coming down?
125. **Smith**
Yes.
126. **Counsel**
How happened you take notice of the letter?
127. **Smith**
Seeing the York stamp.
128. **Counsel**
From these circumstances did you come down here?
129. **Smith**
Yes indeed I did come upon this account.

130. **Counsel**
     When you came to the Castle, did you challenge him or know him?
131. **Smith**
     Yes I did, upon the first view of him, and pointed him out from amongst all the rest of the other prisoners.
132. **Counsel**
     How long was it since you saw him last?
133. **Smith**
     I think about five years.
134. **Counsel**
     Do you know anything more of him?
135. **Smith**
     I think he might be about eleven or twelve years old, when I went to the Excise, and he worked with his father, who was a butcher.
136. **Counsel**
     Was he ever set up in the butcher trade?
137. **Smith**
     Yes, I know he was.
138. **Counsel**
     How long might he live in that way?
139. **Smith**
     I cannot tell he lived at ......* in Essex he left it about six years and after he kept a public house.

* There was such a noise in the Court that the gentleman who took down the trial, could not distinctly hear the name of the place but apprehended it to be Boxhill or some such name.

140. **Counsel**
     Did you afterwards see him?
141. **Smith**
     Yes I saw him afterwards, six miles from thence.
142. **Counsel**
     What became of him then?
143. **Smith**
     I do not know more, only the last time I saw him, I sold him a grey mare, above five years ago before my brother died.
144. **Counsel**
     Do you know no more of him?

145. **Smith**
This I know of him, I have been many times in his company and frequently with him.
146. **Court**
Palmer you are allowed the liberty to ask Mr. Smith any questions.
147. **Prisoner**
I never knew him.
148. **Court**
When Mr. Smith came first to York in February last, he was examined at the Castle by several of His Majesty's Justices of the Peace of this county and he gave them the same account as above.

Mr. Edward Saward of Hempstead in Essex called.

149. **Counsel**
Do you know this Richard Turpin?
150. **Saward**
Yes I do know him, he was born and brought up at the *Bell*, his father kept a public house.
151. **Counsel**
How long have you known him?
152. **Saward**
I have known him these twenty two years. I cannot say know exceeding exact, but about twenty two years upon my soul.

Here the Counsel reproved Saward, and said to him, Friend, you have sworn once already, you need not swear again.

153. **Saward**
I have known him ever since he was a boy and lived at the *Bell*.
154. **Counsel**
How long did he live there?
155. **Saward**
I cannot exactly tell, he lived with his father and I was very great friend with him.
156. **Counsel**
Did you know him after he had set up for himself?
157. **Saward**
Yes I knew him perfectly well then and I have bought a great many good joints of meat from him upon my soul.

Upon this the Judge reprimanded him, and advised him not to speak so rashly, but to consider he was upon oath, and that he should speak seriously.

158. **Counsel**
    Did you know him since he left Hempstead?
159. **Saward**
    I was with him at his house in Hempstead.
160. **Counsel**
    Did you see him there?
161. **Saward**
    I saw him frequently, I cannot tell how often.
162. **Counsel**
    How many years since he left Hempstead.
163. **Saward**
    He came backward and forward.
164. **Counsel**
    How long is it since you saw him last?
165. **Saward**
    About five or six years ago.
166. **Counsel**
    Can you say that assuredly or firmly?
167. **Saward**
    Yes, I never seen him since.
168. **Counsel**
    Did he have any settled dwelling?
169. **Saward**
    Not that I know of.
170. **Counsel**
    Now look at the prisoner, is this Richard Turpin?
171. **Saward**
    Yes, Dick Turpin, the son of John Turpin who keeps the *Bell* at Hempstead.

Turpin denied he knew Edward Saward but he seemed at last to own Smith.

172. **Counsel to Mr. Smith**
    When you spoke to him in the Castle did you know him?
173. **Smith**
    Yes, I did, and he did confess to know me and said unto me two or three times, 'Let us bung our eyes in drink,' and I drank with him, which is this Richard Turpin.

174. **Court to Turpin**
There was a mare and foal lost, what account can you give, how you came by that mare and foal?
175. **Prisoner**
I was going up to Lincolnshire to John Whitehead, there was a mare and foal before his door and I was there drinking.
176. **Counsel**
Does he keep a house and sell ale?
177. **Prisoner**
Yes.
178. **Counsel**
What place was it at?
179. **Prisoner**
Within a mile of Heckington. The man had been at a fair and bought a mare and foal, and he wanted to sell them again.
180. **Counsel**
What time was it?
181. **Prisoner**
In August, I asked the price, and gave him seven guineas for the mare and colt, he gave me back half a crown I stayed all night, and came away next morning, I went to all markets, and wherever I went rode with them without ever being challenged.
182. **Court**
Have you anything more to say?
183. **Prisoner**
I have sent a subpeona for a man and his wife they was present when I bought them.
184. **Counsel**
What is his name?
185. **Prisoner**
I cannot tell, therefore I desire some longer time that these witnesses may be examined I also sent a special messenger with a letter.

Mr. Griffith the gaoler being called, said, the messenger is come back.

186. **Counsel**
What say you to that?

Prisoner was silent.

187. **Court**
    If you have any witnesses you should have had them here before this time, have you any witnesses here present?
188. **Prisoner**
    I have none present, but tomorrow I will have them, I am sure no man can say ill of me in Yorkshire.
189. **Court**
    Have you any witnesses here?
190. **Prisoner**
    Yes, William Thompson Esq. also Mr. Whitehead and Mr. Gill.

All these were called in Court but did not appear.

191. **Court**
    The Jury cannot stay and you see there is none appearing for you.
192. **Prisoner**
    I thought I should have been removed to Essex for I did not expect to be tried in this country, therefore I could not prepare witnesses to my character.

After this The Hon. Sir William Chapple gave his charge to the Jury.

193. **Prisoner**
    The reasons I had for changing my name, were, that I having been long out of trade, and run myself into debt, I changed my name to my mother's which was Palmer.
194. **Counsel**
    What was your name before you came to Lincolnshire?
195. **Prisoner**
    Turpin
196. **Counsel**
    Was it Richard Turpin?
197. **Prisoner**
    Yes, I thought I should have been removed to get my trial in Essex.
198. **Court**
    You have deceived yourself in thinking so.

The Jury without leaving Court brought in their verdict 'Guilty'.

John Palmer, alias Richard Turpin was indicted a second time for stealing a black gelding the property of Thomas Creasy.

199. **Court**
Call Thomas Creasy.
200. **Court**
Sir, was you in possession of a gelding in August last?
201. **Creasy**
Yes I was.
202. **Counsel**
About what time did you miss it?
203. **Creasy**
The eighteenth day of August last, I missed the gelding.
204. **Counsel**
Where did you find him and what colour was he?
205. **Creasy**
I found him at the *Blue Bell* in Beverley.
206. **Counsel**
How came you to hear he was there?
207. **Creasy**
Richard Grassby was the person who told me it was my gelding.
208. **Counsel**
Did you describe the gelding to him?
209. **Creasy**
Yes, and then he told me it was the same.
210. **Counsel**
Upon that what did you do?
211. **Creasy**
I went to the landlord of the house at Beverley and described him to him.
212. **Counsel**
Do you remember what description you gave him of the gelding?
213. **Creasy**
Yes, the description was a black gelding with a little star on the forehead.
214. **Counsel**
What did he (the landlord) do then?
215. **Creasy**
I went with him and he showed me the horse.
216. **Counsel**
Are you sure the gelding he showed you was yours?
217. **Creasy**
Yes I am.

218. **Counsel**
    But are you very sure that was your gelding?
219. **Creasy**
    Yes, yes indeed I am.
220. **Counsel**
    Did you show him to any person?
221. **Creasy**
    I showed him to Carey Gill, the constable at Welton.

Carey Gill was then called.

222. **Court**
    What do you know concerning the prisoner?
223. **Gill**
    He was taken up by me for shooting a cock, upon which I carried him to Beverley Petty Sessions.
224. **Counsel**
    Which way did you carry him, or how did he go?
225. **Gill**
    He rode upon his own horse, and I along with him.
226. **Counsel**
    What month did this happen?
227. **Gill**
    At Micklemas Session, which was October the sixth.
228. **Counsel**
    Do you know what horse he rode upon?
229. **Gill**
    He rode upon a horse which he called his own.
230. **Counsel**
    Did you see the horse?
231. **Gill**
    Yes, it was the same he came from Welton upon.
232. **Court to Thomas Creasy**
    How did you get your horse again?
233. **Creasy**
    I got him from the Justice by his order.
234. **Counsel**
    How many miles is it from your home, you got this horse?
235. **Creasy**
    It was about fifty miles from the Waterside to Welton.

236. **Counsel**
Was it the same horse you heard described?
237. **Creasy**
Yes, it was.
238. **Counsel**
What marks had he?
239. **Creasy**
It was a black gelding with a little star on his forehead and carried a good tail.
240. **Court to James Smith**
How long is it since you have known the prisoner at the bar, look at him again.
241. **Smith**
I have known him from his infancy these twenty-two years and he is the very Richard Turpin which I have known at Hempstead, the son of John Turpin of that town.
242. **Court to Prisoner**
Have you any more to say?
243. **Prisoner**
I bought the horse of Whitehead.

The Jury brought in their verdict of 'Guilty'. When the Judge was going to pass sentence the prisoner was asked, What reason he had to give that sentence of death should not be pronounced upon him, the prisoner replied,

244. It is very hard upon me My Lord because I was not prepared for my defence.
245. **Court**
Why was you not? you knew the time of the Assizes as well as any person present.
246. **Prisoner**
Several persons who came to see me assured me that I should be removed to Essex to be tried there, for which reason I thought it needless to prepare witnesses for my defence.
247. **Judge**
Whoever told you so were highly to blame, and as your country has found you guilty of a crime worthy of death it is my office to pronounce sentence against you.

The prisoner was then sentenced to 'Death'.

II

This is as fair a record of the trial as one could hope to have, and apart from some minor discrepancies would appear to be substantially accurate. It was advertised in the *York Courant* of 17 April 1739 as having been printed by Ward and Chandler in York, and was from that date available at their shop in Temple Bar, London, and at booksellers in Leeds, Wakefield, Hull and Newcastle. Setting aside the matter of whether or not it was the only record of the trial, there can be no doubt that it was the first one to be published.

Annexed to this record were Robert Appleton's account, the letter to Turpin from his father, Turpin's behaviour at the place of execution, and his confession to the hangman at the gallows. But since we are concerned at this point with the trial, it is of some interest to note that a reference to Kyll's shorthand transcript was made in the *York Courant* two weeks before publication, a fact which would seem to prove the authenticity of this particular record and the validity of its content. It has of course been reproduced many times, merely as a means to shew how Turpin came to his end, but it is interesting to look at the evidence to see if the result might have been otherwise, and if there might have been some justification in the sending of Newcastle's letter. Perhaps the most significant thing about this trial is not so much the evidence against Turpin, but his defence, shewn in Lines 41–44, 46–49, 174–198, and 244–247.

Turpin was in a quandary brought about by two factors. He had stolen the horses and been identified as Turpin, and there was sufficient evidence to prove both felony and identity. There could be no defence, for even though Turpin's plea that he obtained the horses from Whitehead (whom Creasy actually knew) was a plausible fiction, there was never any possibility of his getting witnesses to substantiate it as fact. Thus the very most he might have achieved, had he given notice beforehand, was a postponement.

Character witnesses from Yorkshire, even had there been any willing to have come forward, would have been of little help to him; and his plea that he had not had time to prepare witnesses, because he thought he would be removed to Essex, was not one likely to be believed. Officially, as the judge reminded him, he would have been notified of the date of the Assize, and although a number of people probably did tell him he would stand trial in Essex, they could not have been responsible persons upon whose word he should have relied. There can be no doubt that, although his hopes that he would be tried at Chelmsford were kept alive by such stories, there was no reason why he should have believed them.

The truth was that there were no witnesses to come to Turpin's assistance, he had no defence, and for any pretence he made to one he might as well have pleaded guilty and kept his fingers crossed. The result would have been the same.

All Turpin's pretence of innocence of horsestealing was exposed by the stupid blunder born of desperation which he committed very early during the proceedings. He claimed to have been in York Castle when the horses were stolen. It would have been interesting to see what might have happened had he claimed to be a prisoner on the date upon which the indictment stated the horses to have been stolen, but the judge would no doubt have ruled against him and the trial proceeded on the same lines as it did. There is not a great deal one can say about Turpin's pathetic protests, except that they can only have contributed a little to his conviction.

His greatest opportunity to secure release came at a time when both his instinct and desire for survival had deserted him, for in October 1738, when arrested on a trivial charge, the smallest effort on his part might easily have made all the difference between commitment and bail. There was too the chance to escape when Carey Gill the constable escorted him from Welton to Beverley. But these opportunities passed by, he was moved to York, and all hope faded. And even supposing there to have been some chance of his being acquitted under the name of Palmer, Turpin revealed his true identity and reduced his chances to zero. By March 1739 the thought of dying may have made him reconsider his position, but by that time it had become hopeless, a fact clearly illustrated by the way in which his vulnerability was exposed at the trial.

The final point about Turpin's 'defence' concerns the witnesses who did not appear when called; for keeping in mind his habit of distorting the truth to suit his own purposes, it is perhaps ironic that he should invent or select the surnames Thompson, Whitehead and Gill. Henry (not William) Thompson was the master of the man Turpin killed, Whitehead was Thomas Creasy's neighbour and therefore a much more likely candidate as prosecution witness, and Gill (Carey) was the man who arrested Turpin, called to give evidence for the prosecution on the second indictment. There is no evidence of William Thompson's and Mr. Gill's independent existence, but it is appropriate to observe that if Turpin was completely lacking in friends he may well have looked to his enemies for names with which to decorate the fiction of his defence.

III

The prosecution testimony was cruelly efficient, particularly where the evidence of some witnesses dovetailed neatly into that of others to make the perfect box of proof which became Turpin's coffin. And Thomas Place, assisted by Richard Crowle, was painstaking in ensuring nothing of relevance was overlooked.

Line 24, in which Creasy described his mare, was quite enough to establish his ability to distinguish it from all others, and the procedure whereby he was able to convince others of his ownership (without first having sight of the animals) is meticulously drawn out. But on a point of accuracy it is possible that a question from Counsel was omitted between Lines 46 and 47, both of which are Turpin's.

Dawson's evidence, Lines 51 and 53, was damning insofar as it proved that Turpin had sold the stolen horses to him, but although the fact of the sale was clear, the captain's confused recollection of it was such as to even baffle Counsel (line 52), Grassby, Lines 58-69 merely confirmed the testimony of Creasy and Dawson, whilst Goodyear's testimony suggests that Place may have allowed Richard Crowle to tackle him; in this instance the questions could hardly be said to have elicited much in the way of constructive evidence. It did not matter, for having presented the evidence against the prisoner, the prosecution now proceeded, with the assistance of the Hempstead witnesses Smith and Saward, to prove that he was Richard Turpin, robber, highwayman and murderer, against whom there were no previous convictions. And this really was the basis of George Crowle's assurance that there was sufficient proof at York upon which to obtain a conviction.

It is perhaps cynical to say that the prisoner was convicted of being Richard Turpin, but essentially, justice having been seen to be done on the grounds of horse stealing, this was the charge Turpin had to answer. He had made a mockery of law and order, fools of many influential members of the Establishment, and as explicity stated in the indictments, offended against the King, his Crown and Dignity. There cannot be any doubt that even had there been no suspicion of his true identity, John Palmer would have been convicted of horse stealing; but *had* there been any doubt in the minds of the jury, exposing the prisoner in the dock as the most wanted criminal in England was a most effective method of convincing them of his guilt. In the event, this is not what happened; for even when the trial commenced, the jury were well aware that Palmer had been identified as Turpin, and however scrupulous the judge's command of the proceedings (he may for instance have directed the jury to ignore the previous identification on the grounds that it was not proven) the jury, if they had not already accepted the prisoner as Turpin, were prepared to be convinced of the fact. The identification was straightforward, but there are however some few points which need comment.

Comparison between James Smith's testimony and the information he gave a month earlier suggests that the prosecution, having carefully screened the witnesses' informations, then proceeded to brief them with equal care. This would explain how precisely the evidence of one person is complemented by another's. Admittedly the prosecution, by subtle questioning, and being in a position to be able to anticipate the answers, could produce the same effect, but not unless, as illustrated below, certain flaws in testimony had been previously eradicated.

Thus, James Smith's written statement, that he had been constantly in Turpin's company within the last three or four years (in other words within the period of Turpin's criminal activity) became in Line 133, 'It is about five years since I saw him'.[1] More important still is the significant clarification of the written statement, 'Turpin went to school with [me],', as it appears in Lines 116–117.

Counsel
Did you not teach him at school?
Smith
Yes I did, but he was only learning to make letters, and I believe, he was three quarters of a year with me.

With this testimony, the jury could hardly fail to take the point, subsequently made, that here was a man who better than anyone else was exceptionally well qualified to claim that he could recognise Turpin's handwriting. But had the jury been told that Turpin and Smith were merely fellow pupils at the village school, the prosecution would have made no progress at all. James Smith has always been represented as a schoolmaster, but since on this evidence the fact is not established, we may at least ask in what capacity did Smith teach Turpin to make his letters? There is no sure answer here because Smith's age is not known, but from Line 133 where Smith stated Turpin to be eleven or twelve years old when he [Smith] went to the Excise, it may be inferred that Smith was not a schoolmaster, but a boy somewhat older than Turpin and one to whom the schoolmaster had delegated the task of teaching the younger children their letters. This would reconcile Smith's written and verbal testimony and clear him of any suspicion that he might have perjured himself, or that the prosecution had connived with him to that end.

Consideration of Lines 139 and 172–173 is to some extent bound up with the question of whether J. Standen's version of the trial was pirated from the above original or not. Basically the problem is a simple one, was there more than one reporter at the trial? Testimony is not a great help because one would expect it to be substantially the same even if two different people took it down, but in Lines 172–173 there is a departure from Kyll's record in Standen's version. Standen took Lines 171–173 and attributed them to Saward, whereas Kyll shewed them to be in sequence Saward, Counsel, Smith, with a narrative interjection between Lines 171 and 172, which Standen placed after his single entry.

From the introduction to the 4th edition of the Kyll's version it is clear that Standen's was published some time after the 3rd edition of the original, but on what date the 3rd and 4th editions came out is not known. Our knowledge of the date when the editions appeared is largely restricted to the 1st edition being on sale from 17 April 1739, and which apart from being advertised in the *York Courant* of that date (and presumably thereafter or simultaneously in other newspapers) also appeared as Item 20 in 'The Register of Books for April 1739' in the *Gentleman's Magazine.* Our only other clue to date lies in the fact that Standen's version was either copied by, or was a copy of that account which appeared in, the *Political State.*[2]

The account is in the June section, probably published at the beginning of July 1739, and follows a brief synopsis of proceedings at the Assizes at York which ended on 24 March 1739. Such brief coverage of Assizes was a regular feature of the *Political State,* the appearance of such articles being governed by how quickly the information came to hand; and in cases of unusual interest, it was common for a transcript of the proceedings to follow the general synopsis of all cases handled at any particular Assize. In this case however the interval between the report and the event is overlong for the article to have emanated directly from York, and the fact that the synopsis describes Palmer otherwise Turpin as having been capitally convicted of stealing sheep and horses, suggests that this part of the York account was contrived without much regard or knowledge of the March proceedings in that city. The digest version however, if taken from Kyll's, differs in this synopsis because Kyll's version, in the preamble, contains no reference to sheep; similarly there is no reference to sheep in the condensed digest *account* of the trial. In this case there would appear to be no obvious relationship between the synopsis (which was a regular feature) and the trial account (the appearance of which was governed by unusual features). Thus the reference to sheep is a mistake only in the context of the synopsis, and has no common source with the trial account separated from it by a short introduction. 'This John Palmer was the famous Turpin, who has made so much noise on account of the numerous villainies he had committed; and therefore no doubt the following summary account of his trial will be agreeable to the reader.'

A very similar introduction prefaced the 'Letter from York dated March 2nd', which the *Political State* culled from the *General Evening Post,* and the question which still remains is, was the *Political State* the source of Standen's version, or did the *Political State* copy Standen?

There can be very little doubt that the *Political State* reproduced J. Standen's pirated version of Kyll's transcript of the trial. For although we do not know Ward and Chandler's imprint of each of the first three editions, we may be sure that they had a very quick sale and that Standen would have wanted to capitalise on this before demand began to fall off. On this basis, it is probable that Standen's pirate appeared in May 1739, and the strongest argument in support of this theory is the motive of gain. Standen stood to make a quick profit with his pirate edition, especially if he entered the market before Ward and Chandler realised that they would need a 4th edition to satisfy demand. The publishers of the *Political State,* with deadlines to meet and always hungry for ready material, and articles of unusual interest, did not stand to gain much at all. There was probably a limited monthly imprint made to meet an assured demand, and apart from those months when it was possible to fill the space with a complete resumé of a Parliamentary debate on some controversial issue, the editor's main concern would have been to find sufficient material of the right kind to fill the space. Standen's condensed trial account was ideal in interest and length, and saved scouring the newspapers for the equivalent number of smaller items.

Standen pirated John Turpin's letter to York (the original was probably forged), Robert Appleton's account of Turpin in Yorkshire, condensed Kyll's trial account (amending where necessary and putting the proof of identification at the end), and threw in another three forged letters for good measure. By the time Ward and Chandler replied with their 4th edition, in which they castigated Standen, he had possibly sold his imprint and retired from the scene, content in the knowledge that he had made the most of his opportunity. But although the ethics of eighteenth century publishers is not within our brief, there remains some interest in what they did, particularly where it concerns alterations to the text. Thus although both points have previously been examined in a pre-trial context, it is necessary to take a final look at Standen's substitution of Buckhurst Hill (Booker's Hill *sic*) for Kyll's suggested Boxhill (Line 139), and at his attributing Lines 171–173 to Saward.

However Standen arrived at Booker's Hill, it has been demonstrated that there could be no reasonable alternative. If he had left a blank in the testimony and suggested Boxhill, there would have been little doubt at all that his was a pirated version, because if through noise speech becomes indistinct, then no two people are likely to interpret what is heard in the same way. Standen had to substitute something, and it would not have required much effort to have come up with the right answer to thereby confound his critics. Saward's testimony is similar, because on reading Lines 171–173 both continuity and credibility are disturbed.

Smith had already testified that he had identified Turpin from other prisoners in the Castle, an act not likely to have endeared him to the accused. Place confirmed this by writing that Turpin did not confess his identity until the same evening, and even then only to Place himself. Turpin, having married one of Smith's father's maids, was socially inferior to Smith during the period when Smith knew him, and although in a village the size of Hempstead they could hardly avoid meeting there must have been *some* disparity in attitude towards each other, which despite Turpin's pretensions is unlikely to have been resolved at York. Saward on the other hand, Line 155, stated, 'I was very great friends with him', and, on a more intimate level than Smith, 'I was with him at his house in Hempstead', Line 159. So having accepted his denouement and his fate, who else, some day or so after Smith's visit, is Turpin likely to have greeted with the repetitious phrase, 'Let us bung our eyes in drink'? Standen's reconstruction of this part of the evidence must be correct, the only thing which is wrong is that although he put the narrative interjection *after* Line 173, he did not question its content. For why at this point would Turpin deny his friend, acknowledge the man who he had already denied and who had betrayed him, and then, Lines 193–197, admit his identity to the court? In the confusion of the moments when Lines 171–173 were set down by Kyll, something certainly was said about which Kyll was not entirely clear; we may be reasonably certain it was not that which subsequently appeared between Lines 171 and 172.

The evidence upon the second indictment followed the pattern of that given in respect of the first, and in that sense was entirely predictable. A man on trial could call character references and evidence which might prove his innocence, but since Turpin had recourse to neither he really might just as well have not been there. At the end James Smith was recalled, Line 241, and claimed to have known Turpin 22 years, which number curiously enough was the same that Edward Saward claimed to have known Turpin, Line 152. And at the end, being asked if he had anything more to say, Turpin lamely reiterated that he had bought the horse from Whitehead. The jury found him guilty, and in reply to the judge before sentence was passed, he could only repeat that he had expected to be tried in Essex.

As a trial it was not a notable event, there were no sensations, no excitement, and the legendary swashbuckling highwayman gave a dull performance in court. He did restore his image slightly upon the scaffold, and afterwards the mob gave him a send off worthy of a popular hero, but the trial revealed him as an ordinary villain, vulnerable in the face of the law. The *coup de grace* was administered by Sir William Chapple, who informed him 'your country has found you guilty of a crime worthy of death'. It was not of course intended as a merciful thrust, but to a once colourful figure reduced to the commonplace level of criminal society, to be told that conviction on charges of horse stealing was worthy of death was equally effective, even if it was the unkindest cut of all.

IV

On the indictments it was the practice to record the plea, verdict and judgement, and on Turpin's it was abbreviated, 'Puts [himself on his country], Guilty, no goods, [to be] hanged'; but in another volume of the series of *Minute Books,* there appear details normally to be found on the parchment Gaol Delivery (missing in this case) usually filed with the indictments. And here we see Turpin in the same perspective as did the judge, a convicted felon of the same mould as his companion to be on the scaffold. 'John Palmer otherwise Pawmer otherwise $R^{d.}$ Turpin [and] John Stead Being attainted of horse stealing let them be severally hanged by their necks until they be severally dead.'[3]

The Assizes at York ended on Saturday 24 March 1739, a fortnight before Turpin was due to be executed, and although one would have thought the interest of Robert Appleton, Clerk of the Peace for the East Riding, would have come to an end once Turpin had been removed from Beverley to York in October 1738, the Treasury Solicitor's submission on the claim for rewards for Turpin's capture and conviction shews that Appleton played a quite considerable role behind the scenes at the trial.

> There is likewise annexed to the said petition a letter from Robert Appleton to Mr. [George] Crowle dated 24th March 1738 [/9] giving an account of the trouble and expense he was at in sending messengers to serve subpoenas in Lincolnshire and at Hull and other places very distant from York upon the principal witnesses against the offender, and in bringing them to York to give

evidence against him, and in feeing Counsel and paying the charges and other expenses of the prosecution amounting to about 20 1. which he desires might be paid out of the reward, and of which he wrote he would send Mr. Crowle the particulars. And at the bottom of his letter mentions the petitioners to be the several witnesses upon the trial. Mr. Appleton in his letter further says that the criminal owned himself to be Richard Turpin upon the trial.[4]

Crowle subsequently informed Paxton that he did not remember receiving any particulars from Appleton. It is possible that Crowle made some immediate financial settlement which satisfied Appleton, and, since Paxton clearly obtained Appleton's letter from Crowle in support of his plea to be appointed agent for the distribution of the reward, it may have been no more than an oversight that Crowle did not remember receiving details. It was after all some months before the petition for the reward reached Paxton, and since Crowle himself claimed to have paid travelling expenses of various witnesses, and was under obligation to pay for other unspecified services, he possibly regarded Appleton's £20 as being part and parcel of the whole. The letter however, shews the extent to which Appleton was responsible for co-ordinating certain arrangements essential to the smooth progress of Turpin's trial, and taking care of certain financial demands afterwards.

Exactly how the M.P. for Kingston-upon-Hull, the Clerk of the Peace for the East Riding, the Recorder of York and the M.P.'s brother combined in their efforts to dispose of Turpin has not been established, at least not from an administrative point of view. We have seen the separate functions of each, and in some cases how the actions of one or two affected others; but since we have also seen how George Crowle's independent action changed the course of history and legend it may well be that to look to administrative procedure at county level would leave us none the wiser, especially when he may have created a few precedents in the process. However as Crowle was also a Justice of the Peace he and the other three would have had links which would have been much closer than is perhaps evident from the scanty evidence which has been surveyed, and their working relationship in the events which have been described was no doubt integrated to a much greater extent than has been defined.

Written on the same day as Appleton's letter to Crowle, another gentleman's contribution to the account is quite brief, but since it gives some insight into the effect Turpin had on the public at large it has a place here.

From the Diary of Arthur Jessop.[5]
March 24   Very cold wind. I was at Stony Bank. I hear it is not Turpin who is confined at York Castle.

> 25 Mr. Eden preached. I was not at chapel. There is no service at Holmfirth Chapel. Mr. Thompson is ill of the gout.
> 29 Emor Rich of Darrells was here, his daughter continuing very ill and he said that Dr. Cookson of Wakefield is to come and visit her this afternoon.
> April 1 Rain, had no service. Mr. Eden preached at Bull house.
> 2 It is confirmed that it is Turpin who was confined in York Castle, and has took his trial for horse stealing and is condemned.
> 8 Strong blustering cold wind rain hail and snow. I was not at chapel. Mr. Eden preached.

Arthur Jessop was an apothecary of New Mill at Wooldale in the West Riding, a place about five miles south east of Huddersfield. He travelled about all over this vicinity, and it is interesting to find this reference to Turpin mixed with Jessop's routine of weather, sickness, chapel and visits. In his world news did not travel very quickly, but Turpin clearly was a name not unknown to him and one which was of no small interest. We may imagine his fate being discussed in every household Jessop had occasion to visit, but there is no subsequent reference to Turpin's execution and possibly at that point he ceased to be a subject worthy of discussion. From our point of view these entries are of particular relevance when Jessop mentions the prevailing weather conditions, evocative of the winter of 1734/1735, when Turpin robbed with the Gregory gang, a time which he had not forgotten.

V

A week passed by, and since a detailed examination of the correspondence of 24 and 29 March, published about June 1739 by J. Standen, has already been made, no further reference to those letters will be made here; but on 31 March there appeared in a London newspaper another of those reports the contents of which never cease to astound. 'York. March 23rd. Yesterday John Palmer alias Richard Turpin was tried here, and convicted. His necessity in gaol forced him to get a fellow prisoner to write the letter which he signed and which pulled off the mask and discovered him.'[6]

Such news, purporting to have come from York the day after the trial, is quite improbable, even if the author of the information obtained it at second or third hand from the court; and one can only assume that to bolster a meagre account of the conviction this particular fiction was added. In York itself however the reporters were more reliable. 'We hear that the trial of the notorious highwayman Richard Turpin, was taken down in shorthand by the ingenious Mr. Thomas Kyll, Writing-Master in this City; and that the same will be printed very speedily, for the satisfaction of the public.'[7]

Ward and Chandler, if not Kyll himself (we do not know his arrangement with the publishers), must certainly have profited from this advance publicity, and it is conceivable that in anticipation of a spectacular demand for their account of the trial, etc., they were already thinking in terms of a second imprint. But what of Turpin during this time when publishers were thinking in terms of the fat profit to be made from his trial and execution? We look to J. Standen once more for information in this respect, but although certainly he did not pirate this account, that is not to say that he did not invent it:

HIS BEHAVIOUR IN YORK CASTLE

The near approach of death generally causes the most awful apprehensions, even in persons whose lives have been governed with the greatest rectitude, and whose consciences are not burdened with the guilt of any wilful transgressions. It is therefore infinitely surprising that men, who for many years successively, have employed all their talents and endeavours in robbing, plundering and destroying the lives and properties of their fellow creatures, should, without any emotion or concern, be able to look death in the face, contemn the horrors of that gloomy hour, and launch out into the boundless ocean of eternity, without making the least provision for so long and hazardous a voyage. To what causes can this unaccountable phrenzy, or rather stupefaction, be imputed? They must either have worked themselves into a firm persuasion that there is no God to take cognizance of their actions, that there are no rewards or punishments hereafter, or else their consciences, by a long course of vicious practices, are so hardened, that it's impossible for the precepts of religion, and the consideration of a future state, to make any impression upon them. For even the light of nature informs us of the difference between right and wrong; that we have no title to the property of another man; and that in depriving him of it, we do him a positive injury. Justice and injustice are wrote in indelible characters on the minds of man; and whenever he attempts to erase or blot them out, it is a manifest and sensible violence of the conscience; but if this violence be often repeated, conscience will at length lose its active faculty, and in time be quite dormant. This we may reasonably suppose was the case of the unhappy Turpin, who, though one of the most notorious offenders this age has produced, yet, after sentence of death was passed upon him, was as jovial, as merry, and as frolicsome as if he had been perfectly at liberty, and assured of a hundred years of prosperity to come; and went off the stage with as much intrepidity and unconcern, as if he had been taking horse to go a journey.

But to come to some particulars. Turpin being committed prisoner to York Castle, as has been before related, lived in as much pleasure as the liberties of prison would afford, eating, drinking and carousing with anybody that would spend their time with him. Neither did he alter his behaviour even after his condemnation. After it was rumoured abroad, that he was the Turpin who had rendered himself so notorious for his robberies in the southern parts of England, abundance of people from all parts resorted daily to see him. It being about that time a subject very much disputed in all company and conversations, whether this man was the real individual Turpin, the highwayman, or not, a certain young gentleman, who pretended to know him, went one day to see him, to satisfy himself if he was the very man, as reported, and having viewed him very circumspectly, he told the keeper he would lay him a wager of half a guinea, that this man was not Turpin; which Turpin hearing, whispered the Keeper in the ear, 'Lay him the wager; I'll go you halves'.

He continued his mirthful humour to the last, spending his time in joking, drinking and telling stories. He seemed to pay but little regard to the serious remonstrances and admonitions of the reverend clergymen who attended him; and whatever remorse he had upon his conscience for his past villainies, he kept it to himself, not expressing the least concern at the melancholy circumstances he was in.

A few days before his execution, he bought himself a new fustian frock, and a pair of pumps, in order to take his leave of the world in as decent a manner as he possibly could.

We have heard that there was much betting on the identity of the prisoner believed to be Turpin, but the wager now must be on the authenticity of this account of his demeanour after the trial and before execution. Is it possible that having just been sentenced to death Turpin could have been 'jovial, merry, frolicsome, intrepid and unconcerned'? We know that in court, where he was in full view of a considerable number of people, many more than would have been able to see him at one time in his cell, his manner was subdued to the point of dullness. On being returned to his cell, however, with a few drinks inside him, it is conceivable that he affected unconcern and that observers may have found him surprisingly cheerful in the circumstances.

Standen's account is the only one which can be said to relate to Turpin's demeanour between conviction and execution, and being published some months after the events there must remain some doubt about the truth of its content; but having removed the sermon, the rest could be said to be a predictable account of almost any hardened criminal's behaviour.

A final comment on Turpin's behaviour at this time is reflected in what the author of the 'Letter from York' had to say about his post-dénouement/pre-trial demeanour. Even then there was confidence in a hopeless situation, but this undoubtedly stemmed from the money which the 'great concourse of people' who flocked to see him contributed. Apart from food and drink, there was not much he could buy, except as when the day of the execution drew nearer, vanity may well have inspired him to invest in some new clothes suitable for the occasion. This would be consistent with the reliable report of his expenditure in hiring mourners to follow the cart to the scaffold. The reliability of Standen's account of his behaviour in York Castle is largely irrelevant when the general impression it conveys could hardly be far from the truth, but at the same time it would be wrong to regard it as an authentic record. For if Standen could obtain all the rest of the material in his Turpin compendium without moving from Chancery Lane, he is hardly likely to have made a special journey to York to secure the meagre basis to his sermon on how the contrite criminal should prepare to meet his Maker.

VI

From the above and various other instances we have seen how J. Standen capitalised on public interest in Turpin and successfully invaded Ward and Chandler's monopoly on the subject. He did so by pirating sections of their publication and inventing others with which to pad out his own, but in exposing him in the preface to their 4th edition, Ward and Chandler were obliged to confine their protest to the matter of piracy, for they themselves were no innocents when it came to invention. This is particularly evident when we come to the rag bag of incidents purporting to be Turpin's confession:

TURPIN'S CONFESSION

The following account Turpin gave of himself to the topsman the week after his condemnation and repeated the same particulars to him again at the gallows, which being taken down from his own mouth are as follows:
    That he was bred a butcher and served five years of his time very faithfully in White-Chapel but falling into idle company he began to make unlawful measures to support his extravagances and went some time on the highway on

foot, and met with several small booties, his not being detected therein gave him encouragement to steal horses and pursue his new trade in Epping Forest on horseback which he had continued about six years. Having been out one whole day without any booty and being much tired, he laid himself down in the thicket and turned his horse loose, having first taken off the saddle. When he waked, he went to search after his horse and meeting with Mr. Thompson's servant he enquired if he had seen his horse. To which Mr. Thompson's man answered that he knew nothing of Turpin's horse, but that he had found Turpin and accordingly presented his blunderbuss at Turpin, who instantly jumping behind a broad oak, avoided the shot, and instantly fired a carbine at Mr. Thompson's servant and shot him dead on the spot, one slug went through his breast, another through his right thigh, and a third through his groin. This done, he withdrew to a yew tree hard by, where he concealed himself so closely, that though the noise of Mr. Thompson's man's blunderbuss and his own carbine had drawn together a great number of people about the body, yet he continued undiscovered two whole days and one night in the tree, when the company was all dispersed he got out of the forest, and took a black horse out of a close near the road, and there being people working in the field at a distance he threw some money amongst them, and made off, but afterwards the same evening, stole a chesnut mare and turning the black horse loose, made the best of his way for London, some time after he returned to the forest again and attempted to rob Captain Thompson and his lady in an open chaise but the Captain firing a carbine at him, which missed and fired a pistol after the Captain which went through the chaise between him and his lady without any further damage, than tearing the left sleeve of his coat, the Captain driving hard, and being just in sight of a town, Turpin thought it not proper to pursue him any further.

He next stopped a country gentleman whom he bade stop, but the gentleman clapped spurs to his horse and rode off, he rode after him, and fired a pistol, which lodged two balls in his horse's buttocks so that the gentleman was obliged to stop.

After this he stopped a farmer in Epping Forest who had been to London to sell hay, and took from him fifty shillings, and hearing of several coaches coming that way, laid in wait for them but they, being informed of the frequent robberies in those parts, took another road.

Another time meeting a gentleman and lady on horseback in a lane near the forest he stopped them and presented a pistol, at which the lady fell into a swoon, he took from the gentleman seven guineas and some silver and from the lady a watch, a diamond ring, one guinea and fifteen shillings in silver.

He likewise owned that he was a confederate with one King, who was executed in London some time since, and that, once being very near taken, he fired a pistol amongst the crowd, and by mistake, shot the said King into the thigh who was coming to rescue him.

He also confessed the facts of which he was convicted, but said, many things had been laid to his charge of which he was innocent. Though it is very probable he was guilty of several robberies not here mentioned, yet this was the whole confession that the topsman could get from him.

Some might say that neither from Turpin nor the topsman could one have expected a very coherent account of Turpin's exploits, whether it was recounted in his cell or on the scaffold, but fortunately for posterity there has survived a fragment of a confession which Turpin did make and sign. It survives in that by now familiar and extraordinary useful Treasury claim for rewards, and, since the complete and original confession has not survived, must be regarded as uniquely authentic.

> And by the paper annexed which is endorsed to be the Confession of Richard Turpin before he was Executed taken before the Under Sheriff and the Gaoler and Witnessed by them both, it appears that there was a gang of 21 at the house of James Parkinson of Susan Ferry near Waltham the landlord of which was one and they would have had him gone out with them but he always refused to go and that it was then a year since he had seen them there and that they came and went from London frequently—which paper is signed Richard Turpin, and witnessed Richard Sheppard and Thomas Griffith.[8]

It is perhaps wrong to describe this as a fragment of a confession for in the context of Paxton's narrative it could as easily be seen as a complete document; but without the original it cannot be said with certainty that Paxton did not leave anything out. It is somewhat curious however that if complete, Turpin's recollection of his six years of crime should have been confined to the early period when he was with the Gregory gang. An explanation of this may perhaps be found in the phrase, 'it was then a year since he had seen them there', a contraction of time which at first sight might suggest that Turpin's memory was at fault. This was not so for at the trial, he said nothing to indicate that his memory was impaired. Thereafter however, he was drinking, and—perhaps incapable of rational or coherent thought—he may have preferred to dwell on those vivid memories of that most spectactular period of his career, when he was not alone and it still seemed like yesterday.

Ward and Chandler's 'Confession' is singularly unconvincing in that it contains no reference to the Gregory gang, and is for the most part completely erroneous in its outlines of Turpin's pre 1737 activities. Thus for the purpose of a confession it does not commence until Turpin murdered Thomas Morris in May 1737, the account of which amounts to about a third of the whole. This was remembered by someone obviously familiar with the event but somewhat out of touch with the circumstances. The author was similarly out of touch with the timing of the incident which follows where the victims are identified as Captain Thompson and his lady. The circumstances of this attempted robbery are the same as those described in the *London Evening Post* of 21 April 1737, and although the victims were not named in that report there can be no doubt that the 'confession' account stems from the same incident. The same is probably true of the other incidents, in that the necessity of producing a confession within a short space of time obliged the author to forsake reference to newspapers and instead string together his own random recollection of half remembered reports, which process probably explains the references to Matthew King's being executed when he actually died in prison, and Turpin's admission that he shot him when his one concern was to escape rather than get involved with the ambush in which King was trapped.

We may be sure that the topsman was illiterate and that he and Turpin were no doubt as drunk on the days before the execution as they were on the day they met for the first and last time; but in producing their 'confession', it is possible to see that Ward and Chandler may have been inspired to do so by a reference to it in the *York Courant* coverage of the execution.

VII

And so on the morning of Saturday 7 April 1739 Richard Turpin took his last ride, in a cart from York Castle to the place of execution, and in company with a man who like himself had been convicted of horse-stealing.

It is appropriate to recall the entry in Arthur Jessop's diary for the following day, which although descriptive of weather conditions prevailing some 40 miles away and with a night between, is some indication of what they may have been like at York on the appointed day: 'Strong blustering cold wind rain hail and snow.' It was, in any weather, a morning which called for a dram or two to dispel the chill of anticipation, for even in a man who had courted execution for six years, who lived in an age when such a method of leaving this world was not uncommon, the prospect of being taken out and killed must have left some void in a stomach which needed a warmer lining. So fortified against bleak weather and sight of the stark silhouette in the distance, John Stead and Richard Turpin stood manacled in the cart as it trundled slowly through the streets of York. The London newspapers would

The Gregory Gang

perhaps have made more of it, and some other accounts do tell us more, but we must allow the *York Courant* to be our first reporter on this occasion.

> Last Saturday, Richard Turpin and John Stead, were executed at Tyburn for horse stealing. The latter died very penitent, but the former behaved with the greatest assurance to the very last: It was very remarkable, that as he mounted the ladder, his right leg trembled; on which he stamped it down with an air, and with undaunted courage looked round about him, and after speaking a few words to the topsman, he threw himself off the ladder, and expired in about five minutes. Before his death, *he declared himself to be the notorious highwayman* TURPIN, and confessed to the topsman a great number of robberies, which he had committed.[9]

Ward and Chandler's account, which includes a section based on this report, was unable to reconcile Turpin confessing a great number of robberies with the few words he spoke to the topsman, and changed the duration of their conversation to half an hour, thus paving the way for the inclusion of the lengthy confession now discredited. But for the moment the only other point about this report concerns the location of the place of execution, here given as Tyburn, but in more recent times described as Knavesmire. The following explanation should clarify the distinction. 'On the other side of Tyburn is a large common of pasture which has of old been called Knavesmire ... some have fancied it has got this name from its neighbourhood to the gallows.'[10]

For a description of what happened immediately before the execution and in the few days that followed, we are obliged to rely on Ward and Chandler's chapter on the whole proceedings:

The Manner of his behaviour at the place of execution

The morning before Turpin's execution he gave three pounds ten shillings amongst five men, who were to follow the cart as mourners, with hatbands and gloves to several persons more. He also left a gold ring, and two pairs of shoes and clogs, to a married woman at Brough, that he was acquainted with though he at the same time acknowledged a wife and child of his own.

He was carried in a cart to the place of execution, on Saturday April the seventh, 1739, with John Stead, condemned also for horse stealing; he behaved himself with amazing assurance, and bowed to the spectators as he passed. It was remarked, that as he mounted the ladder, his right leg trembled which he stamped down with an air, and with undaunted courage, looking round about him; and after speaking near half an hour to the topsman, threw himself off the ladder, and expired directly.

His corpse was brought back from the gallows at three in the afternoon, and lodged at the *Blue Boar,* at Castle Gate, till ten the next morning, when he was buried in a neat coffin in St. George's churchyard, within Fishergate Postern, and the inscription I.R.1739, R.T. aged 28.* The grave was dug very deep, and the persons whom he appointed his mourners, as above mentioned, took all possible care to secure the body; notwithstanding which, on Tuesday morning, at three in the morning, several persons were discovered moving off the body, which they had taken up, and the mob having got scent where it was carried to, and suspecting it was to be anatomised, went to a garden in which it was deposited, and brought away the body through the streets of the city in a sort of triumph, almost naked, being only laid on a board covered with some straw, and carried on four men's shoulders, and buried in the same grave, having first filled the coffin with slacked lime.

* He confessed to the hangman that he was thirty-three years of age.

This remarkably lucid piece of prose reflects an almost clinical detachment in the way each fact is carefully reassembled and deftly sewn together, but as in a surgical operation the dread subject matter and macabre sequence of events is handled with such delicacy as to amount almost to reverence. The violence and horror are made presentable, the face of death given a slight smile, the villain no longer a villain is laid finally and peacefully at rest.

The absurdity of standing on a ladder for half an hour with a rope around one's neck talking to the man who is waiting to push you off has been exposed, but otherwise one cannot fault this account in its reporting of Turpin's end. Unlike the 'confession' there is neither reason nor means to think or prove that the whole is not authentic, especially since the middle paragraph is essentially the same and may even have been taken from the report in the *York Courant.* With regard to his having had a child, he may have done, for it is no more an unlikely suggestion than that he was acquainted with a married woman at Brough.

The London newspapers tended to dismiss Turpin's end in a couple of lines, a callous rejection of a man who had now ceased to be news, but even the longest accounts, such as that reproduced in the *Gentleman's Magazine,* in its Historical Chronicle for April 1739 (and the one generally quoted) would appear to be merely a resumé of the Ward and Chandler chapters on the execution and confession. And for the same reason that their coverage was published on 17 April, it is not possible to accept even the following as corroboration of the last paragraph, appearing as it did four days later. 'They write from York that an attempt was made by the surgeons of that place to have got the body of Turpin, but the mob hearing that it was dug up, and being informed where it was, went and rescued it and re-interred it, having strewn it over with lime to prevent it being anatomised.'[11]

Did Turpin die courageously? He appears to have been assured, he bowed, and when his leg trembled he stamped it down, then, with bravado, he looked about the crowd and eventually threw himself off the ladder. The very deliberateness of these actions tends to confirm that he was to some extent under the influence of drink, but that he was aware of who and what he was and where he was going, and that since this was *his* moment he must do it in style. If his leg did tremble rather than he slipped because he could hardly stand, then he was afraid, and in any event he clearly did not wish it to be thought that he was afraid and made sure that the spectators would be impressed. But he did not shew any fear in the positive step he took off the ladder, and all things considered, drunk or not, he made a brave enough exit for a man who had no choice in the matter.

Responsible members of society were outraged when villains died unrepentant, but unless convicted of some particularly vile crime the public were less demanding of *their* villains, particularly so in the case of one like Turpin who had kept them entertained for six years. The small matter of murder, committed in self defence, was overlooked. So when it came to dying there was a certain obligation to the public to do so in a manner they might admire, not as the minority for whom he had only contempt would have wanted. So when the mob cheered his leap into oblivion it was not because the villain had met with his just deserts but because he had kept faith with them by dying bravely and unrepentant. He may also in some perverse way, by presenting the crowd with a 'respectable' Saturday morning's entertainment, have absolved them of any bad taste which might have accrued from a cowardly and distasteful spectacle, and restored in them a confidence that it was not unbecoming to witness a public execution, and was therefore in accord with their finer feelings.

It is fortunate that the spectacle is no longer with us, and that no one is more qualified than the next man to speculate on what even the most respectable members of the crowd were thinking or doing at any particular time during that obscene ritual. But whatever the feelings at any given time we do know that on this occasion the villain was a very popular one with the crowd, one whose exploits, body and legend belonged to them alone, to be preserved by them if needs be for ever. And thus, jealously protected, from the day of his execution to this, he has remained.

When the name of a criminal who lived so long ago remains familiar to so many, with each generation which passes, who would deny him one small plot in a churchyard, a small niche in the blank impersonal wall of history, or a small corner in our affections. For however mean and reprehensible he may have been in real life, he has been and will always be largely a creature of our own creation clothed in the romanticism of imagination.

We can put cold facts as follows:

> **Yorkshire** Sir George Cook Bart Sheriff of the said county for the year ending at Michaelmas in the 13th year of King George II
> For conveying under a strong guard to the place of execution the most notorious highwayman Richard Turpin and John Stead and for executing them
> £20 0s. 0d.
> For dieting and guarding them a fortnight
> £0 10s. 0d.[12]

and observe that the sum *allowed* for the execution was only £6 0s. 0d., but indisputable though this information is there will always be odd accounts of Turpin's exploits where it is impossible to draw a dividing line between fact and fiction.

Some attempt has been made in this account to make distinction between the two, to shew how even facts became distorted to be retold as fiction, how fiction was inspired by rumour or motivated by people who wanted to capitalise on the public interest in a man who eluded their grasp like quicksilver. He was legendary in his own lifetime, and inevitably when time buried the truth but the interest still survived, legendary exploits were coupled with the legendary character of a man whose one remarkable attribute was that he somehow contrived to live longer than others like him. In this account we have met all his associates, some of whom have never been heard of before, and it is by being introduced to them one by one and then seeing them fall one by one by the wayside that the essential difference between them and Turpin becomes progressively clearer. Since he was for some time the last of all the gang, and some time later the last of them to go, it is perhaps not so surprising that he should have been the man most likely to be remembered.

VIII

There remains an uncorroborated report with which it is particularly fitting to end this account of our highwayman:

> To the vast crowds who thronged the route down Castlegate, through Micklegate to Knavesmire (to use the words of a witness), 'All the way he bowed repeatedly and with the most astonishing indifference and intrepidity. Arriving at the fatal spot he talked some time to the hangman and presented him with a small ivory whistle'.[13]

There is in York Museum a small ivory whistle which purports to be the same, and one wonders if like King Arthur his restless spirit waits some shrill awakening call, so that he too might ride, 'Down the ribbon of moonlight, over the brow of the hill.'[14]

FOOTNOTES

1. In the second week of May 1737 an Exciseman claimed to have seen Turpin at Barnet. Smith worked for the Excise and the possible connection has already been formulated. If they did meet it would perhaps have been embarrassing for Smith to have mentioned the fact in testimony.
2. *Political State,* Vol.LVII, Jan. to June 1739, pp.537–541.
3. P.R.O./Assizes 41/4.
4. P.R.O./T.53/40 pp.157–158.
5. *Two Yorkshire Diaries,* The Yorkshire Archaeological Society Record Series, Vol.CXVII, 1952 (The Diary of Arthur Jessop), pp.44–45.
6. *Reid's Weekly Journal,* 31 March 1739.
7. *York Courant,* 3 April 1739.
8. P.R.O./T.53/40 p.157.
9. *York Courant,* 10 April 1739.
10. *History and Antiquities of the City of York,* by Francis Drake F.R.S. 1735, p.398.
11. *Ipswich Journal,* 21 April 1739.
12. P.R.O./T.90/147 p.317.
13. *Immortal Turpin,* p.126.
14. Part Two, Verse Six of Alfred Noyes' *The Highwayman.*

APPENDIX ONE

CLAIMS

I

THROUGHOUT the foregoing account a considerable amount of original source material has been obtained from claims for rewards payable upon the capture and conviction of various criminals, and the last of these is that made in respect of Turpin himself. Parts of it having already appeared in extract, the latter part of the Treasury Solicitor's submission is hereafter re-examined in isolation.

It is also appropriate under this heading to touch on other post-Turpin trial claims which could be said to have some relevance to what has gone before, to indicate sources of information for pre-trial claims already quoted, and to provide references to the parallel distribution of Blood Money rewards which previously have only been mentioned in passing.

II

We have seen that Robert Appleton penned his claim for expenses incurred in connection with the trial on the same day that the York Assize ended, viz. 24 March 1739. Appleton sent his account to George Crowle, and two months later, on 29 May, a certificate of conviction (a document without which it would have been difficult to have proceeded with a legitimate claim) was obtained from Sir William Chapple. The next positive step towards establishing a claim was made by the trial witnesses, for their petition to the Lords Commissioners of the Treasury was referred to Nicholas Paxton, the Treasury Solicitor, on 7 August for his consideration.[1]

Paxton's submission in reply, lacking as it does the originally annexed documents from which it was drawn up, does not reflect a very clear picture of the manner in which he obtained all the evidence upon which he based his recommendations; but since the submission is the only evidence which survives on the subject, any consideration of the events which led up to settlement of the claims is governed by the same document. Thus the points which Paxton made were in the following sequence:—

1. Statement of the claim of the seven trial witnesses.
2. Statement of the conditions, etc. in the *London Gazette* advertisement offering reward in respect of the robbery of Joseph Lawrence at Edgware in 1735.
3. The same in respect of the murder of Thomas Morris in 1737.
4. Acknowledgement of issue of the judge's certificate of conviction.
5. Resumé of Turpin's confession.

The remainder of Paxton's submission, with a certain amount of repetition edited out, is reproduced below.

There is likewise annexed to the said petition a letter from Robert Appleton to Mr. Crowle dated 24th March 1738 [/9] giving an account of the trouble and expense he was at in sending messengers to serve subpoenas in Lincolnshire and at Hull and other places very distant from York upon the principal witnesses against the offender, and in bringing them to York to give evidence against him, and in feeing counsel and paying the charges and other expenses of the prosecution amounting to about £20 which he desires might be paid out of the reward, and of which he wrote he would send Mr. Crowle the particulars; and at the bottom of his letter mentions the petitioners to be the several witnesses upon the trial. Mr. Appleton in his letter further says that the criminal owned himself to be Richard Turpin upon the trial.

Not having seen the particulars of Mr. Appleton's charges which he promised to send up, I applied to Mr. Crowle about them (who does not remember to have received them). I likewise desired to know in what manner the distribution of the reward should be made and to whom paid (if your Lordships should be pleased to give any). Upon which I received a letter hereunto annexed from Mr. Crowle dated the 13th instant wherein he takes notice of the expenses of two persons that went twice from Essex to York about the conviction of [Turpin] and without whom he would not have been executed, which he has obliged himself to pay, and that he likewise got leave from the Secretary at War for an Officer in General Harrison's Regiment whose evidence was very material ... and he travelled from Bristol to York. Mr. Crowle observes further that upon the first discovery of Turpin's being in York gaol, it was the Attorney General's opinion that he should be brought up here to be tried which would have been a great expense to the Crown, and then doubtful whether he would have been convicted here but upon the assurances that Mr. Crowle gave the Attorney General that there was sufficient proof against him at York he gave up his opinion and consented to his trial there, by which means a very large sum of money was saved to the Crown.

Mr. Crowle desires that he may be appointed agent for the persons entitled to receive the rewards because he is under engagements to pay almost £100 and he should send the remainder into the country to be distributed by the Bench of Justices.

I am upon the whole of opinion that as the [Lawrence reward of £50 and the Morris reward of £200, &c. are confined to the offender's conviction upon those charges] the petitioners are not entitled to the rewards [for his conviction upon the other indictments at York]; but in regard to the great expense and trouble that has been occasioned by the prosecution in bringing so notorious an offender to Justice at the said Assizes by which a great expense has been saved to the Crown, and as Mr. Crowle is answerable for about £100 to the witnesses that went from Essex and Bristol to the said Assizes I most humbly submit it to your Lordships whether they may not deserve the said rewards or so much thereof as your Lordships shall think proper to defray all charges attending the prosecution and satisfy them for their trouble which may be paid (if your Lordships shall be pleased to order) to Mr. Crowle to answer his engagements on the account aforesaid and to be distributed by the Bench of Justices as is proposed by Mr. Crowle.

Nicho: Paxton 20 December 1739.[2]

The petitioners were Creasy, Goodyear, Dawson, Gill, Smith, Saward and Grassby, the witnesses at the trial; Appleton was not included in the prayer to the Treasury and his letter to Crowle is incidental to the main claim. It is this letter however (which can only have been obtained from Crowle), and Paxton's to Crowle inquiring about the details of Appleton's charges *and* to whom the reward should be distributed, which point to all the items 1 to 5 and Appleton's letter having been sent to the Treasury by Crowle himself. This is a reasonable suggestion, for with the witnesses dispersed after the trial, some other party must have been responsible for the slow accumulation of documents in support of the claim.

And the accumulation was slow when Appleton wrote his letter on 24 March, the judge issued his certificate on 29 May, and these and other documents did not reach the Treasury until August. Had the witnesses themselves been in a position to obtain the evidence in support of their claim, we may be sure that they would not have taken four months to do so; but some, if not all of them, had been promised recovery of their expenses by Crowle, and were presumably obliged to leave the promotion of their case to him. Unfortunately for them Crowle's interest in matters relating to Turpin died when he leapt from the ladder at Tyburn, and there was not the same urgency or application given to their interests as previously rendered to his younger brother.

It has been suggested in this account that the rewards offered might on occasion have provided only a limited incentive to potential witnesses if they were of limited means themselves. This is very well illustrated in this case where three witnesses between them appear to have incurred expenses totalling nearly £100, a sum not reimbursed until some considerable time had elapsed between the trial and the final settlement of their claim. Nor in this instance was there the supplementary benefit of Blood Money normally payable upon *capture* and conviction, Turpin not having been convicted of the offence for which he was originally arrested. So were all the petitioners fairly recompensed for their trouble and expense?

Crowle, M.P. for Kingston upon Hull, no doubt had more pressing interests by this time, and there are some indications in his letter of 13 [December 1739] to Paxton that he was anxious to wash his hands of a business that had dragged on for so long. He did not remember having heard from Appleton again, but it is hardly likely that a man who broached the subject of expenses on the day the Assizes ended would not have followed up with a detailed account. Similarly it seems unlikely that Crowle could have failed to take notice of the expenses of the other four witnesses. *But,* having failed to offer guidance in August, Crowle's reply to Paxton's December letter was really nothing more than a solidly backed request to be appointed agent for the distribution of the reward, a singularly undemanding role when the Bench of Justices was to be asked to distribute 'the remainder'. One wonders if the last condition is a clue to Crowle's part in these proceedings, for from Paxton's summation it is clear that it could have been by no means certain that there would be a remainder.

Crowle does not appear to have shewn much personal interest in this affair until Paxton asked him how the reward should be distributed, at which point he could recall three witnesses to whom he was under engagement to pay nearly £100. But whereas it could be inferred from Appleton's letter that *he* had incurred expenses in bringing the witnesses to York, it is not certain whether these were included in the £20 quoted or whether this sum was merely in respect of the legal costs also mentioned. It seems probable that the comparatively low total was only representative of the legal costs, and that the comprehensive total would have been higher. In any event there appears to be a discrepancy between Appleton's actual expenses and Crowle's promises, if indeed promises they were, and not actual payments which he had to all intents and purposes written off until it seemed possible that they might be recovered from the reward. The only certainty about the settlement is that Crowle was assured of receiving £100 which went either to Dawson, Smith and Saward or into his own pocket to cover his own loss. He does not appear to have been particularly concerned about the remainder, or about who would receive it. It would be impossible on the available evidence to state categorically that part of the reward was misappropriated, even though some points cannot be satisfactorily explained; it would be fairer to say that some of the witnesses may have ended up out of pocket by default, through the agency of a man who may have been more interested in ensuring he did not lose anything by having been involved in Turpin's prosecution.

Three months after Paxton made his submission the Lords Commissioners of the Treasury, after due consideration of the report, thought it, 'reasonable and just that notwithstanding the said Richard Turpin was apprehended and executed at York, for other felonies than those for which the said rewards were advertised, yet that the amount of the said rewards, being £250, should be paid to satisfy all rewards, claims, charges and demands whatsoever made or to be made under colour of the said advertisement for bringing to Justice so desperate and notorious an offender.'[3]

So by their warrant, dated 20 March 1740, George Crowle was appointed agent for the distribution of the reward. It was almost a year since the trial, a long time one might think for such a claim to be settled.

III

In September 1736, Thomas Cavenagh, Keeper of the New Prison at Clerkenwell, submitted his claim for the maintenance of John Wheeler the Evidence.[4] Some two months after Turpin's execution, whilst the evidence in support of the Turpin claim was being collated, Baron Harrington finally signed the order which allowed Cavenagh to be reimbursed for his trouble and expense.

Whitehall 29th June 1739.

Sir,
I desire that out of the money imprested in your hands for carrying on criminal prosecutions, you will pay to Mr. Thomas Cavenagh, Keeper of New Prison, thirty one pounds, and eleven shillings, for the maintenance of John Wheeler, an evidence against Samuel Gregory, and several others, notorious highwaymen, at 1s. per day, from the 8th day of February 1734/5 to the 30th day of September 1736, pursuant to his account enclosed, being in all 601 days [and expenses]. I am &c.
Mr. Paxton
Harrington.[5]

We do not know why Cavenagh had to wait so long for his money when Wheeler had been dead for over a year. The only conceivable explanation is that it had been completely overlooked and that Cavenagh saw fit to submit a reminder when he was himself reminded by Turpin's trial and execution. The only other points worthy of comment are that with the passage of time the respective members of the Gregory Gang had all become, 'notorious highwaymen', and nobody would have considered the possibility of Cavenagh's having added three days too many to his account. For as stated earlier, Wheeler was not taken until 11 February 1735.

IV

During the course of this account much use has been made of information contained in the Treasury Solicitor's reports on claims for rewards which he submitted to the Lords Commissioners of the Treasury. Similar information was also obtained from a few other sources, but only in one or two cases did it prove necessary to make reference to records which shewed when the petitions were passed to the Treasury Solicitor for his opinion, and records which shew how distribution of Blood Money was made have hardly been used at all.

The following chart provides references to those twelve members of the Gregory gang in respect of whose capture or conviction (or both) claims for rewards were made. All the records quoted belong to the Treasury group of classes preserved at the Public Record Office.

Names of the gang members	Claims to Treasury Solicitor	Treasury Solicitor's reports &c.	References to reports in Minutes	Payments of Blood Money rewards
Fielder	T.4/11 p.48	T.53/38 p.159	–	T.53/38 p.18; T.60/16 p.139
Gregory				
Jasper	–	–	–	T.53/38 p.16; T.60/16 p.99
Jeremy[6]	–	T.52/39 p.44	–	–
Samuel	Ibid p.56	T.53/38 p.196	–	T.53/38 p.20; T.60/16 p.175
Haines	Ibid p.59	T.53/39 p.271	–	T.53/38 p.20
Haines[7]	Ibid p.60	–	–	–
Jones	–	T.53/38 p.406	T.29/28 p.3	–
Rose	Ibid p.59	Ibid p.194	–	Ibid p.18; T.60/16 p.139
Rowden	Ibid p.97(2)	T.53/39 p.324	–	–
Schooling	Ibid p.48	T.53/38 p.159	–	T.53/38 p.18; T.60/16 p.139
Turpin	Ibid p.130	T.53/40 p.156	T.29/28 p.196	–
Walker	–	–	–	Ibid; Ibid. p.138
Wheeler	Ibid p.48	T.53/38 p.159	–	–

V

Having dealt with the official claims encountered we come to the unofficial and unsubstantiated claims concerning Turpin, which are of course legion. These are distinct from the fictions written about him during his lifetime and subsequently, which where they appeared to exist in opposition to known or recently discovered facts have been refuted, and could more appropriately be described as claims on his person or his former possessions.

A few have already been examined, i.e. of the latter variety, his portmanteau, but examination of other such claims is bound to be speculative in the extreme, and is unlikely to add anything of value to this account.

Other claims commonly encountered are those of inns, towns, commons and highways, where Turpin rode, stayed or robbed, etc. This type of claim has been studiously avoided, even where there might appear to be some possibility of the claim being true, and the account remains impartial to the point that if the name of any inn, town, common or highway appears in it, it is because there is some good reason and not because tradition has it that it should be so.

There remains therefore of all these multifarious claims one which should be mentioned here, and that is a claim to Turpin's person.

> At the gaol we saw one John Clark, who lay condemned for robbery on the highway. He told us that the person hanged at York was not Turpin, for that he had robbed with him (Turpin) between Maidenhead and Colnbrook, and other places in the last hard weather; that the person then hanged was an accomplice of his and Turpin's, and that they engaged that whichever was caught should take on him the name of Turpin; and that Turpin and he supported that man (named Palmer) in York Castle and was present at his execution; and that Turpin and he waited eight weeks to shoot a man in Epping Forest; but that Turpin was now living, and had taken on him the name of Smith, and he kept an alehouse in the north of England.[8]

Thomas Seccombe, a somewhat eccentric Turpin biographer, quoted this as being from the journal of John Newbery, a noted bookseller who set out from Reading in 1740 upon a tour of England and saw John Clark in Leicester gaol the same year. It is no more than a diverting anecdote which reflects the desire of the nonentity Clark to be identified with the legendary highwayman he had perhaps unsuccessfully tried to emulate, but it is interesting to note that Turpin was then garlanded with the now traditionally English alias of Smith.[9]

VI

The last item in this chapter on claims is included because it is so unusual in its content, but the accusations, like the dating of the document (c. June/July 1735), are not substantiated elsewhere:

> To the Right Hon. Sir. Robert Walpole Chancellor of the Exchequer and first Commissioner of his Majesty's Treasury.

Sheweth

That your Petitioners did about eighteen months ago apprehend Jeremiah Gregory at Hackney for deer stealing and for whom a reward was promised by his Majesty of £50 in the *London Gazette* of the ... day of ...

That your petitioners ventured their lives in taking him as is well known he being a very desperate fellow and had a pistol in his hand when we took him.

That the said Jeremiah Gregory was convicted at Chelmsford for deerstealing by which your petitioners became entitled to the reward promised by his Majesty.

That your petitioners have ever since been kept out of the reward by Mr. Paxton the Solicitor of the Treasury who put us off till the buck season when he promised us the reward if we sent him venison which we did and he received it. We then thought we should have our money but were again put off till the doe season and that we should have it if we sent him more venison and we sent it but had not our money and when we spoke to him he expected we should send him some wood cocks which we likewise sent him but are never the near getting the reward promised by his Majesty.

Your petitioners therefore humbly pray your Honour would sign the order of the conviction that the said reward may be forthwith paid. And your petitioners shall ever pray &c.

Thomas Roades, John Attreidge, John Mugaredg.[10]

It has been suggested that Jeremy Gregory was taken early in 1734, either January or February. William Mason and three Keepers did petition for the reward on 20 June 1734, but for reasons unknown Paxton did not make a report upon the claim in the usual way. There is no evidence that Mason took the matter further, and none that Walpole took any notice of the extraordinary petition above, but as Paxton's position was not affected in any way, the whole affair is and must remain a rather intriguing mystery.

FOOTNOTES

1. P.R.O./T.4/11 (Ind.4625), p.130.
2. P.R.O./T.53/40 pp.156–159 (Paxton's submission &c. complete).
3. *Ibid.*, p.159; T.29/28 p.196 (minute of same).
4. P.R.O./S.P.36/39 ff.145–146.
5. P.R.O./S.P.44/83 p.290 (with copy of Cavenagh's account originally submitted in S.P.36/39 ff.145–146).
6. Not a Treasury Solicitor's report. This was an *ex gratia* payment made upon presumption that a conviction would have been obtained had Jeremy Gregory lived.
7. Petition of Mary Mason and nine others (unnamed) over which the previous petition in respect of Haines took precedence.
8. *Essex Review,* Vol.XI, January 1902, p.31.
9. An error in the *York Courant* of 27 February 1739 implied that Turpin had been committed to York Castle, under the name of Smith.
10. P.R.O./T.1/277 No.56 (undated).

APPENDIX TWO

THE LEGEND OF DICK TURPIN'S RIDE TO YORK

I

THE LEGEND of the ride on Black Bess held sway in popular fancy for about 50 years from the time Harrison Ainsworth dramatised the episode in *Rookwood* in 1834. Throughout this period a romantic Turpin and a noble Bess were inseparable in fiction, in ballads and on the boards, and, as Thomas Hardy illustrated in *Far From the Madding Crowd,* in the circus. Thus we see Turpin in his true perspective, as he was during his own lifetime, during the two hundred or more years since, and as he will no doubt endure in the future, as an entertainer.

There were however a number of people who doubted that Turpin had made such a ride, and once such doubts were voiced in public any serious belief in the story was gradually eroded. The first sign of scepticism appeared in 1860.

DICK TURPIN. Did this famous highwayman, with great jackboots, gold-lace coat, cocked hat, and mounted on his bonny Black Bess, ever ride from London to York in twelve hours? Or, without raising a question as to his costume, or the colour of his horse, did he perform the journey at all?

Popular editions of his *Trial* say he did—storybooks narrate, in a glowing manner, how the five-barred gate was cleared—all *Lives of Highwaymen* make a chapter of the story—old countrymen and red-faced village lads say he did—nine out of ten schoolboys implicity believe in the feat, from the time Turpin left Highgate till he came to York. And Mr. Harrison Ainsworth, in his popular novel of *Rookwood,* has with infinite skill narrated the complete circumstances of the famous ride according to popular belief.

But the late Lord Macaulay had no faith in the story. He was dining one day at the Marquis of Lansdowne's: the subject of Turpin's ride was started, and the old story of the marvellous feat as generally told was alluded to, when Macaulay astonished the company by assuring them that the entire tale from beginning to end was false; that it was founded on a tradition at least three hundred years old; that, like the same anecdote fathered on different men in succeeding generations, it was only told of Turpin because he succeeded the original hero in public taste; and that, if any of the company chose to go with him to his library, he would prove to them the truth of what he had stated in 'black and white'—a favourite phrase with Lord Macaulay.

Might I ask if the old book is known which gives the original of Turpin's ride? And if so what is its title?

Piccadilly.   John Camden Hotten[1]

The reply to Hotten's letter ignored Macaulay's 'three hundred years', but, since it was somewhat nearer the truth than the doubting lord could have been, it is appropriate to quote it here.

A passage in *A Tour Through the Whole Island of Great Britain* attributed to Daniel De Foe, satisfactorily answers I think, the query put by Mr. Hotten in your last number:—

'We see nothing remarkable here but Gad's Hill, a noted place for robbing of seamen, after they have received their pay at Chatham. Here it was that a famous robbery was committed in or about the year 1676, which deserves to be mentioned. It was about four o'clock in the morning, when a gentleman was robbed by one Nicks on a bay mare, just on a declivity of the hill, on the West side. Nicks came away to Gravesend, and, as he said, was stopped by the difficulty of getting the boat near an hour, which was a great discouragement to him; but he made the best use of it, as a kind of 'bate to his horse: from thence he rode cross the country of Essex to Chelmsford. Here he stopped about half an hour to refresh his horse, and gave him some balls; from thence to Braintree, Bocking, Wethersfield; then over the Downs to Cambridge; and from thence, keeping still the cross roads, he went by Fenny Stanton to Godmanchester and Huntingdon, where he and his mare 'bated about an hour; and as he said himself, he slept about half an hour; then holding on the North road and not keeping at full gallop most of the way, he came to York the same afternoon; put off his boots and riding-cloths, and went dressed, as if he had been an inhabitant of the place to the Bowling Green, where among other gentlemen was the Lord Mayor of the City. He singled out his lordship, studied to do some thing particular, that the Mayor might remember him by; and then takes occasion to ask his lordship what o'clock it was, who, pulling out his watch, told him the hour, which was a quarter before or a quarter after eight at night.

Upon a prosecution for this robbery, the whole merit of the case turned upon this single point; the person robbed swore to the man, to the place, and to the time in which the fact was committed; but Nicks, proving by the Lord Mayor that he was as far off as Yorkshire on that day, the jury acquitted him on a bare supposition that it was impossible that the man could be at two places so remote on one and the same day.

W.H.W.[2]

In 1867 another correspondent who signed himself 'Fitzhopkins', was bold enough to suggest that the ride attributed to Turpin had in fact been made by 'Swift' Nicks,[3] and so as the years passed by the idea fell into disrepute, but without anyone offering actual proof of the connection between the ride of highwayman John Nevison *alias* Swift Nicks and that attributed to Turpin. Thus the legend, albeit a little tattered, persisted until the end of the nineteenth century, by which time a new wave of biographers were preparing to pen the 'facts'. In 1895 however there was still a reluctance in some quarters to relinquish what had by then become a sentimental attachment to Black Bess.

> Another cherished declusion is falling beneath the hand of the spoiler ... and now the genuine character of Dick Turpin's Black Bess is questioned. This is the most unkindest cut of all. The famous sable steed, whose counterfeit presentment has figured in innumerable circus performances, is declared to be an invention. A correspondent who has taken up the cudgels on Bess's behalf states, however, that if an invention, it is not an invention of Ainsworth's. As a child he has listened he says, to his mother's stories of Dick Turpin and Black Bess, which she had first hand from her father, and neither of them ever looked into *Rookwood*. Still, it is saddening that a doubt has been cast on the famous quadruped. The gallop from London to York is probably taken from the performances of 'Swift Dick Nevison' ... That may be, but we cannot surrender our sleek-coated favourite altogether without demur.—*Birmingham Weekly Mercury,* March 9.
> Joseph Collinson[4]

Thomas Seccombe, in 1902, and Charles G. Harper, in 1908, both subscribed to the Nevison theory; but although they were right, they found no evidence to back up their claim, even though it existed and was perpetuated in chapbook form throughout the period when the legend attracted most favour.

II

By a process of elimination it was discovered that although there were pre-*Rookwood* references to the ride, none existed in any of the eighteenth-century Turpin chronicles; but, since these references were of a casual nature, there was clearly a root source which existed at the beginning of the nineteenth century. Appropriately enough it was in the Essex Archaeological Society Library, at Hollytrees, Colchester, that this evidence was located in a chapbook tentatively dated 1808, and a copy obtained through the good offices of Mr. J.B. Bennett, the Honorary Librarian.

The Life and Trial of Richard Turpin, A Notorious Highwayman

containing

A Particular Account of His Adventures, from his being first put an Apprentice to a Butcher in Whitechapel, to his execution at York for Horse-stealing.

to which is added

The Life of Sawney Beane, the Man Eater

A New Edition, with Additions.

London: printed by Thomas Maiden, Sherbourn Lane, for J. Roe, 38, Chiswell Street, Finsbury Square; and Anne Lemoine, White Rose Court, Coleman Street. Sold by all booksellers in the United Kingdom. Price sixpence.

The title-page bears no date, but the frontispiece is a print with title, 'Turpin and his Gang placing an Old Lady on the Fire in order to make her discover her Money'. The engraver is stated to be 'S. Sharpe Sc.' And at the foot of the page is the information, 'Published by & for I. Roe. 1808'.

These details are of paramount importance in establishing the pre-*Rookwood* connection with Nevison, and the origin of the legend, for as we shall see, there are numerous other identical accounts to which have been attributed uncertain post-*Rookwood* dates. Thus we need to know if the print dated 1808 really is the frontispiece to the title-page reproduced above.

We have the names and addresses of three people who were involved in the printing of this edition, and London directories for the period from which the following information has been obtained.

1. Thomas Maiden was a printer at 5 Sherbone *or* Sherbourn Lane off Lombard Street in 1800, and appears to have been there continuously from that date until *c.* 1825 at the latest; he does not appear at this or any other address from 1825 onwards, and after 1827, No. 5 Sherbourn Lane disappeared from the directories.

2. John Roe, bookseller and publisher was listed at 90 Houndsditch in 1808, but probably moved in that year to 38 Chiswell Street, at which address he was to be found from 1809 until *c.* 1821; he was not listed at this or any other address from 1822 onwards, and as in the case of Maiden, No. 38 Chiswell Street was not listed in the directories after 1827.

3. Anne Lemoine was more elusive in that she did not appear at all in the London *Post Office* directories. In 1818, a Philip Lemoine, coal merchant was at 11 Craven Street, Strand, but in the following year had been replaced at the same address by an Ann Lemoine. These were however isolated references and it was not until 1827 that Anne Le Moine, Pamphlet Dealer, was located at No. 6 White Rose Court, Coleman Street. But like Maiden and Roe the name and particularly numbered address disappeared from that date onwards. The common denominator which links Maiden, Roe and Lemoine is that the addresses with which they are identified in the chapbook had ceased to exist by 1828, and if not derelict were no longer used as business premises. From this it is certain that the chapbook was published before *Rookwood;* how long before is another question. Roe appears to have retired from publishing

before 1822 and therefore can hardly have worked in conjunction with Maiden from about 1821. Unfortunately the information about Anne Lemoine is inconclusive, and, as a serious business woman, she does not seem to have entered the lists until the two men had retired from them. This does not mean that she was not their associate in earlier years, nor for that matter does the existence of an Ann Lemoine, widow or sister or daughter of Philip Lemoine at an entirely different address really affect speculation upon her status. One could sell coal and still deal in pamphlets, and so far as may be ascertained from the directories, the coal business was soon bankrupt or sold, a possibility that suggests that Ann Lemoine succeeded Philip on a temporary basis which merely interrupted whatever he may have done before and after his retirement from the scene. We do not know that the two women of the same name were the same person, and since the one in which we are interested did not advertise herself until 1827, when she could not have been an associate of Maiden and Roe, the brief appearance of the other is largely irrelevant. It is perhaps sufficient to note that Whiterose Court, Coleman Street was in existence in 1810.

Anne Lemoine does not help us much, but she does not affect the conclusion that the book could not have been published *after* 1821. How then is it possible to reconcile the dated frontispiece with the undated title-page and text? There are two methods by which the matter might be resolved, the first is to consider the likelihood of an isolated 1808 print becoming associated with a later publication, the second to see if the scene as illustrated in the print corresponds to that described in the text.

On the first point it is clear that if the print is an intruder, we have an illustration (for a book dated 1808 which has not been located) itself very rare which has become associated with an equally rare chapbook edition of pre-1822 date. The possibility of this occurring would seem to be extremely remote, and any doubts that print and chapbook might not belong together must surely be dispelled upon consideration of the second point.

The print depicts the unfortunate Widow Shelley of Loughton whom the Gregory gang robbed in 1735. The text states that they, 'Blindfolded the eyes of the old woman and her maid, and tied the legs of her son, a well grown lad, to the bedstead'. The print shews widow and maid blindfolded, and a youth (without blindfold) whose legs are tied to the foot of a four poster bed. The Maiden/Roe edition of Turpin's *Life* is the earliest known account to describe the Widow Shelley incident in this particular manner, and since there is no known edition which could have intervened between the print date and the latest possible date of publication of the associated title-page and text, viz. 1821, there is no hesitation in stating the print to be the frontispiece to an 1808 edition of Turpin's *Life and Trial*.[5]

III

Having established the date of the account and eliminated the eighteenth-century potted biographies, the relevant part of the text which proves the connection with Nevison can now be shewn:

> He had been at Suson, and drank freely at the *Cock* there. Early in the morning he set off, and robbed a gentleman of fifty guineas and a valuable watch, in the environs of London. Apprehensive of being known and pursued, he spurred his horse on, and took the Northern road, and, astonishing to say, reached York the same evening, and was seen playing at bowls in the bowling green with several gentlemen there, which circumstances saved him from the hands of justice for that time.
>
> The gentleman he robbed knew it was Turpin, and caused him to be pursued, and taken at York. He afterwards swore to him, and the horse he rode on, which was the identical one he arrived upon in that city; but on being in the stable, and his rider at play, and all in the space of four and twenty hours, his alibi was admitted; for the magistrates at York could not believe it possible for one horse to cover the ground, being upwards of one hundred and ninety miles, in so short a space of time.
>
> He is reported, upon this occasion, to have used his horse to raw beef upon the bit in his mouth. Some go so far as to say he always rode with fowl's guts tied round it. Be this so or not, it was a race that equalled, if not surpassed, the first achievements of turf velocity at that time.

A man whom only a pardon could have saved would not have needed an alibi, but one might still admit to the possibility of two men making a similar journey to the same place. Too great a strain is placed on one's credibility, however, at the point where they both arrive at the bowling green. The thing that is singularly remarkable about this obvious connection is the fact that, although this particular edition is rare now, it was subsequently copied by a number of other publishers without any amendment to the text. It does therefore seem surprising that those who detected Nevison beneath Turpin's cloak, and were sufficiently interested to do so, did not have access to actual evidence of the connection at a time when it appears to have been in continuous circulation.

Gordon S. Maxwell in 1934 was sure that he had found evidence of the pre-*Rookwood* origins of the ride:

> All these, and many more, are to be found in Mr. Barry Ono's library, the fringes of which I have merely touched upon; and I cannot do better than close

this brief account of that unique collection[6] by quoting a paragraph from an article by this famous collector himself. It is entitled *Dick Turpin Literature,* and the portion that so interested me reads: 'The oldest Turpin relic in my collection is a cheap book, published 1800–1820, but as clean as if just issued. The title is *The Life and Adventures of Richard Turpin, a most notorious Highwayman, comprising a Particular Account of all his robberies, His Ride to York, and his Trial and Execution for Horse Stealing, 1739* ... the antiquity of this little book destroys the theory that W. Harrison Ainsworth invented this legend in *Rookwood.*[7]

Ono was wrong in dating this chapbook 1800–20, and Maxwell misled, for the only book in the *Ono Collection* at the British Museum with the title rendered as above,[8] could not have been published *before* 1840. It was published by 'Ryle & Co., Monmouth Street, Seven Dials', and an examination of directories and rate-books shew that Ryle did not exceed James Catnach at that address until 1840 or later. Thus the next legitimate chronological reference to the ride was made in 1823, in the following manner. 'Many wild and improbable stories are related to him, such as his rapid ride to York, his horse chewing a beef steak all the way.'[9] This is merely a distorted version of the 1808 version wherein the horse's mouth is ravaged by the bit, but it does confirm that the story of the ride to York was already firmly established by 1823, and that Maiden and Roe were responsible.

In the British Museum *General Catalogue* are listed a number of Turpin accounts, given uncertain dates between 1830 and 1855, most of which upon examination turn out to be identical to the 1808 version. They emanated from a number of publishers in different parts of the country, and it is clear that this particular version had a wide distribution over a considerable period of time. But what is most important of all is the fact that the legend was firmly rooted in the public's mind long before Ainsworth penned *Rookwood;* the new factor which he introduced, and which no doubt captured the imagination more than anything else, was the name of Black Bess. For at a time when there was no other means of transport, the identification of the anonymous beast popular in legend and associated with a public hero, brought it instant recognition; the dramatic ride and heart rending circumstances of its death at York assured its immortality.

The literature on the subject is vast, as is evident from the titles provided by Seccombe and Maxwell, and it is clear that if there was an entertainment which stimulated nineteenth century imagination more than any other it was the legend of Turpin and Black Bess in its variously presented forms. But although the pair made a romantic combination, Seccombe in his eulogy was no doubt quite right when he said, 'The last words are due not to our spotted hero, but to our spotless heroine'.[10]

FOOTNOTES

1. *Notes and Queries,* Series 2, Vol.IX, p.386.
2. *Ibid.,* p.433.
3. *Ibid.,* Series 3, Vol.XI, p.440.
4. *Ibid.,* Series 8, Vol.VIII, p.4.
5. Critchett & Woods Post Office Directories for given years and E. Mogg's Street Directory for 1810 (Brit. Mus.); and various directories in P.R.O. Library collection.
6. Now in British Museum. A separate card index, with i.e. 'Ono 98' references, was formerly available in the North Library, but of late (1969) it is apparent that the collection is being or has been assimilated into the general catalogue under new references.
7. *Highwayman's Heath,* by G.S. Maxwell, New Ed. 1949, p.204.
8. Ono 95., but see footnote 6 *supra.*
9. *Retrospective Review.* Baldwyn, London, 1823, p.283.
10. *Essex Review,* Vol.XI, April 1902, p.78.

APPENDIX THREE

THE PORTRAIT TAKEN 'FROM A PRINT IN THE TYBURN CHRONICLE 1742'

THE PORTRAIT depicted in the frontispiece and on the cover of this book is either an idealised impression of Turpin, possibly based on his description, or else the portrait of someone hired to sit for it because he may have fitted the description. It was not, as it purports to have been, taken from a print in the *Tyburn Chronicle* of 1742. Turpin was neither drawn, nor sketched, nor painted, during his lifetime, and this portrait probably dates from about 1840.

None of the early prints which appeared before this date could be termed a portrait, and it is significant that, if one did exist in 1742, it was not associated with any subsequent biography. It is similarly significant that the few, poor-quality early prints have been reproduced *ad nauseum* ever since. But in this case, what of the *Tyburn Chronicle* dated but three years after Turpin's death?

In the 'Monthly Register of Books' which appeared in the *Gentleman's Magazine,* no reference was made in 1742, or for a number of years afterwards, to a *Tyburn Chronicle,* and the earliest known work identifiable by this particular title is the 1768 edition which did, in any case, cover the period of Turpin's existence and include the most notorious villains of that era.

The portrait was discovered in examining material contained in the Barry Ono collection mentioned in the previous appendix, and was found to be the frontispiece to a full length blood and thunder drama called *Dick Turpin* by Henry Downes Miles, published in 1840. The engraver, T.L.S., has been tentatively identified as T.L. Sangar, the only catalogued nineteenth-century engraver with the same initials. His one recorded engraving was made several years after this date, and the identification cannot be certain. Sangar's background is obscure.

Miles was the first serious post-*Rookwood* author to climb on Ainsworth's bandwagon when it was seen that Turpin had become a viable commercial proposition, and it was important that he should make a good impression. His book was long and, as a literary portrait of Turpin himself, something of a travesty, but as an extravagant adventure tale with a deal more pace than *Rookwood* it had some merit for its day, and the inclusion of Turpin was not merely a gimmick designed to spice a turgid drama. So it is possible that Miles commissioned the portrait, and underwrote a claim suggesting antiquity, merely to emphasise the genuine content of the book as implied in the title. And having done so, Miles was no doubt confident that no-one would ever have reason to bother to check his reference.

The face has been described as being of nineteenth-century character, although this observation is valid only in its relation to portraits of that century. Enquiry about the costume proved to be similarly inconclusive, although the detail was insufficient to belie its eighteenth-century appearance. And the signature would appear to be of somewhat later date than that put to his confession, had it survived so long. Of the engraving itself it would be fair to say that it was reasonably competent except where a definite shadow about the collar and shoulders suggests the engraver may not have been very sure of his line.

But with regard to what in any event must surely be a flattering likeness, the portrait does contain elements of Turpin's general description which makes one look twice and perhaps wonder, is that what he might have looked like?

> Cheek bones broad, his face thinner towards the bottom, his visage short, pretty upright and broad about the shoulders.

And with another look it is not too difficult to imagine the stippling about the face to be small-pox scars, and the curl of the lower lip to be a reflection of Turpin's own mean nature. Perhaps we shall never be entirely sure, but in any event, Henry Downes Miles tired of his creation. In the fourth edition of *Dick Turpin,* brought out by a different publisher *c.* 1862, the author claimed to have sold over 20,000 copies; but he had by that time forsaken the portrait frontispiece for a number of more, by that time, conventional illustrations depicting scenes from the novel. If Miles had indeed sold that many copies of his book, then he no longer needed to care unduly about the genuine impression he had originally wished to make.

The final comment upon the Turpin likeness comes from Charles G. Harper's *Half Hours with the Highwaymen,* in which in his chapter on Turpin, he reproduced a line drawing of Turpin with very forbidding appearance, but only crudely representative. Harper, a conscientious albeit naïve biographer, was honest enough to append a cautionary footnote to this drawing, which read, 'From a strictly unauthentic source'.

It is perhaps a line which several generations of other Turpin biographers could have used to good effect, but in the manner of presentation it is not too difficult to imagine that which Turpin himself would have preferred.

Select Chronological Bibliography

1735   Old Bailey Sessions, printed proceedings.

1735   The Ordinary of Newgate's Account of 13 Malefactors executed at Tyburn the 10th [March], and of the Pyrate executed at Execution Dock the 14th, in 3 parts, per 6d. each, printed for J. Applebee. *Not traced.*

1736   A Genuine Account of the Two Surprising Escapes of Daniel Malden taken from his own Mouth in the Old Condemned Hold in Newgate—October 21st 1736, in the Ordinary of Newgate's account of Malefactors executed at Tyburn 2nd of November 1736. J. Applebee. 1736. 6d.

1737   News News, great and wonderful News from London in an uproar; or a Hue and Cry after the great Turpin, with his escape into Ireland.

1739   The trial of Richard Turpin, by Thomas Kyll; an account of Turpin in Yorkshire by Robert Appleton; a letter to Turpin from his father; his behaviour at the place of execution; and his confession. Published 17 April 1739 by Ward and Chandler, York. 6d.

1739   Life of Richard Turpin (General History and Life) by Richard Bayes, at the *Green Man* on Epping Forest, and Others in Essex; the account of Turpin in Yorkshire; condensed version of trial; four letters: John Turpin to Richard Turpin, John Turpin to John Turpin jnr., Richard Turpin to his father, and to his brother-in-law; and Turpin's behaviour in York Castle. J. Standen at *D'Anver's Head* in Chancery Lane.

1739   Life and Trial of Richard Turpin. The fourth edition of Ward and Chandler's April publication but with the life by Richard Bayes as included in J. Standen's edition above. It is not clear which publisher pirated the 'Life', for although Standen pirated some of the first edition, it is not known if Bayes' contribution appeared in the second or third editions brough out by Ward and Chandler.

[1742]   *See* Appendix Three reference to Tyburn Chronicle of this date.

1768   Tyburn Chronicle.

1779	Malefactor's Register or New Newgate and Tyburn Calendar &c.
1808	Life and Trial of Richard Turpin, *with* The Life of Sawney Beane, the Man Eater. Printed by Thomas Maiden for John Roe and Anne Lemoine. London. 6d. Precursor of a new wave of Turpin 'fictions'.
1820	Caulfield's Remarkable Portraits &c.
1824	Newgate Calendar., Vol.I pp.385–394. by Andrew Knapp and William Baldwin. J. Robins & Co., Ivy Lane, Paternoster Row. Except for minor differences in text the same as Caulfield's version above.
[1830]	Life and Trial of Richard Turpin. T. Richardson. Same as 1808 version above, but possibly the first of a number of such copies which appeared in the next three decades. The date of this and subsequent editions by other publishers (as given in the British Museum *General Catalogue*) is uncertain.
1834	Rookwood. William Harrison Ainsworth.
1835	Life of Richard Turpin. John Jones. *Welsh.* Not read but possibly first foreign language edition of Turpin's life.
1840	Richard Turpin. Henry Downes Miles. *See* Appendix Three.
1841–1898	*See* Appendix Two.
1899	Dictionary of National Biography. Entry by T. Seccombe.
1902	Essex Review. Two articles by Thomas Seccombe (as above) in January and April editions.
1908	Half Hours with the Highwaymen, Vol.II by Charles G. Harper. London. Chapman and Hall Ltd.
1934	Highwayman's Heath. Gordon S. Maxwell.
1948	Immortal Turpin. Arty Ash and Julius E. Day. Staples Press, London. 1948.
1949	Highwayman's Heath. Gordon S. Maxwell. New edition by Thomasons, the Middlesex Chronicle, Hounslow.
1962	Knights of the High Toby. by John Barrows. London. Peter Davies.

INDEX

CRIME AND CRIMINALS

affray, 64
affidavits. *See* informations
anatomising, bodies sent or stolen for, 178, 208, 232, 428, 429
Assault, 46, 47, 64, 75; trials for, 46, 47, 151, 156, 168; victims of: Cory, George, 46, 168, Iles, Robert, 47

ASSIZES, SESSIONS & C.
    Beverley, 345-347, 409; *Clerk of Peace*, Appleton, Robert, 324, 333, 334, 339, 343, 344-347, 349, 351, 411, 416, 418, 419, 433, 434-436
    Chelmsford, 26-33, 67, 146, 168, 192, 198, 199, 217, 218, 231, 235-237, 242, 243, 263, 305, 317-320, 328, 376; *Clerk of Assize*, Michell, —, 263; *conspiracy at*, 29-33; *Foreman of Grand Jury*, Child, Sir Caesar, 377
    Gloucester, 241, 243, 244, 263, 301-305
    Hertford, 257, 258, 262, 263, 316
    Kingston-upon-Thames, 6, 76
    Lincoln, 349
    London and Westminster, Hick's Hall, 77, 164, 214; Old Bailey (London), 23, 24; Old Bailey (Middlesex), 23, 47, 92, 93, 124, 125, 142, 144-146, 149-159, 164, 170, 191-193, 195, 196, 198-208, 228, 246, 275, 279, 304, 320, 335-376, 390, report on those condemned at, by [Simon], Mr. Serjeant Urling [Urlin], Deputy Recorder of London, 208; Westminster, Court of King's Bench, 64
    Maiden Assize, 254
    Maidstone, 76
    York, 352, 353, 356, 373, 375-377, 379, 382, 387-391, 393, 411, 415, 433-436; **Turpin's trial at**, *Clerk of Assize*, Simon, Henry, 387; *evidence*, commentary upon, 411-418; *Grand Jury*, 370, 383, 387, 388 (*names*), 390, foreman of, Hildyard, Sir Robert, 388; *Indictments* (Bills), 370, 371, 382, 383, 386-388, 390, 393, validity of dating, 370, validity of use of place names where offences alleged to have been committed, 371; *Judges at. See* Judges: Lee, Chapple; *Petty Jury*, 370, 388, 390 (*names*), 397; *Prosecution for Crown*, Place, Thomas, 374, 393, 413, Crowle, Richard (Junior Counsel), 375, 393, 413, 419, 435; *Shorthand Writer*, Kyll, Thomas, 335, 336, 358, 386, 393, 421; *testimony in published account*, 335, 336, 341, 342, 347, 348, 350-352, 356, 357, 360-363, 367, 368, 386, 393-410; *venue, argument for*, 366, 371-377, 380, 382, 434

Index

bail (sureties), 244, 262, 347, 349, 353
Blood Money, 76, 106, 181, 207, 216, 217, 247, 276, 433, 436, 438 (source refs.)
body snatching, 428, 429
bribery, 186, 189, 440 (alleged)
burglary. *See* Robbery with Violence

cattle stealing, 9, 10, 38
constables. *See* Waltham forest: Officials; *and* Witnesses: Bishop, Gill, Graves and Pullen
conviction, certificates of, 25, 207, 433-435
counterfeiting, uttering counterfeit coins, 5, 6, 34, 167, 168, 175, 215, 232, 237, 240, 241, *trials for*, 6, 243, 244, 301-305, *victims of*, Davis, Elizabeth and Thomas, Dobbs, Ann, 241, 243
Crime, prevention, detection &c., 215-217, 287
CRIMINALS, Arnold, ——, (fugitive), 144; **Arnold**, ——, (another, a convict), 144; **Ashwood**, John, (vagabond, *alias* Turpin), 327; **Beane**, Sawney, (man-eater), 444; **Drake**, West, (thief), 23, 34; **Falconer** *alias* Faulkener, William, (counterfeiter), 5, 6, 34, 167, 168, 175; **Fletcher**, ——, 84; **Gassey** *alias* Gaskey, John, (counterfeiter), 5, 6, 34; **Hughes**, ——, (murderer), 208; **James**, *Black Jack* John, (robber), 173; **Lewis**, ——, (murderer), 208; **Malcolm**, Sarah, (murderess), 232; **Malden**, Daniel, (prison escaper), 238, 240-242, 244-249, 251, 254; **Rogers**, Henry, (murderer), 140; **Rust**, Edward, (brawler), 64; **Stead**, John, (horsestealer), 390, 418, 426, 427, 430; **Sutton**, ——, (condemned person), 208; **Turner**, Nan, (murderess), 84; **Wild**, Jonathan, (thieftaker), 217, 322. *See also* Deerstealers, Gregory Gang, Highwaymen, and Turpin

DEERSTEALERS, 3-5, 7, 9-11, 13-16, 20, 21, 24, 25, 27-35, 37, 38, 56, 63, 65, 88, 114, 139, 142, 378; **Brook**, Edward, 24, 25, 34; **Coster**, John, 5, 26, 28, 31, 34, 40; **Croot**, John, 24, 25, 34; **Downham**, Abraham, 16, 24, 25, 34, 35; **Field** *alias* Fielder, 16, 24, 25, 32, 34, 37; **Fuller**, John, 4, 11, 17, 18, 21, 28, 31, 34, 378; **Fuller**, Nimpous, 30, 31, 40, 378; **Gregory**, Jeremiah or Jeremy, 5, 25-34, 37, 47, 208, 378, 440; **Gregory**, Samuel, 4, 5, 16, 25, 33, 34; **Hicks**, George, 24, 25, 34; **Johnson**, William, 21, 23, 24, 34, 172, 194; **Onion** (Onyon), Philip, 24, 25, 27, 34; **Pateman**, John, 24, 25, 34; **Rogers**, William, 26, 28-34, 40, 378; **Rose**, Joseph, 5, 16, 24-34, 37, 378; **Tanner**, Thomas, 21; **Woodward**, Robert, 16, 24, 25, 34, 35
DEERSTEALING, 3-5, 9, 11, 13-18, 21, 23, 28, 30, 31, 38, 39, 47, 48, 63, 139, 208, 252, 302, 440; *convictions for*, 4, 16, 24, 28, 30, 38, 378; *imprisonment for*, 4, 11, 16-18, 24-26, 28, 32, 38, 39; *laws governing*, 16-18; *pillorying for*, 4, 11, 17, 24, 30, 38, 39, 47, 378, rescue from, 30, 38, 39, 47, 65, 139, 142, 160, 207; *rewards* (including proclamations) published

Crime and Criminals 457

for capture of, 3, 14-16, 18, 21, 27, 37, 114, 216, claims for, 25, 27, 28, 440; *rival factions,* 31, 32, 378; *transportation for,* 18

ESTABLISHMENT, THE, (in opposition to Crime &c.)
 Arnold, Richard, Deputy Secretary at War, 161, 164, 166, 373, 376, 378
 Caroline, Wilhemina Charlotte, Queen Consort to George II, 4, 208, 213, 214, 222, 242
 George II, 4, 16, 18, 65, 103, 104, 108, 113, 119, 140, 160, 161, 214, 252, 306, 308, 327, 328, 364, 374, 381, 382, 389, 413
 Harrington (William Stanhope), Baron, Secretary of State for the Northern Province, 15, 16, 104, 242, 246, 251, 328, 437
 Harrison, Brigadier General ——, 373
 Newcastle (Thomas Pelham-Holles), Duke of, Secretary of State for the Southern Province, 3, 43, 44, 103, 113, 161, 213, 214, 283, 306, 359, 364-366, 372-375, 377, 380-382, 389-391, 411
 Paxton, Nicholas, Treasury Solicitor, 17, 18, 20, 25-28, 185, 207, 373, 418, 419, 425, 433-438, 440, 441
 Place, Thomas, Recorder of York, 44, 283, 359, 362, 364-366, 368, 369, 371, 373-375, 389, 391, 417, 419
 Ryder, Sir Dudley, Attorney General, 213, 214, 365, 372-377, 380-382, 391, 434
 Scrope, John, Secretary to the Treasury, 14, 18
 Stone, Andrew, Under Secretary of State for the Southern Province, 365
 Strickland, Sir William, Secretary at War, 161, 164, 166 (death of)
 Wills, Col. Sir Charles, 164, 167
 Yonge, Sir William, Secretary at War, 166, 373, 374, 380, 434
 See also Enfield Chase: Keepers &c., Judges and Justices, Sheriffs, Treasury, Waltham Forest: Keepers &c.
executions (hanging), 23, 24, 30, 31, 34, 98, 114, 167, 169, 170, 172, 194, 207-209, 219, 251, 319, 320, 327, 426-430, *guards for prevention of rescue at,* 30, 160, 164, 169, 172, 209

false pretences, *obtaining horses by,* 143, *obtaining money by,* 95, 96
fines, 47, 48, 244, 301

Gamekeepers &c. *See* Enfield Chase, Waltham Forest
gibbetting, 113, 114, 167, 169, 178, 208, 209, 218-220, 226, 251; *authority for,* 220; *birds nesting in corpses on gibbet,* 238; *building,* 165; *cost of,* 169, 209; *objections to by public,* 165, 166
GREGORY GANG *or* **ESSEX GANG**
 Barnfield, Thomas, (Receiver), 45, 65, 81, 163, 164, 168, *death of,* 163, 164, 168, 185, 329, *wife,* Ann Barnfield, 163, 329
 Brazier (Brassier) *alias* Cox, Head, Johnson and Rose, Mary, (Receiver), 20,

21, 27, 29, 33, 34, 66, 67, 83, 91-94, 105, 113-117, 121, 125-127, 133, 135, 163, 203, 247, 390; *capture,* 120, 126, 132-134, 138, 155; *commital,* 138, 142, 189; *in prison,* 141, 142, 157, 185, *trial,* 116, 129, 191-193; *transportation, sentenced to,* 192, 207, 208, 228; *transported,* 229, 237, 327, 329

Fielder, John, 47, 56, 59, 60, 63, 70-73, 83, 85, 86, 88, 92-95, 99, 108, 109, 135, 185, 192, 202, 206-208, 238, 246, 252, 317, 390, 438; *capture,* 110-113, 115, 120, 125, 155; *commital,* 111, 115, 118; *execution &c.,* 167, 169, 329; *in prison,* 123, 125, 138, 141; *trial,* 111, 116, 121, 124, 125, 136, 137, 143, 145, 146, 151-160

Gregory, Jasper (*or* Joseph), 36, 44, 46, 48-50, 57, 72, 81, 83, 84, 93, 135, 141, 185, 231, 246, 247, 390, 438; *capture,* 105-107, 117; *execution,* 168, 170-173, 208, 329; *in prison,* 108, 115, 140-142; *trial,* 118, 168, 236

Gregory, Jeremy, 36, 46, 47, 50, 56, 63, 77, 78, 83, 84, 129, 170-173, 206, 207, 214, 222, 228, 438, 441; *alias Lisle,* 172, 178, 190; *capture,* 171, 177-182, 191, 222, 290; *commital,* 178; *death in prison,* 178, 180, 185, 190, 195, 196, 206, 208, 222, 329; *highwayman,* 171, 176, 177, 179, 182; *wounded,* 178, 180, 190, 191

Gregory, Samuel, 35-39, 44-50, 54, 63, 65, 67, 71, 72, 74, 80, 83-86, 88-97, 99, 106, 108, 109, 114-117, 120-123, 125-129, 131, 132, 135, 139, 141, 143, 144, 146, 151, 152, 155, 156, 160, 161, 163, 165, 168-173, 197, 231, 237, 238, 246, 290, 327, 349, 390, 437, 438; *alias Johnson,* 25, 172, 178, 190, 197, 198; *capture,* 129, 161, 163, 177-182, 191, 198, 222; *commital,* 178; *execution,* 144, 198, 207-209, 329; *highwayman,* 169, 170, 176, 177, 179, 182, 226, 228; *in prison,* 145, 160, 181, 185, 195-197, 199; *person mistaken for (John Lyndon alias Samuel Gregory),* 161, 162, 191, 195, 248; *trial,* 116, 146, 176, 181, 198-207; *wounded,* 178-191

Haines, Herbert, 23, 34, 54, 56, 62, 81, 83, 114, 117, 121-123, 126-129, 131, 135, 141, 165, 170-172, 222, 223, 246, 260, 319, 390, 438, 441; *alias Joseph Butler,* 172, 186, 189; *capture,* 185-188, 217, 248; *commital,* 186, 188, 189; *execution,* 219, 220, 329; *in prison,* 198, 199, 217, 218; *mistress of,* Mrs. Carroll, 34, 40, 81, 172, 185-187, 189, 218, 219, her husband, John Carroll, 34, 172, 185-187, 189; *trial,* 199, 217, 218

Jones, John, 48-50, 57, 81, 83, 106, 114, 117, 121-123, 129, 131, 132, 135, 140, 168, 170, 172, 185, 197, 200, 229, 246, 390, 438; *capture and commital,* 228, 230-232, 235, 248; *Highwayman,* 182, 183, 213, 377; *reprieve,* 242, 243; *transported,* 247, 252, 253, 255, 327, 329; *trial,* 235-237

Parkinson, James, 37, 425

Rose, Joseph, 45, 49, 50, 56, 59, 60, 63, 67, 71, 72, 74, 83-86, 88, 91-95, 99, 105, 109, 110, 113-117, 121, 123, 127, 135, 137, 142, 163, 185,

Crime and Criminals

192, 193, 202, 203, 206, 208, 237, 238, 246, 247, 317, 390, 438; *brother-in-law of,* 143; *capture,* 120, 126, 132-134, 138, 140, 155, 158; *commital,* 138, 189; *execution,* 167, 169, 329; *in prison,* 141; *trial,* 116, 121, 124, 125, 136, 137, 142, 143, 145, 146, 151-160

Rowden, Thomas, 4, 6, 34, 54, 62, 72, 81, 83, 114, 117, 121-123, 126-129, 131, 132, 135, 141, 165, 168, 170-172, 200, 217, 263, 290, 390, 438; *alias Daniel Crispe,* 232, 237, 240-244, 263, 270, 301-305, 317, 318; *reprieve,* 328; *transportation,* 328, 329; *trial,* 317-320, 327. *See also* Highwaymen

Rust, Ned (a possibly fictional member), 59, 60, 63, 64, 71, 84, 112

Saunders *alias* Saunderson, Schooling and Bush, William, 46, 47, 50, 77, 78, 83, 84, 94, 95, 99, 108, 119, 135, 185, 192, 208, 214, 222, 246, 252, 390, 438; *capture,* 110-112, 115, 120, 125; *commital,* 111, 115, 118; *execution,* 167, 169, 170, 329; *in prison,* 123, 138, 141; *trial,* 111, 116, 121, 136, 137, 143, 145, 146, 155-160

Turpin, Richard, 39, 44, 46, 50, 51, 54, 58-60, 62-64, 70-73, 79-81, 83-88, 93-95, 98, 109, 113, 114, 117, 120-123, 125-129, 131, 132, 135, 141, 146, 151, 152, 155, 156, 162, 165, 170-172, 174, 179, 199, 200, 202, 217, 233, 260, 263, 317, 380, 381, 390, 438. *See Also* Highwaymen

Walker, Humphrey, 70-73, 78, 81, 83, 84, 94, 99, 113, 114, 117, 120, 121, 123, 135, 137, 138, 185, 192, 208, 238, 246, 247, 317, 390, 438; *capture,* 120, 126, 132-134, 137, 140, 155, 158; *commital,* 138, 189; *death of,* 163, 165, 167, 329; *gibbetting,* 169; *in prison,* 141; *trial,* 116, 121, 124, 125, 136, 137, 143, 145, 146, 155-160

Wheeler, John, 48-50, 54, 62, 67, 71, 72, 74, 80, 83, 85-89, 92-95, 168, 188, 204; *capture,* 110-115, 120, 123, 125, 127, 131, 229, 252; *commital,* 111, 115, 117; *death of,* 327, 329, 363, 377, 437; *in custody,* 123, 125, 128, 139, 141, 181, 182, 185, 219, 246; *Information of,* 135, 140-144, 170, 188, 240, 246, 380, 389, 390; *King's Evidence,* 98, 101, 105-109, 113-121, 123, 127, 129, 130, 133-135, 138-142, 144, 160, 162, 170, 189, 192, 197, 199, 200, 207, 217, 218, 230, 231, 235-237, 240, 241, 270, 277, 305, 317, 319, 380, 381, 437, 438; *release,* 246-249, 253; *testimony at trials,* 146, 152, 156, 159, 192, 193, 202, 203

GENERAL

8, 10, 20, 23, 32, 34-39, 41, 43-56, 58-68, 70-81, 83-97, 103-118, 120-146, 151-160, 163, 165, 168-170, 172, 173, 187, 191-193, 195, 197, 198, 200-209, 215, 217, 219, 220, 223, 229, 231, 233, 235-238, 240, 241, 246-248, 252, 260, 264, 270, 276, 302-304, 307, 317, 318, 320, 325, 327, 333, 377, 378, 380, 382, 420, 425, 437, 438, 446; **capture,** 75-77, 81, 83, 93, 96, 98, 103, 105-114, 120, 121, 125, 129, 132-135, 137, 151, 152, 160, 177-181, 228, 230, 231, warrants for, 132, 140; **descriptions,** *first,* 108, 109, *second,* 123, *third,* 140, 141, *posted on turnpikes,* 144; **escape,** 110, 115, 128, 131, *via sea ports, orders sent to* *prevent,* 140; **flight,** 117, 120, 121, 171, 172, *overseas, attempted,* 49, 50, 172, 176, 185-188 (on ship *Chandos*), 228, 230, 237; **Irish Clan, called,** 107; **others mistaken for,** 125, 139, 144, 161, 162, 179; **rescue, preparations for,** 115, 143, 160, 164, 170-172; **rewards for capture,** *proclamations,* 65, 73, 103-106, 108, 109, 113, 140, 141, 194, 206, 216, 246, 247, 251, 303, 380, 434, *published,* 43, 45, 67, 73, 75, 76, 96, 114, 123, 381, *claimed,* 48, 104, 111, 117, 118, 185, 207, for capture of Fielder and Saunders, 112 (*names*), for capture of Rose, 134 (*names*), for capture of Jeremy and Samuel Gregory, 181 (*names*), for capture of others. *See also* Individuals (captures), *supra,* and Appendix I; **rewards,** *ex gratia payment of,* 171, 180, 207, 222, 441; **trials,** 115-117, 137, 145, 146, 150-159, 168, 174, 192-193, 201-206, 217-218, 235-237, 317-320

VICTIMS, **Asher** (Asser), George, J.P., 66, 67, 113, 125, 175, 191; **Berry** (Bury), ––, 130, 131; **Berry,** Mrs. ––, 130; **Dyde,** Rev. ––, 74, 75, 77, 103, 104, 252; **Emmerton** (Emerson), James, 85-88, 90, 112, 146, 153, 155, 159, 161, 162, 195; **Francis,** Mrs. ––, 94, 95, 138, 156, 157; **Francis,** Sarah, 94, 95, 137, 138, 146, 156-158, 192; **Francis,** ––, Sarah's sister, 94, 138; **Francis,** William, 94-97, 103, 107, 113, 116, 117, 121, 129, 131, 136-138, 145, 146, 155-159, 191-193, 199, 201, 205, 381; **Gladwin** (Gladden), John, 48-50, 73, 106, 123, 140, 168, 230, 231, 236; **Jones,** Edward, 94, 95, 146, 156, 157; **King,** ––, of Ham Farm, 165; **King,** Elizabeth, 52, 54, 64, 217, 218, 260; **Lawrence,** Joseph, Snr., 4, 85-94, 96, 108-113, 115-117, 119, 123, 125-127, 129, 131, 136, 144-146, 151-155, 159-162, 178, 179, 191-193, 196-198, 200-206, 251, 252, 381, 434; **Lawrence,** Joseph, Jnr., 85, 89-91, 132, 134, 159, 202, 223; **Lawrence,** Thomas, 85, 89-91, 111, 112, 115, 116, 125, 132-134, 146, 155, 158-160, 192, 196, 198, 200, 205, 217, 218, 223; **Manning** (Mannington), Stephen, 94, 95, 146, 156, 157; **Mason,** ––, daughter of William, 59-61; **Mason,** Mary, 58, 60, 61, 64, 217, 441; **Mason,** William. *See* Waltham Forest: Keepers; **Pate(s)** (Peats), John 85-88, 111, 112, 119, 134, 153, 159, 160-162, 195; **Richards,** Jonathan, 58, 60, 61, 63, 64, 217; **Roades,** William, 59 (the old man), 60 (Mason's father), 61, 62, 64; **St. John,** Mrs. ––, 126; **Saunders,** ––, 70, 72, 75-77; **Saunders,** Mrs. ––, 70, 71, 75, 76, 79; **Savage,** –– 122; **Sheldon,** ––, 73, 74, 76, 77, 79; **Shelley** (Shirely), Widow ––, 77-81; 84, 103, 104, 252, 319, 445, 446; **Shockley,** John, 48, 49, 106, 168, 236; **Skinner,** Ambrose, Snr., 51-57, 60-62, 64-67, 73, 79, 96, 104, 124, 125, 127, 133, 168, 217, 218, 260, 263, 318, 319, 381; **Skinner,** Ambrose, Jnr., 53, 55, 56, 124, 127, 146, 159, 168, *his wife,* 124, 125, 217, 318, 319; **Spellar,** Henry, 52; **Split** (Splidt, Strype), Peter, 43-46, 79, 103, 105, 194, 251, 380-382, 389, 390; **Styles** (Stiles), Daniel, 52, 64, 218; **Turkle,** ––, 79, 80; **Williams,** Eleanor, 94, 95, 138, 156, 157; **Wooldridge,** Ann, 45, 163;

Crime and Criminals

    Wooldridge, Richard, 45, 46, 65, 103, 104, 163, 164, 251. *See also* Rape: victim of.

Habeas Corpus, 76, 144, 161, 162, 195, 197-199, 218, 235, 236, 304, 305, 317, 318, 352, 365, 366, 379, 383
hanging. *See* Executions
hangman, Jack Ketch, traditional name for, 313
harbouring felons, 163, 280, 282, 283
hard labour, 47, 48
HIGHWAYMEN
    Bonner, ––, 249; **Clark**, John, (Turpin imposter), 439; **Davis**, William (The Golden Farmer), 308; **Goodall**, Toby, 278; **Hind**, Capt. James, 308; **King**, Matthew, 218, 233, 257, 258, 260-265, 268-280, 285, 286, 288, 291, 292, 301, 309, 314, 317, 329, 424-426, (?) *alias Matthew Plear,* 270, 284, 285, *brother (John King),* 272-276, 279, 284, 309, 329, (?) *sister (Elizabeth King),* 54, 218, 260, 272, 284-286, 329, *supposed brother (Robert King),* 271, 274, 275, *traditional name (Tom King),* 233-235, 245, 250, 257, 281; **MacLean**, James, 232; **Nevison**, John, *alias* Swift Nicks, 308, 443-445, 447; **Potter**, Stephen, 257, 258, 260-265, 268-270, 272-274, 276-280, 285, 288, 301, 314, 316-318, 329; **Rowden**, Thomas, 165, 171, 182, 183, 185, 190, 191, 197, 213-215, 222-226, 228-233, 235, 237, 241, 245, 247-249, 270, 377; **Turpin**, Richard, 122, 165, 171, 182, 183, 185, 190, 191, 195, 197, 211, 213-216, 219, 222-226, 228-235, 250-252, 254, 256-266, 268-274, 276-293, 307-314, 317, 320, 326, 329, 340, 347, 348, 350, 365, 377, 378, 393, 401, 418, 427, 430, 431, 439, *believed to be in Holland,* 237, 238, 240-249, 256, 258, 260, 263, *believed to be out of country,* 323, 325; **Wager**, Cocky, 249, 251; **Whitney**, ––, (executed 1694), 308. *See also* Gregory Gang: Gregory, Jeremy and Samuel, Jones
HIGHWAY ROBBERY, 213-216, 223-226, 228, 230, 232, 245, 249, 251, 257, 258, 261-265, 268, 272, 274, 275, 279, 282, 284, 285, 288, 291, 293, 301, 308-314, 316, 317, 321, 349, 363, 364, 377, 424; *laws,* 213, 214; *reward for prevention &c., public subscription for,* 223, 224; *rewards, general,* 213-215, 222, 223, 228, 276, 280; *trial for,* 180; *Victims of,* **Amey**, Rev. ––, 214; **Bone**, James, 226; **Bradele**, ––, 234, 235; **Bradford**, James, 215; **Child**, Sir Caesar, 190, 191, 194, 377; **Durham**, Thomas, 226; **Forde**, ––, 224, 225; **Godfrey**, ––, 223; **Hucks**, William, M.P., 265; **Loan**, ––, 293; **Major**, Joseph, 268-275, 277, 279, 316, 317; **Omar**, ––, 215; **Osborne** (Osbaston), Sir John, 176-179, 196, 206; **Pyecroft**, Mrs. ––, 182, 183; **St John**, ––, 349; **Shirley**, Hon. George, 264; **Spooner**, ––, 176, 177, 179; **Tebb**, ––, 226, 233; **Thompson**, Capt. ––, 264, 265, 424, 426; **Turner**, Sir Charles, 304; **Vane**, ––, 215
Horsestealing, *laws,* 371, *trials for,* Gregory, Samuel, 199-201, 205; Haines, 217, 218; Turpin, 387-418; *victims of,* **Arrowsmith**, ––, 268, 269; **Creasy**, Thomas, *See* Witnesses; **Humphrey** (Humphries), Thomas, 176, 200, 201;

462 *Index*

Major, Joseph. *See* Highway Robbery: Victims; **Richmond, Duke of**, his steward, 308; **Skinner**, Ambrose, 52, 54, 56; **Suffolk (Henry Howard) Earl of**, 169, 170; **Townshend**, Charles, 331, 332, 334, 338, 349, 350, 353. *See also* false pretences, and Turpin
housebreaking. *See* Robbery with Violence
Hue and Cry, 39, 143, 144, 216 (Acts for), 285, 308

Indictments, *departures from norm in dating*, 129, 370; *names of suspected persons remaining on until caught*, 146, 199, 263, 381, 382
Informations (affidavits &c.), *original*, 13-15, 51-53, 60-62, 185, 186, 230, 299, 305, 344, 362
Inquests post mortem, 5, 29, 283, 292, 381, 389-391
Intimidation, 251

JUDGES, Chapple, Sir William, 335, 387, 389, 390, 393, 405, 407, 410-413, 418, 433; **Comyns**, Sir John, 162; **Lee**, Sir William, 387, 388; **Probyn**, Sir Edmund, 162; **Thompson**, Sir William, 112, 263
JUSTICES OF THE PEACE, 24, 25, 30, 64, 105, 139, 161, 177, 178, 181, 240, 244, 246, 256, 300-302, 323, 333, 347, 348, 359, 361-365, 379, 386, 401, 402, 404, 434 (Bench of), 436 (do.), 447; **Adams**, John, 362; **Appleyard**, Capt. ——, (? J.P.), 349, 365; **Asher**. *See* Gregory Gang: Victims; **Bethell**, Hugh, 299, 344-346; **Blackerby**, Nathaniel, 135, 137, 138, 142, 163, 187-189, 231, 304, 305, 390; **Bladen**, Col. Martin, 38, 39, 51, 60, 63-65, 75, 104, 133, 251, 252; **Brocas**, Sir Richard, 186-189; **Burn**, Richard, 22, 220; **Chamberlain**, Anthony, 23; **Constable**, Marmaduke, 299, 344-346; **Crowle**, George, 299, 344-346, 349, 352, 265, 367, 373-379, 381, 382, 418, 419, 433-437; **Delamere**, ——, 332, 334, 343, 348, 349; **Dennet**, Robert, 163, 164, 168; **De Veil**, Col. Thomas, 136; **Dixwell**, Sir Basil, (? J.P.), 327; **Farmer**, Richard, 284; **Fielding**, Henry, 136, 215; **Goodere**, John, 44, 380, 390. *See also* Waltham Forest: Ranger; **Hind (Hynde)**, Robert, 110, 111, 115, 117, 118, 142, *his wife*, 110, 118; **Lade**, Sir John, 75, 76; **Lestock**, Richard, 18; **Mildmay**, Carew. *See* Waltham Forest: Verderer; **Nelthorpe**, George, 362; **Norris**, Henry, 181, 230, 231; **Peck**, John, 357; **Peck**, William, 357; **Pratt**, ——, 144; **Pulson**, J., 305; **Ricards**, (Ricketts), Richard, 274-276, 279, 284; **Robe**, Thomas, 191; **Rolt**, Thomas, 257, 262, 316; **Steward**, Sir Simeon, 205; **Stott**, James, 338; **Stubbing**, Thomas, 362; **Tysson**, Samuel, 46, 230; **Warford**, Thomas, 338

King's Evidences. *See* Criminals: Falconer; Gregory Gang: Wheeler

Magistrates. *See* Justices of the Peace
manslaughter, victim of, Boston John, 5, 28-34, 40
Murder, 21, 23, 34, 65, 78, 84, 88, 140, 194, 220; *trials for*, 23, 24; *victims*

Crime and Criminals

of, **Morris,** Thomas (Mr. Thompson's man), 235, 257, 280-288, 292, 293, 300, 301, 305-307, 310, 312, 329, 364-366, 377, 380, 381, 389, 391, 412, 424, 426, 429, 434; **Tarman,** James, 21, 23

pocket picking, 20, 125; *victims of,* **Graham,** Charles, 20, 27; **Morebeck,** Peter, 20, 27; **Turford,** Ann, 20, 27

PRISONS
    Beverley, House of Correction, 324, 345-347, 349, 351, 379, 382, 395
    Chelmsford, Gaol, 18, 20, 24, 26-28, 33, 34, 37, 56, 105, 107, 108, 115, 140, 141, 144, 199, 217, 219, 237, 291, 318, 329, 332, 338, 340, 355; *escape from prevented,* 353; *Keeper,* Emmerson, — —, 353
    Coventry, Gaol, 304
    Gloucester, Castle, 240-242, 263, 270, 301-305, 317, 318; *Keeper,* 304 (Peters, — —, suggested name of), 305, 319 (Heming *or* Henning, Benjamin, of *official* record)
    Hertford, Gaol, 256-258, 291
    Kent, Eastern Division of, Gaol for, 327
    Leicester, Gaol, 439
    London and Westminster
        Bridewell (Clerkenwell), House of Correction, 47, 56, 63, 83, 115, 181, 182, 274, 275; *clerk,* Walker, William, 78; *Committee inquiring into escape from,* 77, 78, 222; *Committee inquiring into prisoners dying in,* 292; *escape from,* 77, 78, 84, 85, 94, 170, 214, 222; *Keeper,* Creswell, Peter, 76-78, 214; *Turnkey,* Best, Mary, 78
        Compter, 110
        Gatehouse (Westminster), 105, 116, 133, 137, 138, 141, 142, 157, 189, 193; *Keeper of,* 137, 157
        New Gaol (Southwark), 75, 229
        Newgate, 21, 23, 24, 46, 110, 111, 115, 117-119, 123, 125, 134, 138, 141-144, 147, 160-163, 166, 167, 186-189, 194, 196-200, 205, 207-210, 229-232, 236, 237, 239, 244, 254, 275, 277, 294, 304, 316, 317, 320, 326, 330; *death in,* 163-165, 167, 169; *escape from,* 238, 240; *Keeper,* 208; *Old Condemned Hold in,* 317
        New Prison (Clerkenwell), 76, 105, 110, 111, 115, 119, 123, 138, 139, 141, 142, 162, 181, 189, 197, 218, 237, 246-248, 274, 275, 277, 278, 284, 286, 292, 309; *Committee inquiring into prisoners dying in,* 292; *death in,* 275, 292; *Keeper,* Cavannagh, Thomas, 181, 217, 235, 246-248, 292, 305, 437, 441
    Watford, Gaol, 291
    Winchester, Castle, 145, 161, 177, 178, 180, 182, 190, 195-197, 206, 208; *gaoler,* 178, 180; *Keeper,* 162, 197
    York Castle, 278, 306, 343, 349, 351-353, 357, 359, 361-368, 373, 378, 379, 382, 385, 387-389, 391, 397, 402-405, 412, 417, 420, 423, 426,

434, 439, 441; *Gaoler,* Griffith, Thomas, 397, 406, 425; *Governor,* 359, 362, 366; *Keeper,* 420

prisoners, a liability upon county only up to date of conviction, 255

protective custody, expenses for keeping evidence in, 246, 247, 437, 441

rape, *victim of,* **Street,** Dorothy, 85-91, 109, 115, 123, 144, 152, 154, 159, 160, 162, 178, 198; *trial for,* 199-205

receivers. *See* Gregory Gang: Barnfield, Brazier

receiving, 65, 91, 94, 113, 127, 138, 142, 163, 164, 168, 169; trial for, 92, 93, 116, 129, 191-193

recognisances to prosecute, 164, 168, 199, 210, 275, 279, 305, 316, 317

recruiting (illegal), for foreign service, 241, 242, 245, 254

reprieves, 237, 242, 252, 319, 320, 328

Reward, ex gratia payment, apportionment by John (Wallop) Visc. Lymington, *Custos Rotulorum* of Hampshire and town of Southampton, 222

Rewards (general). *See* Deerstealing, Gregory Gang, Highway Robbery, Treasury, and Turpin

Robbery with Violence (usually associated with burglary, housebreaking), *victim of,* **Hale** Jasper, 173. *For remainder of Victims and other aspects related to this heading, See Gregory Gang*

sheepstealing. *See* Turpin

SHERIFFS, 207, 216, 303; *Cravings for Expenses,* 30, 38, 39, 162, 169, 172, 197, 199, 208, 209, 218-220, 236, 252, 253, *255,* 316-318, 328, 329, 430; *Essex,* 26, 28, 30, 38, 39, 219, 263, 357, **Ambrose,** Thomas, 172, **Dawtrey,** William, 252, **Harrison,** John, 106, **Smith,** Hugh, 328, **Trist,** Robert, 328; *Gloucester,* 318; *Hampshire,* **Graham,** Robert, 162, 195, 197; *London and/ or Middlesex,* 143, 160, 164, 181, 217, 218, 235, 236, **Perry,** Micajah, 169, 199, **Salter,** Sir, John, 169, 199; *York,* **Cook,** Sir George, 430, **Sheppard,** Richard, 425

Shooting, *persons affected by or victims of,* Boston, John, 5, 28-34, 40, **Deakins** (Deakin), John, 5, 25, 26, 28, 29, 31, 32, 34, 40, **Hall,** Francis, 299, 344-346, **Robinson,** John, 299, 339, 344-346. *See also* Gregory Gang: Jeremy and Samuel Gregory (capture), King, Matthew (Highwaymen), Morris, Thomas (Murder: victim), and Thompson, Capt. (Highway Robbery: victim); *trials for,* 26-34

smugglers, smuggling, 20, 63, 65, 66, 133, 146, 252, 290. *See also* Turpin

stealing, 23, 378. *See also* pocket-picking; *trials for,* 23, 27, 34, 167, 378; *victim of,* Sharrat (*or* Sharrol), John, 23

Stolen Goods (those taken by highwaymen, being generally small, are not listed), 20, 23, 43, 45, 52, 53, 58, 59, 61, 70, 71, 73, 75, 79-81, 87, 90, 92, 93, 116, 122, 130, 151, 155, 156, 191-193, 200, 201; *Inventories of,* 49, 55, 62, 91, 97, 124; *recovery of,* 127, 129, 132, 133, 137, 138, 155, 163, 164, 193

Crime and Criminals

subpoenas, 418, 434
surgeons, bodies sent to. *See* anatomising

TRANSPORTATION, 98, 114, 208, 228, 229, 236, 237, 242, 252, 253, 255, 319, 320, 327-329, 356, 357; *contractor for,* Forward, Jonathan, of the East India Company, 229, 253, 329; *ships used for,* **Dorsetshire,** William Loney Cmdr., 253, **Forward,** John Magier Cmdr., 329, **John,** John Griffin Cmdr., 229,

TREASURY (as Department responsible for payment &c. of Rewards), 14-16, 28, 104, 106, 217, 252, 293, 302, 435; *agents appointed by for distribution of rewards,* 222, 437; *Lords Commissioners of,* 13, 14, 25, 27, 28, 185, 207, 222 *(names),* 433-438, 440 (Sir Robert Walpole. *See also* Turpin: letter about)

TURPIN, RICHARD. *See also* Gregory Gang, and Highwaymen
alias **Palmer,** otherwise spelt Parmen, Paumer, Pawmer, argument that it could not have been that generally accepted, i.e. Palmer, 382-386; **alias Smith,** 365, 439, 441; **arrest** (final) and commital, 339, 342, 345-349, 351, 373; **ballads,** 310-314, 325; **baptism,** 9, 384; **butcher,** 3, 6, 7, 9, 10, 15, 34, 37, 128, 258, 289, 334, 341, 348, 403, 404, 423; **cattle stealer,** 9, 38; **childhood,** 401; **child of,** 427, 428; **confession** (official), 36-38, 67, 265, 425, 434; **confession** (unofficial), 264, 265, 423-426, 428; **descriptions,** 108, 109, 123, 141, 306, 308, 359, 362, 451; **disinterrment,** 428, 429; **escapes,** attempted or contrived, 9, 38, 113, 114, 197, 256, 257, 259, 260, 277, 278, 309, 334-336, 338, 347, 348, 352, 366; **escapes,** precautions to prevent, 372; **execution** &c., 411, 418, 420, 425-430, 437, 439

Family &c. (uncertain relationships marked ?), *brothers,* **Christopher,** 384, 385, **John,** 355-357, 384, 385, **Thomas** (?), 8, 384, 385, sons of, John, 385, Thomas, 385, wife (Martha Jud), 385; *brothers-in-law,* **Hasler,** Cesar, 385, **Rivernall** (Revinal, Rivinal), Pompadour, 338-341, 355-357, 359-362, 369, 379, 383, 386, 402; *cousins* (?), **Millington,** Betty, 19, 359, **Nott,** Robert, 11, 20, 225, 256-258, 262, 316, 317, 329; *father,* John, 8-10, 19, 331-334, 348, 355-358, 360, 366-368, 384, 386, 401, 403, 405, 410, 411, 416, arrest, 338-341, in prison, 350, 353, 359, release, 355, 377, 378; *grandfather* (?), Nott, ——, 11, 20, 225, 276; *mother,* 128, 362, 382-386, 407; *sisters,* **Dorothy,** 334, 338-340, 348, 357, 359, 362, 379, 384, 385, **Mary** (Maria), 384, 385; *wife,* **Elizabeth** (but variously named), 9, 11, 18-20, 225, 234, 240, 259, 288, 290, 316, 329, 340, 359, 360, 427, friend of (Hannah Elcombe), 256, 262, 316, 329, in prison, 256-258, released, 262

gentleman, living like, 323, 324, 337, 399, 400; **guards,** from Beverley to York, Joshua Milner and George Smith, 349; **horsestealer,** 286, 299-306, 316, 323-325, 331-342, 344, 348-353, 356, 364, 365, 371, 373, 376, 379, 424, 427. *See also* trial *infra;* **imposters.** *See* Criminals: Ashwood, and Highwaymen: Clark; **innkeeper,** 6, 10, 11, 20, 34, 37; **in prison** (York),

Index

before trial, 352-356, 359-368, 370, 372, 374-377, 379-383, 386, 391, 419, after trial, 420-423, wagers on identity in, 365, 393, 422; **legacy to married woman at Brough,** 427, 428; **letter about,** intended as attack on Sir Robert Walpole, 322; **letters from,** 19, 256-259, 338-340, 355-359, 385; **letters, question of authenticity of those published,** 359-365, 386, 402, 420; **Marriage** 8-10, 19, 401, 417; **portmanteau** inscribed R. TVRPIN, 282; **portrait,** 450-452; **prophetic error of recording judgment against instead of person convicted,** 320; **receiver** (of venison), 3, 10, 34, 37; **reward for capture and conviction (for Murder &c.),** 280, 281, 283, 287, 288, 292, 293, 305-307, 364, 365, 380; **reward for capture and conviction (on other charges), claim for,** 373, 376, 418, 419, 422, 425, 433-437; **Robin Hood,** traditional motivation of attributed to, 314; **schooling,** 9, 289, 359, 362, 402, 414; **1733-1734,** analysis of probable activities during, 35-39; **1737-1738,** summary of movements, 324; **sheepstealing,** 9, 323, 333, 334, 338, 350, 352, 364, 365, 415, 416, arrest for, 334, 348; **smuggler,** 3, 9-12; **stealing a kiss,** 250; **transportation, persons asked to intercede to obtain,** Madam Peck and Col. Watson, 356, 357; **Trial,** 3, 6, 7, 11, 18, 44, 118, 289, 290, 335-337, *387-420*. *See also* Assizes: York; **visits home,** 127, 128, 225, 290, 324, 331-334, 338-340; **York, legend of ride to,** 59, 233, 261, 313, *442-449*

whipping, 27, 34, 244
WITNESSES (in its broadest sense. This group includes Constables, Reporters, Observers, Officials and others who were involved in the aforegoing proceedings, but who for the most part do not fit into the various categories defined. Most of the Victims of the varous crimes who testified as witnesses at the trials of persons charged with those crimes, will be found listed as Victims, mainly under Gregory Gang.)
Allen, Arthur, 86, 153; **Arundell,** Richard, 243; **Bailis,** Thomas, 302-305, 319; **Bartram,** Richard, 134, 158; **Baxter,** John, 351, 395; **Bayes,** Richard, 10, 12, 19, 38, 43, 44, 46, 51, 58, 62, 63, 66, 67, 70-74, 79, 80, 90, 113, 133, 174, 233, 235, 245, 254, 257, 258, 268-272, 275-277, 279, 280, 282, 292, 303, 309, 322, 335; **Bishop,** Giles, *constable,* 243; **Bosgrave,** George, 168; **Bowler** (*or* Rowler *or* Rowletts), John, 85, 152, 158, 202; **Bryant,** Mary, 29; **Chandler,** Benjamin, 284, his father, 284, 285; **Corbey** (*or* Gorbey), John, 27; **Creasy,** Thomas, 335-337, 341, 342, 346, 349-353, 363, 376, 387, 388, 394-398, 407-411, 413, 435; **Dawson,** Capt. George, 341, 342, 350, 351, 373, 378, 380, 388, 397-399, 413, 434-436; **Deakins,** Henry, 26, 28, 29, 31-33; **Dowell,** Thomas, 192; **Eyres,** Daniel, 168; **Falconer,** Alice, 6; **Francis** (Frances), Francis, 230, 236; **Freeland,** James, 186-188, 217; **Gardner,** Alice, 192; **Gill,** ——, 356, 407, 412; **Gill,** Carey, *constable,* 346, 347, 352, 388, 409, 412, 435; **Goodyear,** George, 336, 388, 400, 401, 413, 435; **Graham,** Priscilla, 27; **Grant,** John, 279; **Grant,** Margaret, 279, 280, 294; **Grassby,** Richard, 323, 324, 337, 342, 350-352, 388, 395, 396, 398-401,

408, 435; **Graves**, Nicholas, *constable,* 230, 236; **Green**, Abraham, 344-346; **Green**, Dison, 230, 236; **Griffin**, John, 21; **Halmark**, Randall, 23; **Harris**, William, 299, 300, 306, 323, 334, 338-340, 343, 345, 346; **Harrowfield** (Haverfield), George, 134, 158; **Hold(s)worth**, Richard, 272, 275, 276, 285; **Ironmonger**, Joseph, 86, 152, 204; **Johnson**, Prudence, 47; **Lloyd**, --, 120, 132, 133; **Lloyd**, Mary(?) wife of above, 134, 192; **Martin**, Thomas, 80, 153; **Mashin**, John, 236; **Mitchell**, Richard, 192; **Morebeck**, Margaret, 27; **Moreland**, --, 251; **North**, John, 6; **Palmer**, --, 127, 128, 132; **Palmer**, Henry, 185-189, 217; **Peirson**, William, 26, 28, 31-33; **Pullen**, Archelaus, *constable,* 101, 110, 120, 126, 127, 132, 134-136, 138, 155, 158, 192, 198, 200, 205, 216-218; **Poulton**, Dorcas, 243; **Rogers**, John, 243; **Savages**, Robert, 272, 275; **Saward** (Sawood), Edward, 6, 10, 360, 367, 368, 388, 401, 404, 405, 413, 415, 417, 434-436; **Sherman**, John, 272, 275; **Smith**, James, 6-10, 18, 19, 289, 290, 338, 346, 359, 361-365, 367-369, 383, 386, 388, 401-405, 410, 413-415, 417, 432, 434-436; **Stretton**, George, 47; **Taylor**, Richard, 4, 85, 205; **Theed**, Mary, 168, 236; **Thompson**, William, 356, 407, 412; **Tongue**, Philip, 168; **Walten**, George, 217; **Watkins**, Edward, 243; **Westridge**, Charles, 192-194; **Westridge**, Jane (?) wife of above, 134; **Whitehead**, --, 356, 407, 412; **Whitehead**, John, 336, 337, 397, 406, 401-412, 418; **Winter**, James, 23; **Wood**, Richard, 85, 108, 110-112, 151, 152, 159, 160, 204; **Wood**, William, 163; **Woodward**, Abraham, 29; **York**, Lord Mayor of, 443

PLACES, ENGLAND

Aldborough Hatch, Barking, Essex, 51, 251; **Aylesbury,** Bucks., 310; **Banstead Downs,** Surr., 349; **Barking,** Essex, 51-54, 56, 75, 168, 217, 218, 320; **Barnes Common,** Surr., 214, 215, 222-226, 245; **Barnet,** Midd., 288-290, 432; **Barnet Wells,** Midd., 14; **Basingstoke,** Hants., 161; **Bedford,** town and county, 265; **Beverley,** Yorks., 332-335, 346, 347, 349-351, 378, 386, 395, 408, 412, 418, *Blue Bell* at, 346, 352, 408; **Birmingham,** Warw., 301; **Bishop's Stortford,** Herts., 258, 291; **Bocking,** Essex, 443; **Braintree,** Essex, 258, 443; **Brighton** (Brighthelmstone), Suss., 176, 178, 225; **Bristol,** Gloucs., 293, 324, 341, 351, 373, 376, 434, 435; **Brockley,** Kent, 122, 126, 128, 130, 131; **Brough,** Elloughton, Yorks., 293, 299, 300, 306, 307, 321, 323-325, 339, 340, 344, 348, 351, 395, 427, 428, ferry, 301, 306, 324, *Ferry House* at, 300, 306, 323, 334, 340, 343, 345, 346; **Buckhurst Hill** (Booker's Hill, Boxhill, Bucket Hill, Buckworth's Hill), Essex, 7, 8, 10, 284, 285, 289, 290, 403, 416, 417; **Buckinghamshire,** 35, 177; **Bumpstead Helion,** Essex, 362; **Bungay,** Suff., 234, 235, 245; **Cambridge,** 233, 290, 291, 301, 325-327, 443, *Three Tuns* at, 326, Trumpington Street in, 326; **Cambridgeshire,** 290, 292, 293, 323, 325; **Camlet Moat,** Enfield Chase, Midd., 290; **Cannons,** Edgware, Midd., 16; **Canterbury,** Kent, 122, 225, 244; **Charlton,** Kent, 70-74, 76, 122; **Chatham,** Kent, 443; **Chelmsford,** Essex, 30, 64, 144, 170, 171, 198, 199, 208, 217, 219, 236, 237, 243, 253, 302, 305, 316, 317, 320, 327-329, 375, 379, 389, 391, 411, 440, 443, *Black Boy* at, 219, bridge at, 144, 219; **Chester** (Westchester), Cheshire, *White Lion* at, 308; **Chigwell,** Essex, 5, 7, 256, *King's Head* at, 5; **Chingford** (Chinkford), Essex, 5, 26, 31, 38, 46, 48, 50, 75, 106, 107, 126, 127, 130 131, 168, 229, 236, 237; **Chingford** (Chinkford) **Green,** Essex, 48, 140, 231; **Clay Hill,** Enfield, Midd., 225, 259, 288-290, *Rose and Crown* at, 11, 20; **Cliff,** Kent, 130, 131; **Colchester,** Essex, 258; **Colnbrook,** Bucks., 439; **Colney,** Herts., 265; **Conington** (Cunnington) **St. Ives,** Cambs., 265, 270; **Cornwall,** 140; **Coventry,** Warw., 304; **Croydon,** Surr., 72-74, 77, 122, *Half Moon* at, 73, 74; **Debden,** Essex, 127-129, 131, 132; **Derby,** 301, *King's Head* at, 301; **Dover,** Kent, 140; **Earlsbury Farm,** Edgware, Midd., 4, 85, 86, 90, 94, 123, 144; **East Sheen,** Surr., 165; **Edgware,** Midd., 4, 33, 35, 85, 90, 94, 108, 160, 167, 169, 196, 197, 200-202, 205, 208, 218, 220, 237, 238, 251, 434, *Nine Pin and Bowl (Bowl and Skittle)* at, 85, 108, 110, 151, 152, 159, 160, 202, 204; **Edgwarebury,** Midd., 108; **Edgware Road,** Edgware, Midd., 169, 208, 209; **Eggington Heath,** Derbs., 301; **Egham,** Surr., 223; **Elloughton,** Yorks., 344; **Enfield,** Midd., 12, 238, 240, 258, 326

Places, England

ENFIELD CHASE, Midd., 11, 13-16, 225, 288-290; *Bailiff,* Cadwallader, James, 13, 14; *Keepers,* 13, 15, Crew, William, 15, Mason, Turpin, 14, 15, Wood, William, 14, 15; *Ranger,* Chandos (James Brydges), Duke of, 13, 15, 16, 18

Enfield Wash, Midd., 263; **Epping**, Essex, 38, 39, 52, 126-128, 143, 160, 226, 264; **Epping Forest**, *See* Waltham Forest; **Essex**, 8, 43, 45, 67, 68, 71-77, 81, 107, 111, 130, 138, 140, 146, 163, 179, 188, 199, 218, 219, 230, 233, 235, 236, 244, 253, 258, 261, 263-265, 277, 279, 283, 291, 302, 303, 305, 316-319, 325, 326, 329, 346, 347, 353, 359, 362, 364, 365, 367, 380, 381, 383, 386, 389-391, 401, 407, 410, 411, 418, 434, 435, 443, coast, 133; **Fenstanton** (Fenny Stanton), Hunts., 443; **Ferriby** (Ferraby), Yorks., 341, 351, 352, 395, 396; **Finchley**, Midd., 249, 251; **Finchley Common**, Midd., 249, 270; **Gad's Hill**, Kent, 443; **Gloucester**, 232, 237, 301, 330; **Gloucestershire**, 241, 244, 301-305, 317, 319, 320; Godalming (Godliman), Surr., 176, 177, 179; **Godmanchester**, Hunts., 443; **Gravesend**, Kent, 130-132, 165, 185, 186-189, 443; **Great Dunmow**, Essex, 258; **Great Parndon** (Parnedon), Essex, 74, 75, 77, 79, 103; **Guildford**, Surr., 176, *Red Lion* at, 176, 177; **Hadleigh Castle**, Essex, 12; **Hainault Lodge**, Dagenham, Essex, 56, 58, 60-62, 67, 75; **Ham Farm**, Surr., 165; **Hampshire**, 228; **Hampton Court**, Midd., 18; **Hare Street** (near Romford), Essex, 264, 265, 268; **Harrow on the Hill**, Midd., 251; **Harwich**, Essex, 140, 258, 307; **Heckington**, Lincs., 335-337, 340, 346, 350, 352, 371, 394, 406, Common, 335-337, 394, Fen, 351, Waterside, 409; **Hempstead**, Essex, 3, 6, 8-10, 19, 34, 64, 128, 131, 225, 289, 290, 324, 331-334, 338, 339, 346, 350, 355-363, 366, 367, 382, 384, 385, 401, 404, 405, 410, 413, 417, *Blue Bell* or *Bell* at, 331, 338, 340, 359, 360, 367, 368, 404, 405; **Hendon Lane End**, Edgware, Midd., 208; **Hertford**, 224, 257, 281, 291, 292, 305; **Hertfordshire**, 253, 258, 265, 292; **Hindhead** (Hinehead), Surr., 190, *Flying Bull* at, 178, 179; **Hockeril**, Herts., 258; **Holmfirth**, Yorks., Chapel, 420; **Home Counties**, 229, 259, 376; **Hornchurch**, Essex, 290; **Hounslow Heath**, Midd., 223, 224, 288, 293, 313, powder mills on, 310, 313; **Huddersfield**, Yorks., 420; **Hull**, Yorks., 259, 364, 375, 411, 418, 434; **Humber, River**, 287, 290, 301, 306, 316, 324, 325; **Huntingdon**, 513, 443, *Bird in Hand* at, 308; **Huntingdonshire**, 265; **Ilford**, Essex, 251; **Kent**, 67, 68, 71-73, 75, 76, 107, 111, 130, 140, 188, 263, 303, 305, 319; **King's Lynn** (Lynn), Norf., 304, 323, 325; **Kingston Hill**, Surr., 223; **Kingston-upon-Thames**, Surr., 226; **Lea, River**, Essex, 13, 38, 67; **Leeds**, Yorks., 411; **Leicester**, 261, 262, 279, 301, 311, 314, 318; **Leicestershire**, 259-265, 288, 316; **Leigh**, Essex, 20, 66, 67; **Leytonstone**, Leyton (Low Leyton), Essex, 143, 265, 275, 276, *Green Man* at, 12, 268-270, 277, 279, 281, 309, 313, 322; **Lincoln**, 301, 352; **Lincolnshire**, 290, 292, 299, 301, 321, 323, 324, 327, 331, 336, 338, 341, 348, 350, 351, 379, 381, 388, 397, 406, 407, 418, 434; **Liphook**, Hants., 177; **Little Sampford**, Essex, 357

LONDON AND WESTMINSTER, STREETS AND PLACES IN OR NEAR, London, 5, 21, 31, 52, 58, 59, 62, 67, 76, 84-86, 90, 91, 93, 111, 122, 127,

131, 138, 139, 144, 151, 159, 161, 162, 171-173, 176, 182, 186, 188-190, 194-199, 204, 214, 215, 224, 226, 228, 229, 231, 233, 234, 241, 242, 244-246, 248, 249, 251, 252, 262, 265, 270, 283, 285-287, 290, 293, 300, 302-308, 317, 320, 321, 325, 329, 347, 349, 350, 357-359, 364-366, 372-379, 388, 390, 391, 420, 424-426, 428, 442, 444, 445, 447; **London Bridge,** 74, 122, 131, 132, 187-189, 225; *London City,* 172, 213, 214, 225, 229, 306; **London Docks,** 172; **London 'East End',** 23, 33, 83, 84, 113, 120, 122, 125, 283; **London 'West End',** 83. *See also* Westminster

Birchin Lane, *Dial* in, 235; **Black Friars,** 229; **Blackheath,** 224, 226; **Blackwall,** 253, 329; **Bow,** 226; **Bow Street,** 136. *See also* Thieving Lane; **Broadway,** Westminster, *Black Horse* in, 83, 85, 92, 152, 158, 193, 202; **Bromley [? by Bow],** Butcher Row, 321, *Swan* at, 321; **Budge Row,** 21; **Cambridge Heath,** 62, 129; **Chancery Lane,** 423; **Charing Cross,** 224; **Chiswell Street,** Finsbury Square, 445; **Christchurch,** Southwark, 5, 6; **Clapham,** 244, 245; **Clerkenwell St. James,** 292, 295; **Cockpit,** 374; **Commercial Road,** Whitechapel, 172; **Cork Street,** Burlington Gardens, 310, 313; **Craven Street,** Strand, 445; **Custom House,** 140; **Dawes Street,** Westminster, 83, 85, 92, 120, 127, 193; **Deptford,** 122, 130; **Drury Lane,** *White Hart* in, 94, 121, 156, 158; **Drury Lane, Little,** *George* in, 226; **Duck Lane,** 132, 133, 155; **Farmer Street,** St. George in the East, 270, 272, 274, 278, 279; **Gloucester Street,** in Goodman's Fields, 273, 274; **Golden Lane,** 84; **Goodman's Fields,** 273, 274; **Great Ormond Street,** 110, 120; **Greenwich,** 122, 130; **Hackney St. John,** 26, 28, 47, 83, 140, 230, 236, 237, 327, 440; **Hackney Marshes,** 271; **Hick's Hall,** in St. John's Street, 23, 222; **Highgate,** 442; **High Holborn,** Old Leaping Bar (Holborn Bars) in, 92, 160, 164, 167; **Hind Court,** Thames Street, 21; **Hockley in the Hole,** Clerkenwell, 161; **Hog Lane,** Shoreditch, 34, 83, 141; **Holloway,** 293, 310; **Houndsditch,** 445; **Hoxton,** 241, 242; **Inner Temple,** 375, 393; **Islington,** 293, 310; **Kensington Palace,** 208, 214, 215, 222; **King Street,** Bloomsbury, 105, 110, 111, 151, *Punch Bowl* or *House* in, 110-113, 120, 121; **King Street,** Westminster, *Blue Boar's Head* in, 139; **Lewisham,** 122; **Lombard Street,** 445; **Marble Arch,** 167; **Mile End,** 182, 183, 213; **Millbank,** Westminster, 83, 84, 120, 141; **Minories,** 182; **Monmouth Street,** Seven Dials, 448; **New Cross,** Deptford, turnpike at, 130; **Norton Folgate,** Liberty of, Shoreditch, 23; **Old Gravel Lane,** 46, 72, 83, 84, 106, 141, 172, 269, 272, 274, 277, 278; **Old Street,** 79; **Piccadilly,** 443; **Putney,** 223; **Putney Common or Heath,** 226, 233; **Radcliff (Ratcliff) Highway,** 46, 71, 72, 83, 141; **Red House,** 229; **Red Lion Street,** Whitechapel, 269, 271-276, 309; **Roehampton,** 215, 223; **Rope Fields,** *Bun-House* in, 60; **St. George in the East,** 172, 173, 176, 200, 201, 270; **St. James's Palace,** 382; **St. Marylebone** (Marybone, St. Mary la Bonne), 115, 121, 201, 250, Dagot's Farm, 94, Gardens, 250, Park, 94, 156; **St. Sepulchers (Sepulcers),** 272, 275; **Shadwell,** Basin, 46, Church, 72, 141; **Sherbourn (Sherbone) Lane,** 445; **Shoreditch,** 23, 81; **Southwark,** 75, 77, 215, 225, 256, 259, 302; **Southwark, St. George the Martyr,** 166; **State Paper Office,** 381, 389; **Strand,** *Star* in, 214;

Place, England

Temple Bar, 411; **Thieving Lane** *alias* Bow Street, 120, 121, 132-134, 155, 192, 193; **Tothill Fields**, Westminster, 127; **Tothill Street**, St. Margaret Westminster, 120; **Tower of London**, 45, 46, 164; **Tyburn**, 72, 96, 118, 143, 160, 164, 165, 167, 171, 208, 209, 232, 254, 308, 312, 314; **Wandsworth**, 214, 215, 245, 256; **Watling Street** (City), 224; **Well Close Square**, St. George in the East, 269, 270, 272, 274, 278, 309; **Westminster**, 83, 84, 91, 92, 113, 120, 125, 126, 132, 133, 136, 139, 189, 213, 214, 224, 306; **Westminster, St. Margaret**, 124, 136, 159, 168, 191; **Whitechapel**, 9, 10, 72, 83, 120, 141, 172, 182, 183, 196, 197, 213, 245, 261, 269, 272, 275-278, 281, 282, 285, 313, 314, 423, *Red Lion* in, 269-279, 285; **Whitehall**, 13, 35, 75, 103, 107, 108, 140, 164, 213, 242, 248, 292, 306, 328, 372-374, 382, 389, 437; **White Rose Court**, Coleman Street, 445, 446; **Woolwich**, ferry, 72, 74, *George* at, 71, 72

Longbridge, Barking, Essex, 51-54, 56; **Long Sutton**, Lincs., 299, 323, 325, 326, 328, 331-339, 348, 350, 352; **Loughton** (Lawton), Essex, 75, 77-81, 103, 264, 265; **Maidenhead**, Berks., 439; **Maidstone**, Kent, 379; **Manchester**, Lancs., 322; **Markyate (Market) Street**, Herts., 265; **Middlesex**, 67, 71, 76, 107, 111, 136, 138, 140, 179, 188, 189, 199, 229, 265, 288, 316, 320, 330; **Milford Heath**, Surr., 176, 177, 179; **Mortlake**, Surr., 165; **Moulsham**, Essex, 144, 145; **Much Hadham**, Herts., 258; **Newcastle-upon-Tyne**, Northum., 411; **Newmarket**, Cambs., 264; **New Mill**, Wooldale, Yorks., 420; **Newport Pond**, Essex, 64; **Norfolk**, 304, 323, 325; **Northaw Common**, Herts., 224, 225; **North Cave**, Yorks., 323-325; **Ongar**, Essex, 264, 265; **Parkgate**, Ches., 308; **Petersfield**, Hants., 177, 179, 180, 195; **Pinchbeck**, Lincs., 331, 332, 334, 350; **Plaistow**, Westham, Essex, 9, 38, 182; **Plaistow Marshes**, 268, 269; **Pocklington**, Yorks., *fair* at, 351, 395; **Portsmouth**, Hants., 179, 225; **Potters Bar**, Midd., 225; **Puckeridge**, Herts., 256-260, 263, 288, 316; **Rake**, Hants., 177, 180, 181, 195; **Reading**, Berks., 439; **Richmond**, Surr., 214, 215, 226; **Rippleside**, Barking, Essex, 51, 58; **Romford** (Rumford), Essex, 264, 265; **Royston**, Herts., 258; **Saffron Walden**, Essex, 127, 128, 170, 338, 359-362; **Sewardstone** (Susan, Suson, Souson), Essex, 9, 10, 37, 38, 83, *Cock* at, 447, ferry, 37, 38, 67, 83, mill, 37; **Shirley**, Croydon, Surr., 73; **Shoreham**, Suss., 176; **Southampton**, Hants., 176; **South Cave** *alias* Market Cave, Yorks., 324, 351; **Southchurch** (Sechurch, Seachurch), Essex, 20, 33, 68, 125, 133, 165, 191; **Spalding**, Lincs., 378, 379; **Springhead**, Cottingham, Yorks., 375; **Standon**, Herts., 258; **Stanford**, Northants. (Leics. border), 261, 262, 311; **Stanmore**, Midd., 85, 110, *Queen's Head* at, 86, 92, 152, 202, 204; **Stilton**, Hunts., *Bell* at, 309; **Stratford**, Westham, Essex, 144, turnpike, 58, 62; **Stroud**, Gloucs., 231, 240, 241, 243, 244; **Surrey**, 67, 71-73, 76, 77, 107, 111, 138, 140, 188, 223, 263; **Sutton**, Hants., 161; **Thames, River**, 67, 72, 73, 77, 122, 131, 176, 213, 222, 223, 225, 226, estuary, 131, *tides*, 186-188; **Thaxted** (Thacksted), Essex, 8, 127, 128, 143, 289, 306, 384; **Tottenham High Cross**, Midd., 321; **Wakefield**, Yorks, 411, 420; **Wallingford**, Berks., 265; **Waltham Abbey** (Cross *or* Holy Cross), Essex, 9, 10, 30, 37, 38, 263, 280, 282, 283, 390, 425

WALTHAM FOREST, *otherwise* **EPPING FOREST,** Essex, 7, 11, 13-16, 24, 30, 31, 33, 67, 72, 122, 131, 139, 169, 171, 190, 213, 257, 264-266, 274, 276, 278-281, 283, 284, 288, 291, 293, 304, 306, 307, 309, 312, 322, 378, 391, 424, 438; **Court** of Attachments of, 5; **deer** dying in, 48; **gun,** illegal possession of in, 5; **lodge** occupant, Col. Robinson, Chamberlain of the City of London, 14; **Officials,** *Constable,* Barrd, Joseph, 18; *Keepers,* 13, 18, 27, 29, 32, 38, 67, 283, Attreidge, John, 25, 28, 440, Bastick, Joseph, 3, Hebborne (Heyborne), Thomas, 16, 24, 25, Hydes (Hide), Thomas, 3, 16, 24-26, 28, 29, 32, 33, Leigh (Lea), John, 3, Mason, Samuel, 30, Mason, Thomas, 16, 24, 25, Mason William, Snr. 15, 16, 24, 25, 56, 58-65, 67-69, 71, 73 ,76, 79, 88, 96, 104, 129, 133, 139, 160, 217, 218, 263, 318, 319, 440, Mason, William, Jnr. 16, 24, 25, Mugaredg, John, 25, 28, 440, Pater (Painter), Henry, 3, 16, 24, 25, Peckover, John, 3, Roades, Thomas, 25, 28, 440, Stephens, ——, 301, Thompson (Tomson), Henry, 3, 18, 21, 28, 31, 113, 235, 257, 280, 281, 301, 306, 412, 424, Wooton (Wootton), John, 3, 5; *Ranger,* Goodere, John, J.P., 3, 4, 16; *Verderer,* Mildmay, Carew, J.P., 16; *Warden,* Tylney (Richard Child), Earl, 13-16, 18, 38, 56, 61, 63-65; **Places in,** Fairmead (Fair Maid) Bottom, 234, 280, 281; Forest Oak,280; High Beech, 281; King's Oak, 280, 281; Little Wash, 170, 171; New Lodge Walk, 4, 18, 31; *Sign of the Oak,* 301; Three Coney Lane, 64

Walthamstow, Essex, 103, 104; **Wanstead,** Essex, 5, 28, 29, 31, 33; **Watford,** Herts., 43, 44; **Welton,** Yorks, 323-325, 328, 332-334, 337, 338, 340, 341, 344-348, 351, 352, 371, 387, 397, 399, 409, 412; **Westham** (Wittam), Essex, 144, 264; **Wethersfield,** Essex, 443; **Whetstone,** Finchley, Midd. 265; **Wimbledon Common,** Surr., 226; **Winchester** (Winton), Hants., 161, 162, 196-198, 228, 230; **Wivenhoe,** Essex, 191; **Wolverhampton,** Staffs., 161; **Woodford,** Essex, 5, 31, 43-46, 48, 50, 65, 70, 73, 75, 103, 104, 131, 139, 141, 168, 380, 390; **Woodford Row,** Essex, *Loggerheads* at, 43; **Worthy,** Hants., 228; **Yarmouth,** Great, Norfolk, 238, 240, 241; **Yaxton** [but probably **Yaxley**], Hunts., 309, 313; **York,** City of, 8, 19, 232, 278, 283, 338-340, 346, 349, 352, 356, 359-368, 373-383, 389-391, 393, 402, 404, 411-413, 415, 417-420, 423, 426, 428, 434, 435, 439, Bowling Green, 443, 447, *Blue Boar,* 428, Castlegate, 428, 430, Fishergate Postern, 428, Micklegate, 430, St. George's Churchyard, 428, Tyburn *alias* Knavesmire, 314, 427, 430, 435; **Yorkshire,** 281, 287, 290, 292, 299, 304, 307, 314, 323, 324, 327, 328, 331, 333, 334, 339, 342, 344, 346-348, 352, 359, 363, 367, 371, 376, 383, 386, 387, 407, 411, 420, 443

PLACES, OVERSEAS

America, Colonies in, 208, 228, 229, 237, 242, 253, 327, 328
Boulogne (Bullogne), France, 172,
China, 322
Flushing, Netherlands, 241, 242, 248, 249, *Three Dutch Skaters* at, 241, 242
Guernsey, Channel Isles, 176
Hanover, 4, 214
Holland, 172, 186, 217, 232, 237, 238, 240-242, 244-249, 251, 256, 258-260, 263, 290
Ireland, 307, 308, 310-312, 314
Low Countries, 249
Ostend, Belgium, 243, 249
Port South, on Potomac River, 329
Rotterdam, Holland, 241, 242, 248, 256, 259
Tasmania (Van Diemen's Land), 316
Virginia, 253, 329

MISCELLANEA

Admiralty, 140
Army, 1st Foot Guards, Col. Sir Charles Wills commanding, 160, 164, 167, 169; Brigadier General Harrison's Regiment of Foot (at Bristol), 324, 341, 373, 434; recruitment, 161
AUTHORS, Addison, Joseph, 226; **Ainsworth**, William Harrison, 59, 322, 422, 444, 448, 451; Appleton, Robert. *See* Assizes: Beverley, Clerk of Peace; **Ash**, Arty, *and* Day, Julius E., 109, 144, 145, 233, 235, 249, 250, 257, 290, 291, 313, 320, 370, 386; **Bayes**, Richard. *See* Witnesses; **Burn**, Richard, J.P., 20, 220; **D'Anvers**, Caleb, 254; **Davies**, Robert, 335; **Day**, Julius E. *See* Ash *supra;* **Gent**, Thomas, 335; **Grey**, Thomas, 226; **Harper**, Charles G., 59, 60, 63, 71, 214, 444, 452; **Miles**, Henry Downes, 194, 450, 451; **Maxwell**, Gordon S., 447-449; **Newgate, Ordinary of**, 173, 174, 242, 246-248, 251, 254; **Robinson**, W., 11, 12; **Seccombe**, Thomas, 250, 254, 261, 314, 335, 439, 444, 448; **Walford**, Edward, 250, 254; **Walpole**, Horace, 225, 226; **Wroth**, Warwick, 250, 254

Bankruptcy, 276
Bow Street Runners, 134, 136, 215

Diary, of Arthur Jessop, of Wooldale, Yorks., March/April 1739, *names* of persons living near at *places* adjacent, 420

Engravers, **Hogarth**, William, 232; **Sangar**, T.L., 450, 451; **Sharpe**, S., 445
Engraving, Copyright Act governing, 1735, 232
Excise, Exciseman, 288-290, 403, 414, 432

Games and Sports, *cock match,* 177, 179, 180; *fives,* 302; *hazard,* 322
Gin Shops, Report on, 232; Act governing retail of spiritous liquors, 325, 326

Horses, *Black Bess,* 442-448; *Whitestockings,* 260, 268-274, 275-277

Maps, Chapman and Andrés Survey of Essex, 1772, 40

Nepotism, 375
NEWSPAPERS & CO., misleading dates &c. in, practise of using, 162, 221, 251, 274, 275; *Birmingham Weekly Mercury,* 444; *Common Sense,* 321, 322;

Miscellanea

Country Journal (or *Craftsman*), 82, 147, 166, 227, 254, 294, 330; *Daily Courant*, 122-124, 136, 137, 140; *Daily Gazette*, 301, 315, 330; *Daily Gazetteer*, 322; *Daily Journal*, 119, 136; *Daily Post*, 117, 119, 136, 147, 267; *General Evening Post*, 22, 82, 147, 166, 175, 194, 315, 330, 343, 359, 379, 383, 384, 386, 392, 416; *Gentleman's Magazine*, 82, 173, 175, 330, 415, 428, 450; *Grub Street Journal*, 136, 221, 227; *Hooker's Weekly Miscellany*, 147, 166; *Ipswich Gazette*, 227, 254, 369, 392, 432; *Kentish Post and/or Canterbury Newsletter*, 315, 353, 392; *London & Country Journal*, 369, 374, 392; *London Daily Post and/or General Advertiser*, 136, 221, 294; *London Evening Post*, 57, 69, 82, 99, 108, 119, 134, 136, 147, 184, 194, 210, 221, 227, 231, 239, 254, 264, 278, 283, 294, 310, 315, 330, 426; *London Gazette*, 3, 15, 22, 57, 103, 104, 107-109, 119, 123, 124, 127, 136, 137, 140, 141, 147, 179, 185, 186, 189, 221, 251, 252, 292, 308, 315, 365, 434, 440; *London Journal*, 57; *London Magazine*, 175, 194, 295; *Old Whig*, 40, 166, 167, 175, 177, 179-181, 184, 196, 210; *Political State*, 12, 22, 40, 45, 57, 69, 82, 119, 136, 175, 179-181, 184, 210, 220, 221, 254, 267, 294, 295, 306, 310, 315, 330, 343, 353, 379, 383, 392, 415, 416, 432; *Read's* (or *Reid's*) *Weekly Journal*, 57, 69, 82, 99, 110, 131, 136, 147, 166, 179, 184, 267, 294, 295, 369, 432; *Universal Spectator & Weekly Journal*, 82, 119, 392; *Worcester Journal*, 343; *York Courant*, 335, 369, 391, 392, 411, 415, 426-428, 432, 441

Ono, Barry, Collection of Chapbooks &c., 447, 448, 450

Packet — Boats, 243, 245, 308
Physicians, Royal College, of, 232
Poem, *The Highwayman*, by Alfred Noyes, 431, 432
Privy Council, 208, 213, 214
PUBLISHED WORKS, Reference to,
    Alumni Cantabrigienses, Venn, 343
    Charities of Hull, 375
    Collection of Diverting Songs, 1817, 261, 314
    Correspondence of Gray, Walpole, West and Ashton, 227
    Critchett & Woods, Post Office Directories, 449
    Cunningham's Law Directory, 1783, 254
    Dick Turpin, 1840, Henry Downes Miles, 194, 450
    Dictionary of National Biography, 250
    Essex Review, 250, 254, 267, 343, 441, 449
    Far From the Madding Crown, Thomas Hardy, 442
    General History and Life of Richard Turpin, 1739, J. Standen, 335, 355, 358, 368, 415
    Genuine Account of the Two Surprising Escapes of Daniel Malden, 1737, Ordinary of Newgate, 254

Half Hours with the Highwaymen, Charles G. Harper, 69, 71, 221, 452
Highwayman's Heath, Gordon S. Maxwell, 314, 449
History and Antiquities of the City of York, 1735, Francis Drake, F.R.S., 432
Historia Placitorum Coronae, History of the Pleas of the Crown, 1735, Hale, 392
History of Clerkenwell, 1881, W.J. Pinks, 282, 294
Immortal Turpin, 1948, Ash & Day, 99, 119, 136, 141, 145, 147, 221, 227, 233, 239, 245, 254, 267, 294, 315, 330, 383, 384, 386, 392, 432
Newberry, John, Journal, 439
Justice of the Peace and Parish Officer, 1756, Richard Burn, 22, 220
Knights of the High Toby, 1962, John Barrows, 82
Letters of Horace Walpole, 1903, Toynbee, 227
Life and Adventurers of Richard Turpin &c., Ryle & Co., 448
Life and Trial of Richard Turpin &c., 1808, Thomas Maiden & Co., 99, 112, 444-447
Life of Richard Turpin, 1739, Richard Bayes and others in Essex. *See* Authors: Bayes
Life of Thomas Gent, 1832, 335
London, 1927, G.H. Cunningham, 254
London Pleasure Gardens of the 18th C., 1896, Warwick Wroth, 254
Memoirs of the York Press, 1868, Robert Davies, 335
Moggs, E. London Street Directory, 1810, 449
Newgate Calendar, 51
News, News . . . from London, 1737, 308
Notes and Queries, various, 449 (letters)
Old and New London, 1897, Edward Walford, 254
Old Bailey Sessions Proceedings, 99, 151-159, 166, 173, 184, 192-194, 200-206, 210
O Rare Turpin, 1739 (ballad), 315
Ordingary of Newgate's account of 13 Malefactors executed at Tyburn 10 March 1735, contemporary, 173, 307
Pleas of the Crown, 1762, Hawkins, 392
Retrospective Review, 1823, Baldwyn, 449
Rookwood, 1834, William Harrison Ainsworth, 59, 63, 194, 330, 442, 444, 445, 447, 448, 451
St. James Clerkenwell, Registers of Burials, Harleian Society Register Series, 1894, 295
St. Mary Islington, History and Topography of, S. Lewis Jnr., 295
Survey of Essex, 1772, Chapman and André, 40
The Highwayman, Alfred Noyes, 431, 432
Tour Through the Whole Island of Great Britain, attr. De. Foe, 443
Trial of Richard Turpin, 1739, Ward and Chandler, 335, 355, 358, 367, 371, 375, 386, 393, 411-418

Turpin's Behaviour in York Castle, 1739, J. Standen, 421, 422
Turpin's Confession, 1739, Ward and Chandler, 264, 265, 267, 423, 425
Two Yorkshire Diaries, Yorkshire Archaeological Society Record Series, Vol. CXVII, 1952, 419, 420, 426
Tyburn Chronicle, '1742', 450
PUBLISHERS, PRINTERS & CO., *piracy by,* 7, 336, 415-417, 413
  Applebee, J., 173, 254; **Catnach,** James, 448; **Lemoine,** Anne, 445, 446; **Maiden,** Thomas, 445, 446, 448; **Roe,** J., 445, 446, 448; **Ryle & Co.**, 448; **Standen,** J., 415-417, 420, 422, 423; **Ward & Chandler,** 411, 416, 421, 423, 425-428

Quaker General Meeting, London, 293

ROADS, Cambridge Road (Essex), 233; Hertford Road, 291; King's Oak Road (Essex), 234; London Road (Essex), 307; London Road (Hants.), 228; Loughton Road (Essex), 234; Portsmouth Road (Surr.), 223; Tonbridge Road (Kent), 225; Watling Street (Kent), 122, 131

Superstitions, 138

Turnpikes, 52, 56, 90, 144, 263. *See also* London: New Cross, and Stratford, Essex

Weather, descriptions of, 48, 56, 68, 74, 85, 420, 426
Whigs, 322
Wine Licences, 276